DUVALL'S™ Master Study Guide Series United States Tax Code Encyclopedia P-15

2013

Circular E Employers Tax Guide, Publication 15
Encyclopedia of IRS Tax Law and Regulations

Instructors Manual

© Copyright 2013. All rights reserved.
A Ficus Tree Publishing, LLC, Educational-Technical Publication

The International Leader in Construction Technology Home Study

IRS Publication 15 Circular E Employers Tax Guide
DUVALL'S Master Study Guide Series

DUVALL'S Master Study Guide Series, of the United States Tax Code, IRS Publication 15, Employers Tax Guide, Instructor's Manual is a comprehensive, detailed study guide and workbook set forth in multiple-choice question format in such manner as to achieve maximum readability for individuals who have developed scholastic educational reading, comprehension, and retention levels equal to or greater than middle school eighth grade through college freshman and above plateaus of education.

This Work parallels, in generally sequential form, the current edition of the important Internal Revenue Service publication 15. However, this Work is not an official publication of the IRS or the United States Government.

This Work is an independent publication designed and developed over years of classroom lectures. As such, the information and material provided is set forth as Continuing Education material as a teaching aid in multiple-choice question format with answers to meet the needs of qualified instructors engaged in providing highly specialized educational-technical information to Continuing Education students.

The Contents of DUVALL'S Master Study Guide Series, United States Tax Code, IRS Publication 15, IRS Circular E, Employer's Tax Guide; Contents: Include the four initial parts; What's New, Reminders, Calendar and Introduction. The initial parts are important keys to unlocking the door of each annual tax year change. Important information includes the new tax year withholding tables, Social Security and Medicare Tax rates. Contents also include our multiple-choice questions with answers for the Primary Sections of Circular E.

The Primary Sections of IRS Publication 15 Circular E, Employer's Tax Guide are listed as sections 1 to 16 including additional multiple-choice questions for the subject Index of IRS Circular E. The list of the sixteen primary sections of Circular E can be located on the front cover page of the current tax year IRS publication 15. They are: 1. Employer Identification Number; 2. Who are Employees? 3. Family Employees; 4. Employee's Social Security Number (SSN); 5. Wages and Other Compensation; 6. Tips; 7. Supplemental Wages; 8. Payroll Period; 9. Withholding From Employees' Wages; 10. Required Notice to Employees About the Earned Income Credit; 11. Depositing Taxes; 12. Filing Form 941 or Form 944; 13. Reporting Adjustments to Form 941 or Form 944; 14. Federal Unemployment (FUTA) Tax; 15. Special Rules for Various Types of Services and Payments; 16. How To Use the Income Tax Withholding Tables.

The tax tables for each calendar tax year are not included with this study guide. Both the current tax year IRS Publication 15 (Circular E), Employer's Tax Guide and the corresponding tax tables shall be obtained by the individual student. The tax tables for Circular E are contained within each free IRS publication.

© Copyright 2013. All rights reserved. Notice: United States Copyright Laws and International Treaties prohibit unauthorized publication, reproduction, distribution of this Work. Unauthorized use of this copyright in any form, format, publication or document may result in severe civil and criminal penalties. Violations of this copyright are investigated by the United States Department of Justice and carry, upon conviction of fines up to $250,000 and five years confinement. This Work is protected by United States Copyright Laws and International Treaties. Do not Copy, do not reproduce, do not distribute.

A Ficus Tree Publishing Educational-Technical Publications

The International Leader in Construction Technology Home Study

Instructor's Manual • Contents

Page 1.	Title Page
Page 2.	Abstract
Page 3.	Instructor's Manual Contents
Page 4.	Copyright Notice
Page 5.	Copyright Information
Page 6.	Publishers Statement
Page 7.	Instructors Manual Overview, Obtaining IRS information
Page 8.	General Description, Key Words of Test 15E-WN-1
Page 9.	Test 15E-WN-1: What's New-Contents-Index
Page 20.	Test 15E-R1: General information (Reminders is an important test series)
Page 23.	Test 15E-R1: REMINDERS. COBRA, Electronic Filing and Payment
Page 35.	Test 15E-R2: Credit/Debit Card Payments, Employer Responsibilities
Page 45.	Test 15E-R3: Paying Wages, Pensions, Annuities
Page 55.	Test 15E-R4: Pension Plans
Page 65.	Test 15E-R5: Telephone Help, Taxpayer Advocate
Page 77.	Test 15E-C1: Calendar, Current Tax Year Calendar
Page 89.	Test 15E-Intro 1: Introduction, Employers Liability, Federal, State, Local Government Employees, COBRA
Page 107.	Test 15E-S1: Employer Identification Number (EIN)
Page 115.	Test 15E-S2: Who Are Employees?
Page 131.	Test 15E-S2-2: Husband and Wife Business
Page 139.	Test 15E-S3: Family Employees
Page 147.	Test 15E-S4: Employee Social Security Number
Page 159.	Test 15E-S5-1: Wages and Other Compensation
Page 171.	Test 15E-S5-2: Wages and Other Compensation
Page 205.	Test 15E-S6: TIPS
Page 219.	Test 15E-S7: Supplemental Wages
Page 239.	Test 15E-S8: Payroll Period
Page 241.	Test 15E-S9-1: Withholding From Employee's Wages
Page 263.	Test 15E-S9-2: Withholding From Employee's Wages
Page 283.	Test 15E-S9-3: Withholding From Employee's Wages
Page 303.	Test 15E-S10: Required Notice to Employees About the Earned Income Credit (EIC)
Page 307.	Test 15E-S11-1: Depositing Taxes
Page 327.	Test 15E-S11-2: Depositing Taxes
Page 347.	Test 15E-S11-3: Depositing Taxes
Page 365.	Test 15E-S11-4: Depositing Taxes

© Copyright 2013. All rights reserved. Notice: United States Copyright Laws and International Treaties prohibit unauthorized publication, reproduction, distribution of this Work. Unauthorized use of this copyright in any form, format, publication or document may result in severe civil and criminal penalties. Violations of this copyright are investigated by the United States Department of Justice and carry, upon conviction of fines up to $250,000 and five years confinement. This Work is protected by United States Copyright Laws and International Treaties. Do not Copy, do not reproduce, do not distribute.

A Ficus Tree Publishing Educational-Technical Publications

The International Leader in Construction Technology Home Study

Instructor's Manual • Contents-Continued

Page 373.	Test 15E-S12-1: Filing Form 941 or Form 944
Page 395.	Test 15E-S12-2: Filing Form 941 or Form 944
Page 405.	Test 15E-S13-1: Reporting Adjustments to Form 941 or Form 944
Page 429.	Test 15E-S13-2: Reporting Adjustments to Form 941 or Form 944
Page 445.	Test 15E-S14: Federal Unemployment Tax (FUTA)
Page 465.	Test 15E-S15-1: Special Rules for Various Types of Services and Payments
Page 483.	Test 15E-S15-2: Special Rules for Various Types of Services and Payments
Page 505.	Test 15E-S15-3: Special Rules for Various Types of Services and Payments
Page 525.	Test 15E-S15-4: Special Rules for Various Types of Services and Payments
Page 531.	Test 15E-S16-1: How To Use the Income Tax Withholding Tables.
Page 549.	Test 15E-S16-2: How To Use the Income Tax Withholding Tables.
Page 599.	Index Test: I-1(a Key Words Test)

Copyright notice:

United States Copyright Law and International Treaties prohibit unauthorized publication, distribution, or reproduction of this document, unauthorized publication, distribution, or reproduction of the whole, part, portion of this document is a crime and may result in severe civil and criminal penalties. Violations of this copyright are investigated by the United States Department of Justice and carry, upon conviction, of fines up to $250,000 and five years confinement.

No part of this publication may be republished, reproduced, duplicated, digitalized, copied, photocopied, posted, broadcast, or electronically scanned by any means or methods, including without limitation, optical, mechanical, electronic, recording by or in any information storage retrieval system (photocopying is expressly forbidden), without first obtaining written permission from the author and publisher. Purchasers of this document do not have the right or permission to publish, reproduce, reprint, redistribute, digitalize, duplicate, post, broadcast, photocopy, any part, portion or whole of this Work, the information and material contained herein, within this document. Do not copy, do not photocopy.

Although the Code of Federal Regulations, parts thereof, including Department of the Treasury, Internal Revenue Service publications are published in the public domain, the formatting, sequencing, and structuring of such information and materials contained herein are subject to United States and International copyright laws, agreements, regulations and codes.

Further, while every effort has been made to ensure the information contained herein is accurate and complete at the time of printing and publication the possibility of typographic errors, omissions, misprints, and/or oversights may exist. No patent liability is assumed with respect to the use and/or misuse of the information and material contained herein. In addition, it is not the intent of the author or publisher that the information and materials contained herein shall be considered, applied, or referenced as a source document or definitive source for the information and material contained herein. Therefore, neither Ficus Tree Publishing, LLC or the author, nor any person or subsidiary thereof shall be liable for any damages resulting from the use, application, misuse, misapplication or reliance on this publication.

© Copyright 2013. All rights reserved. Notice: United States Copyright Laws and International Treaties prohibit unauthorized publication, reproduction, distribution of this Work. Unauthorized use of this copyright in any form, format, publication or document may result in severe civil and criminal penalties. Violations of this copyright are investigated by the United States Department of Justice and carry, upon conviction of fines up to $250,000 and five years confinement. This Work is protected by United States Copyright Laws and International Treaties. Do not Copy, do not reproduce, do not distribute.

A Ficus Tree Publishing Educational-Technical Publications

The International Leader in Construction Technology Home Study

Caution:

Caution: Always obtain the current official IRS Publication 15 (Circular E), Employer's Tax Guide as the <u>Source Document</u> for reference, research, study, and testing purposes. Contact your local IRS Office to obtain the current edition. You can order employer tax products at www.irs.gov/pub15 . This information is on the front (Cover page) of each IRS Circular E, Employer's Tax Guide. Further, IRS Publication 15, (Circular E), Employer's Tax Guide for your use, for each respective tax year. Including the current tax year Circular E and other IRS important tax publications that are <u>free IRS publication services of the United States Treasury Department</u>.

Important Note: Free IRS Publications are available direct from the IRS. To obtain free IRS Publications of IRS Publication 15, Employer's Tax Guide for each current tax Note: year - Go to IRS Internet website at <u>IRS.gov</u> or call **1-800-829-4933** the IRS Business and Specialty Tax Line with your employment tax questions.

Copyright Information:

ISBN: 978-0-9895390-0-5

Publisher Identification: 2013-p15-MEIM-EIRS-II-00001-00000215

Author: Du Vall, James W.

Title: DUVALL'S™
Master Study Guide Series. United States Tax Code. Encyclopedia P-15
Circular E, Employer's Tax Guide, Publication 15, 2013
Instructors Manual For Study Guides

Source Document: Department of the Treasury, Internal Revenue Service
Publication 15 Catalog Number 10000W (February 05, 2013)
(CIRCULAR E), Employer's Tax Guide For Use in 2013

First printing: November 2013 Instructors Manual Study Guide Series United States Tax Code. Published by Ficus Tree Publishing LLC

This publication is intended solely as an Instructors Manual for study guides developed as lecture tool with guidelines in multiple-choice format with answers provided for the specific publication indicated above. Further, this Work is not, was not, created for or intended to be considered, to be used, applied or presented that this Work is a stand-alone document for any legal entity, professional, or business enterprise. This Work is a Master Study Guide/Workbook Series publication intended for classroom or home study under the supervision of qualified instructors. This Work is not an official publication of the United States Department of the Treasury, the Internal Revenue Service (IRS) or the United States federal government. This Work is a copyrighted, independent publication for educational-technical study purposes only and shall not be considered for or used, applied, misused, misapplied, in any manner other than the stated purpose of the Work.

Printed in the United States of America

© Copyright 2013. All rights reserved. Notice: United States Copyright Laws and International Treaties prohibit unauthorized publication, reproduction, distribution of this Work. Unauthorized use of this copyright in any form, format, publication or document may result in severe civil and criminal penalties. Violations of this copyright are investigated by the United States Department of Justice and carry, upon conviction of fines up to $250,000 and five years confinement. This Work is protected by United States Copyright Laws and International Treaties. Do not Copy, do not reproduce, do not distribute.

A Ficus Tree Publishing Educational-Technical Publications

Publishers Statement:

Instructors Manuals, Student Study Guides, Workbooks, Test Series, Technical Manuals, Technical Papers and similar works by Ficus Tree Publishing, LLC, that are researched, created, developed, published and marketed by Ficus Tree Publishing LLC. for educational purposes, are copyrighted Works protected by United States copyright laws and International copyright agreements.

Therefore, it is hereby stated this Work; The 2013 Edition of Encyclopedia P-E15, Instructor's Manual for Study Guide Series of the United States Tax Code, is a Work authored by James W. Du Vall for the purpose of reading, research, study and problem solving of multiple-choice questions herein identified as DUVALL'S Master Study Guide Series United States Tax Code Encyclopedia P-15, Instructors Manual containing and providing multiple-choice questions with answers as DUVALL'S TESTS with tests created from IRS Publication 15, Catalog Number 10000W, (Circular E), Employer's Tax Guide, is an independent publication. Thus and therefore, this Work, the 2013 Edition of Encyclopedia P-E15, **is not an official publication** of the government of the United States of America, The Department of the Treasury, or the Internal Revenue Service. The Ficus Tree Publishing LLC., DUVALL'S Master Study Guide Series United States Tax Code Encyclopedia P-15, 2013 Edition, is an independent copyright Work.

Further, this Work, is an independent publication, created by the author, is a copyrighted Work according to the United States Code of Federal Regulations (C.F.R.s). This Work is based entirely upon the information and material contained in or otherwise available from the G.P.O. Publication 15 (Circular E), Employer's Tax Guide and the IRS web site.

© Copyright 2013. All rights reserved. Notice: United States Copyright Laws and International Treaties prohibit unauthorized publication, reproduction, distribution of this Work. Unauthorized use of this copyright in any form, format, publication or document may result in severe civil and criminal penalties. Violations of this copyright are investigated by the United States Department of Justice and carry, upon conviction of fines up to $250,000 and five years confinement. This Work is protected by United States Copyright Laws and International Treaties. Do not Copy, do not reproduce, do not distribute.

The International Leader in Construction Technology Home Study

Instructor's Manual Overview
IRS Publication 15 (Circular E), Employer's Tax Guide
Master Study Guide and Workbook Series

The Instructor's Manual for IRS Publication 15 Employer's Tax Guide, is a readable but very tightly detailed, near word for word, sentence by sentence, paragraph by paragraph, study guide and workbook created from the annual publication of the United States, Department of the Treasury, Internal Revenue Service, Publication 15, Catalog Number 10000W (Circular E), Employer's Tax Guide for each specific tax year.

The Work (Instructor's Manual) is presented in simple to read multiple-choice questions presented in the form of detailed Study Guides. The Study Guides are designed to require each student to carry out independent basic reading assignments to solve each multiple-choice question. Thus, it is necessary for the student to read each multiple-choice question broken down into simplified sentences then solve the stated question/problem.

The structure of each test set is intentionally designed to allow the Instructor to assume the initiative when developing his or her study and research habit instructions for the classroom and homework lessons presented by the Instructor. The multiple-choice test sequence structure developed by Ficus Tree Publishing, LLC., for this specific purpose by following word-for-word and generally paralleling the sentence and paragraph structure of the IRS publication.

The Study Guide multiple-choice test sets were initially designed around the 50-minute classroom lecture. Further, research indicates the attention span at the average college freshman during lectures to be in the range of fifteen to twenty minutes. In this, classroom lecture/problem solving for reading and research (not guessing at answers) may be further divided into no more than 10 or 15 multiple-choice, test type questions within each 50-minute classroom hour. This suggestion permits the assignment of 15 to 30 home study in reading, research, and problem solving for students.

The IRS Publication 15, Employer's Tax Guide is a free publication of the Internal Revenue Service. It is suggested each student be required to obtain the current tax year IRS publications in addition to Circular E, Publication 15, Employer's Tax Guide for educational purposes.

Requiring the student to obtain copies of Publication 15, Employer's Tax Guide, and other IRS Publications, for each current tax year directly from the IRS is an important part of this lecture series. This knowledge is an important part of the continuing educational experience of the individual student for research and education.

© Copyright 2013. All rights reserved. Notice: United States Copyright Laws and International Treaties prohibit unauthorized publication, reproduction, distribution of this Work. Unauthorized use of this copyright in any form, format, publication or document may result in severe civil and criminal penalties. Violations of this copyright are investigated by the United States Department of Justice and carry, upon conviction of fines up to $250,000 and five years confinement. This Work is protected by United States Copyright Laws and International Treaties. Do not Copy, do not reproduce, do not distribute.

A Ficus Tree Publishing Educational-Technical Publications

The International Leader in Construction Technology Home Study

Tax Test 15E-WN-1
What's New - Contents - Index

A General Description WN Series Tests

Tax Test 15E-S15-WN-1: Tax Test 15E-WN-1, is a basic introduction test to the study of IRS Circular E, Employer's Tax Guide. In multiple-choice question format with answers, the test questions examine the information provided on the cover page, contents and index of IRS Publication 15. The initial test series is designed to require the student conduct basic study, research and information gathering specifically related to where tax subject information is located. The Work commences with the detailed reading and review of the front cover, page 1 of IRS Circular E. To solve the problems related to this first page requires as stated, a detailed examination of the cover sheet of Circular E.

<u>An Important Notice</u>. The student must obtain a free current copy of IRS Circular E, Publication 15. Employer's Tax Guide for study and research purposes. All page numbers provided within the test questions reference directly to the United States Government current year tax publication of IRS Publication 15, Employer's Tax Guide. IRS Publication 15. The Employer's Tax Guide is a free publication easily obtained from the IRS at the local IRS office or via mail from the IRS. Copies of current IRS publications may be obtained by using the Internet to visit the IRS website. As an employer you are required to follow, comply with, and use the electronic deposit system of the IRS.

Key Words of Tax Test WN Series Tests.
(Note: Key Word page numbers provided for this section reference to IRS Publication 15.)

Test 15E-WN-1

Contents. Page 1- Future Developments. Page 1- Display. Page 1- Implementing the withholding tables. Page 1- Social security and Medicare tax. Page 1- Wage base limit for Medicare tax. Page 1- Index. Page 1 and Page 66- Employer Social security tax rate. Page 1, Contents, Front (page 1), Index. Page 66- Employee Medicare tax rate. What's New, Front cover, page 1, Index, page 66- Employee Social security tax rate. What's New, page 1, Index. Page 66- Payroll Period. Contents, page 1, Index, page 66, Circular E, page 20- Family Employees. Contents. Page 1. Index. Page 66. Circular E. Page 12- Forms 941 and 944. Page 1, Contents. Page 1. Circular E. Page 30- Required Notice to Employees about Earned Income Credit (EIC). Contents. Page 1. Circular E. Page 24- Depositing Taxes. Contents. Page 1. Index. Page 66. Circular E. Page25- Accuracy of Deposits Rule. Index. Page 66. Circular E. Page 28- COBRA. Circular E. Page 10- FUTA. Contents. Page 1. Index. Page 66. Circular E. Page 35- Lookback period. Index. Page 66. Circular E. Page 25- Archer Medical savings accounts. Index. Page 66. Circular E. Page 16.

© Copyright 2013. All rights reserved. Notice: United States Copyright Laws and International Treaties prohibit unauthorized publication, reproduction, distribution of this Work. Unauthorized use of this copyright in any form, format, publication or document may result in severe civil and criminal penalties. Violations of this copyright are investigated by the United States Department of Justice and carry, upon conviction of fines up to $250,000 and five years confinement. This Work is protected by United States Copyright Laws and International Treaties. Do not Copy, do not reproduce, do not distribute.

A Ficus Tree Publishing Educational-Technical Publications

DU VALL'S TESTS™
Master Study Guide Series United States Tax Code
2013 IRS Publication 15 Circular E, Employer's Tax Guide
Instructors Manual
Test 15E-WN-1

WN-1

1. The Contents for the IRS Publication 15 Circular E, Employer's Tax Guide is located on page ___.
    (a)   1
    (b)   7
    (c)   9
    (d)   66
    Answer: See Front page of Circular E, right column, page 1, also see/ (a) 1

2. Future Developments information is listed on page ___ of the IRS Publication 15 Circular E, Employer's Tax Guide.
    (a)   1
    (b)   7
    (c)   9
    (d)   66
    Answer: See Front page of Circular E, right column, page 1, also see Future Developments/ (a) 1

3. For the latest information about developments related to Publication 15 (Circular E), such as legislation enacted after it was published, go to ____.
    (a)   www.irs.gov/publ15
    (b)   www.irs.gov/pub/15
    (c)   www.irs.gov/pub15
    (d)   www.irs.govn/pub15
    Answer: See Front page of Circular E, Future Developments/ (c) www.irs.gov/pub15

4. Get forms and other information faster and easier by Internet ____.
    (a)   IRS.gov
    (a)   IRS.gov.pub15
    (a)   IRS.gov. publications
    (a)   IRS.gov.net
    Answer: See Front page of Circular E, Display/ (a) IRS.gov

5. Employer's should implement the 2013 withholding tables ____,
    (a)   after January 1, 2013
    (b)   as soon as possible,
    (c)   after 1 January 2013
    (d)   after 31 December 2012
    Answer: See Front page of Circular E, lower right hand corner (What's New), page 1/(b) as soon as possible

© Copyright 2013. All rights reserved. Notice: United States Copyright Laws and International Treaties prohibit unauthorized publication, reproduction, distribution of this Work. Unauthorized use of this copyright in any format, publication or document may result in severe civil and criminal penalties. Violations of this copyright are investigated by the United States Department of Justice and carry, upon conviction of fines up to $250,000 and five years confinement. This Work is protected by United States Copyright Laws and International Treaties. Do not Copy, do not reproduce, do not distribute.

A Ficus Tree Publishing Educational-Technical Publications

Tax Test WN-1

6. Employer's should implement the 2013 withholding tables ____, but not later than February ___, 2013.
   (a) after January 1, 2013, 1,
   (b) as soon as possible, 15,
   (c) after 1 January 2013, 5,
   (d) after 31 December 2012, 28,
   Answer: See Front page of Circular E, lower right hand corner (What's New), page 1/(b) as soon as possible, 15,

7. Employer's should implement the 2013 withholding tables ____, but not later than February ___, 2013. Use the 2012 withholding tables until ____ the 2013 withholding tables.
   (a) after January 1, 2013, 1, you receive
   (b) as soon as possible, 15, you implement
   (c) after 1 January 2013, 5, you receive your copy
   (d) after 31 December 2012, 28, you receive notification
   Answer: See Front page of Circular E, lower right hand corner (What's New), page 1/(b) as soon as possible, 15, you implement

8. The Social Security wage base limit for 2013 is $___.
   (a) 87,500
   (b) 102,000
   (c) 110,100
   (d) 113,700
   Answer: See Front page of Circular E, lower right hand corner (What's New), page 1, also see Social Security and Medicare Taxes, Tax rate and social security wage base limit, page 23/(d) 113,700

9. The wage base limit for Medicare tax is $___.
   (a) There is no limit on the amount of wages subject to Medicare tax;
   (b) 25,000
   (c) 52,000
   (d) 110,300
   Answer: See Front page of Circular E, lower right hand corner (What's New), page 1, Tax rate and the social security wage base limit, page 23/ (a) There is no wage base limit for Medicare tax

10. The Index for Circular E is located on page ____ of IRS publication 15.
    (a) 58
    (b) 59
    (c) 66
    (d) 68
    Answer: See Contents, Front page, Circular E/ (c) 66

© Copyright 2013. All rights reserved. Notice: United States Copyright Laws and International Treaties prohibit unauthorized publication, reproduction, distribution of this Work. Unauthorized use of this copyright in any form, format, publication or document may result in severe civil and criminal penalties. Violations of this copyright are investigated by the United States Department of Justice and carry, upon conviction of fines up to $250,000 and five years confinement. This Work is protected by United States Copyright Laws and International Treaties. Do not Copy, do not reproduce, do not distribute.

The International Leader in Construction Technology Home Study

Tax Test 15E-WN-1

11. According to IRS Publication 15, 2013 Circular E, the employer tax rate for social security is ____%.
    - (a) 6.2
    - (b) 7.1
    - (c) 8.4
    - (d) 8.5

    Answer: See Cover, Index & Page 23, Employer tax rate and the social security wage base limit/ (a) 6.2

12. According to the 2013 Circular E, the employee Medicare tax rate is ___%.
    - (a) 1.35
    - (b) 1.45
    - (c) 1.51
    - (d) 3.51

    Answer: See Cover, Index & Page 19, Tax rates and the social security wage base limit/ (b) 1.45

13. Information about family employees can be located on page ___ of Circular E.
    - (a) 3
    - (b) 5
    - (c) 10
    - (d) 12

    Answer: See Contents, front page of Circular E/ (d) 12

14. Information about payroll periods can be located on page ___ of Circular E.
    - (a) 9
    - (b) 10
    - (c) 15
    - (d) 20

    Answer: See Contents, front page Circular E/ (d) 20

15. Information about depositing taxes can be located on page ____ of Circular E.
    - (a) 11
    - (b) 19
    - (c) 20
    - (d) 23

    Answer: See Contents, front page Circular E/ (c) 20

16. Employees are defined on page ____ of Circular E.
    - (a) 3
    - (b) 5
    - (c) 9
    - (d) 11

    Answer: See Contents, front page Circular E/ (d) 11

© Copyright 2013. All rights reserved. Notice: United States Copyright Laws and International Treaties prohibit unauthorized publication, reproduction, distribution of this Work. Unauthorized use of this copyright in any form, format, publication or document may result in severe civil and criminal penalties. Violations of this copyright are investigated by the United States Department of Justice and carry, upon conviction of fines up to $250,000 and five years confinement. This Work is protected by United States Copyright Laws and International Treaties. Do not Copy, do not reproduce, do not distribute.

A Ficus Tree Publishing Educational-Technical Publications

The International Leader in Construction Technology Home Study

Tax Test 15E-WN-1

17. Information about filing of forms 941 and 944 is found on page __, and the Index of Circular E.
    (a) 2
    (b) 27
    (c) 30
    (d) 37
    Answer: See Contents page 1/ (c) 30

18. Required Notice to Employees about the Earned Income Credit (EIC) is discussed on page ___ of Circular E.
    (a) 20
    (b) 24
    (c) 35
    (d) 45
    Answer: See Contents, Circular E/ (b) 24

19. The Accuracy of Deposits Rule, is described on page ___ of Circular E.
    (a) 13
    (b) 19
    (c) 23
    (d) 28
    Answer: See Index page 66/ (d) 28

20. Backup withholding, is discussed on page ___ of Circular E.
    (a) 2
    (b) 4
    (c) 5
    (d) 7
    Answer: See Index, Circular E / (c) 5

21. Change of address is discussed on page ___ of Circular E.
    (a) 3, 6
    (b) 15
    (c) 20
    (d) 29
    Answer: See Index, Circular E/ (a) 3, 6

22. COBRA premium assistance credit is discussed on page ____ of Circular E.
    (a) 5
    (b) 10
    (c) 15
    (d) 23
    Answer: See Index, COBRA/ (b) 10

© Copyright 2013. All rights reserved. Notice: United States Copyright Laws and International Treaties prohibit unauthorized publication, reproduction, distribution of this Work. Unauthorized use of this copyright in any form, format, publication or document may result in severe civil and criminal penalties. Violations of this copyright are investigated by the United States Department of Justice and carry, upon conviction of fines up to $250,000 and five years confinement. This Work is protected by United States Copyright Laws and International Treaties. Do not Copy, do not reproduce, do not distribute.

A Ficus Tree Publishing Educational-Technical Publications

The International Leader in Construction Technology Home Study

Tax Test 15E-WN-1

23. FUTA tax, is discussed on page ____ of Circular E.
    - (a) 6
    - (b) 16
    - (c) 28
    - (d) 35

    Answer: See Cover, Index, Circular E/ (d) 35

24. Information about household employees, is found on page ___ of Circular E.
    - (a) 2
    - (b) 12
    - (c) 25
    - (d) 30

    Answer: See Index, Circular E/ (d) 30

25. International Social Security Agreements, are discussed on page ___ of Circular E.
    - (a) 10
    - (b) 19
    - (c) 24
    - (d) 25

    Answer: See Index, Circular E/ (c) 24

26. **Lookback period**, is discussed on page ___ of Circular E.
    - (a) 7
    - (b) 20
    - (c) 25
    - (d) 27

    Answer: See Index, Circular E/ (c) 25

27. Long-term care insurance, is discussed on page ___ of Circular E.
    - (a) 16
    - (b) 20
    - (c) 30
    - (d) 40

    Answer: See Index, Circular E/(a) 16

28. Medicare tax, is discussed on page ___ of Circular E.
    - (a) 8
    - (b) 10
    - (c) 12
    - (d) 23

    Answer: See Index, Circular E/ (d) 23

© Copyright 2013. All rights reserved. Notice: United States Copyright Laws and International Treaties prohibit unauthorized publication, reproduction, distribution of this Work. Unauthorized use of this copyright in any form, format, publication or document may result in severe civil and criminal penalties. Violations of this copyright are investigated by the United States Department of Justice and carry, upon conviction of fines up to $250,000 and five years confinement. This Work is protected by United States Copyright Laws and International Treaties. Do not Copy, do not reproduce, do not distribute.

A Ficus Tree Publishing Educational-Technical Publications

Tax Test 15E-WN-1

29. Government employers, are discussed on page ___ of Circular E.
    (a) 2
    (b) 4
    (c) 5
    (d) 9
    Answer: See Index, Circular E/ (d) 9
    Tax Test 15E-WN-1

30. Medical savings accounts, are discussed on page ___ of Circular E.
    (a) 5
    (b) 13
    (c) 16
    (d) 18
    Answer: See Index, Circular E/ (c) 16

31. Mileage, is discussed on page ___ of Circular E.
    (a) 7
    (b) 10
    (c) 12
    (d) 15
    Answer: See Index, Circular E/ (d) 15

32. Moving Expenses, are discussed on page ___ of Circular E.
    (a) 3
    (b) 6
    (c) 7
    (d) 16
    Answer: See Index, Circular E/ (d) 16

33. The Monthly deposit schedule, is discussed on page ___ of Circular E.
    (a) 7
    (b) 11
    (c) 15
    (d) 26
    Answer: See Index, Circular E/ (d) 26

34. Noncash wages, are discussed on page ___ of Circular E.
    (a) 9
    (b) 12
    (c) 15
    (d) 27
    Answer: See Index, Circular E/ (c) 15

© Copyright 2013. All rights reserved. Notice: United States Copyright Laws and International Treaties prohibit unauthorized publication, reproduction, distribution of this Work. Unauthorized use of this copyright in any form, format, publication or document may result in severe civil and criminal penalties. Violations of this copyright are investigated by the United States Department of Justice and carry, upon conviction of fines up to $250,000 and five years confinement. This Work is protected by United States Copyright Laws and International Treaties. Do not Copy, do not reproduce, do not distribute.

Tax Test 15E-WN-1

35. Payroll period, is discussed on page ___ of Circular E.
    (a) 13
    (b) 14
    (c) 15
    (d) 20
    Answer: See Index, Circular E/ (d) 20

36. Reconciling Forms W-2 and 941 or 944 are discussed on page ___ of Circular E.
    (a) 15
    (b) 25
    (c) 31
    (d) 35
    Answer: See Index, Circular E/ (c) 31

37. Per Diem reimbursements, are discussed on page ___ of Circular E.
    (a) 3
    (b) 7
    (c) 9
    (d) 15
    Answer: See Circular E, 5. Wages and Other Compensation (reimbursements, per diem or other fixed allowance)/ (d) 15

38. Semiweekly deposit schedule is discussed on page ___ of Circular E.
    (a) 4
    (b) 21
    (c) 26
    (d) 31
    Answer: See Index, Circular E, (c) 26

39. Statutory employees, are discussed on page ___ of Circular E.
    (a) 4
    (b) 9
    (c) 11
    (d) 15
    Answer: See Index, Circular E/ (c) 11

40. Successor Employers, are discussed on pages ___ of Circular E.
    (a) 3, 15
    (b) 19, 29
    (c) 21, 30
    (d) 24, 35
    Answer: See Index, Circular E/ (d) 24, 35

© Copyright 2013. All rights reserved. Notice: United States Copyright Laws and International Treaties prohibit unauthorized publication, reproduction, distribution of this Work. Unauthorized use of this copyright in any form, format, publication or document may result in severe civil and criminal penalties. Violations of this copyright are investigated by the United States Department of Justice and carry, upon conviction of fines up to $250,000 and five years confinement. This Work is protected by United States Copyright Laws and International Treaties. Do not Copy, do not reproduce, do not distribute.

A Ficus Tree Publishing Educational-Technical Publications

Tax Test 15E-WN-1

41. The Trust Fund Recovery Penalty, is discussed on page ___ of Circular E.
    (a) 12
    (b) 17
    (c) 24
    (d) 29
    Answer: See Index, Circular E/ (d) 29

42. Wages, are defined on page ___ of Circular E.
    (a) 7
    (b) 14
    (c) 18
    (d) 21
    Answer: See Index, Circular E/ (b) 14

43. Withholding exemption is discussed on page ___ of Circular E.
    (a) 8
    (b) 14
    (c) 21
    (d) 25
    Answer: See Index, Circular E/ (c) 21

44. Pensions and annuities, are discussed on page ___ of Circular E.
    (a) 5
    (b) 8
    (c) 12
    (d) 16
    Answer: See Index, Circular E, a part of the withholding discussion (W)/ (a) 5

45. The percentage method, is discussed on page ___ of Circular E.
    (a) 12
    (b) 23
    (c) 35
    (d) 42
    Answer: See Index, Circular E (W)/ (d) 42

46. Seasonal Employers, are discussed on page ___ of Circular E.
    (a) 24
    (b) 30
    (c) 41
    (d) 65
    Answer: See Index, Circular E/ (b) 30

Tax Test 15E-WN-1

47. The Formulario W-4 (SP), Certificado de Exención de la Retención del Empleado may be used in place of the Form ___.
    (a) W-4
    (b) W-4A
    (c) W-4B
    (d) W-4S
    Answer See Form W- 4, Forms in Spanish/ (a) W-4

48. For companies engaged in fishing and related activities the employer should see IRS publication ___.
    (a) 440
    (b) 489
    (c) 713
    (d) 334
    Answer: See Circular E, page 37, 15. Special Rules for Various Types of Services and Payments, Fishing and related activities, Tax Guide for Small Business/(d) 334

49. By February 28, you are required to file Copy A of all paper Forms ___ and ____.
    (a) W -1, W -2
    (b) Cancellation of Debt, Earned Income Credit Advance Payment Certificate
    (c) 1099, 1096
    (d) Wage and Tax Statement
    Answer: See Circular E, Calendar, page 8/ (c) 1099, 1096

50. By March 31, File electronic Forms ___, ___, and ___ are required to be filed.
    (a) 1089, 1099, 8027
    (b) 1089, 8027, W - 2
    (c) 1099, 8027, W -2
    (d) 940, 1099, 1028
    Answer: See (c), Circular E, Calendar, page 6/ (c) 1099, 8027, W-2

51. For EFTPS, visit www.eftps.gov or call EFTPS Customer Service at 1 - 800 - 555 - ____.
    (a) 4444
    (b) 4455
    (c) 4466
    (d) 4477
    Answer: See Circular E, Reminders, Electronic Filing and Payment, pp 2,28, 66/ (d) 4477

Tax Test 15E-WN-1

52. If you receive written notification you qualify for the Form 944 Program, Employer's Annual Federal Tax Return, instead of Form ___. If you received this notification, but prefer to file Form 941, you can request to have your filing requirement changed to Form 941.
    (a) 941
    (b) 941A
    (c) 942A
    (d) 944
    Answer: See Cover, Circular E, Filing Form 941 or Form 944, page 30/ (a) 941

53. According to the IRS Circular E Calendar, when filing, if any date falls on a Saturday, Sunday or Federal Holiday, use the ___.
    (a) preceding day
    (b) preceding business day
    (c) following day
    (d) next business day
    Answer: See Calendar (Tip) page 8/ (d) next business day

54. A state wide legal holiday delays a filing due date only if the IRS office where you are required to file is located in that ___.
    (a) state
    (b) county
    (c) city
    (d) country
    Answer: See Calendar (Tip) page 8/ (a) state

55. For any filing due date, you will meet the "file" or "furnish" requirement if the form is properly addressed, contains sufficient postage, and is ___ by the U. S. Postal Service or sent by an IRS designated private delivery service on or before the due date.
    (a) post haste
    (b) postmarked
    (c) First-Class
    (d) Special Delivery
    Answer: See Calendar (Tip) page 8/ (b) postmarked

56. By January 31, the employer shall furnish each employee a completed ___, Wage and Tax Statement.
    (a) 1099
    (b) W-2
    (c) W-4
    (d) 1099-D
    Answer: See Calendar, page 8, (Furnish Forms) By January 31/ (b) W-2

Tax Test 15E-WN-1

57. By January 31, the employer must file Form 940, Employer's Annual Federal Unemployment (FUTA) Tax Return. However if the employer deposited all the FUTA Tax when due, you have an additional ___ calendar days to file.
    (a) 7
    (b) 10
    (c) 15
    (d) 30
    Answer: See Calendar, (File Form 940) By January 31/ (b) 10

58. The employer must ask for a new Form W-4 from each employee who claimed exemption from ____ last year.
    (a) filing for the previous year
    (b) number of dependents
    (c) income tax withholding
    (d) taxes due to financial losses
    Answer: See Calendar, By February 15/ (c) income tax withholding

59. The Exempt Forms ____ expire on February 16.
    (a) W-2
    (b) W-2E
    (c) W-3
    (d) W-4
    Answer: See Calendar, On February 16/ (d) W-4

The International Leader in Construction Technology Home Study

Instructors Manual For Study Guides
"REMINDERS" General Information Tax Test R-1

(Summary of Circular E Study Material)

Reminders is one of the most frequently used parts of Circular E test material but it is also the most frequently overlooked parts by instructors and students alike. In **REMINDERS** from page 2 to page 8 many subjects are summarized in brief paragraph form. The actual wording may vary sufficiently with the later text in a slightly different from the more detailed primary sections of the IRS Circular E, Employers Tax Guide. Thus, the basic information may condensed or abridged slightly (perhaps a minor word change or the addition of a new sentence or paragraph. It is suggested the Instructor provide abundant material from "Reminders" for classroom and home study. Page numbers below from IRS Publication 15. 2013 Edition.

COBRA premium assistance credit	Page 2.
Federal Tax Deposits must be made by electronic funds transfer	Page 2.
You must receive written notice from the IRS to File Form 944	Page 2.
Employers can request to file Forms 941 instead of Form 944	Page 2.
Form 944-SS and Formulario discontinued	Page 3.
Aggregate Form 941 Filers	Page 3.
Aggregate Form 940 Filers	Page 3.
Electronic Filing and Payment	Page 3.
Forms in Spanish	Page 3.
Hiring New employees	Page 3.
Paying Wages, Pensions, or Annuities	Page 4.
Information reporting customer service	Page 4.
Nonpayroll Income Tax Withholding	Page 5.
• Pensions	Page 5.
• Military retirement	Page 5.
• Gambling winnings	Page 5.
• Indian gaming profits	Page 5.
• Certain government payments (unemployment compensation, social security, and Tier 1 railroad retirement benefits, subject to voluntary withholding	Page 5.
• Payments subject to backup withholding	Page 5.
Distributions from nonqualified pension plans and deferred compensation plans	Page 5.
Backup withholding, IRAs, SEP, SIMPLE, 404k, ESOP, MSAs, TIN, W-9, W-9(SP), Recordkeeping,	Page 5.
Paying Wages, Pensions, or Annuities	Page 5.
Employer Responsibilities	Page 5.
New employees	Page 5.
Zero wage returns	Page 5
Information Returns	Page 5.

© Copyright 2013. All rights reserved. Notice: United States Copyright Laws and International Treaties prohibit unauthorized publication, reproduction, distribution of this Work. Unauthorized use of this copyright in any form, format, publication or document may result in severe civil and criminal penalties. Violations of this copyright are investigated by the United States Department of Justice and carry, upon conviction of fines up to $250,000 and five years confinement. This Work is protected by United States Copyright Laws and International Treaties. Do not Copy, do not reproduce, do not distribute.

A Ficus Tree Publishing Educational-Technical Publications

The International Leader in Construction Technology Home Study

Reminders

Form 944-SS and Formulario 944-PR discontinued	Page 5.
Aggregate Form 941 filers	Page 5.
Aggregate Form 940 filers	Page 5.
Change of Address	Page 5.
Electronic Filing and Payment	Page 5.
• Electronic funds withdrawal (EFW)	Page 5.
• Electronic Filing and Payment	Page 5.
• Electronic funds withdrawal (EFW)	Page 5.
• Credit or debit card payments	Page 5.
Forms in Spanish	Page 5.
Hiring New Employees	Page 5.
• New hire reporting	Page 5.
• W-4 request	Page 5.
• Name and social security number	Page 5.
Change of Address	Page 6.
Private Delivery Services	Page 6.
Telephone Help	Page 6.
• Help for people with disabilities	Page 6.
• Recorded tax information (TeleTax)	Page 6.
• Teletax Topics	Page 6.
751. Social Security and Medicare Withholding Rates. (Tasas de retención del seguro social y Medicare, Tema)	Page 6.
752. Form-2—Where, When, and How to File (Dónde, Cuándo y Como Presentar El La Formulario W-2)	Page 6.
753. Form W-4—Employee's Withholding Allowance Certificate (Formulario W-4 (SP)—Certificado de Excensión de Retenciones de Empleado)	Page 6.
755. Employer Identification Number—How to Apply (Como Solicitar Un Numero de Identificación Patronal (EIN)	Page 6.
756. Employment Taxes for Household Employees (Impuestos Patronales para Empleados Domesticos)	Page 6
757. Form 941 and Form 944—Deposit Requirements (Formulario 941 and Formulario 944—Requisitos de Depósito)	Page 7.
758. Form 941—Employer's QUARTERLY Federal Tax return (Formulario 941-PR—Planilla para la Declaracion Federal TRIMESTRAL del Patrono) (Formulario 944-PR—Planilla para la Declaracion Federal ANUAL del Patrono)	Page 7.

© Copyright 2013. All rights reserved. Notice: United States Copyright Laws and International Treaties prohibit unauthorized publication, reproduction, distribution of this Work. Unauthorized use of this copyright in any form, format, publication or document may result in severe civil and criminal penalties. Violations of this copyright are investigated by the United States Department of Justice and carry, upon conviction of fines up to $250,000 and five years confinement. This Work is protected by United States Copyright Laws and International Treaties. Do not Copy, do not reproduce, do not distribute.

A Ficus Tree Publishing Educational-Technical Publications

Reminders

Telephone Help	Page 6.
• Teletax Topics	
759. A Business Credit is Available for Qualified Employers Under "The HIRE ACT" of 2010 (an excellent test type question). (Nueva excenión tributaria y credito comercial para empleadores calificados disponibles bajo la Lay de Incentivos para la Contraction y Recuperación del Empleo del 2010 (HIRE, por sus siglas en ingles)	Page 7.
761. Tips—Withholding and Reporting (Propinas—Declaracion y Retention)	Page 7.
762. Independent Contractor vs. Employee (Contratista Independiente vs. Empleado)	Page 7.
763. The "Affordable Care Act" of 2010 Offers Employers New Tax Deductions and Credits (another excellent test question). (Ley de Cuidado de Salud a Costo Asequible del 2010 ofrece a los empleadores deducciones y creditos tributarios nuevos)	Page 7.

© Copyright 2013. All rights reserved. Notice: United States Copyright Laws and International Treaties prohibit unauthorized publication, reproduction, distribution of this Work. Unauthorized use of this copyright in any form, format, publication or document may result in severe civil and criminal penalties. Violations of this copyright are investigated by the United States Department of Justice and carry, upon conviction of fines up to $250,000 and five years confinement. This Work is protected by United States Copyright Laws and International Treaties. Do not Copy, do not reproduce, do not distribute.

A Ficus Tree Publishing Educational-Technical Publications

DU VALL'S TEST'S™
Instructors Manual Study Guide Series United States Tax Code
IRS Publication 15 Circular E, Employer's Tax Guide Tax Year 2013
Tax Test Reminders Test R-1 [Questions With Answers]

REMINDERS Circular E

1. **COBRA premium assistance credit.** The credit for COBRA premium assistance payments applies for employees involuntarily terminated between ____ and ____, and
   (a) January 1, 2008, August 1, 2009
   (b) June 30, 2008, May 31, 2010
   (c) September 1, 2008, May 31, 2010
   (d) August 1, 2009, May 31, 2012
   Answer: See Circular E, Reminders page 2/ (c) September 1, 2008. May 31, 2010

2. **COBRA premium assistance credit.** The credit for COBRA premium assistance payments applies for employees involuntarily terminated between ____ and ____, and to premiums paid up to ___ months.
   (a) January 1, 2008, August 1, 2009, 14
   (b) June 30, 2008, May 31, 2010, 15
   (c) September 1, 2008, May 31, 2010, 15
   (d) August 1, 2009, May 31, 2012, 18
   Answer: See Circular E, Reminders page 2/ (c) September 1, 2008. May 31, 2010, 15

3. **COBRA premium assistance credit.** The credit for COBRA premium assistance payments applies for employees involuntarily terminated between ____ and ____, and to premiums paid up to ___ months. See COBRA premium assistance credit under ___.
   (a) January 1, 2008, August 1, 2009, 14, Future Developments
   (b) June 30, 2008, May 31, 2010, 15, What's New
   (c) September 1, 2008, May 31, 2010, 15, Introduction
   (d) August 1, 2009, May 31, 2012, 18, Calendar
   Answer: See Circular E, Reminders page 2/ (c) September 1, 2008. May 31, 2010, 15, Introduction

4. You must use electronic funds transfer to make all ___ deposits.
   (a) employee withholding taxes
   (b) withholding tax
   (c) federal tax
   (d) all federal taxes
   Answer: See Circular E, Reminders page 2/ (c) federal tax

Reminders: Federal tax deposits must be made by electronic funds transfer. Page 2.

5. You must use electronic funds transfer to make all___ deposits. Generally, electronic funds transfers are made using the Electronic Federal Taxpayers System (____).
   (a) employee withholding taxes, USPS
   (b) withholding tax, EFICS
   (c) federal tax, EFTPS
   (d) all federal taxes, EUTPS
   Answer: See Circular E, Reminders page 2/ (c) federal tax, EFTPS

6. You must use electronic funds transfer to make all EFTPS deposits. Generally, electronic funds transfers are made using the Electronic Federal Taxpayers System (EFTPS). If you do not want to use EFTPS, you can arrange for your tax professional, financial institution, ____, or other trusted third party to make electronic deposits on your behalf.
   (a) employer service
   (b) payroll service
   (c) financial service
   (d) approved Credit Card Service
   Answer: See Circular E, Reminders page 2/ (b) payroll service

7. You must use electronic funds transfer to make all EFTPS deposits. Generally, electronic funds transfers are made using the Electronic Federal Taxpayers System (EFTPS). If you do not want to use EFTPS, you can arrange for your tax professional, financial institution, ____, or other trusted third party to make electronic deposits on your behalf. Also, you may arrange for your financial institution to initiate a same-day___ payment on your behalf.
   (a) employer service, electronic
   (b) payroll service, wire
   (c) financial service, automatic
   (d) approved Credit Card Service, automatic
   Answer: See Circular E, Reminders page 2/ (b) payroll service, wire

8. You must use electronic funds transfer to make all EFTPS deposits. Generally, electronic funds transfers are made using the Electronic Federal Taxpayers System (EFTPS). If you do not want to use EFTPS, you can arrange for your tax professional, financial institution, ____, or other trusted third party to make electronic deposits on your behalf. Also, you may arrange for your financial institution to initiate a same-day ___ payment on your behalf. EFTPS is a free service provided by the Department of Treasury. Services provided by your tax professional, financial institution, payroll service, or other third party may ___.
   (a) employer service, electronic, have a fee
   (b) payroll service, wire, have a fee
   (c) financial service, automatic, have fees
   (d) approved Credit Card Service, automatic, service fees
   Answer: See Circular E, Reminders page 2/ (b) payroll service, wire, have a fee

© Copyright 2013. All rights reserved. Notice: United States Copyright Laws and International Treaties prohibit unauthorized publication, reproduction, distribution of this Work. Unauthorized use of this copyright in any form, format, publication or document may result in severe civil and criminal penalties. Violations of this copyright are investigated by the United States Department of Justice and carry, upon conviction of fines up to $250,000 and five years confinement. This Work is protected by United States Copyright Laws and International Treaties. Do not Copy, do not reproduce, do not distribute.

The International Leader in Construction Technology Home Study

Reminders: Federal tax deposits must be made by electronic funds transfer.

7. For more information on making federal tax deposits, see *How To Deposit* in section ___.
   (a) 7
   (b) 9
   (c) 11
   (d) 13
   Answer: See Circular E, Reminders page 2/ (c) 11

8. For more information on making federal tax deposits, see *How To Deposit* in section ___. To get more information about EFTPS or to enroll in EFTPS, visit *www.eftps.gov* or call 1-800-555-___.
   (a) 7, 4455
   (b) 9, 4466
   (c) 11, 4477
   (d) 13, 4488
   Answer: See Circular E, Reminders page 2/ (c) 11, 4477

9. For more information on making federal tax deposits, see *How To Deposit* in section ___. To get more information about EFTPS or to enroll in EFTPS, visit *www.eftps.gov* or call 1-800-555-___. Additional information about EFTPS is also available in Publication ___, Electronic Federal Tax Payment System: A Guide To Getting Started.
   (a) 7, 4455, 964
   (b) 9, 4466, 965
   (c) 11, 4477, 966
   (d) 13, 4488, 967
   Answer: See Circular E, Reminders page 2/ (c) 11, 4477, 966

Reminders: You must receive written notice from the IRS to File Form 944. Page 2.

10. If you have been filing Forms ___, Employer's QUARTERLY Federal Tax Return (or Forms 941-SS, Employer's QUARTERLY Federal Tax Return — American Samoa, Guam, the Commonwealth of the Northern Mariana Islands, and the U.S. Virgin Islands, or Formularios 941-PR, Planilla para la Declaracion Federal TRIMESTRAL del Patrono), and believe your employment taxes for the calendar year will be $___ or less, and you would like to file Form 944 instead of Forms 941, you must contact the IRS to request to file Form 944.
    (a) 941, 1,000
    (b) 941, 1,500
    (c) 942, 1,000
    (d) 942, 1,500
    Answer: See Circular E, Reminders page 2/ (a) 941, 1,000

© Copyright 2013. All rights reserved. Notice: United States Copyright Laws and International Treaties prohibit unauthorized publication, reproduction, distribution of this Work. Unauthorized use of this copyright in any form, format, publication or document may result in severe civil and criminal penalties. Violations of this copyright are investigated by the United States Department of Justice and carry, upon conviction of fines up to $250,000 and five years confinement. This Work is protected by United States Copyright Laws and International Treaties. Do not Copy, do not reproduce, do not distribute.

A Ficus Tree Publishing Educational-Technical Publications

Reminders: You must receive written notice from the IRS to File Form 944. Page 2.

11. If you have been filing Forms ___, Employer's QUARTERLY Federal Tax Return (or Forms 941-SS, Employer's QUARTERLY Federal Tax Return — American Samoa, Guam, the Commonwealth of the Northern Mariana Islands, and the U.S. Virgin Islands, or Formularios 941-PR, Planilla para la Declaracion Federal TRIMESTRAL del Patrono), and believe your employment taxes for the calendar year will be $___ or less, and you would like to file Form 944 instead of Forms 941, you must contact the IRS to request to file Form 944. You must receive ___ from the IRS to file Form ___ instead of Form ___ before you may file this form.
    (a) 941, 1,000, written notice, 944, 941
    (b) 941, 1,500, confirmation, 944, 941
    (c) 942, 1,000, permission, 943, 941
    (d) 942, 1,500, notice, 943, 941
    Answer: See Circular E, Reminders page 2/ (a) 941, 1,000, written notice, 944, 941

12. If you have been filing Forms 941, Employer's QUARTERLY Federal Tax Return (or Forms 941- SS, Employer's QUARTERLY Federal Tax Return — American Samoa, Guam, the Commonwealth of the Northern Mariana Islands, and the U.S. Virgin Islands, or Formularios 941-PR, Planilla para la Declaracion Federal TRIMESTRAL del Patrono), and believe your employment taxes for the calendar year will be $1,000 or less, and you would like to file Form 944 instead of Forms 941, you must contact the IRS to request to file Form 944. You must receive written permission from the IRS to file Form 944 instead of Form 941 before you may file this form. For more information on requesting Form ___, visit IRS.gov and enter "____" in the search box.
    (a) 943, request for change from quarterly filling to annual filing
    (b) 943, request to file employment taxes annually
    (c) 944, request to fill taxes annually
    (d) 944, file employment taxes annually
    Answer: See Circular E, Reminders page 2/ (d) 944, file employment taxes annually

Reminders: Employers can request to file Forms 941 instead of Form 944. Page 2.

13. If you received notice from the IRS and have been filing Form ___ but would like to file Forms ___ instead, you must contact the IRS to request to file Forms ___.
    (a) 944, 941, 941
    (b) 944, 941, 943
    (c) 941, 944, 944
    (d) 941, 943, 944
    Answer: See Circular E, Reminders page 2/ (a) 944, 941, 941

Reminders: Employers can request to file Forms 941 instead of Form 944. Page 2.

14. If you received notice from the IRS and have been filing Form ___ but would like to file Forms ___ instead, you must contact the IRS to request to file Forms ___. You must receive written notice from the IRS to file Forms ___ instead of Form ___ before you may file these forms.
    (a) 944, 941, 941, 941, 944
    (b) 944, 941, 943, 941, 943
    (c) 941, 944, 944, 941, 942
    (d) 941, 943, 944, 943, 941
    Answer: See Circular E, Reminders page 2/ (a) 944, 941, 941, 941, 944

15. If you received notice from the IRS and have been filing Form ___ but would like to file Forms ___ instead, you must contact the IRS to request to file Forms ___. You must receive written notice from the IRS to file Forms ___ instead of Form ___ before you may file these forms. For requesting more information on requesting to file Form 944, visit IRS.gov and enter "____" in the search box.
    (a) 944, 941, 941, 941, 944, file employment taxes annually
    (b) 944, 941, 943, 941, 943, file employment taxes semi-annually
    (c) 941, 944, 944, 941, 942, file employment taxes quarterly
    (d) 941, 943, 944, 943, 941, file employment taxes monthly
    Answer: See Circular E, Reminders page 2/ (a) 944, 941, 941, 941, 944, file employment taxes annually

Reminders: Form 944-SS and Formulario 944-PR discontinued. Page 3.

16. Form 944-SS, Employer's ANNUAL Federal Tax Return—American Samoa, Guam, the Commonwealth of the Northern Mariana Islands, and the U.S. Virgin Islands, and Formulario 944-PR, Planilla para la Declaración Federal ANUAL del Patrono, will no longer be issued by the IRS after ___.
    (a) 2011
    (b) 2012
    (c) 2013
    (d) 2014
    Answer: See Circular E, Reminders page 3/ (a) 2011

Reminders: Employers Annual Federal Tax Return

17. Form 944-SS, Employer's ANNUAL Federal Tax Return—American Samoa, Guam, the Commonwealth of the Northern Mariana Islands, and the U.S. Virgin Islands, and Formulario 944-PR, Planilla para la Declaración Federal ANUAL del Patrono, will no longer be issued by the IRS after 2011. Beginning with tax year ___, employers who previously filed Form ___ or Formulario ___ will continue to file annually on Form ___ (or Formulario ___, Declaración Federal ANUAL de Impuestos del Patrono o Empleador, the Spanish language equivalent of Form 944).
    (a) 2011, 944-SS, 944-PR, 944-SP, 944-S
    (b) 2012, 944-SS, 944-PR, 944-SP, 944
    (c) 2013, 944-SS, 944PR, 944-SP, 944-SP
    (d) 2014, 944-SS, 944-PR, 944-SP, 944
    Answer: See Circular E, Reminders page 3/ (b) 2012, 944-SS, 944-PR, 944

18. Form 944-SS, Employer's ANNUAL Federal Tax Return—American Samoa, Guam, the Commonwealth of the Northern Mariana Islands, and the U.S. Virgin Islands, and Formulario 944-PR, Planilla para la Declaración Federal ANUAL del Patrono, will no longer be issued by the IRS after 2011. Beginning with tax year 2012, employers who previously filed Form 944-SS or Formulario 944-PR will continue to file annually on Form 944 (or Formulario 944-SP, Declaración Federal ANUAL de Impuestos del Patrono o Empleador, the Spanish language equivalent of Form 944). Alternatively, 944employers in American Samoa, Guam, the Commonwealth of the Northern Islands, and the U.S. Virgin Islands may request to file Forms ___ instead of Form ___.
    (a) 944-SP, 944-SS
    (b) 944-SS, 944-SP
    (c) 944-SS, 944
    (d) 944, 944-VI
    Answer: See Circular E, Reminders page 3/ (c) 944-SS, 944

19. Employers in Puerto Rico may request to file ___ 941-PR instead of Form 944.
    (a) Form 944-SP
    (b) 944-SS
    (c) Forms
    (d) Formularios
    Answer: See Circular E, Reminders page 3/ (d) Formularious

20. You must receive written notice from the IRS to file Forms 941-___ or Formularios 941-PR instead of Form 944 before you may file these forms.
    (a) Form 944-SP
    (b) SS
    (c) Forms
    (d) Formularios
    Answer: See Circular E, Reminders page 3/ (b) SS

The International Leader in Construction Technology Home Study

Reminders: Aggregate Form 941 filers. (Form 941). Page 3.

21. Agents must complete Schedule ___ (Form 941), Allocation Schedule for Aggregate Form 941.
    (a) SP
    (b) A
    (c) B
    (d) R
    Answer: See Circular E, Reminders page 3/ (d) R

22. Agents must complete Schedule ___ (Form 941), Allocation Schedule for Aggregate Form 941. Allocation Schedule for Aggregate Form 941 Filers, when filing an aggregate Forms 941 may only be filed by agents approved by the IRS under section ___ of the Internal Revenue Code.
    (a) SP, 17
    (b) A, 489
    (c) B, 701
    (d) R, 3504
    Answer: See Circular E, Reminders page 3/ (d) R, 3504

Reminders: Agents

23. Agents must complete Schedule ___ **(Form 941)**, Allocation Schedule for Aggregate Form 941. Allocation Schedule for Aggregate Form 941 Filers, when filing an aggregate Forms 941 may only be filed by agents approved by the IRS under section ___ of the Internal Revenue Code. To request approval to act as an agent for an employer, the agent files Form ___, Employer/payer Appointment of Agent, with the IRS.
    (a) SP, 17, 2675
    (b) A, 489, 2676
    (c) B, 701, 2677
    (d) R, 3504, 2678
    Answer: See Circular E, Reminders page 3/ (d) R, 3504, 2678

Reminders: Aggregate Form 940 filers. (Form 940). Page 3.

24. Agents must complete Schedule ___ **(Form 940)**, Allocation Schedule for Aggregate Form **940**. Allocation Schedule for Aggregate Form **940** Filers, when filing an aggregate Form **940, Employer's Annual Federal Unemployment (FUTA) Tax Return**.
    (a) SP
    (b) A
    (c) B
    (d) R
    Answer: See Circular E, Reminders page 3/ (d) R

Reminders: Aggregate Form 940 filers. (Form 940). Page 3.

25. Agents must complete Schedule ___ (**Form 940**), Allocation Schedule for Aggregate Form 940. Allocation Schedule for Aggregate Form 940 Filers, when filing an aggregate Form 940, **Employer's Annual Federal Unemployment (FUTA) Tax Return**. Aggregate Forms 940 can be filed by agents on behalf of home care service recipients who receive home care services through a program ___ by a federal, state, or local government.
    (a) SP, administered
    (b) A, operated
    (c) B, operated
    (d) R, administered
    Answer: See Circular E, Reminders page 3/ (d) R, administrated

26. Agents must complete Schedule ___ (**Form 940**), Allocation Schedule for Aggregate Form 940. Allocation Schedule for Aggregate Form 940 Filers, when filing an aggregate Form 940, **Employer's Annual Federal Unemployment (FUTA) Tax Return**. Aggregate Forms 940 can be filed by agents on behalf of home care service recipients who receive home care services through a program ___ by a federal, state, or local government. To request approval to act as an agent on behalf of home care service recipients, the agent files a Form ___ with the IRS.
    (a) SP, administered, 2675
    (b) A, operated, 2676
    (c) B, operated, 2677
    (d) R, administered, 2678
    Answer: See Circular E, Reminders page 3/ (d) R, administered, 2678

Reminders: Change of Address—Business. Page 3.

27. Use Form ___, Change of Address—Business, to notify the IRS of an address change.
    (a) 8822-A
    (b) 8822-B
    (c) 8822-C
    (d) 8822-D
    Answer: See Circular E, Reminders page 3/ (b) 8822-B

28. Use Form ___, Change of Address—Business, to notify the IRS of an address change. Do not mail Form ___ with your employment tax return.
    (a) 8822-A, 8822-A
    (b) 8822-B, 8822-B
    (c) 8822-C, 8822-C
    (d) 8822-D, 8822-D
    Answer: See Circular E, Reminders page 3/ (b) 8822-B, 8822-B

© Copyright 2013. All rights reserved. Notice: United States Copyright Laws and International Treaties prohibit unauthorized publication, reproduction, distribution of this Work. Unauthorized use of this copyright in any form, format, publication or document may result in severe civil and criminal penalties. Violations of this copyright are investigated by the United States Department of Justice and carry, upon conviction of fines up to $250,000 and five years confinement. This Work is protected by United States Copyright Laws and International Treaties. Do not Copy, do not reproduce, do not distribute.

The International Leader in Construction Technology Home Study

Reminders: Electronic Filing and Payment. Page 3.

29. Now, more than ever before, businesses can ___ the benefits of filing and paying their federal taxes electronically.
    (a) enjoy
    (b) appreciate
    (c) utilize
    (d) participate in
    Answer: See Circular E, Electronic Filing and Payment. Page 3/ (a) enjoy

30. Now, more than ever before, businesses can ___ the benefits of filing and paying their federal taxes electronically. Whether you rely on a tax professional or handle your own taxes, the IRS offers you ___ programs to make filing and payment easier.
    (a) enjoy, convenient
    (b) appreciate, numerous
    (c) utilize, many
    (d) participate in, free
    Answer: See Circular E, Electronic Filing and Payment. Page 3/ (a) enjoy, convenient

Reminders: Electronic Filing and Payment. Page 3.

31. Now, more than ever before, businesses can enjoy the benefits of filing and paying their federal taxes electronically. Whether you rely on a tax professional or handle your own taxes, the IRS offers you convenient programs to make filing and payment easier. Spend less time and worry on taxes and more time ____ your business.
    (a) operating
    (b) running
    (c) looking after
    (d) recreation
    Answer: See Circular E, Electronic Filing and Payment. Page 3/ (b) running

32. Now, more than ever before, businesses can enjoy the benefits of filing and paying their federal taxes electronically. Whether you rely on a tax professional or handle your own taxes, the IRS offers you convenient programs to make filing and payment easier. Spend less time and worry on taxes and more time ____ your business. Use ___ and the Electronic Federal Tax Payment System (**EFTPS**) to your ___.
    (a) operating, *e-file*, benefit
    (b) running, *e-file*, benefit
    (c) looking after, electronic *e-mail*, profit
    (d) expanding, building, *e-mail*
    Answer: See Circular E, Electronic Filing and Payment. Page 3/ (b) running, *e-file*, benefit

Reminders: Electronic Filing and Payment. Page 3.

33. For *e-file*, visit www____ for additional information.
    (a) www.irsgov/efile
    (b) www.irs.gove/file
    (c) www.irs.gov/efile
    (d) wwwirs.gov/efile
    Answer: See Circular E, Electronic Filing and Payment. Page 3/ (c) www.irs.gov/efile

34. For EFTPS, visit *www.eftps.gov* or call EFTPS Customer Service at 1-800-___-4477.
    (a) 555
    (b) 556
    (c) 557
    (d) 558
    Answer: See Circular E, Electronic Filing and Payment. Page 3/ (a) 555

35. For electronic filing of Forms W-__, visit *www.socialsecurity.gov/employer*.
    (a) 2
    (b) 3
    (c) 4
    (d) 5
    Answer: See Circular E, Electronic Filing and Payment. Page 3/ (a) 2

Reminders: Electronic Filing and Payment (Caution Note). Page 3.

36. If you are filing your tax return or paying your federal taxes electronically, a valid ___ is required at the time the return is filed.
    (a) IRS
    (b) SS
    (c) SSN
    (d) EIN
    Answer: See Circular E, Electronic Filing and Payment. Page 3/ (d) EIN

Reminders: Electronic Filing and Payment (Caution Note)

37. If you are filing your tax return or paying your federal taxes electronically, a valid ___ is required at the time the return is filed. If a valid ___ is not provided, the return or payment will not be processed.
    (a) IRS, IRS
    (b) SS, SS
    (c) SSN, SSN
    (d) EIN, EIN
    Answer: See Circular E, Electronic Filing and Payment. Page 3/ (d) EIN, EIN

The International Leader in Construction Technology Home Study

Reminders: Electronic Filing and Payment (Caution Note).

38. If you are filing your tax return or paying your federal taxes electronically, a valid ___ is required at the time the return is filed. If a valid ___ is not provided, the return or payment will not be processed. this may result in penalties and ___ in processing your return or payment.
    (a) IRS, IRS, fines
    (b) SS, SS, delays
    (c) SSN, SSN, fines
    (d) EIN, EIN, delays
    Answer: See Circular E, Electronic Filing and Payment. Page 3/ (d) EIN, EIN, delays

Reminders: Electronic funds withdrawal (EFW). Page 3.

39. If you file Form 940, Form 941, or Form 944 electronically, you can e-file and e-pay (electronic funds withdrawal) the balance due is a ___ using tax preparation software or through a tax professional.
    (a) easy step
    (b) single step
    (c) simple step
    (d) simplified step
    Answer: See Circular E, Electronic funds withdrawal (EFW). Page 3/ (b) single step

40. If you file Form 940, Form 941, or Form 944 electronically, you can e-file and e-pay (electronic funds withdrawal) the balance due is a ___ using tax preparation software or through a tax professional. However, Do not use ___ to make your federal tax deposits.
    (a) easy step, WEF
    (b) single step, EFW
    (c) simple step, FEW
    (d) simplified step,
    Answer: See Circular E, Electronic funds withdrawal (EFW). Page 3/ (b) single step, EFW

Reminders: Electronic funds withdrawal (EFW). Page 3.

41. If you file Form 940, Form 941, or Form 944 electronically, you can e-file and e-pay (electronic funds withdrawal) the balance due is a ___ using tax preparation software or through a tax professional. However, Do not use ___ to make your federal tax deposits. For More information on paying your taxes using ___, visit the IRS website at www.irs.gov/e-pay. A fee may be charged to file electronically.
    (a) easy step, WEF, MEW
    (b) single step, EFW, EFW
    (c) simple step, FEW, WEF
    (d) simplified step, MEW, EFW
    Answer: See Circular E, Electronic funds withdrawal (EFW). Page 3/ (b) single step, EFW, EFW

© Copyright 2013. All rights reserved. Notice: United States Copyright Laws and International Treaties prohibit unauthorized publication, reproduction, distribution of this Work. Unauthorized use of this copyright in any form, format, publication or document may result in severe civil and criminal penalties. Violations of this copyright are investigated by the United States Department of Justice and carry, upon conviction of fines up to $250,000 and five years confinement. This Work is protected by United States Copyright Laws and International Treaties. Do not Copy, do not reproduce, do not distribute.

A Ficus Tree Publishing Quick Notes Page.

DU VALL'S TEST'S™
Instructors Manual Study Guide Series United States Tax Code
IRS Publication 15 Circular E, Employer's Tax Guide Tax Year 2013
Tax Test Reminders Test 15E-R2 [Questions With Answers]

Reminders: Credit or debit card payments. Page 3.

1. For information on paying your taxes with a credit or debit card, visit the IRS website at ___.
   (a) *www.irs.gov/u-pay*
   (b) *www.irs.gov/e-pay*
   (c) *www.irs.gov/c-pay*
   (d) *www.irs.gov/u-pay2*
   Answer: See Circular E, Electronic Filing and Payment. Page 3/ (b) *www.irs.gov/e-pay*

2. For information on paying your taxes with a credit or debit card, visit the IRS website at *www.irs.gov/e-pay*. However, do not use credit or debit cards to make ___ tax deposits.
   (a) annual
   (b) IRS
   (c) federal
   (d) Federal
   Answer: See Circular E, Electronic Filing and Payment. Page 3/ (c) federal

Reminders: Forms in Spanish. Page 3.

3. You can provide Formulario ___, Certificado de Exención de Retenciones del Empleado, in place of Form W-4, Employee's Withholding Allowance Certificate, to your Spanish-speaking employees.
   (a) W-4(SP)
   (b) W-4(sp)
   (c) W-5(SP)
   (d) W-5(sp)
   Answer: See Circular E, Forms in Spanish. Page 3/ (a) W-4(SP)

4. You can provide Formulario ___, Certificado de Exención de Retenciones del Empleado, in place of Form W-4, Employee's Withholding Allowance Certificate, to your Spanish-speaking employees. For more information, see Publicación ___, El Impuesto Federal sobre los Ingresos (Para Personas Fisicas).
   (a) W-4(SP), 17(SP)
   (b) W-4(sp), 18(SP)
   (c) W-5(SP), 17(sp)
   (d) W-5(sp), 18(sp)
   Answer: See Circular E, Forms in Spanish. Page 3/ (a) W-4(SP), 17(SP)

© Copyright 2013. All rights reserved. Notice: United States Copyright Laws and International Treaties prohibit unauthorized publication, reproduction, distribution of this Work. Unauthorized use of this copyright in any form, format, publication or document may result in severe civil and criminal penalties. Violations of this copyright are investigated by the United States Department of Justice and carry, upon conviction of fines up to $250,000 and five years confinement. This Work is protected by United States Copyright Laws and International Treaties. Do not Copy, do not reproduce, do not distribute.

The International Leader in Construction Technology Home Study

Reminders: Forms in Spanish. Page 3.

5. You can provide Formulario ___, Certificado de Exención de Retenciones del Empleado, in place of Form W-4, Employee's Withholding Allowance Certificate, to your Spanish-speaking employees. For more information, see Publicación ___, El Impuesto Federal sobre los Ingresos (Para Personas Fisicas). For nonemployees, Formulario ___, Solicitud y Certificación del Nùmero de Identificaión del Contribuyente, may be used in place of Form W-9, Request for Taxpayer Identification Number and Certification.
   (a) W-4(SP), 17(SP)
   (b) W-4(sp), 18(SP)
   (c) W-5(SP), 17(sp)
   (d) W-5(sp), 18(sp)
   Answer: See Circular E, Forms in Spanish. Page 3/ (a) W-4(SP), 17(SP)

Reminders: Hiring New Employees. Eligibility for employment. Page 3.

6. You must verify that each new employee is ___ to work in the United States.
   (a) legal
   (b) certified
   (c) eligible
   (d) legally eligible
   Answer: See Circular E, Eligibility for Employment. Page 3/ (d) legally eligible

7. You must verify that each new employee is ___ to work in the United States. This includes completing the U.S. Citizenship and Immigration Services (USCIS) Form ___, Employment Verification.
   (a) legal, I-4
   (b) certified, I-6
   (c) eligible, I-8
   (d) legally eligible, I-9
   Answer: See Circular E, page 3/ (d) legally eligible, I-9

8. You must verify that each new employee is ___ to work in the United States. This includes completing the **U.S. Citizenship and Immigration Services (USCIS)** Form ___, Employment Verification. You can get the form from the USCIS offices or by calling 1-800-___-3676.
   (a) legal, I-4, 375
   (b) certified, I-6, 375
   (c) eligible, I-8, 870
   (d) legally eligible, I-9, 870
   Answer: See Circular E, page 3/ (d) legally eligible, I-9, 870

Reminders: Hiring New Employees. Eligibility for employment. Page 3.

9. You must verify that each new employee is ___ to work in the United States. This includes completing the U.S. Citizenship and Immigration Services (USCIS) Form ___, Employment Verification. You can get the form from the USCIS offices or by calling 1-800-___-3676. Contact the USCIS at ____ or visit the USCIS website at *www.uscis.gov* for more information.
   (a) legal, I-4, 375, 1-866-374-8352
   (b) certified, I-6, 375, 1-800-377-5283
   (c) eligible, I-8, 870, 1-800-376-3582
   (d) legally eligible, I-9, 870, 1-800-375-5283
   Answer: See Circular E, page 3/ (d) legally eligible, I-9, 870, 1-800-375-5283

Reminders: New hire reporting. Page 3.

10. You are required to report any new employee to a designated state new hire ___.
    (a) division
    (b) department
    (c) agency
    (d) registry
    Answer: See Circular E, page 3/ (d) registry

11. You are required to report any new employee to a designated state new hire ___. A new employee is an employee who has not previously been employed by you or was previously employed by you but has been separated from such prior employment for at least ___ consecutive days.
    (a) division, 30
    (b) department, 30
    (c) agency, 60
    (d) registry, 60
    Answer: See Circular E, page 3/ (d) registry, 60

12. You are required to report any new employee to a designated state new hire ___. A new employee is an employee who has not previously been employed by you or was previously employed by you but has been separated from such prior employment for at least ___ consecutive days. Many states accept a copy of Form W-4 with ___ added.
    (a) division, 30, employer-employee information
    (b) department, 30, employee-employer information
    (c) agency, 60, employee information
    (d) registry, 60, employer information
    Answer: See Circular E, page 3/ (d) registry, 60, employer information

Reminders: Hiring New Employees -W-4 request. Page 3.

13. Many states accept a copy of Form W-4 with employer information added. Visit the Office of Child Support Enforcement website at *www.acf.hhs.gov/programs/cse/____* for more information.
    (a)   *new*
    (b)   *newhire*
    (c)   *new emp*
    (d)   *new employee*
    Answer: See Circular E, page 3/ (b) *newhire*

14. Ask each new employee to complete the 2013 Form W-4. See section____.
    (a)   3
    (b)   6
    (c)   9
    (d)   11
    Answer: See Circular E, Hiring new Employees. Page 3/ (c) 9

Reminders: Name and social security number. Page 3.

15. Record each new employee's name and number from his or her social security __.
    (a)   form
    (b)   card
    (c)   information
    (d)   document
    Answer: See Circular E, pages 3 and 4/ (b) card

16. Record each new employee's name and number from his or her social security __. Any employee without a social security card should apply for one. See section__.
    (a)   form, 3
    (b)   card, 4,
    (c)   information, 5
    (d)   document, 7
    Answer: See Circular E, pages 3 and 4/ (b) card, 4

Paying Wages, Pensions, or Annuities
Correcting Form 941 or Form 944

17. If you discover an error on a previously filed Form 941 or Form 944, make the correction using Form ____, Adjusted Employers ____ federal Tax Return or Claim for Refund, or Form 944-X, Adjusted Employer's ANNUAL Federal Tax Return or Claim for Refund.
    (a) 940-X, MONTHLY
    (b) 941-X, QUARTERLY
    (c) 942-X, SEMI-ANNUAL
    (d) 943-Y, ANNUAL
    Answer: See Circular E. Correcting Form 941 or Form 944. Page 4./ (b) 941-X, QUARTERLY

18. Forms ___ and ___ are stand alone forms, meaning taxpayers can file them when an error is discovered.
    (a) 940, 943
    (b) 941, 944
    (c) 940-X, 943-X
    (d) 941-X, 944-X
    Answer: See Circular E. Page 4. Correcting Form 941 or Form 944/ (d) 941-X, 944-X

19. Forms ___ and ___ are used by employers to claim refunds and ___ of employment taxes, rather than Form ___.
    (a) 940, 943, back charges, 844
    (b) 941, 944, relief, 844
    (c) 940-X, 943-X, overpayments, 843
    (d) 941-X, 944-X, abatements, 843
    Answer: See Circular E. Page 4. Correcting Form 941 or Form 944/ (d) 941-X, 944-X, abatements, 843

20. Forms ___ and ___ are used by employers to claim refunds and ___ of employment taxes, rather than Form ___. See section ___ for more information.
    (a) 940, 943, back charges, 844, 12
    (b) 941, 944, relief, 844, 12
    (c) 940-X, 943-X, overpayments, 843, 13
    (d) 941-X, 944-X, abatements, 843, 13
    Answer: See Circular E. Page 4. Correcting Form 941 or Form 944/ (d) 941-X, 944-X, abatements, 843, 13

Paying Wages, Pensions, or Annuities
Correcting Form 941 or Form 944

21. Withhold federal income tax from each wage payment or supplemental unemployment compensation plan benefit payment according to the employee's Form W___ and the correct withholding table.
    (a) 2
    (b) 3
    (c) 4
    (d) 5
    Answer: See Circular E. Page 4. Paying Wages, Pensions, or Annuities. Income tax withholding/ (a) 2

22. Withhold federal income tax from each wage payment or supplemental unemployment compensation plan benefit payment according to the employee's Form W___ and the correct withholding table. If you have **nonresident alien employees**, see *Withholding income tax on the ___ wages of nonresident alien employee's* in section ___.
    (a) 2, 9
    (b) 3, 9
    (c) 4, 10
    (d) 5, 10
    Answer: See Circular E, page 4, Paying Wages, Pensions, or Annuities - Income tax withholding/ (a) 2, 9

23. Withhold from periodic **pension and annuity payments** as if the recipient is married claiming ___ withholding allowances, unless he or she has provided Form W-___, Withholding Certificate for Pension or Annuity Payments,
    (a) zero, 4A
    (b) two, 4C
    (c) three, 4P
    (d) four or more, 4X
    Answer: See Circular E, page 4, Paying Wages, Pensions, or Annuities - Income tax withholding/ (c) three, 4P

Reminders: Income tax withholding

24. Withhold from periodic **pension and annuity payments** as if the recipient is married claiming ___ withholding allowances, unless he or she has provided Form W-___, Withholding Certificate for Pension or Annuity Payments, either electing no withholding or giving a different number of allowances, marital status, or additional ___ to be withheld.
    (a) zero, 4A, number
    (b) two, 4C, number
    (c) three, 4P, amount
    (d) four or more, 4X, amount
    Answer: See Circular E, page 4, Paying Wages, Pensions, or Annuities - Income tax withholding/ (c) three, 4P, amount

Paying Wages, Pensions, or Annuities. Income tax withholding

25. Do not withhold on direct ___ from qualified plans or governmental section ___(b) plans.
    (a) income, 457
    (b) rollovers, 457
    (c) payments, 458
    (d) withholding, 458
    Answer: See Circular E, page 4, Paying Wages, Pensions, or Annuities. Income tax withholding/ (b) rollovers, 457

26. Do not withhold on direct ___ from qualified plans or governmental section ___(b) plans. See section ___ and Publication 15-A, Employer's Supplemental Tax Guide.
    (a) income, 457, 8
    (b) rollovers, 457, 9
    (c) payments, 458, 10
    (d) withholding, 458, 11
    Answer: See Circular E, page 4, Paying Wages, Pensions, or Annuities - Income tax withholding/ (b) rollovers, 457, 9

27. Do not withhold on direct ___ from qualified plans or governmental section ___(b) plans. See section ___ and Publication 15-A, Employer's Supplemental Tax Guide. Publication 15-A includes information about withholding on ___.
    (a) income, 457, 8, personal income tax and dependents
    (b) rollovers, 457, 9, pensions and annuities
    (c) payments, 458, 10, pensions and annuities
    (d) withholding, 458, 11, personal income tax and dependents
    Answer: See Circular E, page 4, Paying Wages, Pensions, or Annuities - Income tax withholding/ (b) rollovers, 457, 9, pensions and annuities

Reminders: Paying Wages, Pensions, or Annuities. Zero wage return

28. If you have not filed a "____" Form 941 or Form 944, or are not a "___" employer, you must continue to file a Form 941 or Form 944 even for periods during which you paid ___ wages.
    (a) final, seasonal, no
    (b) ending, new, employee
    (c) ending, new, employer
    (d) completed, seasonal, no
    Answer: See Circular E, page 4, Paying Wages, Pensions, or Annuities - Zero wage return/ (a) final, seasonal, no

29. If you have not filed a "____" Form 941 or Form 944, or are not a "___" employer, you must continue to file a Form 941 or Form 944 even for periods during which you paid ___ wages. The IRS encourages you to file your "___" Forms 941, or 944 electronically using IRS e-file at *www.irs.gov/efile*.
    (a) final, seasonal, no, Zero Wage
    (b) ending, new, employee, Zero Wages
    (c) ending, new, employer, Zero Wages
    (d) completed, seasonal, no, Zero Wage
    Answer: See Circular E, page 4, Paying Wages, Pensions, or Annuities - Zero wage return/ (a) final, seasonal, no, Zero Wage

Reminders: Employer Responsibilities

"**Employer Responsibilities:** The following list provides a brief summary of your basic responsibilities. Because the individual circumstances for each employer can vary greatly, responsibilities for withholding, depositing, and reporting employment taxes can differ. Each item in this list has a page reference to a more detailed discussion in this publication."

30. The following provides a brief summary of your ___ responsibilities. Because the individual circumstances for each employer can vary greatly, responsibilities for withholding, depositing and reporting ___ taxes can differ.
    (a) mandatory, income
    (b) direct, income
    (c) compulsory, each employee
    (d) basic, employment
    Answer: See Circular E, **Employer Responsibilities, page 4**/ (d) basic, employment

The International Leader in Construction Technology Home Study

Reminders: Employer Responsibilities

31. The following provides a brief summary of your ___responsibilities. Because the individual circumstances for each employer can vary greatly, responsibilities for withholding, depositing and reporting ___ taxes can differ. Each item in this list has a ___ reference to a more detailed discussion in this section.
    (a) mandatory, income, page
    (b) direct, income, section
    (c) compulsory, each employee, section
    (d) basic, employment, page
    Answer: See Circular E, **Employer Responsibilities, page 4**/ (d) basic, employment, page

32. New Employees: Verify work ___ of new employees.
    (a) experience
    (b) papers
    (c) eligibility
    (d) social security card
    Answer: See Circular E. **Employer Responsibilities**: Page 4. New employees/ (c) eligibility.

33. New Employees: Record employees' names and ___ from social security cards.
    (a) SSNs
    (b) USNs
    (c) INSs
    (d) DOB
    Answer: See Circular E. **Employer Responsibilities**: Page 4. New employees/ (a) SSNs.

34. New Employees: Ask employees for Form___.
    (a) W-1
    (b) W-2
    (c) W-3
    (d) W-4
    Answer: See Circular E. **Employer Responsibilities**: Page 4. New employees/ (d) W-4.

35. New Employees: Each Payday: Withhold federal income tax based on each employee's Form ___.
    (a) W-1
    (b) W-2
    (c) W-3
    (d) W-4
    Answer: See Circular E. **Employer Responsibilities**: Page 4. New employees/ (d) W-4.

© Copyright 2013. All rights reserved. Notice: United States Copyright Laws and International Treaties prohibit unauthorized publication, reproduction, distribution of this Work. Unauthorized use of this copyright in any form, format, publication or document may result in severe civil and criminal penalties. Violations of this copyright are investigated by the United States Department of Justice and carry, upon conviction of fines up to $250,000 and five years confinement. This Work is protected by United States Copyright Laws and International Treaties. Do not Copy, do not reproduce, do not distribute.

A Ficus Tree Publishing Educational-Technical Publications

Reminders: Employer Responsibilities

36. New Employees: Each Payday: Withhold ___ share of social security and Medicare taxes.
    (a) employee's
    (b) employers
    (c) taxable
    (d) FUTA
    Answer: See Circular E. **Employer Responsibilities**: Page 4. New employees/ (a) employee's.

37. New Employees: Each Payday: Deposit:
    • Withheld income tax
    • Withheld and ___ social security taxes
    • Withheld and ___ Medicare taxes
    (a) employee, employee
    (b) employee, employer
    (c) employer, employee
    (d) employer, employer
    Answer: See Circular E. **Employer Responsibilities**: Page 4. New employees/ (d) employer, employer.

    Note: *Due date of deposit generally depends on your deposit schedule. (monthly or semiweekly).*

Reminders: Employer Responsibilities. FUTA Tax. Page 4

38. Quarterly (By April 30, July 31, October 31, and January 31):
    Employer's must: Deposit **FUTA** tax if the undeposited amount is over $___.
    (a) 500
    (b) 600
    (c) 1000
    (d) 1500
    Answer: See Circular E, **Employer Responsibilities, page 4**/ (a) 500

39. Employer's must verify the work eligibility of ___ employees.
    (a) all
    (b) new
    (c) permanent
    (d) temporary
    Answer: See Circular E, **Employer Responsibilities, page 4**/ (b) new

DU VALL'S TEST'S™
Instructors Manual Study Guide Series United States Tax Code
IRS Publication 15 Circular E, Employer's Tax Guide Tax Year 2013
Tax Test: Reminders Test R-3 [Questions With Answers]

Reminders: Employer Responsibilities. Page 4.

1. Employer's must: Record new employees' names and SSNs from ___.
   - (a) picture ID cards
   - (b) current drivers licenses
   - (c) social security cards
   - (d) birth records and legal documents

   Answer: See Circular E, **Employer Responsibilities, page 4**/ (c) social security cards

2. Each Payday: Employers must: Withhold employee's share of social security and ___ taxes.
   - (a) income
   - (b) employment
   - (c) withholding
   - (d) Medicare

   Answer: See Circular E, **Employer Responsibilities, page 4**/ (d) Medicare

Paying Wages, Pensions, or Annuities Employer Responsibilities Quarterly (By April 30, July 31, October 31, and January 31)

3. Deposit ___ tax if undeposited amount is over $500.
   - (a) FUTA
   - (b) FICA
   - (c) Medicare
   - (d) COBRA

   Answer: See Circular E, **Employer Responsibilities, page 4**/ (a) FUTA

Paying Wages, Pensions, or Annuities Employer Responsibilities Quarterly (By April 30, July 31, October 31, and January 31)

4. File Form ___ (pay tax with return if not required to deposit)
   - (a) 904
   - (b) 940
   - (c) 941
   - (d) 942

   Answer: See Circular E, **Employer Responsibilities, page 4**/ (c) 941

© Copyright 2013. All rights reserved. Notice: United States Copyright Laws and International Treaties prohibit unauthorized publication, reproduction, distribution of this Work. Unauthorized use of this copyright in any form, format, publication or document may result in severe civil and criminal penalties. Violations of this copyright are investigated by the United States Department of Justice and carry, upon conviction of fines up to $250,000 and five years confinement. This Work is protected by United States Copyright Laws and International Treaties. Do not Copy, do not reproduce, do not distribute.

A Ficus Tree Publishing Educational-Technical Publications

Paying Wages, Pensions, or Annuities Employer Responsibilities Quarterly (By April 30, July 31, October 31, and January 31)

5. Information regarding the depositing of FUTA tax is located on page ___ of the February 2013 Edition of IRS Publication 15, Employer's Tax Guide for use in 2013.
   - (a) 5
   - (b) 25
   - (c) 30
   - (d) 35

   Answer: See Circular E, **Employer Responsibilities, page 4**/ (d) 35

6. Information regarding the filing of Form 941 is located on page ___ of the February 2013 Edition of IRS Publication 15, Employer's Tax Guide for use in 2013.
   - (a) 5
   - (b) 25
   - (c) 30
   - (d) 35

   Answer: See Circular E, **Employer Responsibilities, page 4**/ (c) 30

Paying Wages, Pensions, or Annuities Employer Responsibilities Annually (By January 31 of the current year, for the prior year)

7. File Form ___ if required (pay tax with return if not required to deposit).
   - (a) 941
   - (b) 942
   - (c) 943
   - (d) 944

   Answer: See Circular E, **Employer Responsibilities, page 4**/ (d) 944

8. Information regarding the filing of Form 944 is located on page ___ of the February 2013 Edition of IRS Publication 15, Employer's Tax Guide for use in 2013.
   - (a) 5
   - (b) 25
   - (c) 30
   - (d) 35

   Answer: See Circular E, **Employer Responsibilities, page 4**/ (c) 30

Paying Wages, Pensions, or Annuities Employer Responsibilities
Annually (see: Calendar for due dates)

9. Remind employees to submit a new Form W-___ if they need to change their withholding.
   (a) 2
   (b) 3
   (c) 4
   (d) 5
   Answer: See Circular E, **Employer Responsibilities, page 4**/ (c) 4

10. Ask for a new Form W-4 from employees claiming ___ from income tax withholding.
    (a) exemption
    (b) exemptions
    (c) additional exemptions
    (d) more than 4 exemptions
    Answer: See Circular E, **Employer Responsibilities, page 4**/ (a) exemption

11. Information regarding annually new Form W-4 is located on pages ___ and ___ of the February 2013 Edition of Publication 15, IRS Circular E, Employer's Tax Guide for use in 2013.
    (a) 3, 4
    (b) 19, 20
    (c) 20, 21
    (d) 25, 26
    Answer: See Circular E, **Employer Responsibilities, page 4**/ (c) 20, 21

12. **Annually (see: Calendar for due dates);** Reconcile Forms ___ (or Form ___) with Forms ___ and ___.
    (a) 941, 944, W-2, W-3
    (b) 941, 945, W-2, W-4
    (c) 942, 945, W-3, W-4
    (d) 943, 944, W-2, W-4
    Answer: See Circular E, **Employer Responsibilities, page 4**/ (a) 941, 944, W-2, W-3

13. Information regarding the requirement to reconcile Forms 941 (or Form 944) with Forms W-2 and W-3 is located on page ___ of the February 2013 Edition of IRS Circular E, Publication 15 Employer's Tax Guide to 2013.
    (a) 3
    (b) 19
    (c) 25
    (d) 31
    Answer: See Circular E, **Employer Responsibilities, page 4**/ (d) 31

Paying Wages, Pensions, or Annuities Employer Responsibilities Annually (see: Calendar for due dates)

14. Annually, the employer is required to provide each employee a Form ___.
    (a) 2
    (b) 3
    (c) 4
    (d) 5
    Answer: See Circular E, **Employer Responsibilities, page 4**/ (a) 2

15. Annually, the employer is required to File Copy ___ of Forms W-2 and the transmittal Form W- ___ with the SSA.
    (a) A, 2
    (b) A, 3
    (c) B, 4
    (d) B, 5
    Answer: See Circular E, **Employer Responsibilities, page 4**/ (b) A, 3

16. Furnish each other payee a Form ___(for example, Form 1099-MISC, Miscellaneous Income).
    (a) 1049
    (b) 1079
    (c) 1089
    (d) 1099
    Answer: See Circular E, **Employer Responsibilities, page 4**/ (d) 1099

17. Information related to Form 1099 may be located on page ___ of the February Edition of the 2013 IRS Publication 15 Circular E, Employer's Tax Guide.
    (a) 2
    (b) 4
    (c) 6
    (d) 8
    Answer: See Circular E, **Employer Responsibilities, page 4**/ (d) 8

18. Information to file Forms 1099 and the transmittal Form ___ will be located on page 8 of IRS Circular E Publication 15, Employer's Tax Guide.
    (a) 1079
    (b) 1089
    (c) 1096
    (d) 1099
    Answer: See Circular E, **Employer Responsibilities, page 4**/ (c) 1096

Paying Wages, Pensions, or Annuities Employer Responsibilities Annually (see: Calendar for due dates)

19. The employer is required to file Form ___ for any nonpayroll income tax withholding.
    (a) 940
    (b) 942
    (c) 944
    (d) 945
    Answer: See Circular E, **Employer Responsibilities, page 4** / (d) 945

Reminders: Information Returns. Page 4 and Page 5.

20. You may be required to file ____ returns to report certain types of payments made during the year.
    (a) information
    (b) tax
    (c) reports
    (d) tax reports and
    Answer: See Circular E, page 4, Information Returns / (a) information

21. You may be required to file ____ returns to report certain types of payments made during the year. For example, you must file Form ___-MISC, Miscellaneous Income, to report payments of $600 or more to persons not treated as employees (for example, independent contractors) for services performed for your trade or business.
    (a) information, 1099
    (b) tax, 1099
    (c) reports, 2013
    (d) tax reports and, 2013
    Answer: See Circular E, pages 4 and 5, Information Returns / (a) information, 1099

22. You may be required to file information returns to report certain types of payments made during the year. For example, you must file Form 1099-MISC, Miscellaneous Income, to report payments of $600 or more to persons not treated as employees (for example, independent contractors) for services performed for your trade or business. For details about filing Forms 1099 and for information about required electronic filing, see the ___ for Certain Information Returns for general information and the separate, specific instructions for ___ information return you file (for example, Instructions for Form 1099-MISC).
    (a) Special Instructions, all
    (b) General Instructions, all
    (c) Special Instructions each
    (d) General Instructions, each
    Answer: See Circular E, pages 4 and 5, Information Returns / (d) General Instructions, each

Reminders: Information Returns. Forms 1099. Page 5.

23. Generally, do not use Forms 1099 to report ___ and ___ compensation you paid to employees; report these on Form W-2 Wage and Tax Statement.
    (a) income, wages
    (b) wages, other
    (c) taxes, other
    (d) income, additional
    Answer: See Circular E, page 5, Information Returns / (b) wages, other

24. Generally, do not use Forms 1099 to report wages and other compensation you paid to employees; report these on Form W-2 Wage and Tax Statement. See the General Instructions for Forms W-__ and W-__ for details about filing Form W-2 and for information about required electronic filing.
    (a) 2, 3
    (b) 2, 4
    (c) 3, 4
    (d) 4, 4X
    Answer: See Circular E, page 5, Information Returns / (a) 2, 3

25. If you file ___ or more Forms 1099 you must file them electronically.
    (a) 150
    (b) 250
    (c) 300
    (d) 350
    Answer: See Circular E, page 5, Information Returns / (b) 250

26. If you file ___ or more Forms W-2 you must file them electronically.
    (a) 150
    (b) 250
    (c) 300
    (d) 350
    Answer: See Circular E, page 5, Information Returns / (b) 250

27. SSA ___ Forms W-2 and W-3 filed on ____.
    (a) paper
    (b) computer disks
    (c) electronic media
    (d) magnetic media
    Answer: See Circular E, page 5, Information Returns/ (d) magnetic media

The International Leader in Construction Technology Home Study

Information Returns. Information reporting customer service site Enterprise Computing Center:

28. The IRS operates the Enterprise Computing Center—___,
    (a) Virginia
    (b) Norfolk
    (c) Washington
    (d) Martinsburg
    Answer: See Circular E, page 5, Information Returns/ (d) Martinsburg

29. The IRS operates the Enterprise Computing Center—Martinsburg, a centralized customer service site, to answer questions about ___ on Forms W-2, W-3, 1099, and other information returns.
    (a) misunderstanding
    (b) problems
    (c) filing
    (d) reporting
    Answer: See Circular E, page 5, Information Returns/ (d) reporting.

30. The IRS operates the Enterprise Computing Center—Martinsburg, a centralized customer service site, to answer questions about ___ on Forms W-2, W-3, 1099, and other information returns. If you have questions related to reporting on information returns, call 1-866-455-___ (toll free), 304-263-8700 (toll call), or
    (a) misunderstanding, 7437
    (b) problems, 7437
    (c) filing, 7438
    (d) reporting, 7438
    Answer: See Circular E, page 5, Information Returns/ (d) reporting, 7438

31. The IRS operates the Enterprise Computing Center—Martinsburg, a centralized customer service site, to answer questions about ___ on Forms W-2, W-3, 1099, and other information returns. If you have questions related to reporting on information returns, call 1-866-455-___ (toll free), 304-263-8700 (toll call), or 304-267-3367 (TDD/TTY for persons who are deaf, hard of hearing, or have a speech ___).
    (a) misunderstanding, 7437, difficulty
    (b) problems, 7437, impediment
    (c) filing, 7438, problem
    (d) reporting, 7438, disability
    Answer: See Circular E, page 5, Information Returns/ (d) reporting, 7438, disability

© Copyright 2013. All rights reserved. Notice: United States Copyright Laws and International Treaties prohibit unauthorized publication, reproduction, distribution of this Work. Unauthorized use of this copyright in any form, format, publication or document may result in severe civil and criminal penalties. Violations of this copyright are investigated by the United States Department of Justice and carry, upon conviction of fines up to $250,000 and five years confinement. This Work is protected by United States Copyright Laws and International Treaties. Do not Copy, do not reproduce, do not distribute.

Information Returns. Information reporting customer service site Enterprise Computing Center:

32. The IRS operates the Enterprise Computing Center—Martinsburg, a centralized customer service site, to answer questions about ___ on Forms W-2, W-3, 1099, and other information returns. If you have questions related to reporting on information returns, call 1-866-455-___ (toll free), 304-263-8700 (toll call), or 304-267-3367 (TDD/TTY for persons who are deaf, hard of hearing, or have a speech ___). The center can also be reached by email at *m---irp@irs.gov*.
    (a) misunderstanding, 7437, difficulty, *ee*
    (b) problems, 7437, impediment, *aa*
    (c) filing, 7438, problem, *bb*
    (d) reporting, 7438, disability, *cc*
    Answer: See Circular E, page 5, Information Returns/ (d) reporting, 7438, disability, *cc*

REMINDERS: Nonpayroll Income Tax Withholding. Page 5

33. Nonpayroll federal income tax withholding (reported on Forms ___ and Form ___) must be reported
    (a) W-2, W-4
    (b) 941, 944
    (c) 1099, W-2G
    (d) 1098, 1099
    Answer: See Circular E, page 5, Nonpayroll Income Tax Withholding/ (c) 1099, W-2G

34. Nonpayroll federal income tax withholding (reported on Forms ___ and Form ___) must be reported on Form ___, Annual Return of Withheld Federal Income Tax.
    (a) W-2, W-4, 940
    (b) 941, 944, 941
    (c) 1099, W-2G, 945
    (d) 1098, 1099, 946
    Answer: See Circular E, page 5, Nonpayroll Income Tax Withholding/ (c) 1099, W-2G, 945

35. Nonpayroll federal income tax withholding (reported on Forms 1099 and Form W-2G) must be reported on Form 945, Annual Return of Withheld Federal Income Tax. Separate deposits are required for payroll (Form ___ or Form ___) and nonpayroll (Form ___ withholding.
    (a) 941, 944, 945
    (b) 941, 943, 944
    (c) 941, 943, 940
    (d) 940, W-2, W-4
    Answer: See Circular E, page 5, Nonpayroll Income Tax Withholding/ (a) 941, 944, 945

Nonpayroll Income Tax Withholding

36. Nonpayroll items include:
    • Pensions (including distributions from tax-favored retirement plans, for example, section 401(k), section 403(b), and governmental section ___ plans) and annuities.
    (a) 457(a)
    (b) 457(b)
    (c) 457(c)
    (d) 457(d)
    Answer: See Circular E, page 5, Nonpayroll Income Tax Withholding/ (b) 457(b)

37. Nonpayroll items include:
    • Pensions (including distributions from tax-favored retirement plans, for example, section 401(k), section 403(b), and governmental section 457(b) plans) and annuities.
    • Military retirement
    • Gambling winnings
    • Indian gaming profits
    • Certain government payments such as unemployment compensation, social security, and Tier ___ railroad retirement benefits, subject to voluntary withholding.
    (a) 1
    (b) 2
    (c) 3
    (d) 4
    Answer: See Circular E, page 5, Nonpayroll Income Tax Withholding/ (a) 1

38. Nonpayroll items include:
    • Pensions (including distributions from tax-favored retirement plans, for example, section 401(k), section 403(b), and governmental section 457(b) plans) and annuities.
    • Military retirement
    • Gambling winnings
    • Indian gaming profits
    • Certain government payments such as unemployment compensation, social security, and Tier 1 railroad retirement benefits, subject to voluntary withholding.
    • Payments subject to ___ withholding
    (a) front end
    (b) backup
    (c) special
    (d) conditional
    Answer: See Circular E, page 5, Nonpayroll Income Tax Withholding/ (b) backup

Nonpayroll Income Tax Withholding

39. For details on depositing and reporting nonpayroll income tax withholding, see the instructions for Form __.
    (a) 941
    (b) 942
    (c) 943
    (d) 945
    Answer: See Circular E, page 5, Nonpayroll Income Tax Withholding/ (d) 945

40. All income tax withholding reported on Form W-2 must be reported on Form 941, Form 943, Form 944, or ___.
    (a) Schedule B (Form 1099)
    (b) Schedule M (Form 1089)
    (c) Schedule H (Form 1040)
    (d) Schedule A (Form 1025)
    Answer: See Circular E, page 5, Nonpayroll Income Tax Withholding/ (c) Schedule H (Form 1040)

DU VALL'S TEST'S™
Instructors Manual Study Guide Series United States Tax Code
IRS Publication 15 Circular E, Employer's Tax Guide Tax Year 2013
Tax Test Reminders Test 15E-R4 [Questions With Answers]

Distributions from nonqualified pension plans and deferred compensation plans. Page 5.

1. Because distributions to participants from some non qualified pension plans and deferred compensation plans (including section ___ plans of tax-exempt organizations) are treated as wages and
   (a) 456(a)
   (b) 457(b)
   (c) 458(c)
   (d) 459(d)
   Answer: See Circular E, page 5, Nonpayroll Income Tax Withholding/ (b) 457(b)

2. Because distributions to participants from some non qualified pension plans and deferred compensation plans (including section ___ plans of tax-exempt organizations) are treated as wages and are reported on Form W-2, income tax withheld must be reported on Form 941 or Form 944, not on Form ___.
   (a) 456(a), 943
   (b) 457(b), 945
   (c) 458(c), 946
   (d) 459(d), 1089
   Answer: See Circular E, page 5, Nonpayroll Income Tax Withholding/ (b) 457(b), 945

3. Because distributions to participants from some non qualified pension plans and deferred compensation plans (including section ___ plans of tax-exempt organizations) are treated as wages and are reported on Form W-2, income tax withheld must be reported on Form 941 or Form 944, not on Form ___. However, distributions from such plans to a beneficiary or estate of a deceased employee are not wages and are reported on Forms ___,
   (a) 456(a), 943, 1089-A
   (b) 457(b), 945, 1099-R
   (c) 458(c), 946, 1099-S
   (d) 459(d), 1089, 2103-R
   Answer: See Circular E, Nonpayroll Income Tax Withholding. Page 5./(b) 457(b),945, 1099-R

Distributions from nonqualified pension plans and deferred compensation plans. Page 5.

4. Because distributions to participants from some non qualified pension plans and deferred compensation plans (including section ___ plans of tax-exempt organizations) are treated as wages and are reported on Form W-2, income tax withheld must be reported on Form 941 or Form 944, not on Form ___. However, distributions from such plans to a beneficiary or estate of a deceased employee are not wages and are reported on Forms ___, Distributions From Pensions, Annuities, Retirement or Profit-Sharing Plans, IRAs, Insurance Contracts, etc.; income tax withheld must be reported on Form ___.
   (a) 456(a), 943, 1089-A, 941
   (b) 457(b), 945, 1099-R, 945
   (c) 458(c), 946, 1099-S, 944
   (d) 459(d), 1089, 2103-R, 945
   Answer: See Circular E, page 5, Nonpayroll Income Tax Withholding/ (b) 457(b), 945, 1099-R, 945

Reminders: Nonpayroll Income Tax Withholding - Backup withholding. Page 5.

5. You generally must withhold ___% of certain taxable if the payee fails to furnish you with his or her correct taxpayer identification number (TIN)
   (a) 22
   (b) 27.5
   (c) 28
   (d) 34.6
   Answer: See Circular E, page 5, Nonpayroll Income Tax Withholding/ (c) 28

6. You generally must withhold ___% of certain taxable if the payee fails to furnish you with his or her correct taxpayer identification number (TIN). This withholding is referred to a "___".
   (a) 22, backup withholding
   (b) 27.5, tax reserve
   (c) 28, backup withholding
   (d) 34.6, reserve
   Answer: See Circular E, page 5, Nonpayroll Income Tax Withholding/ (c) 28, backup withholding

7. Payments subject to backup withholding include interest, dividends, patronage dividends, rents, royalties, commissions, ___ compensation, and certain other payments you make in the course of your trade or business.
   (a) employer
   (b) employee
   (c) nonemployee
   (d) non-employer
   Answer: See Circular E, page 5, Nonpayroll Income Tax Withholding/ (c) nonemployee

Nonpayroll Income Tax Withholding - Backup withholding

8. Payments subject to backup withholding include interest, dividends, patronage dividends, rents, royalties, commissions, ___ compensation, and certain other payments you make in the course of your trade or business. In addition, transactions by brokers and barter exchanges and certain made by ___ operators are subject to backup withholding.
   (a) employer, real estate
   (b) employee, commercial airline
   (c) nonemployee, fishing boat
   (d) non-employer, aircraft
   Answer: See Circular E, page 5, Nonpayroll Income Tax Withholding/ (c) nonemployee, fishing boat

Nonpayroll Income Tax Withholding
Backup withholding Caution Note

9. Backup withholding does not apply wages, pensions, annuities, IRAs (including simplified employee pension (SEP) and ___ retirement plans),
   (a) UNION
   (b) MUNICIPAL
   (c) GOVERNMENTAL
   (d) SIMPLE
   Answer: See Circular E, page 5, Nonpayroll Income Tax Withholding, Caution Note/ (d) SIMPLE

10. Backup withholding does not apply wages, pensions, annuities, IRAs (including simplified employee pension (SEP) and ___ retirement plans), section ___(k) distributions from an employee stock ownership plan (ESOP), medical savings accounts, long-term-care benefits, or real estate transactions.
    (a) UNION, 401
    (b) MUNICIPAL, 402
    (c) GOVERNMENTAL, 403
    (d) SIMPLE, 404
    Answer: See Circular E, page 5, Nonpayroll Income Tax Withholding, Caution Note/ (d) SIMPLE, 404

11. You can use Form W-___ or Formulario W-___ (SP) to request payees to furnish a TIN and to certify the number is correct.
    (a) 2, 2
    (b) 4, 4
    (c) 7, 7
    (d) 9, 9
    Answer: See Circular E, page 5, Nonpayroll Income Tax Withholding, Caution Note/ (d) 9, 9

REMINDERS: RECORDKEEPING

12. Keep all records of employment taxes for at least ___ years.
    (a) 3
    (b) 4
    (c) 5
    (d) 7
    Answer: See Circular E, page 5, Recordkeeping/ (b) 4

13. Keep all records of employment taxes **for at least 4 years**. These should be available for ___ review.
    (a) Accounting
    (b) Audit
    (c) IRS
    (d) Comparison
    Answer: See Circular E, page 5, Recordkeeping/ (c) IRS

14. Keep all records of employment taxes **for at least 4 years**. These should be available for ___ review. Your records ___ include the following information.
    (a) Accounting, must
    (b) Audit, shall
    (c) IRS, should
    (d) Comparison, shall
    Answer: See Circular E, page 5, Recordkeeping/ (c) IRS, should

15. Keep all records of employment taxes **for at least 4 years**. These should be available for IRS review. Your records should include the following information.
    • Your ___ identification number (EIN).
    (a) employee
    (b) employer
    (c) employees
    (d) employers
    Answer: See Circular E, page 5, Recordkeeping/ (b) employer

16. Keep all records of employment taxes **for at least 4 years**. These should be available for IRS review. Your records should include the following information.
    • Amounts and ___ of all wage, annuity, and pension payments.
    (a) withholding
    (b) deductions
    (c) taxes
    (d) dates
    Answer: See Circular E, page 5, Recordkeeping/ (d) dates

REMINDERS: RECORDKEEPING

17. Keep all records of employment taxes **for at least 4 years**. These should be available for IRS review. Your records should include the following information.
    • Amounts of ___ reported to you by your employees.
    (a) tips
    (b) dependents
    (c) deduction
    (d) other income
    Answer: See Circular E, page 5, Recordkeeping/ (a) tips

18. Keep all records of employment taxes **for at least 4 years**. These should be available for IRS review. Your records should include the following information.
    • Records of allocated ___.
    (a) tips
    (b) dependents
    (c) deduction
    (d) other income
    Answer: See Circular E, page 5, Recordkeeping/ (a) tips

19. Keep all records of employment taxes **for at least 4 years**. These should be available for IRS review. Your records should include the following information.
    • The **fair market value** of ___ wages paid.
    (a) supplemental
    (b) incidental
    (c) in-kind
    (d) other income
    Answer: See Circular E, page 5, Recordkeeping/ (c) in-kind

20. Keep all records of employment taxes **for at least 4 years**. These should be available for IRS review. Your records should include the following information.
    • Names, addresses, social security numbers, and ___ of employees and recipients.
    (a) occupations
    (b) trade
    (c) job
    (d) work classification
    Answer: See Circular E, page 5, Recordkeeping/ (a) occupations

REMINDERS: RECORDKEEPING

21. Keep all records of employment taxes **for at least 4 years**. These should be available for IRS review. Your records should include the following information.
    • Any employee copies of Forms W-2 and ___ returned to you as undeliverable.
    (a) W-2a
    (b) W-2c
    (c) W2-g
    (d) WF4U-F
    Answer: See Circular E, page 5, Recordkeeping/ (b) W-2c

22. Keep all records of employment taxes **for at least 4 years**. These should be available for IRS review. Your records should include the following information.
    • Dates of ___ for each employee.
    (a) hire
    (b) employment
    (c) filing
    (d) payroll
    Answer: See Circular E, page 6, Recordkeeping/ (b) employment

23. Keep all records of employment taxes **for at least 4 years**. These should be available for IRS review. Your records should include the following information.
    • Periods for which employees and recipients were paid while absent due to sickness or ___.
    (a) leave
    (b) termination
    (c) vacation
    (d) injury
    Answer: See Circular E, page 6, Recordkeeping/ (d) injury

24. Keep all records of employment taxes **for at least 4 years**. These should be available for IRS review. Your records should include the following information.
    • Periods for which employees and recipients were paid while absent due to sickness or ___ and the weekly rate of payments you or ___ payers made to them.
    (a) leave, supplemental
    (b) termination, unemployment
    (c) vacation, benefits
    (d) injury, third party
    Answer: See Circular E, page 6, Recordkeeping/ (d) injury, third party

REMINDERS: RECORDKEEPING

25. Keep all records of employment taxes **for at least 4 years**. These should be available for IRS review. Your records should include the following information.
    • Copies of employees' and recipients' income tax withholding certificates (Forms W-4, W-4P,
    W-4(SP), W4-___, and W-4___).
    (a) A, B
    (b) J, K
    (c) S, V
    (d) X, Y
    Answer: See Circular E, page 6, Recordkeeping/ (c) S, V

26. Keep all records of employment taxes **for at least 4 years**. These should be available for IRS review. Your records should include the following information.
    • Copies of employees' Earned Income Credit Advance Payment Certificates (Forms W-__ and W-__).
    (a) 2, 2(SP)
    (b) 3, 3(SP)
    (c) 4, 4(SP)
    (d) 5, 5(SP)
    Answer: See Circular E, page 6, Recordkeeping/ (d) 5, 5(SP)

27. Keep all records of employment taxes **for at least 4 years**. These should be available for IRS review. Your records should include the following information.
    • Dates and amounts of tax deposits you made and acknowledgement numbers for deposits made by ___.
    (a) you
    (b) others
    (c) employees
    (d) EFTPS
    Answer: See Circular E, page 6, Recordkeeping/ (d) EFTPS

28. Keep all records of employment taxes **for at least 4 years**. These should be available for IRS review. Your records should include the following information.
    • Copies of returns filed and ___ numbers
    (a) confirmation
    (b) tax code
    (c) sequence numbers
    (d) IRS sequence numbers
    Answer: See Circular E, page 6, Recordkeeping/ (a) confirmation

REMINDERS: RECORDKEEPING

29. Keep all records of <u>employment taxes for at least 4 years</u>. These should be available for IRS review. Your records should include the following information.
    • Records of fringe benefits and expense reimbursements provided to your employees, including ___.
    (a) sanitation
    (b) substantiation
    (c) substation
    (d) substandard
    Answer: See Circular E, page 6, Recordkeeping/ (b) substantiation

Reminders: Change of Address. Page 6.

30. To notify the IRS of a new business mailing address or business ___, file Form 8822-B. Do not mail Form 8822-B with your ___ tax return.
    (a) name, employment
    (b) ownership, employer
    (c) location, employment
    (d) owner, employer
    Answer: See Circular E, page 6, Change of Address/ (c) location, employment

Reminders: Private Delivery Services. Page 6.

31. You can use certain private delivery services designated by the IRS to mail ___ and payments.
    (a) tax returns
    (b) your tax
    (c) your taxes
    (d) your income tax returns
    Answer: See Circular E, page 6, Private Delivery Services/ (a) tax returns

32. You can use certain private delivery services designated by the IRS to mail ___ and payments. The list includes ___ the following:
    (a) tax returns, only
    (b) tax, a few of
    (c) taxes, all
    (d) income tax returns, only
    Answer: See Circular E, page 6, Private Delivery Services/ (a) tax returns, only

The International Leader in Construction Technology Home Study

Reminders: Private Delivery Services. Page 6.

33. You can use certain private delivery services designated by the IRS to mail returns and payments. The list includes only three of the following: Identify the incorrect answer.
    (a) DHL Express (DHL)
    (b) Federal Express (FedEx)
    (c) United Parcel Service (UPS)
    (d) U. S. Postal Service (USPS)
    Answer: See Circular E, page 6, Private Delivery Services/ (d) U.S. Postal Service (USPS)

34. You can use DHL Express ____ private delivery services designated by the IRS to mail returns and payments.
    (a) DHL Express (DHL): Priority Overnight
    (b) DHL Express (DHL): Same Day Service
    (c) DHL Express (DHL): Standard Overnight
    (d) DHL Express (DHL): Worldwide Express
    Answer: See Circular E, page 6, Private Delivery Services/ (b) DHL Express (DHL): Same Day Service

35. You can use Federal Express (FedEx): ____ private delivery services designated by the IRS to mail returns and payments.
    (a) Federal Express (FedEx): FedEx Priority Overnight
    (b) Federal Express (Fed Ex): Same Day Service
    (c) Federal Express (Fed Ex): Worldwide Express
    (d) Federal Express (Fed Ex): Worldwide Express Plus
    Answer: See Circular E, page 6, Private Delivery Services/ (a) Federal Express (FedEx): FedEx Priority Overnight

36. For the IRS mailing address to use if you are using a private delivery service, go to IRS.gov and enter "____" in search box.
    (a) private delivery
    (b) private courier
    (c) PDS
    (d) private delivery service
    Answer: See Circular E, page 6, Private Delivery Services/ (d) private delivery service

37. For the IRS mailing address to use if you are using a private delivery service, go to IRS.gov and enter "____" in search box. Your private delivery service can tell you how to get written proof of the ___ date.
    (a) private delivery, mailing
    (b) private courier, delivery
    (c) PDS, delivery
    (d) private delivery service, mailing
    Answer: See Circular E, page 6, Private Delivery Services/ (d) private delivery service, mailing

© Copyright 2013. All rights reserved. Notice: United States Copyright Laws and International Treaties prohibit unauthorized publication, reproduction, distribution of this Work. Unauthorized use of this copyright in any form, format, publication or document may result in severe civil and criminal penalties. Violations of this copyright are investigated by the United States Department of Justice and carry, upon conviction of fines up to $250,000 and five years confinement. This Work is protected by United States Copyright Laws and International Treaties. Do not Copy, do not reproduce, do not distribute.

A Ficus Tree Publishing Educational-Technical Publications

Reminders: Private Delivery Services. Page 6.

38. For the IRS mailing address to use if you are using a private delivery service, go to IRS.gov and enter "private delivery service" in search box. Your private delivery service can tell you how to get written proof of the mailing date.
    CAUTION Private delivery services ___ deliver items to P.O. boxes.
    (a) do not
    (b) cannot
    (c) can not
    (d) will not
    Answer: See Circular E, page 6, Private Delivery Services/ (c) cannot

39. For the IRS mailing address to use if you are using a private delivery service, go to IRS.gov and enter "private delivery service" in search box. Your private delivery service can tell you how to get written proof of the mailing date.
    CAUTION Private delivery services ___ deliver items to P.O. boxes. You must use the U.S. Postal Service to mail any ___ to an IRS P.O. box address.
    (a) do not, package
    (b) cannot, item
    (c) does not, documents
    (d) will not, parcel
    Answer: See Circular E, page 6, Private Delivery Services/ (c) cannot, item

DU VALL'S TEST'S™
Instructors Manual Study Guide Series United States Tax Code
IRS Publication 15 Circular E, Employer's Tax Guide Tax Year 2013
Tax Test. Reminders Test R-5 [Multiple-Choice Questions With Answers]

Reminders: Telephone Help. Page 6.

1. **Tax questions**. You can call the IRS Business and Specialty with your employment tax questions at 1-800-___-4933.
    - (a) 305
    - (b) 495
    - (c) 828
    - (d) 989

    Answer: See Circular E, page 6, Telephone Help/ (c) 829

2. **Help for people with disabilities**. You may call 1-800-829-4059 (TDD/TTY for persons who are deaf, hard of hearing, or have a speech ___) with any tax question or to order forms and publications.
    - (a) disability
    - (b) problem
    - (c) impediment
    - (d) difficulty

    Answer: See Circular E, page 6, Telephone Help/ (a) disability

3. **Help for people with disabilities**. You may call 1-800-829-4059 (TDD/TTY for persons who are deaf, hard of hearing, or have a speech ___) with any tax question or to order forms and publications. You may also use this number for ___ with unresolved tax problems.
    - (a) disability, assistance
    - (b) problem, help
    - (c) impediment, help
    - (d) difficulty, assistance

    Answer: See Circular E, page 6, Telephone Help/ (a) disability, assistance

Recorded tax information (Tele Tax). Page 6.

4. **Recorded tax information (Tele Tax)**. The IRS Tele Tax service provides ___ tax information on topics that answer many individual and business federal tax problems.
    - (a) recorded
    - (b) important
    - (c) current
    - (d) updated

    Answer: See Circular E, page 6, Telephone Help/ (a) recorded

© Copyright 2013. All rights reserved. Notice: United States Copyright Laws and International Treaties prohibit unauthorized publication, reproduction, distribution of this Work. Unauthorized use of this copyright in any form, format, publication or document may result in severe civil and criminal penalties. Violations of this copyright are investigated by the United States Department of Justice and carry, upon conviction of fines up to $250,000 and five years confinement. This Work is protected by United States Copyright Laws and International Treaties. Do not Copy, do not reproduce, do not distribute.

A Ficus Tree Publishing Educational-Technical Publications

Reminders. Recorded tax information (Tele Tax). Page 6.

5. **Recorded tax information (Tele Tax).** The IRS Tele Tax service provides ___ tax information on topics that answer many individual and business federal tax problems. You can listen to up to ___ topics on each call you make.
    (a) recorded, three
    (b) important, four
    (c) current, five
    (d) updated, six
    Answer: See Circular E, page 6, Telephone Help/ (a) recorded, three

6. **Recorded tax information (Tele Tax).** The IRS Tele Tax service provides ___ tax information on topics that answer many individual and business federal tax problems. You can listen to up to ___ topics on each call you make.
    (a) recorded, three
    (b) important, four
    (c) current, five
    (d) updated, six
    Answer: See Circular E, page 6, Telephone Help/ (a) recorded, three

7. **Recorded tax information (Tele Tax).** The IRS Tele Tax service provides ___ tax information on topics that answer many individual and business federal tax problems. You can listen to up to ___ topics on each call you make. Touch-Tone service is available 24 hours a day, 7 days a week. TeleTax is also available on the IRS website at ___.
    (a) recorded, three, *www.irs.gov/taxtopics*
    (b) important, four, *www.irs.gov/taxesirs*
    (c) current, five, *www.irs.gov/taxtopics2013*
    (d) updated, six, *www.irs.gov/taxsand topic*
    Answer: See Circular E, page 6, Telephone Help/ (a) recorded, three, *www.irs.gov/taxtopics*.

8. **Recorded tax information (Tele Tax).** The IRS Tele Tax service provides recorded tax information on topics that answer many individual and business federal tax problems. You can listen to up to three topics on each call you make. Touch-Tone service is available 24 hours a day, 7 days a week. TeleTax is also available on the IRS website at *www.irs.gov/taxtopics*. A list of employment tax topics is provided below. Select by ___, the topic you want to hear and call 1-800-929-4477.
    (a) topic
    (b) number
    (c) subject
    (d) your question
    Answer: See Circular E, page 6, Telephone Help/ (b) number

Reminders. Recorded tax information (Tele Tax). Page 6.

9. **Recorded tax information (Tele Tax).** The IRS Tele Tax service provides recorded tax information on topics that answer many individual and business federal tax problems. You can listen to up to three topics on each call you make. Touch-Tone service is available 24 hours a day, 7 days a week. TeleTax is also available on the IRS website at *www.irs.gov/taxtopics*. A list of employment tax topics is provided below. Select by number, the topic you want to hear and call 1-800-929-4477. For the directory of all topics select Topic ___.
   (a) topic, 122
   (b) number, 123
   (c) subject, 124
   (d) your question, 135
   Answer: See Circular E, page 6, Telephone Help/ (b) number, 123

10. Teletax Topics subject Social Security and Medicare Withholding Rates (Tasas de retención del seguro social y Medicare, Terna) is listed as Topic No. ___.
    (a) 751
    (b) 752
    (c) 753
    (d) 755
    Answer: See Circular E, page 6, Telephone Help/ (a) 751

11. Teletax Topics subject Form W-2 — Where, When, and How to File (Dónde, Cuándo y Cómo Presentar El La Forulario W-2) is listed as Topic No. ___.
    (a) 751
    (b) 752
    (c) 753
    (d) 755
    Answer: See Circular E, page 6, Telephone Help/ (b) 752

12. Teletax Topics subject Form W-4 — Employee's Withholding Certificate (Formulario W-4(SP)—Certificado de Excensión de Retenciones del Empleado) is listed as Topic No. ___.
    (a) 751
    (b) 752
    (c) 753
    (d) 755
    Answer: See Circular E, page 6, Telephone Help/ (c) 753

Reminders. Recorded tax information (Tele Tax). Page 6.

13. Teletax Topics subject Employer Identification Number (EIN)—How to Apply (Como Solicitar Un Numero de Identificación Patronal (EIN) is listed as Topic No. ___.
    (a) 751
    (b) 752
    (c) 753
    (d) 755
    Answer: See Circular E, page 6, Telephone Help/ (d) 755

14. Teletax Topics subject Employer Taxes for Household Employees (Impuestos Patronales para Empleados Domesticos) is listed as Topic No. ___.
    (a) 756
    (b) 757
    (c) 758
    (d) 759
    Answer: See Circular E, page 6, Telephone Help/ (a) 756

15. Teletax Topics subject Form 941 and Form 944—Deposit Requirements (Form 941 and Form 944—Deposit requirements (Formulario 941 and Formulario 944—reqistos de Depósito) is listed as Topic No. ___.
    (a) 756
    (b) 757
    (c) 758
    (d) 759
    Answer: See Circular E, page 7, Telephone Help/ (b) 757

16. Teletax Topics subject Form 941—Employer's QUARTERLY Federal Tax Return and Form 944—Employers ANNUAL Federal Tax Return (Formulario 942-PR—Planilla para la Declaración Federal TRIMESTRAL del Patrono) (Forulario 944-PR—Planilla para la Declaración Federal ANUAL del Patrono) is listed as Topic No. ___.
    (a) 756
    (b) 757
    (c) 758
    (d) 759
    Answer: See Circular E, page 7, Telephone Help/ (c) 758

17. Teletax Topics subject A Business Credit is Available for Qualified Employers Under "The Hire Act" of 2010 (Nueva excenión tributaria y credito comercial para empleadores calificados disponibles bajo la Ley de Incentivos para la Contratación y Recuperación del 2010 (HIRE, por sus siglas en ingles)) is listed as Topic No. ___.
    (a) 756
    (b) 757
    (c) 758
    (d) 759
    Answer: See Circular E, page 7, Telephone Help/ (d) 759

© Copyright 2013. All rights reserved. Notice: United States Copyright Laws and International Treaties prohibit unauthorized publication, reproduction, distribution of this Work. Unauthorized use of this copyright in any form, format, publication or document may result in severe civil and criminal penalties. Violations of this copyright are investigated by the United States Department of Justice and carry, upon conviction of fines up to $250,000 and five years confinement. This Work is protected by United States Copyright Laws and International Treaties. Do not Copy, do not reproduce, do not distribute.

The International Leader in Construction Technology Home Study

Reminders. Recorded tax information (Tele Tax). Page 7.

18. Teletax Topics subject Tips—Withholding and Reporting (Propinas—Declaración y Retención) is listed as Topic No. ___.
    (a) 759
    (b) 761
    (c) 762
    (d) 763
    Answer: See Circular E, page 7, Telephone Help/ (b) 761

19. Teletax Topics subject Independent Contractor vs. Employee (Contratista Independiente vs. Empleado) is listed as Topic No. ___.
    (a) 759
    (b) 761
    (c) 762
    (d) 763
    Answer: See Circular E, Reminders page 7, Telephone Help/ (c) 762

20. Teletax Topics subject The "Affordable Care Act" of 2010 Offers Employers New Tax Deductions and Credits (Ley de Cuidado de Salud a Costo Asequible del 2010 ofrece a los empleadores deducciones y creditos tributarios nuevos) is listed as Topic No. ___.
    (a) 759
    (b) 761
    (c) 762
    (d) 763
    Answer: See Circular E, page 7, Telephone Help/ (c) 763

21. Additional employment tax information. Visit the IRS website at *www.irs.gov/businesses* and click on the Employment Taxes under ____.
    (a) Employment Taxes
    (b) Business Taxes
    (c) Businesses Topics
    (d) Employment Topics
    Answer: See Circular E, page 7, Telephone Help/ (c) Businesses Topics

Reminders: Ordering Employer Tax Products. Page 7

22. You can order employer tax products and information returns on line at ____.
    (a) *www.irs.gov/business*
    (b) *www.irs.gov/businesses*
    (c) *www.irs.gov/businessesinfo*
    (d) *www.irs.gov/businessesdocs*
    Answer: See Circular E, page 7, Ordering Employer Tax Products/ (b) *www.irs.gov/businesses*

© Copyright 2013. All rights reserved. Notice: United States Copyright Laws and International Treaties prohibit unauthorized publication, reproduction, distribution of this Work. Unauthorized use of this copyright in any form, format, publication or document may result in severe civil and criminal penalties. Violations of this copyright are investigated by the United States Department of Justice and carry, upon conviction of fines up to $250,000 and five years confinement. This Work is protected by United States Copyright Laws and International Treaties. Do not Copy, do not reproduce, do not distribute.

Reminders: Ordering Employer Tax Products. Page 7

23. To order 2012 and 2013 forms, click on the *Online Ordering for Information Returns and Employer Returns* link. You may also order employer tax products and information returns by calling 1-800-TAX-FORM (1-800-829-____).
    (a) 3676
    (b) 3677
    (c) 3678
    (d) 3679
    Answer: See Circular E, page 7, Ordering Employer Tax Products/ (a) 3676

24. Instead of ordering paper Forms W-__ and W-__, consider filing them electronically using the Social Security Administration's (SSA) free e-file service.
    (a) 2, 3
    (b) 2, 4
    (c) 3, 4
    (d) 3, 5
    Answer: See Circular E, page 7, Ordering Employer Tax Products/ (a) 2, 3

25. Visit the SSA's Employer W-2 Filing Instructions & Information website at *www.socialsecurity.gov/employer* to register for ___.
    (a) Business Services Online
    (b) Businesses and Services Online
    (c) Businesses & Services Online
    (d) Employer Business Services Online
    Answer: See Circular E, Reminders page 7, Ordering Employer Tax Products/ (a) Business Services Online

26. Visit the SSA's Employer W-2 Filing Instructions & Information website at *www.socialsecurity.gov/employer* to register for ___. You will be able to create Forms W-2 online and submit them to the SSA by typing your wage information into easy-to-use ___ fields.
    (a) Business Services Online, fill-in
    (b) Businesses and Services Online, file-in
    (c) Businesses & Services Online, file-in
    (d) Employer Business Services Online, fill-in
    Answer: See Circular E, Reminders page 7, Ordering Employer Tax Products/ (a) Business Services Online, fill-in

The International Leader in Construction Technology Home Study

Reminders: Ordering Employer Tax Products. Page 7

27. Visit the SSA's Employer W-2 Filing Instructions & Information website at *www.socialsecurity.gov/employer* to register for Business Services Online. You will be able to create Forms W-2 online and submit them to the SSA by typing your wage information into easy-to-use fill-in fields. In addition, you can print out completed copies of Forms W-2 to file with state or ___,
    (a) local tax agencies
    (b) local governmental agencies
    (c) local governments
    (d) federal agencies
    Answer: See Circular E, page 7, Ordering Employer Tax Products/ (c) local governments

28. Visit the SSA's Employer W-2 Filing Instructions & Information website at *www.socialsecurity.gov/employer* to register for Business Services Online. You will be able to create Forms W-2 online and submit them to the SSA by typing your wage information into easy-to-use fill-in fields. In addition, you can print out completed copies of Forms W-2 to file with state or local governments, distribute to your employees, and keep for your records. Forms W-3 will be created for you based on your Forms W-___.
    (a) 1
    (b) 2
    (c) 4
    (d) 5
    Answer: See Circular E, page 7, Ordering Employer Tax Products/ (b) 2

REMINDERS: Taxpayer Advocate Service Is Here To Help You

29. The Taxpayer Advocate Service (TAS) is your ___ at the IRS.
    (a) direct link
    (b) quickest link
    (c) link
    (d) voice
    Answer: See Circular E, page 7, / (d) voice

30. The Taxpayer Advocate Service (TAS) is your ___ at the IRS. We help taxpayers whose problems with the IRS are causing financial ___;
    (a) direct link, stress
    (b) quickest link, problems
    (c) link, concerns
    (d) voice, difficulties
    Answer: See Circular E, page 7, / (d) voice, difficulties

REMINDERS: Taxpayer Advocate Service Is Here To Help You

31. The Taxpayer Advocate Service (TAS) is your ___ at the IRS. We help taxpayers whose problems with the IRS are causing financial ___; who have tried but haven't been able to ___ their problems with the IRS; and those who ___ an IRS system or procedure is not working as it should.
    (a) direct link, stress, conclude, are annoyed
    (b) quickest link, problems, resolve, know
    (c) link, concerns, solve, feel
    (d) voice, difficulties, resolve, believe
    Answer: See Circular E, page 7, /(d) voice, difficulties, believe

32. You can contact TAS by calling the TAS toll-free number at 1-877-777-4778 to ___ whether you are ___ for assistance.
    (a) find out, eligible
    (b) ascertain, qualified
    (c) determine, eligible
    (d) learn, qualified
    Answer: See Circular E, page 7, / (c) determine, eligible

33. You can also call or write to your local taxpayer advocate, whose phone number and address are listed in your local telephone directory and in Publication ___, Taxpayer Advocate Service Assistance (And Application for Taxpayer Assistance Order), or ask an IRS employee to complete it on your behalf.
    (a) 1545
    (b) 1546
    (c) 1547
    (d) 1548
    Answer: See Circular E, Reminders page 7, Ordering Employer Tax Products/ (b) 1546

34. For more information, go to ____.
    (a) www.irs.gov/taxhelp
    (b) www.irs.gov/taxassistance
    (c) www.irs.gov/advocate
    (d) www.irs.gov/assistance
    Answer: See Circular E, Reminders page 7, Ordering Employer Tax Products/ (c) www.irs.gov/advocate

Reminders: Filing Addresses. Page 7.

35. Generally, your filing address for Forms 940, 941, 943, 944, 945 or ___ depends on the location of your residence or principal place of business and
    (a) AT-1
    (b) BT-1
    (c) AT-9
    (d) CT-1
    Answer: See Circular E, page 7, Filing Addresses/ (d) CT-1

36. Generally, your filing address for Forms 940, 941, 943, 944, 945 or ___ depends on the location of your residence or principal place of business and whether or not you are ___ a payment with your return.
    (a) AT-1, enclosing
    (b) BT-1, adding
    (c) AT-9, enclosing
    (d) CT-1, including
    Answer: See Circular E, page 7, Filing Addresses/ (d) CT-1, including

37. Generally, your filing address for Forms 940, 941, 943, 944, 945 or ___ depends on the location of your residence or principal place of business and whether or not you are ___ a payment with your return. There are separate filing addresses for these returns if you are a ___ organization or government entity.
    (a) AT-1, enclosing, not-for-profit
    (b) BT-1, adding, non-profit
    (c) AT-9, enclosing, tax-exempt
    (d) CT-1, including, tax-exempt
    Answer: See Circular E, page 7, Filing Addresses/ (d) CT-1, including, tax-exempt

38. See the separate instructions for Forms 940, 941, 943, 944, 946 or ___ for the filing address.
    (a) AT-1
    (b) BT-1
    (c) AT-9
    (d) CT-1
    Answer: See Circular E, page 7, Filing Addresses/ (d) CT-1

Reminders: Photographs Of Missing Children

The Internal Revenue Service is a proud partner with the National Center for Missing and Exploited Children. Photographs of missing children selected by the Center may appear in this publication on pages that would otherwise be blank. You can help bring these children home by looking at the photographs and calling 1-800-THE-LOST (1-800-843-5678) if you recognize a child.

© Copyright 2013. All rights reserved. Notice: United States Copyright Laws and International Treaties prohibit unauthorized publication, reproduction, distribution of this Work. Unauthorized use of this copyright in any form, format, publication or document may result in severe civil and criminal penalties. Violations of this copyright are investigated by the United States Department of Justice and carry, upon conviction of fines up to $250,000 and five years confinement. This Work is protected by United States Copyright Laws and International Treaties. Do not Copy, do not reproduce, do not distribute.

Reminders: Comments and Suggestions. Page 8.

38. We welcome your comments about this publication and your suggestions for future editions. You can write to use at the following address.
    Internal Revenue Service
    Business, Exempt Organizations, and International Tax Forms & Publications Branch
    SE: __:CAR:MP:T:B
    1111 Constitution Ave. NW, IR-6528
    Washington, DC 20224
    (a) N
    (b) S
    (c) E
    (d) W
    Answer: See Circular E, Comments and Suggestions, page 8, /(d) W

39. We respond to many letters by telephone. Therefore, it would be helpful if you would include your ___ phone number, including the area code, in your correspondence.
    (a) contact
    (b) daytime
    (c) home
    (d) business
    Answer: See Circular E, Comments and Suggestions, page 8, /(b) daytime

40. You can email us at *taxforms@irs.gov*. Please put 'Publication ___' on the subject line.
    (a) 13
    (b) 14
    (c) 15
    (d) 16
    Answer: See Circular E, Comments and Suggestions, page 8, /(c) 15

41. You can email us at *taxforms@irs.gov*. Please put 'Publication ___' on the subject line. You can also send us comments from ___.
    (a) 13, *www.irs.gov/formspubs*.
    (b) 14, *www.irs.gov/formspubs*.
    (c) 15, *www.irs.gov/formspubs*.
    (d) 16, *www.irs.gov/formspubs*.
    Answer: See Circular E, Comments and Suggestions, page 8, /(c) 15, *www.irs.gov/formspubs*.

Reminders: Comments and Suggestions. Page 8.

42. You can email us at *taxforms@irs.gov*. Please put 'Publication 15' on the subject line. You can also send us comments from *www.irs.gov/formspubs*. Click on More Information and then ___ Comment on Tax Forms and Publications.
    (a) turn on
    (b) click on
    (c) switch on
    (d) go to
    Answer: See Circular E, Comments and Suggestions, page 8, /(b) click on

43. Although we cannot respond individually to each comment received, we do appreciate your feedback and ___ consider your comments as we revise our tax products.
    (a) will
    (b) review
    (c) do
    (d) discuss and
    Answer: See Circular E, Comments and Suggestions, page 8, /(a) will

A Ficus Tree Publishing Quick Notes Page

The International Leader in Construction Technology Home Study

Instructor's Manual for Circular E Tax Calendar Tax Test C-1

Calendar. General Description. Page 8

Tax Test 15E-C-1. The Tax Calendar for each successive tax year is generally a constant. By constant it is meant to be reasonably fixed and unchanging with few variables. Depositing on the mandatory calendar due dates is essential and necessary

Calendar. Key Words. Page 8. Page 9.

Tax Test 15E-C-1. Deposits on Business Days Only (also Section11) January 31. February 15. February 16. February 28. March 31. By April 30, July 31, October 31, and January 31. Before December 1. legal holiday, statewide legal holiday, depositing on next business day, filing date, Private Delivery Services, FUTA tax, Nonpayroll federal income tax, Deposit FUTA tax, file New Forms W-4,

DU VALL'S TEST'S™
Instructors Manual Study Guide Series United States Tax Code
IRS Publication 15 Circular E, Employer's Tax Guide Tax Year 2013
Tax Calendar Test C-1 [Questions With Answers]

Tax Calendar: Page 8

1. The following is a list of important dates. Also see Publication ___, Tax Calendars.
    (a) 507
    (b) 508
    (c) 509
    (d) 510
   Answer: See Circular E, Calendar, page 8, /(c) 509

Calendar-TIP, Page 8

2. If any date shown below for filing a return, furnishing a form, or depositing taxes falls on a Saturday, Sunday, or legal holiday, use the next ___ day.
    (a) week
    (b) Mon
    (c) Fri
    (d) business
   Answer: See Circular E, Calendar, TIP, page 8, /(d) business

© Copyright 2013. All rights reserved. Notice: United States Copyright Laws and International Treaties prohibit unauthorized publication, reproduction, distribution of this Work. Unauthorized use of this copyright in any form, format, publication or document may result in severe civil and criminal penalties. Violations of this copyright are investigated by the United States Department of Justice and carry, upon conviction of fines up to $250,000 and five years confinement. This Work is protected by United States Copyright Laws and International Treaties. Do not Copy, do not reproduce, do not distribute.

A Ficus Tree Publishing Educational-Technical Publications

Calendar: TIP Page 8

3. A **statewide legal holiday delays** a filing due date only if the IRS office where you are required to file is ____.
   (a) closed
   (b) not accessible
   (c) in that specific state
   (d) located in that state
   Answer: See Circular E, Calendar, TIP, page 8, /(d) located in that state

4. However, a **statewide legal holiday does not delay** the due date of ___.
   (a) tax deposits
   (b) income tax deposits
   (c) federal tax deposits
   (d) federal income tax deposits
   Answer: See Circular E, Calendar, TIP, page 8, /(c) federal tax deposits

5. See <u>Deposits on Business Days Only</u> in section ___.
   (a) 10
   (b) 11
   (c) 12
   (d) 13
   Answer: See Circular E, Calendar, TIP, page 8, /(b) 11

6. For any filing due date, you will meet the "file" or "__" requirement if the envelope containing the return or form is properly addressed, contains ___ postage, and is postmarked by the U.S. Postal Service on or before the due date, or
   (a) furnish, sufficient
   (b) meet, adequate
   (c) provide, sufficient
   (d) furnish, correct
   Answer: See Circular E, Calendar, TIP, page 8, /(a) furnish, sufficient

7. For any filing due date, you will meet the "file" or "___" requirement if the envelope containing the return or form is properly addressed, contains ___ postage, and is postmarked by the U.S. Postal Service on or before the due date, or sent by an IRS-___ private delivery service on or before the due date.
   (a) furnish, sufficient, designated
   (b) meet, adequate, certified
   (c) provide, sufficient, approved
   (d) furnish, correct, certified
   Answer: See Circular E, Calendar, TIP, page 8, /(a) furnish, sufficient, designated

The International Leader in Construction Technology Home Study

Calendar: TIP Page 8

8   See <u>Private Delivery Services</u> under ___ for more information.
    (a)   What's New
    (b)   Reminders
    (c)   Introduction
    (d)   Tips
Answer: See Circular E, Calendar, TIP, page 8, /(b) Reminders

Calendar-By January 31. Page 8.

9.   By January 31: Furnish Forms ___ and ___.
    (a)   1089, W-2
    (b)   1089, W-4
    (c)   1099, W-2
    (d)   1099, W-4
Answer: See Circular E, Calendar, By January 31, page 8, /(c) 1099, W-2

10.   By January 31: Furnish Forms ___ and ___. Furnish each employee a completed Form ___.
    (a)   1089, W-2, W-4,
    (b)   1089, W-4, W-2,
    (c)   1099, W-2, W-2,
    (d)   1099, W-4, W-4,
Answer: See Circular E, Calendar, By January 31, page 8, /(c) 1099, W-2, W-2

11.   By January 31: Furnish Forms ___ and ___. Furnish each employee a completed Form ___. Furnish each other employee a completed Form 1099 (For example, Form 1099___).
    (a)   1089, W-2, W-4, IRS-X
    (b)   1089, W-4, W-2, IRS-X.
    (c)   1099, W-2, W-2, MISC.
    (d)   1099, W-4, W-4, MISC
Answer: See Circular E, Calendar, By January 31, page 8, /(c) 1099, W-2, W-2, MISC.

12.   By January 31 File Form ___ or Form ___.
    (a)   940, 941
    (b)   941, 942
    (c)   941, 943
    (d)   941, 944
Answer: See Circular E, Calendar, By January 31, page 8, /(d) 941, 944

© Copyright 2013. All rights reserved. Notice: United States Copyright Laws and International Treaties prohibit unauthorized publication, reproduction, distribution of this Work. Unauthorized use of this copyright in any form, format, publication or document may result in severe civil and criminal penalties. Violations of this copyright are investigated by the United States Department of Justice and carry, upon conviction of fines up to $250,000 and five years confinement. This Work is protected by United States Copyright Laws and International Treaties. Do not Copy, do not reproduce, do not distribute.

A Ficus Tree Publishing Educational-Technical Publications

Calendar-By January 31. Page 8.

13. File Form ___ for the ___ quarter of the previous calendar year and deposit any undeposited income, social security, and Medicare taxes.
    (a)   941, first
    (b)   940, second
    (c)   941, third
    (d)   941, fourth
    Answer: See Circular E, Calendar, By January 31, page 8, /(d) 941, fourth

14. File Form ___ for the ___ quarter of the previous calendar year and deposit any undeposited income, social security, and Medicare taxes. You may pay these taxes with Form ___ if your total tax liability for the quarter is less than $___.
    (a)   941, first, 940, 1,000
    (b)   940, second, 940, 1,500
    (c)   941, third, 941, 2,000
    (d)   941, fourth, 941, 2,500
    Answer: See Circular E, Calendar, By January 31, page 8, /(d) 941, fourth, 941, 2,500

15. File Form 941 for the fourth quarter of the previous calendar year and deposit any undeposited income, social security, and Medicare taxes. You may pay these taxes with Form 941 if your total tax liability for the quarter is less than $2,500. File Form ___ for the previous calendar year instead of Form 941 if the IRS has notified you in writing to file Form ___ and pay any undeposited income, social security and Medicare taxes.
    (a)   942, 942
    (b)   943, 943
    (c)   944, 944
    (d)   945, 945
    Answer: See Circular E, Calendar, By January 31, page 8, /(c) 944, 944

16. File Form 941 for the fourth quarter of the previous calendar year and deposit any undeposited income, social security, and Medicare taxes. You may pay these taxes with Form 941 if your total tax liability for the quarter is less than $2,500. File Form 944 for the previous calendar year instead of Form 941 if the IRS has notified you in writing to file Form 944 and pay any undeposited income, social security and Medicare taxes. You may pay these taxes with Form 944 if your total tax liability for the year is less than $___.
    (a)   2,000
    (b)   2,500
    (c)   3,000
    (d)   5,000
    Answer: See Circular E, Calendar, By January 31, page 8, /(b) 2,500

Calendar-By January 31. Page 8.

17. File Form 941 for the fourth quarter of the previous calendar year and deposit any undeposited income, social security, and Medicare taxes. You may pay these taxes with Form 941 if your total tax liability for the quarter is less than $2,500. File Form 944 for the previous calendar year instead of Form 941 if the IRS has notified you in writing to file Form 944 and pay any undeposited income, social security and Medicare taxes. You may pay these taxes with Form 944 if your total tax liability for the year is less than $2,500. For additional rules on when you can pay your taxes with your return, see *Payment with return* in section ___.
    (a) 10
    (b) 11
    (c) 12
    (d) 13
    Answer: See Circular E, Calendar, By January 31, page 8, /(b) 11

18. If you timely deposited all taxes when due, you have 10 additional calendar days from January 31 to file the ___ return.
    (a) complete
    (b) completed
    (c) appropriate
    (d) adjusted
    Answer: See Circular E, Calendar, By January 31, page 8, /(c) appropriate

Calendar-By January 31. FUTA TAX. Page 8.

19. File Form ___ to report any **FUTA** tax.
    (a) 940
    (b) 941
    (c) 943
    (d) 945
    Answer: See Circular E, Calendar, By January 31, page 8, /(a) 940

NOTE: FUTA defined is the Federal Unemployment Tax Act (26 U.S.C. ch. 23). 26 U.S.C. is the United States Code of Federal Regulations the CFR's.

20. File Form ___ to report any **FUTA** tax. However, if you deposited all taxes when due, you have ___ additional days to file.
    (a) 940, 10
    (b) 941, 14
    (c) 943, 15
    (d) 945, 30
    Answer: See Circular E, Calendar, By January 31, page 8, /(a) 940, 10

Calendar-By January 31. Nonpayroll Federal Income Tax. Page 8.

21. File Form ___ to report any nonpayroll tax withheld in 2012.
    (a) 940
    (b) 941
    (c) 943
    (d) 945
    Answer: See Circular E, Calendar, By January 31, page 8, /(d) 945

22. File Form ___ to report any nonpayroll tax withheld in 2012. If you deposited all taxes when due, you have 10 additional calendar days to file. See *Nonpayroll Income Tax Withholding* under ___ for more information.
    (a) 940, Nonpayroll Tax Withholding
    (b) 941, Contents
    (c) 943, Information
    (d) 945, Reminders
    Answer: See Circular E, Calendar, By January 31, page 8, /(d) 945, Reminders

Calendar-By February 15 Page 8

23. By February 15 request a new Form W-___ from ___ employees.
    (a) 2, new
    (b) 4, exempt
    (c) 5, all
    (d) 1099, new
    Answer: See Circular E, Calendar, By February 15, page 8, /(b) 4, exempt

24. By February 15 request a new Form W-4 from exempt employees. Ask for a new Form ___ from each employee who claimed ___ from income tax withholding.
    (a) 2, exempt
    (b) 4, exemption
    (c) 5, new
    (d) 1099, new
    Answer: See Circular E, Calendar, By February 15, page 8, /(b) 4, exemption

Calendar. On February 16, Page 8.

25. Forms W-___ claiming exemption from withholding ___.
    (a) 4, exempt
    (b) 4, exemption
    (c) 4, expire
    (d) 1099, expire
    Answer: See Circular E, Calendar, On February 16, page 8, /(c) 4, expire

The International Leader in Construction Technology Home Study

Calendar. On February 16, Page 8.

26. Forms W-4 claiming exemption from withholding expire. Any Form W-4 claiming exemption from withholding for the previous year has now ___.
    (a) become invalid
    (b) discontinued
    (c) become inactive
    (d) expired
    Answer: See Circular E, Calendar, On February 16, page 8, /(d) expired

27. Forms W-4 claiming exemption from withholding expire. Any Form W-4 claiming exemption from withholding for the previous year has now expired. Begin withholding for any ___ who previously claimed exemption but has not given you a new Form W-___ for the ___ year.
    (a) employee, 2, current
    (b) employee, 4, current
    (c) person, 2, present
    (d) employee, 4, present
    Answer: See Circular E, Calendar, On February 16, page 8, /(b) employee, 4, current

28. If the employee does not give you a new W-4, withhold tax based on the ___ Form W-4 for the employee that **does not** claim exemption from withholding or, if one does not exist, as if he or she is ___ with zero withholding allowances.
    (a) prior, single
    (b) existing, single
    (c) last valid, single
    (d) prior, married
    Answer: See Circular E, Calendar, On February 16, page 8, /(c) last valid, single

29. If the employee does not give you a new W-4, withhold tax based on the ___ Form W-4 for the employee that **does not** claim exemption from withholding or, if one does not exist, as if he or she is ___ with zero withholding allowances. See section ___ for more information.
    (a) prior, single, 8
    (b) existing, single, 9
    (c) last valid, single, 9
    (d) prior, married, 9
    Answer: See Circular E, Calendar, On February 16, page 8, /(c) last valid, single, 9

30. If the employee furnishes a new Form W-4 claiming exemption from withholding after February 15, you ___ the exemption to future wages, but
    (a) may apply
    (b) may not apply
    (c) shall not apply
    (d) must apply
    Answer: See Circular E, Calendar, On February 16, page 8, /(a) may apply

© Copyright 2013. All rights reserved. Notice: United States Copyright Laws and International Treaties prohibit unauthorized publication, reproduction, distribution of this Work. Unauthorized use of this copyright in any form, format, publication or document may result in severe civil and criminal penalties. Violations of this copyright are investigated by the United States Department of Justice and carry, upon conviction of fines up to $250,000 and five years confinement. This Work is protected by United States Copyright Laws and International Treaties. Do not Copy, do not reproduce, do not distribute.

A Ficus Tree Publishing Educational-Technical Publications

Calendar. On February 16, Page 8.

31. If the employee furnishes a new Form W-4 claiming exemption from withholding after February 15, you ___ the exemption to future wages, but ___ the exemption to future wages, but ___ refund taxes withheld while the exempt status was not in place.
    (a)   may apply, do not
    (b)   may not apply, shall not
    (c)   shall not apply, cannot
    (d)   must apply, must not
    Answer: See Circular E, Calendar, On February 16, page 8, /(a) may apply, do not

Calendar. By February 28, Page 8.

32. File Forms ___ and ___.
    (a)   941, 944
    (b)   944, 941
    (c)   1096, 1099
    (d)   1099, 1096
    Answer: See Circular E, Calendar, By February 28, page 8, /(d) 1099, 1096

33. File Copy ___ with Forms 1099 with Form 1096, Annual Summary and Transmittal of U.S. Information returns , with the IRS.
    (a)   A
    (b)   B
    (c)   C
    (d)   D
    Answer: See Circular E, Calendar, By February 28, page 8, /(a) A

Calendar. By February 28, Page 8.

34. File Copy A with all Forms 1099 with Form 1096, Annual Summary and Transmittal of U.S. Information returns, with the IRS. For electronically filed returns see, see *By ___*, later.
    (a)   *March 1*
    (b)   *March 10*
    (c)   *March 15*
    (d)   *March 31*
    Answer: See Circular E, Calendar, By February 28, page 8, /(d) *March 31*

35. File paper Forms W-___ and W-___.
    (a)   2, 3
    (b)   2, 4
    (c)   2, 5
    (d)   3, 4
    Answer: See Circular E, Calendar, By February 28, page 8, /(a) 2, 3.

© Copyright 2013. All rights reserved. Notice: United States Copyright Laws and International Treaties prohibit unauthorized publication, reproduction, distribution of this Work. Unauthorized use of this copyright in any form, format, publication or document may result in severe civil and criminal penalties. Violations of this copyright are investigated by the United States Department of Justice and carry, upon conviction of fines up to $250,000 and five years confinement. This Work is protected by United States Copyright Laws and International Treaties. Do not Copy, do not reproduce, do not distribute.

The International Leader in Construction Technology Home Study

Calendar. By February 28, Page 8.

36. File paper Forms W-__ and W-__. File Copy __ of all Forms W-2 with Form W-3, Transmittal of ___ and ___ Statements, with the Social Security Administration (SSA).
    (a)   2, 3, A, Wage, Tax
    (b)   2, 4, B, Tax, Wage
    (c)   2, 5, C, Income, Earnings
    (d)   3, 4, D, Earnings, Income
    Answer: See Circular E, Calendar, By February 28, page 8, /(a) 2, 3, A, Wage, Tax.

37. File paper Forms W-2 and W-3. File Copy A of all Forms W-2 with Form W-3, Transmittal of Wage and Tax Statements, with the Social Security Administration (SSA). For electronically filed returns, see *By___*, later.
    (a)   *March 1*
    (b)   *March 10*
    (c)   *March 15*
    (d)   *March 31*
    Answer: See Circular E, Calendar, By February 28, page 8, /(d) *March 31*

38. By February 28 File paper form ___, Employer's Annual Information Return of Tip Income and Allocated Tips, with the IRS. See section __. For electronically filed returns, see *By March31* below.
    (a)   8027, 6
    (b)   8028, 7
    (c)   8029, 8
    (d)   941, 9
    Answer: See Circular E, Calendar, By February 28, pages 8 and 9, /(a) 8027, 6

Calendar. By March 31, Page 9.

39. File electronic Forms 1099, ___, and W-2.
    (a)   8027
    (b)   8028
    (c)   8029
    (d)   W-3
    Answer: See Circular E, Calendar, By March 31, page 9, /(a) 8027

40. File electronic Forms 1099, and ___ with the IRS. File Electronic Forms ___ with the SSA.
    (a)   8027, W-2
    (b)   8028, W-3
    (c)   8029, W-4
    (d)   W-3, W-6
    Answer: See Circular E, Calendar, By March 31, page 9, /(a) 8027, W-2

© Copyright 2013. All rights reserved. Notice: United States Copyright Laws and International Treaties prohibit unauthorized publication, reproduction, distribution of this Work. Unauthorized use of this copyright in any form, format, publication or document may result in severe civil and criminal penalties. Violations of this copyright are investigated by the United States Department of Justice and carry, upon conviction of fines up to $250,000 and five years confinement. This Work is protected by United States Copyright Laws and International Treaties. Do not Copy, do not reproduce, do not distribute.

A Ficus Tree Publishing Educational-Technical Publications

Calendar. By March 31, Page 9.

41. For information on reporting Form W-2 to the SSA electronically, visit the Social Security Administration's ___ W-2 Filing Instructions & Information webpage at *www.socialsecurity.gov/employer*.
    (a) Employee
    (b) Employer
    (c) SS
    (d) IRS
    Answer: See Circular E, Calendar, By March 31, page 9, /(b) Employer

42. For information on filing ___ returns with the IRS, see Publication ___, Specifications for Filing Forms 1097, 1098, 1099, 3921, 3922, 5498, 8935, and W-2G Electronically, and
    (a) Medicare, 1218
    (b) Medicare, 1219
    (c) information, 1220
    (d) social security, 1220
    Answer: See Circular E, Calendar, By March 31, page 9, /(c) information, 1220

43. For information on filing ___ returns with the IRS, see Publication ___, Specifications for Filing Forms 1097, 1098, 1099, 3921, 3922, 5498, 8935, and W-2G Electronically, and Publication 1239, Specifications for Filing Form ____, Employer's Annual Information Return of Tip Income and Allocated Tips, Electronically.
    (a) Medicare, 1218, 8025
    (b) Medicare, 1219, 8026
    (c) information, 1220, 8027
    (d) social security, 1220, 8028
    Answer: See Circular E, Calendar, By March 31, page 9, /(c) information, 1220, 8027

Calendar By April 30, July 31, October 31, and January 31 Deposit FUTA taxes.

44. Deposit FUTA tax due if it is more than $____.
    (a) 500
    (b) 750
    (c) 1,000
    (d) 1,500
    Answer: See Circular E, Calendar, By April 30, July 31, October 31, and January 31 page 9, /(a) 500

Calendar By April 30, July 31, October 31, and January 31
File Form 941

45. File form 941 and deposit any ___ income, social security, and Medicare taxes.
    (a) due
    (b) unreported
    (c) undeposited
    (d) ending
    Answer: See Circular E, Calendar, By April 30, July 31, October 31, and January 31, page 9, /(c) undeposited

46. File form 941 and deposit any ___ income, social security, and Medicare taxes. You may pay these taxes with Form 941 if your ___ liability for the quarter is less than $2,500.
    (a) due, tax
    (b) unreported, total
    (c) undeposited, total tax
    (d) ending, amount due
    Answer: See Circular E, Calendar, By April 30, July 31, October 31, and January 31, page 9, /(c) undeposited, total tax

47. File form 941 and deposit any ___ income, social security, and Medicare taxes. You may pay these taxes with Form 941 if your ___ liability for the quarter is less than $2,500. If you ___ deposited all taxes when due, you have 10 additional days from the due dates above to file the return.
    (a) due, tax, timely
    (b) unreported, total, promptly
    (c) undeposited, total tax, timely
    (d) ending, amount due, promptly
    Answer: See Circular E, Calendar, By April 30, July 31, October 31, and January 31, page 9, /(c) undeposited, total tax

Calendar Before December 1 - New Forms W-4

48. Remind employees to submit a new Form W-4 if their marital status or withholding ___ have changes or will change for the next year.
    (a) deductions
    (b) allowances
    (c) tax base
    (d) number of dependents
    Answer: See Circular E, Calendar, Before December 1, page 9, /(b) allowances

A Ficus Tree Publishing Quick Notes Page

© Copyright 2013. All rights reserved. Notice: United States Copyright Laws and International Treaties prohibit unauthorized publication, reproduction, distribution of this Work. Unauthorized use of this copyright in any form, format, publication or document may result in severe civil and criminal penalties. Violations of this copyright are investigated by the United States Department of Justice and carry, upon conviction of fines up to $250,000 and five years confinement. This Work is protected by United States Copyright Laws and International Treaties. Do not Copy, do not reproduce, do not distribute.

A Ficus Tree Publishing Educational-Technical Publications

The International Leader in Construction Technology Home Study

Instructor's Manual for Circular E
Introduction
Tax Test 15E-Intro-1

Introduction. Tax Test 15E-Intro-1. General Description. Page 9.

Tax Test 15E-Intro-1 is the Introductions section of Circular E, Employer's **15E-Intro-1.** Tax Guide. Test Question (1) of Test 15E-Intro-1 discusses in test format the Employer takes the credit of form 941, line 12a or Form 944, line 9a, once the 35% of the premium is paid by or on behalf of the assistance eligible individual Test question (1) is a prime example of the typical structure of the professional level test. On any examination always expect questions related to standards, dimensions, quantities, percentages, Form numbers, times, dates, and periods of time. It is possible to memorized specific points of information but it is equally important to know where such information is located and to be able to apply such information quickly, accurately, and correctly. This is more information about COBRA and another way of saving funds by reducing tax liability for you as the employer.

Introduction Tax Test 15 Intro-1. Key Words.

Tax Test 15 Intro-1. Income tax, Social security tax, Medicare tax, FUTA tax, Employer's liability, Federal Government employers, State and local government employers, Disregarded entities and qualified subchapter S subsidiaries, own employment tax obligation, ERISA, Cobra premium assistance credit, American Recovery and Reinvestment Act, ARRA. Employee Retirement Income Security Act, Federal Employees Health Benefits Program, FEHBP. Consolidated Omnibus Budget Reconciliation Act of 1985.

DU VALL'S TEST'S™
Instructors Manual Study Guide Series United States Tax Code
IRS Publication 15 Circular E, Employer's Tax Guide Tax Year 2013
Introduction Test Intro-1 [Multiple-Choice Questions With Answers]

Introduction: Page 9

1. This publication explains your ___ as an employer.
    (a) financial obligations
    (b) tax allowances
    (c) tax rights
    (d) tax responsibilities
    Answer: See Circular E, Introduction, page 9, /(d) tax responsibilities

© Copyright 2013. All rights reserved. Notice: United States Copyright Laws and International Treaties prohibit unauthorized publication, reproduction, distribution of this Work. Unauthorized use of this copyright in any form, format, publication or document may result in severe civil and criminal penalties. Violations of this copyright are investigated by the United States Department of Justice and carry, upon conviction of fines up to $250,000 and five years confinement. This Work is protected by United States Copyright Laws and International Treaties. Do not Copy, do not reproduce, do not distribute.

A Ficus Tree Publishing Educational-Technical Publications

Introduction: Page 9

2. This publication explains your ___ as an employer. It explains the requirements for withholding, depositing, reporting, paying and ___ employment taxes.
   (a) financial obligations, tax rights of
   (b) tax allowances, correcting
   (c) tax rights, mandatory taxes
   (d) tax responsibilities, correcting
   Answer: See Circular E, Introduction, page 9, /(d) tax responsibilities, correcting

3. This publication explains your ___ as an employer. It explains the requirements for withholding, depositing, reporting, paying and ___ employment taxes. It explains the forms you must give to your employees, those your employees must give to you, and those you ___ to the IRS and SSA.
   (a) financial obligations, tax rights of, are required to send
   (b) tax allowances, correcting, shall send
   (c) tax rights, mandatory taxes, are required to send
   (d) tax responsibilities, correcting, must send
   Answer: See Circular E, Introduction, page 9, /(d) tax responsibilities, correcting, must send

4. This publication explains your tax responsibilities as an employer. It explains the requirements for withholding, depositing, reporting, paying and correcting employment taxes. It explains the forms you must give to your employees, those your employees must give to you, and those you must send to the IRS and SSA. This guide also has the ___ you need to figure the taxes to withhold from each employee for 2013.
   (a) tables
   (b) tax tables
   (c) information
   (d) tax information
   Answer: See Circular E, Introduction, page 9, /(b) tax tables

5. This publication explains your tax responsibilities as an employer. It explains the requirements for withholding, depositing, reporting, paying and correcting employment taxes. It explains the forms you must give to your employees, those your employees must give to you, and those you must send to the IRS and SSA. This guide also has the ___ you need to figure the taxes to withhold from each employee for 2013. References to "___" in this guide apply only to "___" income tax.
   (a) tables, taxes, current year
   (b) tax tables, income tax, federal
   (c) information, taxes, current year
   (d) tax information, income tax, federal
   Answer: See Circular E, Introduction, page 9, /(b) tax tables, income tax, federal

Introduction: Page 9

6. Contact your state or local tax ___ to determine if their rules are different.
   (a) agency
   (b) service
   (c) office
   (d) department
   Answer: See Circular E, Introduction, page 9, /(d) department

7. Additional employment tax information is available in Publication ___.
   (a) 15A
   (b) 16A
   (c) 17A
   (d) 18A
   Answer: See Circular E, Introduction, page 9 /(a) 15A

8. Additional employment tax information is available in Publication ___. Publication ___ includes specialized information ___ the basic employment tax information provided in this publication.
   (a) 15A, 15A, supplementing
   (b) 16A, 15A, supplementing
   (c) 17A, 17A, adding credibility
   (d) 18A, 18A, clarifying
   Answer: See Circular E, Introduction, page 9, /(a) 15A, 15A, supplementing

9. Publication 15-B, Employer's Tax Guide to Fringe Benefits, contains information about the employment tax ___ and valuation of various types of noncash compensation
   (a) deductions
   (b) treatment
   (c) requirements
   (d) withholding
   Answer: See Circular E, Introduction, page 9, /(b) treatment

10. Most employers must withhold (except ___), deposit, report and pay the following employment taxes.
    (a) COBRA
    (b) FICA
    (c) FUTA
    (d) HSAS
    Answer: See Circular E, Introduction, page 9, /(c) FUTA

Introduction: Page 9

11. Most employers must withhold (except ___), deposit, report and pay the following employment taxes. These are exceptions to these requirements. See <u>section</u> ___ for guidance.
    (a) COBRA, 13
    (b) FICA, 14
    (c) FUTA, 15
    (d) HSAS, 16
    Answer: See Circular E, Introduction, page 9, /(c) FUTA, 15

12. Most employers must withhold (except ___), deposit, report and pay the following employment taxes. These are exceptions to these requirements. See <u>section</u> ___ for guidance. Railroad retirement taxes are ___ in the Instructions for Form CT-1.
    (a) COBRA, 13, discussed
    (b) FICA, 14, detailed
    (c) FUTA, 15, explained
    (d) HSAS, 16, discussed
    Answer: See Circular E, Introduction, page 9, /(c) FUTA, 15, explained

Introduction. Employers Liability. Page 9

13. Employer's are responsible for ___ tax returns are filed and deposits and payments are made, even if
    (a) correct
    (b) ensuring
    (c) insuring
    (d) accurate
    Answer: See Circular E, Introduction, page 9, /(b) ensuring

14. Employer's are responsible for ___ tax returns are filed and deposits and payments are made, even if the employer ___ a third party to perform those functions.
    (a) correct, employs
    (b) ensuring, retains
    (c) insuring, contracts
    (d) accurate, contracts with
    Answer: See Circular E, Introduction, page 9, /(b) ensuring, retains

Authors note: (Payroll management services, Independent Contractor services, or other similar third party private payment services). Contact the IRS for additional information for additional information. See IRS Publication 15A and 15B.

Introduction. Employers Liability. Page 9

15. Employer's are responsible for ___ tax returns are filed and deposits and payments are made, even if the employer ___ a third party to perform those functions. The employer remains ___ if the third party fails to perform a required action.
    (a) correct, employs, responsible
    (b) ensuring, retains, liable
    (c) insuring, contracts, liable
    (d) accurate, contracts with, responsible
    Answer: See Circular E, Introduction, page 9, /(b) ensuring, retains, liable

16. Employer's are responsible for ___ tax returns are filed and deposits and payments are made, even if the employer ___ a third party to perform those functions. The employer remains ___ if the third party fails to perform a required action. Employers who enroll in ___ will be able to view ___ deposits and payments made on their behalf.
    (a) correct, employs, responsible, IRSTPS
    (b) ensuring, retains, liable, EFTPS
    (c) insuring, contracts, liable, SSNTPS
    (d) accurate, contracts with, responsible, USTPS
    Answer: See Circular E, Introduction, page 9, /(b) ensuring, retains, liable, EFTPS

Introduction Page 9 - Federal Government employers.

17. The information in this guide applies to federal agencies, except for the rules requiring deposit of federal taxes only at ___ or through the FedTax option of
    (a) FICA
    (b) Federal Reserve banks
    (c) EFIS direct deposit
    (d) FUTA
    Answer: See Circular E, Introduction, page 9, Federal Government employees/(b) Federal Reserve banks,

18. The information in this guide applies to federal agencies, except for the rules requiring deposit of federal taxes only at ___ or through the FedTax option of the Government___ Accounting Link Systems (GOALS).
    (a) FICA, Off-Line
    (b) Federal Reserve banks, On-Line
    (c) EFIS direct deposit, On-Line
    (d) FUTA, Off Line
    Answer: See Circular E, Introduction, page 9, Federal Government employees/(b) Federal Reserve banks, On-Line

Introduction Page 9 - Federal Government employers.

19. See the Treasury Financial Manual (I TFM 3-____) for more information.
    (a) 4000
    (b) 5000
    (c) 6000
    (d) 7000
    Answer: See Circular E, Introduction, page 9, Federal Government employees/(a) 4000

20. See the Treasury Financial Manual (I TFM 3-____) for more information. You can access the Treasury Financial Manual online at *www.fms.treas.gov/___*.
    (a) 4000, *tms*
    (b) 5000, *fmf*
    (c) 6000, *f2g*
    (d) 7000, *f6f*
    Answer: See Circular E, Introduction, page 9, Federal Government employees/(a) 4000, *tms*

Introduction Page 9 - State and local government employees.

21. Payments to employees for services in the employ of state and local government employers are generally subject to federal income tax withholding but not ___ tax.
    (a) FICA
    (b) COBRA
    (c) FUTA
    (d) Medicare
    Answer: See Circular E, Introduction, page 9, State and local government employees/(c) FUTA

22. Payments to employees for services in the employ of state and local government employers are generally subject to federal income tax withholding but not ___ tax. Most elected and appointed public officials of state or local governments are employees under ___,
    (a) FICA, Constitutional Law
    (b) COBRA, States Rights Law
    (c) FUTA, common law rules
    (d) Medicare, Presidential Decree
    Answer: See Circular E, Introduction, page 9, State and local government employees/(c) FUTA, common law rule

Introduction Page 9 - State and local government employees.

23. Payments to employees for services in the employ of state and local government employers are generally subject to federal income tax withholding but not ___ tax. Most elected and appointed public officials of state or local governments are employees under ___, See chapter ___ of Publication ___, Federal-State Reference Guide.
    (a) FICA, Constitutional Law, 1, 962
    (b) COBRA, States Rights Law, 2, 962
    (c) FUTA, common law rules, 3, 963
    (d) Medicare, Presidential Decree, 4, 963
    Answer: See Circular E, Introduction, page 9, State and local government employees/(c) FUTA, common law rules, 3, 963

24. Payments to employees for services in the employ of state and local government employers are generally subject to federal income tax withholding but not FUTA tax. Most elected and appointed public officials of state or local governments are employees under common law rules, See chapter 3 of Publication 963, Federal-State Reference Guide. In addition, wages with certain ___ are subject to social security and Medicare taxes.
    (a) waivers
    (b) conditions
    (c) agreements
    (d) exceptions
    Answer: See Circular E, Introduction, page 9, State and local government employees/(d) exceptions

25. Payments to employees for services in the employ of state and local government employers are generally subject to federal income tax withholding but not FUTA tax. Most elected and appointed public officials of state or local governments are employees under common law rules, See chapter 3 of Publication 963, Federal-State Reference Guide. In addition, wages with certain ___ are subject to social security and Medicare taxes. See *section* ___ for more information on exceptions.
    (a) waivers, 12
    (b) conditions, 13
    (c) agreements, 14
    (d) exceptions, 15
    Answer: See Circular E, Introduction, page 9, State and local government employees/(d) exceptions, 15

Introduction Page 9 - State and local government employees.

26. If an election worker is employed in another capacity with the same government entity, see Revenue Ruling 2000-6 on page __ of Internal Revenue Bulletin 2000-6 at www.irs.gov/pub/irs-irbs/irb00-06.pdf.
    (a)   512
    (b)   513
    (c)   514
    (d)   515
    Answer: See Circular E, Introduction, page 9, State and local government employees/(a) 512

27. You can get information on reporting and social security coverage from ___.
    (a)   the IRS help center
    (b)   Taxpayer Advocate Service
    (c)   your local IRS office
    (d)   the Social Security Regional Offices
    Answer: See Circular E, Introduction, page 9, State and local government employees/(c) your local IRS office

28. If you have any questions about coverage under section ___ (Social Security Act) agreement, contact the appropriate state official.
    (a)   217
    (b)   218
    (c)   219
    (d)   220
    Answer: See Circular E, Introduction, page 9, State and local government employees/(b) 218

29. If you have any questions about coverage under section ___ (Social Security Act) agreement, contact the appropriate state official. To find your State Social Security Administrator, visit the National ___ of State Social Security Administrators website at www.ncsssa.org.
    (a)   217, Association
    (b)   218, Conference
    (c)   219, Board
    (d)   220, Congress
    Answer: See Circular E, Introduction, page 9, State and local government employees/(b) 218, Conference

Disregarded Entities and Qualified Subchapter S Subsidiaries

30. The IRS has published final regulations section 301.7.701-2(c)(2)(iv), under which __Subs and eligible single-owner disregarded entities are treated as separate entities for employment tax purposes.
    (a) S
    (b) K
    (c) W
    (d) Q
    Answer: See Circular E, Introduction, page 9, Disregarded entities and qualified subchapter S subsidiaries/(d) Q

31. The IRS has published final regulations section 301.7.701-2(c)(2)(iv), under which __Subs and eligible single-owner disregarded entities are treated as separate entities for employment tax purposes. Under these regulations, eligible ___ entities that have not elected to be taxed as corporations must report and pay employment taxes on wages paid after December 31, 2008,
    (a) S, dual-member
    (b) K, dual-member
    (c) W, single-member
    (d) Q, single-member
    Answer: See Circular E, Introduction, page 9, Disregarded entities and qualified subchapter S subsidiaries/(d) Q, single-member

32. The IRS has published final regulations section 301.7.701-2(c)(2)(iv), under which __Subs and eligible single-owner disregarded entities are treated as separate entities for employment tax purposes. Under these regulations, eligible ___ entities that have not elected to be taxed as corporations must report and pay employment taxes on wages paid after December 31, 2008, using the entities own names and ___.
    (a) S, dual-member, SENs
    (b) K, dual-member, SENs
    (c) W, single-member, EINs
    (d) Q, single-member, EINs
    Answer: See Circular E, Introduction, page 9, Disregarded entities and qualified subchapter S subsidiaries/(d) Q, single-member, EINs,

33. The disregarded entity will be responsible for its **own employment tax obligations** on wages paid after December 31, ___.
    (a) 2008
    (b) 2009
    (c) 2010
    (d) 2011
    Answer: See Circular E, Introduction, page 9 and page 10, Disregarded entities and qualified subchapter S subsidiaries/(a) 2008

Disregarded Entities and Qualified Subchapter S Subsidiaries

34. The disregarded entity will be responsible for its **own employment tax obligations** on wages paid after December 31, ___. For wages paid before January 1, ___, see Publication 15 (Circular E) (For use in ___).
    (a) 2008, 2009, 2008
    (b) 2009, 2010, 2009
    (c) 2010, 2011, 2010
    (d) 2011, 2012, 2011
    Answer: See Circular E, Introduction, page 9 and page 10, Disregarded entities and qualified subchapter S subsidiaries/(a) 2008, 2009, 2008

COBRA Introduction - COBRA Premium Assistance Credit

35. COBRA is defined as ___.
    (a) insurance
    (b) employee paid insurance
    (c) employer paid insurance
    (d) premium assistance credit
    Answer: (a) Insurance. See Circular E, Introduction, page 10, COBRA premium assistance credit.

36. The Consolidated Omnibus Budget Reconciliation Act of ___ (COBRA) provides certain former employees, retirees, spouses, former spouses, and dependent children the right to ___ of health coverage at group rates.
    (a) insurance
    (b) employee paid insurance
    (c) employer paid insurance
    (d) premium assistance credit, temporary continuation
    Answer: See Circular E, Introduction, page 10, COBRA premium assistance credit/(d) premium assistance credit, temporary continuation

37. COBRA generally covers multiemployer health plans and health plans maintained by ___ employers (other than churches) with
    (a) individual
    (b) multiple
    (c) private-sector
    (d) corporations
    Answer: See Circular E, Introduction, page 10, COBRA premium assistance credit/(c) private-sector

COBRA Premium Assistance Credit. (ERISA)

38. COBRA generally covers multiemployer health plans and health plans maintained by ____ employers (other than churches) with ____ or more full and part-time employees.
    (a) individual, 10
    (b) multiple, 15
    (c) private-sector, 20
    (d) corporations, 25
    Answer: See Circular E, Introduction, page 10, COBRA premium assistance credit/(c) private-sector, 20

39. **COBRA** generally covers multiemployer health plans and health plans maintained by ____ employers (other than churches) with ____ or more full and part-time employees. Parallel requirements apply to these plans under the Employee Retirement Income Security Act of ____ (**ERISA**).
    (a) individual, 10, 1955
    (b) multiple, 15, 1971
    (c) private-sector, 20, 1974
    (d) corporations, 25, 2013
    Answer: See Circular E, Introduction, page 10, COBRA premium assistance credit/(c) private-sector, 20, 1974

40. COBRA generally covers multiemployer health plans and health plans maintained by private-sector employers (other than churches) with 20 or more full and part-time employees. Parallel requirements apply to these plans under the Employee Retirement Income Security Act of 1974 (ERISA). Under the Public Health Service Act, COBRA requirements apply to health plans covering ____ or ____ employees. Similar requirements apply under the Federal Employees Health Benefits Program and under ____ state laws.
    (a) state, local government, some
    (b) union, nonunion, all
    (c) nonunion, union, many
    (d) blue collar, white collar, a few
    Answer: See Circular E, Introduction, page 10, COBRA premium assistance credit/(a) state, local government, some

41. For the premium assistance (or subsidy) discussed below, these requirements are all referred to as ____ requirements.
    (a) IRS Publication 15
    (b) Publication 15
    (c) ERISA
    (d) COBRA
    Answer: See Circular E, Introduction, page 10, COBRA premium assistance credit/(d) COBRA

American Recovery and Reinvestment Act of 2009 (ARRA)

42. Under the American Recovery and Reinvestment Act of ___ (ARRA), employers are allowed a credit
    (a) 2009
    (b) 2010
    (c) 2011
    (d) 2012
    Answer: See Circular E, Introduction, page 10, COBRA premium assistance credit/(a) 2009

43. Under the **American Recovery and Reinvestment Act** of ___ (**ARRA**), employers are allowed a credit against "___" (referred to in this publication as "___" for providing COBRA premium assistance to eligible individuals.
    (a) 2009, payroll taxes, employment taxes
    (b) 2010, employment taxes, payroll taxes
    (c) 2011, payroll taxes, employers tax
    (d) 2012, employment taxes, payroll taxes
    Answer: See Circular E, Introduction, page 10, COBRA premium assistance credit/(a) 2009, payroll taxes, employment taxes

COBRA Premium Assistance Credit. (ERISA) Page 10

44. For periods of COBRA continuation coverage beginning after ____, a group health plan must treat an assistance eligible individual as having paid the required COBRA continuation coverage premium if
    (a) January 31, 2009
    (b) February 16, 2009
    (c) March 1, 2009
    (d) April 30, 2009
    Answer: See Circular E, Introduction, page 10, COBRA premium assistance credit/(b) February 16, 2009

45. For periods of COBRA continuation coverage beginning after ____, a group health plan must treat an assistance eligible individual as having paid the required COBRA continuation coverage premium if the individual elects COBRA coverage and pays ___% of the amount of the premium.
    (a) January 31, 2009, 30
    (b) February 16, 2009, 35
    (c) March 1, 2009, 37
    (d) April 30, 2009, 42
    Answer: See Circular E, Introduction, page 10, COBRA premium assistance credit/(b) February 16, 2009, 35

COBRA Premium Assistance Credit. (ERISA) Page 10

46. An assistance eligible individual is a _____ who is eligible for COBRA continuation coverage during the period beginning September 1, 2008 and ending ____,
    (a) qualified beneficiary, January 31, 2009
    (b) employee, February 16, 2009
    (c) employee, April 1, 2010
    (d) qualified beneficiary, May 31, 2010
    Answer: See Circular E, Introduction, page 10, COBRA premium assistance credit/(d) May 31, 2010

47. An assistance eligible individual is a qualified beneficiary who is eligible for COBRA continuation coverage during the period beginning September 1, 2008 and ending ____, due to the ___ from employment of a covered employee during the period and elects continuation COBRA coverage.
    (a) January 31, 2009, termination
    (b) February 16, 2009, termination
    (c) April 1, 2010, involuntary termination
    (d) May 31, 2010, involuntary termination
    Answer: See Circular E, Introduction, page 10, COBRA premium assistance credit/(d) May 31, 2010, involuntary termination

48. An assistance eligible individual is a qualified beneficiary who is eligible for COBRA continuation coverage during the period beginning September 1, 2008 and ending ____, due to the ___ from employment of a covered employee during the period and elects continuation COBRA coverage. The assistance for coverage can last up to ___ months.
    (a) January 31, 2009, termination, 12
    (b) February 16, 2009, termination, 12
    (c) April 1, 2010, involuntary termination, 15
    (d) May 31, 2010, involuntary termination, 15
    Answer: See Circular E, Introduction, page 10, COBRA premium assistance credit/(d) May 31, 2010, involuntary termination, 15

49. Administrators of the group health plans (or other entities) that provide COBRA continuation coverage ___ notice to assistance eligible individuals of the COBRA premium assistance.
    (a) must provide
    (b) will provide
    (c) shall provide
    (d) in addition shall provide
    Answer: See Circular E, Introduction, page 10, COBRA premium assistance credit/(a) must provide

COBRA Premium Assistance Credit. (ERISA) Page 10

50. The ___% of the premium not paid by the assistance eligible individuals is reimbursed to the employer is ___ to the employer maintaining the group health plan.
    (a) 50, billed
    (b) 55, charged
    (c) 60, returned
    (d) 65, reimbursed
    Answer: See Circular E, Introduction, page 10, COBRA premium assistance credit/(d) 65, reimbursed

51. The ___% of the premium not paid by the assistance eligible individuals is reimbursed to the employer is ___ to the employer maintaining the group health plan. The reimbursement is made through a ___ against the employer's tax liabilities.
    (a) 50, billed, debit
    (b) 55, charged, deduction
    (c) 60, returned, charge
    (d) 65, reimbursed, credit
    Answer: See Circular E, Introduction, page 10, COBRA premium assistance credit/(d) 65, reimbursed, credit

52. The ___% of the premium not paid by the assistance eligible individuals is reimbursed to the employer is ___ to the employer maintaining the group health plan. The reimbursement is made through a ___ against the employer's tax liabilities. The employer takes the credit on Form 941 line ___, or Form 944 line ___,
    (a) 50, billed, debit, 9a, 12a
    (b) 55, charged, deduction, 9a, 12a
    (c) 60, returned, charge, 12a, 9a
    (d) 65, reimbursed, credit, 12a, 9a
    Answer: See Circular E, Introduction, page 10, COBRA premium assistance credit/(d) 65, reimbursed, credit, 12a, 9a

53. The employer takes the credit on Form 941 line ___, or Form 944 line ___, once the ___% of the premium is paid by or on behalf of the assistance eligible individual.
    (a) 9a, 11a, 30
    (b) 12a, 9a, 35
    (c) 12a, 10a, 35
    (d) 10a, 12a, 37
    Answer: See Circular E, Introduction, page 10, COBRA premium assistance credit/(b) 12a, 9a, 35

© Copyright 2013. All rights reserved. Notice: United States Copyright Laws and International Treaties prohibit unauthorized publication, reproduction, distribution of this Work. Unauthorized use of this copyright in any form, format, publication or document may result in severe civil and criminal penalties. Violations of this copyright are investigated by the United States Department of Justice and carry, upon conviction of fines up to $250,000 and five years confinement. This Work is protected by United States Copyright Laws and International Treaties. Do not Copy, do not reproduce, do not distribute.

COBRA Premium Assistance Credit. (ERISA) Page 10

54. The employer takes the credit on Form 941 line ___, or Form 944 line ___, once the ___% of the premium is paid by or on behalf of the assistance eligible individual. The credit is treated as a ___ made on the first day of the return period (quarter or year).
    (a)   9a, 11a, 30, liability
    (b)   12a, 9a, 35, deposit
    (c)   12a, 10a, 35, payment
    (d)   10a, 12a, 35, liability
    Answer: See Circular E, Introduction, page 10, COBRA premium assistance credit/(b) 12a, 9a, 35, deposit

55. The employer takes the credit on Form 941 line 12a or Form 944 line 9a, once the 35% of the premium is paid by or on behalf of the assistance eligible individual. The credit is treated as a deposit made on the first day of the return period (quarter or year). In the case of a multiemployer plan, the credit is claimed by the ___ rather than the ___.
    (a)   business, owner
    (b)   plan, employer
    (c)   insurance company, employer
    (d)   employee, employer
    Answer: See Circular E, Introduction, page 10, COBRA premium assistance credit/(b) plan, employer

56. The employer takes the credit on Form 941 line 12a or Form 944 line 9a, once the 35% of the premium is paid by or on behalf of the assistance eligible individual. The credit is treated as a deposit made on the first day of the return period (quarter or year). In the case of a multiemployer plan, the credit is claimed by the plan rather than the employer. In the case of an insured plan subject to state law continuation coverage requirements, the credit is claimed by the ___, rather than the employer. Anyone claiming the credit for COBRA premium assistance ___ maintain the following information to support their claim, including the following.
    (a)   business, must
    (b)   plan, shall
    (c)   insurance company, must
    (d)   employee, shall
    Answer: See Circular E, Introduction, page 10, COBRA premium assistance credit/(c) insurance company, must

COBRA Premium Assistance Credit. (ERISA) Page 10

57. Anyone claiming the credit for COBRA premium assistance must maintain the following information to support their claim, including the following.
    • Information on the receipt of the assistance eligible individuals' ___% share of the premium, including dates and amounts.
    (a) 30
    (b) 33
    (c) 35
    (d) 37
    Answer: See Circular E, Introduction, page 10, COBRA premium assistance credit/(c) 35

58. Anyone claiming the credit for COBRA premium assistance must maintain the following information to support their claim, including the following. • Information on the receipt of the assistance eligible individuals' ___% share of the premium, including dates and amounts.
    • In the case of an insurance plan, a copy of ___ or other supporting statement from the insurance carrier and proof of ___ payment of the full premium to the insurance carrier required under COBRA.
    (a) 30, invoice, timely
    (b) 33, payment, complete
    (c) 35, invoice, timely
    (d) 37, payment proof, complete
    Answer: See Circular E, Introduction, page 10, COBRA premium assistance credit/(c) 35, invoice, timely

59. Anyone claiming the credit for COBRA premium assistance must maintain the following information to support their claim, including the following. • Information on the receipt of the assistance eligible individuals' 35% share of the premium, including dates and amounts. • In the case of an insurance plan, a copy of invoice or other supporting statement from the insurance carrier and proof of timely payment of the full premium to the insurance carrier required under COBRA.
    • In the case of a ___ plan, proof of the premium amount and proof of the coverage provided to the assistance eligible individuals.
    (a) self-insured
    (b) self-insuring
    (c) corporation
    (d) combination corporation
    Answer: See Circular E, Introduction, page 10, COBRA premium assistance credit/(a) self-insured

COBRA Premium Assistance Credit. (ERISA) Page 10

60. Anyone claiming the credit for COBRA premium assistance must maintain the following information to support their claim, including the following.
    • Attestation of involuntary termination, including the date of the involuntary termination for each covered employee whose involuntary termination is the basis for eligibility for the ___.
    (a) request
    (b) subsidy
    (c) refund
    (d) credit
    Answer: See Circular E, Introduction, page 10, COBRA premium assistance credit/(b) subsidy

61. Anyone claiming the credit for COBRA premium assistance must maintain the following information to support their claim, including the following. • Attestation of involuntary termination, including the date of the involuntary termination for each covered employee whose involuntary termination is the basis for eligibility for the ___.
    • Proof of each assistance eligible individual's eligibility for COBRA coverage and the ___ of COBRA coverage.
    (a) request, continuity
    (b) subsidy, election
    (c) refund, participation
    (d) credit, enrollment
    Answer: See Circular E, Introduction, page 10, COBRA premium assistance credit/(b) subsidy, election

62. Anyone claiming the credit for COBRA premium assistance must maintain the following information to support their claim, including the following. • Attestation of involuntary termination, including the date of the involuntary termination for each covered employee whose involuntary termination is the basis for eligibility for the ___. • Proof of each assistance eligible individual's eligibility for COBRA coverage and the ___ of COBRA coverage.
    • A record of the SSNs of all covered employees, the amount of the subsidy ___ with the respect to each covered employee, and
    (a) request, continuity, credit
    (b) subsidy, election, reimbursed
    (c) refund, participation, requested
    (d) credit, enrollment, deducted
    Answer: See Circular E, Introduction, page 10, COBRA premium assistance credit/(b) subsidy, election, reimbursed

COBRA Premium Assistance Credit. (ERISA) Page 10

63. Anyone claiming the credit for COBRA premium assistance must maintain the following information to support their claim, including the following. • Attestation of involuntary termination, including the date of the involuntary termination for each covered employee whose involuntary termination is the basis for eligibility for the ___. • Proof of each assistance eligible individual's eligibility for COBRA coverage and the ___ of COBRA coverage. • A record of the SSNs of all covered employees, the amount of the subsidy ___ with the respect to each covered employee, and whether the ___ was for one individual or two or more individuals.

(a) request, continuity, credit, request
(b) subsidy, election, reimbursed, subsidy
(c) refund, participation, requested, refund
(d) credit, enrollment, deducted, credit

Answer: See Circular E, Introduction, page 10, COBRA premium assistance credit/(b) subsidy, election, reimbursed, subsidy

For more information, visit IRS.gov and enter "COBRA" in the search box.

Instructor's Manual Tests For Section 1
Employer Identification Number (EIN)
The Primary Sections of IRS Circular E
General Description

Tax Test 15E-S1. Tax Test 15E-S1. **Section 1. Employer Identification Number (EIN).** The E.I.N. or Employer Identification Number is to identify for record keeping purposes each employer. It serves a purpose similar in many respects to a Social Security Number, the SSN or any other numerical system of identification. Common test type questions may appear in the forms as follow below.

How many digits make up the EIN number? What purpose does the EIN serve? What is the arrangement of the digits? What is a "Successor Employer"? What are the restrictions placed on a "Successor Employer? Section 1, is a primary section seldom sees changes to text or structure. However, Section 1, though small is frequently a base for Circular E test type questions. Examples of test type questions are provided in Tax test 15E-S1-1.

Section 1 - Employer Identification Number (EIN)
Section 1. Employer Identification Number (EIN)

DU VALL'S TEST'S™
Instructors Manual Study Guide Series United States Tax Code
IRS Publication 15 Circular E, Employer's Tax Guide Tax Year 2013
Tax Test 15E-S1-1 [Multiple-Choice Questions With Answers]

1. Employer Identification Number (EIN) page 10

1. Employer Identification Number
1. If you are required to report ___ taxes or give tax statements to employees or ___, you need an employer identification number (EIN).
    (a) office staff, annual statements
    (b) income, the IRS
    (c) employment, annuitants
    (d) quarterly, the IRS
    Answer: See Circular E, 1. Employer Identification Number (EIN), page 10/(c) employment, annuitants

© Copyright 2013. All rights reserved. Notice: United States Copyright Laws and International Treaties prohibit unauthorized publication, reproduction, distribution of this Work. Unauthorized use of this copyright in any form, format, publication or document may result in severe civil and criminal penalties. Violations of this copyright are investigated by the United States Department of Justice and carry, upon conviction of fines up to $250,000 and five years confinement. This Work is protected by United States Copyright Laws and International Treaties. Do not Copy, do not reproduce, do not distribute.

A Ficus Tree Publishing Educational-Technical Publications

1. Employer Identification Number (EIN)

1. Employer Identification Number
2. The EIN is a ___-digit number.
   (a) seven
   (b) eight
   (c) nine
   (d) ten
   Answer: See Circular E, 1. Employer Identification Number (EIN), page 10/(c) nine

1. Employer Identification Number
3. The EIN is a ___-digit number. The digits are arranged as follows: ___.
   (a) seven, 00-0000000
   (b) eight, 00-000000
   (c) nine, 00-0000000
   (d) ten, 000-0000000
   Answer: See Circular E, 1. Employer Identification Number (EIN), page 10/
   (c) nine, 00-0000000

1. Employer Identification Number
4. The EIN is a ___-digit number. The digits are arranged as follows: ___. It is used to identify the tax accounts of employers and certain others who have no ___.
   (a) seven, 00-0000000, employees
   (b) eight, 00-000000, employers
   (c) nine, 00-0000000, employees
   (d) ten, 000-0000000, employers
   Answer: See Circular E, 1. Employer Identification Number (EIN), page 10/
   (c) nine, 00-0000000, employees

1. Employer Identification Number
5. Use your EIN on all items you send to the IRS and ___.
   (a) SSA
   (b) ICC
   (c) COBRA
   (d) FCC
   Answer: See Circular E, 1. Employer Identification Number (EIN), page 10/(a) SSA

1. Employer Identification Number
6. For more information, see Publication ___, Employer Identification Number: Understanding Your EIN.
   (a) 1634
   (b) 1635
   (c) 1636
   (d) 1637
   Answer: See Circular E, 1. Employer Identification Number (EIN), page 10/(b) 1635

1. Employer Identification Number (EIN)

1. Employer Identification Number
7. If you do not have an EIN, you may apply for one on-line. Go to the IRS.gov and click on the ___ for an EIN Online link under Tools.
   (a) New
   (b) New Employer
   (c) Apply
   (d) Application
   Answer: See Circular E, 1. Employer Identification Number (EIN), page 10/(c) Apply

1. Employer Identification Number
8. If you do not have an EIN, you may apply for one on-line. Go to the IRS.gov and click on the ___ for an EIN Online link under Tools. You may also apply for an EIN by calling ____, or
   (a) New, 1-800-829-4931
   (b) New Employer, 1-800-829-4932
   (c) Apply, 1-800-829-4933
   (d) Application, 1-800-829-4934
   Answer: See Circular E, 1. Employer Identification Number (EIN), page 10/(c) Apply, 1-800-829-4933

1. Employer Identification Number
9. If you do not have an EIN, you may apply for one on-line. Go to the IRS.gov and click on the ___ for an EIN Online link under Tools. You may also apply for an EIN by calling ___, or you can fax or mail Form ___, Application for Employer Identification Number, to the IRS.
   (a) New, 1-800-829-4931, SS-3
   (b) New Employer, 1-800-829-4932, SS-3
   (c) Apply, 1-800-829-4933, SS-4
   (d) Application, 1-800-829-4934, SS-4
   Answer: See Circular E, 1. Employer Identification Number (EIN), page 10/(c) Apply, 1-800-829-4933, SS-4

1. Employer Identification Number
10. If you do not have an EIN, you may apply for one on-line. Go to the IRS.gov and click on the ___ for an EIN Online link under Tools. You may also apply for an EIN by calling ___, or you can fax or mail Form ___, Application for Employer Identification Number, to the IRS. Do not use a ___ in place of an EIN.
    (a) New, 1-800-829-4931, SS-3, your personal income tax number
    (b) New Employer, 1-800-829-4932, SS-3, personal income tax number
    (c) Apply, 1-800-829-4933, SS-4, social security number (SSN)
    (d) Application, 1-800-829-4934, SS-4, Social Security Number
    Answer: See Circular E, 1. Employer Identification Number (EIN), page 10/(c) Apply, 1-800-829-4933, SS-4, social security number (SSN)

© Copyright 2013. All rights reserved. Notice: United States Copyright Laws and International Treaties prohibit unauthorized publication, reproduction, distribution of this Work. Unauthorized use of this copyright in any form, format, publication or document may result in severe civil and criminal penalties. Violations of this copyright are investigated by the United States Department of Justice and carry, upon conviction of fines up to $250,000 and five years confinement. This Work is protected by United States Copyright Laws and International Treaties. Do not Copy, do not reproduce, do not distribute.

1. Employer Identification Number (EIN)

1. Employer Identification Number
11.   You should have only one ___.
   (a)   SSN
   (b)   EIN
   (c)   tax number
   (d)   Employer Tax Number
   Answer: See Circular E, 1. Employer Identification Number (EIN), page 10/(b) EIN

1. Employer Identification Number
12.   You should have only one ___. If you have more than one and are not sure which one to use, call 1-800-929-4933 or 1-800-829-4059 (TDD/TTY for persons who are ___, hard of hearing, or have a speech disability).
   (a)   SSN, deaf
   (b)   EIN, deaf
   (c)   tax number, blind
   (d)   Employer Tax Number, blind
   Answer: See Circular E, 1. Employer Identification Number (EIN), page 10/(b) EIN, deaf

1. Employer Identification Number
13.   You should have only one EIN. If you have more than one and are not sure which one to use, call 1-800-929-4933 or 1-800-829-4059 (TDD/TTY for persons who are deaf, hard of hearing, or have a speech disability). Give the numbers you have, the name and ___ to which each was assigned, and
   (a)   the name of the individual
   (b)   identity
   (c)   correct address
   (d)   address
   Answer: See Circular E, 1. Employer Identification Number (EIN), page 10/(d) address

1. Employer Identification Number
14.   You should have only one EIN. If you have more than one and are not sure which one to use, call 1-800-929-4933 or 1-800-829-4059 (TDD/TTY for persons who are deaf, hard of hearing, or have a speech disability). Give the numbers you have, the name and ___ to which each was assigned, and to which each was assigned, and the address of your ___ place of business. The IRS will tell you which number to use.
   (a)   the name of the individual, registered
   (b)   identity, official
   (c)   correct address, primary
   (d)   address, main
   Answer: See Circular E, 1. Employer Identification Number (EIN), page 10/(d) address, main

© Copyright 2013. All rights reserved. Notice: United States Copyright Laws and International Treaties prohibit unauthorized publication, reproduction, distribution of this Work. Unauthorized use of this copyright in any form, format, publication or document may result in severe civil and criminal penalties. Violations of this copyright are investigated by the United States Department of Justice and carry, upon conviction of fines up to $250,000 and five years confinement. This Work is protected by United States Copyright Laws and International Treaties. Do not Copy, do not reproduce, do not distribute.

1. Employer Identification Number (EIN) Successor employer

1. Employer Identification Number

15. If you took over another employer's business (see <u>Successor employer</u> in section ___), do not use that employer's EIN.
    - (a) 9
    - (b) 10
    - (c) 11
    - (d) 12

    Answer: See Circular E, 1. Employer Identification Number (EIN), page 11/(a) 9

1. Employer Identification Number

16. If you took over another employer's business (see <u>Successor employer</u> in section ___), do not use that employer's EIN. If you have applied for an EIN but do not have your EIN by the time it is due, file a ___ return and write "Applied For" and the date you applied for it in the space shown for the number.
    - (a) 9, paper
    - (b) 10, electronic
    - (c) 11, temporary
    - (d) 12, substitute

    Answer: See Circular E, 1. Employer Identification Number (EIN), page 11/(a) 9, paper

A Ficus Tree Publishing Quick Notes Page.

© Copyright 2013. All rights reserved. Notice: United States Copyright Laws and International Treaties prohibit unauthorized publication, reproduction, distribution of this Work. Unauthorized use of this copyright in any form, format, publication or document may result in severe civil and criminal penalties. Violations of this copyright are investigated by the United States Department of Justice and carry, upon conviction of fines up to $250,000 and five years confinement. This Work is protected by United States Copyright Laws and International Treaties. Do not Copy, do not reproduce, do not distribute.

A Ficus Tree Publishing Educational-Technical Publications

The International Leader in Construction Technology Home Study

Instructor's Manual for Tax Test 15E-S2
Section 2
Tax Test 15E-S2-1. Who are Employees?
Tax Test 15E-S2-2. Husband And Wife Business

General Description

Tax Test 15E-S2-1. Section 2. Who Are Employees? Who is a common law employee or a statute law employee. What is the status of an employee under common law as to an employee under statute law. Generally, people in business for themselves are not employees (think Doctor, Lawyer or similar occupation). How is a full-time life insurance person who sells primarily for one company classified. What is the definition of a statutory nonemployee. How is a H-2A agricultural worker classified. Treating employees as nonemployees. You will generally be liable for social security and Medicare taxes if you do not deduct and withhold them because you treat an employees as a nonemployee.

Tax Test 15E-S2-2. Section 2. Husband-Wife Business. If you and your spouse jointly own and operate a business and share in the profits and losses, you are partners in a partnership. There are exceptions to this basic rule. The exceptions do exist providing material for test type questions.

Key Words

Tax Test 15E-S2-1and S2-2. Employee status under common law. Statutory employees. An agent. A full-time life insurance salesperson. A homeworker. A traveling or city salesperson. Statutory nonemployees. H-2A agricultural workers. treating employees as nonemployees. Section 3509 rates. Relief provisions. IRS help. Voluntary Classification Settlement Program (VCSP). Husband-Wife Business. Exception. Qualified joint venture. Community Income.

Section 2 - Who are Employees 15E-S2-1. Who Are Employees? Page 11

© Copyright 2013. All rights reserved. Notice: United States Copyright Laws and International Treaties prohibit unauthorized publication, reproduction, distribution of this Work. Unauthorized use of this copyright in any form, format, publication or document may result in severe civil and criminal penalties. Violations of this copyright are investigated by the United States Department of Justice and carry, upon conviction of fines up to $250,000 and five years confinement. This Work is protected by United States Copyright Laws and International Treaties. Do not Copy, do not reproduce, do not distribute.

A Ficus Tree Publishing Educational-Technical Publications

A Ficus Tree Publishing Quick Notes Page

The International Leader in Construction Technology Home Study

DU VALL'S TEST'S™
Instructors Manual Study Guide Series United States Tax Code
IRS Publication 15 Circular E, Employer's Tax Guide Tax Year 2013
Tax Test 15E-S2-1 [Multiple-Choice Questions With Answers]

15E-S2-1. Who Are Employees? Common Law

2. Who Are Employees?
1. Generally, employees are defined either under ___ or under ___ for certain situations.
    (a) statute law, common law
    (b) common law, statute
    (c) self-employed, Independent
    (d) Independent Contractors, full-time employees
    Answer: See Circular E, 2. Who are Employees, page 11/(b) common law, statute
    15E-S2-1. Who Are Employees? Common Law

2. Who are employees?
2. Generally, employees are defined either under ___ or under ___ for certain situations. See Publication ___ for details on statutory employees and nonemployees.
    (a) statute law, common law, 15
    (b) common law, statute, 15A
    (c) self-employed, Independent, 15B
    (d) Independent Contractors, full-time employees, 15C
    Answer: See Circular E, 2. Who are Employees, page 11/(b) common law, statute, 15A

2. Employee status under common law.
3. Generally, a worker who performs services for you is you have the right to ____ what will be done and how it will be done.
    (a) direct
    (b) specify
    (c) control
    (d) designate
    Answer: See Circular E, 2. Who are Employees, page 11/(c) control

2. Employee status under common law.
4. Generally, a worker who performs services for you is you have the right to ____ what will be done and how it will be done. This is so even when you give the employee ___.
    (a) direct, hourly wages
    (b) specify, specific instructions
    (c) control, freedom of action
    (d) designate, specific tasks
    Answer: See Circular E, 2. Who are Employees, page 11/(c) control, freedom of action,

© Copyright 2013. All rights reserved. Notice: United States Copyright Laws and International Treaties prohibit unauthorized publication, reproduction, distribution of this Work. Unauthorized use of this copyright in any form, format, publication or document may result in severe civil and criminal penalties. Violations of this copyright are investigated by the United States Department of Justice and carry, upon conviction of fines up to $250,000 and five years confinement. This Work is protected by United States Copyright Laws and International Treaties. Do not Copy, do not reproduce, do not distribute.

A Ficus Tree Publishing Educational-Technical Publications

Who Are Employees? Common Law

2. Employee status under common law.
5. Generally, a worker who performs services for you is you have the right to ___ what will be done and how it will be done. This is so even when you give the employee ___. What matters is that you have the right to ___ of how the services are performed.
    (a) direct, hourly wages, control the work
    (b) specify, specific instructions, control the work
    (c) control, freedom of action, control the details
    (d) designate, specific tasks, control the actual task
Answer: See Circular E, 2. Who are Employees, page 11/(c) control, freedom of action, control the details

2. Employee status under common law.
6. See Publication 15-A for more information on how to determine whether an individual providing services is an ___ or an employee.
    (a) independent contractor
    (b) statutory employee
    (c) private contractor
    (d) nonemployee
Answer: See Circular E, 2. Who are Employees, page 11/(a) independent contractor

2. Employee status under common law.
7. Generally, people in business for themselves are ___.
    (a) proprietors
    (b) not employees
    (c) the private contractor
    (d) a nonemployee
Answer: See Circular E, 2. Who are Employees, page 11/(b) not employees

2. Employee status under common law.
8. Generally, people in business for themselves are ___. **For example**, doctors, lawyers, ___, and others in an ___ trade in which they offer their services to the public are usually not employees.
    (a) proprietors, engineers, independent
    (b) not employees, veterinarians, independent
    (c) the private contractor, independent contractors, professional
    (d) a nonemployee, engineers, professional
Answer: See Circular E, 2. Who are Employees, page 11/(b) not employees, veterinarians, independent

The International Leader in Construction Technology Home Study

Who Are Employees? Common Law

2. Employee status under common law.
9. Generally, people in business for themselves are not employees. **For example**, doctors, lawyers, veterinarians, and others in an independent trade in which they offer their services to the public are usually not employees. However, if the business is ____, corporate officers who work in the business ___ employees of the corporation.
   (a) a corporation, are not
   (b) incorporated, may be
   (c) a corporation, are
   (d) incorporated, are
   Answer: See Circular E, 2. Who are Employees, page 11/(d) incorporated, are

2. Employee status under common law.
10. If an employer-employee relationship exists, it ___ what it is called.
   (a) does not matter
   (b) is unimportant
   (c) is important
   (d) must comply with
   Answer: See Circular E, 2. Who are Employees, page 11/(a) it does not matter

2. Employee status under common law.
11. If an employer-employee relationship exists, it ___ what it is called. The employee may be called an ___ or independent contractor.
   (a) does not matter, agent
   (b) is unimportant, relative
   (c) is important, family member
   (d) must comply with, employee
   Answer: See Circular E, 2. Who are Employees, page 11/(a) it does not matter, agent

2. Employee status under common law.
12. If an employer-employee relationship exists, it ___ what it is called. The employee may be called an ___ or independent contractor. It also does not matter how ___ are measured or ___, what they are called, or if the employee works full or part time.
   (a) does not matter, agent, payments, paid
   (b) is unimportant, relative, wages, paid
   (c) is important, family member, wages, compensated
   (d) must comply with, employee, wages, compensated
   Answer: See Circular E, 2. Who are Employees, page 11/(a) it does not matter, agent, payments, paid

© Copyright 2013. All rights reserved. Notice: United States Copyright Laws and International Treaties prohibit unauthorized publication, reproduction, distribution of this Work. Unauthorized use of this copyright in any form, format, publication or document may result in severe civil and criminal penalties. Violations of this copyright are investigated by the United States Department of Justice and carry, upon conviction of fines up to $250,000 and five years confinement. This Work is protected by United States Copyright Laws and International Treaties. Do not Copy, do not reproduce, do not distribute.

A Ficus Tree Publishing Educational-Technical Publications

S2-1. Who Are Employees? Statutory Employees

2. Statutory employees.
13. If someone who works for you is ____ under the common law rules discussed earlier,
    (a) an employee
    (b) not an employee
    (c) a subordinate
    (d) a manager
    Answer: See Circular E, 2. Who are Employees, page 11/(b) not an employee

2. Statutory employees.
14. If someone who works for you is ____ under the common law rules discussed earlier, do not withhold ___ from his or her pay, unless
    (a) an employee, Medicare tax
    (b) not an employee, federal income tax
    (c) a subordinate, social security tax
    (d) a manager, Medicare and social security taxes
    Answer: See Circular E, 2. Who are Employees, page 11/(b) not an employee, federal income tax

2. Statutory employees.
15. If someone who works for you is ____ under the common law rules discussed earlier, do not withhold ___ from his or her pay, unless
    (a) an employee, Medicare tax, backup withholding
    (b) not an employee, federal income tax, backup withholding
    (c) a subordinate, social security tax, child support payments
    (d) a manager, Medicare and social security taxes, child support payments
    Answer: See Circular E, 2. Who are Employees, page 11/(b) not an employee, federal income tax, backup withholding

2. Statutory employees.
16. Although the following persons may not be ___, they are considered employees by ___ for social security, Medicare and FUTA tax purposes under certain conditions.
    (a) employees, the IRS
    (b) statute law employees, statute
    (c) common law employees, statute
    (d) employees, federal tax law
    Answer: See Circular E, 2. Who are Employees, page 11/(c) common law employees, statute

S2-1. Who Are Employees? Statutory Employees

2. Statutory employees.
17. Although the following persons may not be common law employees, they are considered employees by statute for social security, Medicare and FUTA tax purposes under certain conditions.
    • An agent (or ___) driver who delivers food, beverages (other than milk), laundry, or dry cleaning for someone else.
    (a)   sales person
    (b)   salesman
    (c)   representative
    (d)   commission
    Answer: See Circular E, 2. Who are Employees, page 11/(d) commission

2. Statutory employees.
18. Although the following persons may not be common law employees, they are considered employees by statute for social security, Medicare and FUTA tax purposes under certain conditions.
    • An full-time life insurance salesperson who sells ___ for one company.
    (a)   primarily
    (b)   policies
    (c)   contracts
    (d)   for a commission
    Answer: See Circular E, 2. Who are Employees, page 11/(a) primarily

2. Statutory employees.
19. Although the following persons may not be common law employees, they are considered employees by statute for social security, Medicare and FUTA tax purposes under certain conditions. • A homeworker who works by ___ of the person for whom the work is done, with materials furnished by and returned to that person or someone that person designates.
    (a)   salary
    (b)   guidelines
    (c)   the supervision
    (d)   direct supervision
    Answer: See Circular E, 2. Who are Employees, page 11/(b) guidelines

S2-1. Who Are Employees? Statutory Employees

2. Statutory employees.
20. Although the following persons may not be common law employees, they are considered employees by statute for social security, Medicare and FUTA tax purposes under certain conditions.
    • A traveling or city salesperson (other than an agent-driver or commission driver) who works full time (except for ___) for one firm getting orders from customers.
    (a) outside sales
    (b) direct sales
    (c) sideline sales activity
    (d) direct sales supervision activity
    Answer: See Circular E, 2. Who are Employees, page 11/(c) sideline sales activity

2. Statutory employees.
21. Although the following persons may not be common law employees, they are considered employees by statute for social security, Medicare and FUTA tax purposes under certain conditions.
    • A traveling or city salesperson (other than an agent-driver or commission driver) who works full time (except for ___) for one firm getting orders from customers. The orders must be for merchandise for ___ or supplies for use in the customer's business.
    (a) outside sales, resale
    (b) direct sales, retail
    (c) sideline sales activity, resale
    (d) direct sales supervision activity, retail
    Answer: See Circular E, 2. Who are Employees, page 11/(c) sideline sales activity, resale

2. Statutory employees.
22. Although the following persons may not be common law employees, they are considered employees by statute for social security, Medicare and FUTA tax purposes under certain conditions.
    • A traveling or city salesperson (other than an agent-driver or commission driver) who works full time (except for ___) for one firm getting orders from customers. The orders must be for merchandise for ___ or supplies for use in the customer's business. The customers must be retailers, wholesalers, contractors, or operators of hotels, restaurants, or other businesses dealing with food or ___.
    (a) outside sales, resale, lodging
    (b) direct sales, retail, shelter
    (c) sideline sales activity, resale, lodging
    (d) direct sales supervision activity, retail, logging
    Answer: See Circular E, 2. Who are Employees, page 11/(c) sideline sales activity, resale, lodging

S2-1. Who Are Employees? Statutory Nonemployees

2. Statutory employees-Statutory nonemployees
23. There are ___ different statutory employee designations in Part 2. Who Are Employees?
    (a) two
    (b) three
    (c) four
    (d) five
    Answer: See Circular E, Who Are Employees? Statutory employees, Page 11/ (a) two (statutory employees, statutory nonemployee)

2. Statutory nonemployees.
24. Direct sellers, qualified real estate agents, and certain ___ sitters are, by law, considered nonemployees.
    (a) dog
    (b) pet
    (c) house
    (d) companion
    Answer: See Circular E, 2. Who are Employees, page 11/(d) companion

2. Statutory nonemployees.
25. Direct sellers, qualified real estate agents, and certain ___ sitters are, by law, considered nonemployees. They are generally treated as ___ for all federal tax purposes, including income and employment taxes.
    (a) dog, self-employed
    (b) pet, household employees
    (c) house, independent contractors
    (d) companion, self-employed
    Answer: See Circular E, 2. Who are Employees, page 11/(d) companion, self-employed

S2-1. Who Are Employees? H-2A agricultural workers, page 11.

2. H-2A agricultural workers
26. On Form W-2, do not check box ___ (Statutory employees),
    (a) 11
    (b) 12
    (c) 13
    (d) 14
    Answer: See Circular E, 2. Who are Employees, page 11/(c) 13

S2-1. Who Are Employees? H-2A agricultural workers, page 11.

2. H-2A agricultural workers

27. On Form W-2, do not check box ___ (Statutory employees), as H-2A workers are not ___ employees.
    (a) 11, permanent
    (b) 12, industrial
    (c) 13, statutory
    (d) 14, nonemployees
    Answer: See Circular E, 2. Who are Employees, page 11/(c) 13, statutory

S2-1. Who Are Employees? Treating employees as nonemployees

2. Treating employees as nonemployees

28. You will generally be liable for social security and Medicare taxes and withheld income tax if you do not deduct and withhold them because you treat an employee as a ___.
    (a) family member
    (b) corporate officer
    (c) full partner
    (d) nonemployee
    Answer: See Circular E, Who Are Employees? Statutory nonemployees, page 11/ (d) nonemployee

2. Treating employees as nonemployees

28. You will generally be liable for social security and Medicare taxes and withheld income tax if you do not deduct and withhold them because you treat an employee as a___. You may be able to calculate your liability using special section ___ rates for the
    (a) family member, 3508
    (b) corporate officer, 3509
    (c) full partner, 3508
    (d) nonemployee, 3509
    Answer: See Circular E, Who Are Employees? Statutory nonemployees, page 11/ (d) nonemployee, 3509

2. Treating employees as nonemployees

29. You will generally be liable for social security and Medicare taxes and withheld income tax if you do not deduct and withhold them because you treat an employee as a___. You may be able to calculate your liability using special section ___ rates for the ___ share of social security and Medicare taxes and the federal income tax withholding.
    (a) family member, 3508, employer
    (b) corporate officer, 3509, employer
    (c) full partner, 3508, employee
    (d) nonemployee, 3509, employee
    Answer: See Circular E, Who Are Employees? Statutory nonemployees, page 11/ (d) nonemployee, 3509, employee

S2-1. Who Are Employees? Treating employees as nonemployees

2. Treating employees as nonemployees
30. You will generally be liable for social security and Medicare taxes and withheld income tax if you do not deduct and withhold them because you treat an employee as a nonemployee. You may be able to calculate your liability using special section 3509 rates for the employee share of social security and Medicare taxes and the federal income tax withholding. The applicable rates depend on whether you filed the required Forms ___.
    (a) 1099
    (b) 1098
    (c) 941
    (d) 944
    Answer: See Circular E, Who Are Employees? Statutory nonemployees, page 11/ (a) 1099

2. Treating employees as nonemployees
31. You will generally be liable for social security and Medicare taxes and withheld income tax if you do not deduct and withhold them because you treat an employee as a nonemployee. You may be able to calculate your liability using special section 3509 rates for the employee share of social security and Medicare taxes and the federal income tax withholding. The applicable rates depend on whether you filed the required Forms ___. You cannot recover the ___ share of social security, or
    (a) 1099, employee
    (b) 1098, employer
    (c) 941, employee
    (d) 944, employer
    Answer: See Circular E, Who Are Employees? Statutory nonemployees, page 11/
    (a) 1099, employee

2. Treating employees as nonemployees
32. You will generally be liable for social security and Medicare taxes and withheld income tax if you do not deduct and withhold them because you treat an employee as a nonemployee. You may be able to calculate your liability using special section 3509 rates for the employee share of social security and Medicare taxes and the federal income tax withholding. The applicable rates depend on whether you filed the required Forms ___. You cannot recover the ___ share of social security, or Medicare tax, or income tax withholding from the employee if the tax is paid under section ___.
    (a) 1099, employee, 3509
    (b) 1098, employer, 3508
    (c) 941, employee, 3509
    (d) 944, employer, 3508
    Answer: See Circular E, Who Are Employees? Statutory nonemployees, page 11/ (a) 1099, employee, 3509

S2-1. Who Are Employees? Treating employees as nonemployees

2. Treating employees as nonemployees

33. You will generally be liable for social security and Medicare taxes and withheld income tax if you do not deduct and withhold them because you treat an employee as a nonemployee. You may be able to calculate your liability using special section 3509 rates for the employee share of social security and Medicare taxes and the federal income tax withholding. The applicable rates depend on whether you filed the required Forms ___. You cannot recover the ___ share of social security, or Medicare tax, or income tax withholding from the employee if the tax is paid under section ___. You are liable for the income tax ___ regardless of whether the employee paid income taxes on the wages.
    (a) 1099, employee, 3509, withholding
    (b) 1098, employer, 3508, withheld
    (c) 941, employee, 3509, payment
    (d) 944, employer, 3508, due
    Answer: See Circular E, Who Are Employees? Statutory nonemployees, page 11/ (a) 1099, employee, 3509, withholding

2. Treating employees as nonemployees

34. You will generally be liable for social security and Medicare taxes and withheld income tax if you do not deduct and withhold them because you treat an employee as a nonemployee. You may be able to calculate your liability using special section 3509 rates for the employee share of social security and Medicare taxes and the federal income tax withholding. The applicable rates depend on whether you filed the required Forms ___. You cannot recover the ___ share of social security, or Medicare tax, or income tax withholding from the employee if the tax is paid under section ___. You are liable for the income tax ___ regardless of whether the employee paid income taxes on the wages. You continue to owe the full ___ share of social security and Medicare taxes.
    (a) 1099, employee, 3509, withholding, employer
    (b) 1098, employer, 3508, withheld, employee
    (c) 941, employee, 3509, payment, business
    (d) 944, employer, 3508, due, employer
    Answer: See Circular E, Who Are Employees? Statutory nonemployees, page 11/ (a) 1099, employee, 3509, withholding, employer

S2-1. Who Are Employees? Treating employees as nonemployees

2. Treating employees as nonemployees
35. You will generally be liable for social security and Medicare taxes and withheld income tax if you do not deduct and withhold them because you treat an employee as a nonemployee. You may be able to calculate your liability using special section 3509 rates for the employee share of social security and Medicare taxes and the federal income tax withholding. The applicable rates depend on whether you filed the required Forms 1099. You cannot recover the employee share of social security, or Medicare tax, or income tax withholding from the employee if the tax is paid under section 3509. You are liable for the income tax withholding regardless of whether the employee paid income taxes on the wages. The employee remains liable for the ___ share of social security and Medicare taxes.
    (a) withholding
    (b) withheld
    (c) employee
    (d) employer
    Answer: See Circular E, Who Are Employees? Treating employees as nonemployees, page 11/ (c) employee

2. Treating employees as nonemployees
36. You will generally be liable for social security and Medicare taxes and withheld income tax if you do not deduct and withhold them because you treat an employee as a nonemployee. You may be able to calculate your liability using special section 3509 rates for the employee share of social security and Medicare taxes and the federal income tax withholding. The applicable rates depend on whether you filed the required Forms 1099. You cannot recover the employee share of social security, or Medicare tax, or income tax withholding from the employee if the tax is paid under section 3509. You are liable for the income tax withholding regardless of whether the employee paid income taxes on the wages. The employee remains liable for the ___ share of social security and Medicare taxes. See Internal Revenue Code section 3509 for details. Also see the Instructions for Form ___.
    (a) withholding, 941-A
    (b) withheld, 941-C
    (c) employee, 941-X
    (d) employer, 941-Z
    Answer: See Circular E, Who Are Employees? Treating employees as nonemployees, page 11/ (c) employee, 941-X

S2-1. Who Are Employees? Treating employees as nonemployees

2. Treating employees as nonemployees
37. Section 3509 rates are not available if you ____ the requirement to withhold taxes from the employee or is you withheld income taxes but not social security or Medicare taxes.
    (a) intentionally disregarded
    (b) completely disregarded
    (c) disregarded
    (d) willfully disregarded
    Answer: See Circular E, Who Are Employees? Treating employees as nonemployees, page 11/ (a) intentionally disregarded

2. Treating employees as nonemployees
38. Section 3509 rates are not available if you ____ the requirement to withhold taxes from the employee or is you withheld income taxes but not social security or Medicare taxes. Section ___ is not available for reclassifying statutory employees. See *Statutory employees*, earlier in this section.
    (a) intentionally disregarded, 3509
    (b) completely disregarded, 3509
    (c) disregarded, 3508
    (d) willfully disregarded, 3508
    Answer: See Circular E, Who Are Employees? Treating employees as non employees, page 11/ (a) intentionally disregarded, 3508

2. Treating employees as nonemployees
39. If the employer issued information returns, the section ___ rates are:
    (a) 3508
    (b) 3509
    (c) 3510
    (d) 3511
    Answer: See Circular E, Who Are Employees? Treating employees as non employees, page 11/ (b) 3509

2. Treating employees as nonemployees
40. If the employer issued information returns, the section 3509 rates are:
    • For social security taxes; employer rate of ___% plus ___% of the employee rate (see instructions for Form ___).
    (a) 6.2, 15, 940-X
    (b) 6.2, 18, 940-X
    (c) 6.2, 20, 941-X
    (d) 6.3, 20, 941-X
    Answer: See Circular E, Who Are Employees? treating employees as nonemployees, page 11/ (c) 6.2, 20, 941-X

S2-1. Who Are Employees? Treating employees as nonemployees

2. Treating employees as nonemployees
41. If the employer issued information returns, the section 3509 rates are:
    • For Medicare taxes; employer rate of ___% plus ___% of the employee rate of ___%, for a total rate of ___% of wages.
    (a) 1.45, 15, 1.45, 1.70
    (b) 1.45, 15, 1.45, 1.72
    (c) 1.45, 15, 1.45, 1.73
    (d) 1.45, 20, 1.45, 1.74
    Answer: See Circular E, Who Are Employees? treating employees as nonemployees, page 11/ (d) 1.45, 20, 1.45, 1.74.

2. Treating employees as nonemployees
42. If the employer issued information returns, the section 3509 rates are:
    • For Additional Medicare Tax; ___% of the employee rate of ___%.
    (a) 20, 0.9
    (b) 20, 10
    (c) 25, 0.9
    (d) 25, 10
    Answer: See Circular E, Who Are Employees? treating employees as nonemployees, page 11/ (a) 20, 0.9.

2. Treating employees as nonemployees
43. If the employer issued information returns, the section 3509 rates are:
    • For income tax withholding, the rate is ___% of wages.
    (a) 1.25
    (b) 1.5
    (c) 1.75
    (d) 2.0
    Answer: See Circular E, Who Are Employees? treating employees as nonemployees, page 11/ (b) 1.5

2. Treating employees as nonemployees
44. If the employer did not issue required information returns, the section 3509 rates are:
    • For social security taxes; the employer rate of 6.2% plus ___% of the employee rate (see the Instructions for Form 941-X).
    (a) 30
    (b) 35
    (c) 40
    (d) 45
    Answer: See Circular E, Who Are Employees? treating employees as nonemployees, page 11/(c) 40

S2-1. Who Are Employees? Treating employees as nonemployees

2. Treating employees as nonemployees
45. If the employer did not issue required information returns, the section 3509 rates are:
    • For **Medicare** taxes; employer rate of 1.45% plus ___% of the employee rate of ___%, for a total rate of ___% of wages.
    (a)   30, 1.25, 2.01
    (b)   35, 1.35, 2.02
    (c)   40, 1.45, 2.03
    (d)   45, 1.50, 2.05
    Answer: See Circular E, Who Are Employees? treating employees as nonemployees, page 11/(c) 40, 1.45, 2.03

2. Treating employees as nonemployees
46. If the employer did not issue required information returns, the section 3509 rates are:
    • For **Additional** Medicare Tax; ___% of the employee rate of ___%.
    (a)   30, 0.5
    (b)   35, 0.8
    (c)   40, 0.9
    (d)   45, 0.9
    Answer: See Circular E, Who Are Employees? treating employees as nonemployees, page 12/(c) 40, 0.9

2. Treating employees as nonemployees
47. If the employer did not issue required information returns, the section 3509 rates are:
    • For **income tax** withholding the rate is ___% of wages.
    (a)   3.0
    (b)   3.5
    (c)   4.0
    (d)   4.5
    Answer: See Circular E, Who Are Employees? treating employees as nonemployees, page 12/(a) 3.0

S2-1. Who Are Employees? Relief Provisions. Page 12.

2. Relief provisions
48. If you have a reasonable basis for not treating a ___ as an employee, you may be relieved from having to pay employment taxes for that worker.
    (a)   employee
    (b)   worker
    (c)   independent contractor
    (d)   agent
    Answer: See Circular E, Who Are Employees? Relief provisions, page 12/ (b) worker

S2-1. Who Are Employees? Relief Provisions

2. Relief provisions
49. If you have a reasonable basis for not treating a worker as an employee, you may be relieved from having to pay employment taxes for that worker. To get this relief under the relief provisions, you must file all required federal tax returns, including information returns on a basis consistent with your ___ of the worker.
    (a) employment
    (b) classification
    (c) treatment
    (d) supervision
    Answer: See Circular E, Who Are Employees? Relief provisions, page 12/ (c) treatment

2. Relief provisions
50. If you have a reasonable basis for not treating a worker as an employee, you may be relieved from having to pay employment taxes for that worker. To get this relief under the relief provisions, you must file all required federal tax returns, including information returns on a basis consistent with your treatment of the worker. You (or your predecessor) must not have treated any worker holding a ___ similar position as an employee for any periods beginning after ___.
    (a) substantially, 1977
    (b) identical or, 1987
    (c) comparable, 2010
    (d) parallel, 2012
    Answer: See Circular E, Who Are Employees? Relief provisions, page 12/ (a) substantially, 1977

2. Relief provisions
51. If you have a reasonable basis for not treating a worker as an employee, you may be relieved from having to pay employment taxes for that worker. To get this relief under the relief provisions, you must file all required federal tax returns, including information returns on a basis consistent with your treatment of the worker. You (or your predecessor) must not have treated any worker holding a ___ similar position as an employee for any periods beginning after ___. See Publication 1976, Do You Qualify for Relief Under Section ___.
    (a) substantially, 1977, 530
    (b) identical or, 1987, 540
    (c) comparable, 2010, 550
    (d) parallel, 2012, 530
    Answer: See Circular E, Who Are Employees? Relief provisions, page 12/ (a) substantially, 1977, 530

S2-1. Who Are Employees? Relief Provisions. Page 12.

2. IRS Help.
53. If you want the IRS to determine whether a workers is an employee, file Form ___, Determination of Worker Status for Purposes of Federal Employment Taxes and Income Tax Withholding.
    (a)   SS-5
    (b)   SS-6
    (c)   SS-7
    (d)   SS-8
Answer: See Circular E, Who Are Employees? Relief provisions, page 12/ (d) SS-8

2. **VCSP**, Page 12
54. Employers who are currently treating their workers (or a class or group of workers) as ___ or other nonemployees and want to ___ reclassify their for future tax periods may workers as employees may
    (a)   nonemployees, comply and
    (b)   independent contractors, voluntarily
    (c)   independent contractors, comply and
    (d)   agents, voluntarily
Answer: See Circular E, Who Are Employees? Relief provisions, page 12/ (b) independent contractors, voluntarily

2. **VCSP**, Page 12
55. Employers who are currently treating their workers (or a class or group of workers) as ___ or other nonemployees and want to ___ reclassify their for future tax periods may workers as employees may be ___ to participate in the VCSP if certain requirements are met.
    (a)   nonemployees, comply and, permitted
    (b)   independent contractors, voluntarily, eligible
    (c)   independent contractors, comply and, allowed
    (d)   agents, voluntarily, eligible,
Answer: See Circular E, Who Are Employees? Relief provisions, page 12/ (b) independent contractors, voluntarily, eligible

2. **VCSP**, Page 12
56. To apply, use Form ___, Application for **V**oluntary **C**lassification **S**ettlement **P**rogram (**VCSP**). For more information visit IRS.gov and enter "VCSP" in the search box.
    (a)   8952
    (b)   8953
    (c)   8954
    (d)   8955
Answer: See Circular E, Who Are Employees? Relief provisions, page 12/ (a) 8952

© Copyright 2013. All rights reserved. Notice: United States Copyright Laws and International Treaties prohibit unauthorized publication, reproduction, distribution of this Work. Unauthorized use of this copyright in any form, format, publication or document may result in severe civil and criminal penalties. Violations of this copyright are investigated by the United States Department of Justice and carry, upon conviction of fines up to $250,000 and five years confinement. This Work is protected by United States Copyright Laws and International Treaties. Do not Copy, do not reproduce, do not distribute.

The International Leader in Construction Technology Home Study

Instructor's Manual for Tax Test 15E-S2-2
Section 15E-S2-2 Test
Who Are Employees? Husband-Wife Business

General Description

Tax Test 15E-S2-2. Information related to the Husband-Wife Business tax rules discussion commences with Tax Test 15E-S2-2. This is a detailed, important test series that should not be overlooked. Keep in mind; The partnership (Husband and Wife Business) is considered the employer of any employees and is liable for any employment taxes. If you or your spouse jointly own and operate a business and share in the profits and losses, you are partners in a partnership. Carefully examine the requirements of a Qualified Joint Venture.

DU VALL'S TEST'S™
Instructors Manual Study Guide Series United States Tax Code
IRS Publication 15 Circular E, Employer's Tax Guide Tax Year 2013
Tax Test 15E-S2-2 [Multiple-Choice Questions With Answers]

15E-S2-2. Who Are Employees? Husband-Wife Business

2. Husband-Wife Business, page 12
1. If you or your spouse jointly own and operate a business and share in the profits and losses, you are ___,
   - (a) incorporated as a partnership
   - (b) a private corporation
   - (c) a joint venture
   - (d) partners in a partnership

   Answer: See Circular E, Who Are Employees? Husband-Wife Business, page 12/ (d) partners in a partnership

2. Husband-Wife Business, page 12
2. If you or your spouse jointly own and operate a business and share in the profits and losses, you are ___, whether or not you have a formal ___.
   - (a) incorporated as a partnership, agreement
   - (b) a private corporation, legal agreement
   - (c) a joint venture, legal agreement
   - (d) partners in a partnership, partnership agreement

   Answer: See Circular E, Who Are Employees? Husband-Wife Business, page 12/ (d) partners in a partnership, partnership agreement

© Copyright 2013. All rights reserved. Notice: United States Copyright Laws and International Treaties prohibit unauthorized publication, reproduction, distribution of this Work. Unauthorized use of this copyright in any form, format, publication or document may result in severe civil and criminal penalties. Violations of this copyright are investigated by the United States Department of Justice and carry, upon conviction of fines up to $250,000 and five years confinement. This Work is protected by United States Copyright Laws and International Treaties. Do not Copy, do not reproduce, do not distribute.

A Ficus Tree Publishing Educational-Technical Publications

Husband-Wife Business

2. Husband-Wife Business, page 12

3. If you or your spouse jointly own and operate a business and share in the profits and losses, you are partners in a partnership, whether or not you have a formal partnership agreement. See Publication ___, Partnerships, for more details.
   (a) 540
   (b) 541
   (c) 542
   (d) 543
   Answer: See Circular E, Who Are Employees? Husband-Wife Business, page 12/ (b) 541

2. Husband-Wife Business, page 12

4. The partnership is considered the employer of any employees, and is ___ for any employment taxes due on wages paid to its employees.
   (a) responsible
   (b) held accountable
   (c) liable
   (d) legally responsible
   Answer: See Circular E, Who Are Employees? Husband-Wife Business, page 12/ (c) liable

2. Husband-Wife Business, Exception—Qualified joint venture. Page 12

5. For tax years beginning after ___, the Small Business and Work Opportunity Tax Act of ___ (Public Law 110-28) provides that
   (a) January 1, 2003, 2005
   (b) December 31, 2006, 2007
   (c) June 30, 2009, 2010
   (d) December 31, 2012, 2013
   Answer: See Circular E, Who Are Employees? Husband-Wife Business, page 12/ (b) December 31, 2006, 2007

2. Husband-Wife Business, Exception—Qualified joint venture. Page 12

6. For tax years beginning after ___, the Small Business and Work Opportunity Tax Act of ___ (Public Law 110-28) provides that a "qualified joint venture," whose only members are a husband and wife filing a ___ tax return, can elect not to be
   (a) January 1, 2003, 2005, small business,
   (b) December 31, 2006, 2007, joint income,
   (c) June 30, 2009, 2010, limited liability company,
   (d) December 31, 2012, 2013, corporate,
   Answer: See Circular E, Who Are Employees? Husband-Wife Business, page 12/ (b) December 31, 2006, 2007, joint income,

Husband-Wife Business

2. Husband-Wife Business, Exception—Qualified joint venture. Page 12
7. For tax years beginning after ___, the Small Business and Work Opportunity Tax Act of ___ (Public Law 110-28) provides that a "qualified joint venture," whose only members are a husband and wife filing a ___ tax return, can elect not to be treated as a partnership for ___.
   (a) January 1, 2003, 2005, small business, federal tax purposes
   (b) December 31, 2006, 2007, joint income, federal tax purposes
   (c) June 30, 2009, 2010, limited liability company, tax purposes
   (d) December 31, 2012, 2013, corporate, tax purposes
   Answer: See Circular E, Who Are Employees? Husband Wife Business, page 12/ (b) December 31, 2006, 2007, joint income, federal tax purposes

2. Husband-Wife Business, Exception—Qualified joint venture. Page 12
8. A qualified joint venture conducts a trade or business where: • the only members of a joint venture are a husband and wife who ___,
   (a) file separate tax returns
   (b) file a partnership return
   (c) file a joint income tax return
   (d) file a corporate tax return
   Answer: See Circular E, Who Are Employees? Husband-Wife Business, page 12/ (c) file a joint income tax return

2. Husband-Wife Business, Exception—Qualified joint venture. Page 12
9. A qualified joint venture conducts a trade or business where: • the only members of a joint venture are a husband and wife who file a joint income tax return, • Both spouses ___ Participate (see Material participation in the Instructions for Schedule C (Form ___) line G) in the
   (a) jointly participate, 941
   (b) jointly participate, 1040
   (c) participate, 941
   (d) materially participate, 1040
   Answer: See Circular E, Who Are Employees? Husband-Wife Business, page 12/ (d) materially participate, 1040

2. Husband-Wife Business, Exception—Qualified joint venture. Page 12
10. A qualified joint venture conducts a trade or business where: • Both spouses ___ Participate (see Material participation in the Instructions for Schedule C (Form ___) line G) in the trade or business. (mere joint ownership of ___ is not enough).
    (a) jointly participate, 941, assets
    (b) jointly participate, 1040, property
    (c) participate, 941, assets
    (d) materially participate, 1040, property
    Answer: See Circular E, Who Are Employees? Husband-Wife Business, page 12/ (d) materially participate, 1040, property

Husband-Wife Business

2. Husband-Wife Business, Exception—Qualified joint venture. Page 12

11. A qualified joint venture conducts a trade or business where: • the only members of a joint venture are a husband and wife who file a joint income tax return, • Both spouses ___ to not be treated as a partnership and
    - (a) agree
    - (b) elect
    - (c) decide
    - (d) choose

    Answer: See Circular E, Who Are Employees? Husband-Wife Business, page 12/ (b) elect

2. Husband-Wife Business, Exception—Qualified joint venture. Page 12

12. A qualified joint venture conducts a trade or business where: • the only members of a joint venture are a husband and wife who file a joint income tax return, • Both spouses ___ to not be treated as a partnership and • The business is co-owned by both spouses and is not held in the name of a state law entity such as a partnership or ___.
    - (a) agree, partnership
    - (b) elect, limited liability company (LLC).
    - (c) decide, incorporated company
    - (d) choose, corporation

    Answer: See Circular E, Who Are Employees? Husband-Wife Business, page 12/ (b) elect, Limited Liability Company (LLC)

2. Husband-Wife Business, Exception—Qualified joint venture. Page 12

13. To make the ___, all items of income, gain, loss, deduction, and credit must be divided between spouses,
    - (a) agreement
    - (b) election
    - (c) decision
    - (d) choice

    Answer: See Circular E, Who Are Employees? Husband-Wife Business, page 12/ (b) election

2. Husband-Wife Business, Exception—Qualified joint venture. Page 12

14. To make the ___, all items of income, gain, loss, deduction, and credit must be divided between spouses, in accordance with each spouse's interest in the venture, and reported on separate Schedules ___ or ___ as
    - (a) agreement, B, E
    - (b) election, C, F
    - (c) decision, D, G
    - (d) choice, F, H

    Answer: See Circular E, Who Are Employees? Husband-Wife Business, page 12/(b) election, C, F

Husband-Wife Business

2. Husband-Wife Business, Exception—Qualified joint venture. Page 12
15. To make the ___, all items of income, gain, loss, deduction, and credit must be divided between spouses, in accordance with each spouse's interest in the venture, and reported on separate Schedules ___ or ___ as ___.
    (a) agreement, B, E, owners
    (b) election, C, F, sole proprietors
    (c) decision, D, G, dual owners
    (d) choice, F, H, equal owners
    Answer: See Circular E, Who Are Employees? Husband-Wife Business, page 12/ (b) election, C, F, sole proprietors

2. Husband-Wife Business, Exception—Qualified joint venture. Page 12
16. Each spouse must also file a separate Schedule ___ to pay self-employment taxes, as applicable.
    (a) CD
    (b) EM
    (c) SE
    (d) JD
    Answer: See Circular E, Who Are Employees? Husband-Wife Business, page 12/ (c) SE

2. Husband-Wife Business, Exception—Qualified joint venture. Page 12
17. Spouses using the qualified joint venture rules are treated as ___ for federal tax purposes and generally do not need an EIN.
    (a) owners
    (b) partners
    (c) husband and wife
    (d) sole proprietors
    Answer: See Circular E, Who Are Employees? Husband-Wife Business, page 12/ (d) sole proprietors

2. Husband-Wife Business, Exception—Qualified joint venture. Page 12
18. If employment taxes are owed by the qualified joint venture, either spouse may report and pay the employment taxes using the ___ of that spouse's sole proprietorship.
    (a) EIN
    (b) SSN
    (c) IRS
    (d) CAA
    Answer: See Circular E, Who Are Employees? Husband-Wife Business, page 12/ (a) EIN

Husband-Wife Business

2. Husband-Wife Business, Exception—Qualified joint venture. Page 12
19. Generally, filing as a qualified joint venture will not ___ the spouse's total tax owed on the joint income tax return.
    (a) alter
    (b) increase
    (c) change
    (d) add to
    Answer: See Circular E, Who Are Employees? Husband-Wife Business, page 12/ (b) increase

2. Husband-Wife Business, Exception—Qualified joint venture. Page 12
20. However, it gives each spouse credit for ___ earning on which retirement benefits are based and for Medicare coverage without filing a partnership return.
    (a) total
    (b) calculated
    (c) social security
    (d) computed
    Answer: See Circular E, Who Are Employees? Husband-Wife Business, page 12/ (c) social security

2. Husband-Wife Business, Exception—Qualified joint venture. Page 12
21. Note. If your spouse is your employee, not your partner, you must ___ social security and Medicare taxes for him or her.
    (a) withhold
    (b) pay
    (c) deduct
    (d) also pay
    Answer: See Circular E, Who Are Employees? Husband-Wife Business, page 12/ (b) pay

2. Husband-Wife Business, Exception—Qualified joint venture. Page 12
22. Note. If your spouse is your employee, not your partner, you must ___ social security and Medicare taxes for him or her. For more information on qualified joint ventures, visit IRS.gov, enter "qualified joint venture" in the search box, the select Election for Husband and Wife ___.
    (a) withhold, Incorporated Businesses
    (b) pay, Unincorporated Businesses
    (c) deduct, Incorporated Businesses
    (d) also pay, Unincorporated Businesses
    Answer: See Circular E, Who Are Employees? Husband-Wife Business, page 12/ (b) pay, Unincorporated Businesses

Husband-Wife Business

2. Husband-Wife Business, Exception—Community Income. Page 12
23. If you or your spouse ____ an unincorporated business as community property under the community property laws of a state, foreign country, or U.S. Possession, you can treat the business either as a ___ (of a spouse who carried on the business) or a ___.
    (a) wholly own, limited liability company, unincorporated business
    (b) jointly own, partnership, limited corporation
    (c) wholly own, sole proprietorship, partnership
    (d) jointly own, unincorporated business, limited liability company
    Answer: See Circular E, Who Are Employees? Husband-Wife Business, page 12/ (c) wholly own, sole proprietorship, partnership

2. Husband-Wife Business, Exception—Community Income. Page 12
24. If you or your spouse wholly own an unincorporated business as community property under the community property laws of a state, foreign country, or U.S. Possession, you can treat the business either as a sole proprietorship (of a spouse who carried on the business) or a partnership. You may still ___ to be taxed as a qualified joint venture instead of a partnership. See *Exception—Qualified_____joint venture* above.
    (a) file an exception
    (b) decide
    (c) choose
    (d) make an election
    Answer: See Circular E, Who Are Employees? Husband-Wife Business, page 12/ (d) make an election

A Ficus Tree Publishing LLC. Quick Notes Page

Instructor's Manual for Tax Test 15E-S3
Section 3 - Family Employees

General Description

Tax Test 15E-S3.
Section 3. Introduces Family Employees. Important questions for Section 3 include: Child employed by parent; Payments for the services of a child 18; Covered services of a child or spouse; Parent employed by son or daughter; Social security and Medicare taxes.

Key Words From Section 3. Family Employees. Page 12.

Tax Test 15E-S3.
Section 3. Family Employees. Child employed by parents. One spouse employed by another. Covered services of a child or spouse. Parent employed by son or daughter. FUTA tax.

DU VALL'S TEST'S™
Instructors Manual Study Guide Series United States Tax Code
IRS Publication 15 Circular E, Employer's Tax Guide Tax Year 2013
Tax Test 15E-S3 [Multiple-Choice Questions With Answers]

Section 3. Family Employees Page 12.

3. Family Employees - Child employed by parents. Page 12.
1. Payments for the services of a child under age ___ who works for his or her parent in a trade or business, are not subject to ___ and ___ taxes if the trade or business is a sole proprietorship or a partnership in which each partner is a parent of the child.
    (a) 14, FICA, FUTA
    (b) 15, social security, Medicare
    (c) 16, FUTA, social security
    (d) 18, social security, Medicare
   Answer: See Circular E Part 3. Family Employees, Child employed by parents, page 12, (*remember this is federal tax law not state law*; do not confuse them)/ (d) 18, social security, Medicare

Section 3. Family Employees - Child employed by parents

3. Family Employees - Child employed by parents. Page 12.
2. Payments for the services of a child under age ___ who works for his or her parent in a trade or business, are not subject to ___ and ___ taxes if the trade or business is a sole proprietorship or a partnership in which each partner is a parent of the child. If these payments are for work other than in a trade or business, such as domestic work in the parent's home, they are not subject to social security and Medicare taxes until the child reaches age ___.
   (a)   14, FICA, FUTA, 18
   (b)   15, social security, Medicare, 18,
   (c)   16, FUTA, social security, 21
   (d)   18, social security, Medicare, 21
   Answer: See Circular E Part 3. Family Employees, Child employed by parents, page 12, (*remember this is federal tax law not state law*; do not confuse them)/ (d) 18, social security, Medicare, 21

3. Family Employees - Child employed by parents. Page 12.
3. However, see <u>Covered services of a child or spouse</u>, later in this section. Payments for the services of a child under ___ who works for his or her parent, whether or not in a trade or business are not subject to ___ tax.
   (a)   18, FUTA
   (b)   18, FICA
   (c)   21, FUTA
   (d)   21, FICA
   Answer: See Circular E Part 3. Family Employees, Child employed by parents, page 12, (*remember this is federal tax law not state law*; do not confuse them)/ (c) 21, FUTA

3. Family Employees - Child employed by parents. Page 12.
4. Payments for the services of a child of any age who works for his or her parent are generally subject to income tax withholding unless the payment are for domestic work in the parent's ___,
   (a)   home
   (b)   business
   (c)   trade
   (d)   profession
   Answer: See Circular E Part 3. Family Employees, Child employed by parents, page 12, (*remember this is federal tax law not state law*; do not confuse them)/ (a) home

Section 3. Family Employees - Child employed by parents

3. Family Employees - Child employed by parents. Page 12.
5. Payments for the services of a child of any age who works for his or her parent are generally subject to income tax withholding unless the payment are for domestic work in the parent's ___, or unless the payments are for work other than in a trade or business are less than $___ in the quarter or
  (a) home, 50
  (b) business, 50
  (c) trade, 100
  (d) profession, 100
  Answer: See Circular E Part 3. Family Employees, Child employed by parents, page 12, (*remember this is federal tax law not state law*; do not confuse them)/ (a) home, 50,

3. Family Employees - Child employed by parents. Page 12.
6. Payments for the services of a child of any age who works for his or her parent are generally subject to income tax withholding unless the payment are for domestic work in the parent's ___, or unless the payments are for work other than in a trade or business are less than $___ in the quarter or the ___ is not regularly employed to do such work.
  (a) home, 50, child
  (b) business, 50, person
  (c) trade, 100, child
  (d) profession, 100, person
  Answer: See Circular E Part 3. Family Employees, Child employed by parents, page 12, (*remember this is federal tax law not state law*; do not confuse them)/ (a) home, 50, child

3. Family Employees - One spouse employed by another

3. Family Employees - One spouse employed by another. Pages 12 and 13.
7. The wages for the services of an individual who works for his or her spouse in a trade or business are subject to withholding and social security and Medicare taxes, but not ___ tax.
  (a) FICA
  (b) FUTA
  (c) VCSP
  (d) WPA
  Answer: See Circular E Part 3. Family Employees, One spouse employed by another, pages 12, 13 (*remember this is federal tax law not state law*; do not confuse them)/ (b) FUTA

3. Family Employees - One spouse employed by another

3. Family Employees - One spouse employed by another. Pages 12 and 13.
8.   The wages for the services of an individual who works for his or her spouse in a trade or business are subject to withholding and social security and Medicare taxes, but not FUTA tax. However, the payments for services of one spouse employed by another in other than a trade or business, such as domestic service in a private home, are not subject to ___.
   (a)   social security, Medicare and FUTA taxes
   (b)   social security and Medicare taxes
   (c)   social security and FICA
   (d)   FUTA and FICA
   Answer: See Circular E Part 3. Family Employees, One spouse employed by another, pages 12, 13 (*remember this is federal tax law not state law*; do not confuse them)/ (a) social security, Medicare and FUTA taxes.

Section 3. Family Employees - Covered services of a child or spouse

3. Covered services of a child or spouse.
9.   The wages for the services of a child or spouse are subject to income tax withholding as well as social security, Medicare and FUTA taxes if he or she works for:
   • A ___, even if it is controlled by the child's parent or the individual's spouse.
   (a)   joint venture
   (b)   partnership
   (c)   corporation
   (d)   business
   Answer: See Circular E Part 3. Family Employees, Covered services of a child or spouse, page 13, (*remember this is federal tax law not state law*; do not confuse them)/ (c) corporation

3. Covered services of a child or spouse.
10.   The wages for the services of a child or spouse are subject to income tax withholding as well as social security, Medicare and FUTA taxes if he or she works for:
   • A partnership, even if the child's parent is a partner, unless ___.
   (a)   the parent is the sole proprietor
   (b)   each parent is considered a sole proprietor
   (c)   each partner is a parent of the child
   (d)   the child is the legal owner of the business
   Answer: See Circular E Part 3. Family Employees, Covered services of a child or spouse, page 13, (*remember this is federal tax law not state law*; do not confuse them)/ (c) each partner is parent of the child

Section 3. Family Employees - Covered services of a child or spouse

3. Covered services of a child or spouse.
11. The wages for the services of a child or spouse are subject to income tax withholding as well as social security, Medicare and FUTA taxes if he or she works for:
 • A partnership, even if the individual's ___ is a partner; or
 (a) the parent is the sole proprietor
 (b) each parent is considered a sole proprietor
 (c) each partner is a parent of the child
 (d) spouse
 Answer: See Circular E Part 3. Family Employees, Covered services of a child or spouse, page 13, (*remember this is federal tax law not state law*; do not confuse them)/ (d) spouse

3. Covered services of a child or spouse.
12. The wages for the services of a child or spouse are subject to income tax withholding as well as social security, Medicare and FUTA taxes if he or she works for:
 • An estate, even if it is the estate of a ___.
 (a) deceased parent
 (b) deceased spouse
 (c) deceased family member
 (d) relative
 Answer: See Circular E Part 3. Family Employees, Covered services of a child or spouse, page 13, (*remember this is federal tax law not state law*; do not confuse them)/ (a) deceased parent

Family Employees - Parent employed by son or daughter

3. Parent employed by son or daughter.
13. When the employer is a son or daughter employing his or her parent the following rules apply;
 • Payments for the services of a parent in the son's or daughter's (the ___) trade or business are subject to income tax withholding and social security and Medicate taxes.
 (a) business
 (b) trade
 (c) employer's
 (d) employee's
 Answer: See Circular E Part 3. Family Employees, Parent employed by son or daughter, page 13, (*remember this is federal tax law not state law*; do not confuse them)/ (c) employer's

Family Employees - Parent employed by son or daughter

3. Parent employed by son or daughter.
14. When the employer is a son or daughter employing his or her parent the following rules apply;
    • Payments for the services of a parent not in the son's or daughter's (the employer's) trade or business are generally not subject to ____.
    (a) taxes
    (b) income taxes
    (c) social security taxes
    (d) social security and Medicare taxes
    Answer: See Circular E Part 3. Family Employees, Parent employed by son or daughter, page 13, (*remember this is federal tax law not state law*; do not confuse them)/ (d) social security and Medicare taxes

3. Parent employed by son or daughter - CAUTION NOTE.
15. Social security and Medicare taxes do apply to payments do apply to payments made to a parent for domestic services if all of the following apply:
    • The parent is employed by his or her son or daughter; • The son or daughter (the employer) has a child or ___ living in the home;
    (a) stepchild
    (b) another parent
    (c) other parent
    (d) related individual
    Answer: See Circular E Part 3. Family Employees, Parent employed by son or daughter, page 13, (*remember this is federal tax law not state law*; do not confuse them)/ (a) stepchild

3. Parent employed by son or daughter - CAUTION NOTE.
16. Social security and Medicare taxes do apply to payments do apply to payments made to a parent for domestic services if all of the following apply:
    • The parent is employed by his or her son or daughter; • The son or daughter (the employer) has a child or ___ living in the home; • The son or daughter (the employer) is a widow or widower, divorced, or living with a spouse who, because of a mental or physical condition, cannot care for the child or stepchild for at least ___continuous weeks in a calendar quarter; and
    (a) stepchild, 4
    (b) another parent, 16
    (c) other parent, 12
    (d) related individual, 26
    Answer: See Circular E Part 3. Family Employees, Parent employed by son or daughter, page 13, (*remember this is federal tax law not state law*; do not confuse them)/ (a) stepchild, 4

Section 3. Family Employees - Parent employed by son or daughter

3. Parent employed by son or daughter - CAUTION NOTE.
17. Social security and Medicare taxes do apply to payments do apply to payments made to a parent for domestic services if all of the following apply:
    • The parent is employed by his or her son or daughter; • The son or daughter (the employer) has a child or stepchild living in the home; • The son or daughter (the employer) is a widow or widower, divorced, or living with a spouse who, because of a mental or physical condition, cannot care for the child or stepchild for at least 4 continuous weeks in a calendar quarter; and • The child or stepchild is either under age ___ or requires the personal care of an adult for at least ___ continuous weeks in a calendar quarter due to a mental or physical condition.
    - (a) 14, 8
    - (b) 16, 8
    - (c) 18, 4
    - (d) 21, 4

    Answer: See Circular E 3. Family Employees, Parent employed by son or daughter, page 13, (*remember this is federal tax law not state law*; do not confuse them)/ (c) 18, 4

3. Parent employed by son or daughter - CAUTION NOTE.
18. Social security and Medicare taxes do apply to payments do apply to payments made to a parent for domestic services if all of the following apply: Payments made to a parent employed by his or her child are not subject to ___, regardless of the type of services provided.
    - (a) FICA
    - (b) social security tax
    - (c) Medicare tax
    - (d) FUTA tax

    Answer: See Circular E 3. Family Employees, Parent employed by son or daughter, page 13, (*remember this is federal tax law not state law*; do not confuse them)/ (d) FUTA tax

Instructor's Manual for Tax Test 15E-S4
Section 4. Employees Social Security Number

General Description of Tax Test 15E-S4.

Section 4. Tax Test 15E-S4 Employee's Social Security Number (SSN) also includes information regarding Individual taxpayer identification numbers (ITINs) for aliens and the requirement for verification of social security numbers. Tax Test 15E-S4 continues to parallel the construction and text of IRS Publication 15, Employer's Tax Guide. In addition note the reference to Form W-2 and the employer's requirement to obtain the correct and current information for the tax records. Note also, the requirement for the employer to view (to show you) the social security card of the employee. It is stated that it is the employer's responsibility to record the correct name, SSN, and address of the employee. Instructions in the form of Tax Test questions provide basic information for Applying for a social security card. Instructions are also provided in multiple-choice test format for obtaining a social security number. The correct recording of the employee's name and SSN is specific with the burden of providing correct information on the employer. Individual taxpayer identification numbers (ITINs) are required for aliens. Information for the verification of social security numbers is provided in multiple-choice test format.

Key Words of Tax Test 15E-S4 follow below.

Not valid for employment, Applying for Social Security Card, Applying for Social Security Number, Correctly record employees name and social security number, Individual Taxpayer Identification Number (**ITIN**), Individual Taxpayer Identification Numbers (**ITINs**) for Aliens, Verification of Social Security Numbers, Registering for SSNVA (Social Security Number Verification Service, One-time activation code.

© Copyright 2013. All rights reserved. Notice: United States Copyright Laws and International Treaties prohibit unauthorized publication, reproduction, distribution of this Work. Unauthorized use of this copyright in any form, format, publication or document may result in severe civil and criminal penalties. Violations of this copyright are investigated by the United States Department of Justice and carry, upon conviction of fines up to $250,000 and five years confinement. This Work is protected by United States Copyright Laws and International Treaties. Do not Copy, do not reproduce, do not distribute.

A Ficus Tree Publishing Educational-Technical Publications

DU VALL'S TEST'S™
Instructors Manual Study Guide Series United States Tax Code
IRS Publication 15 Circular E, Employer's Tax Guide Tax Year 2013
Tax Test 15E-S4 [Multiple-Choice Questions With Answers]

Section 4. Employee's Social Security Number (SSN) Page 13

4. Employee's Social Security Number (SSN)
1. You are required to get each employee's name and SSN and to enter them on Form ___. This requirement also applies to resident and nonresident alien employees.
   (a) W-2
   (b) W-4
   (c) W-5
   (d) 1099
   Answer: See 4. Employee's Social Security Number (SSN) page 13/ (a) W-2

4. Employee's Social Security Number (SSN)
2. You are required to get each employee's name and SSN and to enter them on Form ___. This requirement also applies to resident and nonresident alien employees. You should ask your employee to ___ his or her social security card.
   (a) W-2, show you
   (b) W-4, present
   (c) W-5, provide a copy
   (d) 1099, show you
   Answer: See 4. Employee's Social Security Number (SSN) page 13/ (a) W-2, show you

4. Employee's Social Security Number (SSN)
3. You are required to get each employee's name and SSN and to enter them on Form ___. This requirement also applies to resident and nonresident alien employees. You should ask your employee to ___ his or her social security card. The employee ___ show the card if it is available.
   (a) W-2, show you, will
   (b) W-4, present, must
   (c) W-5, provide a copy, shall
   (d) 1099, show you, is required to
   Answer: See 4. Employee's Social Security Number (SSN) page 13/ (a) W-2, show you, will

Section 4. Employee's Social Security Number (SSN)

4. Employee's Social Security Number (SSN) CAUTION
4. Do not accept a social security card that says "___."
   - (a) EXPIRED
   - (b) Not valid
   - (c) Not valid for employment
   - (d) Temporary

   Answer: See 4. Employee's Social Security Number (SSN) page 13/ (c) Not valid for employment

4. Employee's Social Security Number (SSN)
5. Do not accept a social security card that says "___."A social security number issued with this ___ does not permit employment.
   - (a) EXPIRED, statement
   - (b) Not valid, legend
   - (c) Not valid for employment, legend
   - (d) Temporary, statement

   Answer: See 4. Employee's Social Security Number (SSN), Caution, page 13/ (c) Not valid for employment, legend

4. Employee's Social Security Number (SSN)
6. You may, but are not required to, ____ the social security card if the employee provides it.
   - (a) check
   - (b) copy
   - (c) photocopy
   - (d) duplicate

   Answer: See 4. Employee's Social Security Number (SSN) page 13/ (c) photocopy

4. Employee's Social Security Number (SSN)
7. You may, but are not required to, ____ the social security card if the employee provides it. If you do not provide the correct employee name and SSN on Form ___, you may owe a penalty unless
   - (a) check, 1099
   - (b) copy, W-2
   - (c) photocopy, W-2
   - (d) duplicate, 1099

   Answer: See 4. Employee's Social Security Number (SSN) page 13/ (c) photocopy, W-2

Section 4. Employee's Social Security Number (SSN)

4. Employee's Social Security Number (SSN)
8.   You may, but are not required to, photocopy the social security card if the employee provides it. If you do not -provide the correct employee name and SSN on Form W-2, you may owe a penalty unless you have ___.
   (a)   acceptable reasons
   (b)   reasonable cause
   (c)   specific reason
   (d)   acceptable cause
   Answer: See 4. Employee's Social Security Number (SSN) page 13/ (b) reasonable cause

4. Employee's Social Security Number (SSN)
9.   You may, but are not required to, photocopy the social security card if the employee provides it. If you do not -provide the correct employee name and SSN on Form W-2, you may owe a penalty unless you have reasonable cause. See Publication ___, Reasonable Cause Regulations & Requirements for Missing and Incorrect Name/TINs, for information on the requirements to solicit the employee's, SSN.
   (a)   1584
   (b)   1585
   (c)   1586
   (d)   1587
   Answer: See 4. Employee's Social Security Number (SSN) page 13/ (c) 1586

Applying for a Social Security Card

4. Applying for a social security card.
10.   Any employee who is legally ___ to work in the United States and does not have a social security card can get one by completing Form ___, Application for a Social Security Card, and submitting the necessary documentation.
   (a)   eligible, SS-3
   (b)   qualified, SS-4
   (c)   eligible, SS-5
   (d)   qualified, SS-6
   Answer: See 4. Employee's Social Security Number (SSN) page 13/ (c) eligible, SS-5

Applying for a Social Security Card

4. Applying for a social security card.
11. Any employee who is legally eligible to work in the United States and does not have a social security card can get one by completing Form SS-5, Application for a Social Security Card, and submitting the necessary documentation. You can get this form at SSA offices, by calling ___, or from the SSA website at *www.socialsecurity.gov/online/ss-5.html*.
    (a) 1-800-772-1210
    (b) 1-800-772-1211
    (c) 1-800-772-1212
    (d) 1-800-772-1213
    Answer: See 4. Employee's Social Security Number (SSN) page 13/ (d) 1-800-772-1213

4. Applying for a social security card.
12. Any employee who is legally eligible to work in the United States and does not have a social security card can get one by completing Form SS-5, Application for a Social Security Card, and submitting the necessary documentation. You can get this form at SSA offices, by calling ___, or from the SSA website at *www.socialsecurity.gov/online/ss-5.html*. The employee must complete and ___ Form SS-5, it cannot be filed by the employer.
    (a) 1-800-772-1210, certify
    (b) 1-800-772-1211, certify
    (c) 1-800-772-1212, endorse
    (d) 1-800-772-1213, sign
    Answer: See 4. Employee's Social Security Number (SSN) page 13/ (d) 1-800-772-1213, sign

4. Applying for a social security number.
13. If you file Form W-2 on paper and your employee applied for an SSN but does not have one when you must file Form W-2, enter "___" on the form.
    (a) Processing
    (b) Application Submitted
    (c) Applied For
    (d) Submitted
    Answer: See 4. Employee's Social Security Number (SSN) page 13/ (c) Applied For

4. Applying for a social security number.
14. If you file Form W-2 on paper and your employee applied for an SSN but does not have one when you must file Form W-2, enter "___" on the form. If you are filing electronically, enter all ___ (000-00-000) in the social security number field.
    (a) Processing , numbers
    (b) Application Submitted, numbers
    (c) Applied For, zeros
    (d) Submitted, digits
    Answer: See 4. Employee's Social Security Number (SSN) page 13/ (c) Applied For, zeros

Applying for a Social Security Number

4. Applying for a social security number.
15. If you file Form W-2 on paper and your employee applied for an SSN but does not have one when you must file Form W-2, enter "Applied For" on the form. If you are filing electronically, enter all zeros (000-00-000) in the social security number field. When the employee receives the SSN, file Copy ___ of Form ___, Corrected Wage and Tax Statement.
    (a)   A, W-2c
    (b)   B, W-2c
    (c)   C, W-2c
    (d)   D, W-2d
    Answer: See 4. Employee's Social Security Number (SSN) page 13/ (c) A, W-2c

4. Applying for a social security number.
16. If you file Form W-2 on paper and your employee applied for an SSN but does not have one when you must file Form W-2, enter "Applied For" on the form. If you are filing electronically, enter all zeros (000-00-000) in the social security number field. When the employee receives the SSN, file Copy ___ of Form ___, Corrected Wage and Tax Statement. Furnish Copies B, C and __ of Form W-2c to the employee.
    (a)   A, W-2c, two
    (b)   B, W-2c, three
    (c)   C, W-2c, 2
    (d)   D, W-2d, 3
    Answer: See 4. Employee's Social Security Number (SSN) page 13/ (c) A, W-2c, 2

4. Applying for a social security number.
17. Up to ___ Forms W-2c for each Form ___, Transmittal of Corrected Wage and Tax Statements may now be filed over the Internet, with no limit on the number of sessions.
    (a)   10
    (b)   15
    (c)   20
    (d)   25
    Answer: See 4. Employee's Social Security Number (SSN) page 13/ (d) 25

4. Applying for a social security number.
18. For more information, visit the SSA's Employer ___ Filing Instructions & Information webpage at (a) W-2
    (b)   W-3
    (c)   W-4
    (d)   W-5
    Answer: See 4. Employee's Social Security Number (SSN) page 13/ (a) W-2

Applying for a Social Security Number

4. Applying for a social security number.
19. For more information, visit the SSA's Employer ___ Filing Instructions & Information webpage at *www.socialsecurity.gov/employer*. Advise your employee to correct the SSN on his or her original Form ___.
    (a)   W-2, W-2
    (b)   W-3, W-3
    (c)   W-4, W-4
    (d)   W-5, W-5
    Answer: See 4. Employee's Social Security Number (SSN) page 13/ (a) W-2, W-2

Correctly record the employees name and SSN

4. Correctly record the employee's name and SSN.
20   Record the name and number of ___ as they are shown on the employee's social security card.
    (a)   each employee
    (b)   every employee
    (c)   all employee's
    (d)   each worker
    Answer: See 4. Employee's Social Security Number (SSN) page 13/ (a) each employee

4. Correctly record the employee's name and SSN.
21.   Record the name and number of each employee as they are shown on the employee's social security card. If an employee's name is not correct as shown on the card because of a marriage or divorce, the employee should ___.
    (a)   notify the nearest social security office
    (b)   request a different card for the Social Security Administration
    (c)   tear up the card
    (d)   request a corrected card from the SSA
    Answer: See 4. Employee's Social Security Number (SSN) Correctly record the employee's name and SSN. Page 13/ (d) request a corrected card from the SSA

4. Correctly record the employee's name and SSN.
22.   Record the name and number of each employee as they are shown on the employee's social security card. If an employee's name is not correct as shown on the card because of a marriage or divorce, the employee should request a corrected card from the SSA. Continue to report the employee's wages ___ until the employee shows you an updated social security card with the new name.
    (a)   notify the IRS
    (b)   under the old name
    (c)   notify the SSA
    (d)   continue to withhold all taxes based upon the prior Form
    Answer: See 4. Employee's Social Security Number (SSN) Correctly record the employee's name and SSN. Page 13/ (b) under the old name

Correctly record the employees name and SSN

4. Correctly record the employee's name and SSN. Page 14

23. If the SSA issues the employee a replacement card after a name change, or a new card with a different social security number after a change in ___ work status, file a Form W-2c to correct the name/SSN reported for the most recently filed Form W-2.
    - (a) a wife's
    - (b) a husband's
    - (c) the individual's
    - (d) alien

    Answer: See 4. Employee's Social Security Number (SSN) page 14, Correctly record the employee's name and SSN/ (d) alien

4. Correctly record the employee's name and SSN.

24. If the SSA issues the employee a replacement card after a name change, or a new card with a different social security number after a change in ___ work status, file a Form W-2c to correct the name/SSN reported for the most recently filed Form W-2. It is ___ to correct other years if the previous name and number were used for years before the most recent Form W-2.
    - (a) a wife's, required
    - (b) a husband's, necessary
    - (c) the individual's, mandatory
    - (d) alien, not necessary

    Answer: See 4. Employee's Social Security Number (SSN) page 14, Correctly record the employee's name and SSN/ (d) alien, not necessary

4. IRS individual taxpayer identification numbers (ITINs) for aliens

4. IRS individual taxpayer identification numbers (ITINs) for aliens.

25. Do not accept an ITIN in place of an ___ for employee identification or for work.
    - (a) SSN
    - (b) CNN
    - (c) ATM
    - (d) ICC

    Answer: See 4. IRS individual taxpayer identification numbers for (ITINS) for aliens/ (a) SSN

4. IRS individual taxpayer identification numbers (ITINs) for aliens

4. IRS individual taxpayer identification numbers (ITINs) for aliens.
26. Do not accept an ITIN in place of an ___ for employee identification or for work. An ITIN is only available to resident and nonresident aliens who are not eligible for U.S. employment and need identification for ___ purposes.
    (a)   SSN, other
    (b)   CNN, similar
    (c)   ATM, other
    (d)   ICC, similar
Answer: See 4. IRS individual taxpayer identification numbers for (ITINS) for aliens/ (a) SSN, other

4. IRS individual taxpayer identification numbers (ITINs) for aliens.
27. You can identify an ITIN because it is a ___-digit number, beginning
    (a)   eight
    (b)   nine
    (c)   ten
    (d)   twelve
Answer: See 4. IRS individual taxpayer identification numbers for (ITINS) for aliens/ (b) nine

4. IRS individual taxpayer identification numbers (ITINs) for aliens.
28. You can identify an ITIN because it is a ___-digit number, beginning with the number ___ with either a "7" or "8" as the fourth digit and is
    (a)   eight, 8
    (b)   nine, 9
    (c)   ten, 7
    (d)   twelve, 9
Answer: See 4. IRS individual taxpayer identification numbers for (ITINS) for aliens/ (b) nine, 9

4. IRS individual taxpayer identification numbers (ITINs) for aliens.
29. You can identify an ITIN because it is a ___-digit number, beginning with the number ___ with either a "7" or "8" as the fourth digit and is formatted like an SSN (for example, ___-7N-NNNN).
    (a)   eight, 8, 8NN
    (b)   nine, 9, 9NN
    (c)   ten, 7, 7NN
    (d)   twelve, 9, 9NN
Answer: See 4. IRS individual taxpayer identification numbers for (ITINS) for aliens/ (b) nine, 9, 9NN

4. IRS individual taxpayer identification numbers (ITINs) for aliens

4. IRS individual taxpayer identification numbers (ITINs) for aliens. Caution

30. An individual with an ITIN who later becomes eligible to work in the United States must obtain ___.
    (a) a social security card
    (b) a social security number
    (c) both a and b
    (d) an SSN
    Answer: See 4. IRS individual taxpayer identification numbers (ITINs) for aliens, Caution, p 14/ (d) an SSN

4. IRS individual taxpayer identification numbers (ITINs) for aliens. Caution

31. An individual with an ITIN who later becomes eligible to work in the United States must obtain an SSN. If the individual is currently eligible to work in the United States, ___ the individual to apply for an SSN and follow the instructions under Applying for a social security number, ___.
    (a) instruct, earlier
    (b) notify, without delay
    (c) tell, as soon as possible
    (d) suggest, without delay
    Answer: See Section 4. IRS individual taxpayer identification numbers (ITINs) Caution, p 14/ (a) instruct, earlier

4. IRS individual taxpayer identification numbers (ITINs) for aliens. Caution

32. An individual with an ITIN who later becomes eligible to work in the United States must obtain an SSN. If the individual is currently eligible to work in the United States, ___ the individual to apply for an SSN and follow the instructions under Applying for a social security number, ___. Do not use an ITIN in place of an SSN on Form ___.
    (a) instruct, earlier, W-2
    (b) notify, without delay, W-3
    (c) tell, as soon as possible, 1099
    (d) suggest, without delay, W-2
    Answer: See 4. IRS individual taxpayer identification numbers (ITINs) Caution, p 14/ (a) instruct, earlier, W-2

Section 4. Verification of social security numbers

4. IRS individual taxpayer identification numbers (ITINs) for aliens.
33. Employers and authorized reporting agents can use the Social Security Number Verification Service (SSNVS) to instantly verify up to ___ names and SSNs (per screen) at a time, or
    (a) 10
    (b) 25
    (c) 50
    (d) 300
    Answer: See 4. Employee's Social Security Numbers (SSN), Verification of social security numbers, page 14/ (a) 10

4. IRS individual taxpayer identification numbers (ITINs) for aliens.
34. Employers and authorized reporting agents can use the Social Security Number Verification Service (SSNVS) to instantly verify up to ___ names and SSNs (per screen) at a time, or submit an electronic file of up to ___ names and SSNs and usually receive the results the next business day. Visit *www.socia security.gov/employer/ssnv.htm* for more information.
    (a) 10, 250,000
    (b) 25, 300,000
    (c) 50, 500,000
    (d) 300, 750,000
    Answer: See 4. Employee's Social Security Numbers (SSN), Verification of social security numbers, page 14/ (a) 10, 250,000

Section 4. Registering for SSNVS. Page 14.

4. Registering for SSNVS.
35. You must register online and receive ___ from your employer to use SSNVS.
    (a) permission
    (b) authorization
    (c) the codes
    (d) the user code
    Answer: See 4. Employee's Social Security Numbers (SSN). Registering for SSNVS, page 14/ (b) authorization

4. Registering for SSNVS.
36. You must register online and receive ___ from your employer to use SSNVS. To register, visit SSA's website at *www.ssa.gov/employer* and click on the ___ link.
    (a) permission, Social Security Services
    (b) authorization, Business Services Online
    (c) the codes, IRS Services
    (d) the user code, Social Security Business Services
    Answer: See 4. Employee's Social Security Numbers (SSN). Registering for SSNVS, page 14/ (b) authorization, Business Services Online

Section 4. Registering for SSNVS

4. Registering for SSNVS.
37. You must register online and receive ___ from your employer to use SSNVS. To register, visit SSA's website at *www.ssa.gov/employer* and click on the ___ link. Follow the registration instructions to obtain a user identification (ID) and ___.
   (a) permission, Social Security Services, code
   (b) authorization, Business Services Online, password
   (c) the codes, IRS Services, code
   (d) the user code, Social Security Business Services, password
   Answer: See 4. Employee's Social Security Numbers (SSN). Registering for SSNVS, page 14/ (b) authorization, Business Services Online, password

4. Registering for SSNVS.
38. You will need to provide the following information about yourself and your company. Name, SSN, Date of birth, ___, EIN, Company name, address, and telephone number, Email address.
   (a) Type of business
   (b) Classification of business type
   (c) Type of employer
   (d) Number of employee's
   Answer: See 4. Employee's Social Security Numbers (SSN). Registering for SSNVS, page 14/ (c) Type of employer

4. Registering for SSNVS.
39. You will need to provide the following information about yourself and your company. Name, SSN, Date of birth, ___, EIN, Company name, address, and telephone number, Email address. When you have completed the online registration process, SSA will mail a ___ activation code to your employer. You must enter the activation code online to use SSNVS.
   (a) Type of business, user code
   (b) Classification of business type, user code
   (c) Type of employer, one-time
   (d) Number of employee's, one-time
   Answer: See 4. Employee's Social Security Numbers (SSN). Registering for SSNVS, page 14/ (c) Type of employer, one-time

The International Leader in Construction Technology Home Study

Instructor's Manual for Tax Test 15E-S5 Section 5 Wages and Other Compensation

General Description

Tax Test 15E-S5. In Tax Test 15E-S5, Circular E, Section 5. Wages and Other Compensation. Section 5, first paragraph, immediately provides additional information describing and defining the extent of wages and other compensation. The statement "Wages subject to federal employment taxes generally include all pay you give to an employee for services performed." The paragraph then further clarifies the introductory sentence by stating "The pay may be in cash or in other forms", proceeding to identify and include salaries, vacation allowances, bonuses, commissions, and fringe benefits in addition to wages. The focus of Section 5 is thereby directed toward taxes due on wages and other sources of other compensation.

It is important to note the reference in the second paragraph "More information", in bold print, to accompanying IRS publications 15-A and 15-B. The title of Publication 15-B is Employer's Tax Guide to Fringe Benefits.

Key Words

Tax Test 15E-S5. The title of Section 5. Page numbers provided with this paragraph apply only to the IRS publication of Circular E, Employer's Tax Guide, not to this work. Bold print headings in IRS Circular E publication 15, generally identify key word and index information of the section or part. Section 5. Key Words: Wages. Other compensation. More information. Employee business expense reimbursement. Accountable plan. Nonaccountable plan. Per diem. Per diem or other fixed allowances. Wages not paid in money. Moving expenses. Meal and lodging. 50% test. Health insurance plans. S corporation employees. 2%.Health Savings Accounts. Medical saving accounts. HSA. MSA. Archer medical saving account (MSA). Medical care reimbursements. Differential wage payments. Fringe benefits. Nontaxable fringe benefits. When fringe benefits are treated as paid. Valuation of fringe benefits. Withholding on fringe benefits. Depositing taxes on fringe benefits. Sick pay.

© Copyright 2013. All rights reserved. Notice: United States Copyright Laws and International Treaties prohibit unauthorized publication, reproduction, distribution of this Work. Unauthorized use of this copyright in any form, format, publication or document may result in severe civil and criminal penalties. Violations of this copyright are investigated by the United States Department of Justice and carry, upon conviction of fines up to $250,000 and five years confinement. This Work is protected by United States Copyright Laws and International Treaties. Do not Copy, do not reproduce, do not distribute.

A Ficus Tree Publishing Educational-Technical Publications

DUVALL'S TEST'S™
Instructors Manual Study Guide Series United States Tax Code
IRS Publication 15 Circular E, Employer's Tax Guide Tax Year 2013
Tax Test 15E-S5-1 [Multiple-Choice Questions With Answers]

Section 15E-S5-1. Wages and Other Compensation Page 14

5. Wages and Other Compensation
1. Wages subject to Federal employment taxes generally include ___.
    (a) withholding, social security, Medicare
    (b) all pay you give an employee for services performed
    (c) all wages you give an employee for services preformed
    (d) all wages that are determined to be taxable
    Answer: See 5. Wages and Other Compensation, page 14/ (b) all pay you give an employee for services performed

5. Wages and Other Compensation
2. The pay may be in cash or in other forms. It includes vacation allowances, bonuses, salaries, commissions and ___.
    (a) salaries
    (b) fringe benefits
    (c) overtime
    (d) stand-by time
    Answer: See Section 5. Wages and Other Compensation, page 14/ (b) fringe benefits

5. Wages and Other Compensation
3. The pay may be in cash or in other forms. It includes vacation allowances, bonuses, salaries, commissions and ___. It does not matter how you ___ or make the payments.
    (a) salaries, decide
    (b) fringe benefits, measure
    (c) overtime, measure
    (d) stand-by time, disburse
    Answer: See 5. Wages and Other Compensation, page 14/ (b) fringe benefits, measure

5. Wages and Other Compensation
4. Amounts an employer pays as a ___ for signing or ratifying a contract in connection with the establishment of an employer-employee relationship and the amount paid to an employee for cancellation of an employment contract and relinquishment of contract rights are wages ___ social security, Medicare, and FUTA taxes and income tax withholding.
    (a) bonus, not subject to
    (b) bonus, subject to
    (c) benefit, subject to
    (d) bonus, not subject to
    Answer: See 5. Wages and Other Compensation. Page 11/ (b) bonus, subject to

Wages and Other Compensation

5. Wages and Other Compensation

5. Amounts an employer pays as a bonus for signing or ratifying a contract in connection with the establishment of an employer-employee relationship and the amount paid to an employee for cancellation of an employment contract and relinquishment of contract rights are wages subject to social security, Medicare, and FUTA taxes and income tax withholding. Also, compensation paid to a former employee for services performed while still employed is wages ___.
    (a) subject to tax
    (b) subject to taxation
    (c) subject to employment taxes
    (d) earned
    Answer: See 5. Wages and Other Compensation. Page 14/ (c) subject to employment taxes

5. Wages and Other Compensation - More information

6. See section ___ for discussion of tips and section ___ for a discussion of supplemental wages.
    (a) 3, 4
    (b) 4, 5
    (c) 5, 6
    (d) 6, 7
    Answer: See 5. Wages and Other Compensation, More information. Page 14/ (d) 6, 7

Wages and Other Compensation. More Information

5. Wages and Other Compensation - More information

7. See section ___ for discussion of tips and section ___ for a discussion of supplemental wages. Also, see section ___ for ___ to general rules for wages.
    (a) 3, 4, 12, special conditions
    (b) 4, 5, 13, exceptions
    (c) 5, 6, 14, exceptions
    (d) 6, 7, 15, exceptions
    Answer: See 5. Wages and Other Compensation, More information. Page 14/ (d) 6, 7, 15, exceptions

Wages and Other Compensation. More Information

5. Wages and Other Compensation - More information
8. See section 6 for discussion of tips and section 7 for a discussion of supplemental wages. Also, see section 15 for exceptions to general rules for wages. Publication ___A provides additional information on wages, including nonqualified ___compensation, and other compensation.
   (a) 15, deferred
   (b) 16, deferred
   (c) 15, deferrals
   (d) 16, deferrals
   Answer: See 5. Wages and Other Compensation, More information. Page 14/ (a) 15, deferred

5. Wages and Other Compensation - More information
9. Publication ___A provides additional information on wages, including nonqualified ___compensation, and other compensation. Publication 15 ___ provides information on other forms of ___, including:
   (a) A, income
   (b) B, compensation
   (c) C, wages
   (d) D, compensation
   Answer: See 5. Wages and Other Compensation, More information. Page 14/ (d) B, compensation

5. Wages and Other Compensation - More information
10. Publication 15B provides information on other forms of compensation, including: Accident and health benefits, Achievement awards, Adoption assistance, ____.
    (a) Athletic achievement
    (b) Achievement compensation
    (c) Adoption financial assistance
    (d) Athletic facilities
    Answer: See 5. Wages and Other Compensation, More information. Page 14/ (d) Athletic facilities

5. Wages and Other Compensation - More information
11. Publication 15B provides information on other forms of compensation, including: De minimis (minimal) benefits, Dependent care assistance, ___, Employee discounts.
    (a) Educational funding
    (b) Educational grants
    (c) Educational assistance
    (d) Financial assistance
    Answer: See 5. Wages and Other Compensation, More information. Page 14/ (c) Educational assistance

Wages and Other Compensation. More Information

5. Wages and Other Compensation - More information

12. Publication 15B provides information on other forms of compensation, including: Employee stock options, ___, Group-term life insurance coverage, Health Savings Accounts.
    (a) Employer provided transportation
    (b) Employer-provided cell phones
    (c) Employee family care
    (d) Employee family vacations
    Answer: See 5. Wages and Other Compensation, More information. Page 14/ (b) Employer-provided cell phones

5. Wages and Other Compensation - More information

13. Publication 15B provides information on other forms of compensation, including: Lodging on your business premises, Meals, ___, No-additional-cost services
    (a) Hand tools and equipment
    (b) Recreational equipment compensation
    (c) Moving expense reimbursements
    (d) Relocation expense compensation
    Answer: See 5. Wages and Other Compensation, More information. Page 14/ (c) Moving expense reimbursements

5. Wages and Other Compensation - More information

14. Publication 15B provides information on other forms of compensation, including: Retirement planning services, Transportation (commuting) benefits, Tuition reduction, and ___.
    (a) Food services
    (b) Housing
    (c) Recreational expense benefits
    (d) Working condition benefits
    Answer: See 5. Wages and Other Compensation, More information. Pages 14 and 15/ (d) Working condition benefits

Wages and Other Compensation
Employee business expense reimbursements

5. Wages and Other Compensation - Employee business expense reimbursements

15. A reimbursement or allowance arrangement is a system by which you pay the advances, reimbursements, and ____ for your employees' business expenses.
    (a) charges
    (b) costs
    (c) expenses
    (d) expenditures
    Answer: See 5. Wages and Other Compensation, Employee business expense reimbursements, Page 15/ (a) charges

© Copyright 2013. All rights reserved. Notice: United States Copyright Laws and International Treaties prohibit unauthorized publication, reproduction, distribution of this Work. Unauthorized use of this copyright in any form, format, publication or document may result in severe civil and criminal penalties. Violations of this copyright are investigated by the United States Department of Justice and carry, upon conviction of fines up to $250,000 and five years confinement. This Work is protected by United States Copyright Laws and International Treaties. Do not Copy, do not reproduce, do not distribute.

Wages and Other Compensation
Employee business expense reimbursements

5. Wages and Other Compensation - Employee business expense reimbursements
16. How you report a reimbursement or allowance amount depends whether you have an ___ or a ___ plan.
    (a) debit, credit
    (b) accountable, nonaccountable
    (c) nonaccountable, accountable
    (d) credit, cash
    Answer: See 5. Wages and Other Compensation, Employee business expense reimbursements, Page 15/ (b) accountable, nonaccountable

5. Wages and Other Compensation - Employee business expense reimbursements
17. How you report a reimbursement or allowance amount depends whether you have an ___ or a ___ plan. If a single payment includes both wages and reimbursement, you must ___ the amount of the reimbursement.
    (a) debit, credit, state or provide
    (b) accountable, nonaccountable, specify
    (c) nonaccountable, accountable, specify
    (d) credit, cash, state or provide
    Answer: See 5. Wages and Other Compensation, Employee business expense reimbursements, Page 15/ (b) accountable, nonaccountable, specify

5. Wages and Other Compensation - Employee business expense reimbursements
18. These rules apply to all ordinary and necessary employee business expenses that would otherwise qualify for ___.
    (a) a business deduction
    (b) a income tax liability
    (c) a deduction got the employee
    (d) a deduction for the employer
    Answer: See 5. Wages and Other Compensation, Employee business expense reimbursements, Page 15/ (c) a deduction for the employee

Employee business expense reimbursements. Accountable Plan

5. Wages and Other Compensation - Accountable plan.
19. To be an accountable plan, your reimbursement or ___ arrangements must require your employees to meet all ___ of the following rules.
    (a) payment, two
    (b) expense, three
    (c) refund, two
    (d) allowance, three
    Answer: See 5. Wages and Other Compensation. Accountable plan, page 15/ (d) allowance, three

Employee business expense reimbursements. Accountable Plan

5. Wages and Other Compensation - Accountable plan.
20. To be an accountable plan, your reimbursement or allowance arrangements must require your employees to meet all three of the following rules. 1. They must have ____ or incurred deductable expenses while performing services as your employee.
    (a) purchased
    (b) bought
    (c) paid
    (d) spent
    Answer: See 5. Wages and Other Compensation. Accountable plan, page 15/ (c) paid

5. Wages and Other Compensation - Accountable plan.
21. To be an accountable plan, your reimbursement or allowance arrangements must require your employees to meet all three of the following rules. 1. They must have ____ or incurred deductable expenses while performing services as your employee. The reimbursement or advance must be paid for the ___ and must not be an amount that would have otherwise been paid by the employee.
    (a) purchased, item
    (b) bought, expense
    (c) paid, expense
    (d) spent, item
    Answer: See 5. Wages and Other Compensation. Accountable plan, page 15/ (c) paid, expense

5. Wages and Other Compensation - Accountable plan.
22. To be an accountable plan, your reimbursement or allowance arrangements must require your employees to meet all three of the following rules.
    1. They must have paid or incurred deductable expenses while performing services as your employee. The reimbursement or advance must be paid for the expense and must not be an amount that would have otherwise been paid by the employee.
    2. They must __ these expenses to you within a reasonable period of time.
    (a) document
    (b) substantiate
    (c) certify
    (d) prove
    Answer: See 5. Wages and Other Compensation. Accountable plan, page 15/ (b) substantiate

Employee business expense reimbursements. Accountable Plan

5. Wages and Other Compensation - Accountable plan.
23. To be an accountable plan, your reimbursement or allowance arrangements must require your employees to meet all three of the following rules.
    1. They must have paid or incurred deductable expenses while performing services as your employee. The reimbursement or advance must be paid for the expense and must not be an amount that would have otherwise been paid by the employee.
    2. They must __ these expenses to you within a reasonable period of time.
    3. They must __ any amounts in excess of substantiated expenses within a reasonable period of time.
    (a) document, refund
    (b) substantiate , return
    (c) certify, return
    (d) prove, refund
    Answer: See 5. Wages and Other Compensation. Accountable plan, page 15/ (b) substantiate, return

5. Wages and Other Compensation - Accountable plan.
24. Amounts paid under an ___ plan are not wages and are not subject to the withholding and payment of income, social security, Medicare, and FUTA taxes.
    (a) accountable
    (b) nonaccountable
    (c) reimbursement
    (d) expense
    Answer: See 5. Wages and Other Compensation. Accountable plan, page 15/ (a) accountable

5. Wages and Other Compensation - Accountable plan.
25. If the expenses covered by this arrangement are not substantiated (or amounts in excess of substantiated expenses are not returned within a reasonable period of time) the amount paid under the arrangement in excess of the substantiated expenses is treated as paid under a ___.
    (a) accountable plan
    (b) nonaccountable plan
    (c) tax liability expense
    (d) tax liability payment due
    Answer: See 5. Wages and Other Compensation. Accountable plan, page 15/ (b) nonaccountable plan

Employee business expense reimbursements. Accountable Plan

5. Wages and Other Compensation - Accountable plan.
26. If the expenses covered by this arrangement are not substantiated (or amounts in excess of substantiated expenses are not returned within a reasonable period of time) the amount paid under the arrangement in excess of the substantiated expenses is treated as paid under a ___. This amount is subject to the withholding and payment of income, social security, Medicare, and FUTA taxes for the ___ period following the end of a reasonable period of time.
    (a) accountable plan, quarter
    (b) nonaccountable plan, first
    (c) tax liability expense, annual
    (d) tax liability payment due, annual
    Answer: See 5. Wages and Other Compensation. Accountable plan, page 15/ (b) nonaccountable plan, first

5. Wages and Other Compensation - Accountable plan.
27. A reasonable period of time depends on the ___ and ___.
    (a) employer, employee
    (b) accounting system, auditing
    (c) facts, circumstances
    (d) circumstances, facts
    Answer: See 5. Wages and Other Compensation. Accountable plan, page 15/ (c) facts, circumstances

5. Wages and Other Compensation - Accountable plan.
28. A reasonable period of time depends on the facts and circumstances. Generally, it is considered reasonable if your employees receive their advance within ___ days of the time they incur the expenses,
    (a) 7
    (b) 10
    (c) 15
    (d) 30
    Answer: See 5. Wages and Other Compensation. Accountable plan, page 15/ (d) 30

5. Wages and Other Compensation - Accountable plan.
29. A reasonable period of time depends on the facts and circumstances. Generally, it is considered reasonable if your employees receive their advance within ___ days of the time they incur the expenses, adequately account for the expenses within ___ days after the expenses were paid or
    (a) 10, 14
    (b) 15, 30
    (c) 30, 60
    (d) 45, 90
    Answer: See 5. Wages and Other Compensation. Accountable plan, page 15/ (c) 30, 60

Employee business expense reimbursements - Accountable Plan

5. Wages and Other Compensation - Accountable plan.
30. A reasonable period of time depends on the facts and circumstances. Generally, it is considered reasonable if your employees receive their advance within ___days of the time they incur the expenses, adequately account for the expenses within ___days after the expenses were paid or incurred , and return any amounts in excess of expenses within ___days after the expenses were paid or incurred.
    (a) 15, 30,60
    (b) 30, 60, 90
    (c) 30, 60, 120
    (d) 45, 90, 120
    Answer: See 5. Wages and Other Compensation. Accountable plan, page 15/ (c) 30, 60, 120

5. Wages and Other Compensation - Accountable plan.
31. Also, it is considered reasonable if you give your employees a ___statement (at least quarterly) that asks them to either return or adequately account for outstanding amounts and the do so within ___days.
    (a) weekly, 30
    (b) monthly, 60
    (c) quarterly, 90
    (d) periodic, 120
    Answer: See 5. Wages and Other Compensation. Accountable plan, page 15/ (d) periodic, 120

Employee business expense reimbursements. Nonaccountable Plan

5. Wages and Other Compensation - Nonaccountable plan.
32. Payments to your employees for travel and other expenses of your business under a nonaccountable plan are ___ and are treated as ___ wages and
    (a) wages, supplemental
    (b) income, deferred
    (c) income, earned
    (d) income, payroll
    Answer: See 5. Wages and Other Compensation. Nonaccountable plan, page 15/ (a) wages, supplemental

Employee business expense reimbursements. Nonaccountable Plan

5. Wages and Other Compensation - Nonaccountable plan.
33. Payments to your employees for travel and other expenses of your business under a nonaccountable plan are ___ and are treated as ___ wages and subject to the withholding and payment of income, social security, Medicare, and FUTA taxes. Your payments are treated as ___ under a nonaccountable plan if:
   (a) wages, supplemental, paid
   (b) income, deferred, income
   (c) income, earned, taxable
   (d) income, payroll, taxable
   Answer: See 5. Wages and Other Compensation. Nonaccountable plan, page 15/ (a) wages, supplemental, paid

5. Wages and Other Compensation - Nonaccountable plan.
34. Payments to your employees for travel and other expenses of your business under a nonaccountable plan are wages and are treated as supplemental wages and subject to the withholding and payment of income, social security, Medicare, and FUTA taxes. Your payments are treated as paid under a nonaccountable plan if: • Your employee is not required to or ___ substantiate timely those expenses to you with receipts or documentation.
   (a) disregards
   (b) does not
   (c) ignores
   (d) refuses to
   Answer: See 5. Wages and Other Compensation. Nonaccountable plan, page 15/ (b) does not

5. Wages and Other Compensation - Nonaccountable plan.
35. Payments to your employees for travel and other expenses of your business under a nonaccountable plan are wages and are treated as supplemental wages and subject to the withholding and payment of income, social security, Medicare, and FUTA taxes. Your payments are treated as paid under a nonaccountable plan if:
   • Your employee is not required to or does not substantiate timely those expenses to you with receipts or documentation.
   • You advance an amount to your employee for business expenses and your employee ___ or does
     not return timely any amount he or she does not use for business expenses.
   (a) fails
   (b) does not
   (c) is not required to
   (d) has not
   Answer: See 5. Wages and Other Compensation. Nonaccountable plan, page 15/ (c) is not required to

Employee business expense reimbursements. Nonaccountable Plan

5. Wages and Other Compensation - Nonaccountable plan.

36. Payments to your employees for travel and other expenses of your business under a nonaccountable plan are wages and are treated as supplemental wages and subject to the withholding and payment of income, social security, Medicare, and FUTA taxes. Your payments are treated as paid under a nonaccountable plan if:
    - Your employee is not required to or does not substantiate timely those expenses to you with receipts or documentation.
    - You advance an amount to your employee for business expenses and your employee ___ or does
      not return timely any amount he or she does not use for business expenses.
    - You advance or pay an amount to your employee regardless of whether you reasonably expect to have ___ expenses related to your business, or

    (a) fails, business
    (b) does not, personal
    (c) is not required to, business
    (d) has not, additional

    Answer: See 5. Wages and Other Compensation. Nonaccountable plan, page 15/ (c) is not required to, business

5. Wages and Other Compensation - Nonaccountable plan.

37. Payments to your employees for travel and other expenses of your business under a nonaccountable plan are wages and are treated as supplemental wages and subject to the withholding and payment of income, social security, Medicare, and FUTA taxes. Your payments are treated as paid under a nonaccountable plan if:
    - Your employee is not required to or does not substantiate timely those expenses to you with receipts or documentation.
    - You advance an amount to your employee for business expenses and your employee is not required to or does not return timely any amount he or she does not use for business expenses.
    - You advance or pay an amount to your employee regardless of whether you reasonably expect to have ___ expenses related to your business, or
    - You pay an amount as a ___ you would have otherwise paid as wages.

    (a) bonus
    (b) salary
    (c) gift
    (d) reimbursement

    Answer: See 5. Wages and Other Compensation. Nonaccountable plan, page 15/ (d) reimbursement

Employee Business Expense Reimbursements - Nonaccountable Plan

5. Wages and Other Compensation - Nonaccountable plan.

38.   See <u>section</u> ___ for more information on supplemental wages.
- (a) 5
- (b) 7
- (c) 9
- (d) 11

Answer: See 5. Wages and Other Compensation. Nonaccountable plan, page 15/ (b) 7

DUVALL'S TEST'S™
Instructors Manual Study Guide Series United States Tax Code
IRS Publication 15 Circular E, Employer's Tax Guide Tax Year 2013
Tax Test 15E-S5-2 [Multiple-Choice Questions With Answers]

Wages and Other Compensation. Per diem or other fixed allowance

5. Wages and Other Compensation - Per diem or other fixed allowance
1. You may reimburse your employees by ___, miles, or some other fixed allowance under the applicable revenue procedure.
    (a) travel
    (b) travel expenses
    (c) travel days
    (d) mileage
    Answer: See 5. Wages and Other Compensation. Per diem or other fixed allowance, page 15/ (c) travel days

5. Wages and Other Compensation - Per diem or other fixed allowance
2. You may reimburse your employees by travel days, miles, or some other fixed allowance under the applicable revenue procedure. In these cases, your employee is considered to have ___ if your reimbursement does not exceed rates established by the Federal Government.
    (a) substantiated to you
    (b) accounted to you
    (c) certified to you
    (d) provided documentation,
    Answer: See 5. Wages and Other Compensation. Per diem or other fixed allowance, page 15/ (b) accounted to you

5. Wages and Other Compensation - Per diem or other fixed allowance.
3. The **2012** standard mileage rate for auto expenses was 55.5 cents per mile. The **2013** standard mileage rate for auto expenses is ___ cents per mile.
    (a) 55.0
    (b) 56.0
    (c) 56.5
    (d) 57.0
    Answer: See Section 5. Per diem or other fixed allowance, Wages and other Compensation, page 15/ (c) 56.5

© Copyright 2013. All rights reserved. Notice: United States Copyright Laws and International Treaties prohibit unauthorized publication, reproduction, distribution of this Work. Unauthorized use of this copyright in any form, format, publication or document may result in severe civil and criminal penalties. Violations of this copyright are investigated by the United States Department of Justice and carry, upon conviction of fines up to $250,000 and five years confinement. This Work is protected by United States Copyright Laws and International Treaties. Do not Copy, do not reproduce, do not distribute.

A Ficus Tree Publishing Educational-Technical Publications

Wages and Other Compensation. Per diem or other fixed allowance

5. Wages and Other Compensation - Per diem or other fixed allowance.
4. The government per diem rates for meals and lodging in the continental United States are listed in Publication ___, Per Diem Rates.
   (a) 1044
   (b) 1442
   (c) 1492
   (d) 1542
   Answer: See Section 5. Per diem or other fixed allowance, Wages and other Compensation, page 15/ (d) 1542

5. Wages and Other Compensation - Per diem or other fixed allowance.
5. The government per diem rates for meals and lodging in the continental United States are listed in Publication ___, Per Diem Rates. Other than the amount of these expenses, your employees' business expenses must be ___ (for example, the business purpose of the travel or the number of business miles driven).
   (a) 1044, reasonably accurate
   (b) 1442, verified
   (c) 1492, documented
   (d) 1542, substantiated
   Answer: See Section 5. Per diem or other fixed allowance, Wages and other Compensation, page 15/ (d) 1542, substantiated

5. Wages and Other Compensation - Per diem or other fixed allowance.
6. If the per diem or allowance paid exceeds the amounts substantiated, you must report the ___ as wages.
   (a) excess amount
   (b) excessive amount
   (c) exceeded amount
   (d) difference
   Answer: See Section 5. Per diem or other fixed allowance, Wages and other Compensation, page 15/ (a) excess amount

5. Wages and Other Compensation - Per diem or other fixed allowance.
7. If the per diem or allowance paid exceeds the amounts substantiated, you must report the excess amount as wages. This excess amount is ___ income tax withholding and payment of social security, Medicare, and FUTA taxes.
   (a) taxable
   (b) earned income thus
   (c) subject to
   (d) taxable wages, thus
   Answer: See Section 5. Per diem or other fixed allowance, Wages and other Compensation, page 15/ (c) subject to

Wages and Other Compensation. Per diem or other fixed allowance

5. Wages and Other Compensation - Per diem or other fixed allowance.
8. If the per diem or allowance paid exceeds the amounts substantiated, you must report the excess amount as wages. This excess amount is ___ income tax withholding and payment of social security, Medicare, and FUTA taxes. Show the amount equal to the substantiated amount (for example, the nontaxable portion) in box 12 of Form W-2 using code "__".
   (a) taxable, J
   (b) earned income thus, K
   (c) subject to, L
   (d) taxable wages, thus, M
   Answer: See Section 5. Per diem or other fixed allowance, Wages and other Compensation, page 15/ (c) subject to, L

Wages and Other Compensation. Wages not paid in money

5. Wages and Other Compensation - Wages not paid in money.
9. If in the course of your trade or business you pay your employees in a medium that is neither cash or a readily negotiable instrument, such as a check, you are said to pay them "___."
   (a) in kind
   (b) en escrow
   (c) et all
   (d) taxable wages
   Answer: See Section 5. Wages and other Compensation, Wages not paid in money. Page 15/ (a) in kind

5. Wages and Other Compensation - Wages not paid in money.
10. Payments in kind may be in the form of goods, ___, food, clothing, or services.
    (a) lodging
    (b) entertainment
    (c) books and manuals
    (d) study aids
    Answer: See Section 5. Wages and other Compensation, Wages not paid in money. Page 15/ (a) lodging

© Copyright 2013. All rights reserved. Notice: United States Copyright Laws and International Treaties prohibit unauthorized publication, reproduction, distribution of this Work. Unauthorized use of this copyright in any form, format, publication or document may result in severe civil and criminal penalties. Violations of this copyright are investigated by the United States Department of Justice and carry, upon conviction of fines up to $250,000 and five years confinement. This Work is protected by United States Copyright Laws and International Treaties. Do not Copy, do not reproduce, do not distribute.

Wages and Other Compensation. Wages not paid in money

5. Wages and Other Compensation - Wages not paid in money.
11.   Payments in kind may be in the form of goods, ___, food, clothing, or services. Generally, the *__fair market value__* of such payments at the time they are ___ is subject to federal income tax withholding and social security, Medicare and FUTA taxes.
   (a)   lodging, provided
   (b)   entertainment, incurred
   (c)   books and manuals, obtained
   (d)   study aids, incurred
   Answer: See Section 5. Wages and other Compensation, Wages not paid in money. Page 15/ (a) lodging, provided

5. Wages and Other Compensation - Wages not paid in money.
12.   Payments in kind may be in the form of goods, ___, food, clothing, or services. Generally, the *__fair market value__* of such payments at the time they are ___ is subject to federal income tax withholding and social security, Medicare and FUTA taxes. However, noncash payments for household work, agricultural labor, and service not in the employer's trade or business are ___ social security, Medicare, and FUTA taxes.
   (a)   lodging, provided, exempt from
   (b)   entertainment, incurred, are not exempt from
   (c)   books and manuals, obtained, taxable such as
   (d)   study aids, incurred, taxable such as
   Answer: See Section 5. Wages and other Compensation, Wages not paid in money. Page 15/ (a) lodging, provided, exempt from

5. Wages and Other Compensation - Wages not paid in money.
13.   Payments in kind may be in the form of goods, lodging, food, clothing, or services. Generally, the *__fair market value__* of such payments at the time they are provided is subject to federal income tax withholding and social security, Medicare and FUTA taxes. However, noncash payments for household work, agricultural labor, and service not in the employer's trade or business are exempt from social security, Medicare, and FUTA taxes. Withhold income tax on these payments only if you and the employee ___.
   (a)   notified by the IRS
   (b)   agree to do so
   (c)   cannot agree to do so
   (d)   do not agree to do so
   Answer: See Section 5. Wages and other Compensation, Wages not paid in money. Page 15/ (b) agree to do so

The International Leader in Construction Technology Home Study

Wages and Other Compensation. Wages not paid in money

5. Wages and Other Compensation - Wages not paid in money.

14. Payments in kind may be in the form of goods, lodging, food, clothing, or services. Generally, the *fair market value* of such payments at the time they are provided is subject to federal income tax withholding and social security, Medicare and FUTA taxes. However, noncash payments for household work, agricultural labor, and service not in the employer's trade or business are exempt from social security, Medicare, and FUTA taxes. Withhold income tax on these payments only if you and the employee ___. Nonetheless, noncash payments for agricultural labor, such as ___ wages, are treated as cash payments subject to employment taxes if the substance of the transaction is a cash payment.
    (a) notified by the IRS, communal
    (b) agree to do so, commodity
    (c) cannot agree to do so, community
    (d) do not agree to do so, contractual
    Answer: See 5. Wages and other Compensation, Wages not paid in money. Page 15/ (b) agree to do so, commodity

Wages and Other Compensation. Moving Expenses

5. Wages and Other Compensation - Moving expenses.

15. Reimbursed and employer-paid ___ moving expenses (those that would otherwise be deductible by the employee) paid under an ___ are not includible in the employee's income unless
    (a) qualified, nonaccountable plan
    (b) approved, accountable plan
    (c) qualified, accountable plan
    (d) approved, nonaccountable plan
    Answer: See 5. Wages and other Compensation. Moving expenses. Page 16/ (c) qualified, accountable plan

5. Wages and Other Compensation - Moving expenses.

16. Reimbursed and employer-paid qualified moving expenses (those that would otherwise be deductible by the employee) paid under an accountable plan are not includible in the employee's income unless you have knowledge the employee ___ expenses in a prior year. Reimbursed and employer-paid ___ moving expenses are includible in income and are subject to employment taxes and income tax withholding.
    (a) claimed, nonqualified
    (b) credited, non-approved
    (c) debited, non-acceptable
    (d) deducted, nonqualified
    Answer: See 5. Wages and other Compensation. Moving expenses. Page 16/ (d) deducted, nonqualified

Wages and Other Compensation. Moving Expenses

5. Wages and Other Compensation - Moving expenses.
17. For more information on moving expenses, see Publication ___, Moving Expenses.
    (a) 521
    (b) 522
    (c) 523
    (d) 524
    Answer: See 5. Wages and other Compensation. Moving expenses. Page 16/ (a) 521

Wages and Other Compensation. Meals and Lodging

5. Wages and Other Compensation - Meals and lodging.
18. The ___ of meals is not taxable income tax withholding and social security, Medicare, and FUTA taxes if the meals are furnished for the employer's convenience and on the employer's premises.
    (a) cost
    (b) value
    (c) price
    (d) expense
    Answer: See 5. Wages and other Compensation. Meals and lodging. Page 16/ (b) value

5. Wages and Other Compensation - Meals and lodging
19. The value of lodging ___ subject to income tax withholding and social security, Medicare, and FUTA taxes if the lodging is furnished for the employer's convenience, on the employer's premises, as a condition of employment.
    (a) are
    (b) is not
    (c) is
    (d) are not
    Answer: Section 5. Wages and Other Compensation, Meals and lodging, page16/ (b) is not

5. Wages and Other Compensation - Meals and lodging
20. "For the convenience of the employer" means that you have a substantial business reason for providing the meals and lodging other than to provide additional ___ to the employee.
    (a) wages
    (b) income
    (c) compensation
    (d) remuneration
    Answer: See 5. Wages and Other Compensation, Meals and lodging, page 16. (note the example)/ (c) compensation

Wages and Other Compensation. Meals and Lodging

5. Wages and Other Compensation - Meals and lodging
21. "For the convenience of the employer" means that you have a substantial business reason for providing the meals and lodging other than to provide additional ___ to the employee. For example, meals you provide at the place of work so that the employee is available for ___ during his or her lunch period are generally considered to be for your convenience.
    (a) wages, standby
    (b) income, emergencies
    (c) compensation, emergencies
    (d) remuneration, standby
    Answer: See 5. Wages and Other Compensation, Meals and lodging, page 16 (note the example)/ (c) compensation, emergencies

5. Wages and Other Compensation - Meals and lodging
22. "For the convenience of the employer" means that you have a substantial business reason for providing the meals and lodging other than to provide additional ___ to the employee. For example, meals you provide at the place of work so that the employee is available for ___ during his or her lunch period are generally considered to be for your convenience. However, whether meals or lodging are provided for the convenience of the employer depend on all the ___ and ___.
    (a) wages, standby, circumstances, facts
    (b) income, emergencies, conditions, necessity
    (c) compensation, emergencies, facts, circumstances
    (d) remuneration, standby, necessity, conditions
    Answer: See 5. Wages and Other Compensation, Meals and lodging, page 16 (note the example)/ (c) compensation, emergencies, facts, circumstances

5. Wages and Other Compensation - Meals and lodging
23. "For the convenience of the employer" means that you have a substantial business reason for providing the meals and lodging other than to provide additional ___ to the employee. For example, meals you provide at the place of work so that the employee is available for ___ during his or her lunch period are generally considered to be for your convenience. However, whether meals or lodging are provided for the convenience of the employer depend on all the ___ and ___. A written statement that the meals or lodging are for your convenience is ___.
    (a) wages, standby, circumstances, facts, acceptable
    (b) income, emergencies, conditions, necessity, sufficient
    (c) compensation, emergencies, facts, circumstances, not sufficient
    (d) remuneration, standby, necessity, conditions, unacceptable
    Answer: See 5. Wages and Other Compensation, Meals and lodging, page 16 (note the example)/ (c) compensation, emergencies, facts, circumstances, not sufficient

Section 5. 15E-S2. Wages and Other Compensation. 50% Test

5. Wages and Other Compensation - 50% Test.

24. If over ___% of the employees who are provided meals on an employer's premises receive these meals for the convenience of the employer, all meals provided on the premises are treated as furnished for the convenience of the employer.
    (a) 12½
    (b) 25
    (c) 33
    (d) 50
    Answer: See 5. Wages and Other Compensation, 50% test, page 16/ (d) 50

5. Wages and Other Compensation - 50% test.

25. If over ___% of the employees who are provided meals on an employer's premises receive these meals for the convenience of the employer, all meals provided on the premises are treated as furnished for the convenience of the employer. If this ___% test is met, the value of the meals is excludable from income for all employees and is not subject to income tax withholding or employment taxes.
    (a) 12½, 12½
    (b) 25, 25
    (c) 33, 33
    (d) 50, 50
    Answer: See 5. Wages and Other Compensation, 50% test, page 16/ (d) 50, 50

5. Wages and Other Compensation - 50% test.

26. If over ___% of the employees who are provided meals on an employer's premises receive these meals for the convenience of the employer, all meals provided on the premises are treated as furnished for the convenience of the employer. If this ___% test is met, the value of the meals is excludable from income for all employees and is not subject to income tax withholding or employment taxes. For more information, see Publication ___.
    (a) 12½, 12½, 15-A
    (b) 25, 25, 15-A
    (c) 33, 33, 15-B
    (d) 50, 50, 15-B
    Answer: See 5. Wages and Other Compensation, 50% test, page 16/ (d) 50, 50, 15-B

Wages and Other Compensation. Health Insurance Plans

5. Wages and Other Compensation - Health insurance plans.

27. If you pay the cost of an accident or health insurance plan for your employees, including an employee's spouse and dependents, your payments ___ wages and ___ subject to social security, Medicare, and FUTA taxes, or federal income tax withholding.
    (a) are, are
    (b) are not, are not
    (c) are taxable, are taxable
    (d) are not taxable, are taxable
    Answer: See 5. Wages and Other Compensation, Health insurance plans, page 16/ (b) are not, are not

5. Wages and Other Compensation - Health insurance plans.

28. If you pay the cost of an accident or health insurance plan for your employees, including an employee's spouse and dependents, your payments ___ wages and ___ subject to social security, Medicare, and FUTA taxes, or federal income tax withholding. Generally, this ___ also applies to qualified long-term care insurance contracts.
    (a) are, are, exclusion
    (b) are not, are not, exclusion
    (c) are taxable, are taxable, requirement
    (d) are not taxable, are taxable, requirement
    Answer: See 5. Wages and Other Compensation, Health insurance plans, page 16/ (b) are not, are not, exclusion

5. Wages and Other Compensation - Health insurance plans.

29. If you pay the cost of an accident or health insurance plan for your employees, including an employee's spouse and dependents, your payments are not wages and are not subject to social security, Medicare, and FUTA taxes, or federal income tax withholding. Generally, this exception also applies to qualified long-term care insurance contracts. However, for income tax withholding, the value of health insurance benefits must be included in the wages of ___ corporation employees who own more than ___% of the ___ corporation (___% shareholders).
    (a) S, 2, S, 2
    (b) S, 5, S, 5
    (c) C, 5, C, 5
    (d) M, 10, M 10
    Answer: See 5. Wages and Other Compensation, Health insurance plans, page 16/ (a) S, 2, S, 2

Wages and Other Compensation. Health Insurance Plans

5. Wages and Other Compensation - Health insurance plans.
30.   If you pay the cost of an accident or health insurance plan for your employees, including an employee's spouse and dependents, your payments are not wages and are not subject to social security, Medicare, and FUTA taxes, or federal income tax withholding. Generally, this exception also applies to qualified long-term care insurance contracts. However, for income tax withholding, the value of health insurance benefits must be included in the wages of ___ corporation employees who own more than ___% of the ___corporation (___% shareholders). For social security, Medicare, and FUTA taxes, the health insurance benefits are ___ from the wages only for employees and their dependents or for a class or classes of employees and their dependents.
    (a)   S, 2, S, 2, excluded
    (b)   S, 5, S, 5, included
    (c)   C, 5, C, 5, excluded
    (d)   M, 10, M 10, included
    Answer: See 5. Wages and Other Compensation, Health insurance plans, page 16/ (a) S, 2, S, 2, excluded

5. Wages and Other Compensation - Health insurance plans.
31.   For social security, Medicare, and FUTA taxes, the health insurance benefits are ___ from the wages only for employees and their dependents or for a class or classes of employees and their dependents. See Announcement ___ for more information.
    (a)   null, 2013-A
    (b)   included, 92-15
    (c)   excluded, 92-16
    (d)   an entitlement, 92-17
    Answer: See 5. Wages and Other Compensation, Health insurance plans, page 16/ (c) excluded, 92-16

5. Wages and Other Compensation - Health insurance plans.
32.   For social security, Medicare, and FUTA taxes, the health insurance benefits are ___ from the wages only for employees and their dependents or for a class or classes of employees and their dependents. See Announcement ___ for more information. You can find Announcement ___ on page 53 of Internal Revenue Bulletin ___.
    (a)   null, 2013-A, 2013-B, 1992-5
    (b)   included, 92-15, 92-16, 1992-4
    (c)   excluded, 92-16, 92-16, 1992-5
    (d)   an entitlement, 92-17, 92-16, 1992-5
    Answer: See 5. Wages and Other Compensation, Health insurance plans, page 16/ (c) excluded, 92-16, 92-16, 1992-5

Health Savings Accounts and Medical Saving Accounts

5. Wages and Other Compensation - Health Savings Accounts and medical savings accounts.
33. A Health Saving Account is abbreviated as a HCA, however, a **Archer** medical savings account would be abbreviated in Circular E as ___.
 (a) AMS
 (b) MSA
 (c) HMO
 (d) H_2O
 Answer: See 5. Wages and Other Compensation, Health Savings Accounts and medical savings accounts, page 16/ (b) MSA (Medical Saving Account)

5. Wages and Other Compensation - Health Savings Accounts Medical Savings Accounts.
34. Your contributions to an employee's Health Saving Account (HSA) or ___ medical saving account (MSA) are not subject to social security, Medicare, or FUTA taxes, or federal income tax withholding if
 (a) Archer
 (b) Baker
 (c) Charlie
 (d) Fox
 Answer: See 5. Wages and Other Compensation, Health Savings Accounts and medical savings accounts, page 16/ (a) Archer

5. Wages and Other Compensation - Health Savings Accounts medical savings accounts.
35. Your contributions to an employee's Health Savings Account (HSA) or ___ medical savings account are not subject to social security, Medicare or FUTA taxes, or withholding taxes if it is reasonable to believe at the time of payment of the contributions that they will be ___ from the income of the employee.
 (a) Archer, excludable
 (b) Davis-Bacon Act, includable
 (c) Copeland Act, extraneous to and
 (d) Modified IRA-M, excludable
 Answer: See 5. Wages and Other Compensation, Archer medical savings accounts, page 16/ (a) Archer, excludable

Health Savings Accounts and Medical Savings Accounts

5. Wages and Other Compensation - Health Savings Accounts and medical savings accounts.

36. Your contributions to an employee's Health Savings Account (HSA) or Archer medical savings account are not subject to social security, Medicare or FUTA taxes, or withholding taxes if it is reasonable to believe at the time of payment of the contributions that they will be excludable from the income of the employee. To the extent it is not reasonable to believe they will excludable, your contributions ___ these taxes.
    (a) will be included with
    (b) will not be included with
    (c) are subject to
    (d) are not subject to
    Answer: See Section 5. Wages and Other Compensation, Archer medical savings accounts, pg 16/ (c) are subject to

5. Wages and Other Compensation - Health Savings Accounts - medical savings accounts.

37. Employee contributions to their HSAs and _____ through a payroll deduction plan must be included in wages and are subject social security, Medicare, and FUTA taxes, and income tax withholding.
    (a) MDAs
    (b) MSAs
    (c) MBAs
    (d) MCLs
    Answer: See 5. Wages and Other Compensation, Archer medical savings accounts, page 16/ (b) MSAs

5. Wages and Other Compensation - Health Savings Accounts medical savings accounts.

38. Employee contributions to their HSAs and ___ through a payroll deduction plan must be included in wages and are subject social security, Medicare, and FUTA taxes, and income tax withholding. However, ___ contributions made under a salary reduction arrangement in a section 125 ___ plan   and are not subject to employment taxes or withholding.
    (a) MDAs, MBA, cafeteria
    (b) MSAs, HSA, cafeteria
    (c) MBAs, INC, restaurant
    (d) MCLs, BBC, cafeteria
    Answer: See 5. Wages and Other Compensation, Archer medical savings accounts, page 16/ (b) MSAs, HSA, cafeteria

Section 5. 15E-S5-2 Health Savings Accounts and Medical Saving Accounts. Page 16

(**Important:** Know the definition of a cafeteria plan. Know the definition of an Archer Account.)

Health Savings Accounts and Medical Savings Accounts

5. Wages and Other Compensation - Health Savings Accounts-Medical Savings Accounts.
39. Employee contributions to their HSAs and ___ through a payroll deduction plan must be included in wages and are subject social security, Medicare, and FUTA taxes, and income tax withholding. However, ___ contributions made under a salary reduction arrangement in a section 125 ___ plan and are not subject to employment taxes or withholding. For more information, see the instructions for Form ___, Health Savings Accounts (HSAs).
(a)   MDAs, MBA, cafeteria, 8888
(b)   MSAs, HSA, cafeteria, 8889
(c)   MBAs, INC, restaurant, 8890
(d)   MCLs, BBC, cafeteria, 8891
Answer: See 5. Wages and Other Compensation, Archer medical savings accounts, page 16/ (b) MSAs, HSA, cafeteria, 8889

5. Health Savings Accounts. Medical Care Reimbursements

5. Wages and Other Compensation - Medical care reimbursements
40. Medicare care reimbursements. Generally, medical care reimbursements paid for an employee under an employer's ___ medical reimbursement plan are not wages and are not subject to social security, Medicare, and FUTA, or income tax withholding.
(a)   self-insured
(b)   insurance
(c)   health
(d)   company
Answer: See 5. Wages and Other Compensation, Medical care reimbursements, page 16/ (a) self-insured

5. Wages and Other Compensation - Medical care reimbursements
41. Medicare care reimbursements. Generally, medical care reimbursements paid for an employee under an employer's ___ medical reimbursement plan are not wages and are not subject to social security, Medicare, and FUTA, or income tax withholding. See Publication ___ for an exception for highly compensated employees.
(a)   self-insured, 15B
(b)   insurance, 15C
(c)   health, 15A
(d)   company, 15
Answer: See 5. Wages and Other Compensation, Medical care reimbursements, page 16/ (a) self-insured, 15B

Wages and Other Compensation. Differential Wage Payments

5. Wages and Other Compensation - Differential wage payments
42. Differential wage payments are any payments made by an employer to an individual for a period during which the individual is performing service in the uniformed services while on active duty for a period of more than ___ days and
   (a) 15
   (b) 30
   (c) 45
   (d) 90
   Answer: See 5. Wages and Other Compensation. Differential wage payments, page 16/
   (b) 30

5. Wages and Other Compensation - Differential wage payments
43. Differential wage payments are any payments made by an employer to an individual for a period during which the individual is performing service in the uniformed services while on active duty for a period of more than ___ days and represent all or the portion of the ___ the individual would have received from the employer if the individual were performing services for the employer.
   (a) 15, income
   (b) 30, wages
   (c) 45, earnings
   (d) 90, income
   Answer: See 5. Wages and Other Compensation. Differential wage payments, page 16/
   (b) 30, wages

5. Wages and Other Compensation - Differential wage payments
44. Differential wage payments are wages for ___ but are not subject to social security, Medicare, or FUTA taxes.
   (a) military service
   (b) deferred military service
   (c) tax withholding
   (d) income tax withholding
   Answer: See 5. Wages and Other Compensation. Differential wage payments, page 16/
   (d) income tax withholding

5. Wages and Other Compensation - Differential wage payments
45. Differential wage payments are wages for ___ but are not subject to social security, Medicare, or FUTA taxes. Employers should report differential wage payment in box 1 of Form W- ___.
   (a) military service, 1
   (b) deferred military service, 3
   (c) tax withholding, 4
   (d) income tax withholding, 2
   Answer: See 5. Wages and Other Compensation. Differential wage payments, page 16/
   (d) income tax withholding , 2

© Copyright 2013. All rights reserved. Notice: United States Copyright Laws and International Treaties prohibit unauthorized publication, reproduction, distribution of this Work. Unauthorized use of this copyright in any form, format, publication or document may result in severe civil and criminal penalties. Violations of this copyright are investigated by the United States Department of Justice and carry, upon conviction of fines up to $250,000 and five years confinement. This Work is protected by United States Copyright Laws and International Treaties. Do not Copy, do not reproduce, do not distribute.

Wages and Other Compensation. Differential Wage Payments

5. Wages and Other Compensation - Differential wage payments
46. Differential wage payments are wages for ___ but are not subject to social security, Medicare, or FUTA taxes. Employers should report differential wage payment in box 1 of Form W- ___. For more information about the ___ of differential wage payments, visit IRS.gov and enter
   (a) military service, 1, treatment
   (b) deferred military service, 3, tax requirements
   (c) tax withholding, 4, tax rules
   (d) income tax withholding, 2, tax treatment
   Answer: See 5. Wages and Other Compensation. Differential wage payments, page 16/
   (d) income tax withholding , 2, tax treatment

5. Wages and Other Compensation - Differential wage payments
47. Differential wage payments are wages for income tax withholding but are not subject to social security, Medicare, or FUTA taxes. Employers should report differential wage payment in box 1 of Form W- 2. For more information about the tax treatment of differential wage payments, visit IRS.gov and enter "____" in the search box.
   (a) employees in uniform services
   (b) employees in military service
   (c) employees in a combat zone
   (d) employees in national service
   Answer: See 5. Wages and Other Compensation. Differential wage payments, page 16/
   (c) employees in a combat zone

A Ficus Tree Publishing Quick Notes Page

© Copyright 2013. All rights reserved. Notice: United States Copyright Laws and International Treaties prohibit unauthorized publication, reproduction, distribution of this Work. Unauthorized use of this copyright in any form, format, publication or document may result in severe civil and criminal penalties. Violations of this copyright are investigated by the United States Department of Justice and carry, upon conviction of fines up to $250,000 and five years confinement. This Work is protected by United States Copyright Laws and International Treaties. Do not Copy, do not reproduce, do not distribute.

A Ficus Tree Publishing Educational-Technical Publications

DUVALL'S TEST'S™
Instructors Manual Study Guide Series United States Tax Code
IRS Publication 15 Circular E, Employer's Tax Guide Tax Year 2013
Tax Test 15E-S5-3 [Multiple-Choice Questions With Answers]

Section 5. 15E-S5-3 Wages and Other Compensation Nontaxable Fringe Benefits

5. Wages and Other Compensation - Fringe benefits.
1. Fringe benefits. You generally must include fringe benefits in the employee's ___ (but see **Nontaxable fringe benefits** next).
   (a) gross income
   (b) gross wages
   (c) total income
   (d) total wages
   Answer: See 5. Wages and Other Compensation. Fringe Benefits, page 16/ (a) gross income

5. Wages and Other Compensation - Fringe benefits.
2. Fringe benefits. You generally must include fringe benefits in the employee's ___ (but see **Nontaxable fringe benefits** next). The benefits are subject to income tax withholding and ___ taxes.
   (a) gross income, employment
   (b) gross wages, unemployment
   (c) total income, Medicare
   (d) total wages, social security
   Answer: See 5. Wages and Other Compensation. Fringe Benefits, page 16/ (a) gross income, employment

5. Wages and Other Compensation - Fringe benefits.
3. Fringe benefits. You generally must include fringe benefits in the employee's ___ (but see **Nontaxable fringe benefits** next). The benefits are subject to income tax withholding and ___ taxes. Fringe benefits include cars you provide, free or discounted commercial flights, vacations, discounts or property or services, memberships in country clubs or other ___ clubs, and tickets to entertainment or sporting events.
   (a) gross income, employment, social
   (b) gross wages, unemployment, business
   (c) total income, Medicare, political
   (d) total wages, social security, health
   Answer: See 5. Wages and Other Compensation. Fringe Benefits, page 16/ (a) gross income, employment, social

Wages and Other Compensation Nontaxable Fringe Benefits

5. Wages and Other Compensation - Fringe benefits.
4.   Fringe benefits. You generally must include fringe benefits in the employee's ___ (but see **Nontaxable fringe benefits** next). The benefits are subject to income tax withholding and ___ taxes. Fringe benefits include cars you provide, free or discounted commercial flights, vacations, discounts or property or services, memberships in country clubs or other ___ clubs, and tickets to entertainment or sporting events. In general, the amount you must include is the amount by which the ____ of the benefits is more than the sum of what the employee paid for
   (a)   gross income, employment, social, fair market value
   (b)   gross wages, unemployment, business, actual expense
   (c)   total income, Medicare, political, the total expense
   (d)   total wages, social security, health, actual expense
   Answer: See 5. Wages and Other Compensation. Fringe Benefits, page 16/ (a) gross income, employment, social, fair market value,

5. Wages and Other Compensation - Fringe benefits.
5.   Fringe benefits. You generally must include fringe benefits in the employee's ___ (but see **Nontaxable fringe benefits** next). The benefits are subject to income tax withholding and ___ taxes. Fringe benefits include cars you provide, free or discounted commercial flights, vacations, discounts or property or services, memberships in country clubs or other ___ clubs, and tickets to entertainment or sporting events. In general, the amount you must include is the amount by which the ____ of the benefits is more than the sum of what the employee paid for it plus any amount the law __.
   (a)   gross income, employment, social, fair market value, excludes
   (b)   gross wages, unemployment, business, actual expense, perm1ts
   (c)   total income, Medicare, political, the total expense, allows
   (d)   total wages, social security, health, actual expense, excludes
   Answer: See 5. Wages and Other Compensation. Fringe Benefits, page 16/ (a) gross income, employment, social, fair market value, excludes

Wages and Other Compensation Nontaxable Fringe Benefits

5. Wages and Other Compensation - Fringe benefits.

6. Fringe benefits. You generally must include fringe benefits in the employee's ___ (but see **Nontaxable fringe benefits** next). The benefits are subject to income tax withholding and ___ taxes. Fringe benefits include cars you provide, free or discounted commercial flights, vacations, discounts or property or services, memberships in country clubs or other ___ clubs, and tickets to entertainment or sporting events. In general, the amount you must include is the amount by which the ___ of the benefits is more than the sum of what the employee paid for it plus any amount the law ___ . There are other special rules you and your employees may use to value certain fringe benefits. See Publication___ for more information.
   (a) gross income, employment, social, fair market value, excludes, 15B
   (b) gross wages, unemployment, business, actual expense, permits, 15C
   (c) total income, Medicare, political, the total expense, allows, 15A
   (d) total wages, social security, health, actual expense, excludes, 15

   Answer: See 5. Wages and Other Compensation. Fringe Benefits, page 16/ (a) gross income, employment, social, fair market value, excludes, 15B

5. Wages and Other Compensation - Nontaxable Fringe benefits.

7. Nontaxable Fringe benefits. Some fringe benefits are not taxable (or are ___ taxable) if certain conditions are met.
   (a) differed
   (b) deferred
   (c) diminished
   (d) minimally

   Answer: See 5. Wages and Other Compensation. Nontaxable Fringe Benefits, page 16/ (d) minimally

5. Wages and Other Compensation - Nontaxable Fringe benefits.

8. Nontaxable Fringe benefits. Some fringe benefits are not taxable (or are ___ taxable) if certain conditions are met. See Publication 15___ for details.
   (a) differed, 15
   (b) deferred, C
   (c) diminished, A
   (d) minimally, B

   Answer: See 5. Wages and Other Compensation. Nontaxable Fringe Benefits, page 16/ (d) minimally, B

Wages and Other Compensation Nontaxable Fringe Benefits

5. Wages and Other Compensation - Nontaxable Fringe benefits.
9. Nontaxable Fringe benefits. Some fringe benefits are not taxable (or are minimally taxable) if certain conditions are met. See Publication 15B for details. The following are some examples of nontaxable fringe benefits.
    1. Services provided to your employees at ___.
    (a) fair market value
    (b) no cost to you
    (c) no additional cost to you
    (d) no taxable cost to you
    Answer: See 5. Wages and Other Compensation. Nontaxable Fringe Benefits, page 17/
    (c) no additional cost to you

5. Wages and Other Compensation - Nontaxable Fringe benefits.
10. Nontaxable Fringe benefits. Some fringe benefits are not taxable (or are minimally taxable) if certain conditions are met. See Publication 15B for details. The following are some examples of nontaxable fringe benefits.
    1. Services provided to your employees at no additional cost to you.
    2. Qualified employee ___.
    (a) bonus
    (b) discounts
    (c) benefits
    (d) services
    Answer: See 5. Wages and Other Compensation. Nontaxable Fringe Benefits, page 17/
    (b) discounts

5. Wages and Other Compensation - Nontaxable Fringe benefits.
11. Nontaxable Fringe benefits. Some fringe benefits are not taxable (or are minimally taxable) if certain conditions are met. See Publication 15B for details. The following are some examples of nontaxable fringe benefits.
    1. Services provided to your employees at no additional cost to you.
    2. Qualified employee discounts.
    3. Working condition fringes that are property or services the employee could ___ as a business expense if she or he had paid for it.
    (a) deduct
    (b) claim
    (c) credit
    (d) include
    Answer: See 5. Wages and Other Compensation. Nontaxable Fringe Benefits, page 17/
    (a) deduct

Wages and Other Compensation Nontaxable Fringe Benefits

5. Wages and Other Compensation - Nontaxable Fringe benefits.
12. Nontaxable Fringe benefits. Some fringe benefits are not taxable (or are minimally taxable) if certain conditions are met. See Publication 15B for details. The following are some examples of nontaxable fringe benefits.
    1. Services provided to your employees at no additional cost to you.
    2. Qualified employee discounts.
    3. Working condition fringes that are property or services the employee could ___ as a business expense if she or he had paid for it. Examples include a company car for business use and ___.
    (a)   deduct, subscriptions to business magazines
    (b)   claim, club memberships
    (c)   credit, personal recreational equipment
    (d)   include, subscriptions and memberships to health clubs
    Answer: See 5. Wages and Other Compensation. Nontaxable Fringe Benefits, page 17/
    (a) deduct, subscriptions to business magazines.

5. Wages and Other Compensation - Nontaxable Fringe benefits.
13. Nontaxable Fringe benefits. Some fringe benefits are not taxable (or are minimally taxable) if certain conditions are met. See Publication 15B for details. The following are some examples of nontaxable fringe benefits.
    1. Services provided to your employees at no additional cost to you.
    2. Qualified employee discounts.
    3. Working condition fringes that are property or services the employee could ___ as a business expense if she or he had paid for it. Examples include a company car for business use and ___.
    4. Certain minimal value ___ (including an occasional cab ride when an employee must work overtime and meals you provide at ___ you run for your employees if the meals are not furnished at below cost).
    (a)   deduct, subscriptions to business magazines, fringes, eating places
    (b)   claim, club memberships, fringe benefits, luncheons
    (c)   credit, personal recreational equipment, fringe benefits, cafeterias
    (d)   include, subscriptions and memberships to health clubs, programs, food services
    Answer: See 5. Wages and Other Compensation. Nontaxable Fringe Benefits, page 17/
    (a) deduct, subscriptions to business magazine, fringes, eating places

Wages and Other Compensation Nontaxable Fringe Benefits

5. Wages and Other Compensation - Nontaxable Fringe benefits.
14. Nontaxable Fringe benefits. Some fringe benefits are not taxable (or are minimally taxable) if certain conditions are met. See Publication 15B for details. The following are some examples of nontaxable fringe benefits.
   5. Qualified transportation ___ subject to specified conditions and dollar limitations (including transportation in a commuter highway vehicle, any transit pass, and qualified parking).
   (a) fringe benefits
   (b) perks
   (c) benefits
   (d) fringes
   Answer: See 5. Wages and Other Compensation. Nontaxable Fringe Benefits, page 17/
   (d) fringes

5. Wages and Other Compensation - Nontaxable Fringe benefits.
15. Nontaxable Fringe benefits. Some fringe benefits are not taxable (or are minimally taxable) if certain conditions are met. See Publication 15B for details. The following are some examples of nontaxable fringe benefits.
   6. Qualified moving expense reimbursement. See ___, earlier in this section, for details.
   (a) *Moving espense*
   (b) *Moving expenses*
   (c) *Moving*
   (d) *Allowable reimbursement expenses*
   Answer: See 5. Wages and Other Compensation. Nontaxable Fringe Benefits, page 17/
   (b) *Moving expenses*

5. Wages and Other Compensation - Nontaxable Fringe benefits.
16. Nontaxable Fringe benefits. Some fringe benefits are not taxable (or are minimally taxable) if certain conditions are met. See Publication 15B for details. The following are some examples of nontaxable fringe benefits.
   7. The use of ___ athletic facilities, if substantially all of the use is by employees, their spouses, and their dependent children.
   (a) off-site
   (b) in-house
   (c) on-site
   (d) on-premises
   Answer: See 5. Wages and Other Compensation. Nontaxable Fringe Benefits, page 17/
   (d) on-premises

Wages and Other Compensation Nontaxable Fringe Benefits

5. Wages and Other Compensation - Nontaxable Fringe benefits.
17. Nontaxable Fringe benefits. Some fringe benefits are not taxable (or are minimally taxable) if certain conditions are met. See Publication 15B for details. The following are some examples of nontaxable fringe benefits.
    8. Qualified tuition reduction an ___ provides to its employees for education.
    (a)   educational facility
    (b)   approved college or university
    (c)   educational organization
    (d)   approved commercial business entity
    Answer: See 5. Wages and Other Compensation. Nontaxable Fringe Benefits, page 17/
    (c) educational organization

5. Wages and Other Compensation - Nontaxable Fringe benefits.
18. Nontaxable Fringe benefits. Some fringe benefits are not taxable (or are minimally taxable) if certain conditions are met. See Publication 15B for details. The following are some examples of nontaxable fringe benefits.
    8. Qualified tuition reduction an ___ provides to its employees for education. For more information, see Publication ___, Tax Benefits for Education.
    (a)   educational facility, 15C
    (b)   approved college or university, 15A
    (c)   educational organization, 970
    (d)   approved commercial business entity, 15B
    Answer: See 5. Wages and Other Compensation. Nontaxable Fringe Benefits, page 17/
    (c) educational organization, 970

5. Wages and Other Compensation - Nontaxable Fringe benefits.
19. Nontaxable Fringe benefits. Some fringe benefits are not taxable (or are minimally taxable) if certain conditions are met. See Publication 15B for details. The following are some examples of nontaxable fringe benefits.
    8. Qualified tuition reduction an ___ provides to its employees for education. For more information, see Publication ___, Tax Benefits for Education.
    9. Employer-provided cell phones primarily for a ___ business reason.
    (a)   educational facility, 15C, compensated
    (b)   approved college or university, 15A, compensatory
    (c)   educational organization, 970, noncompensatory
    (d)   approved commercial business entity, 15B, compensatory
    Answer: See 5. Wages and Other Compensation. Nontaxable Fringe Benefits, page 17/
    (c) educational organization, 970, noncompensatory

Wages and Other Compensation Nontaxable Fringe Benefits

5. Wages and Other Compensation - Nontaxable Fringe benefits.
20. Nontaxable Fringe benefits. Some fringe benefits are not taxable (or are minimally taxable) if certain conditions are met. See Publication 15B for details. The following are examples of nontaxable fringe benefits. **IRS** Publication 15 (Circular E), Employer's Tax Guide for use in 2013 provides ___ examples of Nontaxable Fringe Benefits on pages 16 and 17.
    (a) six
    (b) seven
    (c) eight
    (d) nine
    Answer: See 5. Wages and Other Compensation. Nontaxable Fringe Benefits, page 17/
    (d) nine

5. Wages and Other Compensation - Nontaxable Fringe benefits.
21. Nontaxable Fringe benefits. Some fringe benefits are not taxable (or are minimally taxable) if certain conditions are met. See Publication 15B for details. The following are examples of nontaxable fringe benefits. **IRS** Publication 15 (Circular E), Employer's Tax Guide for use in 2013 provides nine examples of Nontaxable Fringe Benefits on pages 16 and 17. However, do not ___ the following fringe benefits from the income of highly compensated employees unless the benefit is available to other employees on a ___ basis.
    (a) include, nondiscriminatory
    (b) exclude, nondiscriminatory
    (c) include, discriminatory
    (d) exclude. discriminatory
    Answer: See 5. Wages and Other Compensation. Nontaxable Fringe Benefits, page 17/
    (b) exclude, nondiscriminatory

5. Wages and Other Compensation - Nontaxable Fringe benefits.
22. However, do not exclude the following fringe benefits from the income of highly compensated employees unless the benefit is available to other employees on a nondiscriminatory basis.
    • No-additional- ___.
    (a) cost-services
    (b) tax-liability
    (c) service-tax-liability
    (d) tax-deferred-liability
    Answer: See 5. Wages and Other Compensation. Nontaxable Fringe Benefits, page 17/
    (a) cost-services

Wages and Other Compensation Nontaxable Fringe Benefits

5. Wages and Other Compensation - Nontaxable Fringe benefits.
23. However, do not exclude the following fringe benefits from the income of highly compensated employees unless the benefit is available to other employees on a nondiscriminatory basis.
 • Qualified employee ___.
 (a) plans
 (b) services
 (c) discounts
 (d) benefits
 Answer: See 5. Wages and Other Compensation. Nontaxable Fringe Benefits, p. 17/ (c) discounts

5. Wages and Other Compensation - Nontaxable Fringe benefits.
24. However, do not exclude the following fringe benefits from the income of highly compensated employees unless the benefit is available to other employees on a nondiscriminatory basis.
 • Meals provided at an employer operated ___ facility.
 (a) lunch
 (b) food
 (c) dining
 (d) eating
 Answer: See 5. Wages and Other Compensation. Nontaxable Fringe Benefits, p. 17/ (d) eating

5. Wages and Other Compensation - Nontaxable Fringe benefits.
25. However, do not exclude the following fringe benefits from the income of highly compensated employees unless the benefit is available to other employees on a nondiscriminatory basis.
 • Reduced tuition for education. For more information, including the definition of a highly compensated employee, see Publication ___.
 (a) 975
 (b) 970
 (c) 15A
 (d) 15B
 Answer: See 5. Wages and Other Compensation. Nontaxable Fringe Benefits, p. 17/ (d) 15B

When fringe benefits are treated as paid

5. Wages and Other Compensation - When fringe benefits are treated as paid.
26.   You may choose to treat certain ___ fringe benefits as paid by the ___, by the quarter, or on any other basis you choose as long as you treat the benefits as paid at least once ___.
   (a)   noncash, pay period, a year
   (b)   cash, employer, every five years
   (c)   noncash, week, a quarter
   (d)   noncash, bi-weekly, month
   Answer: See 5. Wages and Other Compensation. Fringe benefits treated as paid, p. 17/ (a) noncash, pay period, a year

5. Wages and Other Compensation - When fringe benefits are treated as paid.
27.   You may choose to treat certain noncash fringe benefits as paid by the pay period, by the quarter, or on any other basis you choose as long as you treat the benefits as paid at least once a year. You do not have to make a ___ of the payment dates or notify the IRS of the dates you choose.
   (a)   choice
   (b)   specific choice
   (c)   clear choice
   (d)   formal choice
   Answer: See 5. Wages and Other Compensation. Fringe benefits treated as paid, p. 17/ (d) formal choice

5. Wages and Other Compensation - When fringe benefits are treated as paid.
28.   You may choose to treat certain noncash fringe benefits as paid by the pay period, by the quarter, or on any other basis you choose as long as you treat the benefits as paid at least once a year. You do not have to make a ___ of the payment dates or notify the IRS of the dates you choose. You ___ have to make this choice for all employees.
   (a)   choice, shall
   (b)   specific choice, are required to
   (c)   clear choice, must
   (d)   formal choice, do not
   Answer: See 5. Wages and Other Compensation. Fringe benefits treated as paid, p. 17/ (d) formal choice, do not

When fringe benefits are treated as paid

5. Wages and Other Compensation - When fringe benefits are treated as paid.
29. You may choose to treat certain noncash fringe benefits as paid by the pay period, by the quarter, or on any other basis you choose as long as you treat the benefits as paid at least once a year. You do not have to make a ___ of the payment dates or notify the IRS of the dates you choose. You ___ have to make this choice for all employees.
   (a)   choice, shall
   (b)   specific choice, are required to
   (c)   clear choice, must
   (d)   formal choice, do not
   Answer: See 5. Wages and Other Compensation. Fringe benefits treated as paid, p. 17/
   (d) formal choice, do not

5. Wages and Other Compensation - When fringe benefits are treated as paid.
30. You may choose to treat certain noncash fringe benefits as paid by the pay period, by the quarter, or on any other basis you choose as long as you treat the benefits as paid at least once a year. You do not have to make a ___ of the payment dates or notify the IRS of the dates you choose. You ___ have to make this choice for all employees. You may change methods as often as you like, as long as you treat all benefits provided in a calendar year as paid by ___ of the calendar year.
   (a)   choice, shall, January 1
   (b)   specific choice, are required to, April 15
   (c)   clear choice, must, June 15
   (d)   formal choice, do not, December 31
   Answer: See 5. Wages and Other Compensation. Fringe benefits treated as paid, p. 17/
   (d) formal choice, do not, December 31

5. Wages and Other Compensation - When fringe benefits are treated as paid.
31. You may choose to treat certain noncash fringe benefits as paid by the pay period, by the quarter, or on any other basis you choose as long as you treat the benefits as paid at least once a year. You do not have to make a ___ of the payment dates or notify the IRS of the dates you choose. You ___ have to make this choice for all employees. You may change methods as often as you like, as long as you treat all benefits provided in a calendar year as paid by ___ of the calendar year. See Publication 15B for more information, including a discussion of the special accounting rule for fringe benefits provided during ___ and ___.
   (a)   choice, shall, January 1, June, August
   (b)   specific choice, are required to, April 15, April, August
   (c)   clear choice, must, June 15, November, December
   (d)   formal choice, do not, December 31, November, December
   Answer: See 5. Wages and Other Compensation. Fringe benefits treated as paid, p. 17/
   (d) formal choice, do not, December 31, November, December

Wages and Other Compensation. Valuation of Fringe Benefits

5. Wages and Other Compensation - Valuation of fringe benefits.
32. Generally, you must determine the value of fringe benefits no later than ___ of the next year.
    (a) January 31
    (b) February 10
    (c) March 31
    (d) April 15
    Answer: See 5. Wages and Other Compensation. Valuation of fringe benefits, p.17/ (a) January 31

5. Wages and Other Compensation - Valuation of fringe benefits.
33. Generally, you must determine the value of fringe benefits no later than ___ of the next year. Before ___, you may reasonably estimate the value of the fringe benefits for purposes of ___ and ___ on time.
    (a) January 31, January 31, withholding, depositing
    (b) February 10, February 1, monthly, quarterly deposits
    (c) March 31, March 15, employee tax payments, required deposits
    (d) April 15, April 15, employee tax payments, required deposits
    Answer: See 5. Wages and Other Compensation. Valuation of fringe benefits, p.17/ (a) January 31, January 31, withholding, depositing

Wages and Other Compensation. Withholding on Fringe Benefits

5. Wages and Other Compensation - Withholding on fringe benefits.
34. You may add the value of fringe benefits to ___ wages for a payroll period and figure withholding taxes on the total, or
    (a) the employee
    (b) weekly
    (c) average
    (d) regular
    Answer: See 5. Wages and Other Compensation. Withholding on fringe benefits, p.17/ (d) regular

5. Wages and Other Compensation - Withholding on fringe benefits.
35. You may add the value of fringe benefits to ___ wages for a payroll period and figure withholding taxes on the total, or you may withhold federal income tax on the value of the fringe benefits at the optional flat ___% supplemental wage rate.
    (a) the employee, 13
    (b) weekly, 22.5
    (c) average, 25
    (d) regular, 25
    Answer: See 5. Wages and Other Compensation. Withholding on fringe benefits, p.17/ (d) regular, 25

Wages and Other Compensation - Withholding on Fringe Benefits

5. Wages and Other Compensation - Withholding on fringe benefits.
36. You may add the value of fringe benefits to ___ wages for a payroll period and figure withholding taxes on the total, or you may withhold federal income tax on the value of the fringe benefits at the optional flat ___% supplemental wage rate. However, see *Withholding on supplemental wages when the employee receives more than $1 million of supplemental wages during the calendar year* in section ___.
   (a) the employee, 13, 4
   (b) weekly, 22.5, 5
   (c) average, 25, 6
   (d) regular, 25, 7
   Answer: See 5. Wages and Other Compensation. Withholding on fringe benefits, p.17/
   (d) regular, 25

5. Wages and Other Compensation - Withholding on fringe benefits.
37. You may choose not to withhold ___ tax on the value of an employee's personal use of a vehicle you provide.
   (a) social security
   (b) Medicare
   (c) income
   (d) fringe benefit
   Answer: See 5. Wages and Other Compensation. Withholding on fringe benefits, p.17/
   (c) income

5. Wages and Other Compensation - Withholding on fringe benefits.
38. You may choose not to withhold ___ tax on the value of an employee's personal use of a vehicle you provide. You must, however, withhold ___ and ___ taxes on the use of the vehicle.
   (a) social security, Medicare, FUTA
   (b) Medicare, social security, FUTA
   (c) income, social security, Medicare
   (d) fringe benefit, FUTA, social security
   Answer: See 5. Wages and Other Compensation. Withholding on fringe benefits, p.17/
   (c) income, social security, Medicare

5. Wages and Other Compensation - Withholding on fringe benefits.
39. You may choose not to withhold ___ tax on the value of an employee's personal use of a vehicle you provide. You must, however, withhold ___ and ___ taxes on the use of the vehicle. See Publication ___ for more information on this election.
   (a) social security, Medicare, FUTA, 15A
   (b) Medicare, social security, FUTA, 15A
   (c) income, social security, Medicare, 15B
   (d) fringe benefit, FUTA, social security, 15C
   Answer: See 5. Wages and Other Compensation. Withholding on fringe benefits, p.17/
   (c) income, social security, Medicare, 15B

© Copyright 2013. All rights reserved. Notice: United States Copyright Laws and International Treaties prohibit unauthorized publication, reproduction, distribution of this Work. Unauthorized use of this copyright in any form, format, publication or document may result in severe civil and criminal penalties. Violations of this copyright are investigated by the United States Department of Justice and carry, upon conviction of fines up to $250,000 and five years confinement. This Work is protected by United States Copyright Laws and International Treaties. Do not Copy, do not reproduce, do not distribute.

Wages and Other Compensation - Depositing Taxes on Fringe Benefits

5. Wages and Other Compensation - Depositing taxes on fringe benefits.
40.   Once you choose when fringe benefits are paid, you must deposit taxes ___, you treat the fringe benefit as paid.
        (a)   in the same manner
        (b)   in the same period
        (c)   in the same deposit period
        (d)   electronically
        Answer: See 5. Wages and Other Compensation. Depositing taxes on fringe benefits, p.17/ (c) in the same deposit period

5. Wages and Other Compensation - Depositing taxes on fringe benefits.
41.   Once you choose when fringe benefits are paid, you must deposit taxes ___, you treat the fringe benefit as paid. To avoid a penalty, depositing the taxes ___ the general deposit rules for that deposit period.
        (a)   in the same manner, according to
        (b)   in the same period, following
        (c)   in the same deposit period, following
        (d)   electronically, according to
        Answer: See 5. Wages and Other Compensation. Depositing taxes on fringe benefits, page 17/ (c) in the same deposit period

5. Wages and Other Compensation - Depositing taxes on fringe benefits.
42.   If you determine by ___ you overestimated the value of the fringe benefit at the time you withheld and deposited it, you may ___ a refund for overpayment or
        (a)   January 31, claim
        (b)   April 15, claim
        (c)   June 1, file for
        (d)   November 1, file for
        Answer: See 5. Wages and Other Compensation. Depositing taxes on fringe benefits, p.17/ (a) January 31, claim

5. Wages and Other Compensation - Depositing taxes on fringe benefits.
43.   If you determine by ___ you overestimated the value of the fringe benefit at the time you withheld and deposited it, you may ___ a refund for overpayment or have it applied to your next ___ return. See *Valuation of fringe benefits* above.
        (a)   January 31, claim, employment tax
        (b)   April 15, claim, quarterly
        (c)   June 1, file for, tax
        (d)   November 1, file for, tax
        Answer: See 5. Wages and Other Compensation. Depositing taxes on fringe benefits, p.17/ (a) January 31, claim, employment tax

Wages and Other Compensation - Depositing Taxes on Fringe Benefits

5. Wages and Other Compensation - Depositing taxes on fringe benefits.
44. If you determine by January 31 you overestimated the value of the fringe benefit at the time you withheld and deposited it, you may claim a refund for overpayment or have it applied to your next employment tax return. See *Valuation of fringe benefits* above. If you underestimated the value and deposited too little, you may be subject to a ____ penalty.
    (a) unlawful deposit
    (b) failure-to-deposit
    (c) serious
    (d) inadequate funds
    Answer: See 5. Wages and Other Compensation. Depositing taxes on fringe benefits, p.17/ (b) failure-to-deposit

5. Wages and Other Compensation - Depositing taxes on fringe benefits.
45. If you determine by January 31 you overestimated the value of the fringe benefit at the time you withheld and deposited it, you may claim a refund for overpayment or have it applied to your next employment tax return. See *Valuation of fringe benefits* above. If you underestimated the value and deposited too little, you may be subject to a ____ penalty. See section ___ for information on deposit penalties.
    (a) unlawful deposit, 11
    (b) failure-to-deposit, 11
    (c) serious, 11
    (d) inadequate funds, 12
    Answer: See 5. Wages and Other Compensation. Depositing taxes on fringe benefits, p.17/ (b) failure-to-deposit, 11

5. Wages and Other Compensation - Depositing taxes on fringe benefits.
46. If you determine by January 31 you overestimated the value of the fringe benefit at the time you withheld and deposited it, you may claim a refund for overpayment or have it applied to your next employment tax return. See *Valuation of fringe benefits* above. If you underestimated the value and deposited too little, you may be subject to a failure-to-deposit penalty. See section 11 for information on deposit penalties.
    If you deposited the required amount of taxes but withheld a lesser amount from the employee, you can ___ from the employee, the social security, Medicare, or income taxes on his or her behalf, and included in the employee's Form W-2.
    (a) demand
    (b) recover
    (c) obtain
    (d) withhold
    Answer: See 5. Wages and Other Compensation. Depositing taxes on fringe benefits, p.17/ (b) recover

Wages and Other Compensation - Depositing Taxes on Fringe Benefits

5. Wages and Other Compensation - Depositing taxes on fringe benefits.
47.   If you determine by January 31 you overestimated the value of the fringe benefit at the time you withheld and deposited it, you may claim a refund for overpayment or have it applied to your next employment tax return. See ***Valuation of fringe benefits*** above. If you underestimated the value and deposited too little, you may be subject to a failure-to-deposit penalty. See <u>section 11</u> for information on deposit penalties.
If you deposited the required amount of taxes but withheld a lesser amount from the employee, you can ___ from the employee, the social security, Medicare, or income taxes on his or her behalf, and included in the employee's Form W-2. However, you must recover the income taxes before ___ of the following year.
    (a)   demand, January 1
    (b)   recover, April 1
    (c)   obtain, November 1
    (d)   withhold, December 31
Answer: See 5. Wages and Other Compensation. Depositing taxes on fringe benefits, p.17/ (b) recover, April 1

Wages and Other Compensation - Sick Pay

5. Wages and Other Compensation - Sick pay.
48.   Sick pay. In general, sick pay is any amount you pay under a ___ to an employee who is unable to work because of sickness or injury.
    (a)   contract
    (b)   insurance
    (c)   plan
    (d)   insurance plan
Answer: See 5. Wages and Other Compensation. Sick pay, page 17/ (c) plan

5. Wages and Other Compensation - Sick pay.
49.   Sick pay. In general, sick pay is any amount you pay under a ___ to an employee who is unable to work because of sickness or injury. These amounts are sometimes paid by a ___,
    (a)   contract, hospitalization plan
    (b)   insurance, medical plan
    (c)   plan, third party
    (d)   insurance plan, Archer plan
Answer: See 5. Wages and Other Compensation. Sick pay, page 17/ (c) plan, third party

Wages and Other Compensation - Sick Pay

5. Wages and Other Compensation - Sick pay.
50. Sick pay. In general, sick pay is any amount you pay under a ___ to an employee who is unable to work because of sickness or injury. These amounts are sometimes paid by a ___, such as an insurance company or an employees' ___.
    (a) contract, hospitalization plan, fund
    (b) insurance, medical plan, fund
    (c) plan, third party, trust
    (d) insurance plan, Archer plan, workers' compensation plan
    Answer: See 5. Wages and Other Compensation. Sick pay, page 17/ (c) plan, third party, trust

5. Wages and Other Compensation - Sick pay.
51. Sick pay. In general, sick pay is any amount you pay under a ___ to an employee who is unable to work because of sickness or injury. These amounts are sometimes paid by a ___, such as an insurance company or an employees' ___. In either case, these payments are subject to social security, Medicare and ___ taxes.
    (a) contract, hospitalization plan, fund, COBRA
    (b) insurance, medical plan, fund, FICA
    (c) plan, third party, trust, FUTA
    (d) insurance plan, Archer plan, workers' compensation plan, FEMA
    Answer: See 5. Wages and Other Compensation. Sick pay, page 17/ (c) plan, third party, trust, FUTA

5. Wages and Other Compensation - Sick pay.
52. Sick pay. In general, sick pay is any amount you pay under a plan to an employee who is unable to work because of sickness or injury. These amounts are sometimes paid by a third party, such as an insurance company or an employees' trust. In either case, these payments are subject to social security, Medicare and FUTA taxes. Sick pay becomes exempt from these taxes after the end of ___ calendar months after the employee last worked for the employer.
    (a) 3
    (b) 6
    (c) 9
    (d) 12
    Answer: See 5. Wages and Other Compensation. Sick pay, page 17/ (b) 6

Wages and Other Compensation - Sick Pay

5. Wages and Other Compensation - Sick pay.
53. Sick pay. In general, sick pay is any amount you pay under a plan to an employee who is unable to work because of sickness or injury. These amounts are sometimes paid by a third party, such as an insurance company or an employees' trust. In either case, these payments are subject to social security, Medicare and FUTA taxes. Sick pay becomes exempt from these taxes after the end of ___ calendar months after the employee last worked for the employer. The payments are ___ subject to federal income tax.
    (a) 3, usually
    (b) 6, always
    (c) 9, generally
    (d) 12, not
    Answer: See 5. Wages and Other Compensation. Sick pay, page 17/ (b) 6, always

5. Wages and Other Compensation - Sick pay.
54. Sick pay. In general, sick pay is any amount you pay under a plan to an employee who is unable to work because of sickness or injury. These amounts are sometimes paid by a third party, such as an insurance company or an employees' trust. In either case, these payments are subject to social security, Medicare and FUTA taxes. Sick pay becomes exempt from these taxes after the end of ___ calendar months after the employee last worked for the employer. The payments are ___ subject to federal income tax. See Publication ___ for more information.
    (a) 3, usually, 15-A
    (b) 6, always, 15-A
    (c) 9, generally, 15-B
    (d) 12, not, 15-B
    Answer: See 5. Wages and Other Compensation. Sick pay, page 17/ (b) 6, always, 15-A

The International Leader in Construction Technology Home Study

Instructor's Manual for Tax Test 15E-S6 Section 6. Tips

General Description

Tax Test 15E-S6. Tax Test 15E-S6 in Publication 15E, Employer's Tax Guide provides a brief but important discussion of the IRS regulations as applied to tips your employees may receive for their services while employed by the Employer. Section 6, Publication 15 E, Circular E, further states the responsibility of the Employer's responsibility of collecting taxes on tips, the payment of taxes on tips, reporting tips, and the Tip Rate Determination and Education Program.

Key Words

Tips. Less than $20. More than $20. Form 4070. Form 4070-A. Publication 1244. Collecting taxes on tips. Ordering rule. Reporting tips. Revenue Ruling 2012-18. Allocated Tips. Tip Rate Determination and Education Program.

DU VALL'S TEST'S™
Instructors Manual Study Guide Series United States Tax Code
IRS Publication 15. Circular E, Employer's Tax Guide Tax Year 2013
Tax Test 15E-S6 [Multiple-Choice Questions With Answers]

Section 6. 15E-S6. Tips. Page 17.

6.Tips.
1. Tips your employee receives from customers are generally subject to ___.
   (a) taxes
   (b) withholding
   (c) withholding taxes
   (d) FICA
   Answer: See Section 6. Tips, page 17/ (b) withholding

6.Tips.
2. Tips your employee receives from customers are generally subject to ___. Your employee must report cash tips to you by the ___ of the month after the month the tips are received.
   (a) taxes, 1st
   (b) withholding, 10th
   (c) withholding taxes, 15th
   (d) FICA, 30th
   Answer: See Section 6. Tips, page 17/ (b) withholding, 10th

© Copyright 2013. All rights reserved. Notice: United States Copyright Laws and International Treaties prohibit unauthorized publication, reproduction, distribution of this Work. Unauthorized use of this copyright in any form, format, publication or document may result in severe civil and criminal penalties. Violations of this copyright are investigated by the United States Department of Justice and carry, upon conviction of fines up to $250,000 and five years confinement. This Work is protected by United States Copyright Laws and International Treaties. Do not Copy, do not reproduce, do not distribute.

A Ficus Tree Publishing Educational-Technical Publications

Tips

6.Tips.
3. The report should include tips you paid over to the employees for ___ customers, and
(a) charge
(b) cash
(c) all
(d) regular
Answer: See Section 6. Tips, page 17/ (a) charge

6.Tips.
4. The report should include tips you paid over to the employees for ___ customers, tips the employee received ___ from customers, and tips received from other employees under any ___ arrangement.
(a) charge, directly, tip-sharing
(b) cash, indirectly, cooperation
(c) all, directly, tip-sharing
(d) regular, personally, sharing
Answer: See Section 6. Tips, page 17/ (a) charge, directly, tip-sharing

6.Tips.
5. The report should include tips you paid over to the employees for charge customers, tips the employee received directly from customers, and tips received from other employees under any tip-sharing arrangement. Both directly and ___ tipped employees must report tips to you.
(a) salaried
(b) hourly
(c) indirectly
(d) temporary
Answer: See Section 6. Tips, page 17/ (c) indirectly

6.Tips.
6. The report should include tips you paid over to the employees for charge customers, tips the employee received directly from customers, and tips received from other employees under any tip-sharing arrangement. Both directly and ___ tipped employees must report tips to you. No report is required for months when tips are less than $___.
(a) salaried, 10
(b) hourly, 15
(c) indirectly, 20
(d) temporary, 50
Answer: See Section 6. Tips, pages 17 and 18/ (c) indirectly, 20

Tips

6. Tips.
7. The report should include tips you paid over to the employees for charge customers, tips the employee received directly from customers, and tips received from other employees under any tip-sharing arrangement. Both directly and indirectly tipped employees must report tips to you. No report is required for months when tips are less than $20. Your employee reports the tips on Form ___, Employee's Report of Tips to Employer, or on a similar statement.
(a) 4040
(b) 4050
(c) 4060
(d) 4070
Answer: See Section 6. Tips, page 18/ (d) 4070

6. Tips.
8. The report should include tips you paid over to the employees for charge customers, tips the employee received directly from customers, and tips received from other employees under any tip-sharing arrangement. Both directly and indirectly tipped employees must report tips to you. No report is required for months when tips are less than $20. Your employee reports the tips on Form ___, Employee's Report of Tips to Employer, or on a similar statement. The statement must be ___ by the employee and must include:
(a) 4040, cosigned
(b) 4050, witnessed
(c) 4060, initialed
(d) 4070, signed
Answer: See Section 6. Tips, page 18/ (d) 4070, signed

6. Tips.
9. The report should include tips you paid over to the employees for charge customers, tips the employee received directly from customers, and tips received from other employees under any tip-sharing arrangement. Both directly and indirectly tipped employees must report tips to you. No report is required for months when tips are less than $20. Your employee reports the tips on Form 4070, Employee's Report of Tips to Employer, or on a similar statement. The statement must be signed by the employee and must include:
• The employee's name, address and SSN,
• Your name and address,
• The month or ___ the report covers, and
(a) date
(b) quarter
(c) period
(d) time
Answer: See Section 6. Tips, page 18/ (c) period

Tips

6. Tips

10. The report should include tips you paid over to the employees for charge customers, tips the employee received directly from customers, and tips received from other employees under any tip-sharing arrangement. Both directly and indirectly tipped employees must report tips to you. No report is required for months when tips are less than $20. Your employee reports the tips on Form 4070, Employee's Report of Tips to Employer, or on a similar statement. The statement must be signed by the employee and must include:
    • The employee's name, address and SSN,
    • Your name and address,
    • The month or ___ the report covers, and
    • The total of ___ received during the month or period.
    (a) date, tips
    (b) quarter, earnings
    (c) period, tips
    (d) time, income
    Answer: See Section 6. Tips, page 18/ (c) period, tips

6.Tips.

11. Both Forms ___ and ___, Employee's Daily Record of Tips, are included in Publication ___, Employee's Daily Record of Tips and report to Employer.
    (a) 4070, 4070-A, 1244
    (b) 4070, 4070-A, 1245
    (c) 4070, 4070-A, 1246
    (d) 4070-A, 4070-B, 1244
    Answer: See Section 6. Tips, page 18/ (a) 4070, 4070-A, 1244

6.Tips.

12. (TIP) You are permitted to establish a system for electronic tip reporting by employees. See Regulations section ___.
    (a) 31.6053-1(c)
    (b) 31.6053-1(d)
    (c) 31.6053-1(e)
    (d) 31.6053-1(f)
    Answer: See Section 6. Tips, page 18/ (b) 31.6053-1(d)

Collecting taxes on tips

6.Tips.

13. **Collecting taxes on tips.** You must collect income tax, employee social security tax, and employee Medicare tax on ___.
    (a) the employee's tip income.
    (b) the employees total income
    (c) the employee's tips
    (d) all employee tip income
    Answer: See Section 6. Tips, page 18/ (c) the employee's tips

Collecting taxes on tips

6.Tips.
14. **Collecting taxes on tips.** The withholding rules for withholding an employee's share of Medicare tax on tips also applies to withholding the Additional Medicare Tax once the wages and tips exceed $___ in the calendar year.
   (a) 85,000
   (b) 100,000
   (c) 150,000
   (d) 200,000
   Answer: See Section 6. Tips, page 18/ (d) 200,000

6.Tips.
15. **Collecting taxes on tips.** The withholding rules for withholding an employee's share of Medicare tax on tips also applies to withholding the Additional Medicare Tax once the wages and tips exceed $___ in the calendar year.
   (a) 85,000
   (b) 100,000
   (c) 150,000
   (d) 200,000
   Answer: See Section 6. Tips, page 18/ (d) 200,000

6.Tips.
16. **Collecting taxes on tips.** The withholding rules for withholding an employee's share of Medicare tax on tips also applies to withholding the Additional Medicare Tax once the wages and tips exceed $___ in the calendar year. If an employee reports to you in writing $___ or more in tips in a month, the tips are also subject to ___ tax.
   (a) 85,000, 10, FICA
   (b) 100,000, 10, FUTA
   (c) 150,000, 20, FICA
   (d) 200,000, 20, FUTA
   Answer: See Section 6. Tips, page 18/ (d) 200,000, 20, FUTA

6.Tips.
17. **Collecting taxes on tips.** The withholding rules for withholding an employee's share of Medicare tax on tips also applies to withholding the Additional Medicare Tax once the wages and tips exceed $200,000 in the calendar year. If an employee reports to you in writing $20 or more in tips in a month, the tips are also subject to FUTA tax. You can collect these taxes from the employee's wages or from ___.
   (a) other funds he or she makes available
   (b) other funds he or she become available
   (c) other funds he or she has available
   (d) other funds he or she that are available
   Answer: See Section 6. Tips, page 18/ (a) other funds he or she makes available.

© Copyright 2013. All rights reserved. Notice: United States Copyright Laws and International Treaties prohibit unauthorized publication, reproduction, distribution of this Work. Unauthorized use of this copyright in any form, format, publication or document may result in severe civil and criminal penalties. Violations of this copyright are investigated by the United States Department of Justice and carry, upon conviction of fines up to $250,000 and five years confinement. This Work is protected by United States Copyright Laws and International Treaties. Do not Copy, do not reproduce, do not distribute.

Collecting taxes on tips

6.Tips.

18. **Collecting taxes on tips**. The withholding rules for withholding an employee's share of Medicare tax on tips also applies to withholding the Additional Medicare Tax once the wages and tips exceed $200,000 in the calendar year. If an employee reports to you in writing $20 or more in tips in a month, the tips are also subject to FUTA tax. You can collect these taxes from the employee's wages or from ___. See ***Tips treated as supplemental wages*** in section ___ for more information.
    (a) other funds he or she makes available, 7
    (b) other funds he or she become available, 7
    (c) other funds he or she has available, 8
    (d) other funds he or she that are available, 8
    Answer: See Section 6. Tips, page 18/ (a) other funds he or she makes available, 7.

6.Tips.

19. **Collecting taxes on tips**. The withholding rules for withholding an employee's share of Medicare tax on tips also applies to withholding the Additional Medicare Tax once the wages and tips exceed $200,000 in the calendar year. If an employee reports to you in writing $20 or more in tips in a month, the tips are also subject to FUTA tax. You can collect these taxes from the employee's wages or from ___. See ***Tips treated as supplemental wages*** in section ___ for more information. Stop collecting the employee social security tax when his or her wages and tips for tax year 2013 reach $___;
    (a) other funds he or she makes available, 7, 113,700
    (b) other funds he or she become available, 7, 115,700
    (c) other funds he or she has available, 8, 115,800
    (d) other funds he or she that are available, 8, 115,900
    Answer: See Section 6. Tips, page 18/ (a) other funds he or she makes available, 7, 113,700

6.Tips.

20. **Collecting taxes on tips**. The withholding rules for withholding an employee's share of Medicare tax on tips also applies to withholding the Additional Medicare Tax once the wages and tips exceed $200,000 in the calendar year. If an employee reports to you in writing $20 or more in tips in a month, the tips are also subject to FUTA tax. You can collect these taxes from the employee's wages or from ___. See ***Tips treated as supplemental wages*** in section ___ for more information. Stop collecting the employee social security tax when his or her wages and tips for tax year 2013 reach $___; collect the income and employee Medicare taxes for the ___ year on all wages and tips.
    (a) other funds he or she makes available, 7, 113,700, whole
    (b) other funds he or she become available, 7, 115,700, entire
    (c) other funds he or she has available, 8, 115,800, remainder of
    (d) other funds he or she that are available, 8, 115,900, entire
    Answer: See Section 6. Tips, page 18/ (a) other funds he or she makes available, 7, 113,700, whole

Collecting taxes on tips

6. Tips.

21. **Collecting taxes on tips.** You are responsible for the employer social security tax on wages and tips until the wages (including tips) ___.
    (a) max out
    (b) reach the limit
    (c) reach the allowable SS level.
    (d) reach the allowable social security level.
    Answer: See Section 6. Tips, page 18/ (b) reach the limit

6. Tips

22. **Collecting taxes on tips.** You are responsible for the employer social security tax on wages and tips until the wages (including tips) ___. You are responsible for the employer Medicare tax for the whole year on all wages and tips. File Form ___ or Form ___ to report withholding and employment taxes on tips.
    (a) max out, 940, 942
    (b) reach the limit, 941, 944
    (c) reach the allowable SS level, 943, 945
    (d) reach the allowable social security level, 944, 946
    Answer: See Section 6. Tips, page 18/ (b) reach the limit, 941, 944

6. Tips

23. **Ordering rule.** If, by the ___ of the month after the month for which you received an employee's report on tips, you do not have enough employee funds available to deduct the employee tax, you no longer have to collect it.
    (a) 1st
    (b) 7th
    (c) 10th
    (d) 15th
    Answer: See Section 6. Tips, Ordering rule, page 18/ (c) 10th

6. Tips

24. **Ordering rule.** If, by the ___ of the month after the month for which you received an employee's report on tips, you do not have enough employee funds available to deduct the employee tax, you no longer have to collect it. If there are not enough funds available, withhold taxes in the following order.
    1. Withhold on regular wages and other compensation.
    2. Withhold social security and Medicare taxes on tips.
    3. Withhold income tax on ___.
    (a) 1st, tips
    (b) 7th, supplemental income
    (c) 10th, tips
    (d) 15th, supplemental income
    Answer: See Section 6. Tips, Ordering rule, page 18/ (c) 10th, supplemental income

6. Tips

25. **Reporting tips.** Report tips and any collected and uncollected social security and Medicare taxes on Form __ and on Form ___, lines
    (a) W-2, 941
    (b) W-2, 942
    (c) W-3, 942
    (d) W-4, 943
    Answer: See Section 6. Tips, Reporting tips, page 18/ (a) W-2, 941

Tips. Reporting Tips

6. Tips

26. **Reporting tips.** Report tips and any collected and uncollected social security and Medicare taxes on Form __ and on Form ___, lines 5b, 5c, and 5d (Form ___, lines 4b and 4c).
    (a) W-2, 941, 944
    (b) W-2, 942, 941
    (c) W-3, 942, 943
    (d) W-4, 943, 945
    Answer: See Section 6. Tips, Reporting tips, page 18/ (a) W-2, 941, 944

6. Tips

27. **Reporting tips.** Report an adjustment on Form ___, line ___ Form 944, line 6),
    (a) 941, 8
    (b) 941, 9
    (c) 942, 8
    (d) 943, 9
    Answer: See Section 6. Tips, Reporting tips, page 18/ (b) 941, 9

6. Tips

28. **Reporting tips.** Report an adjustment on Form 941, line 9, (Form 944, line 6), for the ___.
    (a) uncollected tax
    (b) uncollected taxes
    (c) uncollected social security
    (d) uncollected social security and Medicare taxes
    Answer: See Section 6. Tips, Reporting tips, page 18/ (d) uncollected social security and Medicare taxes

Tips. Reporting Tips

6. Tips

29. **Reporting tips.** Report an adjustment on Form 941, line 9, (Form 944, line 6), for the uncollected social security and Medicare taxes. Enter the amount of uncollected social security and Medicare taxes in box ___ of Form W-2 with codes "___" and "___."
    (a)   12, A, B
    (b)   12, B, C
    (c)   13, A, B
    (d)   13, a, b
    Answer: See Section 6. Tips, Reporting tips, page 18/ (a), 12, A, B

6. Tips

30. **Reporting tips.** Report an adjustment on Form 941, line 9, (Form 944, line 6), for the uncollected social security and Medicare taxes. Enter the amount of uncollected social security and Medicare taxes in box ___ of Form W-2 with codes "___" and "___." See section ___ and the General Instructions for Forms W-2 and W-3.
    (a)   12, A, B, 13
    (b)   12, B, C, 14
    (c)   13, A, B, 13
    (d)   13, a, b, 13
    Answer: See Section 6. Tips, Reporting tips, page 18/ (a), 12, A, B, 13

Tips. Reporting Tips. Revenue Ruling

6. Tips

31. **Reporting tips.** Revenue Ruling ___ provides guidance for employers regarding social security and Medicare taxes imposed on tips,
    (a)   2010-18
    (b)   2011-18
    (c)   2012-18
    (d)   2013-18
    Answer: See Section 6. Tips, Reporting tips, page 18/ (c), 2012-18

6. Tips

32. **Reporting tips.** Revenue Ruling ___ provides guidance for employers regarding social security and Medicare taxes imposed on tips, including information on the reporting of the employer share of social security and Medicare taxes under section ___,
    (a)   2010-18,   3121(o)
    (b)   2011-18, 3121(p)
    (c)   2012-18, 3121(q)
    (d)   2013-18, 3121(r)
    Answer: See Section 6. Tips, Reporting tips, page 18/ (c), 2012-18, 3121(q),

© Copyright 2013. All rights reserved. Notice: United States Copyright Laws and International Treaties prohibit unauthorized publication, reproduction, distribution of this Work. Unauthorized use of this copyright in any form, format, publication or document may result in severe civil and criminal penalties. Violations of this copyright are investigated by the United States Department of Justice and carry, upon conviction of fines up to $250,000 and five years confinement. This Work is protected by United States Copyright Laws and International Treaties. Do not Copy, do not reproduce, do not distribute.

Tips. Reporting Tips. Revenue Ruling

6. Tips

33. **Reporting tips.** Revenue Ruling ___ provides guidance for employers regarding social security and Medicare taxes imposed on tips, including information on the reporting of the employer share of social security and Medicare taxes under section ___,
    (a) 2010-18, 3121(o)
    (b) 2011-18, 3121(p)
    (c) 2012-18, 3121(q)
    (d) 2013-18, 3121(r)
    Answer: See Section 6. Tips, Reporting tips, page 18/ (c), 2012-18, 3121(q),

6. Tips

34. **Reporting tips.** Revenue Ruling ___ provides guidance for employers regarding social security and Medicare taxes imposed on tips, including information on the reporting of the employer share of social security and Medicare taxes under section ___, the difference between tips and service charges, and the section ___ credit.
    (a) 2010-18, 3121(o), 44B
    (b) 2011-18, 3121(p), 44C
    (c) 2012-18, 3121(q), 45B
    (d) 2013-18, 3121(r), 45C
    Answer: See Section 6. Tips, Reporting tips, page 18/ (c), 2012-18, 3121(q), 45B

6. Tips

35. **Reporting tips.** Revenue Ruling ___ provides guidance for employers regarding social security and Medicare taxes imposed on tips, including information on the reporting of the employer share of social security and Medicare taxes under section ___, the difference between tips and service charges, and the section ___ credit. See Revenue Ruling 2012-18, ___ I.R.B. ___, available at ***www.irs.gov/irb/2012-12.IRD/ar07.html***.
    (a) 2010-18, 3121(o), 44B, 2012-24, 1032
    (b) 2011-18, 3121(p), 44C, 2012-25, 1023
    (c) 2012-18, 3121(q), 45B, 2012-26, 1032
    (d) 2013-18, 3121(r), 45C, 2012-26, 1023
    Answer: See Section 6. Tips, Reporting tips, page 18/ (c), 2012-18, 3121(q), 45B, 2012-26, 1032

Tips. Reporting Tips. Allocated Tips

6. Tips

36. **Allocated tips.** if you operate a large food or beverage establishment, you must ___ allocated tips under certain circumstances.
    (a) deduct from
    (b) report
    (c) withhold
    (d) pay taxes
    Answer: See Section 6. Tips, Allocated tips, page 18/ (b) report

Tips. Reporting Tips. Allocated Tips

6. Tips
37. **Allocated tips.** if you operate a large food or beverage establishment, you must report allocated tips under certain circumstances. However, do not withhold income, social security or ___ taxes on allocated tips.
    (a)   Medicare
    (b)   FUTA
    (c)   FICA
    (d)   COBRA
    Answer: See Section 6. Tips, Allocated tips, page 18/ (a) Medicare

6. Tips
38. **Allocated tips.** A large food or beverage establishment is one that provides food or beverages for ___ on the premises, where tipping is customary, and
    (a)   lunch or supper
    (b)   dinner
    (c)   dining
    (d)   consumption
    Answer: See Section 6. Tips, Allocated tips, page 18/ (d) consumption

6. Tips
39. **Allocated tips.** A large food or beverage establishment is one that provides food or beverages for ___ on the premises, where tipping is customary, and where there were ___ more than ___ employees on a typical business day during the preceding year.
    (a)   lunch or supper, normally, 10
    (b)   dinner, generally, 12
    (c)   dining, usually, 12
    (d)   consumption, normally, 10
    Answer: See Section 6. Tips, Allocated tips, page 18/ (d) consumption, normally, 10

6. Tips
40. **Allocated tips.** The tips may be allocated by one of ___ methods—
    (a)   two
    (b)   three
    (c)   four
    (d)   five
    Answer: See Section 6. Tips, Allocated tips, page 18/ (b) three

Tips. Reporting tips. Allocated Tips

6. Tips

41. **Allocated tips.** The tips may be allocated by one of ___ methods—hours worked, gross receipts, or ____ agreement.
    (a) two, employer-employee agreement
    (b) three, good faith
    (c) four, contract
    (d) five, employment
    Answer: See Section 6. Tips, Allocated tips, page 18/ (b) three, good faith

6. Tips

42. **Allocated tips.** The tips may be allocated by one of three methods—hours worked, gross receipts, or good faith agreement. For information about these allocation methods, including the requirement to file Form ___ electronically if ___ or more forms are filed, see
    (a) 8025, 150
    (b) 8026, 200
    (c) 8027, 250
    (d) 8028, 300
    Answer: See Section 6. Tips, Allocated tips, page 18/ (c) 8027, 250

6. Tips

43. **Allocated tips.** The tips may be allocated by one of three methods—hours worked, gross receipts, or good faith agreement. For information about these allocation methods, including the requirement to file Form ___ electronically if ___ or more forms are filed, see the Instructions for Form ___.
    (a) 8025, 150, 8025
    (b) 8026, 200, 8026
    (c) 8027, 250, 8027
    (d) 8028, 300, 8028
    Answer: See Section 6. Tips, Allocated tips, page 18/ (c) 8027, 250, 8027

Tips. Reporting tips. Allocated Tips

6. Tips

44. **Allocated tips.** The tips may be allocated by one of three methods—hours worked, gross receipts, or good faith agreement. For information about these allocation methods, including the requirement to file Form 8027 electronically if 250 or more forms are filed, see the Instructions for Form 8027. For information on filing Form 8027 electronically with the IRS, see Publication ___.
    (a) 1239
    (b) 1240
    (c) 1241
    (d) 1242
    Answer: See Section 6. Tips, Allocated tips, page 18/ (a) 1239

© Copyright 2013. All rights reserved. Notice: United States Copyright Laws and International Treaties prohibit unauthorized publication, reproduction, distribution of this Work. Unauthorized use of this copyright in any form, format, publication or document may result in severe civil and criminal penalties. Violations of this copyright are investigated by the United States Department of Justice and carry, upon conviction of fines up to $250,000 and five years confinement. This Work is protected by United States Copyright Laws and International Treaties. Do not Copy, do not reproduce, do not distribute.

Tips. Tip Rate Determination and Education Program

6. Tips

45. **Tip Rate Determination.** Employers may ___ in the Tip Rate Determination and Education Program.
    (a) join
    (b) participate
    (c) choose to
    (d) apply to join
    Answer: See Section 6. Tips, Tip Rate Determination, page 18/ (b) participate

6. Tips

46. **Tip Rate Determination.** Employers may participate in the Tip Rate Determination and Education Program. The program primarily consists of ___ voluntary agreements
    (a) two
    (b) three
    (c) four
    (d) six
    Answer: See Section 6. Tips, Tip Rate Determination, page 18/ (a) two

6. Tips

47. **Tip Rate Determination.** Employers may participate in the Tip Rate Determination and Education Program. The program primarily consists of ___ voluntary agreements developed to ___ tip income reporting by helping taxpayers to understand and meet their tip reporting responsibilities.
    (a) two, improve
    (b) three, stabilize
    (c) four, record
    (d) six, report
    Answer: See Section 6. Tips, Tip Rate Determination, page 18/ (a) two, improve

6. Tips

48. **Tip Rate Determination.** Employers may participate in the Tip Rate Determination and Education Program. The program primarily consists of two voluntary agreements developed to improve tip income reporting by helping taxpayers to understand and meet their tip reporting responsibilities. The two agreements are the Tip Rate Determination Agreement (TRDA) and the ___ (TRAC).
    (a) Tip Rate Accounting Commitment
    (b) Tip Reporting Accounting Commitment
    (c) Tip Reporting Alternative Commitment
    (d) Tip Rate Alternative Commitment
    Answer: See Section 6. Tips, Tip Rate Determination, page 18/ (c) Tip Reporting Alternative Commitment

Tips. Tip Rate Determination

6. Tips

49. **Tip Rate Determination.** Employers may participate in the Tip Rate Determination and Education Program. The program primarily consists of two voluntary agreements developed to improve tip income reporting by helping taxpayers to understand and meet their tip reporting responsibilities. The two agreements are the Tip Rate Determination Agreement (TRDA) and the ___ (TRAC). A tip agreement in the Gaming Industry Tip Compliance Agreement (____), is available for the gaming (casino) industry.
    (a) Tip Rate Accounting Commitment, GONNA
    (b) Tip Reporting Accounting Commitment, GETCA
    (c) Tip Reporting Alternative Commitment, GITCA
    (d) Tip Rate Alternative Commitment, GOTCHA
    Answer: See Section 6. Tips, Tip Rate Determination, page 18/ (c) Tip Reporting Alternative Commitment, GITCA

6. Tips

50. **Tip Rate Determination.** Employers may participate in the Tip Rate Determination and Education Program. The program primarily consists of two voluntary agreements developed to improve tip income reporting by helping taxpayers to understand and meet their tip reporting responsibilities. The two agreements are the Tip Rate Determination Agreement (TRDA) and the Tip Reporting Alternative Commitment (TRAC). A tip agreement in the Gaming Industry Tip Compliance Agreement (GITCA), is available for the gaming (casino) industry. To get more information about TRDA and TRAC agreements, see Publication ___ Tips on Tips.
    (a) 3141
    (b) 3142
    (c) 3143
    (d) 3144
    Answer: See Section 6. Tips, Tip Rate Determination, page 18/ (d) 3144

51. **Tip Rate Determination.** Employers may participate in the Tip Rate Determination and Education Program. The program primarily consists of two voluntary agreements developed to improve tip income reporting by helping taxpayers to understand and meet their tip reporting responsibilities. The two agreements are the Tip Rate Determination Agreement (TRDA) and the Tip Reporting Alternative Commitment (TRAC). A tip agreement in the Gaming Industry Tip Compliance Agreement (GITCA), is available for the gaming (casino) industry. To get more information about TRDA and TRAC agreements, see Publication ___ Tips on Tips. Additionally, visit IRS.gov and enter "___ tips" in the search box to get more information about GITCA, TRDA, or TRAC agreements.
    (a) 3141, ALA
    (b) 3142, LSU
    (c) 3143, FSU
    (d) 3144, MSU
    Answer: See Section 6. Tips, Tip Rate Determination, page 18/ (d) 3144, MSU

© Copyright 2013. All rights reserved. Notice: United States Copyright Laws and International Treaties prohibit unauthorized publication, reproduction, distribution of this Work. Unauthorized use of this copyright in any form, format, publication or document may result in severe civil and criminal penalties. Violations of this copyright are investigated by the United States Department of Justice and carry, upon conviction of fines up to $250,000 and five years confinement. This Work is protected by United States Copyright Laws and International Treaties. Do not Copy, do not reproduce, do not distribute.

The International Leader in Construction Technology Home Study

Instructor's Manual for Tax Test 15E-S7
Section 7. Supplemental Wages

General Description. Section 7. Supplemental Wages. 15E-S7.

Tax Test 15E-S7: Tax Test 15E-S7. This is the detailed examination of wage payments that are not regular wages. Additional information and study material contained within Test 15E-S7 includes the following: Withholding on Supplemental Wages when an employee receives more than $1 million of supplemental wages during the calendar year. Withholding on supplemental wages to an employee who does not receive $1 million in supplementary wages in a calendar year.

Key Words. Section 7. Supplemental Wages. 15E-S7.

Tax Test 15E-S7: Section 7 Supplemental Wages. Withholding on Supplemental Wages (Excess of 1 Million Dollars). Supplemental Wages Combined with regular wages. Supplemental wages identified separately from regular wages. Vacation pay. Withhold a flat 25% (no other percentage allowed). Tips treated as supplemental wages. Examples.

DU VALL'S TEST'S™
Instructors Manual Study Guide Series United States Tax Code
IRS Publication 15 Circular E, Employer's Tax Guide Tax Year 2013
Tax Test 15E-S7 [Multiple-Choice Questions With Answers]

Section 7. 15E-S7. Supplemental Wages Page 18

7. Supplemental Wages
1. **Supplemental Wages.** Supplemental wages are ___ to an employee that are not wages.
    - (a) benefits
    - (b) wage payments
    - (c) income
    - (d) taxable income

    Answer: See Section 7. Supplemental Wages, page 18/ (b) wage payments

7. Supplemental Wages
2. **Supplemental Wages.** Supplemental wages are ___ to an employee that are not wages. They include, but are not limited to, bonuses, commissions, overtime pay, payments for accumulated sick leave, ___, awards, prizes, back pay, retroactive pay increases, and payments for nondeductible moving expenses.
    - (a) benefits, vacations
    - (b) wage payments, severance pay
    - (c) income, severance pay
    - (d) taxable income, vacations

    Answer: See Section 7. Supplemental Wages, page 18/ (b) wage payments, severance pay

© Copyright 2013. All rights reserved. Notice: United States Copyright Laws and International Treaties prohibit unauthorized publication, reproduction, distribution of this Work. Unauthorized use of this copyright in any form, format, publication or document may result in severe civil and criminal penalties. Violations of this copyright are investigated by the United States Department of Justice and carry, upon conviction of fines up to $250,000 and five years confinement. This Work is protected by United States Copyright Laws and International Treaties. Do not Copy, do not reproduce, do not distribute.

A Ficus Tree Publishing Educational-Technical Publications

Supplemental Wages

7. Supplemental Wages
3. **Supplemental Wages.** Supplemental wages are ___ to an employee that are not wages. They include, but are not limited to, bonuses, commissions, overtime pay, payments for accumulated sick leave, ___, awards, prizes, back pay, retroactive pay increases, and payments for nondeductible moving expenses.
    (a) benefits, vacations
    (b) wage payments, severance pay
    (c) income, severance pay
    (d) taxable income, vacations
    Answer: See Section 7. Supplemental Wages, page 18/ (b) wage payments, severance pay

7. Supplemental Wages
4. **Supplemental Wages.** Supplemental wages are ___ to an employee that are not wages. They include, but are not limited to, bonuses, commissions, overtime pay, payments for accumulated sick leave, ___, awards, prizes, back pay, retroactive pay increases, and payments for nondeductible moving expenses.
    (a) benefits, vacations, accountable plan
    (b) wage payments, severance pay, nonaccountable plan
    (c) income, severance pay, Archer account
    (d) taxable income, vacations, Cafeteria plan
    Answer: See Section 7. Supplemental Wages, page 18/ (b) wage payments, severance pay, nonaccountable plan

7. Supplemental Wages
5. **Supplemental Wages.** Supplemental wages are ___ to an employee that are not wages. They include, but are not limited to, bonuses, commissions, overtime pay, payments for accumulated sick leave, ___, awards, prizes, back pay, retroactive pay increases, and payments for nondeductible moving expenses.
    (a) benefits, vacations, accountable plan
    (b) wage payments, severance pay, nonaccountable plan
    (c) income, severance pay, Archer account
    (d) taxable income, vacations, Cafeteria plan
    Answer: See Section 7. Supplemental Wages, page 18/ (b) wage payments, severance pay, nonaccountable plan

Supplemental Wages

7. Supplemental Wages

6. **Supplemental Wages.** Supplemental wages are wage payments to an employee that are not wages. They include, but are not limited to, bonuses, commissions, overtime pay, payments for accumulated sick leave, severance pay, awards, prizes, back pay, retroactive pay increases, and payments for nondeductible moving expenses. How you withhold on supplemental wages depend on whether the supplemental payment is identified as a ___.
   - (a) regular pay supplement
   - (b) separate payment from regular wages.
   - (c) benefit payment or MSA
   - (d) taxable income or Cafeteria plan

   Answer: See Section 7. Supplemental Wages, page 18/ (b) separate payment from regular wages

7. Supplemental Wages

7. **Supplemental Wages.** See Regulations section ____ for additional guidance for wages paid after January 1, ___.
   - (a) 31.3402(g)-1, 2007
   - (b) 31.3403(g)-1, 2010
   - (c) 31.3404(h)-1, 2011
   - (d) 31.3405(h)-1, 2012

   Answer: See Section 7. Supplemental Wages, page 18/ (a) 31.3402(g)-1, 2007

7. Supplemental Wages

8. **Supplemental Wages.** See Regulations section ____ for additional guidance for wages paid after January 1, ___. Also see Revenue Ruling 2008-29, 2008-24 I.R.B. ___, available at *www.irs.gov/irb/2008-24_IRB/ar08.html*.
   - (a) 31.3402(g)-1, 2007
   - (b) 31.3403(g)-1, 2010
   - (c) 31.3404(h)-1, 2011
   - (d) 31.3405(h)-1, 2012

   Answer: See Section 7. Supplemental Wages, page 18/ (a) 31.3402(g)-1, 2007

Section 7. Supplemental Wages. Withholding on supplemental wages when an employee receives more than $1 million of supplementary wages from you during the calendar year. Page 19.

7. Supplemental Wages-Withholding

9. **Supplemental Wages - Withholding.** Special rules apply to the extent supplemental wages paid to any ___ during the calendar year exceed $1 million.
   - (a) employee
   - (b) executive employed by you
   - (c) one employee
   - (d) management employee

   Answer: See Section 7. Supplemental Wages, Withholding, page 19/ (c) one employee

Supplemental Wages

7. Supplemental Wages-Withholding

10. **Supplemental Wages - Withholding.** If a supplemental wage payment. together with other supplemental wage payments made to the employee during the calendar year, exceeds $1 million, the excess is subjected to withholding at ___% (or the highest rate of income tax for the year).
    (a) 25.8
    (b) 33.9
    (c) 39.6
    (d) 51.5
    Answer: See Section 7. Supplemental Wages, Withholding, page 19/ (c) 39.6

7. Supplemental Wages-Withholding

11. **Supplemental Wages - Withholding.** If a supplemental wage payment. together with other supplemental wage payments made to the employee during the calendar yea, exceeds $1 million, the excess is subjected to withholding at ___% (or the highest rate of income tax for the year). Withhold using the ___% rate without regard to the employee's Form W-___.
    (a) 25.8, 25.8, 2
    (b) 33.9, 33.9, 3
    (c) 39.6, 39.6, 4
    (d) 51.5, 51.5, 4
    Answer: See Section 7. Supplemental Wages, Withholding, page 19/ (c) 39.6, 39.9, 4

Section 7. 15E-S7. Supplemental Wages. Withholding on supplemental wages when an employee receives more than $1 million of supplementary wages from you during the calendar year. Page 19.

7. Supplemental Wages-Withholding

12. **Supplemental Wages - Withholding.** If a supplemental wage payment. together with other supplemental wage payments made to the employee during the calendar year, exceeds $1 million, the excess is subjected to withholding at 39.6% (or the highest rate of income tax for the year). Withhold using the 39.6% rate without regard to the employee's Form W-4. In determining supplemental wages paid to the employee during the year, include payment from all businesses under ___, available at www.irs.gov/
    (a) direct control, I.R.S. Publication 422
    (b) corporate control, I.R.B. 422
    (c) your control, I.R.S. Publication 423
    (d) common control, I.R.B. 423
    Answer: See Section 7. Supplemental Wages, Withholding, page 19/ (d) common control, I.R.B. 423

Section 7. 15E-S7. Supplemental Wages. Withholding on supplemental wages when an employee receives more than $1 million of supplementary wages from you during the calendar year. Page 19.

Supplemental Wages

7. Supplemental Wages-Withholding
13. **Supplemental Wages - Withholding.** If a supplemental wage payment. together with other supplemental wage payments made to the employee during the calendar year, exceeds $1 million, the excess is subjected to withholding at 39.6% (or the highest rate of income tax for the year). Withhold using the 39.6% rate without regard to the employee's Form W-4. In determining supplemental wages paid to the employee during the year, i include payment from all businesses under ___, available at *www.irs.gov/irb/2006-___. IRB/ar09.html*.
    - (a) direct control, I.R.S. Publication 422, *34*
    - (b) corporate control, I.R.B. 422, *35*
    - (c) your control, I.R.S. Publication 423, *36*
    - (d) common control, I.R.B. 423, *37*

    Answer: See Section 7. Supplemental Wages, Withholding, page 19/ (d) common control, I.R.B. 423, *37*

Section 7. Supplemental Wages Page 19. Withholding on supplemental wages to an employee who does not receive $1 million of supplementary wages from you during the calendar year.

14. **Supplemental Wages - Withholding.** If the supplemental wages paid to the employee are less than or ___ $1 million, the following rules apply in determining the amount of income tax to be withheld.
    - (a) equal to
    - (b) over three-quarters of
    - (c) over two thirds of
    - (d) over one-half of

    Answer: See Section 7. Supplemental Wages, page 19/ (a) equal to

Supplemental Wages. Combined with regular wages

7. Supplemental Wages- Supplemental wages combined with regular wages.
15. **Supplemental Wages.** If you pay supplemental wages with regular wages but ___, withhold federal income tax as if the total were a single payment for a regular payroll period.
    - (a) do not specify the amount
    - (b) do not specify the amount of each
    - (c) do not specify the total amount of each
    - (d) do not specify the total amount of wages paid

    Answer: See Section 7. Supplemental Wages, page 19/ (b) do not specify the amount of each

Supplemental Wages identified separately from regular wages

7. Supplemental Wages- Supplemental wages identified separately from regular wages.
16. **Supplemental Wages.** If you pay supplemental wages with regular wages separately (or combine them in a single payment and specify the amount of each), the federal income tax withholding depends ___ on whether you withhold income tax from your employee's regular wages.
 (a) entirely
 (b) solely
 (c) partly
 (d) partially
 Answer: See Section 7. Supplemental Wages, page 19/ (c) partly

7. Supplemental Wages- Supplemental wages identified separately from regular wages.
17. **Supplemental Wages.** If you pay supplemental wages with regular wages separately (or combine them in a single payment and specify the amount of each), the federal income tax withholding depends ___ on whether you withhold income tax from your employee's regular wages.
 1. If you withheld income tax from an employee's regular wages in the current or ___, you can use one or more of the following methods for the supplemental wages.
 (a) entirely, immediately preceding tax year
 (b) solely, immediately preceding tax quarter
 (c) partly, immediately preceding calendar year
 (d) partially, annual tax period
 Answer: See Section 7. Supplemental Wages, page 19/ (c) partly, immediately preceding calendar year

7. Supplemental Wages- Supplemental wages identified separately from regular wages.
18. **Supplemental Wages.** If you pay supplemental wages with regular wages separately (or combine them in a single payment and specify the amount of each), the federal income tax withholding depends ___ on whether you withhold income tax from your employee's regular wages.
 1. If you withheld income tax from an employee's regular wages in the current or ___, you can use one or more of the following methods for the supplemental wages.
 a. Withhold a flat ___% (no other percentage allowed).
 (a) entirely, immediately preceding tax year, 25
 (b) solely, immediately preceding tax quarter, 15
 (c) partly, immediately preceding calendar year, 25
 (d) partially, annual tax period , 15
 Answer: See Section 7. Supplemental Wages, page 19/ (c) partly, immediately preceding calendar year, 25

Supplemental wages identified separately from regular wages

7. Supplemental Wages- Supplemental wages identified separately from regular wages.
19.   **Supplemental Wages.** If you pay supplemental wages with regular wages separately (or combine them in a single payment and specify the amount of each), the federal income tax withholding depends partly on whether you withhold income tax from your employee's regular wages.
   1. If you withheld income tax from an employee's regular wages in the current or immediately preceding calendar year, you can use one or more of the following methods for the supplemental wages.
   a. Withhold a flat 25% (no other percentage allowed).
   b. If the supplemental wages are paid ___ with regular wages, ___ the supplemental wages to alternatively, either
   (a)   concurrently, subtract
   (b)   consecutively, add
   (c)   consecutively, subtract
   (d)   concurrently, add
   Answer: See Section 7. Supplemental Wages, page 19/ (d) concurrently, add

7. Supplemental Wages- Supplemental wages identified separately from regular wages.
20.   **Supplemental Wages.** If you pay supplemental wages with regular wages separately (or combine them in a single payment and specify the amount of each), the federal income tax withholding depends partly on whether you withhold income tax from your employee's regular wages.
   1. If you withheld income tax from an employee's regular wages in the current or immediately preceding calendar year, you can use one or more of the following methods for the supplemental wages.
   a. Withhold a flat 25% (no other percentage allowed).
   b. If the supplemental wages are paid ___ with regular wages, ___ the supplemental wages to alternatively, either to the concurrently paid regular wages. If there are no ___ paid regular wages, add the supplemental wages to
   (a)   concurrently, subtract, concurrently
   (b)   consecutively, add, currently
   (c)   consecutively, subtract, current
   (d)   concurrently, add, concurrently,
   Answer: See Section 7. Supplemental Wages, page 19/ (d) concurrently, add, concurrently,

Supplemental wages identified separately from regular wages

7. Supplemental Wages-Supplemental wages identified separately from regular wages.

21. **Supplemental Wages.** If you pay supplemental wages with regular wages separately (or combine them in a single payment and specify the amount of each), the federal income tax withholding depends partly on whether you withhold income tax from your employee's regular wages.

   1. If you withheld income tax from an employee's regular wages in the current or immediately preceding calendar year, you can use one or more of the following methods for the supplemental wages.

   a. Withhold a flat 25% (no other percentage allowed).

   b. If the supplemental wages are paid ___ with regular wages, ___ the supplemental wages to alternatively, either to the concurrently paid regular wages. If there are no ___ paid regular wages, add the supplemental wages to alternatively, either the ___ wages paid or to

   (a) concurrently, subtract, concurrently, tax period
   (b) consecutively, add, currently, annual
   (c) consecutively, subtract, current, supplemental
   (d) concurrently, add, concurrently, regular

   Answer: See Section 7. Supplemental Wages, page 19/ (d) concurrently, add, concurrently, regular

7. Supplemental Wages-Supplemental wages identified separately from regular wages.

22. **Supplemental Wages.** If you pay supplemental wages with regular wages separately (or combine them in a single payment and specify the amount of each), the federal income tax withholding depends partly on whether you withhold income tax from your employee's regular wages.

   1. If you withheld income tax from an employee's regular wages in the current or immediately preceding calendar year, you can use one or more of the following methods for the supplemental wages.

   a. Withhold a flat 25% (no other percentage allowed).

   b. If the supplemental wages are paid concurrently with regular wages, add the supplemental wages to alternatively, either to the concurrently paid regular wages. If there are no concurrently paid regular wages, add the supplemental wages to alternatively, either the regular wages paid or to be paid for the current payroll period or the regular wages paid for ___.

   (a) the preceding payroll period
   (b) the annual payroll period
   (c) the quarterly payroll period
   (d) the semi-annual payroll period

   Answer: See Section 7. Supplemental Wages, page 19/ (a) the preceding payroll period

Supplemental wages identified separately from regular wages

7. Supplemental Wages- Supplemental wages identified separately from regular wages.
23.   **Supplemental Wages.** If you pay supplemental wages with regular wages separately (or combine them in a single payment and specify the amount of each), the federal income tax withholding depends partly on whether you withhold income tax from your employee's regular wages.
   1. If you withheld income tax from an employee's regular wages in the current or immediately preceding calendar year, you can use one or more of the following methods for the supplemental wages.
   1. a. Withhold a flat ___% (no other percentage allowed).
   (a)   10
   (b)   15
   (c)   20
   (d)   25
   Answer: See Section 7. Supplemental wages, page 19/(d) 25.

7. Supplemental Wages- Supplemental wages identified separately from regular wages.
24.   **Supplemental Wages.** If you pay supplemental wages with regular wages separately (or combine them in a single payment and specify the amount of each), the federal income tax withholding depends partly on whether you withhold income tax from your employee's regular wages.
   1. b. If the supplemental wages are paid concurrently with regular wages, add the supplemental wages to alternatively, either to the concurrently paid regular wages. If there are no concurrently paid regular wages, add the supplemental wages to alternatively, either the regular wages paid or to be paid for the current payroll period or the regular wages paid for ___. Figure the income tax withholding as if the ___ of the regular wages and supplemental wages is a single payment.
   (a)   the preceding payroll period, total
   (b)   the annual payroll period, combined
   (c)   the quarterly payroll period, total
   (d)   the semi-annual payroll period, combined
   Answer: See Section 7. Supplemental Wages, page 19/ (a) the preceding payroll period, total

Supplemental wages identified separately from regular wages

7. Supplemental wages identified separately from regular wages

25. **Supplemental Wages.** If you pay supplemental wages with regular wages separately (or combine them in a single payment and specify the amount of each), the federal income tax withholding depends partly on whether you withhold income tax from your employee's regular wages.

    1b. If the supplemental wages are paid concurrently with regular wages, add the supplemental wages to alternatively, either to the concurrently paid regular wages. If there are no concurrently paid regular wages, add the supplemental wages to alternatively, either the regular wages paid or to be paid for the current payroll period or the regular wages paid for ___. Figure the income tax withholding as if the ___ of the regular wages and supplemental wages is a single payment. Subtract the tax withheld from the ___.
    - (a) the preceding payroll period, total, regular wages
    - (b) the annual payroll period, combined, supplemental wages
    - (c) the quarterly payroll period, total, annual wages
    - (d) the semi-annual payroll period, combined, combined annual wages

    Answer: See Section 7. Supplemental Wages, page 19/ (a) the preceding payroll period, total, regular wages

Supplemental wages identified separately from regular wages

26. **Supplemental Wages.** If you pay supplemental wages with regular wages separately (or combine them in a single payment and specify the amount of each), the federal income tax withholding depends partly on whether you withhold income tax from your employee's regular wages.

    1b. If the supplemental wages are paid concurrently with regular wages, add the supplemental wages to alternatively, either to the concurrently paid regular wages. If there are no concurrently paid regular wages, add the supplemental wages to alternatively, either the regular wages paid or to be paid for the current payroll period or the regular wages paid for the preceding payroll period. Figure the income tax withholding as if the total of the regular wages and supplemental wages is a single payment. Subtract the tax withheld from the regular wages. Withhold the ___ tax from the supplemental wages.
    - (a) additional
    - (b) remaining
    - (c) penalty
    - (d) excess

    Answer: See Section 7. Supplemental Wages, page 19/ (b) remaining

Supplemental wages identified separately from regular wages

27. **Supplemental Wages.** If you pay supplemental wages with regular wages separately (or combine them in a single payment and specify the amount of each), the federal income tax withholding depends partly on whether you withhold income tax from your employee's regular wages.
    1b. If the supplemental wages are paid concurrently with regular wages, add the supplemental wages to alternatively, either to the concurrently paid regular wages. If there are no concurrently paid regular wages, add the supplemental wages to alternatively, either the regular wages paid or to be paid for the current payroll period or the regular wages paid for the preceding payroll period. Figure the income tax withholding as if the total of the regular wages and supplemental wages is a single payment. Subtract the tax withheld from the regular wages. Withhold the ___ tax from the supplemental wages. If there were other payments of supplemental wages paid during the payroll period made before the current payment of supplemental of supplemental wages, ___ all the payments supplemental wages paid during the payroll period with the regular wages paid during the payroll period, calculate
    (a) additional, merge
    (b) remaining, aggregate
    (c) penalty, combine
    (d) excess, combine
    Answer: See Section 7. Supplemental Wages, page 19/ (b) remaining, aggregate

28. **Supplemental Wages.** If you pay supplemental wages with regular wages separately (or combine them in a single payment and specify the amount of each), the federal income tax withholding depends partly on whether you withhold income tax from your employee's regular wages.
    1b. If the supplemental wages are paid concurrently with regular wages, add the supplemental wages to alternatively, either to the concurrently paid regular wages. If there are no concurrently paid regular wages, add the supplemental wages to alternatively, either the regular wages paid or to be paid for the current payroll period or the regular wages paid for the preceding payroll period. Figure the income tax withholding as if the total of the regular wages and supplemental wages is a single payment. Subtract the tax withheld from the regular wages. Withhold the ___ tax from the supplemental wages. If there were other payments of supplemental wages paid during the payroll period made before the current payment of supplemental of supplemental wages, ___ all the payments supplemental wages paid during the payroll period with the regular wages paid during the payroll period, calculate the tax on the total and ___ the tax already withheld from the regular wages and previous supplemental wage payments, and withhold the remaining tax
    (a) additional, merge, add
    (b) remaining, aggregate, subtract
    (c) penalty, combine, multiply
    (d) excess, combine, divide
    Answer: See Section 7. Supplemental Wages, page 19/ (b) remaining, aggregate, subtract

Supplemental wages identified separately from regular wages

29. **Supplemental Wages.** If you pay supplemental wages with regular wages separately (or combine them in a single payment and specify the amount of each), the federal income tax withholding depends partly on whether you withhold income tax from your employee's regular wages.
    2. If you did not withhold income tax from the employee's regular wages in the current or immediate preceding calendar year, use method ___ above.
    (a) 1
    (b) 1-a
    (c) 1-b
    (d) 2
    Answer: See Section 7. Supplemental Wages, page 19/ (c) 1-b

7. Supplemental Wages- Supplemental wages identified separately from regular wages.
30. **Supplemental Wages.** If you pay supplemental wages with regular wages separately (or combine them in a single payment and specify the amount of each), the federal income tax withholding depends partly on whether you withhold income tax from your employee's regular wages.
    2. If you did not withhold income tax from the employee's regular wages in the current or immediate preceding calendar year, use method 1-b above. This would occur, for example, when the ___ of the employee's withholding allowances claimed on Form W-4 is more than the wages.
    (a) amount
    (b) income
    (c) total
    (d) value
    Answer: See Section 7. Supplemental Wages, page 19/ (d) value

7. Supplemental Wages- Supplemental wages identified separately from regular wages.
31. **Supplemental Wages.** Regardless of the ___ you use to withhold income tax on supplemental wages, they are subject to social security, Medicare, and ___ taxes.
    (a) tax system, COBRA
    (b) system, ARCHER
    (c) procedure, FICA
    (d) method, FUTA
    Answer: See Section 7. Supplemental Wages, page 19/ (d) method, FUTA

Section 7. Supplemental Wages — IRS Examples. Page 19 and 20.

2013 IRS Example 1.
You pay John Peters a base salary on the 1st of each month. He is single and claims one withholding allowance. In January he is paid **$1,000**. Using the wage bracket tables (**Single Persons—Monthly** Payroll Period, page 58. **For Wages Paid through December 2013**), you withhold **$51** from this amount. See page 58, (And the wages are at least **$1,000** but less than **$1,040**), from the (And the number of withholding allowance claimed is—) the column claiming one withholding allowance = **$51**).

In February, he received salary of $1,000 plus a commission of $2,000, which you combine with regular wages and do not separately identify. You figure the withholding based on the total of **$3,000**. The correct withholding from the tables is $340. Go to page **59**. Locate from the column "And the wages are" the amount of "At least **3,000** but less than **3,040**", from the column claiming one withholding allowance the amount of income tax to withhold is **340**.

A Similar Comparison Problem from Tax Year 2012, Test 15E-5 was written as following: Note the minor differences in the same type of example-problems.
2012 IRS Example 1.
You pay John Peters a base salary on the 1st of each month. He is single and claims one withholding allowance. <u>In January</u> he is paid **$1,000**. Using the wage bracket table information (**Wage Bracket Method**) located on page 50, from Single Persons — Monthly Payroll Period, (For Wages paid through December 2012), column heading (And the wages are - At least **$1,000** but less than **$1,040**, with one deduction you withhold **$52** from the amount John is paid. This amount matches Example 1. page 16.
<u>In February</u> He (John Peters) receives salary of **$1,000** plus a commission of **$2,000** (supplemental wages) which you combine with regular wages and do not separately identify obtaining at total income for February of **$3,000**. Return to the tax tables to verify the amount stated in Example 1. From page 51 Single Persons — Monthly Payroll Period and read (At least **$3,000** but less than **$3,040**) with one deduction .From the table the amount of income tax to be withheld is **$342**. From Example 1, Page *16*, the tax amount given for February 2012 is **$342**. We have verified the answer for Example1 as accurate. Answer: See Part 7. Supplemental Wages, Example 1, page 15 (Use table for Single Persons Monthly Payroll Period located on (page *51*) for wage amount at least **$3,000** but less than **$3,040**)/ (c), **342**

It is in column 1 - Highlight it. Test type multiple-choice questions from Circular E, Tax Year current for tax year 2012 was based on Example 1 and was written as for 2012 as follows: The examples continue on the following page.

Section 7. Supplemental Wages — IRS Examples. Page 19 and 20.

Continuing the example.
1. **In tax year 2012** You pay John Peters a base salary on the 1st of each month. He is single and claims one withholding allowance. In January John is paid $1,000. Underline the wage bracket method determine his tax for January 2012.
   - (a) $48
   - (b) $49.75
   - (c) $50.50
   - (d) $52

   Answer: ___, from the wage bracket method for tax year 2012 the answer is $52. The tax changes each year are generally minor. However, they do and will change for each tax year.

2012 Tax Table example problem. Solve the amount of $1,500.
You pay John Peters a base salary on the first of each month. He is single and claims one withholding allowance. In January he is paid **$1,500**. Using the wage bracket method determine his tax for January **2012**.
   - (a) 104
   - (b) 110
   - (c) 114
   - (d) 115

   Answer:____. See Tables Page 50 (more than $1,480 but less than $1,520)/ (c) 114

2013 Tax Table problem. (Same problem but for tax year 2013).
Solve: You pay John Peters a base salary on the first of each month. He is single and claims one withholding allowance. In January he is paid $1,500. Using the wage bracket method determine his tax for January 2013.
   - (a) 104
   - (b) 110
   - (c) 112
   - (d) 115

   Answer:____. See Tables Page 50 (more than $1,480 but less than $1,520)/ (c) 112

Solution: Go to page 58. **Single** persons—**Monthly** Payroll Period (For Wages paid through December 2103). Go to the left column "And the wages are—" At least 1.480 but less than 1,520. Go to column 1 under "And the number of withholding allowances claimed is—". The tax on $1,500 is $112.

Note **one** important basic fact related to IRS Tax Laws and Regulations. Changes are, for the most part usually minor adjustments from year to year. For **Self study work**: Use this same example for John Peters and create additional tax problems for the income amounts of $1,250, 1,675, 1,735, 2,125, 2,500, 2,855, 3,150. Follow this by adding to your problems the additional **Monthly Commissions** of $2,500, 2,800, 3,100, 3,500, 3,850, 3,895 and 4,000. When you have completed this basic assignment, rework the allowances for the following allowances: 0, 2, 3, 4, and 5.

Section 7. Supplemental Wages — IRS Examples. Page 19

2013 IRS Example 2.
You pay Sharon Warren a base salary on the 1st of each month. She is single and claims one allowance. Her May 1, pay is $2,000. Using the wage bracket tables, you withhold $192 (page 58) at least $2000 but less than $2040 with one dependent for tax year 2013 is $190) **Verify this amount from the 2013 tax tables, page 58 Single Persons Monthly Payroll Period.**
On May 14, she receives a bonus of $1,000. Electing to use supplemental payment method (1-b) page 19, you:
(1) Add the bonus amount to the amount of wages from the most recent pay date ($2,000 + $1,000 = $3,000)
 (2) Determine the amount of the withholding on the combined $3,000 amount for tax year 3013 to be $340= (at least $3000 but less than $3040). **page 59**, Monthly Payroll Period.
 (3) Subtract the amount withheld from the wages on the most recent pay date (May 1) from the combined withholding amount ($340 - $190 = $150)
 (4) Withhold $_____ from the bonus payment
  (a) 150
  (b) 390
  (c) 658
  (d) 856
  Answer: See (a), 150, Part 7. Supplemental Wages, Example 2, page 16. Use the Wage Bracket Table for Single Persons - Monthly Payroll Period for wages paid, Wages at least $3,000 but less than $3,040, page 51)/ (a), 150

2012 IRS Example 2. Comparison Example. IRS Example 2.
You pay Sharon Warren a base salary on the 1st of each month. She is single and claims one allowance. Her May 1, pay is $2,000.
 Using the wage bracket tables, you withhold $192 (page 50) at least $2000 but less than $2040 with one dependent is $192) **Verify this amount from the 2012 tax tables only.** On May 14, she receives a bonus of $1,000. Electing to use supplemental payment method (1-b), you:
 (1) Add the bonus amount to the amount of wages from the most recent pay date ($2,000 + $1,000 = $3,000)
 (2) Determine the amount of the withholding on the combined $3,000 amount to be $342 (at least $3000 but less than $3040). From tax tables tax year 2012, page 51, Monthly Payroll Period.
 (3) Subtract the amount withheld from the wages on the most recent pay date May 1 from the combined withholding amount ($342 - $192 = $150)
 (4) Withhold $___ from the bonus payment
  (a) 150
  (b) 390
  (c) 658
  (d) 856
 Answer: See 2012 tax tables, section 7. Supplemental Wages, Example 2, page 16. Use the Wage Bracket Table for Single Persons - Monthly Payroll Period for wages paid, Wages at least $3,000 but less than $3,040, page 51)/ (a), 150 .

Section 7. Supplemental Wages — IRS Examples. Page 19

2013 IRS Example 3.
The facts are the same as in Example 2, except you elect to use the flat rate method of withholding on the bonus. You withhold 25% of $1,000, or $250, from Sharon's bonus payment.
Solution/explanation: See **Supplemental wages identified separately from regular wages,** page 19, middle of left column.
1. If you withheld income tax from an employee's regular wages in the current or immediately preceding calendar year, you can use one of the following methods for the supplemental wages.
    a. **Withhold a flat 25%** (no other percentage is allowed).

2013 IRS Example 4 pages 19 and 20.
The facts are the same as in Example 2, except you elect to pay Sharon a second bonus of $2,000 on May 28. Using supplemental wage withholding method 1-b, page 19, you ;

(1)   Add the bonus amount to the amount of wages from the most recent pay date ($2,000 + $1,000 + $2,000 = $5,000).

(2)   Determine the amount of the withholding on the combined $5,000 amount for tax year 2013 to be $789 (From Monthly Tax Table page 59 bottom of page, **Wage Bracket Table** (at least $5,000 but less than $5,040, one withholding allowance).

(3)   Subtract the amount withheld from the wages on the most recent pay date (May 1) from the combined withholding amount ($789 - $190 - $150 = $449).

(4)   Withhold $_____ from the second bonus payment.
    (a)   150
    (b)   489
    (c)   658
    (d)   856
Answer: See (b), 489, section 7. Supplemental Wages, Example 4, page 18. Again, use the Wage Bracket Table for Single Persons - Monthly Payroll Period for wages paid, Wages at least $5,000 but less than $5,040, page 59) bottom of page/ (b), 489

Create additional work problems using the **Wage Bracket Tables** for the number of withholding allowances using the same bonus amounts but for 2, 3, 4, 6 allowances.

7. Supplemental Wages- Tips treated as supplemental wages. Page 20.

7. Supplemental Wages- Tips treated as supplemental wages.
32.   Withhold income tax on tips from wages earned by the employee or from ___.
    (a)   other funds the employee makes available
    (b)   other funds that are available
    (c)   other funds the employee has available
    (d)   other employee funds that are available
Answer: See Section 7. Supplemental Wages, page 20/ (a) or from other funds the employee makes available

7. Supplemental Wages- Tips treated as supplemental wages. Page 20.

7. Supplemental Wages- Tips treated as supplemental wages.
33. If an employee receives regular wages and reports tips, ___ income tax withholding as if the tips were ___ wages.
    (a) calculate, supplemental
    (b) figure, supplemental
    (c) enter, regular
    (d) figure, regular
    Answer: See Section 7. Supplemental Wages, page 20/ (b) figure, supplemental

7. Supplemental Wages- Tips treated as supplemental wages.
34. If you have not withheld income tax from the regular wages, add the tips to the ___ wages.
    (a) supplemental
    (b) total
    (c) regular
    (d) quarterly
    Answer: See Section 7. Supplemental Wages, page 20/ (c) regular

7. Supplemental Wages- Tips treated as supplemental wages.
35. If you have not withheld income tax from the regular wages, add the tips to the ___ wages. Then withhold income tax on ___.
    (a) supplemental, total
    (b) total, annual wages
    (c) regular, total
    (d) quarterly, supplemental wages
    Answer: See Section 7. Supplemental Wages, page 20/ (c) regular, total

7. Supplemental Wages- Tips treated as supplemental wages.
36. If you withheld income tax from the regular wages, you can withhold on tips by ___ discussed earlier in this section under
    (a) section 7 Supplemental Wages —Tips
    (b) tax rules
    (c) methods
    (d) method 1-a or 1-b
    Answer: See Section 7. Supplemental Wages, page 20/ (d) method 1-a or 1-b

7. Supplemental Wages- Tips treated as supplemental wages.

7. Supplemental Wages- Tips treated as supplemental wages.
37. If you withheld income tax from the regular wages, you can withhold on tips by ___ discussed earlier in this section under ___ wages identified separately from regular wages.
    (a)   section 7 Supplemental Wages —Tips, Supplemental
    (b)   tax rules, regular
    (c)   methods, Regular
    (d)   method 1-a or 1-b, Supplemental
Answer: See Section 7. Supplemental Wages, page 20/ (d) method 1-a or 1-b, Supplemental

7. Supplemental Wages- Vacation pay

7. Supplemental Wages- Vacation pay.
38. Vacation pay is subject to withholding as if it were ___.
    (a)   a regular wage payment
    (b)   a supplemental wage payment
    (c)   a supplemental wage benefit
    (d)   income
Answer: See Section 7. Supplemental Wages, Vacation pay, page 20/ (a) a regular wage payment

7. Supplemental Wages- Vacation pay.
39. When vacation pay is in addition to regular wages for the vacation period, treat is as ___.
    (a)   a regular wage payment
    (b)   a supplemental wage payment
    (c)   a supplemental wage benefit
    (d)   income
Answer: See Section 7. Supplemental Wages, Vacation pay, page 20/ (b) a supplemental wage payment

7. Supplemental Wages- Vacation pay.
40. If the vacation pay is for a time longer than your usual pay period, ___.
    (a)   use method 3-c
    (b)   expand it over the pay periods for which you pay it
    (c)   spread it over the pay periods for which you pay it
    (d)   condense it over the pay periods for which you pay it
Answer: See Section 7. Supplemental Wages, Vacation pay, page 20/ (c) spread it over the pay periods for which you pay it

7. Supplemental Wages. Vacation Pay. Page 20.

7. Supplemental Wages- Vacation pay.
41. Vacation pay is subject to withholding as if it were a ___wage payment.
    (a) bonus
    (b) additional
    (c) regular
    (d) supplemental
    Answer: See Part 7. Supplemental Wages, Vacation pay, page 20/ (c), regular

7. Supplemental Wages- Vacation pay.
42. When vacation pay is in addition to regular wages for the vacation period, treat it as a ____wage payment.
    (a) bonus
    (b) additional
    (c) regular
    (d) supplemental
    Answer: See (d), supplemental, Part 7. Supplemental Wages, Vacation pay, page 20/ (d), supplemental

7. Supplemental Wages- Vacation pay.
43. If the vacation pay is for a time longer than your usual payroll period, ____it over the pay periods for which you pay it.
    (a) spread
    (b) extend
    (c) condense
    (d) average
    Answer: See Part 7. Supplemental Wages, Vacation pay, page 20/ (a), spread

Instructor's Manual for Tax Test 15E-S8
Section 8. Payroll Period

General Description. 15E-S8. Section 8. Payroll Period.

Tax Test 15E-S8. Tax Test 15E-S8. Section 8. Payroll Period is a very brief Section. However, do not disregard or ignore Section 8. The information will confused with other parts of Circular E that discuss Payroll Periods. know there similar information is located. Generally, professional examinations require exact word-for-word answers.

Key Words. 15E-S8. Section 8. Payroll Period.

Payroll Period. No regular payroll period. Employee paid for a period less than 1 week.

© Copyright 2013. All rights reserved. Notice: United States Copyright Laws and International Treaties prohibit unauthorized publication, reproduction, distribution of this Work. Unauthorized use of this copyright in any form, format, publication or document may result in severe civil and criminal penalties. Violations of this copyright are investigated by the United States Department of Justice and carry, upon conviction of fines up to $250,000 and five years confinement. This Work is protected by United States Copyright Laws and International Treaties. Do not Copy, do not reproduce, do not distribute.

A Ficus Tree Publishing Educational-Technical Publications

DU VALL'S TEST'S™
Instructors Manual Study Guide Series United States Tax Code
IRS Publication 15 Circular E, Employer's Tax Guide Tax Year 2013
Tax Test 15E-S8 [Multiple-Choice Questions With Answers]

Section 8. Payroll Period Page 20

8. Payroll Period.
1. Your payroll period is a period of ___ for which you usually pay ___.
   (a) activity, your employees
   (b) work, income
   (c) employment, wages
   (d) service, wages
   Answer: See Section 7. Supplemental Wages, Vacation pay, page 20/ (d) service, wages

8. Payroll Period.
2. When you have a regular payroll period, withhold income tax for that time period even if your employee ___.
   (a) takes his or her vacation during that period
   (b) does not work the full period
   (c) receives extra bonuses during the period
   (d) is laid off in the second period
   Answer: See Part 8. Payroll period, page 20/ (b), does not work the full period

8. Payroll Period.
3. When you do not have a regular payroll period, withhold the tax as if you paid wages for daily or miscellaneous payroll period. Figure the number of days (including ___ and ___) in the period covered by the wage payment.
   (a) weekends
   (b) Saturdays and Sundays
   (c) Sundays and holidays
   (d) overtime
   Answer: See Part 8. Payroll period, page 20/ (c), Sundays and holidays

8. Payroll Period.
4. If the wages are unrelated to a specific length of time (for example, commissions paid on completion of a sale), ___ the number of days from the payment period to the latest of:
   (a) count back
   (b) deduct
   (c) add
   (d) subtract
   Answer: See Part 8. Payroll period, page 16/ (a) count back

Section 8. Payroll Period Page 20

8. Payroll Period.

5. If the wages are unrelated to a specific length of time (for example, commissions paid on completion of a sale), count back the number of days from the payment period to the latest of:
   - The last wage payment made during the same calendar year
   - The date employment began, if during the same calendar year, or
   - _____ 1, of the same year

   (a) January
   (b) April
   (c) June
   (d) December

   Answer: See Part 8. Payroll period, page 20/ (a), January

8. Payroll Period.

6. When you pay an employee for a period of less than 1 week, and the employee signs a statement under penalties of perjury that he or she is not working for any other employer during the same week for wages subject to withholding, figure withholding based on a ___payroll period.

   (a) hourly
   (b) daily
   (c) weekly
   (d) estimated

   Answer: See Part 8. Payroll period, page 20/ (c), weekly

8. Payroll Period.

7. If the employee later begins working for another employer for wages subject to withholding, the employee must notify you within ___days. You then figure withholding based on the daily or miscellaneous period.

   (a) 5
   (b) 7
   (c) 10
   (d) 15

   Answer: See Part 8. Payroll period, page 20/ (c) 10

The International Leader in Construction Technology Home Study

Instructor's Manual for Tax Test 15E-S9
Section 9. Withholding From Employee's Wages

General Description. 15E-9. Page 20.

Tax Test 15E-S9. Tax Test 15E-S9 is a substantial, important section. This section requires diligent study and research on the part of the student. It is suggested that continuous, ongoing review, of the material provided herein be conducted.

Key Words. 15E-9. Page 20.

Tax Test 15E-S9. Section 9 Withholding From Employees Wages. **Employee's Withholding Allowance Certificate**. Effective Date of Form W-4. Income Tax Withholding. Using Form W-4 to figure withholding. Form in Spanish. Electronic system to receive Form W-4. Successor employer. Completing Form W-4. Exemption from federal income tax withholding. Invalid Forms W-4. single with zero withholding allowances. Withholding income taxes on the wages of nonresident alien employees. Withholding adjustment for nonresident alien employees. Amount to Add. Table 5. Percentage Method. Wage Bracket Method. Supplemental wage payment. Nonresident alien employee's Form W-4. Form 8233. IRS review of requested Forms W-4. **Initial lock-in letter**. Employee not performing services. Termination and re-hire of employees. Modification notice. New Form W-4 after notice. Substitute Forms W-4. Invalid Forms W-4. Amount exempt from levy on wages, salary, and other income. Social Security and Medicare Services. **Tax rates and the social security wage base limit**. The employee tax rate for social security is. The employer tax rate for social security remains. There is no wage base limit for. Additional Medicare Tax Withholding. Additional Medicare tax is only imposed on the employee. Successor employer. Withholding of social security and Medicare taxes on nonresident aliens. International social security agreements. Religious exemptions. Foreign persons treated as American employers. Part-Time Workers. FUTA Publication 15-A.

© Copyright 2013. All rights reserved. Notice: United States Copyright Laws and International Treaties prohibit unauthorized publication, reproduction, distribution of this Work. Unauthorized use of this copyright in any form, format, publication or document may result in severe civil and criminal penalties. Violations of this copyright are investigated by the United States Department of Justice and carry, upon conviction of fines up to $250,000 and five years confinement. This Work is protected by United States Copyright Laws and International Treaties. Do not Copy, do not reproduce, do not distribute.

A Ficus Tree Publishing Educational-Technical Publications

A Ficus Tree Publishing Quick Notes Page

DU VALL'S TEST'S™
Instructors Manual Study Guide Series United States Tax Code
IRS Publication 15 Circular E, Employer's Tax Guide Tax Year 2013
Tax Test 15E-S9-1[Multiple-Choice Questions With Answers]

Section 9. Withholding From Employees' Wages. Page 20.

9. Withholding From Employee's Wages.
1. To know how much income tax to withhold from employees' wages, you should have a Form ___, **Employee's Withholding Allowance Certificate** on file for each employee.
    (a) W-2
    (b) W-3
    (c) W-4
    (d) 1049
    Answer: See Part 9. Withholding From Employee's Wages, Income Tax Withholding, page 20/(c), W-4

9. Withholding From Employee's Wages.
2. Encourage your employees to file an updated Form W-4 for ___,
    (a) W-2, this tax year
    (b) W-3, each tax year
    (c) W-4, 2013
    (d) 1049, 2014
    Answer: See Part 9. Withholding From Employee's Wages, Income Tax Withholding, page 20/(c), W-4, 2013

9. Withholding From Employee's Wages.
3. Encourage your employees to file an updated Form W-4 for ___, especially if they owed taxes or received a large refund when filing their ___ tax return.
    (a) W-2, 2012, 2013
    (b) W-3, 2012, 1013
    (c) W-4, 2013, 2012
    (d) 1049, 2013, 2012
    Answer: See Part 9. Withholding From Employee's Wages, Income Tax Withholding, page 20/(c), W-4, 2013, 2012

9. Withholding From Employee's Wages.
4. Advise your employees to use the IRS Withholding Calculator on the IRS website at *www.irs.gov/individuals* for help in determining ___ on their Forms W-4.
    (a) deductions
    (b) allowances
    (c) the number of allowances allowed
    (d) how many withholding allowances to claim
    Answer: See Part 9. Withholding From Employee's Wages, Income Tax Withholding, page 20/ (d) how many withholding allowances to claim

© Copyright 2013. All rights reserved. Notice: United States Copyright Laws and International Treaties prohibit unauthorized publication, reproduction, distribution of this Work. Unauthorized use of this copyright in any form, format, publication or document may result in severe civil and criminal penalties. Violations of this copyright are investigated by the United States Department of Justice and carry, upon conviction of fines up to $250,000 and five years confinement. This Work is protected by United States Copyright Laws and International Treaties. Do not Copy, do not reproduce, do not distribute.

Section 9. Withholding From Employees' Wages. Page 20.

9. Withholding From Employee's Wages.
5.   Ask all new employees to give you a signed Form ____ when they _____.
    (a)   W-2, are hired
    (b)   W-4, start work
    (c)   W-5, at the commencement of the payroll period
    (d)   1049, initially apply for employment
    Answer: See Part 9. Withholding From Employee's Wages, Income Tax Withholding, page 20/(b), W-4, start work

9. Withholding From Employee's Wages.
6.   Make the form effective with the first wage payment. If a new employee does not give you a completed Form ___, withhold taxes as if he or she is single with ___ allowances.
    (a)   W-4, no withholding
    (b)   W-5, one withholding
    (c)   1049, no withholding
    (d)   1089, one withholding
    Answer: See Part 9. Withholding From Employees Wages, Income Tax Withholding, page 20/ (a), W-4, no withholding

9. Withholding From Employee's Wages.
7.   You can provide Formulario___, Certificado de Exención de Retention del Empleado, in place of Form W-4.
    (a)   W-4(S)
    (b)   W-4(SP)
    (c)   W-4(PSP)
    (d)   W-4(RSP)
    Answer: See Part 9. Withholding From Employee's Wages, Income Tax Withholding page 20/ (b) W-4(SP)

9. Withholding From Employee's Wages.
8.   For more information see Publicacion ____ (SP),
    (a)   15 (SP)
    (b)   15d(SP)
    (c)   16
    (d)   17
    Answer: See Part 9. Withholding From Employee's Wages, Forms in Spanish Page 20/ (d) 17

Withholding From Employee's Wages

9. Withholding From Employee's Wages.
9. For more information see Publicacion ____ (SP), El Impuesto Federal ___ los Ingresos (Para Personas Fisicas).
   (a) 15 (SP), somber
   (b) 15d(SP), somber
   (c) 16, sobre
   (d) 17, sobre
   Answer: See Part 9. Withholding From Employee's Wages, Form in Spanish Page 20/ (d) 17, sobre

9. Withholding From Employee's Wages.
10. For more information see Publicacion ____ (SP), El Impuesto Federal ___ los Ingresos (Para Personas Fisicas). The ___ discussed in this section that apply to Form W-4 also apply to Formulario W-4(SP).
   (a) 15 (SP), slumber,
   (b) 15d(SP), sober, regulations
   (c) 16, sobre, rules
   (d) 17, sobre, rules
   Answer: See Part 9. Withholding From Employee's Wages, Form in Spanish Page 20/ (d) 17, sobre, rules

Withholding From Employee's Wages
Electronic system to receive Form W-4

9. Withholding From Employee's Wages.
11. You may establish a system to electronically receive Form W-4 from your employees. See Regulations section ___ for more information.
   (a) 30.3400(f)(5)-1(c)
   (b) 31.3400(f)(5)-1(c)
   (c) 31.3401(f)(5)-1(c)
   (d) 31.3402 (f)(5)-1(c)
   Answer: See Part 9. Withholding From Employees Wages, Income Tax Withholding, page 20/ (d) 31.3402(f) (5)-1 (c)

9. Withholding From Employee's Wages - Effective Date of Form W-4

9. Withholding From Employee's Wages.
12. A Form W-4 remains in effect until the employee ___.
   (a) gives you a new one
   (b) provides a new one
   (c) submits a new one
   (d) leaves your employment
   Answer: See Part 9. Withholding From Employees Wages, Income Tax Withholding, page 20/ (a) gives you a new one

Withholding From Employee's Wages

9. Withholding From Employee's Wages - Effective date of Form W-4
13. When you receive a new Form W-4 from an employee, do not ___ withholding for pay periods before the effective date of the new form.
    (a) correct
    (b) adjust
    (c) change
    (d) alter
    Answer: See Part 9. Withholding From Employees Wages, Income Tax Withholding, page 20/ (b) adjust

9. Withholding From Employee's Wages - Effective date of Form W-4
14. If an employee gives you a Form W-4 that replaces an existing Form W-4 begin withholding no later than the start of the first ___ ending on or after
    (a) pay period
    (b) quarter
    (c) payroll period
    (d) payment of wages
    Answer: See Part 9. Withholding From Employees Wages, Income Tax Withholding, page 20/ (c) payroll period

9. Withholding From Employee's Wages - Effective date of Form W-4
15. If an employee gives you a Form W-4 that replaces an existing Form W-4 begin withholding no later than the start of the first ___ ending on or after the ___ from the date you received the replacement Form W-4.
    (a) pay period, first week
    (b) quarter, fifth day
    (c) payroll period, 30th day
    (d) payment of wages, first quarter
    Answer: See Part 9. Withholding From Employees Wages, Income Tax Withholding, page 20/ (c) payroll period, 30th day

9. Withholding From Employee's Wages - Effective date of Form W-4
16. If an employee gives you a Form W-4 that replaces an existing Form W-4 begin withholding no later than the start of the first payroll period ending on or after the 30th day from the date you received the replacement Form W-4. For exceptions, see ***Exemption from federal income tax withholding, IRS review of requested Forms W-4,*** and ___ , later in this section.
    (a) ***replacement Forms W-4***
    (b) ***outdated Forms W-4***
    (c) ***obsolete Forms W-4***
    (d) ***invalid Forms W-4***
    Answer: See Part 9. Withholding From Employees Wages, Income Tax Withholding, page 20/(d***) invalid Forms W-4***

9. Withholding From Employee's Wages - Effective date of Form W-4

9. Withholding From Employee's Wages - !CAUTION!
17. A Form W-4 that makes a change for the next calendar year ___.
    (a) will not take effect in the current calendar year
    (b) shall not take effect in the current calendar year
    (c) shall take effect in the current calendar year
    (d) will take effect in the current calendar year
    Answer: See Part 9. Withholding From Employees Wages, Income Tax Withholding, page 20/ (a) will not take effect in the current calendar year

9. Withholding From Employee's Wages. Successor Employer. Page 20.

9. Withholding From Employee's Wages - Successor employer
18. If you are a successor employer (see *Successor employer*, later in this section), secure new Forms __ from the transferred employees unless the "Alternative Procedure" in section 5 of Revenue Procedure 2004-53 applies.
    (a) W-2
    (b) W-3
    (c) W-4
    (d) W-5
    Answer: See Part 9. Withholding From Employees Wages, Successor employer, page 20/ (c) W-4.

Note the reference to Revenue Procedure 2004-53, 2004-34 I.R.B. 320.
Available at ww.irs.gov/irb/2004-34_ar13.html.
Define [irb] = Internal Revenue Bulletin

9. Withholding From Employee's Wages - Successor employer (see Successor employer, later in this section).

19. If you are a successor employer (see *Successor employer*, later in this section) secure new Forms __ from the transferred employees unless the "Alternative Procedure" in section 5 of Revenue Procedure 2004-53 applies. See Revenue Procedure 2004-53, 2004-34 I.R.B. ___, available at *www.irs.gov/irb/2004-34_IRB/ar13.html*.
    (a) W-2, 318
    (b) W-3, 319
    (c) W-4, 320
    (d) W-5, 321
    Answer: See Part 9. Withholding From Employees Wages, Successor employer, page 20/ (c) W-4, 320

Withholding From Employee's Wages. Completing Form W-4

9. Withholding From Employee's Wages - Successor employer
20. The amount of any federal income tax withholding must be based on _____ status and withholding allowances.
    (a) the individual's
    (b) married
    (c) dependent
    (d) marital
    Answer: See Completing Form W-4, Part 9. Withholding From Employee's Wages, page 21 (d) marital

9. Withholding From Employee's Wages - Completing Form W-4

9. Withholding From Employee's Wages - Completing Form W-4
21. Your employees may not base their withholding amounts on a fixed dollar amount or ____.
    (a) estimated income
    (b) estimates
    (c) percentage
    (d) percent
    Answer: See Completing Form W-4, Part 9. Withholding From Employees Wages, pg 21/ (c) percentage

9. Withholding From Employee's Wages - Completing Form W-4
22. However, an employee may specify a dollar amount to be withheld in addition to the amount of withholding based on ___ and withholding allowances claimed on Form W-4.
    (a) deductions
    (b) percentage
    (c) filing status
    (d) dependent status
    Answer: See Completing Form W-4, Part 9. Withholding From Employees, page 21/ (c) filing status

9. Withholding From Employee's Wages - Completing Form W-4
23. Employees may claim fewer withholding allowances than they are entitled to claim. They may wish to claim fewer allowances to ___ they will have enough withholding or to offset the tax on other sources of taxable income not subject to withholding.
    (a) ensure
    (b) guarantee
    (c) provide
    (d) assure
    Answer: See (a) ensure, Completing Form W-4, Part 9. Withholding From Employees, page 21/ (a) ensure

9. Withholding From Employee's Wages - Completing Form W-4

9. Withholding From Employee's Wages - Completing Form W-4

24. Do not ___ any withholding or estimated tax payments from your employees in addition to withholding based on their Form W-4.
    (a) accept
    (b) collect
    (c) provide
    (d) assure
    Answer: See (a) ensure, Completing Form W-4, Part 9. Withholding From Employees, page 21/ (a) accept

9. Withholding From Employee's Wages - Completing Form W-4

25. Do not ___ any withholding or estimated tax payments from your employees in addition to withholding based on their Form W-4. If they require additional withholding, they should submit a new Form W-4 and, if necessary, pay estimated tax by filing Form ___. Estimated Tax for individuals, or
    (a) accept, 1040-ES
    (b) collect, 1045-EZ
    (c) provide, 1045-ES
    (d) assure, 1040-ES
    Answer: See (a) ensure, Completing Form W-4, Part 9. Withholding From Employees, page 21/ (a) accept, 1040-ES

9. Withholding From Employee's Wages - Completing Form W-4

26. Do not ___ any withholding or estimated tax payments from your employees in addition to withholding based on their Form W-4. If they require additional withholding, they should submit a new Form W-4 and, if necessary, pay estimated tax by filing Form ___. Estimated Tax for individuals, or by using the Electronic Federal Tax Payment System (EFTPS) to make ___ tax payments.
    (a) accept, 1040-ES, estimated
    (b) collect, 1045-EZ, your
    (c) provide, 1045-ES, additional
    (d) assure, 1040-ES, the necessary
    Answer: See (a) ensure, Completing Form W-4, Part 9. Withholding From Employees, page 21/ (a) accept, 1040-ES, estimated

Withholding From Employee's Wages
Exemption from Federal Income Tax Withholding

9. Withholding From Employee's Wages - Exemption from federal income tax withholding.
27. Generally, an employee may claim exemption from federal income tax withholding because he or she had no income tax liability last year and expects none this year. See the Form W-4 instructions for more information. However, the wages are still subject to social security and Medicate taxes. See also ___ , later in this section.
   (a) <u>IRS Exceptions</u>
   (b) <u>IRS Rule 2113</u>
   (c) <u>Invalid Forms W-4</u>
   (d) <u>Invalid Forms W-4b</u>
   Answer: See Part 9. Withholding From Employees, Exemption from federal income tax withholding, page 21/ (c) <u>Invalid Forms W-4</u>

9. Withholding From Employee's Wages - Exemption from federal income tax withholding.
28. A Form W-4 claiming exemption from withholding is effective when it is filed with the ___ and only for that calendar year.
   (a) IRS
   (b) employer
   (c) Treasury Department
   (d) employee
   Answer: See Part 9. Withholding From Employees, Exemption from federal income tax withholding, page 21/ (b) employer

9. Withholding From Employee's Wages - Exemption from federal income tax withholding.
29. To continue to be exempt from withholding in the next calendar year, an employee must give you a new Form W-4 by ___.
   (a) January 15
   (b) February 15
   (c) March 15
   (d) April 15
   Answer: See Part 9. Withholding From Employees, Exemption from federal income tax withholding, page 21/ See (b) February 15

9. Withholding From Employee's Wages - Exemption from federal income tax withholding.
30. If the employee does not give you an new Form W-4 by February 15, began withholding based upon the last Form W-4 for the employee that did not claim an exemption, or, if one was not filed, the withhold tax as if he or she is ___.
   (a) single with zero withholding allowances
   (b) single without withholding allowances
   (c) single with one withholding allowance
   (d) married with one withholding allowance
   Answer: See Part 9. Withholding From Employees, Exemption from federal income tax withholding page 21/ (a) single with zero withholding allowances

© Copyright 2013. All rights reserved. Notice: United States Copyright Laws and International Treaties prohibit unauthorized publication, reproduction, distribution of this Work. Unauthorized use of this copyright in any form, format, publication or document may result in severe civil and criminal penalties. Violations of this copyright are investigated by the United States Department of Justice and carry, upon conviction of fines up to $250,000 and five years confinement. This Work is protected by United States Copyright Laws and International Treaties. Do not Copy, do not reproduce, do not distribute.

Withholding From Employee's Wages
Exemption from Federal Income Tax Withholding

9. Withholding From Employee's Wages - Exemption from federal income tax withholding.

31. If the employee does not give you an new Form W-4 by February 15, began withholding based upon the last Form W-4 for the employee that did not claim an exemption, or, if one was not filed, the withhold tax as if he or she is ___. If the employee provides a new Form W-4 claiming exemption from withholding on ___ or later, you may
    (a) single with zero withholding allowances, February 16
    (b) single without withholding allowances, March 1
    (c) single with one withholding allowance, March 14
    (d) married with one withholding allowance, April 1
    Answer: See Part 9. Withholding From Employees, Exemption from federal income tax withholding page 21/ (a) single with zero withholding allowances, February 16

9. Withholding From Employee's Wages - Exemption from federal income tax withholding.

32. If the employee does not give you an new Form W-4 by February 15, began withholding based upon the last Form W-4 for the employee that did not claim an exemption, or, if one was not filed, the withhold tax as if he or she is ___. If the employee provides a new Form W-4 claiming exemption from withholding on ___ or later, you may apply it to ___ wages but do not refund any taxes already withheld.
    (a) single with zero withholding allowances, February 16, future
    (b) single without withholding allowances, March 1, current
    (c) single with one withholding allowance, March 14, monthly
    (d) married with one withholding allowance, April 1, quarterly
    Answer: See Part 9. Withholding From Employees, Exemption from federal income tax withholding page 21/ (a) single with zero withholding allowances, February 16, future

Withholding From Employee's Wages
Withholding income taxes of nonresident alien employees

Withholding income taxes on the wages of nonresident alien employees.

33. In general, you must withhold federal income taxes on the ___ of nonresident alien employees.
    (a) earnings
    (b) wages
    (c) income
    (d) supplementary
    Answer: See Part 9. Withholding From Employees, Exemption from federal income tax withholding page 21/ (b) wages

Withholding From Employee's Wages
Withholding income taxes of nonresident alien employees

9. Withholding From Employee's Wages Withholding income taxes on the wages of nonresident alien employees.

34. In general, you must withhold federal income taxes on the wages of ___. However, see Publication ___, Withholding Tax on Nonresident Aliens and Foreign Entities, for exceptions to this general rule.
    (a) resident alien employees, 514
    (b) nonresident alien employees, 515
    (c) all your employees, 516
    (d) all regular, statutory and any extraneous employees, 516
    Answer: See Withholding income taxes on the wages of nonresident alien employees, page 21 (b) nonresident alien employees, 515

9. Withholding From Employee's Wages - Withholding income taxes on the wages of nonresident alien employees.

35. In general, you must withhold federal income taxes on the wages of ___. However, see Publication ___, Withholding Tax on Nonresident Aliens and Foreign Entities, for exceptions to this general rule. Also, see section __ of Publication ___ (Circular A), Agricultural Employer's Tax Guide, for
    (a) resident alien employees, 514, 3, 50
    (b) nonresident alien employees, 515, 3, 51
    (c) all your employees, 516, 3, 52
    (d) all regular, statutory and any extraneous employees, 517, 4, 52
    Answer: See Withholding income taxes on the wages of nonresident alien employees, page 21 (b) nonresident alien employees, 515, 3, 51

9. Withholding From Employee's Wages - Withholding income taxes on the wages of nonresident alien employees.

36. In general, you must withhold federal income taxes on the wages of ___. However, see Publication ___, Withholding Tax on Nonresident Aliens and Foreign Entities, for exceptions to this general rule. Also, see section __ of Publication ___ (Circular A), Agricultural Employer's Tax Guide, for ___ on H-2A visa workers
    (a) resident alien employees, 514, 3, 50, information
    (b) nonresident alien employees, 515, 3, 51, guidance
    (c) all your employees, 516, 3, 52, information, guidance
    (d) all regular, statutory and any extraneous employees, 517, 4, 52
    Answer: See Withholding income taxes on the wages of nonresident alien employees, page 21 (b) nonresident alien employees, 515, 3, 51, guidance

© Copyright 2013. All rights reserved. Notice: United States Copyright Laws and International Treaties prohibit unauthorized publication, reproduction, distribution of this Work. Unauthorized use of this copyright in any form, format, publication or document may result in severe civil and criminal penalties. Violations of this copyright are investigated by the United States Department of Justice and carry, upon conviction of fines up to $250,000 and five years confinement. This Work is protected by United States Copyright Laws and International Treaties. Do not Copy, do not reproduce, do not distribute.

Withholding From Employee's Wages
Withholding income taxes of nonresident alien employees

9. Withholding From Employee's Wages - Withholding income taxes on the wages of nonresident alien employees.

37. For 2013, apply the ___ discussed below to figure the amount of income to withhold from the wages of nonresident employees ___ services within the United States.
    (a) procedure, performing
    (b) steps, engaged in
    (c) method, engaged in
    (d) rules, work or
    Answer: See Withholding income taxes on the wages of nonresident alien employees, page 21 (a) procedure, performing

9. Withholding From Employee's Wages - Withholding income taxes on the wages of nonresident alien employees.

38. TIP. Nonresident alien students from India and ___ apprentices from India are not subject to this procedure.
    (a) construction
    (b) engineering
    (c) electrical
    (d) business
    Answer: See Withholding income taxes on the wages of nonresident alien employees, page 21 (d) business

9. Withholding From Employee's Wages - Withholding income taxes on the wages of nonresident alien employees.

39. For 2013, apply the procedure discussed below to ___ the amount of income tax to withhold from the wages of nonresident alien employees performing services within the United States.
    (a) determine
    (b) compute
    (c) establish
    (d) figure
    Answer: See Withholding adjustment for nonresident aliens. Page 21/ (d) figure

9. Withholding From Employee's Wages - Withholding income taxes on the wages of nonresident alien employees.

40. **Instructions**. To figure how much income tax to withhold from the wages paid to nonresident alien employee ___ in the United States, use the following steps.
    (a) working
    (b) employed
    (c) performing services
    (d) employed by you
    Answer: See Instructions, Withholding adjustment for nonresident aliens. Withholding adjustment for nonresident alien employees. Page 21/ (c) performing services

© Copyright 2013. All rights reserved. Notice: United States Copyright Laws and International Treaties prohibit unauthorized publication, reproduction, distribution of this Work. Unauthorized use of this copyright in any form, format, publication or document may result in severe civil and criminal penalties. Violations of this copyright are investigated by the United States Department of Justice and carry, upon conviction of fines up to $250,000 and five years confinement. This Work is protected by United States Copyright Laws and International Treaties. Do not Copy, do not reproduce, do not distribute.

Withholding From Employee's Wages
Withholding income taxes of nonresident alien employees

9. Withholding From Employee's Wages - Withholding income taxes on the wages of nonresident alien employees.
41. *Step 1*. Add to the wages paid to the nonresident alien employee for the payroll period the amount shown in the ____ payroll period.
    (a)   following chart for the applicable
    (b)   in the table below
    (c)   in the chart below for the applicable
    (d)   chart for the corresponding
Answer: See Instructions, Step 1. Withholding adjustment for nonresident aliens. Withholding From Employees. Page 21/ (c) in the chart below for the applicable

9. Withholding From Employee's Wages - Withholding income taxes on the wages of nonresident alien employees.
42. **Amount to Add to the Nonresident Alien Employee's Wages for Calculating Income Tax Withholding Only.** See page 21, 2013 IRS Circular E, Publication 15.

          Payroll Period   **Add Additional**
Solve: From page 21 provide correct amount for each:
(a)   Weekly $ _____
(b)   Biweekly $ _____
(c)   Semimonthly $ _____
(d)   Monthly $ _____
(e)   Quarterly $ _____
(f)   Semiannually $ _____
(g)   Annually $ _____
(h)   Daily or Miscellaneous
        (each day of the payroll period) $ _____

Answer: See Instructions, Step 1. Withholding adjustment for nonresident aliens. Withholding From Employees. Page 21/ (a) following chart lists the applicable amounts. From the list, enter the correct amount.

$8.50
$84.60
$91.70
$183.30
$550.00
$1100.00
$2200.00

Withholding From Employee's Wages
Withholding income taxes of nonresident alien employees

9. Withholding From Employee's Wages - Withholding income taxes on the wages of nonresident alien employees.

43. *Step 2*. Use the amount figured in Step 1 and the number of withholding allowances claimed (generally, limited to ___) to figure income tax withholding.
    (a) zero allowances
    (b) one allowance
    (c) zero
    (d) one
    Answer: See Step 2, Withholding adjustment for nonresident aliens, Withholding From Employees. Page 21/ (b) one allowance

9. Withholding From Employee's Wages - Withholding income taxes on the wages of nonresident alien employees.

44. Determine the value of withholding allowances by ___ the number claimed by the appropriate amount from *Table 5 Percentage Method—2013 Amount for One Withholding Allowance* shown on page 42.
    (a) the employee for
    (b) adding
    (c) multiplying
    (d) subtracting
    Answer: See Step 2. Withholding adjustment for nonresident aliens, Withholding From Employees, page 21/ (c) multiplying

9. Withholding From Employee's Wages - Withholding income taxes on the wages of nonresident alien employees.

45. Determine the value of withholding allowances by ___ the number claimed by the appropriate amount from *Table 5 Percentage Method—2013 Amount for One Withholding Allowance* shown on page 42. If you are using the Percentage Method Tables for Income Tax Withholding, provided on pages ___-___, use the amount figured in Step 1 by the value of withholding allowances and use that reduced amount to figure the income tax withholding.
    (a) the employee for, 42, 43
    (b) adding, 43, 44
    (c) multiplying, 44, 45
    (d) subtracting, 45, 46
    Answer: See Step 2. Withholding adjustment for nonresident aliens, Withholding From Employees, page 21/ (c) multiplying, 44, 45

Withholding From Employee's Wages
Withholding income taxes of nonresident alien employees

9. Withholding From Employee's Wages - Withholding income taxes on the wages of nonresident alien employees.

46. Determine the value of withholding allowances by multiplying the number claimed by the appropriate amount from *Table 5 Percentage Method—2013 Amount for* One Withholding *Allowance* shown on page 42. If you are using the Percentage Method Tables for Income Tax Withholding, provided on pages 44-45, use the amount figured in Step 1 by the value of withholding allowances and use that reduced amount to figure the income tax withholding.
    If you are using the *Wage Bracket Method for Income Tax Withholding*, provided on pages 46-65, use the amount figured Step 1 and the number of withholding allowances to ___ income tax withholding.
    (a) figure
    (b) calculate
    (c) determine
    (d) compute
    Answer: See Section 9. Withholding From Employee's Wages-Withholding income taxes of nonresident alien employees. Step 2, Page 21/ (a) figure

9. Withholding From Employee's Wages - Withholding income taxes on the wages of nonresident alien employees.

47. The amounts added under the charts above are added to wages solely for ___ income tax withholding on the wages of the nonresident alien employee.
    (a) figuring
    (b) calculating
    (c) determining
    (d) computing
    Answer: See Step 2, Withholding adjustment for nonresident aliens, Part 9. Withholding From Employees, page 21/ (b) calculating

9. Withholding From Employee's Wages - Withholding income taxes on the wages of nonresident alien employees.

48. The amounts from the chart above ___ in any box on the employee's Form W-2 and do not increase the income tax liability of the employee.
    (a) shall not be included
    (b) should not be included
    (c) shall be included
    (d) should be included
    Answer: See Step 2. Withholding adjustment for nonresident aliens, Withholding From Employees, page 21/ (b) should not be included

Withholding From Employee's Wages
Withholding income taxes of nonresident alien employees

9. Withholding From Employee's Wages - Withholding income taxes on the wages of nonresident alien employees.

49. Also, these chart amounts ___ the social security, Medicare, or FUTA tax liability of the ___ or the ___.
    (a) do not increase, employer, employee
    (b) increase, employee, employer
    (c) should not, employer, employee
    (d) will not, employer, employee
    Answer: See Step 2, Withholding adjustment for nonresident aliens, Withholding From Employees, page 21/ (a) do not increase, employer, employee

9. Withholding From Employee's Wages - Withholding income taxes on the wages of nonresident alien employees.

50. This ___ only applies to nonresident alien employees who have wages subject to income tax withholding.
    (a) rule
    (b) requirement
    (c) section
    (d) procedure
    Answer: See Step 2, Withholding adjustment for nonresident aliens, Withholding From Employees, page 22/ (d) procedure

9. Withholding From Employee's Wages - Withholding income taxes on the wages of nonresident alien employees.

51. **IRS Example Page 22.** An Employer using the percentage method of withholding pays wages of $500 for a biweekly payroll period to a married nonresident alien employee. The nonresident alien has properly completed Form __, entering the marital status as "single" with one withholding allowance and indication status as a nonresident alien on line 6 of Form __,
    (a) W-2, W-2
    (b) W-2, W-3
    (c) W-3, W-4
    (d) W-4, W-4
    Answer: See Withholding adjustment for nonresident aliens, Withholding From Employees, page 22/ (d) W-4, W-4, Example

Withholding From Employee's Wages
Withholding income taxes of nonresident alien employees

9. Withholding From Employee's Wages - Withholding income taxes on the wages of nonresident alien employees.

52. **IRS Example Page 22.** An Employer using the percentage method of withholding pays wages of $500 for a biweekly payroll period to a married nonresident alien employee. The nonresident alien has properly completed Form W-4, entering the marital status as "single" with one withholding allowance and indication status as a nonresident alien on line 6 of Form W-4, (see *Nonresident alien employee's Form W-4*, later in this section). The employer determines the wages to be used in the withholding tables by adding to the $500 amount of $___ from the chart under *Step 1* ($___ total).
    (a) 8.50, 508.50
    (b) 42.30, 542.30
    (c) 84.60, 584.60
    (d) 91.70, 591.70
    Answer: See Withholding adjustment for nonresident aliens, Withholding From Employees, page 22/ (c) 84.60, 584.60

9. Withholding From Employee's Wages - Withholding income taxes on the wages of nonresident alien employees.

53. **IRS Example Page 22.** An Employer using the percentage method of withholding pays wages of $500 for a biweekly payroll period to a married nonresident alien employee. The nonresident alien has properly completed Form W-4, entering the marital status as "single" with one withholding allowance and indication status as a nonresident alien on line 6 of Form W-4, (see *Nonresident alien employee's Form W-4*, later in this section). The employer determines the wages to be used in the withholding tables by adding to the $500 amount of $___ from the chart under *Step 1* ($___ total).
    (a) 8.50, 508.50
    (b) 42.30, 542.30
    (c) 84.60, 584.60
    (d) 91.70, 591.70
    Answer: See Withholding adjustment for nonresident aliens, Withholding From Employees, page 22/ (c) 84.60, 584.60

© Copyright 2013. All rights reserved. Notice: United States Copyright Laws and International Treaties prohibit unauthorized publication, reproduction, distribution of this Work. Unauthorized use of this copyright in any form, format, publication or document may result in severe civil and criminal penalties. Violations of this copyright are investigated by the United States Department of Justice and carry, upon conviction of fines up to $250,000 and five years confinement. This Work is protected by United States Copyright Laws and International Treaties. Do not Copy, do not reproduce, do not distribute.

A Ficus Tree Publishing Educational-Technical Publications

Section 9. Withholding From Employee's Wages-Withholding income taxes of nonresident alien employees. Page 22

9. Withholding From Employee's Wages - Withholding income taxes on the wages of nonresident alien employees.

54. **IRS Example Page 22.** An Employer using the percentage method of withholding pays wages of $500 for a biweekly payroll period to a married nonresident alien employee. The nonresident alien has properly completed Form W-4, entering the marital status as "single" with one withholding allowance and indication status as a nonresident alien on line 6 of Form W-4, (see *Nonresident alien employee's Form W-4*, later in this section). The employer determines the wages to be used in the withholding tables by adding to the $500 amount of $84.50 from the chart under *Step 1* ($584.60 total). The employer then applies the ___ tables to determine the income tax withholding for nonresident aliens (see *Step 2*).
    (a) correct
    (b) applicable
    (c) 2013 tax
    (d) IRS tax
    Answer: See Withholding adjustment for nonresident aliens, Withholding From Employees, page 22/ (b) applicable

9. Withholding From Employee's Wages - Withholding income taxes on the wages of nonresident alien employees.

55. **IRS Example Page 22.** An Employer using the percentage method of withholding pays wages of $500 for a biweekly payroll period to a married nonresident alien employee. The nonresident alien has properly completed Form W-4, entering the marital status as "single" with one withholding allowance and indication status as a nonresident alien on line 6 of Form W-4, (see *Nonresident alien employee's Form W-4*, later in this section). The employer determines the wages to be used in the withholding tables by adding to the $500 amount of $84.50 from the chart under *Step 1* ($584.60 total). The employer then applies the ___ tables to determine the income tax withholding for nonresident aliens (see *Step 2*). Reminder: If you use the Percentage Method Tables for Income Tax Withholding, ___ the amount figured in Step 1 by the ___ of the withholding allowances and use that reduced amount to figure income tax withholding.
    (a) correct, increase, value
    (b) applicable, reduce, value
    (c) 2013 tax, reduce, amount
    (d) IRS tax, increase, value
    Answer: See Withholding adjustment for nonresident aliens, Withholding From Employees, page 22/ (b) applicable, reduce, value

Withholding From Employee's Wages
Withholding income taxes of nonresident alien employees

9. Withholding From Employee's Wages - Withholding income taxes on the wages of nonresident alien employees.
56.   **IRS Example Page 22.** The $84.60 added to the wages for calculating income tax withholding is not reported on Form W- __, and
- (a) 1
- (b) 2
- (c) 3
- (d) 4

Answer: See Withholding adjustment for nonresident aliens, Withholding From Employees, page 22/ (b) 2

9. Withholding From Employee's Wages - Withholding income taxes on the wages of nonresident alien employees.
57.   **IRS Example Page 22.** The $84.60 added to the wages for calculating income tax withholding is not reported on Form W- __, and does not increase the tax ___ of the employee.
- (a) 1, rate
- (b) 2, liability
- (c) 3, burden
- (d) 4, responsibility

Answer: See Withholding adjustment for nonresident aliens, Withholding From Employees, page 22/ (b) 2, liability

9. Withholding From Employee's Wages - Withholding income taxes on the wages of nonresident alien employees.
58.   **IRS Example Page 22.** The $84.60 added to the wages for calculating income tax withholding is not reported on Form W- __, and does not increase the tax ___ of the employee. The $___ added amount also does not affect the social security tax, Medicare tax, or FUTA tax liability of the employer or the employee.
- (a) 1, rate, 42.30
- (b) 2, liability, 84.60
- (c) 3, burden, 91.70
- (d) 4, responsibility, 183.30

Answer: See Withholding adjustment for nonresident aliens, Withholding From Employees, page 22/ (b) 2, liability, 84.60

Withholding income taxes of nonresident alien employees
Supplemental wage payment

9. Withholding From Employee's Wages - Supplemental wage payment.
59. Supplemental wage payment. This procedure for determining the amount of income tax withholding does not apply to a supplemental wage payment (see section ___) if
  (a) 7
  (b) 8
  (c) 9
  (d) 10
  Answer: See Withholding From Employees, page 22/ (a) 7

9. Withholding From Employee's Wages - Supplemental wage payment.
60. Supplemental wage payment. This procedure for determining the amount of income tax withholding does not apply to a supplemental wage payment (see *section* ___) if the ___% mandatory flat rate withholding applies or if the
  (a) 7, 39.6
  (b) 8, 39.7
  (c) 9, 39.8
  (d) 10, 39.9
  Answer: See Withholding From Employees, page 22/ (a) 7, 39.6

9. Withholding From Employee's Wages - Supplemental wage payment.
61. Supplemental wage payment. This procedure for determining the amount of income tax withholding does not apply to a supplemental wage payment (see *section* ___) if the ___% mandatory flat rate withholding applies or if the ___% optional flat rate withholding applies is being used to calculate income tax withholding on the supplemental wage payment.
  (a) 7, 39.6, 25
  (b) 8, 39.7, 28
  (c) 9, 39.8, 31
  (d) 10, 39.9, 33
  Answer: See Withholding From Employees, page 22/ (a) 7, 39.6, 25

A Ficus Tree Publishing Quick Notes Page.

DU VALL'S TEST'S™
Instructors Manual Study Guide Series United States Tax Code
IRS Publication 15 Circular E, Employer's Tax Guide Tax Year 2013
Tax Test 15E-S9-2[Multiple-Choice Questions With Answers]

Withholding From Employee's Wages
Nonresident alien employee's Form W-4

9. Withholding From Employee's Wages - Nonresident alien employee's Form W-4.
1. When completing Forms W-4, nonresident aliens are required to:
   • Not claim exemption from income tax withholding.
   • Request withholding as if they are single, regardless of their actual marital status.
   • Claim ___ (if the nonresident alien is a resident of Canada, Mexico, or South Korea, or a student
      business apprentice from India) he or she may
   (a)   no allowances
   (b)   only one allowance
   (c)   more than four allowances
   (d)   more than ten allowances
   Answer: See Withholding From Employees, page 22/ (b) only one allowance

9. Withholding From Employee's Wages - Nonresident alien employee's Form W-4.
2. When completing Forms W-4, nonresident aliens are required to:
   • Not claim exemption from income tax withholding.
   • Request withholding as if they are single, regardless of their actual marital status.
   • Claim ___ (if the nonresident alien is a resident of Canada, Mexico, or South Korea, or a student
      business apprentice from India) he or she may claim more than one allowance) and
   • Write "Nonresident Alien" or "NRA" above the dotted line on line ___ of Form W-4.
   (a)   no allowances, 5
   (b)   only one allowance, 6
   (c)   more than four allowances, 7
   (d)   more than ten allowances, 8
   Answer: See Withholding From Employees, page 22/ (b) only one allowance, 6

Withholding From Employee's Wages
Nonresident alien employee's Form W-4

9. Withholding From Employee's Wages - Nonresident alien employee's Form W-4.
3. Nonresident alien employee's Form W-4. When completing Forms W-4, nonresident aliens are required to:
   • Not claim exemption from income tax withholding.
   • Request withholding as if they are single, regardless of their actual marital status.
   • Claim only one allowance (if the nonresident alien is a resident of Canada, Mexico ___, he or she may claim more than one allowance), and
   • Write "Nonresident Alien" or "NRA" above the dotted line on line 6 of Form W-4.
   (a) South Korea
   (b) Japan
   (c) the Philippines
   (d) France
   Answer: See Withholding From Employees, page 22/ (a) South Korea

9. Withholding From Employee's Wages - Nonresident alien employee's Form W-4.
4. As defined and used in the 2013 IRS (Circular E) Employer's Tax Guide the abbreviation "NRA" means.
   (a) National Rifle Association
   (b) National Republican Association
   (c) National Realtor's Association
   (d) Nonresident Alien
   Answer: See Withholding From Employee's, page 22/ (d) Nonresident Alien

9. Withholding From Employee's Wages - Nonresident alien employee's Form W-4.
5. If you maintain an electronic Form W-4 system, you should provide a ___ for nonresident aliens to enter nonresident alien status
   (a) space
   (b) line
   (c) column
   (d) field
   Answer: See Withholding From Employee's, page 22/ (d) field

9. Withholding From Employee's Wages - Nonresident alien employee's Form W-4.
6. If you maintain an electronic Form W-4 system, you should provide a ___ for nonresident aliens to enter nonresident alien status in lieu of writing "Nonresident Alien" or "NRA" above the dotted line on line ___.
   (a) space, 3
   (b) line, 4
   (c) column, 5
   (d) field, 6
   Answer: See Withholding From Employee's, page 22/ (d) field, 6

© Copyright 2013. All rights reserved. Notice: United States Copyright Laws and International Treaties prohibit unauthorized publication, reproduction, distribution of this Work. Unauthorized use of this copyright in any form, format, publication or document may result in severe civil and criminal penalties. Violations of this copyright are investigated by the United States Department of Justice and carry, upon conviction of fines up to $250,000 and five years confinement. This Work is protected by United States Copyright Laws and International Treaties. Do not Copy, do not reproduce, do not distribute.

Withholding From Employee's Wages. TIP

9. Withholding From Employee's Wages - TIP Page 22

7. A nonresident alien may request additional withholding at his or her option for ___, although
   (a) tax purposes
   (b) a tax cushion
   (c) other purposes
   (d) personal reasons
   Answer: See TIP, Withholding From Employee's, page 22/ (c) other purposes, TIP, Nonresident alien employee's Form W-4

9. Withholding From Employee's Wages - TIP Page 22

8. A nonresident alien may request additional withholding at his or her option for ___, although such additions should not be necessary for withholding to ___ federal income tax liability related to employment.
   (a) tax purposes, meet
   (b) a tax cushion, provide
   (c) other purposes, cover
   (d) personal reasons, cover
   Answer: See TIP, Withholding From Employee's, page 22/ (c) other purposes, cover

9. Withholding From Employee's Wages - TIP Page 22

9. A nonresident alien may request additional withholding at his or her option for ___, although such additions should not be necessary for withholding to ___ federal income tax liability related to employment.
   (a) tax purposes, meet
   (b) a tax cushion, provide
   (c) other purposes, cover
   (d) personal reasons, cover
   Answer: See TIP, Withholding From Employee's, page 22/ (c) other purposes, cover

Withholding From Employee's Wages. TIP. Form 8233.

9. Withholding From Employee's Wages - Form 8233

10. If a nonresident alien employee claims a ___ exemption from withholding, the employee must submit Form 8233,
    (a) alien treaty
    (b) Treasury Department treaty
    (c) International
    (d) tax treaty
    Answer: See Withholding From Employees, page 22/ (d) tax treaty

Withholding From Employee's Wages. TIP. Form 8233

9. Withholding From Employee's Wages - Form 8233
11. If a nonresident alien employee claims a ___ exemption from withholding, the employee must submit Form 8233, Exemption from withholding on ___ for Independent (and Certain Dependent) Personal Services of a Nonresident Alien Individual, with respect to the income exempt under the treaty, instead of Form W-4.
    (a) alien treaty, Income
    (b) Treasury Department treaty, Income
    (c) International, Wages
    (d) tax treaty, Compensation
    Answer: See Withholding From Employees, page 22/ (d) tax treaty, Compensation

9. Withholding From Employee's Wages - Form 8233
12. If a nonresident alien employee claims a ___ exemption from withholding, the employee must submit Form 8233, Exemption from withholding on ___ for Independent (and Certain Dependent) Personal Services of a Nonresident Alien Individual, with respect to the income exempt under the treaty, instead of Form W-4. See Publication ___ for details.
    (a) alien treaty, Income, 512
    (b) Treasury Department treaty, Income, 513
    (c) International, Wages, 514
    (d) tax treaty, Compensation, 515
    Answer: See Withholding From Employees, page 22/ (d) tax treaty, Compensation, 515

Withholding From Employee's Wages
IRS review of requested Forms W-4

9. Withholding From Employee's Wages - IRS review of requested Forms W-4.
13. When requested by the IRS, you must ___ original Forms W-4 available for inspection by an IRS employee.
    (a) make
    (b) provide
    (c) copy
    (d) present
    Answer: See Withholding From Employees. IRS review of requested Forms W-4. Page 22/ (a) make

Withholding From Employee's Wages
IRS review of requested Forms W-4

9. Withholding From Employee's Wages - IRS review of requested Forms W-4.
14. When requested by the IRS, you must ___ original Forms W-4 available for inspection by an IRS ___.
    (a) make, employee
    (b) provide, agent
    (c) copy, inspector
    (d) present, auditor
    Answer: See Withholding From Employees. IRS review of requested Forms W-4. Page 22/ (a) make, employee

9. Withholding From Employee's Wages - IRS review of requested Forms W-4.
15. When requested by the IRS, you must ___ original Forms W-4 available for inspection by an IRS ___. You may also be ___ to send certain Forms W-4 to the IRS.
    (a) make, employee, directed
    (b) provide, agent, required
    (c) copy, inspector, instructed
    (d) present, auditor, required
    Answer: See Withholding From Employees. IRS review of requested Forms W-4. Page 22/ (a) make, employee, directed

9. Withholding From Employee's Wages - IRS review of requested Forms W-4.
16. When requested by the IRS, you must ___ original Forms W-4 available for inspection by an IRS ___. You may also be ___ to send certain Forms W-4 to the IRS. You may receive a ___ from the IRS requiring you to submit a copy of Form W-4 for one or more of your named employees.
    (a) make, employee, directed, notice
    (b) provide, agent, required, instruction
    (c) copy, inspector, instructed, directive
    (d) present, auditor, required, order
    Answer: See Withholding From Employees. IRS review of requested Forms W-4. Page 22/(a) make, employee, directed, notice

Withholding From Employee's Wages
IRS review of requested Forms W-4

9. Withholding From Employee's Wages - IRS review of requested Forms W-4.
17. When requested by the IRS, you must make original Forms W-4 available for inspection by an IRS employee. You may also be directed to send certain Forms W-4 to the IRS. You may receive a notice from the IRS requiring you to submit a copy of Form W-4 for one or more of your named employees. Send the requested copy or copies of Form W-4 to the IRS at the address ___ directed by the notice.
   (a) provided
   (b) provided and in the manner
   (c) self addressed envelope
   (d) of the local IRS auditor
   Answer: See Withholding From Employees. IRS review of requested Forms W-4. Page 22/ (b) provided and in the manner

9. Withholding From Employee's Wages - IRS review of requested Forms W-4.
18. When requested by the IRS, you must make original Forms W-4 available for inspection by an IRS employee. You may also be directed to send certain Forms W-4 to the IRS. You may receive a notice from the IRS requiring you to submit a copy of Form W-4 for one or more of your named employees. Send the requested copy or copies of Form W-4 to the IRS at the address provided and in the manner directed by the notice. The IRS may also require you to submit copies of Form W-4 to the IRS as directed by a ___ procedure or notice published in the Internal Revenue Bulletin.
   (a) audit
   (b) auditing
   (c) revenue
   (d) investigative
   Answer: See Withholding From Employees. IRS review of requested Forms W-4. Page 22/ (c) revenue

9. Withholding From Employee's Wages - IRS review of requested Forms W-4.
19. When requested by the IRS, you must make original Forms W-4 available for inspection by an IRS employee. You may also be directed to send certain Forms W-4 to the IRS. You may receive a notice from the IRS requiring you to submit a copy of Form W-4 for one or more of your named employees. Send the requested copy or copies of Form W-4 to the IRS at the address provided and in the manner directed by the notice. The IRS may also require you to submit copies of Form W-4 to the IRS as directed by a revenue procedure or notice published in the Internal Revenue Bulletin. When we refer to Form W-4, the same rules apply to Formulario W-4(SP), its ___ translation.
   (a) business
   (b) International
   (c) Latin
   (d) Spanish
   Answer: See Withholding From Employees. IRS review of requested Forms W-4. Page 22/ (d) Spanish

Withholding From Employee's Wages
IRS review of requested Forms W-4

9. Withholding From Employee's Wages - IRS review of requested Forms W-4.
20. After submitting a copy of a requested Form W-4 to the IRS, continue to withhold federal income tax based on that Form W-4 if it is ___
    (a) valid
    (b) current
    (c) up to date
    (d) in compliance to IRS law
    Answer: See Withholding From Employees. IRS review of requested Forms W-4. Page 22/ (a) valid

9. Withholding From Employee's Wages - IRS review of requested Forms W-4.
21. After submitting a copy of a requested Form W-4 to the IRS, continue to withhold federal income tax based on that Form W-4 if it is ___ (see *Invalid Forms W-4*, later in this section). However, if the IRS later notifies you ___ the employee is not entitled to claim exemption from withholding or a claimed ___ of withholding allowances, withhold
    (a) valid, in writing, number
    (b) current, certified letter, deduction
    (c) up to date, certified, dependent
    (d) in compliance to IRS law, in writing, number
    Answer: See Withholding From Employees. IRS review of requested Forms W-4. Page 22/ (a) valid, in writing, number

9. Withholding From Employee's Wages - IRS review of requested Forms W-4.
22. After submitting a copy of a requested Form W-4 to the IRS, continue to withhold federal income tax based on that Form W-4 if it is valid (see *Invalid Forms W-4*, later in this section). However, if the IRS later notifies you in writing the employee is not entitled to claim exemption from withholding or a claimed number of withholding allowances, withhold federal income tax based on the effective date, marital status, and maximum number of withholding allowances specified in the ___
    (a) letter
    (b) notice
    (c) rejection
    (d) correspondence
    Answer: See Withholding From Employees. IRS review of requested Forms W-4. Page 22/ (b) notice

Withholding From Employee's Wages
IRS review of requested Forms W-4

9. Withholding From Employee's Wages - IRS review of requested Forms W-4.

23. After submitting a copy of a requested Form W-4 to the IRS, continue to withhold federal income tax based on that Form W-4 if it is valid (see *Invalid Forms W-4*, later in this section). However, if the IRS later notifies you in writing the employee is not entitled to claim exemption from withholding or a claimed number of withholding allowances, withhold federal income tax based on the effective date, marital status, and maximum number of withholding allowances specified in the ___ (commonly referred to as a "___").
    (a) letter, formal rejection
    (b) notice, lock-in letter
    (c) rejection, IRS rejection
    (d) correspondence, IRS denial letter
    Answer: See Withholding From Employees. IRS review of requested Forms W-4. Page 22/ (b) notice, lock-in letter

Withholding From Employee's Wages. Initial lock-in letter

9. Withholding From Employee's Wages - Initial lock-in letter.

24. The IRS also uses information reported on Form ___ to identify employees with withholding compliance problems.
    (a) W-2
    (b) W-3
    (c) W-4
    (d) W-5
    Answer: See Withholding From Employees. Initial lock-in letter. Page 22/ (a) W-2

9. Withholding From Employee's Wages - Initial lock-in letter.

25. The IRS also uses information reported on Form ___ to identify employees with withholding compliance problems. In some cases, if a ___ under-withholding problem is found to exist for a particular employee, the IRS may issue
    (a) W-2, serious
    (b) W-3, critical
    (c) W-4, intentional
    (d) W-5, willful
    Answer: See Withholding From Employees. Initial lock-in letter. Page 22/ (a) W-2, serious

Withholding From Employee's Wages. Initial lock-in letter

9. Withholding From Employee's Wages - Initial lock-in letter.
26. The IRS also uses information reported on Form ___ to identify employees with withholding compliance problems. In some cases, if a ___ under-withholding problem is found to exist for a particular employee, the IRS may issue a lock-in letter to the employer ___ the maximum number of withholding allowances and marital status permitted for a specific employee.
    (a) W-2, serious, specifying
    (b) W-3, critical, stating
    (c) W-4, intentional, mandating
    (d) W-5, willful, mandating
    Answer: See Withholding From Employees. Initial lock-in letter. Page 22/ (a) W-2, serious, specifying

9. Withholding From Employee's Wages - Initial lock-in letter.
27. The IRS also uses information reported on Form W-2 to identify employees with withholding compliance problems. In some cases, if a serious under-withholding problem is found to exist for a particular employee, the IRS may issue a lock-in letter to the employer specifying the maximum number of withholding allowances and marital status permitted for a specific employee. You must furnish this notice to the employee within ___ business days of receipt if the employee is employed by you as of the date of the notice.
    (a) 5
    (b) 10
    (c) 15
    (d) 30
    Answer: See Withholding From Employees. Initial lock-in letter. Page 22/ (b) 10

9. Withholding From Employee's Wages - Initial lock-in letter.
28. The IRS also uses information reported on Form W-2 to identify employees with withholding compliance problems. In some cases, if a serious under-withholding problem is found to exist for a particular employee, the IRS may issue a lock-in letter to the employer specifying the maximum number of withholding allowances and marital status permitted for a specific employee. You must furnish this notice to the employee within ___ business days of receipt if the employee is employed by you as of the date of the notice. Begin withholding based on the notice of the date ___ in the notice.
    (a) 5, stated
    (b) 10, specified
    (c) 15, given
    (d) 30, provided
    Answer: See Withholding From Employees. Initial lock-in letter. Page 22/ (b) 10, specified

Withholding From Employee's Wages
Employee not performing services

9. Withholding From Employee's Wages - Employee not performing services.
29. If you receive a notice for an employee who is not performing services for you, you must ___ and withhold based on the notice if any of the following apply.
    (a)   notify the IRS immediately
    (b)   locate and furnish the notice to the employee
    (c)   still furnish the notice to the employee
    (d)   shall furnish the notice to the employee
Answer: See Withholding From Employees. Initial lock-in letter. Page 22/ (c) still furnish the notice to the employee

9. Withholding From Employee's Wages - Employee not performing services.
30. If you receive a notice for an employee who is not performing services for you, you must still furnish the notice to the employee and withhold based on the notice if any of the following apply.
• You are paying wages for the employee's ___ services and the wages are subject to income tax withholding on or after the date specified in the notice.
    (a)   past
    (b)   completed
    (c)   previous
    (d)   prior
Answer: See Withholding From Employees. Initial lock-in letter. Page 22/ (d) prior

9. Withholding From Employee's Wages - Employee not performing services.
31. If you receive a notice for an employee who is not performing services for you, you must still furnish the notice to the employee and withhold based on the notice if any of the following apply.
• You are paying wages for the employee's ___ services and the wages are subject to income tax withholding on or after the date specified in the notice.
• You reasonably expect the employee to resume services within ___ months of the date of service.
    (a)   past, 3
    (b)   completed, 6
    (c)   previous, 9
    (d)   prior, 12
Answer: See Withholding From Employees. Initial lock-in letter. Page 22/ (d) prior, 12

Withholding From Employee's Wages
Employee not performing services

9. Withholding From Employee's Wages - Employee not performing services.
32. If you receive a notice for an employee who is not performing services for you, you must still furnish the notice to the employee and withhold based on the notice if any of the following apply.
   - You are paying wages for the employee's ___ services and the wages are subject to income tax withholding on or after the date specified in the notice.
   - You reasonably expect the employee to resume services within ___ months of the date of service.
   - The employee is on leave of absence that does not exceed ___ months or the employee has a right reemployment after the leave of absence.
   (a) past, 3, 6
   (b) completed, 6, 9
   (c) previous, 9, 12
   (d) prior, 12, 12
   Answer: See Withholding From Employees. Initial lock-in letter. Page 22/ (d) prior, 12, 12

Withholding From Employee's Wages
Termination and re-hire of employees

9. Withholding From Employee's Wages - Termination and re-hire of employees.
33. If you must furnish and withhold based on the notice and the employment relationship is ___ after the date of the notice, you must continue to withhold based on the notice if you continue to pay any wages subject to income tax withholding.
   (a) terminated
   (b) discharged
   (c) laid-off
   (d) fired
   Answer: See Withholding From Employees. Termination and re-hire of employee. Page 22/ (a) terminated

9. Withholding From Employee's Wages - Termination and re-hire of employees.
34. If you must furnish and withhold based on the notice and the employment relationship is ___ after the date of the notice, you must continue to withhold based on the notice if you continue to pay any wages subject to income tax withholding. You must also withhold based on the notice or ___ notice if the employee resumes the employment relationship with you within ___ months after the termination of the employment relationship.
   (a) terminated, modification, 12
   (b) discharged, rehire, 9
   (c) laid-off, re-employment, 6
   (d) fired, rehire, 3
   Answer: See Withholding From Employees. Termination and re-hire of employee. Pages 22 and 23/ (a) terminated, modification, 12

Withholding From Employee's Wages. Modification notice

9. Withholding From Employee's Wages - Modification notice.

35. After issuing the notice specifying the maximum number of withholding allowances and marital status permitted, the IRS may issue a ___ notice (modification notice) that ___ the original notice.
    (a) updates, modifies
    (b) changes, alters
    (c) subsequent, modifies
    (d) current, changes
    Answer: See Withholding From Employees. Modification notice. Page 23/ (c) subsequent, modifies

9. Withholding From Employee's Wages - Modification notice.

36. After issuing the notice specifying the maximum number of withholding allowances and marital status permitted, the IRS may issue a subsequent notice (modification notice) that modifies the original notice. The modification notice may change the marital status and/or the number of ___ allowances permitted.
    (a) deductions
    (b) dependents
    (c) tax
    (d) withholding
    Answer: See Withholding From Employees. Modification notice. Page 23/ (d) withholding

9. Withholding From Employee's Wages - Modification notice.

37. After issuing the notice specifying the maximum number of withholding allowances and marital status permitted, the IRS may issue a subsequent notice (modification notice) that modifies the original notice. The modification notice may change the marital status and/or the number of ___ allowances permitted. You must withhold federal income tax based on the ___ specified in the modification notice.
    (a) deductions, specified date
    (b) dependents, date
    (c) tax, actual date
    (d) withholding, effective date
    Answer: See Withholding From Employees. Modification notice. Page 23/ (d) withholding, effective date

Withholding From Employee's Wages - New Form W-4 after notice

9. Withholding From Employee's Wages - New Form W-4 after notice.
38. After the IRS issues a notice or modification notice, if the employee provides you with a new Form W-4 claiming ___ from withholding or claims a marital status, a number of withholding allowances, and any additional withholding that results in less withholding than would result under the IRS notice or modification notice,
   (a) complete exemption
   (b) partial exemption
   (c) partial or complete exemption
   (d) all IRS requirements
   Answer: See Withholding From Employees. New Form W-4 after notice. Page 23/ (a) complete exemption

9. Withholding From Employee's Wages - New Form W-4 after notice.
39. After the IRS issues a notice or modification notice, if the employee provides you with a new Form W-4 claiming ___ from withholding or claims a marital status, a number of withholding allowances, and any additional withholding that results in less withholding than would result under the IRS notice or modification notice, ___ the new Form W-4.
   (a) complete exemption, disregard
   (b) partial exemption, accept, instructs
   (c) partial or complete exemption, disregard
   (d) all IRS requirements, accept
   Answer: See Withholding From Employees. New Form W-4 after notice. Page 23/ (a) complete exemption, disregard

9. Withholding From Employee's Wages - New Form W-4 after notice.
40. After the IRS issues a notice or modification notice, if the employee provides you with a new Form W-4 claiming ___ from withholding or claims a marital status, a number of withholding allowances, and any additional withholding that results in less withholding than would result under the IRS notice or modification notice, ___ the new Form W-4. You must withhold based upon the notice or modification notice unless the IRS ___ you to withhold based on the new Form W-4.
   (a) complete exemption, disregard, notifies
   (b) partial exemption, accept, instructs
   (c) partial or complete exemption, disregard, instructs
   (d) all IRS requirements, accept, informs
   Answer: See Withholding From Employees. New Form W-4 after notice. Page 23/ (a) complete exemption, disregard, notifies

Withholding From Employee's Wages - New Form W-4 after notice

9. Withholding From Employee's Wages - New Form W-4 after notice.
41. After the IRS issues a notice or modification notice, if the employee provides you with a new Form W-4 claiming complete exemption from withholding or claims a marital status, a number of withholding allowances, and any additional withholding that results in less withholding than would result under the IRS notice or modification notice, disregard the new Form W-4. You must withhold based upon the notice or modification notice unless the IRS notifies you to withhold based on the new Form W-4. If the employee wants to put a new Form W-4 into effect that results in less withholding than required, the employee must ___ the IRS.
    (a)   speak to the IRS Auditor at
    (b)   contact
    (c)   request a meeting with
    (d)   petition
    Answer: See Withholding From Employees. New Form W-4 after notice. Page 23/ (b) contact

9. Withholding From Employee's Wages - New Form W-4 after notice.
42. If, after you receive an IRS notice or modification notice, your employee gives you a new Form W-4 that ___ from federal income tax withholding and claims a marital status, a number of withholding allowances, and any additional withholding that results in more withholding than would result under the notice or modification notice, you must
    (a)   claims additional exemptions
    (b)   demands additional exemptions
    (c)   does not claim exemption
    (d)   requests additional exemptions
    Answer: See Withholding From Employees. New Form W-4 after notice. Page 23/ (c) does not claim exemption

9. Withholding From Employee's Wages - New Form W-4 after notice.
43. If, after you receive an IRS notice or modification notice, your employee gives you a new Form W-4 that ___ from federal income tax withholding and claims a marital status, a number of withholding allowances, and any additional withholding that results in more withholding than would result under the notice or modification notice, you must withhold tax based on the new Form W-4. Otherwise, ___ any subsequent Forms W-4 provided by the employee and withhold based on the IRS notice or modification notice.
    (a)   claims additional exemptions, disregard
    (b)   demands additional exemptions, refuse
    (c)   does not claim exemption, disregard
    (d)   requests additional exemptions, ignore
    Answer: See Withholding From Employees. New Form W-4 after notice. Page 23/ (c) does not claim exemption

Withholding From Employee's Wages - New Form W-4 after notice

9. Withholding From Employee's Wages - New Form W-4 after notice.
44. For additional information about these rules, see Treasury Decision ___, 2007-35 I.R.B. 455, available at *www.irs.gov/irb/2007-35/ar10.html*.
    (a)   9334
    (b)   9335
    (c)   9336
    (d)   9337
Answer: See Withholding From Employees. New Form W-4 after notice. Page 23/ (d) 9337

Withholding From Employee's Wages. Substitute Forms W-4

9. Withholding From Employee's Wages - Substitute Forms W-4.
45. You are encouraged to have your employees use the ___ version of Form W-4 to claim withholding allowances or exemption from withholding.
    (a)   IRS
    (b)   official
    (c)   correct
    (d)   acceptable
Answer: See Withholding From Employees. Substitute Forms W-4. Page 23/ (b) official

9. Withholding From Employee's Wages - Substitute Forms W-4.
46. You are encouraged to have your employees use the ___ version of Form W-4 to claim withholding allowances or exemption from withholding. Call the IRS at 1-800-TAX-FORM (1-800-829-3676) or visit ___ to obtain copies of Form W-4.
    (a)   IRS, IRS. Form W-4
    (b)   official, IRS.gov
    (c)   correct, IRS.gov
    (d)   acceptable, *Forms/W-4*
Answer: See Withholding From Employees. Substitute Forms W-4. Page 23/ (b) official, IRS.gov

9. Withholding From Employee's Wages - Substitute Forms W-4.
47. You may use a ___ version of Form W-4 to meet your business needs.
    (a)   temporary
    (b)   alternate
    (c)   substitute
    (d)   approved alternate
Answer: See Withholding From Employees. Substitute Forms W-4. Page 23/ (c) substitute

© Copyright 2013. All rights reserved. Notice: United States Copyright Laws and International Treaties prohibit unauthorized publication, reproduction, distribution of this Work. Unauthorized use of this copyright in any form, format, publication or document may result in severe civil and criminal penalties. Violations of this copyright are investigated by the United States Department of Justice and carry, upon conviction of fines up to $250,000 and five years confinement. This Work is protected by United States Copyright Laws and International Treaties. Do not Copy, do not reproduce, do not distribute.

Withholding From Employee's Wages. Substitute Forms W-4

9. Withholding From Employee's Wages - Substitute Forms W-4.
48. You may use a ___ version of Form W-4 to meet your business needs. However, your substitute Form W-4 must contain ___ that is identical to the official Form W-4 and your form must meet all current IRS rules for substitute forms.
    (a)   temporary, information
    (b)   alternate, wording
    (c)   substitute, language
    (d)   approved alternate, verbiage
Answer: See Withholding From Employees. Substitute Forms W-4. Page 23/ (c) substitute, language

9. Withholding From Employee's Wages - Substitute Forms W-4.
49. You may use a ___ version of Form W-4 to meet your business needs. However, your substitute Form W-4 must contain ___ that is identical to the official Form W-4 and your form must meet all current IRS rules for substitute forms. At the time you provide your substitute form to the employee, you must provide him or her with all tables, instructions and ___ from the current Form W-4.
    (a)   temporary, information, worksheets
    (b)   alternate, wording, formulas
    (c)   substitute, language, worksheets
    (d)   approved alternate, verbiage, formulas
Answer: See Withholding From Employees. Substitute Forms W-4. Page 23/ (c) substitute, language, worksheets

9. Withholding From Employee's Wages - Substitute Forms W-4.
50. You cannot accept substitute Forms W-4 developed by ___.
    (a)   others
    (b)   employees
    (c)   independent contractors
    (d)   alien employees developed by other nations
Answer: See Withholding From Employees. Substitute Forms W-4. Page 23/ (b) employees

9. Withholding From Employee's Wages - Substitute Forms W-4.
51. An employee who submits an employee-developed substitute Form W-4 after October 11, ___, will be treated as failing to furnish a Form W-4.
    (a)   2007
    (b)   2009
    (c)   2011
    (d)   2013
Answer: See Withholding From Employees. Substitute Forms W-4. Page 23/ (a) 2007
Section 9. Withholding From Employee's Wages. Substitute Forms W-4. Page 23.

Withholding From Employee's Wages. Substitute Forms W-4

9. Withholding From Employee's Wages - Substitute Forms W-4.
52. An employee who submits an employee-developed substitute Form W-4 after October 11, ___, will be treated as failing to furnish a Form W-4. However, continue to honor any valid employee-developed Forms W-4 you accepted before October 11, ___.
    - (a) 2007, 2007
    - (b) 2009, 2009
    - (c) 2011, 2011
    - (d) 2013, 2009

    Answer: See Withholding From Employees. Substitute Forms W-4. Page 23/ (a) 2007, 2007

Withholding From Employee's Wages. Invalid Forms W-4

9. Withholding From Employee's Wages - Invalid Forms W-4.
53. Any unauthorized change or ___ to Form W-4 makes it invalid.
    - (a) alteration
    - (b) modification
    - (c) addition
    - (d) obliterate

    Answer: See Withholding From Employees. Invalid Forms W-4. Page 23/ (c) addition

9. Withholding From Employee's Wages - Substitute Forms W-4.
54. Any unauthorized change or ___ to Form W-4 makes it invalid. This includes taking out any __ by which the employee certifies the form is correct.
    - (a) alteration, amending
    - (b) modification, obliteration
    - (c) addition, language
    - (d) obliterate, blocking out

    Answer: See Withholding From Employees. Invalid Forms W-4. Page 23/ (c) addition, language

9. Withholding From Employee's Wages - Invalid Forms W-4.
55. Any unauthorized change or ___ to Form W-4 makes it invalid. This includes taking out any ___ by which the employee certifies the form is correct. A form W-4 is also invalid if, by the date an employee gives it to you, he or she indicates in any way it is ___.
    - (a) alteration, amending, misleading
    - (b) modification, obliteration, incorrect
    - (c) addition, language, false
    - (d) obliterate, blocking out, willfully deceiving

    Answer: See Withholding From Employees. Invalid Forms W-4. Page 23/ (c) addition, language, false

Withholding From Employee's Wages. Invalid Forms W-4

9. Withholding From Employee's Wages - Invalid Forms W-4.

56. Any unauthorized change or addition to Form W-4 makes it invalid. This includes taking out any language by which the employee certifies the form is correct. A form W-4 is also invalid if, by the date an employee gives it to you, he or she indicates in any way it is false. An employee who submits a false Form W-4 may be subject to a $___ penalty.
    (a) 500
    (b) 1,000
    (c) 2,500
    (d) 5,000
    Answer: See Withholding From Employees. Invalid Forms W-4. Page 23/ (a) 500

9. Withholding From Employee's Wages - Invalid Forms W-4.

57. Any unauthorized change or addition to Form W-4 makes it invalid. This includes taking out any language by which the employee certifies the form is correct. A form W-4 is also invalid if, by the date an employee gives it to you, he or she indicates in any way it is false. An employee who submits a false Form W-4 may be subject to a $___ penalty. You may treat a Form W-4 as invalid if the employee wrote "___" on line 7 and also entered a number on line 5 or an amount on line 6.
    (a) 500, exempt
    (b) 1,000, inapplicable
    (c) 2,500, NA
    (d) 5,000, exempt
    Answer: See Withholding From Employees. Invalid Forms W-4. Page 23/ (a) 500, exempt

9. Withholding From Employee's Wages - Invalid Forms W-4.

58. When you get an invalid Form W-4, do not use it to figure federal income tax withholding. Tell the employee it is invalid and ___.
    (a) refuse to accept the Form
    (b) ask for another one
    (c) notify the IRS
    (d) provide the employee with approved blank approved Form W-4
    Answer: See Withholding From Employees. Invalid Forms W-4. Page 23/ (b) ask for another one

9. Withholding From Employee's Wages - Invalid Forms W-4.

59. If the employee does not give you a valid one (*a valid Form W-4*), withhold as if the employee ___.
    (a) is single and claiming no withholding allowances
    (b) was single and claiming additional withholding allowances
    (c) was single and claiming no withholding allowances
    (d) is single and claiming no additional withholding allowances
    Answer: See Withholding From Employees. Invalid Forms W-4. Page 23/ (c) was single and claiming no withholding allowances

© Copyright 2013. All rights reserved. Notice: United States Copyright Laws and International Treaties prohibit unauthorized publication, reproduction, distribution of this Work. Unauthorized use of this copyright in any form, format, publication or document may result in severe civil and criminal penalties. Violations of this copyright are investigated by the United States Department of Justice and carry, upon conviction of fines up to $250,000 and five years confinement. This Work is protected by United States Copyright Laws and International Treaties. Do not Copy, do not reproduce, do not distribute.

Withholding From Employee's Wages. Invalid Forms W-4

9. Withholding From Employee's Wages - Invalid Forms W-4.

60.   If the employee does not give you a valid one (*a valid Form W-4*), withhold as if the employee ___. However, if you have ___ Form W-4 for this worker that is valid, withhold as you did before.
  (a)   is single and claiming no withholding allowances, a current
  (b)   was single and claiming additional withholding allowances, a current valid
  (c)   was single and claiming no withholding allowances, an earlier
  (d)   is single and claiming no additional withholding allowances, a earlier
  Answer: See Withholding From Employees. Invalid Forms W-4. Page 23/ (c) was single and claiming no withholding allowances, an earlier

A Ficus Tree Publishing Quick Notes Page.

DU VALL'S TEST'S™
Instructors Manual Study Guide Series United States Tax Code
IRS Publication 15 Circular E, Employer's Tax Guide Tax Year 2013
Tax Test 15E-S9-3[Multiple-Choice Questions With Answers]

Section 9. Withholding From Employee's Wages. Amounts exempt from levy on wages, salary, and other income. Page 23.

9. Withholding From Employee's Wages - Amounts exempt from levy on wages, salary, and other income.

1. If you receive a Notice of ___ on Wages, Salary, and Other Income
   - (a) Levy
   - (b) Lien
   - (c) Debt
   - (d) Withhold

   Answer: See Withholding From Employees. Amounts exempt from levy on wages, salary, and other income. Page 23/ (a) Levy

9. Amounts exempt from levy on wages, salary, and other income.

2. If you receive a Notice of ___ on Wages, Salary, and Other Income (Forms 668-W(___), 668-W (c) (___), or 668-W(___)), you must withhold amounts as described in the instructions for these forms.
   - (a) Levy, ACS, DO, ICS
   - (b) Lien, ACS, DO, IRS
   - (c) Debt, ACS, DE, IRS
   - (d) Withhold, ACP, DE, IRS

   Answer: See Withholding From Employees. Amounts exempt from levy on wages, salary, and other income. Page 23/ (a) Levy, ACS, DO, ICS

9. Amounts exempt from levy on wages, salary, and other income.

3. If you receive a Notice of ___ on Wages, Salary, and Other Income (Forms 668-W(___), 668-W (c) (___), or 668-W(___)), you must withhold amounts as described in the instructions for these forms. Publication ___, Tables for Figuring Amount Exempt From Levy on Wages, Salary, and Other Income-Forms 668-W(ACS), 668-W(c)(DO), and 668-W(ICS), shows the exempt amount.
   - (a) Levy, ACS, DO, ICS, 1494
   - (b) Lien, ACS, DO, IRS, 1492
   - (c) Debt, ACS, DE, IRS, 1490
   - (d) Withhold, ACP, DE, IRS, 1984

   Answer: See Withholding From Employees. Amounts exempt from levy on wages, salary, and other income. Page 23/ (a) Levy, ACS, DO, ICS, 1494

© Copyright 2013. All rights reserved. Notice: United States Copyright Laws and International Treaties prohibit unauthorized publication, reproduction, distribution of this Work. Unauthorized use of this copyright in any form, format, publication or document may result in severe civil and criminal penalties. Violations of this copyright are investigated by the United States Department of Justice and carry, upon conviction of fines up to $250,000 and five years confinement. This Work is protected by United States Copyright Laws and International Treaties. Do not Copy, do not reproduce, do not distribute.

A Ficus Tree Publishing Educational-Technical Publications

Withholding From Employee's Wages
Amounts exempt from levy on wages, salary, and other income.

9. Amounts exempt from levy on wages, salary, and other income.

4. If you receive a Notice of ___ on Wages, Salary, and Other Income (Forms 668-W(___), 668-W (c) (___), or 668-W(___)), you must withhold amounts as described in the instructions for these forms. Publication ___, Tables for Figuring Amount Exempt From Levy on Wages, Salary, and Other Income-Forms 668-W(ACS), 668-W(c)(DO), and 668-W(ICS), shows the exempt amount. If a levy issued in a prior year is still in effect and the taxpayer submits a new ___, use the current year Publication 1494 to compute the exempt amount.

    (a) Levy, ACS, DO, ICS, 1494, Statement of Exemptions and Filing Status
    (b) Lien, ACS, DO, IRS, 1492, Statement of Exemption and Filing Status
    (c) Debt, ACS, DE, IRS, 1490, Statement of Exemptions and Tax Filing Status
    (d) Withhold , ACP, DE, IRS, 1984, Statement of Exemptions and Tax Filing Status

Answer: See Withholding From Employees. Amounts exempt from levy on wages, salary, and other income. Page 23/ (a) Levy, ACS, DO, ICS, 1494, Statement of Exemptions and Filing Status

Withholding From Employee's Wages
Social Security and Medicare Taxes

9. Withholding From Employee's Wages - Social Security and Medicare Taxes.

5. FICA is identified and defined in section 9 of IRS Circular E, Employer's Tax Guide as ___.

    (a) The Federal Insurance Control Act
    (b) The Federal Insurance Contributions Act
    (c) Federal Insured Contributions Act
    (d) The IRS Federal Insurance Contributions Act

Answer: See Withholding From Employees. Social Security and Medicare Taxes. Page 23/ (b) The Federal Insurance Contributions Act

9. Withholding From Employee's Wages - Social Security and Medicare Taxes.

6. The Federal Insurance Contributions Act (FICA) ___ for a federal system of old-age, survivors, disability, and hospital insurance. The old-age, survivors, and disability insurance ___ is financed by the social security tax.

    (a) provides, part
    (b) establishes, fund
    (c) is an enablement, reserve
    (d) is a tax, fund

Answer: See Withholding From Employees. Social Security and Medicare Taxes. Page 23/ (a) provides, part

Withholding From Employee's Wages
Social Security and Medicare Taxes

9. Withholding From Employee's Wages - Social Security and Medicare Taxes.
7. The Federal Insurance Contributions Act (FICA) ___ for a federal system of old-age, survivors, disability, and hospital insurance. The old-age, survivors, and disability insurance ___ is financed by the social security tax. The hospital insurance ___ is financed by the Medicare tax.
   (a) provides, part, part
   (b) establishes, fund, fund
   (c) is an enablement, reserve, funding
   (d) is a tax, fund, part
   Answer: See Withholding From Employees. Social Security and Medicare Taxes. Page 23/ (a) provides, part, part

9. Withholding From Employee's Wages - Social Security and Medicare Taxes.
8. The Federal Insurance Contributions Act (FICA) ___ for a federal system of old-age, survivors, disability, and hospital insurance. The old-age, survivors, and disability insurance ___ is financed by the social security tax. The hospital insurance ___ is financed by the Medicare tax. Each of these taxes is ___ separately.
   (a) provides, part, part, reported
   (b) establishes, fund, fund, collected
   (c) is an enablement, reserve, funding, taxed
   (d) is a tax, fund, part, recorded
   Answer: See Withholding From Employees. Social Security and Medicare Taxes. Page 23/ (a) provides, part, part, reported

9. Withholding From Employee's Wages - Social Security and Medicare Taxes.
9. Generally, you are required to withhold social security and Medicare taxes from your employees' wages and pay ___ share of these taxes.
   (a) the employer's
   (b) an additional
   (c) the mandatory
   (d) the stated
   Answer: See Withholding From Employees. Social Security and Medicare Taxes. Page 23/ (a) the employer's

Withholding From Employee's Wages
Social Security and Medicare Taxes

9. Withholding From Employee's Wages - Social Security and Medicare Taxes.
10. Generally, you are required to withhold social security and Medicare taxes from your employees' wages and pay ___ share of these taxes. Certain types of wages and ___ are not subject to social security and Medicare taxes.
    (a)   the employer's, compensation
    (b)   an additional, income
    (c)   the mandatory, supplemental income
    (d)   the stated, other compensation
Answer: See Withholding From Employees. Social Security and Medicare Taxes. Page 23/ (a) the employer's, compensation

9. Withholding From Employee's Wages - Social Security and Medicare Taxes.
11. Generally, you are required to withhold social security and Medicare taxes from your employees' wages and pay ___ share of these taxes. Certain types of wages and ___ are not subject to social security and Medicare taxes. See <u>section</u> ___ and <u>section</u> ___ for details.
    (a)   the employer's, compensation, 5, 15
    (b)   an additional, income, 6, 16
    (c)   the mandatory, supplemental income, 7, 17
    (d)   the stated, other compensation, 8, 18
Answer: See Withholding From Employees. Social Security and Medicare Taxes. Page 23/ (a) the employer's, compensation, 5, 15

9. Withholding From Employee's Wages - Social Security and Medicare Taxes.
12. Generally, employee wages are subject to social security and Medicare taxes regardless of the employee's age or whether he or she is ___ social security benefits.
    (a)   provided
    (b)   receiving
    (c)   receiving compensated
    (d)   a recipient of
Answer: See Withholding From Employees. Social Security and Medicare Taxes. Page 23/ (b) receiving

9. Withholding From Employee's Wages - Social Security and Medicare Taxes.
13. Generally, employee wages are subject to social security and Medicare taxes regardless of the employee's age or whether he or she is ___ social security benefits. If the employee reports tips, see <u>section</u> ___.
    (a)   provided, 6
    (b)   receiving, 7
    (c)   receiving compensated, 8
    (d)   a recipient of, 9
Answer: See Withholding From Employees. Social Security and Medicare Taxes. Page 23/ (b) receiving, 6

© Copyright 2013. All rights reserved. Notice: United States Copyright Laws and International Treaties prohibit unauthorized publication, reproduction, distribution of this Work. Unauthorized use of this copyright in any form, format, publication or document may result in severe civil and criminal penalties. Violations of this copyright are investigated by the United States Department of Justice and carry, upon conviction of fines up to $250,000 and five years confinement. This Work is protected by United States Copyright Laws and International Treaties. Do not Copy, do not reproduce, do not distribute.

Section 9. Withholding From Employee's Wages.
Tax rates and the social security wage base limit Page 23.
(This is a very important section - study this section in detail).

9. Withholding From Employee's Wages - Tax rates and the social security wage base limit.
14. Social security and Medicare taxes have ___ rates
    (a) annual changes to the
    (b) varying
    (c) different
    (d) variable
    Answer: See Withholding From Employees. Tax rates and the social security wage base limit. Page 23/ (c) different

9. Withholding From Employee's Wages - Tax rates and the social security wage base limit.
15. Social security and Medicare taxes have ___ rates and only the social security has a ___.
    (a) annual changes to the, a limit
    (b) varying, limits
    (c) different, wage base limit
    (d) variable, limitations
    Answer: See Withholding From Employees. Tax rates and the social security wage base limit. Page 23/ (c) different, wage base limit

9. Withholding From Employee's Wages - Tax rates and the social security wage base limit.
16. Social security and Medicare taxes have different rates and only the social security has a wage base limit. The wage base limit is the ___ subject to the tax the year.
    (a) total
    (b) average
    (c) minimum
    (d) maximum
    Answer: See Withholding From Employees. Tax rates and the social security wage base limit. Page 23/ (d) maximum

9. Withholding From Employee's Wages - Tax rates and the social security wage base limit.
17. Social security and Medicare taxes have different rates and only the social security has a wage base limit. The wage base limit is the ___ subject to the tax the year.
    (a) total
    (b) average
    (c) minimum
    (d) maximum
    Answer: See Withholding From Employees. Tax rates and the social security wage base limit. Page 23/ (d) maximum

© Copyright 2013. All rights reserved. Notice: United States Copyright Laws and International Treaties prohibit unauthorized publication, reproduction, distribution of this Work. Unauthorized use of this copyright in any form, format, publication or document may result in severe civil and criminal penalties. Violations of this copyright are investigated by the United States Department of Justice and carry, upon conviction of fines up to $250,000 and five years confinement. This Work is protected by United States Copyright Laws and International Treaties. Do not Copy, do not reproduce, do not distribute.

A Ficus Tree Publishing Educational-Technical Publications

Withholding From Employee's Wages
Tax rates and the social security wage base limit.

9. Withholding From Employee's Wages - Tax rates and the social security wage base limit.
18. Social security and Medicare taxes have different rates and only the social security has a wage base limit. The wage base limit is the ___ subject to the tax the year. Determine the amount of withholding for social security and Medicare taxes by ___ each payment by the employee tax rate.
    (a)   total, combining
    (b)   average, adding
    (c)   minimum, combining
    (d)   maximum, multiplying
    Answer: See Withholding From Employees. Tax rates and the social security wage base limit. Page 23/ (d) maximum, multiplying

9. Withholding From Employee's Wages - Tax rates and the social security wage base limit.
19. Social security and Medicare taxes have different rates and only the social security has a wage base limit. The wage base limit is the ___ subject to the tax the year. Determine the amount of withholding for social security and Medicare taxes by ___ each payment by the employee tax rate. There are no ___ for social security and Medicare taxes.
    (a)   total, combining, withholding
    (b)   average, adding, allowances
    (c)   minimum, combining, tax allowances
    (d)   maximum, multiplying, withholding allowances
    Answer: See Withholding From Employees. Tax rates and the social security wage base limit. Page 23/ (d) maximum, multiplying, withholding allowances

9. Withholding From Employee's Wages - Tax rates and the social security wage base limit.
20. The employee tax rate for social security is ___% for 2013.
    (a)   5.8
    (b)   6.2
    (c)   6.3
    (d)   6.4
    Answer: See Withholding From Employees. Tax rates and the social security wage base limit. Page 23/ (b) 6.2

9. Withholding From Employee's Wages - Tax rates and the social security wage base limit.
21. The employer tax rate for social security remains unchanged at ___% for 2013.
    (a)   5.8
    (b)   6.2
    (c)   6.3
    (d)   6.4
    Answer: See Withholding From Employees. Tax rates and the social security wage base limit. Page 23/ (b) 6.2

© Copyright 2013. All rights reserved. Notice: United States Copyright Laws and International Treaties prohibit unauthorized publication, reproduction, distribution of this Work. Unauthorized use of this copyright in any form, format, publication or document may result in severe civil and criminal penalties. Violations of this copyright are investigated by the United States Department of Justice and carry, upon conviction of fines up to $250,000 and five years confinement. This Work is protected by United States Copyright Laws and International Treaties. Do not Copy, do not reproduce, do not distribute.

Withholding From Employee's Wages
Tax rates and the social security wage base limit

9. Withholding From Employee's Wages - Tax rates and the social security wage base limit.
22. The social security wage base limit is $___.
    (a) 113,275
    (b) 113,480
    (c) 113,700
    (d) 114,050
    Answer: See Withholding From Employees. Tax rates and the social security wage base limit. Page 23/ (c) 113,700

9. Withholding From Employee's Wages - Tax rates and the social security wage base limit.
23. The 2013 employee tax rate for Medicare is ___% (amount withheld)
    (a) 1.30
    (b) 1.35
    (c) 1.40
    (d) 1.45
    Answer: See Withholding From Employees. Tax rates and the social security wage base limit. Page 23/ (d) 1.45

9. Withholding From Employee's Wages - Tax rates and the social security wage base limit.
24. The 2013 employee tax rate for Medicare is ___% (amount withheld) each for the employee and the employer (___% total).
    (a) 1.45, 2.9
    (b) 1.55, 3.05
    (c) 2.0, 3.15
    (d) 2.9, 3.17
    Answer: See Withholding From Employees. Tax rates and the social security wage base limit. Page 23/ (d) 1.45, 2.9

9. Withholding From Employee's Wages - Tax rates and the social security wage base limit.
25. There is no wage base limit for ___ tax
    (a) Medicare
    (b) Medicaid
    (c) Medicate
    (d) Medical
    Answer: See Withholding From Employees. Tax rates and the social security wage base limit. Page 23/ (a) Medicare

Withholding From Employee's Wages
Tax rates and the social security wage base limit

9. Withholding From Employee's Wages - Tax rates and the social security wage base limit.

26. There is no wage base limit for ___ tax; all ___ wages are subject to ___ tax.
    - (a) Medicare, covered, Medicare
    - (b) Medicaid, paid, Medicaid
    - (c) Medicate, earned income, Medicate
    - (d) Medical, earned income, Medical

    Answer: See Withholding From Employees. Tax rates and the social security wage base limit. Page 23/ (a) Medicare, covered, Medicare

Withholding From Employee's Wages
Additional Medicare Tax withholding

9. Withholding From Employee's Wages - Additional Medicare Tax withholding.

27. In addition to withholding Medicare tax at 1.45%, you must withhold a ___% Additional Medicare Tax from wages you pay to an employee in excess of $___ in a calendar year.
    - (a) 0.7, 100,000
    - (b) 0.7, 150,000
    - (c) 0.9, 200,000
    - (d) 0.9, 225,000

    Answer: See Withholding From Employees. Additional Medicare Tax withholding. Page 24/ (c) 0.9, 200,000

9. Withholding From Employee's Wages - Additional Medicare Tax withholding.

28. You are required to begin withholding Additional Medicare Tax in the pay period in which you pay wages in excess of $___ to an employee and continue to withhold it in ___ pay period until the end of the calendar year.
    - (a) 100,000, each
    - (b) 200,000, each
    - (c) 300,000, all
    - (d) 400,000, all

    Answer: See Withholding From Employees. Additional Medicare Tax withholding. Page 24/ (b) 200,000, each

Withholding From Employee's Wages
Additional Medicare Tax withholding

9. Withholding From Employee's Wages - Additional Medicare Tax withholding.

29. You are required to begin withholding Additional Medicare Tax in the pay period in which you pay wages in excess of $200,000 to an employee and continue to withhold it in each pay period until the end of the calendar year. Additional Medicare Tax is only imposed on the ___.
    (a) employee
    (b) employer
    (c) individual
    (d) individuals
    Answer: See Withholding From Employees. Additional Medicare Tax withholding. Page 24/ (a) employee

9. Withholding From Employee's Wages - Additional Medicare Tax withholding.

30. You are required to begin withholding Additional Medicare Tax in the pay period in which you pay wages in excess of $200,000 to an employee and continue to withhold it in each pay period until the end of the calendar year. Additional Medicare Tax is only imposed on the ___. There is ___ of Additional Medicare Tax.
    (a) employee, no employer share
    (b) employer, no employer participation
    (c) individual, a similar employer share
    (d) individuals, an employer share
    Answer: See Withholding From Employees. Additional Medicare Tax withholding. Page 24/ (a) employee, no employer share

9. Withholding From Employee's Wages - Additional Medicare Tax withholding.

31. You are required to begin withholding Additional Medicare Tax in the pay period in which you pay wages in excess of $200,000 to an employee and continue to withhold it in each pay period until the end of the calendar year. Additional Medicare Tax is only imposed on the employee. There is no employer share of Additional Medicare Tax. All wages that are subject to Medicare tax are subject to Additional Medicare Tax withholding if paid in excess of the $200,000 withholding ___. For more information on what wages are subject to Medicare tax, see the chart, ***Special Rules for Various Types of Services and Payments***, in section ___.
    (a) limit, 13
    (b) range, 14
    (c) threshold, 15
    (d) plateau, 16
    Answer: See Withholding From Employees. Additional Medicare Tax withholding. Page 24/ (c) threshold, 15

Withholding From Employee's Wages. Successor employer

9. Withholding From Employee's Wages - Successor employer.
32. When corporate acquisitions meet certain requirements, wages paid by the predecessor are treated as ___ by the successor for the purposes of
  (a) deposited tax payments
  (b) deposited
  (c) earned
  (d) paid
  Answer: See Withholding From Employees. Successor employer. Page 24/ (d) paid

9. Withholding From Employee's Wages - Successor employer.
33. When corporate acquisitions meet certain requirements, wages paid by the predecessor are treated as ___ by the successor for the purposes of applying the social security wage base and for applying the Additional Medicare Tax withholding threshold (that is, $200,000 in a ___ year).
  (a) deposited tax payments, tax period
  (b) deposited, calendar period
  (c) earned, calendar period
  (d) paid, calendar year
  Answer: See Withholding From Employees. Successor employer. Page 24/ (d) paid, calendar year

9. Withholding From Employee's Wages - Successor employer.
34. When corporate acquisitions meet certain requirements, wages paid by the predecessor are treated as ___ by the successor for the purposes of applying the social security wage base and for applying the Additional Medicare Tax withholding threshold (that is, $200,000 in a ___). You should determine whether or not you should file Schedule D (Form ___), Report of Discrepancies Caused by Acquisitions, Statutory ___, or Consolidations, by reviewing the instructions for Schedule D (Form 941).
  (a) deposited tax payments, tax period, 940, Mergers
  (b) deposited, calendar period, 940, Acquisitions
  (c) earned, calendar period.940. Mergers
  (d) paid, calendar year, 941, Mergers
  Answer: See Withholding From Employees. Successor employer. Page 24/ (d) paid, calendar year, 941, Mergers

Withholding From Employee's Wages. Successor employer

9. Withholding From Employee's Wages - Successor employer.
35. When corporate acquisitions meet certain requirements, wages paid by the predecessor are treated as paid by the successor for the purposes of applying the social security wage base and for applying the Additional Medicare Tax withholding threshold (that is, $200,000 in a calendar year). You should determine whether or not you should file Schedule D (Form 941), Report of Discrepancies Caused by Acquisitions, Statutory Mergers, or Consolidations, by reviewing the instructions for Schedule D (Form 941). See Regulations section 31.3121___ for more information.
    (a)   (a)(1)-1(b)
    (b)   (a)(1)-2(b)
    (c)   (a)(1)-3(b)
    (d)   (a)(1)-4(b)
    Answer: See Withholding From Employees. Successor employer. Page 24/ (a) (a)(1)-1(b)

9. Withholding From Employee's Wages - Successor employer.
36. When corporate acquisitions meet certain requirements, wages paid by the predecessor are treated as paid by the successor for the purposes of applying the social security wage base and for applying the Additional Medicare Tax withholding threshold (that is, $200,000 in a calendar year). You should determine whether or not you should file Schedule D (Form 941), Report of Discrepancies Caused by Acquisitions, Statutory Merger, or Consolidations, by reviewing the instructions for Schedule D (Form 941). See Regulations section 31.3121___ for more information. Also see Revenue Procedure 2004-53, 2004-34 I.R.B. ___ available at *www.irs.gov/irb2004-34 IRB /ar13.html*.
    (a)   (a)(1)-1(b), 320
    (b)   (a)(1)-2(b), 320
    (c)   (a)(1)-3(b), 321
    (d)   (a)(1)-4(b), 322
    Answer: See Withholding From Employees. Successor employer. Page 24/ (a) (a)(1)-1(b), 320

Withholding From Employee's Wages. Successor employer. Example

9. Withholding From Employee's Wages - Successor employer. Example.
Early in 2013, you bought all the assets of a plumbing business from Mr. Martin. Mr. Brown, who had been employed by Mr. Martin and received $___ in wages before the date of purchase, continued to work for you. The wages you paid to Mr. Brown are subject to social security taxes on the first $111,700 ($113,700 minus $2,000). Medicare tax is due on all wages you pay him during the ___.

You should include the $___ Mr. Brown received while employed by Mr. Martin in determining whether Mr. Brown's wages exceed the $200,000 for Additional Medicare Tax withholding threshold.
(a) 2,000, calendar year, 2,000
(b) 2,000, second quarter, 2,000
(c) 2,000, third quarter, 2,000
(d) 200,000, fourth quarter, 200,000
Answer: See Withholding From Employees. Successor employer. Page 24/ (a) 2,000, calendar year, 2,000

Withholding From Employee's Wages
Withholding of social security and Medicare taxes on nonresident aliens

9. Withholding From Employee's Wages - Withholding of social security and Medicare taxes on nonresident aliens.
37. In general, if you pay wages to nonresident alien employees, you must withhold federal social security and Medicare taxes as you would for ___.
    (a) any individual employee
    (b) a U.S. citizen
    (c) all foreign nationals
    (d) all foreign nationals expect those specifically exempt
    Answer: See Withholding From Employees. Withholding of social security and Medicare taxes on nonresident aliens. Page 24/(b) a U.S. citizen

9. Withholding From Employee's Wages - Withholding of social security and Medicare taxes on nonresident aliens.
38. In general, if you pay wages to nonresident alien employees, you must withhold federal social security and Medicare taxes as you would for ___. However, see Publication ___ for exceptions to this general rule.
    (a) any individual employee, 514
    (b) a U.S. citizen, 515
    (c) all foreign nationals, 516
    (d) all foreign nationals expect those specifically exempt, 515
    Answer: See Withholding From Employees. Withholding of social security and Medicare taxes on nonresident aliens. Page 24/(b) a U.S. citizen, 515

© Copyright 2013. All rights reserved. Notice: United States Copyright Laws and International Treaties prohibit unauthorized publication, reproduction, distribution of this Work. Unauthorized use of this copyright in any form, format, publication or document may result in severe civil and criminal penalties. Violations of this copyright are investigated by the United States Department of Justice and carry, upon conviction of fines up to $250,000 and five years confinement. This Work is protected by United States Copyright Laws and International Treaties. Do not Copy, do not reproduce, do not distribute.

Withholding From Employee's Wages
International social security agreements

9. Withholding From Employee's Wages - International social security agreements.
39. The United States has social security agreements, also known as ___, with many countries that eliminate ___ and dual coverage.
    (a) intergovernmental treaties, duplication of taxation
    (b) intergovernmental employment treaties, duplication of taxation
    (c) totalization agreements, dual taxation
    (d) intergovernmental agreements, duplicate taxation
    Answer: See Withholding From Employees. International social security agreements.
    Page 24/(c) totalization agreements, dual taxation

9. Withholding From Employee's Wages - International social security agreements.
40. The United States has social security agreements, also known as ___, with many countries that eliminate ___ and dual coverage. Compensation subject to social security and Medicare taxes may be exempt under ___ of these agreements.
    (a) intergovernmental treaties, duplication of taxation, many
    (b) intergovernmental employment treaties, duplication of taxation, one
    (c) totalization agreements, dual taxation, one
    (d) intergovernmental agreements, duplicate taxation, most
    Answer: See Withholding From Employees. International social security agreements.
    Page 24/(c) totalization agreements, dual taxation, one

9. Withholding From Employee's Wages - International social security agreements.
41. The United States has social security agreements, also known as ___, with many countries that eliminate ___ and dual coverage. Compensation subject to social security and Medicare taxes may be exempt under ___ of these agreements. You can get more information and a list of ___ countries from the SSA at *ww.socialsecurity.gov/international*.
    (a) intergovernmental treaties, duplication of taxation, many, member
    (b) intergovernmental employment treaties, duplication of taxation, one, member
    (c) totalization agreements, dual taxation, one, agreement
    (d) intergovernmental agreements, duplicate taxation, most, participating
    Answer: See Withholding From Employees. International social security agreements.
    Page 24/(c) totalization agreements, dual taxation, one, agreement

Withholding From Employee's Wages
International social security agreements

9. Withholding From Employee's Wages - International social security agreements.

42. The United States has social security agreements, also known as ___, with many countries that eliminate ___ and dual coverage. Compensation subject to social security and Medicare taxes may be exempt under ___ of these agreements. You can get more information and a list of ___ countries from the SSA at ***www.socialsecurity.gov/international*** or see section ___ of Publication 15-A.
   - (a) intergovernmental treaties, duplication of taxation, many, member, 5
   - (b) intergovernmental employment treaties, duplication of taxation, one, member, 6
   - (c) totalization agreements, dual taxation, one, agreement, 7
   - (d) intergovernmental agreements, duplicate taxation, most, participating, 8

   Answer: See Withholding From Employees. International social security agreements. Page 24/(c) totalization agreements, dual taxation, one, agreement, 7

Withholding From Employee's Wages. Religious exemption

9. Withholding From Employee's Wages - Religious exemption.

43. An exemption from social security and Medicare taxes is available to members of a recognized religious sect opposed to ___.
    - (a) taxes
    - (b) income taxes
    - (c) government regulations
    - (d) insurance

    Answer: See Withholding From Employees. Religious exemption. Page 24/(d) insurance

9. Withholding From Employee's Wages - Religious exemption.

44. An exemption from social security and Medicare taxes is available to members of a recognized religious sect opposed to ___. This exemption is available only if both the employee and the employer are members of the same ___.
    - (a) taxes, congregation
    - (b) income taxes, religion
    - (c) government regulations, church
    - (d) insurance, sect

    Answer: See Withholding From Employees. Religious exemption. Page 24/(d) insurance, sect

9. Withholding From Employee's Wages - Religious exemption.

45. For more information, see Publication ___, Social Security and Other Information for Members of the Clergy and Religious Workers.
    - (a) 517
    - (b) 518
    - (c) 519
    - (d) 520

    Answer: See Withholding From Employees. Religious exemption. Page 24/(a) 517

© Copyright 2013. All rights reserved. Notice: United States Copyright Laws and International Treaties prohibit unauthorized publication, reproduction, distribution of this Work. Unauthorized use of this copyright in any form, format, publication or document may result in severe civil and criminal penalties. Violations of this copyright are investigated by the United States Department of Justice and carry, upon conviction of fines up to $250,000 and five years confinement. This Work is protected by United States Copyright Laws and International Treaties. Do not Copy, do not reproduce, do not distribute.

Withholding From Employee's Wages
Foreign persons treated as American employers

9. Withholding From Employee's Wages - Foreign persons treated as American employers.
46. Under IRC section ___, for services performed after July 31, ___, a foreign person
    (a) 3121(v), 2013
    (b) 3121(z), 2012
    (c) 3121(x), 2010
    (d) 3121(z), 2008
    Answer: See Withholding From Employees. Foreign persons treated as American employers. P 24 /(d) 3121(z), 2008

9. Withholding From Employee's Wages - Foreign persons treated as American employers.
47. Under IRC section ___, for services performed after July 31, ___, a foreign person who meets ___ of the following conditions is generally treated as an American employer for purposes of paying FICA taxes on wages paid to an employee who is a United States citizen or ___.
    (a) 3121(v), 2013, the two listed
    (b) 3121(z), 2012, each
    (c) 3121(x), 2010, all
    (d) 3121(z), 2008, both
    Answer: See Withholding From Employees. Foreign persons treated as American employers. P 24 /(d) 3121(z), 2008, both

9. Withholding From Employee's Wages - Foreign persons treated as American employers.
48. Under IRC section ___, for services performed after July 31, ___, a foreign person who meets ___ of the following conditions is generally treated as an American employer for purposes of paying FICA taxes on wages paid to an employee who is a United States citizen or ___.
    (a) 3121(v), 2013, the two listed, approved
    (b) 3121(z), 2012, each, retired citizen
    (c) 3121(x), 2010, all, dependent
    (d) 3121(z), 2008, both, resident
    Answer: See Withholding From Employees. Foreign persons treated as American employers. P 24 /(d) 3121(z), 2008, both, resident

Withholding From Employee's Wages
Foreign persons treated as American employers

9. Withholding From Employee's Wages - Foreign persons treated as American employers.
49. Under IRC section 3121(z), for services performed after July 31, 2008, a foreign person who meets both of the following conditions is generally treated as an American employer for purposes of paying FICA taxes on wages paid to an employee who is a United States citizen or resident.
1. The foreign person is a member of a ___ controlled group of entities.
(a) international
(b) global
(c) domestically
(d) multi-national
Answer: See Withholding From Employees. Foreign persons treated as American employers. P 24 /(c) domestically

9. Withholding From Employee's Wages - Foreign persons treated as American employers.
50. Under IRC section 3121(z), for services performed after July 31, 2008, a foreign person who meets both of the following conditions is generally treated as an American employer for purposes of paying FICA taxes on wages paid to an employee who is a United States citizen or resident.
1. The foreign person is a member of a ___ controlled group of entities.
2. The employee of the foreign person performs services in connection with a ___ between the U.S. Government (or instrumentality of the U. S. Government) and any member of
(a) international, agreement
(b) global, charter
(c) domestically, contract
(d) multi-national, treaty
Answer: See Withholding From Employees. Foreign persons treated as American employers. P 24 (c) domestically, contract

Withholding From Employee's Wages
Foreign persons treated as American employers

9. Withholding From Employee's Wages - Foreign persons treated as American employers.

51. Under IRC section 3121(z), for services performed after July 31, 2008, a foreign person who meets both of the following conditions is generally treated as an American employer for purposes of paying FICA taxes on wages paid to an employee who is a United States citizen or resident.
    1. The foreign person is a member of a ___ controlled group of entities.
    2. The employee of the foreign person performs services in connection with a ___ between the U.S. Government (or instrumentality of the U. S. Government) and any member of the ___ controlled group of entities.
    (a) international, agreement, internationally
    (b) global, charter, international
    (c) domestically, contract, domestically
    (d) multi-national, treaty, domestically
    Answer: See Withholding From Employees. Foreign persons treated as American employers. P 24 (c) domestically, contract, domestically

9. Withholding From Employee's Wages - Foreign persons treated as American employers.

52. Ownership of more than ___% constitutes control.
    (a) 30
    (b) 33
    (c) 50
    (d) 51
    Answer: See Withholding From Employees. Foreign persons treated as American employers. P 24 /(c) 50

Withholding From Employee's Wages. Part-Time Workers

9. Withholding From Employee's Wages - Part Time Workers.

53. For federal income tax withholding and social security, Medicare, and ___ tax purposes there are no
    (a) FICA
    (b) COBRA
    (c) FUTA
    (d) CFR's
    Answer: See Withholding From Employees. Part-Time Workers. Page 24/(c) FUTA

Withholding From Employee's Wages. Part-Time Workers

9. Withholding From Employee's Wages - Part Time Workers.

54. For federal income tax withholding and social security, Medicare, and ___ tax purposes there are no differences among full-time employees, part-time employees, and employees hired for ___.
    (a) FICA, farm labor
    (b) COBRA, migratory work
    (c) FUTA, short periods
    (d) CFR's, common labor employment
    Answer: See Withholding From Employees. Part-Time Workers. Page 24/(c) FUTA, short periods

9. Withholding From Employee's Wages - Part Time Workers.

55. For federal income tax withholding and social security, Medicare, and FUTA purposes there are no differences among full-time employees, part-time employees, and employees hired for short periods. It does not matter whether the worker ___ or has the maximum amount of social security withheld by another employer.
    (a) is a new hire
    (b) has two jobs
    (c) is employed in another trade
    (d) has another job
    Answer: See Withholding From Employees. Part-Time Workers. Page 24/(d) has another job

9. Withholding From Employee's Wages - Part Time Workers.

56. For federal income tax withholding and social security, Medicare, and FUTA purposes there are no differences among full-time employees, part-time employees, and employees hired for short periods. It does not matter whether the worker ___ or has the maximum amount of social security withheld by another employer. Income tax withholding may be figured ___ as for full-time workers.
    (a) is a new hire, exactly
    (b) has two jobs, in the same manner
    (c) is employed in another trade, the same
    (d) has another job, the same way
    Answer: See Withholding From Employees. Part-Time Workers. Page 24/(d) has another job, the same way

Withholding From Employee's Wages. Part-Time Workers

9. Withholding From Employee's Wages - Part Time Workers.

57. For federal income tax withholding and social security, Medicare, and FUTA purposes there are no differences among full-time employees, part-time employees, and employees hired for short periods. It does not matter whether the worker ___ or has the maximum amount of social security withheld by another employer. Income tax withholding may be figured ___ as for full-time workers. Or it may be figured by the part-year employment method explained in section 9 of Publication ___.
    (a) is a new hire, exactly, 14-A
    (b) has two jobs, in the same manner, 14-B
    (c) is employed in another trade, the same, 15
    (d) has another job, the same way, 15-A

    Answer: See Withholding From Employees. Part-Time Workers. Page 24/(d) has another job, the same way, 15-A

A Ficus Tree Publishing LLC., Quick Notes Page.

Instructor's Manual for Tax Test 15E-S10
Required Notice To Employees About The Earned Income Credit (EIC)

Section 10. General Description

Tax Test 15E-S10. Tax Test 15E-S10 is a very brief study of **IRS Section 10. Required Notice to Employees About the Earned Income Credit (EIC).**

Section 10. Key Words.

Tax Test 15E-S10. Required notice. Earned Income Credit. EIC. no federal income tax withheld. more than tax they owe. Notice 797. Copy B. Possible Federal Tax Refund Due to EIC. Form W-2. Substitute Form W-2. February 7.

DU VALL'S TEST'S™
Instructors Manual Study Guide Series United States Tax Code
IRS Publication 15 Circular E, Employer's Tax Guide Tax Year 2013
Tax Test 15E-S10-1 [Multiple-Choice Questions With Answers]

Required Notice to Employees About the Earned Income Credit (EIC)

10. Required Notice to Employees About the Earned Income Credit.
1. You must notify employees who have no federal income tax withheld that they may be able to a tax refund because of the ___.
   - (a) EIC
   - (b) IRS
   - (c) SSA
   - (d) NARA

   Answer: See 10. Required Notice to Employees About the Earned Income Credit (EIC). Section 10, page 24/(a) EIC

10. Required Notice to Employees About the Earned Income Credit.
2. You must notify employees who have no federal income tax withheld that they may be able to a tax refund because of the EIC. Although you do not have to notify employees who claim exemption from withholding on Form W-4 about EIC, you are encouraged to notify employees whose wages for 2012 were less than $45,060 ($50,270 if married and filing jointly) that they may be able to claim the ___ for 2012.
   - (a) refund
   - (b) tax refund
   - (c) bonus refund
   - (d) credit

   Answer: See Required Notice to Employees About the Earned Income Credit (EIC), Section 10 page 24/ (d) credit

© Copyright 2013. All rights reserved. Notice: United States Copyright Laws and International Treaties prohibit unauthorized publication, reproduction, distribution of this Work. Unauthorized use of this copyright in any form, format, publication or document may result in severe civil and criminal penalties. Violations of this copyright are investigated by the United States Department of Justice and carry, upon conviction of fines up to $250,000 and five years confinement. This Work is protected by United States Copyright Laws and International Treaties. Do not Copy, do not reproduce, do not distribute.

A Ficus Tree Publishing Educational-Technical Publications

Required Notice to Employees About the Earned Income Credit (EIC)

10. Required Notice to Employees About the Earned Income Credit.

3. You must notify employees who have no federal income tax withheld that they may be able to a tax refund because of the EIC. Although you do not have to notify employees who claim exemption from withholding on Form W-4 about EIC, you are encouraged to notify employees whose wages for 2012 were less than $45,060 ($50,270 if married and filing jointly) that they may be able to claim the ___ for 2012. This because eligible employees may get a refund of the amount of EIC that is more than the tax ___.
   (a) refund, they owe
   (b) tax refund, they paid
   (c) bonus refund, that was withheld
   (d) credit, that was deposited
   Answer: See Required Notice to Employees About the Earned Income Credit (EIC), Section 10, page 24/ (d) credit, they owe

10. Required Notice to Employees About the Earned Income Credit.

4. You must notify employees who have no federal income tax withheld that they may be able to a tax refund because of the EIC. Although you do not have to notify employees who claim exemption from withholding on Form W-4 about EIC, you are encouraged to notify employees whose wages for 2012 were less than $45,060 ($50,270 if married and filing jointly) that they may be able to claim the credit for 2012. This because eligible employees may get a refund of the amount of EIC that is more than the tax they owe.

   You will meet this notification requirement if you issue the employee Form W-2 with the EIC notice on the back of Copy B, or a substitute Form W-2 with the same statement. You will also meet the requirement by providing Notice 797, Possible Federal Tax Refund Due to the Earned Income Credit (ECI), or your own statement that contains the same wording.

   If a substitute for Form W - ___ is given to the employee on time but does not have the required statement, you must notify the employee within ___ of the date the substitute Form W - ___ is given.
   (a) 1, seven-days, 1
   (b) 2, 1 week, 2
   (c) 3, 1 week, 3
   (d) 4, 10 days, 4
   Answer: See Section 10. Required Notice to Employees About the Earned Income Credit (EIC) pages 24 and 25/(b) 2, 1 week, 2

Required Notice to Employees About the Earned Income Credit (EIC)

10. Required Notice to Employees About the Earned Income Credit.

5. If a substitute for Form W - 2 is given to the employee on time but does not have the required statement, you must notify the employee within 1 week of the date the substitute Form W - 2 is given. If Form W-2 is required but is not given on time, you must give the employee Notice ___ or a written statement by the date Form W-2 is given.
   (a) 767
   (b) 777
   (c) 787
   (d) 797
   Answer: See Section 10 Required Notice to Employees About the Earned Income Credit (EIC) page 25/ (d) 797

10. Required Notice to Employees About the Earned Income Credit.

6. If a substitute for Form W - 2 is given to the employee on time but does not have the required statement, you must notify the employee within 1 week of the date the substitute Form W - 2 is given. If Form W-2 is required but is not given on time, you must give the employee Notice ___ or a written statement by the date Form W-2 is given. If Form W-2 is not required, you must notify the employee by February ___, 2012.
   (a) 4
   (b) 5
   (c) 6
   (d) 7
   Answer: See Section 10. Required Notice to Employees About the Earned Income Credit (EIC) page 25/ (d) 797, 7

A Ficus Tree Publishing Quick Notes Page.

The International Leader in Construction Technology Home Study

Instructor's Manual for Tax Test 15E-S11
Section 11. Depositing Taxes

General Description. Section 11. Depositing Taxes. Page 25.

Tax Test 15E-S11. Tax Test 15E-S11-1, introduces material and information pertaining to IRS Circular E, Employer's Tax Guide, Section 11. Depositing Taxes. Section 11. Depositing Taxes is a large, important, comprehensive, section of IRS Circular E, Employer's Tax Guide.

Key Words. Section 11. Depositing Taxes. Page 25.

Tax Test 15E-S11. Depositing Taxes. How To Deposit. COBRA. credit against employment taxes. Form 941. line 12a. Payment with return. Form 944. Accuracy of Deposits Rule. Employer's Tax Liability. Monthly Schedule Depositor. Semi-weekly rules. $100,000 Next day deposit rule. current quarter. fourth quarter tax liability. less than $2,500. $2,500 or more. failure-to-deposit penalties. Separate deposit requirements for nonpayroll. Form 945 tax liabilities. When to deposit. Two Deposit Schedules. Rules do not apply to FUTA. Do not combine deposits. nonpayroll liabilities. Lookback Period. Lookback Period Calendar. Adjustments and the lookback rule. Deposit Period. Monthly deposit schedule. Semiweekly Deposit Schedule. deposit period spanning two quarters. Examples of Monthly and Semiweekly Schedules. Deposits on Business Days Only. Legal Holiday. $100,000 Next-Day Deposit Rule. once you accumulate. Accuracy of deposits Rule. Makeup Date for Deposit Shortfall. Monthly. Semiweekly. **How To Deposit**. Electronic deposit requirement. When you receive your EIN. Deposit Record. Depositing on time. Same-day payment options. How to claim credit for overpayments. **Deposit Penalties**. Penalties may apply if. proper and timely deposit. late deposit penalty. Special rule for former Form 944 filers. Order in which deposits are applied. **Trust fund recovery penalty**. Willfully. A responsible person. Separate accounting when deposits are not made or withheld taxes are not paid. Averaged. Averaged failure-to-deposit- penalty. FDT. prior period errors.

© Copyright 2013. All rights reserved. Notice: United States Copyright Laws and International Treaties prohibit unauthorized publication, reproduction, distribution of this Work. Unauthorized use of this copyright in any form, format, publication or document may result in severe civil and criminal penalties. Violations of this copyright are investigated by the United States Department of Justice and carry, upon conviction of fines up to $250,000 and five years confinement. This Work is protected by United States Copyright Laws and International Treaties. Do not Copy, do not reproduce, do not distribute.

A Ficus Tree Publishing Educational-Technical Publications

A Ficus Tree Publishing Quick Notes Page

Know and understand "Lookback" and "Lookback Period"

DU VALL'S TEST'S™
Instructors Manual For Study Guide Series United States Tax Code
IRS Publication 15 Circular E, Employer's Tax Guide Tax Year 2013
Tax Test 15E-S11-1 [Multiple-Choice Questions With Answers]

Section 11. Depositing Taxes. Page 25.

Section 11. Depositing Taxes.
1. In general, you must deposit income tax withheld and ___ the employer and employee social security and Medicare taxes.
   - (a) all
   - (b) all withheld taxes for
   - (c) both
   - (d) any additional taxes for

   Answer: See Section 11. Depositing Taxes, page 25/ (c) both

11. Depositing Taxes.
2. In general, you must deposit income tax withheld and ___ the employer and employee social security and Medicare taxes. You must use ___ to make all federal deposits.
   - (a) all, electronic banking transfer
   - (b) all withheld taxes for, IRS electronic transfer procedures
   - (c) both, electronic funds transfer
   - (d) any additional taxes for, the paperless electronic funds transfer

   Answer: See Section 11. Depositing Taxes, page 25/ (c) both, electronic funds transfer

11. Depositing taxes.
3. In general, you must deposit income tax withheld and ___ the employer and employee social security and Medicare taxes. You must use ___ to make all federal deposits. See *How To Deposit*, later in this section, for electronic deposit ___.
   - (a) all, electronic banking transfer, information
   - (b) all withheld taxes for, IRS electronic transfer procedures, processing
   - (c) both, electronic funds transfer, requirements
   - (d) any additional taxes for, the paperless electronic funds transfer, procedures

   Answer: See Section 11. Depositing Taxes, page 25/ (c) both, electronic funds transfer, requirements.

11. Depositing Taxes. Tip
4. The credit against ___ taxes for COBRA assistance payments you take on Form 941, line 12a, or Form 944, line ___ is treated as a deposit of taxes on the first day of your return period.
   - (a) employment, 9a
   - (b) employment, 9b
   - (c) payroll, 7a
   - (d) payroll, 7b

   Answer: See Section 11. Depositing Taxes, Tip, page 25/ (a) employment, 9a

Depositing Taxes

11. Depositing Taxes. Tip
5. The credit against employment taxes for COBRA assistance payment you take on Form 941, line ___ or Form 944, line ___, is treated as a deposit of taxes on the first day of your return period.
   (a)   11a, 12a
   (b)   12a, 11a
   (c)   11b, 12b
   (d)   12b, 11b
   Answer: See Section 11. Depositing Taxes, Tip, page 25/ (b) 12a, 11a

11. Depositing Taxes. Tip
6. The credit against ___ taxes for COBRA assistance payments you take on Form 941, line 12a, or Form 944, line ___ is treated as a deposit of taxes on the first day of your return period. See **COBRA ___ assistance credit** under Introduction for more information.
   (a)   employment, 9a, premium
   (b)   employment, 9b, premium
   (c)   payroll, 7a, financial
   (d)   payroll, 7b, financial
   Answer: See Section 11. Depositing Taxes, Tip, page 25/ (a) employment, 9a, premium

Depositing Taxes Payment with return

11. Depositing Taxes. Payment with return.
7. You may make a payment with Form 941 or Form ___ instead of ___ without incurring a penalty, if
   (a)   943, direct deposit
   (b)   944, depositing
   (c)   945, waiting
   (d)   946, postponing
   Answer: See Section 11. Depositing Taxes. Payment with return. Page 25/ (b) 944, depositing

11. Depositing Taxes. Payment with return.
8. You may make a payment with Form 941 or Form ___ instead of ___ without incurring a penalty, if one of the following applies.
   • Your Form 941 total tax liability for either the current quarter or the preceding is less than $___,
   (a)   943, direct deposit, 2.380
   (b)   944, depositing, 2,500
   (c)   945, waiting, 3,000
   (d)   946, postponing, 3,100
   Answer: See Section 11. Depositing Taxes. Payment with return. Page 25/ (b) 944, depositing, 2,500

© Copyright 2013. All rights reserved. Notice: United States Copyright Laws and International Treaties prohibit unauthorized publication, reproduction, distribution of this Work. Unauthorized use of this copyright in any form, format, publication or document may result in severe civil and criminal penalties. Violations of this copyright are investigated by the United States Department of Justice and carry, upon conviction of fines up to $250,000 and five years confinement. This Work is protected by United States Copyright Laws and International Treaties. Do not Copy, do not reproduce, do not distribute.

Depositing Taxes

11. Depositing Taxes. Payment with return.

9. You may make a payment with Form 941 or Form ___ instead of ___ without incurring a penalty, if one of the following applies.
   • Your Form 941 total tax liability for either the current quarter or the preceding is less than $___, and you did not incur a $___ next-day deposit obligation during the current quarter.
   (a) 943, direct deposit, 2,380, 52,000
   (b) 944, depositing, 2,500, 100,000
   (c) 945, waiting, 3,000, 150,000
   (d) 946, postponing, 3,100, 200,000
   Answer: See Section 11. Depositing Taxes. Payment with return. Page 25/ (b) 944, depositing, 2,500, 100,000

11. Depositing Taxes. Payment with return.

10. You may make a payment with Form 941 or Form 944 instead of depositing without incurring a penalty, if one of the following applies.
    • Your Form 941 total tax liability for either the current quarter or the preceding is less than $___, and you did not incur a $___ next-day deposit obligation during the current quarter. If you are not sure your total tax liability for the current quarter will be less than $___,
    (a) waiting, 2,500, 200,000, 2,500
    (b) direct deposit, 2,380, 52,000, 2,380
    (c) depositing, 2,500, 100,000, 2,500
    (d) waiting, 3,000, 150,000, 3000
    Answer: See Section 11. Depositing Taxes. Payment with return. Page 25/ (b) depositing, 2,500, 100,000, 2,500

11. Depositing Taxes. Payment with return.

11. You may make a payment with Form 941 or Form 944 instead of depositing without incurring a penalty, if one of the following applies.
    • Your Form 941 total tax liability for either the current quarter or the preceding is less than $2,500, and you did not incur a $100,000 next-day deposit obligation during the current quarter. If you are not sure your total tax liability for the current quarter will be less than $2,500, (and your liability for the preceding quarter was not less than $2,500), make deposits using the semi-weekly or monthly rules so you won't be subject to ___.
    (a) penalties
    (b) IRS penalties
    (c) deposit penalties
    (d) failure-to-deposit penalties
    Answer: See Section 11. Depositing Taxes. Payment with return. Page 25/ (d) failure-to-deposit penalties

11. Depositing Taxes. Payment with return.

11. Depositing Taxes. Payment with return.
12. You may make a payment with Form 941 or Form 944 instead of depositing without incurring a penalty, if one of the following applies.
    • You are a monthly schedule depositor (defined later) and make a ___ in accordance with the ***Accuracy of Deposits Rule*** discussed later in this section.
    (a) payment
    (b) deposit
    (c) timely deposit
    (d) late deposit
    Answer: See Section 11. Depositing Taxes. Payment with return. Page 25/ (a) payment

11. Depositing Taxes. Payment with return.
13. You may make a payment with Form 941 or Form 944 instead of depositing without incurring a penalty, if one of the following applies.
    • You are a monthly schedule depositor (defined later) and make a ___ in accordance with the ***Accuracy of Deposits Rule*** discussed later in this section. This payment may be $___ or more.
    (a) payment, 2,500
    (b) deposit, 2,500
    (c) timely deposit, 3,000
    (d) late deposit, 2,500
    Answer: See Section 11. Depositing Taxes. Payment with return. Page 25/ (a) payment, 2.500

11. Depositing Taxes. Payment with return.
14. Employers who have been notified to File Form ___ can pay their fourth quarter tax liability with Form 944 if the fourth quarter tax liability is less than $___.
    (a) 943, 2,200
    (b) 944, 2,500
    (c) 945, 2,750
    (d) 946, 3,000
    Answer: See Section 11. Depositing Taxes. Payment with return. Page 25/(b) 944, 2,500

11. Depositing Taxes. Payment with return.
15. Employers who have been notified to File Form 944 can pay their fourth quarter tax liability with Form 944 if the fourth quarter tax liability is less than $2,500. Employers must have deposited any tax liability due for the first, second and third quarters according to deposit rules to avoid __ during those quarters.
    (a) penalties
    (b) additional penalties
    (c) IRS Audit
    (d) failure to deposit rules for deposits
    Answer: See Section 11. Depositing Taxes. Payment with return. Page 25/(d) failure to deposit penalties for deposits

Depositing Taxes
Separate deposit requirements for nonpayroll (Form 945) tax liabilities

11. Separate deposit requirements for nonpayroll (Form 945) tax liabilities.
16. Separate deposits are required for nonpayroll and payroll income tax ___.
    (a) wages
    (b) income
    (c) withholding
    (d) failure to deposit
    Answer: See Section 11. Depositing Taxes. Separate deposit requirements for nonpayroll (Form 945) tax liabilities. Page 25/(c) withholding

11. Separate deposit requirements for nonpayroll (Form 945) tax liabilities.
17. Separate deposits are required for nonpayroll and payroll income tax withholding. Do not combine deposits for Forms ___ (or Form) and Form ___ tax liabilities.
    (a) 942, 943, 944
    (b) 941, 943, 944
    (c) 941, 944, 943
    (d) 941, 944, 945
    Answer: See Section 11. Depositing Taxes. Separate deposit requirements for nonpayroll (Form 945) tax liabilities. Page 25/(d) 941, 944, 945

11. Separate deposit requirements for nonpayroll (Form 945) tax liabilities.
18. Generally, the deposit rules for nonpayroll ___ are the same as discussed below, except
    (a) liabilities
    (b) withholding
    (c) taxes
    (d) income
    Answer: See Section 11. Depositing Taxes. Separate deposit requirements for nonpayroll (Form 945) tax liabilities. Page 25/(a) liabilities

11. Separate deposit requirements for nonpayroll (Form 945) tax liabilities.
19. Generally, the deposit rules for nonpayroll ___ are the same as discussed below, except the rules apply to an ___ rather than a quarterly return period. Thus, the $___ threshold for the deposit requirement discussed earlier applies to Form 945 on an annual basis.
    (a) liabilities, annual, 2,500
    (b) withholding, semi-annual, 3,000
    (c) taxes, quarterly, 3.500
    (d) income, monthly, 5,000
    Answer: See Section 11. Depositing Taxes. Separate deposit requirements for nonpayroll (Form 945) tax liabilities. Page 25/(a) liabilities, annual, 2,500

© Copyright 2013. All rights reserved. Notice: United States Copyright Laws and International Treaties prohibit unauthorized publication, reproduction, distribution of this Work. Unauthorized use of this copyright in any form, format, publication or document may result in severe civil and criminal penalties. Violations of this copyright are investigated by the United States Department of Justice and carry, upon conviction of fines up to $250,000 and five years confinement. This Work is protected by United States Copyright Laws and International Treaties. Do not Copy, do not reproduce, do not distribute.

A Ficus Tree Publishing Educational-Technical Publications

Separate deposit requirements for nonpayroll (Form 945) tax liabilities

11. Separate deposit requirements for nonpayroll (Form 945) tax liabilities.
20. Generally, the deposit rules for nonpayroll ___ are the same as discussed below, except the rules apply to an ___ rather than a quarterly return period. Thus, the $___ threshold for the deposit requirement discussed earlier applies to Form 945 on an annual basis. See the separate instructions for Form ___ for more information.
   (a) liabilities, annual, 2,500, 945
   (b) withholding, semi-annual, 3,000, 944
   (c) taxes, quarterly, 3.500, 943
   (d) income, monthly, 5,000, 941
   Answer: See Section 11. Depositing Taxes. Separate deposit requirements for nonpayroll (Form 945) tax liabilities. Page 25/(a) liabilities, annual, 2,500, 945

Section 11. Depositing Taxes. When To Deposit

11. Depositing Taxes. When to deposit.
21. There are ___ deposit schedules.
   (a) five
   (b) four
   (c) three
   (d) two
   Answer: See Section 11. Depositing Taxes. When to Deposit. Page 25/(d) two

11. Depositing Taxes. When to deposit.
22. There are two deposit schedules—monthly and ___ — for determining when deposit social security, Medicare, and ___ taxes.
   (a) weekly, payroll
   (b) semi-weekly, withheld
   (c) quarterly, nonpayroll
   (d) semi-annually, employment
   Answer: See Section 11. Depositing Taxes. When to Deposit. Page 25/(b) semi-weekly, withheld

11. Depositing Taxes. When to deposit.
23. There are two deposit schedules—monthly and ___ — for determining when deposit social security, Medicare, and ___ taxes. These schedules tell you when a ___ is due after a tax liability arises (for example, when you have a payday).
   (a) weekly, payroll, tax
   (b) semi-weekly, withheld, deposit
   (c) quarterly, nonpayroll, tax payment
   (d) semi-annually, employment, tax
   Answer: See Section 11. Depositing Taxes. When to Deposit. Page 25/(b) semi-weekly, withheld, deposit

Section 11. Depositing Taxes. When To Deposit

11. Depositing Taxes. When to deposit.
24. Before the beginning of each calendar year, you must determine which of the ___ deposit schedules you are required to use.
   (a) two
   (b) three
   (c) four
   (d) approved
   Answer: See Section 11. Depositing Taxes. When to Deposit. Page 25/(a) two

11. Depositing Taxes. When to deposit.
25. Before the beginning of each calendar year, you must determine which of the ___ deposit schedules you are required to use. The deposit schedule you must use is based on the total tax liability you reported on Form ___ during the **lookback period** discussed next.
   (a) two, 941
   (b) three, 942
   (c) four, 943
   (d) approved, 944
   Answer: See Section 11. Depositing Taxes. When to Deposit. Page 25/(a) two, 941

11. Depositing Taxes. When to deposit.
26. Before the beginning of each calendar year, you must determine which of the ___ deposit schedules you are required to use. The deposit schedule you must use is based on the total tax liability you reported on Form ___ during the **lookback period** discussed next. Your deposit schedule is not determined by how often you pay your employees or ___.
   (a) two, 941, make deposits
   (b) three, 942, pay taxes
   (c) four, 943, pay employer taxes
   (d) approved, 944, pay employer taxes based upon your employees productivity
   Answer: See Section 11. Depositing Taxes. When to Deposit. Page 25/(a) two, 941, make deposits

Section 11. Depositing Taxes. When To Deposit. Forms 944 and 945.

11. Depositing Taxes. When to deposit.
27. See special rules for Forms ___ and ___, later in this section.
   (a) 940, 941
   (b) 941, 942
   (c) 942, 943
   (d) 944, 945
   Answer: See Section 11. Depositing Taxes. When to Deposit. Page 25/(d) 944, 945

Section 11. Depositing Taxes. When To Deposit. Forms 944 and 945.

11. Depositing Taxes. When to deposit.
28. See special rules for Forms ___ and ___, later in this section. Also see *Application of Monthly and ___ Schedules*, later in this section.
    (a) 940, 941, *Semi-annually*
    (b) 941, 942, *Quarterly*
    (c) 942, 943, *Weekly*
    (d) 944, 945, *Semiweekly*
    Answer: See Section 11. Depositing Taxes. When to Deposit. Page 25/(d) 944, 945, *Semiweekly*

11. Depositing Taxes. When to deposit. Caution!
29. These rules do not apply to federal FUTA tax. See **section** ___ for information on depositing FUTA tax.
    (a) 12
    (b) 13
    (c) 14
    (d) 15
    Answer: See section 11. Depositing Taxes, When To Deposit, Caution! Page 25/ (c) 14

11. Depositing Taxes. When To Deposit. Lookback Period.

11. Depositing Taxes. Lookback period.
30. If you are a Form 941 filer, your deposit schedule is determined from the total taxes reported of Forms 941, line ___, in
    (a) 7
    (b) 8
    (c) 9
    (d) 10
    Answer: See section 11. Depositing Taxes, When To Deposit, Lookback period. Page 25/ (d) 10

11. Depositing Taxes. Lookback period.
31. If you are a Form 941 filer, your deposit schedule is determined from the total taxes reported of Forms 941, line ___, in a ___-quarter lookback period.
    (a) 7, First
    (b) 8, Second
    (c) 9, Third
    (d) 10, 4
    Answer: See section 11. Depositing Taxes, When To Deposit, Lookback period. Page 25/ (d) 10

11. Depositing Taxes. When To Deposit. Lookback Period.

11. Depositing Taxes. Lookback period.
32. If you reported $___ or less of taxes for the lookback period, you are a ___ schedule depositor.
 (a) 30,000, weekly
 (b) 40,000, semi-monthly
 (c) 50,000, monthly
 (d) 75,000, quarterly
 Answer: See section 11. Depositing Taxes, When To Deposit, Lookback period. Page 25/ (c) 50,000, monthly

11. Depositing Taxes. Lookback period.
33. If you reported more than $___ , you are a ___ schedule depositor.
 (a) 30,000, weekly
 (b) 40,000, semi-weekly
 (c) 50,000, monthly
 (d) 75,000, quarterly
 Answer: See section 11. Depositing Taxes, When To Deposit, Lookback period. Page 25/ (c) 50,000, monthly

11. Depositing Taxes. Lookback period.
34. The lookback period begins ___ and ends ___.
 (a) Jan. 1, 2012 through Mar. 31, 2012
 (b) Apr. 1, 2012 through June 30, 2012
 (c) July 1, June 30
 (d) Oct. 1, 2011 through Dec. 31, 2011
 Answer: See section 11. Depositing Taxes, When To Deposit, Lookback period. Page 25/ (c) July 1, June 30

11. Depositing Taxes. Lookback Period for any Calendar Year.

11. Depositing Taxes. Lookback period for any Calendar Year.
35. The lookback period begins ___ and ends ___.
 (a) January 1, December 31
 (b) April 1, April 15
 (c) April 1, March 31
 (d) July 1, June 30
 Answer: See Part 11. Depositing Taxes, When To Deposit, Lookback period, page / (d) July 1, June 30

Depositing Taxes. When To Deposit.
Lookback Period for Calendar Year 2013
Table 1. Lookback Period for Calendar Year 2013

11. Depositing Taxes. Lookback period.
36. The lookback period for Calendar Year 2013 begins ___ and ends ___.
   (a) Jan. 1, 2012 through Mar. 31, 2012
   (b) Apr. 1, 2012 through June 30, 2012
   (c) July 1, 2011 through Sep. 30, 2011
   (d) Oct. 1, 2011 through Dec. 31, 2011
   Answer: See section 11. Depositing Taxes, When To Deposit, Lookback period. Page 25/
   (c) July 1, 2011 through Sep. 30, 2011

11. Depositing Taxes. Lookback period.
37. The fourth quarter of the lookback period for Calendar Year 2013 begins ___ and ends ___.
   (a) Jan. 1, 2012 through Mar. 31, 2012
   (b) Apr. 1, 2012 through June 30, 2012
   (c) July 1, 2011 through Sep. 30, 2011
   (d) Oct. 1, 2011 through Dec. 31, 2011
   Answer: See section 11. Depositing Taxes, When To Deposit, Lookback period. Page 25/
   (b) Apr. 1, 2012 through June 30, 2012

11. Depositing Taxes. Lookback period.
38. The second quarter of the calendar year lookback period for 2013 begins ___.
   (a) Jan. 1, 2013
   (b) Apr. 1, 2013
   (c) July 1 and ends June 30
   (d) Oct. 1, 2012 through Dec. 31, 2012
   Answer: See section 11. Depositing Taxes, When To Deposit, Lookback period. Page 25/
   (d) Oct. 1, 2011 through Dec. 31, 2011

11. Depositing Taxes. Lookback period.
39. The third quarter of the calendar year lookback period for 2013 begins ___.
   (a) Jan. 1, 2013
   (b) Apr. 1, 2013
   (c) July 1 and ends June 30
   (d) Oct. 1, 2012 through Dec. 31, 2012
   Answer: See section 11. Depositing Taxes, When To Deposit, Lookback period. Page 25/
   (d) Oct. 1, 2011 through Dec. 31, 2011

The International Leader in Construction Technology Home Study

Section 11. Depositing Taxes. When To Deposit.
Lookback Period for Calendar Year 2013. Page 25.
Table 1. Lookback Period for Calendar Year 2013

11. Depositing Taxes. Lookback period.
40.   The first quarter of the lookback period for Calendar Year 2013 begins ___ and ends ___.
   (a)   Jan. 1, 2012, Mar. 31, 2012
   (b)   Apr. 1, 2012, June 30, 2012
   (c)   July 1, 2011, Sep. 30, 2011
   (d)   Oct. 1, 2011, Dec. 31, 2011
   Answer: See section 11. Depositing Taxes, When To Deposit, Lookback period. Page 25/ (c) July 1, 2011, Sep. 30, 2011

11. Depositing Taxes. Lookback period. Caution!
41.   The lookback period for a 2013 Form 941filer is who filed Form 944 in either 2011 or 2012 is calendar year ___.
   (a)   2010
   (b)   2011
   (c)   2012
   (d)   2013
   Answer: See section 11. Depositing Taxes, When To Deposit, Lookback period. Caution. Page 25/ (b) 2011

11. Depositing Taxes. Lookback period.
42.   If you are a Form 944 filer for the current year or either of the preceding ___ years, your deposit schedule for a calendar year is determined from
   (a)   2
   (b)   3
   (c)   4
   (d)   5
   Answer: See section 11. Depositing Taxes, When To Deposit, Lookback period, Page 25/ (a) 2

© Copyright 2013. All rights reserved. Notice: United States Copyright Laws and International Treaties prohibit unauthorized publication, reproduction, distribution of this Work. Unauthorized use of this copyright in any form, format, publication or document may result in severe civil and criminal penalties. Violations of this copyright are investigated by the United States Department of Justice and carry, upon conviction of fines up to $250,000 and five years confinement. This Work is protected by United States Copyright Laws and International Treaties. Do not Copy, do not reproduce, do not distribute.

A Ficus Tree Publishing Educational-Technical Publications

Section 11. Depositing Taxes. Lookback Period. (Form 941)

11. Depositing Taxes. Lookback period. (Form 941)
43. If you are a Form 944 filer for the current year or either of the preceding ___years, your deposit schedule for a calendar year is determined from the total taxes reported during the ___ preceding calendar year (either on your **Form 941** for all ___ of that year or your Form 944 for that year).
    (a) 2, second, 4 quarters
    (b) 3, third, 4 quarters
    (c) 4, fourth, 4 quarters
    (d) 5, first, 4 quarters
    Answer: See section 11. Depositing Taxes, When To Deposit, Lookback period. Page 25/
    (a) 2, second,4 quarters

Section 11. Depositing Taxes. When To Deposit Lookback Period (Form 944)
Table 1. Lookback Period for Calendar Year 2013

11. Depositing Taxes. Lookback period. (Form 944)
44. If you are a **Form 944** filer for the current year or either of the preceding ___years, your deposit schedule for a calendar year is determined from the total taxes reported during the ___ preceding calendar year (either on your Form 941for all ___ of that year or your **Form 944** for that year).
    (a) 2, second, 4 quarters
    (b) 3, third, 4 quarters
    (c) 4, fourth, 4 quarters
    (d) 5, first, 4 quarters
    Answer: See section 11. Depositing Taxes, When To Deposit, Lookback period. Page 25/
    (a) 2, second,4 quarters

11. Depositing Taxes. Lookback period.
45. If you are a **Form 944** filer for the current year or either of the preceding **2 years**, your deposit schedule for a calendar year is determined from the total taxes reported during the second preceding calendar year (either on your **Form 941**for all 4 quarters of that year or your **Form 944** for that year). If you reported $___ **or less** of taxes for the lookback period, you are a **monthly** schedule depositor.
    (a) 10,000
    (b) 25,000
    (c) 50,000
    (d) 75,000
    Answer: See section 11. Depositing Taxes, When To Deposit, Lookback period. Page 25/
    (c) 50,000

When To Deposit. Lookback Period (Form 944)

11. Depositing Taxes. Lookback period.
46. If you are a **Form 944** filer for the current year or either of the preceding 2 years, your deposit schedule for a calendar year is determined from the total taxes reported during the second preceding calendar year (either on your **Form 941** for all 4 quarters of that year or your **Form 944** for that year). If you reported **less** than $___ or less of taxes for the lookback period, you are a monthly schedule depositor. If you reported **more** than $___ you are a **semiweekly** schedule depositor.
    (a) 10,000, 10,000
    (b) 25,000, 25,000
    (c) 50,000, 50,000
    (d) 75,000, 75,000
    Answer: See section 11. Depositing Taxes, When To Deposit, Lookback period. Page 25/ (c) 50,000, 50,000

11. Depositing Taxes. Lookback period.
47. If you are a **Form 945** filer, your deposit schedule is determined from the total taxes reported on line ___ of your **Form 945** for the **second** preceding year.
    (a) 3
    (b) 4
    (c) 5
    (d) 6
    Answer: See section 11. Depositing Taxes, When To Deposit, Lookback period. Page. 25/ (a) 3

Depositing Taxes. When To Deposit. Lookback Period. Form 945 filer

11. Depositing Taxes. Lookback period.
48. If you are a **Form 945** filer, your deposit schedule is determined from the total taxes reported on line ___ of your **Form 945** for the **second** preceding year. The lookback period for 2013 for a **Form 945** filer is calendar year ___.
    (a) 3, 2011
    (b) 4, 2012
    (c) 5, 2013
    (d) 6, 2010
    Answer: See section 11. Depositing Taxes, When To Deposit, Lookback period. Page 25/ (a) 3, 2011

Section 11. Depositing Taxes. Adjustments and the lookback rule.

11. Depositing Taxes. Adjustments and the lookback rule.
49. Adjustments made on **Form ___**, **Form ___**, and **Form ___** do not affect the amount of tax liability for previous periods for purposes of the lookback rule.
 (a) 941, 944, 945
 (b) 941-a, 944-a, 945-a
 (c) 941-b, 944-b, 945-b
 (d) 941-x, 944-x, 945-x
 Answer: See section 11. Depositing Taxes, When To Deposit, Lookback period. Page 26/ (d) 941-x, 944-x, 945-x

11. Depositing Taxes. Adjustments and the lookback rule. Example:
50. Example. An employer originally reported a tax liability of $45,000 for the lookback period. The employer discovered, during January 2013, that the tax reported for one of the lookback period quarters was <u>understated</u> by $10,000 and <u>corrected this error</u> by filing **Form ___**.
 (a) 941
 (b) 941-a
 (c) 941-b
 (d) 941-x
 Answer: See section 11. Depositing Taxes, When To Deposit, Lookback period. Example. Page 26/ (d) 941-x

Section 11. Depositing Taxes. Adjustments and the lookback rule. Example: Page 26.

11. Depositing Taxes. Adjustments and the lookback rule. Example:
51. Example. An employer originally reported a tax liability of $45,000 for the lookback period. The employer discovered, during January 2013, that the tax reported for one of the lookback period quarters was <u>understated</u> by $10,000 and <u>corrected this error</u> by filing **Form 941-x**. This employer is a ___ depositor for 2013 because the lookback period tax liabilities are based on the amounts originally reported, and they were $50,000 or less.
 (a) weekly schedule
 (b) semi-weekly schedule
 (c) monthly schedule
 (d) quarterly schedule
 Answer: See section 11. Depositing Taxes, When To Deposit, Lookback period. Example. Page 26/ (c) monthly schedule

Section 11. Depositing Taxes. Deposit period. Page 26.

11. Depositing Taxes. Deposit period.
52. The term deposit period refers to the period during which tax liabilities are ___ for each required due date.
    (a) compiled
    (b) accumulated
    (c) recorded
    (d) posted
    Answer: See section 11. Depositing Taxes. Deposit period. Page 26/ (b) accumulated

11. Depositing Taxes. Deposit period.
53. The term deposit period refers to the period during which tax liabilities are ___ for each required due date. For monthly schedule depositors, the deposit period is a ___ month.
    (a) compiled, standard
    (b) accumulated, calendar
    (c) recorded, typical
    (d) posted, 30 day
    Answer: See section 11. Depositing Taxes. Deposit period. Page 26/ (b) accumulated, calendar

11. Depositing Taxes. Deposit period.
54. The term deposit period refers to the period during which tax liabilities are accumulated for each required due date. For monthly schedule depositors, the deposit period is a calendar month. The deposit periods for semiweekly schedule depositors are ___ through ___ and ___ through ___.
    (a) Thursday, Saturday, Sunday, Tuesday
    (b) Monday, Thursday, Friday, Sunday
    (c) Wednesday, Friday, Saturday, Tuesday
    (d) Sunday, Wednesday, Thursday, Saturday
    Answer: See section 11. Depositing Taxes. Deposit period. Page 26/ (c) Wednesday, Friday, Saturday, Tuesday

Section 11. Depositing Taxes. Monthly Deposit Schedule. Page 26.

11. Depositing Taxes. Monthly Deposit Schedule.(Form 941)
55. You are a monthly schedule depositor for a calendar year if the total taxes on **Form 941**, line ___, for the 4 quarters in your lookback period were $___ or less.
    (a) 8, 10,000
    (b) 9, 25,000
    (c) 10, 50,000
    (d) 11, 100,000
    Answer: See section 11. Depositing Taxes. Monthly Deposit Schedule. Page 26/ (c) 10, 50,000

Section 11. Depositing Taxes. Monthly Deposit Schedule. Page 26.

11. Depositing Taxes. Monthly Deposit Schedule.(Form 941)
56. You are a monthly schedule depositor for a calendar year if the total taxes on **Form 941**, line ___, for the 4 quarters in your lookback period were $___ or less. Under the monthly deposit schedule, deposit employment taxes on payments made during the month by the __day of the following month.
    (a) 8, 10,000, 5th
    (b) 9, 25,000, 10th
    (c) 10, 50,000, 15th
    (d) 11, 100,000, 30th
    Answer: See section 11. Depositing Taxes. Monthly Deposit Schedule. Page 26/ (c) 10, 50,000, 15th

11. Depositing Taxes. Monthly Deposit Schedule.(Form 941)
57. You are a monthly schedule depositor for a calendar year if the total taxes on **Form 941**, line 10, for the 4 quarters in your lookback period were $50,000 or less. Under the monthly deposit schedule, deposit employment taxes on payments made during the month by the 15th day of the following month. See also, *Deposits on Business Days Only* and the *$___ Next-Day Deposit Rule*, later in this section.
    (a) 50,000
    (b) 100,000
    (c) 150,000
    (d) 200,000
    Answer: See section 11. Depositing Taxes. Monthly Deposit Schedule. Page 26/ (b) 100,000

11. Depositing Taxes. Monthly Deposit Schedule.(Form 941)
58. You are a monthly schedule depositor for a calendar year if the total taxes on **Form 941**, line 10, for the 4 quarters in your lookback period were $50,000 or less. Under the monthly deposit schedule, deposit employment taxes on payments made during the month by the 15th day of the following month. See also, *Deposits on Business Days Only* and the *$___ Next-Day Deposit Rule*, later in this section. Monthly schedule depositors should not file Form ___ or Form ___ on a monthly basis.
    (a) 50,000, 940, 943
    (b) 100,000, 941, 944
    (c) 150,000, 943, 945
    (d) 200,000, 943, 945
    Answer: See section 11. Depositing Taxes. Monthly Deposit Schedule. Page 26/ (b) 100,000, 941, 944

Section 11. Depositing Taxes. Monthly Deposit Schedule. New employers. Page 26.

11. Depositing Taxes. Monthly Deposit Schedule. New employers.
59. Your tax liability for any quarter in the lookback period before you started or acquired your business is ___.
    (a) the total amount of your assets
    (b) the amount of your net business worth
    (c) zero
    (d) $10,000
    Answer: See section 11. Depositing Taxes. Monthly Deposit Schedule. New employers Page 26/ (c) zero

11. Depositing Taxes. Monthly Deposit Schedule. New employers.
60. Your tax liability for any quarter in the lookback period before you started or acquired your business is ___. Therefore, you are a ___ schedule depositor for the first calendar year of your business.
    (a) the total amount of your assets, weekly
    (b) the amount of your net business worth, semiweekly
    (c) zero, monthly
    (d) $10,000, quarterly
    Answer: See section 11. Depositing Taxes. Monthly Deposit Schedule. New employers Page 26/ (c) zero, monthly

11. Depositing Taxes. Monthly Deposit Schedule. New employers.
61. Your tax liability for any quarter in the lookback period before you started or acquired your business is ___. Therefore, you are a ___ schedule depositor for the first calendar year of your business. However, see the *$___ Next-Day Deposit Rule*, later in this section.
    (a) the total amount of your assets, weekly, 50,000
    (b) the amount of your net business worth, semiweekly, 50,000
    (c) zero, monthly, 100,000
    (d) $10,000, quarterly, 200,000
    Answer: See section 11. Depositing Taxes. Monthly Deposit Schedule. New employers Page 26/(c) zero, monthly, 100,000

A Ficus Tree Publishing Quick Notes Page

DU VALL'S TEST'S™
Instructors Manual Study Guide Series United States Tax Code
IRS Publication 15 Circular E, Employer's Tax Guide Tax Year 2013
Tax Test 15E-S11-2 [Multiple-Choice Questions With Answers]

Section 11. Depositing Taxes. Semiweekly Deposit Schedule. Page 26

11. Depositing Taxes. Semiweekly Deposit Schedule.
1. You are a semiweekly depositor for a calendar year if your total taxes on Form 941, line ___, during your lookback period were more than $50,000.
   - (a)   10
   - (b)   11
   - (c)   12
   - (d)   13

   Answer: See section 11. Depositing Taxes. Semiweekly Deposit Schedule. P. 26/ (a) 10

11. Depositing Taxes. Semiweekly Deposit Schedule.
2. You are a semiweekly depositor for a calendar year if your total taxes on Form 941, line ___, during your lookback period were more than $50,000. Under the semiweekly deposit schedule, deposit employment taxes for payments made on Wednesday, Thursday, and/or Friday by the following ___.
   - (a)   10, Wednesday
   - (b)   11, Thursday
   - (c)   12, Friday
   - (d)   13, Monday

   Answer: See section 11. Depositing Taxes. Semiweekly Deposit Schedule. Page 26/ (a) 10, Wednesday

11. Depositing Taxes. Semiweekly Deposit Schedule.
3. You are a semiweekly depositor for a calendar year if your total taxes on Form 941, line ___, during your lookback period were more than $50,000. Under the semiweekly deposit schedule, deposit employment taxes for payments made on Wednesday, Thursday, and/or Friday by the following ___. Deposit taxes for payments made on Saturday, Sunday, Monday, and /or Tuesday by the following ___.
   - (a)   10, Wednesday, Friday
   - (b)   11, Thursday, Monday
   - (c)   12, Friday, Tuesday
   - (d)   13, Monday, Wednesday

   Answer: See section 11. Depositing Taxes. Semiweekly Deposit Schedule. Page 26/ (a) 10, Wednesday, Friday

Section 11. Depositing Taxes. Semiweekly Deposit Schedule. Page 26

11. Depositing Taxes. Semiweekly Deposit Schedule.
4. You are a semiweekly depositor for a calendar year if your total taxes on Form 941, line ___, during your lookback period were more than $50,000. Under the semiweekly deposit schedule, deposit employment taxes for payments made on Wednesday, Thursday, and/or Friday by the following ___. Deposit taxes for payments made on Saturday, Sunday, Monday, and /or Tuesday by the following ___. See also, Deposits on ___ , later in this section.
   (a)   10, Wednesday, Friday, Business Days Only
   (b)   11, Thursday, Monday, Week Days Only
   (c)   12, Friday, Tuesday, business days only
   (d)   13, Monday, Wednesday, Banking Days Only
Answer: See section 11. Depositing Taxes. Semiweekly Deposit Schedule. Page 26/ (a) 10, Wednesday, Friday, Business Days Only

11. Depositing Taxes. Semiweekly Deposit Schedule. Note.
5. Semiweekly depositors must complete Schedule ___ (Form 941), Report of Tax Liability for Semiweekly Schedule Depositors, and submit it with Form 941.
   (a)   A
   (b)   B
   (c)   C
   (d)   D
Answer: See section 11. Depositing Taxes. Semiweekly Deposit Schedule. **Note.** Page 26/ (b) B

11. Depositing Taxes. Semiweekly Deposit Schedule. Note.
6. Semiweekly depositors must complete Schedule ___ (Form 941), Report of Tax Liability for Semiweekly Schedule Depositors, and submit it with Form 941. If you file Form 944 and are a semiweekly schedule depositor, complete Form ___, Annual Record of Federal Tax Liability, and submit it with your return (instead of Schedule ___).
   (a)   A, 944-A, A
   (b)   B, 945-A, B
   (c)   C, 946-C, C
   (d)   D, 948-D, D
Answer: See section 11. Depositing Taxes. Semiweekly Deposit Schedule. **Note.** Page 26/ (b) B, 945-B, B

The International Leader in Construction Technology Home Study

Section 11. Depositing Taxes. Table 2. Semiweekly Deposit Schedule.

11. Depositing Taxes. Table 2. Semiweekly Deposit Schedule.
7. If a payday falls on a Wednesday, Thursday and/or Friday, then deposit taxes by the following ___.
   (a) Monday
   (b) Tuesday
   (c) Wednesday
   (d) Thursday
   Answer: See section 11. Depositing Taxes. Table 2. Semiweekly Deposit Schedule. Page 26/ (c) Wednesday

11. Depositing Taxes. Table 2. Semiweekly Deposit Schedule.
8. If a payday falls on a Saturday, Sunday, Monday, and or Tuesday, then deposit taxes by the following ___.
   (a) Tuesday
   (b) Wednesday
   (c) Thursday
   (d) Friday
   Answer: See section 11. Depositing Taxes. Table 2. Semiweekly Deposit Schedule. Page 26/ (d) Friday

11. Depositing Taxes. Semiweekly Deposit period spanning 2 quarters.

11. Depositing Taxes. Semiweekly Deposit period spanning 2 quarters.
9. If you have more than one pay date during a semiweekly period and the pay dates fall in different calendar quarters, you will need to make ___ for ___.
   (a) different deposits, separate liabilities
   (b) separate deposits, separate liabilities
   (c) timely deposits, separate liabilities
   (d) weekly deposits, separate liabilities
   Answer: See section 11. Depositing Taxes. Table 2. Semiweekly Deposit Schedule. Page 26/ (b) Separate deposits, separate liabilities

11. Depositing Taxes. Semiweekly Deposit period spanning 2 quarters. Example.
10. **Example**. If you have a pay date on Saturday, March 30, 2013 (first quarter), and another pay date on Tuesday, April 2, 2013 (second quarter), two separate deposits would be required even though the pay dates fall within the same semiweekly period. Both deposits would be due ___, April 5, 2013
    (a) Monday
    (b) Wednesday
    (c) Thursday
    (d) Friday
    Answer: See section 11. Depositing Taxes. Semiweekly Deposit Schedule. **Example**. Page 26/ (d) Friday

© Copyright 2013. All rights reserved. Notice: United States Copyright Laws and International Treaties prohibit unauthorized publication, reproduction, distribution of this Work. Unauthorized use of this copyright in any form, format, publication or document may result in severe civil and criminal penalties. Violations of this copyright are investigated by the United States Department of Justice and carry, upon conviction of fines up to $250,000 and five years confinement. This Work is protected by United States Copyright Laws and International Treaties. Do not Copy, do not reproduce, do not distribute.

A Ficus Tree Publishing Educational-Technical Publications

Section 11. Depositing Taxes. Deposit period spanning 2 quarters. Summary of Steps to Determine Your Deposit Schedule. (Example)

11. Depositing Taxes. Semiweekly Deposit period spanning 2 quarters. Summary of Steps to Determine Your Deposit Schedule. (Example)

11. 1. Identify your lookback period (see <u>Lookback period</u> earlier in this section).
2. Add the total taxes you reported on Form ___, line___, during the lookback period.
3. Determine if you are a monthly or semiweekly schedule depositor.
If the total taxes you reported in the lookback period were $50,000 or less, then you are a Monthly Schedule Depositor. If the total taxes you reported in the lookback period were more than $50,000, then you are a Semiweekly Schedule Depositor.
(a) 941, 10
(b) 941, 11
(c) 944, 10
(d) 944, 11
Answer: See section 11. Depositing Taxes. Semiweekly Deposit Schedule. **Example**.
Page 26/ (a) 941, 10

Depositing Taxes. Examples of Monthly and Semiweekly Schedules.

11. Depositing Taxes. Example.

12. Rose Co. reported **Form 941** taxes as follows:
2012 Lookback Period.
3rd Quarter 2010 ($12,000)
4th Quarter 2010 ($12,000)
1st Quarter 2011 ($12,000)
2nd Quarter 2011 <u>($12,000)</u>
   $48,000

2013 Lookback Period.
3rd Quarter 2011 ($12,000)
4th Quarter 2011 ($12,000)
1st Quarter 2012 ($12,000)
2nd Quarter 2012 <u>($15,000)</u>
   $51,000

Rose Co. is a monthly schedule depositor for 2012 because its tax liability for the 4 quarters in its lookback period (third quarter 2010 through second quarter 2011) was not more than $___.
However, for 2013, Rose Co. is a semiweekly schedule because the total taxes exceeded $___ for the four quarters in its lookback period (third quarter 2011 through second quarter 2012).
(a) 25,000, 25,000
(b) 30,000, 30,000
(c) 40,000, 40,000
(d) 50,000, 50,000
Answer: See section 11. Depositing Taxes. Semiweekly Deposit Schedule. **Example**.
Page 26/ (d) 50,000, 50,000

Section 11. Depositing Taxes. Deposits on Business Days Only. Page 27.

11. Depositing Taxes. Deposits on Business Days Only.
13. If a deposit is required to be made on a day that is not a business day, the deposit is considered ___ if it is made by the close of the next business day.
    (a) as due
    (b) overdue
    (c) timely
    (d) late
    Answer: See section 11. Depositing Taxes. Deposits on Business Days Only. Page 27/ (c) timely

11. Depositing Taxes. Deposits on Business Days Only.
14. If a deposit is required to be made on a day that is not a business day, the deposit is considered ___ if it is made by the close of the next business day. A business day is any day other than a Saturday, Sunday, or ___.
    (a) as due, religious holiday
    (b) overdue, a holiday
    (c) timely, legal holiday
    (d) late, national holiday
    Answer: See section 11. Depositing Taxes. Deposits on Business Days Only. Page 27/ (c) timely, legal holiday

11. Depositing Taxes. Deposits on Business Days Only.
15. If a deposit is required to be made on a day that is not a business day, the deposit is considered ___ if it is made by the close of the next business day. A business day is any day other than a Saturday, Sunday, or ___. For example, if a deposit is required to be made on Friday and Friday is a legal holiday, the deposit will be considered ___ if it is made by the following Monday (if ___).
    (a) as due, religious holiday, paid, that day is not a holiday
    (b) overdue, a holiday, timely, that day is a business day
    (c) timely, legal holiday, timely, that Monday is a business day
    (d) late, national holiday, timely, that Monday is a business day
    Answer: See section 11. Depositing Taxes. Deposits on Business Days Only. Page 27/ (c) timely, legal holiday, timely, that Monday is a business day).

Section 11. Depositing Taxes.
Deposits on Business Days Only. Semiweekly schedule depositors.

11. Depositing Taxes. Semiweekly schedule depositors.
16. Semiweekly depositors have at least ___ to make a deposit.
    (a)　　two business days
    (b)　　three business days
    (c)　　five business days
    (d)　　seven business days
    Answer: See section 11. Depositing Taxes. Deposits on Business Days Only. Page 27/ (b) three business days

11. Depositing Taxes. Semiweekly schedule depositors.
17. Semiweekly depositors have at least ___ to make a deposit. If any of the ___ after the end of a semiweekly period is a legal holiday, you
    (a)　　two business days, two weekdays
    (b)　　three business days, three weekdays
    (c)　　five business days, five weekdays
    (d)　　seven business days, seven days, full week
    Answer: See section 11. Depositing Taxes. Deposits on Business Days Only. Page 27/ (b) three business days, three weekdays

11. Depositing Taxes. Semiweekly schedule depositors.
18. Semiweekly depositors have at least ___ to make a deposit. If any of the ___ after the end of a semiweekly period is a legal holiday, you will have an ___ for each day that is a legal holiday to make the required deposit.
    (a)　　two business days, two weekdays, extra day
    (b)　　three business days, three weekdays, additional day
    (c)　　five business days, five weekdays, additional day
    (d)　　seven business days, seven days, full week extra day
    Answer: See section 11. Depositing Taxes. Deposits on Business Days Only. Page 27/ (b) three business days, three weekdays, additional day

11. Depositing Taxes. Semiweekly schedule depositors.
19. Semiweekly depositors have at least ___ to make a deposit. If any of the ___ after the end of a semiweekly period is a legal holiday, you will have an ___ for each day that is a legal holiday to make the required deposit. For example, if a semiweekly schedule depositor accumulated taxes for payments made on Friday and the following Monday is a legal holiday, the deposit normally due on Wednesday may be made on ___ (this allows ___ business days to make the deposit).
    (a)　　two business days, two weekdays, extra day, Thursday, 2
    (b)　　three business days, three weekdays, additional day, Thursday, 3
    (c)　　five business days, five weekdays, additional day, the following Monday, five
    (d)　　seven business days, seven days, full week extra day, the following Monday, 7
    Answer: See section 11. Depositing Taxes. Deposits on Business Days Only. Page 27/ (b) three business days, three weekdays, additional day, Thursday, 3

The International Leader in Construction Technology Home Study

Depositing Taxes. Deposits on Business Days Only. Legal holiday.

11. Depositing Taxes. Deposits on Business Days Only. Legal holiday
20. The term "legal holiday" means any legal holiday in the District of Columbia. Legal holidays for 2013 are listed below. The IRS Publication 15, Circular E, Employers Tax Guide for use in 2013 lists ___ "legal holidays" for the District of Columbia.
    (a) 11
    (b) 12
    (c) 13
    (d) 14
    Answer: See section 11. Depositing Taxes. Deposits on Business Days Only. Legal holiday. Page 27/ (a) 11

Depositing Taxes. Application of Monthly and Semiweekly Schedules.

11. Depositing Taxes. Application of Monthly and Semiweekly Schedules.
21. The terms "monthly schedule depositor" and "semiweekly schedule depositor" do not refer to ___ or even how often you are required to make deposits.
    (a) the payroll intervals of your business
    (b) the frequency you pay your employees
    (c) how often your business pays its employees
    (d) when your business pays its employees
    Answer: See section 11. Depositing Taxes. Application of Monthly and Semiweekly Schedules. Page 27/ (c) how often your business pays its employees

11. Depositing Taxes. Application of Monthly and Semiweekly Schedules.
22. The terms "monthly schedule depositor" and "semiweekly schedule depositor" do not refer to ___ or even how often you are required to make deposits. The terms identify ___ you must follow when an employment tax liability arises.
    (a) the payroll intervals of your business, the IRS deposit rules
    (b) the frequency you pay your employees, the deposit rules
    (c) how often your business pays its employees, which set of deposit rules
    (d) when your business pays its employees, the deposit rules
    Answer: See section 11. Depositing Taxes. Application of Monthly and Semiweekly Schedules. Page 27/ (c) how often your business pays its employees, which set of deposit rules

© Copyright 2013. All rights reserved. Notice: United States Copyright Laws and International Treaties prohibit unauthorized publication, reproduction, distribution of this Work. Unauthorized use of this copyright in any form, format, publication or document may result in severe civil and criminal penalties. Violations of this copyright are investigated by the United States Department of Justice and carry, upon conviction of fines up to $250,000 and five years confinement. This Work is protected by United States Copyright Laws and International Treaties. Do not Copy, do not reproduce, do not distribute.

A Ficus Tree Publishing Educational-Technical Publications

Depositing Taxes. Application of Monthly and Semiweekly Schedules.

11. Depositing Taxes. Application of Monthly and Semiweekly Schedules.
23.   The terms "monthly schedule depositor" and "semiweekly schedule depositor" do not refer to ___ or even how often you are required to make deposits. The terms identify ___ you must follow when an employment tax liability arises. The deposit rules are based on the ___ (for example, cash basis);
   (a)   the payroll intervals of your business, the IRS deposit rules, actual payroll amounts
   (b)   the frequency you pay your employees, the deposit rules, payroll tax amount
   (c)   how often your business pays its employees, which set of deposit rules, dates
   (d)   when your business pays its employees, the deposit rules, total tax amount
   Answer: See section 11. Depositing Taxes. Application of Monthly and Semiweekly Schedules. Page 27/ (c) how often your business pays its employees, which set of deposit rules, dates

11. Depositing Taxes. Application of Monthly and Semiweekly Schedules.
24.   The terms "monthly schedule depositor" and "semiweekly schedule depositor" do not refer to how often your business pays its employees or even how often you are required to make deposits. The terms identify which set of deposit rules you must follow when an employment tax liability arises. The deposit rules are based on the dates (for example, cash basis); not on when tax liabilities are ___ for accounting purposes.
   (a)   calculated
   (b)   figured
   (c)   totaled
   (d)   accrued
   Answer: See section 11. Depositing Taxes. Application of Monthly and Semiweekly Schedules. Page 27/ (d) accrued

11. Depositing Taxes. Application of Monthly and Semiweekly Schedules. Monthly schedule example
25.   Spruce Co. is a monthly schedule depositor with ___ employees.
   (a)   seasonal
   (b)   migrant
   (c)   migratory
   (d)   semiskilled
   Answer: See section 11. Depositing Taxes. Application of Monthly and Semiweekly Schedules. Monthly schedule example. Page 27/ (a) seasonal

Section 11. Depositing Taxes.
Application of Monthly and Semiweekly Schedules.
Monthly schedule example.

11. Depositing Taxes. Application of Monthly and Semiweekly Schedules. Monthly schedule example.

26. Spruce Co. is a monthly schedule depositor with ___ employees. It paid wages each Friday during January but did not pay any wages during February. Under the ___ deposit schedule, Spruce Co. must deposit the combined tax liabilities for the four January paydays by ___.
    (a) seasonal, monthly, February 15
    (b) migrant, monthly, February 15
    (c) migratory, seasonal, March 1
    (d) semiskilled, seasonal, March 1
    Answer: See section 11. Depositing Taxes. Application of Monthly and Semiweekly Schedules. Monthly schedule example. Page 27/ (a) seasonal, monthly, February 15

11. Depositing Taxes. Application of Monthly and Semiweekly Schedules. Monthly schedule example

27. Spruce Co. is a monthly schedule depositor with seasonal employees. It paid wages each Friday during January but did not pay any wages during February. Under the monthly deposit schedule, Spruce Co. must deposit the combined tax liabilities for the four January paydays by February 15. Spruce Co. does not have a deposit requirement for February (due by ___) because no wages were paid, and therefore, it did not have a tax liability for February.
    (a) February 15
    (b) February 20
    (c) March 1
    (d) March 15
    Answer: See section 11. Depositing Taxes. Application of Monthly and Semiweekly Schedules. Monthly schedule example. Page 27/ (d) March 15

11. Depositing Taxes. Application of Monthly and Semiweekly Schedules. Semiweekly schedule example.

28. Green, Inc. is a semiweekly schedule depositor and pays wages once each month on the last ___ of the month.
    (a) day
    (b) week
    (c) calendar day
    (d) Friday
    Answer: See section 11. Depositing Taxes. Application of Monthly and Semiweekly Schedules. Semiweekly schedule example. Page 27/ (d) Friday

11. Depositing Taxes.
Application of Monthly and Semiweekly Schedules.
Semiweekly schedule example.

11. Depositing Taxes. Application of Monthly and Semiweekly Schedules. Semiweekly schedule example.

29. Green, Inc. is a semiweekly schedule depositor and pays wages once each month on the last ___ of the month. Although Green, Inc., has a semiweekly deposit schedule, it will deposit ___ because it pays wages only once a month.
    (a) day, each week
    (b) week, weekly
    (c) calendar day, semiweekly
    (d) Friday, just once a month
    Answer: See section 11. Depositing Taxes. Application of Monthly and Semiweekly Schedules. Semiweekly schedule example. Page 27/ (d) Friday, just once a month

11. Depositing Taxes. Application of Monthly and Semiweekly Schedules. Semiweekly schedule example

30. Green, Inc. is a semiweekly schedule depositor and pays wages once each month on the last ___ of the month. Although Green, Inc., has a semiweekly deposit schedule, it will deposit ___ because it pays wages only once a month. The deposit, however, will be made under the ___ schedule as follows: Green, Inc.'s tax liability
    (a) day, each week, monthly
    (b) week, weekly, monthly
    (c) calendar day, semiweekly, semiweekly
    (d) Friday, just once a month, semiweekly
    Answer: See section 11. Depositing Taxes. Application of Monthly and Semiweekly Schedules. Semiweekly schedule example. Page 27/ (d) Friday, just once a month, semiweekly

11. Depositing Taxes. Application of Monthly and Semiweekly Schedules. Semiweekly schedule example

31. Green, Inc. is a semiweekly schedule depositor and pays wages once each month on the last Friday of the month. Although Green, Inc., has a semiweekly deposit schedule, it will deposit just once a month because it pays wages only once a month. The deposit, however, will be made under the semiweekly schedule as follows: Green, Inc.'s tax liability for the April 26, 2013 (Friday), payday must be deposited by ___.
    (a) April 30, 2013 (Tuesday)
    (b) May 1, 2013 (Wednesday)
    (c) May 2, 2013 (Thursday)
    (d) May 3, 2013 (Friday)
    Answer: See section 11. Depositing Taxes. Application of Monthly and Semiweekly Schedules. Semiweekly schedule example. Page 27/ (b) May 1, 2013(Wednesday)

Section 11. Depositing Taxes.
Application of Monthly and Semiweekly Schedules.
Semiweekly schedule example

11. Depositing Taxes. Application of Monthly and Semiweekly Schedules. Semiweekly schedule example

32. Under the semiweekly deposit schedule, liabilities for wages paid on Wednesday through Friday must be deposited by the following ___.
    (a) Tuesday
    (b) Wednesday
    (c) Thursday
    (d) Friday
    Answer: See section 11. Depositing Taxes. Application of Monthly and Semiweekly Schedules. Semiweekly schedule example. Page 27/ (b) Wednesday

Section 11. Depositing Taxes. $100,000 Next-Day Deposit Rule. Page 27.

11. Depositing Taxes. $100,000 Next-Day Deposit Rule

33. If you accumulate $100,000 or more in taxes on any day during a monthly or semiweekly deposit period (see ___, earlier in this section), you must deposit the tax by the ___, whether you are a monthly or semi-weekly schedule depositor.
    (a) Depositing Taxes, before the end of the week
    (b) Deposits on Business Days Only, next business day
    (c) *Deposit period*, next business day
    (d) *Deposit period*, next day
    Answer: See section 11. Depositing Taxes. $100,000 Next-Day Deposit Rule. Page 27/ (c) *Deposit period*, next business day

11. Depositing Taxes. $100,000 Next-Day Deposit Rule

34. For purposes of the $100,000 rule, do not continue ___ a tax liability after the end of a deposit period.
    (a) withholding
    (b) collecting
    (c) building
    (d) accumulating
    Answer: See section 11. Depositing Taxes. $100,000 Next-Day Deposit Rule. Page 27/ (d) accumulating

© Copyright 2013. All rights reserved. Notice: United States Copyright Laws and International Treaties prohibit unauthorized publication, reproduction, distribution of this Work. Unauthorized use of this copyright in any form, format, publication or document may result in severe civil and criminal penalties. Violations of this copyright are investigated by the United States Department of Justice and carry, upon conviction of fines up to $250,000 and five years confinement. This Work is protected by United States Copyright Laws and International Treaties. Do not Copy, do not reproduce, do not distribute.

11. Depositing Taxes. $100,000 Next-Day Deposit Rule

11. Depositing Taxes. $100,000 Next-Day Deposit Rule
35. For purposes of the $100,000 rule, do not continue ___ a tax liability after the end of a deposit period. For example, if a semiweekly schedule depositor has accumulated a liability of $95,000 on a Tuesday (of a Saturday-through-Tuesday deposit period) and accumulated a $10,000 on Wednesday, the next-day deposit rule ___.
   (a) withholding, will apply
   (b) collecting, will not apply
   (c) building, does apply
   (d) accumulating, does not apply
   Answer: See section 11. Depositing Taxes. $100,000 Next-Day Deposit Rule. Page 27/
   (d) accumulating, does not apply

11. Depositing Taxes. $100,000 Next-Day Deposit Rule
36. For purposes of the $100,000 rule, do not continue ___ a tax liability after the end of a deposit period. For example, if a semiweekly schedule depositor has accumulated a liability of $95,000 on a Tuesday (of a Saturday-through-Tuesday deposit period) and accumulated a $10,000 on Wednesday, the next-day deposit rule ___. Thus, $95,000 must be deposited by Friday and $10,000 must be deposited by the following ___.
   (a) withholding, will apply, Thursday
   (b) collecting, will not apply, Monday
   (c) building, does apply, Tuesday
   (d) accumulating, does not apply, Wednesday
   Answer: See section 11. Depositing Taxes. $100,000 Next-Day Deposit Rule. Page 27/
   (d) accumulating, does not apply, Wednesday

11. Depositing Taxes. $100,000 Next-Day Deposit Rule
37. However, once you accumulate at least $100,000 in a deposit period, stop accumulating at the end of ___.
   (a) the deposit period
   (b) the pay period
   (c) that day
   (d) that deposit period
   Answer: See section 11. Depositing Taxes. $100,000 Next-Day Deposit Rule. Page 27/
   (c) that day

Section 11. Depositing Taxes. $100,000 Next-Day Deposit Rule. Page 27.

11. Depositing Taxes. $100,000 Next-Day Deposit Rule
38. However, once you accumulate at least $100,000 in a deposit period, stop accumulating at the end of ___ and begin to accumulate ___ on the next day.
   (a) the deposit period, again
   (b) the pay period, again
   (c) that day, anew
   (d) that deposit period, anew
   Answer: See section 11. Depositing Taxes. $100,000 Next-Day Deposit Rule. Page 27/
   (c) that day, anew

11. Depositing Taxes. $100,000 Next-Day Deposit Rule
39. For example, Fir Co. is a semiweekly schedule depositor. On Monday, Fir Co. accumulates taxes of $110,000 and must deposit this amount on ___.
   (a) Tuesday, the next business day
   (b) Wednesday, at midweek
   (c) Thursday, within 24 to 48 hours of accumulation
   (d) Friday, the end of the deposit period
   Answer: See section 11. Depositing Taxes. $100,000 Next-Day Deposit Rule. Page 27/
   (a) Tuesday, the next business day

11. Depositing Taxes. $100,000 Next-Day Deposit Rule
40. For example, Fir Co. is a semiweekly schedule depositor. On Monday, Fir Co. accumulates taxes of $110,000 and must deposit this amount on Tuesday, the next business day. On Tuesday, Fir Co. accumulates additional taxes of $30,000. Because the $30,000 is not added to the previous $110,000 and is less than $100,000, Fir Co. must deposit the $30,000 by ___ (following the semiweekly deposit schedule).
   (a) Monday
   (b) Wednesday
   (c) Friday
   (d) The following Tuesday
   Answer: See section 11. Depositing Taxes. $100,000 Next-Day Deposit Rule. Page 27/
   (c) Friday

11. Depositing Taxes. $100,000 Next-Day Deposit Rule - Caution!
41. If you are a monthly schedule depositor and accumulate a $100,000 tax liability on any day, you become a ___ schedule depositor on the ___.
   (a) Quarterly, next day
   (b) Quarterly, end of the deposit period
   (c) semiweekly, end of the deposit period
   (d) semiweekly, next day
   Answer: See section 11. Depositing Taxes. $100,000 Next-Day Deposit Rule. Caution! Page 27/ (d) semiweekly, next day

Section 11. Depositing Taxes. $100,000 Next-Day Deposit Rule. Page 27.

11. Depositing Taxes. $100,000 Next-Day Deposit Rule - Caution!
42.   If you are a monthly schedule depositor and accumulate a $100,000 tax liability on any day, you become a ___ schedule depositor on the ___ and remain so for at least the rest of the calendar year and ___.
   (a)   Quarterly, next day, for the next year
   (b)   Quarterly, end of the deposit period, for the next year
   (c)   semiweekly, end of the deposit period, for the next year
   (d)   semiweekly, next day, for the following calendar year
   Answer: See section 11. Depositing Taxes. $100,000 Next-Day Deposit Rule. Caution! Page 27/ (d) semiweekly, next day, for the following calendar year

Depositing Taxes. $100,000 Next-Day Deposit Rule. Example. Page 27.

11. Depositing Taxes. $100,000 Next-Day Deposit Rule - Example
43.   Elm, Inc., started its business on May 1, 2013. On May 8, it paid wages for the first time and accumulated a tax liability of $___.
   (a)   40,000
   (b)   50,000
   (c)   75,000
   (d)   100,000
   Answer: See section 11. Depositing Taxes. $100,000 Next-Day Deposit Rule. Example. Page 27/ (a) 40,000

11. Depositing Taxes. $100,000 Next-Day Deposit Rule - Example
44.   Elm, Inc., started its business on May 1, 2013. On May 8, it paid wages for the first time and accumulated a tax liability of $___. On Friday, may 10, 2013, Elm, Inc., paid wages and accumulated a liability of $60,000, bringing its total accumulated tax liability to $___.
   (a)   40,000, 100,000
   (b)   50,000, 150,000
   (c)   75,000, 175,000
   (d)   100,000, 200,000
   Answer: See section 11. Depositing Taxes. $100,000 Next-Day Deposit Rule. Example. Page 27/ (a) 40,000, 100,000

Depositing Taxes. $100,000 Next-Day Deposit Rule. Example. Page 27.

11. Depositing Taxes. $100,000 Next-Day Deposit Rule - Example
45.　　Elm, Inc., started its business on May 1, 2013. On May 8, it paid wages for the first time and accumulated a tax liability of $40,000. On Friday, may 10, 2013, Elm, Inc., paid wages and accumulated a liability of $60,000, bringing its total accumulated tax liability to $100,000___. Because this was the first year of its business, the tax liability for its lookback period is considered to be___.
(a)　　40,000
(b)　　50,000
(c)　　100,000
(d)　　zero
Answer: See section 11. Depositing Taxes. $100,000 Next-Day Deposit Rule. Example. Page 27/ (d) zero

11. Depositing Taxes. $100,000 Next-Day Deposit Rule - Example
46.　　Elm, Inc., started its business on May 1, 2013. On May 8, it paid wages for the first time and accumulated a tax liability of $40,000. On Friday, May 10, 2013, Elm, Inc., paid wages and accumulated a liability of $60,000, bringing its total accumulated tax liability to $100,000___. Because this was the first year of its business, the tax liability for its lookback period is considered to be___, and it would be a ___ schedule depositor based on the lookback rules.
(a)　　40,000, semiweekly
(b)　　50,000, quarterly
(c)　　100,000, annual
(d)　　zero, monthly
Answer: See section 11. Depositing Taxes. $100,000 Next-Day Deposit Rule. Example. Pages 27and 28/ (d) zero, monthly

11. Depositing Taxes. $100,000 Next-Day Deposit Rule - Example
47.　　Elm, Inc., started its business on May 1, 2013. On May 8, it paid wages for the first time and accumulated a tax liability of $40,000. On Friday, May 10, 2013, Elm, Inc., paid wages and accumulated a liability of $60,000, bringing its total accumulated tax liability to $100,000___. Because this was the first year of its business, the tax liability for its lookback period is considered to be zero, and it would be a monthly schedule depositor based on the lookback rules. However, since Elm, Inc., accumulated a $100,000 liability on May 10, it became a ___ schedule depositor for the remainder of 3013 and for 2014.
(a)　　weekly
(b)　　semiweekly
(c)　　monthly
(d)　　quarterly
Answer: See section 11. Depositing Taxes. $100,000 Next-Day Deposit Rule. Example. Page 28/ (b) semiweekly

Depositing Taxes. $100,000 Next-Day Deposit Rule. Example. Page 27.

11. Depositing Taxes. $100,000 Next-Day Deposit Rule - Example
48. Elm, Inc., started its business on May 1, 2013. On May 8, it paid wages for the first time and accumulated a tax liability of $40,000. On Friday, May 10, 2013, Elm, Inc., paid wages and accumulated a liability of $60,000, bringing its total accumulated tax liability to $100,000___. Because this was the first year of its business, the tax liability for its lookback period is considered to be zero, and it would be a monthly schedule depositor based on the lookback rules. However, since Elm, Inc., accumulated a $100,000 liability on May 10, it became a ___ schedule depositor for the remainder of 3013 and for 2014. Elm, Inc, is required to deposit the $100,000 by ____, the next business day.
    (a) weekly, Friday, May 10
    (b) semiweekly, Monday, May 13
    (c) monthly, Wednesday, May 15
    (d) quarterly, Friday, May 17
    Answer: See section 11. Depositing Taxes. $100,000 Next-Day Deposit Rule. Example. Page 28/ (b) semiweekly, Monday, May 13

Section 11. Depositing Taxes. Accuracy of Deposits Rule. Page 28.

11. Depositing Taxes. Accuracy of Deposits Rule.
49. You are required to deposit ___% of your tax liability on or before the deposit due date.
    (a) 70
    (b) 80
    (c) 90
    (d) 100
    Answer: See section 11. Accuracy of Deposits Rule. Page 28/ (d) 100

11. Depositing Taxes. Accuracy of Deposits Rule.
50. You are required to deposit ___% of your tax liability on or before the deposit due date. However, penalties will not be applied for depositing less than ___ if both of the following conditions are met.
    (a) 70, half
    (b) 80, two-thirds
    (c) 90, three-quarters
    (d) 100, 100%
    Answer: See section 11. Accuracy of Deposits Rule. Page 28/ (d) 100, 100%

Section 11. Depositing Taxes. Accuracy of Deposits Rule. Page 28.

11. Depositing Taxes. Accuracy of Deposits Rule.
51. You are required to deposit 100% of your tax liability on or before the deposit due date. However, penalties will not be applied for depositing less than 100% if both of the following conditions are met.
    • Any deposit ___ does not exceed the greater of $100 or ___% of the amount of taxes otherwise required to be deposited.
    (a) shortfall, 2
    (b) shortage, 2
    (c) amount, 10
    (d) made, 25
    Answer: See section 11. Accuracy of Deposits Rule. Page 28/ (a) shortfall, 2

11. Depositing Taxes. Accuracy of Deposits Rule.
52. You are required to deposit 100% of your tax liability on or before the deposit due date. However, penalties will not be applied for depositing less than 100% if both of the following conditions are met.
    • Any deposit ___ does not exceed the greater of $100 or ___% of the amount of taxes otherwise required to be deposited.
    • The deposit is ___ or ___ by the shortfall makeup date as described below.
    (a) shortfall, 2, paid, deposited
    (b) shortage, 2, deposited, paid
    (c) amount, 10, made, submitted
    (d) made, 25, made, deposited
    Answer: See section 11. Accuracy of Deposits Rule. Page 28/ (a) shortfall, 2, paid, deposited

Section 11. Depositing Taxes. Accuracy of Deposits Rule. Makeup Date for Deposit Shortfall. Page 28.

11. Depositing Taxes. Accuracy of Deposits Rule. Makeup Date for Deposit Shortfall
53. 1. Monthly schedule depositor. Deposit the ___ or ___ with your return by the due date of your return for the period in which the shortfall occurred.
    (a) shortfall, pay it
    (b) shortage, combine
    (c) shortage, include it
    (d) amount, submit it
    Answer: See section 11. Accuracy of Deposits Rule. Makeup date for deposit Shortfall. Page 28/(a) shortfall, pay it

Section 11. Depositing Taxes. Accuracy of Deposits Rule. Makeup Date for Deposit Shortfall. Page 28.

11. Depositing Taxes. Accuracy of Deposits Rule. Makeup Date for Deposit Shortfall

54. **1. Monthly schedule depositor.** Deposit the shortfall or pay it with your return by the due date of your return for the period in which the shortfall occurred. You may pay the ___ with your return even if the amount is $___ or more.
    (a)   shortfall, 1,500
    (b)   shortfall, 2,500
    (c)   shortage, 2,800
    (d)   deficit, 3,000
    Answer: See section 11. Accuracy of Deposits Rule. Makeup date for deposit Shortfall. Page 28/ (b) shortfall, 2,500

11. Depositing Taxes. Accuracy of Deposits Rule. Makeup Date for Deposit Shortfall

55. **2. Semiweekly schedule depositor.** Deposit by the earlier of:
    a. The first ___ or ___ (whichever comes first) that falls on or after the 15th of of the month following the month in which the shortfall occurred.
    (a)   Monday, Wednesday
    (b)   Tuesday, Thursday
    (c)   Wednesday, Friday
    (d)   Friday, Monday
    Answer: See section 11. Accuracy of Deposits Rule. Makeup date for deposit Shortfall. Page 28/ (c) Wednesday, Friday

11. Depositing Taxes. Accuracy of Deposits Rule. Makeup Date for Deposit Shortfall

56. **2. Semiweekly schedule depositor.** Deposit by the earlier of:
    a. The first ___ or ___ (whichever comes first) that falls on or after the 15th of the month following the month in which the shortfall occurred.
    b. The due date of your ___ (for the return period of the tax liability.
    (a)   Monday, Wednesday, tax deposit
    (b)   Tuesday, Thursday, tax return
    (c)   Wednesday, Friday, return
    (d)   Friday, Monday, deposit
    Answer: See section 11. Accuracy of Deposits Rule. Makeup date for deposit Shortfall. Page 28/ (c) Wednesday, Friday, return

© Copyright 2013. All rights reserved. Notice: United States Copyright Laws and International Treaties prohibit unauthorized publication, reproduction, distribution of this Work. Unauthorized use of this copyright in any form, format, publication or document may result in severe civil and criminal penalties. Violations of this copyright are investigated by the United States Department of Justice and carry, upon conviction of fines up to $250,000 and five years confinement. This Work is protected by United States Copyright Laws and International Treaties. Do not Copy, do not reproduce, do not distribute.

Section 11. Depositing Taxes. Accuracy of Deposits Rule. Makeup Date for Deposit Shortfall (Example). Page 28.

11. Depositing Taxes. Accuracy of Deposits Rule. Makeup Date for Deposit Shortfall (Example).

57. For example, if a semiweekly schedule depositor has a deposit ___ during July 2013, the ___ makeup date is August 16, 2013 (___).
    (a) shortfall, shortfall, Monday
    (b) falls short, falls short, Tuesday
    (c) shortfall, downfall, Thursday
    (d) shortfall, shortfall, Friday
    Answer: See section 11. Accuracy of Deposits Rule. Makeup date for deposit Shortfall. (Example) Page 28/ (d) shortfall, shortfall, Friday

11. Depositing Taxes. Accuracy of Deposits Rule. Makeup Date for Deposit Shortfall (Example)

58. For example, if a semiweekly schedule depositor has a deposit shortfall during July 2013, the shortfall makeup date is August 16, 2013 (Friday). However, if the shortfall occurred on the required April 3, 2013 (___) deposit due date for a March ___, 2013 (Friday) pay date, the return due date for the March ___, 2013 pay date (April ___, 2013 would come before the
    (a) Monday, 27, 27, 31
    (b) Tuesday, 28, 28, 31
    (c) Wednesday, 29, 29, 30
    (d) Thursday, 30, 30, 30
    Answer: See section 11. Accuracy of Deposits Rule. Makeup date for deposit Shortfall. (Example) Page 28/ (c) Wednesday, 29, 29, 30

11. Depositing Taxes. Accuracy of Deposits Rule. Makeup Date for Deposit Shortfall (Example)

59. For example, if a semiweekly schedule depositor has a deposit shortfall during July 2013, the shortfall makeup date is August 16, 2013 (Friday). However, if the shortfall occurred on the required April 3, 2013 (Wednesday) deposit due date for a March 29, 2013 (Friday) pay date, the return due date for the March 29, 2013 pay date (April 30, 2013) would come before the May ___, 2013(Wednesday) <u>shortfall makeup date</u>.
    (a) 10
    (b) 15
    (c) 18
    (d) 31
    Answer: See section 11. Accuracy of Deposits Rule. Makeup date for deposit Shortfall. (Example) Page 28/ (b) 15

Section 11. Depositing Taxes. Accuracy of Deposits Rule. Makeup Date for Deposit Shortfall (Example)

11. Depositing Taxes. Accuracy of Deposits Rule. Makeup Date for Deposit Shortfall (Example)

60. For example, if a semiweekly schedule depositor has a deposit shortfall during July 2013, the shortfall makeup date is August 16, 2013 (Friday). However, if the shortfall occurred on the required April 3, 2013 (Wednesday) deposit due date for a March 29, 2013 (Friday) pay date, the return due date for the March 29, 2013 pay date (April 30, 2013) would come before the May ___, 2013(Wednesday) <u>shortfall makeup date</u>. In this case, the shortfall must be deposited by ___.
    (a)   10, April 15, 2013
    (b)   15, April 30, 2013
    (c)   18, May 1, 2013
    (d)   31, May 7, 2013
    Answer: See section 11. Accuracy of Deposits Rule. Makeup date for deposit Shortfall. (Example) Page 28/ (b) 15, April 30, 2013

DU VALL'S TEST'S™
Instructor's Manual Study Guide Series United States Tax Code
IRS Publication 15 Circular E, Employer's Tax Guide Tax Year 2013
Tax Test 15E-S11-3 [Multiple-Choice Questions With Answers]

Section 11. Depositing Taxes. How To Deposit. Page 28.

11. Depositing Taxes. How To Deposit
1. You must deposit ___ taxes, including Form 945 taxes, by electronic funds transfer.
   - (a) all
   - (b) income
   - (c) employment
   - (d) employer

   Answer: See section 11. Depositing Taxes. How To Deposit. Page 28/ (c) employment

11. Depositing Taxes. How To Deposit
2. You must deposit ___ taxes, including Form 945 taxes, by electronic funds transfer. See Payment with return, earlier in ___,
   - (a) all, Publication 15
   - (b) income, Publication 15 A
   - (c) employment, this section
   - (d) employer, this part

   Answer: See section 11. Depositing Taxes. How To Deposit. Page 28/ (c) employment, this section

11. Depositing Taxes. How To Deposit
3. You must deposit employment taxes, including Form 945 taxes, by electronic funds transfer. See Payment with return, earlier in this section, for exceptions explaining ___ taxes may be paid with a tax return instead of being deposited.
   - (a) how
   - (b) why
   - (c) when
   - (d) the steps

   Answer: See section 11. Depositing Taxes. How To Deposit. Page 28/ (c) when

11. Depositing Taxes. How To Deposit. Electronic deposit requirement.
4. You must use funds transfer to make ___ federal tax deposits.
   - (a) every
   - (b) all
   - (c) certified
   - (d) direct

   Answer: See section 11. Depositing Taxes. How To Deposit. Electronic deposit requirement. Page 28/ (b) all

© Copyright 2013. All rights reserved. Notice: United States Copyright Laws and International Treaties prohibit unauthorized publication, reproduction, distribution of this Work. Unauthorized use of this copyright in any form, format, publication or document may result in severe civil and criminal penalties. Violations of this copyright are investigated by the United States Department of Justice and carry, upon conviction of fines up to $250,000 and five years confinement. This Work is protected by United States Copyright Laws and International Treaties. Do not Copy, do not reproduce, do not distribute.

A Ficus Tree Publishing Educational-Technical Publications

Section 11. Depositing Taxes. How To Deposit. Electronic Deposit Requirement. Page 28.

11. Depositing Taxes. How To Deposit. Electronic deposit requirement.
5. You must use funds transfer to make ___ federal tax deposits (such as deposits of employment tax, excise tax, and ___ tax).
    (a) every, business and professional
    (b) all, corporate income
    (c) certified, individual
    (d) direct, sales
    Answer: See section 11. Depositing Taxes. How To Deposit. Electronic deposit requirement. Page 28/ (b) all, corporate income

11. Depositing Taxes. How To Deposit. Electronic deposit requirement.
6. You must use funds transfer to make ___ federal tax deposits (such as deposits of employment tax, excise tax, and ___ tax). Generally, ___ fund transfers are made using the Electronic Federal Tax Payment System (EFTPS).
    (a) every, business and professional, electronic
    (b) all, corporate income, electronic
    (c) certified, individual, digital
    (d) direct, sales, digital
    Answer: See section 11. Depositing Taxes. How To Deposit. Electronic deposit requirement. Page 28/ (b) all, corporate income, electronic

11. Depositing Taxes. How To Deposit. Electronic deposit requirement.
7. If you do not want to use EFTPS, you can arrange for your tax professional, ___, payroll service, or other trusted third party to make electronic deposits on your behalf.
    (a) financial institution
    (b) national bank
    (c) credit union
    (d) insured financial institution
    Answer: See section 11. Depositing Taxes. How To Deposit. Electronic deposit requirement. Page 28/ (a) financial institution

11. Depositing Taxes. How To Deposit. Electronic deposit requirement.
8. EFTPS is a free service provided by the ___.
    (a) IRS
    (b) NASA
    (c) Department of Consumer Services
    (d) Department of Treasury
    Answer: See section 11. Depositing Taxes. How To Deposit. Electronic deposit requirement. Page 28/ (d) Department of Treasury

Section 11. Depositing Taxes. How To Deposit. Electronic deposit requirement. Page 28.

11. Depositing Taxes. How To Deposit. Electronic deposit requirement.
9. To get more information or to enroll in EFTPS, call 1-800-555-___.
   (a) 4455
   (b) 4466
   (c) 4477
   (d) 4488
   Answer: See section 11. Depositing Taxes. How To Deposit. Electronic deposit requirement. Page 28/ (c) 4477

11. Depositing Taxes. How To Deposit. Electronic deposit requirement.
10. You can also visit the EFTPS website at ___.
    (a) *www.elfs.gov*
    (b) *www.selfs.gov*
    (c) *www.flsa.gov*
    (d) *www.eftps.gov*
    Answer: See section 11. Depositing Taxes. How To Deposit. Electronic deposit requirement. Page 28/ (d) *www.eftps.gov*

11. Depositing Taxes. How To Deposit. Electronic deposit requirement.
11. Additional information about EFTPS is also available in Publication ___.
    (a) 966
    (b) 967
    (c) 968
    (d) 969
    Answer: See section 11. Depositing Taxes. How To Deposit. Electronic deposit requirement. Page 28/ (a) 966

Section 11. Depositing Taxes. When you receive your EIN. Page 28.

11. Depositing Taxes. How To Deposit. When you receive your EIN.
12. If you are a new employer that indicated a federal tax ___ when requesting an EIN, you will be pre-enrolled in EFTPS.
    (a) responsibility
    (b) obligation
    (c) schedule
    (d) mandatory deposit
    Answer: See section 11. Depositing Taxes. How To Deposit. Electronic deposit requirement. Page 28/ (b) obligation

Section 11. Depositing Taxes. How To Deposit.
When you receive your EIN. Page 28.

11. Depositing Taxes. How To Deposit. When you receive your EIN.
13.   If you are a new employer that indicated a federal tax ___ when requesting an EIN, you will be pre-enrolled in EFTPS. You will receive information about ___ Enrollment in your Employer Identification Number (EIN) Package and an additional mailing containing your EFTPS personal identification number (PIN) and instructions for activating your PIN.
(a)   responsibility, IRS
(b)   obligation, Express
(c)   schedule, IRS
(d)   mandatory deposit, EFTPS
Answer: See section 11. Depositing Taxes. How To Deposit. When you receive your EIN. Page 28/ (b) obligation, Express

11. Depositing Taxes. How To Deposit. When you receive your EIN.
14.   Call the toll-free number locate in your "How to Activate Your ___" brochure to
(a)   EFTPS
(b)   IRS account
(c)   Enrollment
(d)   Account
Answer: See section 11. Depositing Taxes. How To Deposit. When you receive your EIN. Page 28/ (c) Enrollment

11. Depositing Taxes. How To Deposit. When you receive your EIN.
15.   Call the toll-free number locate in your "How to Activate Your ___" brochure to and begin making your ___ tax deposits.
(a)   EFTPS, employee
(b)   IRS account, employer
(c)   Enrollment, payroll
(d)   Account, electronic
Answer: See section 11. Depositing Taxes. How To Deposit. When you receive your EIN. Page 28/ (c) Enrollment, payroll

11. Depositing Taxes. How To Deposit. When you receive your EIN.
16.   Call the toll-free number locate in your "How to Activate Your ___" brochure to and begin making your ___ tax deposits. Be sure to tell your payroll ___ about your EFTPS enrollment.
(a)   EFTPS, employee, service
(b)   IRS account, employer, accountant
(c)   Enrollment, payroll, provider
(d)   Account, electronic, accountant
Answer: See section 11. Depositing Taxes. How To Deposit. When you receive your EIN. Page 28/ (c) Enrollment, payroll, provider

Section 11. Depositing Taxes. How To Deposit. Deposit Record. Page 28.

11. Depositing Taxes. How To Deposit. Deposit record.
17. For your records, and Electronic Funds Transfer (EFT) ___ Number will be provided with each successful payment.
    (a)   Trace
    (b)   Track
    (c)   Tracking
    (d)   Tracing
    Answer: See section 11. Depositing Taxes. How To Deposit. Deposit record. Page 28/ (a) Trace

11. Depositing Taxes. How To Deposit. Deposit record.
18. For your records, and Electronic Funds Transfer (EFT) ___ Number will be provided with each successful payment. The number can be used as a ___ or to trace the payment.
    (a)   Trace, receipt
    (b)   Track, record
    (c)   Tracking, recording
    (d)   Tracing, control
    Answer: See section 11. Depositing Taxes. How To Deposit. Deposit record. Page 28/ (a) Trace, receipt

Section 11. Depositing Taxes. How To Deposit. Depositing on time.

11. Depositing Taxes. How To Deposit. Depositing on time.
19. For deposits made by EFTPS to be on time, you must ___ the deposit by ___ the day before the deposit is due.
    (a)   initiate, 7 p.m. Eastern time
    (b)   initiate, 8 p.m. Eastern time
    (c)   complete, 8 p.m. Eastern Standard Time
    (d)   complete, 7 p.m. Pacific Standard Time
    Answer: See section 11. Depositing Taxes. How To Deposit. Depositing on time. Page 28/ (b) initiate, 8 p.m. Eastern time

11. Depositing Taxes. How To Deposit. Depositing on time.
20. For deposits made by EFTPS to be on time, you must ___ the deposit by ___ the day before the deposit is due. If you use a third party to make a deposit on your behalf, they may have ___.
    (a)   initiate, 7 p.m. Eastern time, different cutoff hours
    (b)   initiate, 8 p.m. Eastern time, different cutoff times
    (c)   complete, 8 p.m. Eastern Standard Time, variable cutoff times
    (d)   complete, 7 p.m. Pacific Standard Time, they must comply with the approved cutoff time
    Answer: See section 11. Depositing Taxes. How To Deposit. Depositing on time. Page 28/ (b) initiate, 8 p.m. Eastern time, different cutoff times

Depositing Taxes. How To Deposit. Same-day payment option

11. Depositing Taxes. How To Deposit. Same-day payment option.
21. If you fail to ___ a deposit transaction on EFTPS by 8 p.m. Eastern Time the ___, you can still make your deposit on time by using the Federal Tax Application (FTA).
   (a) start, day preceding the deposit due date
   (b) send, due date for depositing
   (c) initiate, day before the deposit is due
   (d) promptly send, due date for depositing
   Answer: See section 11. Depositing Taxes. How To Deposit. Same-day payment option. Page 28/ (c) initiate, the day before the deposit is due

11. Depositing Taxes. How To Deposit. Same-day payment option.
22. If you fail to ___ a deposit transaction on EFTPS by 8 p.m. Eastern Time the ___, you can still make your deposit on time by using the Federal Tax Application (FTA). To use the same-day payment method, you need to make arrangements with your financial institution ___.
   (a) start, day preceding the deposit due date, 30 days prior to the due date
   (b) send, due date for depositing, prior to the due date
   (c) initiate, day before the deposit is due, ahead of time
   (d) promptly send, due date for depositing, ahead of time
   Answer: See section 11. Depositing Taxes. How To Deposit. Same-day payment option. Page 28/ (c) initiate, the day before the deposit is due, ahead of time

11. Depositing Taxes. How To Deposit. Same-day payment option.
23. If you fail to initiate a deposit transaction on EFTPS by 8 p.m. Eastern Time the day before the deposit is due, you can still make your deposit on time by using the Federal Tax Application (FTA). To use the same-day payment method, you need to make arrangements with your financial institution ahead of time. Please check with your financial institution regarding availability, ___, and costs.
   (a) requirements
   (b) time frame for submittal
   (c) time frame for submittal of financial data
   (d) deadlines
   Answer: See section 11. Depositing Taxes. How To Deposit. Same-day payment option. Page 28/ (d) deadlines

11. Depositing Taxes. How To Deposit. Same-day payment option.

11. Depositing Taxes. How To Deposit. Same-day payment option.
24. If you fail to initiate a deposit transaction on EFTPS by 8 p.m. Eastern Time the day before the deposit is due, you can still make your deposit on time by using the **Federal Tax Application (FTA)**. To use the same-day payment method, you need to make arrangements with your financial institution ahead of time. Please check with your financial institution regarding availability, ___, and costs. Your financial institution may charge you a fee for ___ made this way.
   (a) requirements, services
   (b) time frame for submittal, services
   (c) time frame for submittal of financial data, transactions
   (d) deadlines, payments
   Answer: See section 11. Depositing Taxes. How To Deposit. Same-day payment option. Page 28/ (d) deadlines, payments

11. Depositing Taxes. How To Deposit. Same-day payment option.
25. If you fail to initiate a deposit transaction on EFTPS by 8 p.m. Eastern Time the day before the deposit is due, you can still make your deposit on time by using the Federal Tax Application (FTA). To use the same-day payment method, you need to make arrangements with your financial institution ahead of time. Please check with your financial institution regarding availability, ___, and costs. Your financial institution may charge you a fee for ___ made this way. To learn more To learn more about the ___ you will need to provide to your financial institution to
   (a) requirements, services, data
   (b) time frame for submittal, services, procedures
   (c) time frame for submittal of financial data, transactions, procedure
   (d) deadlines, payments, information
   Answer: See section 11. Depositing Taxes. How To Deposit. Same-day payment option. Page 28/ (d) deadlines, payments, information

11. Depositing Taxes. How To Deposit. Same-day payment option.
26. If you fail to initiate a deposit transaction on EFTPS by 8 p.m. Eastern Time the day before the deposit is due, you can still make your deposit on time by using the Federal Tax Application (FTA). To use the same-day payment method, you need to make arrangements with your financial institution ahead of time. Please check with your financial institution regarding availability, ___, and costs. Your financial institution may charge you a fee for ___ made this way. To learn more To learn more about the ___ you will need to provide to your financial institution to make a same-day ___ payment, visit www.eftps.gov to download the
   (a) requirements, services, data, electronic
   (b) time frame for submittal, services, procedures, electronic
   (c) time frame for submittal of financial data, transactions, procedure, e-mail
   (d) deadlines, payments, information, wire
   Answer: See section 11. Depositing Taxes. How To Deposit. Same-day payment option. Page 28/ (d) deadlines, payments, information, wire

© Copyright 2013. All rights reserved. Notice: United States Copyright Laws and International Treaties prohibit unauthorized publication, reproduction, distribution of this Work. Unauthorized use of this copyright in any form, format, publication or document may result in severe civil and criminal penalties. Violations of this copyright are investigated by the United States Department of Justice and carry, upon conviction of fines up to $250,000 and five years confinement. This Work is protected by United States Copyright Laws and International Treaties. Do not Copy, do not reproduce, do not distribute.

11. Depositing Taxes. How To Deposit. Same-day payment option.

11. Depositing Taxes. How To Deposit. Same-day payment option.
27. If you fail to initiate a deposit transaction on EFTPS by 8 p.m. Eastern Time the day before the deposit is due, you can still make your deposit on time by using the Federal Tax Application (FTA). To use the same-day payment method, you need to make arrangements with your financial institution ahead of time. Please check with your financial institution regarding availability, ___, and costs. Your financial institution may charge you a fee for ___ made this way. To learn more To learn more about the ___ you will need to provide to your financial institution to make a same-day ___ payment, visit *www.eftps.gov* to download the ***Same-Day Payment___***.
   (a) requirements, services, data, electronic, *spreadsheet*
   (b) time frame for submittal, services, procedures, electronic, *spreadsheet*
   (c) time frame for submittal of financial data, transactions, procedure, e-mail,
   (d) deadlines, payments, information, wire, *worksheet*
   Answer: See section 11. Depositing Taxes. How To Deposit. Same-day payment option. Page 28/ (d) deadlines, payments, information, wire, *worksheet*

Section 11. Depositing Taxes. How To Deposit. How to claim credit for overpayments.

11. Depositing Taxes. How To Deposit. How to claim credit for overpayments.
28. If you deposit more than the ___ amount of taxes for a ___, you can choose on **Form 941** for that **quarter** (or on **Form 944** for that **year**) to
   (a) right, quarter
   (b) correct, deposit period
   (c) correct, quarter
   (d) required, deposit period
   Answer: See section 11. Depositing Taxes. How To Deposit. How to claim credit for overpayments. Page 28/ (a) right, quarter

11. Depositing Taxes. How To Deposit. How to claim credit for overpayments.
29. If you deposit more than the right amount of taxes for a quarter, you can choose on **Form 941** for that **quarter** (or on **Form 944** for that **year**) to have the overpayment refunded or applied as a ___ to your next return.
   (a) prepayment
   (b) post-payment
   (c) credit
   (d) debit
   Answer: See section 11. Depositing Taxes. How To Deposit. How to claim credit for overpayments. Page 28/ (c) credit

Section 11. Depositing Taxes. How To Deposit.
How to claim credit for overpayments.

11. Depositing Taxes. How To Deposit. How to claim credit for overpayments.

30. If you deposit more than the right amount of taxes for a quarter, you can choose on **Form 941** for that **quarter** (or on **Form 944** for that **year**) to have the overpayment refunded or applied as a ___ to your next return. Do not ask ___ to request a refund from the IRS for you.
    (a) prepayment, the government
    (b) post-payment, your local tax agency
    (c) credit, EFTPS
    (d) debit, your financial institution
    Answer: See section 11. Depositing Taxes. How To Deposit. How to claim credit for overpayments. Page 28/ (c) credit, EFTPS

Section 11. Depositing Taxes. Deposit Penalties. TIP. Page 28.

11. Depositing Taxes. Deposit Penalties. TIP.

31. Although the deposit penalties information provided below refers specifically to **Form 941**, these rules also apply to **Form** ___ and **Form** ___ (if the employer required to file **Form** ___ does not qualify for the exception to the deposit requirements discussed under *Payment with return*, earlier in this section).
    (a) 941, 943, 945
    (b) 945, 944, 944
    (c) 945, 943, 941
    (d) 954, 944, 943
    Answer: See section 11. Depositing Taxes. Page 28/ (b) 945, 944, 944

11. Depositing Taxes. Deposit Penalties.

32. Penalties may apply if you do not make required deposits ___ or for less than the required amount.
    (a) in a timely manner
    (b) when due
    (c) on time
    (d) according to the IRS calendar date
    Answer: See section 11. Depositing Taxes. Page 28/ (c) on time

Section 11. Depositing Taxes. Deposit Penalties.

11. Depositing Taxes. Deposit Penalties.
33. Penalties may apply if you do not make required deposits ___ or for less than the required amount. The penalties do not apply if any failure to make a proper and timely deposit was due to ___ and not to willful neglect.
    (a)   in a timely manner, posting error
    (b)   when due, accounting error
    (c)   on time, reasonable cause
    (d)   according to the IRS calendar date, posting error
    Answer: See section 11. Depositing Taxes. Pages 28 and 29/ (c) on time, reasonable cause

11. Depositing Taxes. Deposit Penalties.
34. The IRS may also waive penalties if you ___ fail to deposit in the first quarter you were required to deposit any ___ tax, or
    (a)   inadvertently, employment
    (b)   unintentionally, employment
    (c)   forget and, withholding
    (d)   unintentionally, withholding
    Answer: See section 11. Depositing Taxes. Page 29/ (a) inadvertently, employment

11. Depositing Taxes. Deposit Penalties.
35. The IRS may also waive penalties if you ___ fail to deposit in the first quarter you were required to deposit any ___ tax, or in the first quarter during which your ___ of deposits changed, if you timely filed your employment tax return.
    (a)   inadvertently, employment, frequency
    (b)   unintentionally, employment, schedule
    (c)   forget and, withholding, schedule
    (d)   unintentionally, withholding, date
    Answer: See section 11. Depositing Taxes. Page 29/ (a) inadvertently, employment, frequency

11. Depositing Taxes. Deposit Penalties.
36. For amounts not properly or timely deposited, the penalty rates are as follows. Deposits made 1 to 5 days late. ___%
    (a)   1
    (b)   2
    (c)   3
    (d)   3½
    Answer: See section 11. Depositing Taxes. Page 29/ (b) 2

Section 11. Depositing Taxes. Deposit Penalties. Page 29.

11. Depositing Taxes. Deposit Penalties.
37. For amounts not properly or timely deposited, the penalty rates are as follows. Deposits made 6 to 15 days late. ___%
    (a) 2
    (b) 3
    (c) 4
    (d) 5
    Answer: See section 11. Depositing Taxes. Page 29/ (d) 5

11. Depositing Taxes. Deposit Penalties.
38. For amounts not properly or timely deposited, the penalty rates are as follows. Deposits made 16 or more days late. Also applies to amounts paid within 10 days of the date of the first notice the IRS sent asking for the tax due. ___%
    (a) 7½
    (b) 10
    (c) 15
    (d) 18
    Answer: See section 11. Depositing Taxes. Page 29/ (b) 10

11. Depositing Taxes. Deposit Penalties.
39. Amounts (that should have been deposited) paid directly to the IRS, or paid with your tax return. But see *Payment with return*, earlier in this section for an exception. ___%.
    (a) 7½
    (b) 10
    (c) 15
    (d) 18
    Answer: See section 11. Depositing Taxes. Page 29/ (b) 10

11. Depositing Taxes. Deposit Penalties.
40. Amounts still unpaid more than 10 days after the date of the first notice the IRS sent asking for the tax due or the day on which you received notice and **demand** for **immediate payment**, whichever is earlier. ___%.
    (a) 7½
    (b) 10
    (c) 15
    (d) 18
    Answer: See section 11. Depositing Taxes. Page 29/ (c) 15

Section 11. Depositing Taxes. Deposit Penalties.

11. Depositing Taxes. Deposit Penalties.
41. Amounts still unpaid more than 10 days after the date of the first notice the IRS sent asking for the tax due or the day on which you received notice and **demand** for **immediate payment**, whichever is earlier. ___%. Late deposit penalty amounts are determined using ___ days, starting from the due date of the liability.
- (a) 7½, regular
- (b) 10, working
- (c) 15, calendar
- (d) 18, calendar

Answer: See section 11. Depositing Taxes. Page 29/ (c) 15, calendar

Section 11. Depositing Taxes. Special rule for former Form 944 Filers. Page 29.

11. Depositing Taxes. Special rule for former Form 944 Filers.
42. If you filed Form 944 for the prior year and Forms ___ for the current year, the failure-to-deposit penalty will not apply to a deposit of
- (a) 941
- (b) 942
- (c) 943
- (d) 945

Answer: See section 11. Depositing Taxes. Special rule for former Form 944 filers. Page 29/ (a) 941

11. Depositing Taxes. Deposit Penalties. Special rule for former Form 944 Filers.
43. If you filed Form 944 for the prior year and Forms 941 for the current year, the failure-to-deposit penalty will not apply to a deposit of ___ taxes for January of the current year if the taxes are deposited in full by March ___ of the current year.
- (a) withholding, 1
- (b) employment, 10
- (c) employment, 15
- (d) withholding, 31

Answer: See section 11. Depositing Taxes. Special rule for former Form 944 filers, Page 29/ (c) employment, 15

Deposit Penalties. Order in which deposits are applied.

11. Depositing Taxes. Order in which deposits are applied.
44. Deposits generally are applied to the ___ tax liability within
- (a) recent
- (b) most delinquent
- (c) most recent
- (d) current

Answer: See section 11. Depositing Taxes. Order in which deposits are applied. Page 29/ (c) most recent

Deposit Penalties. Order in which deposits are applied.

11. Depositing Taxes. Order in which deposits are applied.
45. Deposits generally are applied to the ___ tax liability within the quarter. If you receive a failure-to-deposit penalty notice, you may ___ are to be applied in order to
    (a) recent, suggest how your deposits
    (b) most delinquent, designate the method
    (c) most recent, designate how your deposits
    (d) current, designate the method
    Answer: See section 11. Depositing Taxes. Order in which deposits are applied. Page 29/
    (c) most recent, designate how your deposits

11. Depositing Taxes. Order in which deposits are applied.
46. Deposits generally are applied to the ___ tax liability within the quarter. If you receive a failure- to-deposit penalty notice, you may ___ are to be applied in order to ___ the amount of the penalty if
    (a) recent, suggest how your deposits, reduce
    (b) most delinquent, designate the method, mitigate
    (c) most recent, designate how your deposits, minimize
    (d) current, designate the method, neutralize
    Answer: See section 11. Depositing Taxes. Order in which deposits are applied. Page 29/
    (c) most recent, designate how your deposits, minimize

11. Depositing Taxes. Order in which deposits are applied.
47. Deposits generally are applied to the ___ tax liability within the quarter. If you receive a failure-to-deposit penalty notice, you may ___ are to be applied in order to ___ the amount of the penalty if you do so within ___ days of the date of the notice.
    (a) recent, suggest how your deposits, reduce, 30
    (b) most delinquent, designate the method, mitigate, 60
    (c) most recent, designate how your deposits, minimize, 90
    (d) current, designate the method, neutralize, 90
    Answer: See section 11. Depositing Taxes. Order in which deposits are applied. Page 29/
    (c) most recent, designate how your deposits, minimize, 90

11. Depositing Taxes. Order in which deposits are applied.
48. Deposits generally are applied to the most recent tax liability within the quarter. If you receive a failure-to-deposit penalty notice, you may designate how your deposits are to be applied in order to minimize the amount of the penalty if you do so within ___ days of the date of the notice. Follow the instructions on the ___ notice you received. For more information on designating deposits, see Revenue Procedure ___.
    (a) 15, official, 2013-58
    (b) 30, IRS, 2010-59
    (c) 60, penalty, 2007-59
    (d) 90, penalty, 2001-58
    Answer: See section 11. Depositing Taxes. Order in which deposits are applied. Page 29/
    (d) 90, penalty, 2001-58

© Copyright 2013. All rights reserved. Notice: United States Copyright Laws and International Treaties prohibit unauthorized publication, reproduction, distribution of this Work. Unauthorized use of this copyright in any form, format, publication or document may result in severe civil and criminal penalties. Violations of this copyright are investigated by the United States Department of Justice and carry, upon conviction of fines up to $250,000 and five years confinement. This Work is protected by United States Copyright Laws and International Treaties. Do not Copy, do not reproduce, do not distribute.

A Ficus Tree Publishing Educational-Technical Publications

Deposit Penalties. Order in which deposits are applied.

11. Depositing Taxes. Order in which deposits are applied.
49. You can find Revenue Procedure ___ on page ___ of Internal Revenue Bulletin 2001-50 at *www.irs.gov/pub/irs-irbs/irb01-50.pdf*.
 (a) 2000-58, 578
 (b) 2001-58, 579
 (c) 2010-59, 579
 (d) 2013-59, 579
 Answer: See section 11. Depositing Taxes. Order in which deposits are applied. Page 29/ (b) 2001-58, 579

Deposit penalties Order in which deposits are applied. Example.

11. Depositing Taxes. Order in which deposits are applied. Example.
50. Cedar, Inc. is required to make a deposit of $1,000 on June 15 and $1,500 on July 15. It does not make the deposit on June 15. On July 15, Cedar, Inc. deposits $2,000. Under the deposits rule, which applies deposits to the most recent tax liability, $___ of the deposit is applied to the ___ deposit and
 (a) 1,000, June 15
 (b) 1,500, July 15
 (c) 2,000, July 15
 (d) 2,000, August 1
 Answer: See section 11. Depositing Taxes. Order in which deposits are applied. Example. Page 29/ (b) 1,500, July 15

11. Depositing Taxes. Order in which deposits are applied. Example.
51. Cedar, Inc. is required to make a deposit of $1,000 on June 15 and $1,500 on July 15. It does not make the deposit on June 15. On July 15, Cedar, Inc. deposits $2,000. Under the deposits rule, which applies deposits to the most recent tax liability, $___ of the deposit is applied to the ___ deposit and the remaining ___ is applied to the ___ deposit.
 (a) 1,000, June 15, balance, July
 (b) 1,500, July 15 $500, June
 (c) 2,000, July 15, funds, July
 (d) 2,000, August 1, payment, August
 Answer: See section 11. Depositing Taxes. Order in which deposits are applied. Example. Page 29/ (b) 1,500, July 15

The International Leader in Construction Technology Home Study

11. Depositing Taxes. Order in which deposits are applied. Example.

11. Depositing Taxes. Order in which deposits are applied. Example.
52. Cedar, Inc. is required to make a deposit of $1,000 on June 15 and $1,500 on July 15. It does not make the deposit on June 15. On July 15, Cedar, Inc. deposits $2,000. Under the deposits rule, which applies deposits to the most recent tax liability, $1,500 of the deposit is applied to the July 15 deposit and the remaining $500 is applied to the June deposit. Accordingly, $___ of the June 15 liability remains undeposited.
   (a) 500
   (b) 1,000
   (c) 1,500
   (d) 2,000
   Answer: See section 11. Depositing Taxes. Order in which deposits are applied. Example. Page 29/ (a) 500

11. Depositing Taxes. Order in which deposits are applied. Example.
53. Cedar, Inc. is required to make a deposit of $1,000 on June 15 and $1,500 on July 15. It does not make the deposit on June 15. On July 15, Cedar, Inc. deposits $2,000. Under the deposits rule, which applies deposits to the most recent tax liability, $1,500 of the deposit is applied to the July 15 deposit and the remaining $500 is applied to the June deposit. Accordingly, $___ of the June 15 liability remains undeposited. The penalty on this ___ will apply as explained earlier.
   (a) 500, underdeposit
   (b) 1,000, undeposited amount
   (c) 1,500, undeposited, balance
   (d) 2,000, undeposited tax due
   Answer: See section 11. Depositing Taxes. Order in which deposits are applied. Example. Page 29/ (a) 500, underdeposit

Section 11. Depositing Taxes. Trust fund recovery penalty. Page 29.

11. Depositing Taxes. Trust fund recovery penalty.
54. If federal income, social security, or Medicare taxes that must be withheld are not withheld or are not deposited or paid to the ___, the ___ may apply.
   (a) IRS, penalties
   (b) IRS tax deposit file, penalties
   (c) Income Tax withholding fund, recovery penalty
   (d) United States Treasury, trust fund recovery penalty
   Answer: See section 11. Depositing Taxes. Trust fund recovery penalty. Page 29/ (d) United States Treasury, trust fund recovery penalty

Section 11. Depositing Taxes. Trust fund recovery penalty.

11. Depositing Taxes. Trust fund recovery penalty.
55. If federal income, social security, or Medicare taxes that must be withheld are not withheld or are not deposited or paid to the ___, the ___ may apply. The penalty is the full amount of the ___ trust fund tax.
    (a) IRS, penalties, penalties, unpaid
    (b) IRS tax deposit file, penalties, uncollected
    (c) Income Tax withholding fund, recovery penalty, uncollected
    (d) United States Treasury, trust fund recovery penalty, unpaid
    Answer: See section 11. Depositing Taxes. Trust fund recovery penalty. Page 29/ (d) United States Treasury, trust fund recovery penalty, unpaid

11. Depositing Taxes. Trust fund recovery penalty.
56. If federal income, social security, or Medicare taxes that must be withheld are not withheld or are not deposited or paid to the United States Treasury, the trust fund recovery penalty may apply. The penalty is the full amount of the unpaid trust fund tax. This penalty may apply to ___ if these unpaid taxes cannot be immediately collected from the employer or business.
    (a) you
    (b) the officers
    (c) the stockholders
    (d) the employees
    Answer: See section 11. Depositing Taxes. Trust fund recovery penalty. Page 29/ (a) you

11. Depositing Taxes. Trust fund recovery penalty.
57. If federal income, social security, or Medicare taxes that must be withheld are not withheld or are not deposited or paid to the United States Treasury, the trust fund recovery penalty may apply. The penalty is the full amount of the unpaid trust fund tax. This penalty may apply to ___ if these unpaid taxes cannot be immediately collected from the employer or business. The trust fund recovery penalty may be imposed on all persons who are determined by the IRS to be responsible for collecting, accounting for, and paying over these taxes, and who ___ in not doing so.
    (a) you, acted willfully
    (b) the officers, knowingly
    (c) the stockholders, wantonly
    (d) the employees, illegally
    Answer: See section 11. Depositing Taxes. Trust fund recovery penalty. Page 29/ (a) you, acted willfully

Section 11. Depositing Taxes. A responsible person. Page 29.

11. Depositing Taxes. A responsible person.
58. A responsible person can be an officer or ___ of a corporation, a partner or employee of a partnership, an accountant, a volunteer director/trustee, or the employee of a sole proprietorship, or any other person or entity that is responsible for collecting, accounting for, and paying over trust fund taxes.
    (a) individual
    (b) person
    (c) employee
    (d) entity
    Answer: See section 11. Depositing Taxes. A responsible person. Page 29/ (c) employee

11. Depositing Taxes. A responsible person.
59. A responsible person can be an officer or ___ of a corporation, a partner or employee of a partnership, an accountant, a volunteer director/trustee, or the employee of a sole proprietorship, or any other person or entity that is responsible for collecting, accounting for, and paying over trust fund taxes. A responsible person also may include ___ for the business or otherwise has authority to cause the spending of business funds.
    (a) individual, purchasing
    (b) person, sales staff
    (c) employee, one who signs checks
    (d) entity, independent contractors
    Answer: See section 11. Depositing Taxes. A responsible person. Page 29/ (c) employee, one who signs checks

A Ficus Tree Publishing Quick Notes Page.

DU VALL'S TEST'S™
Instructor's Manual Study Guide Series United States Tax Code
IRS Publication 15 Circular E, Employer's Tax Guide Tax Year 2013
Tax Test 15E-S11-4 [Multiple-Choice Questions With Answers]

Section 11. Depositing Taxes. Willfully. Page 29.

11. Depositing Taxes. Willfully.
1. Willfully means ___, consciously, and intentionally.
    (a) deceitfully
    (b) voluntarily
    (c) knowingly
    (d) unlawfully
    Answer: See section 11. Depositing Taxes. Willfully. Page 29/ (b) voluntarily

11. Depositing Taxes. Willfully.
2. Willfully means ___, consciously, and intentionally. A responsible person acts willfully if the person ___ the required actions of collecting, accounting for or paying over trust fund taxes are not taking place, or
    (a) deceitfully, is aware
    (b) voluntarily, knows
    (c) knowingly, colludes with
    (d) unlawfully, conspires with
    Answer: See section 11. Depositing Taxes. Willfully. Page 29/ (b) voluntarily, knows

11. Depositing Taxes. Willfully.
3. Willfully means ___, consciously, and intentionally. A responsible person acts willfully if the person ___ the required actions of collecting, accounting for or paying over trust fund taxes are not taking place, or ___ disregards obvious and known risks to the government's right to receive trust fund taxes.
    (a) deceitfully, is aware, unlawfully
    (b) voluntarily, knows, recklessly
    (c) knowingly, colludes with, intentionally
    (d) unlawfully, conspires with, intentionally
    Answer: See section 11. Depositing Taxes. Willfully. Page 29/ (b) voluntarily, knows, recklessly

© Copyright 2013. All rights reserved. Notice: United States Copyright Laws and International Treaties prohibit unauthorized publication, reproduction, distribution of this Work. Unauthorized use of this copyright in any form, format, publication or document may result in severe civil and criminal penalties. Violations of this copyright are investigated by the United States Department of Justice and carry, upon conviction of fines up to $250,000 and five years confinement. This Work is protected by United States Copyright Laws and International Treaties. Do not Copy, do not reproduce, do not distribute.

A Ficus Tree Publishing Educational-Technical Publications

Section 11. Depositing Taxes. Separate accounting when deposits are not made or withheld taxes are not paid.

11. Depositing Taxes. Separate accounting when deposits are not made or withheld taxes are not paid.

4. Separate accounting may be required if you do not ___ withheld social security, Medicare, or income taxes; deposit required taxes; make required payments; or file tax returns.
   (a) pay
   (b) deposit
   (c) pay over
   (d) comply and deposit
   Answer: See section 11. Depositing Taxes. Separate accounting when deposits are not made or withheld taxes are not paid. Page 29/ (c) pay over

11. Depositing Taxes. Separate accounting when deposits are not made or withheld taxes are not paid.

5. Separate accounting may be required if you do not ___ withheld social security, Medicare, or income taxes; deposit required taxes; make required payments; or file tax returns. In this case, you would receive written notice from the IRS ___ to deposit taxes into a special trust account for the U.S. Government.
   (a) pay, instructing you
   (b) deposit, warning you
   (c) pay over, requiring you
   (d) comply and deposit, mandating you
   Answer: See section 11. Depositing Taxes. Separate accounting when deposits are not made or withheld taxes are not paid. Page 29/ (c) pay over, requiring you

11. Depositing Taxes. Separate accounting when deposits are not made or withheld taxes are not paid. Caution!

6. You may be ___ if you do not comply with the special bank deposit requirements for the special trust account for the U.S. Government.
   (a) charged with a federal offense
   (b) indicted by the federal government
   (c) charged with criminal penalties
   (d) arrested and charges with criminal penalties
   Answer: See section 11. Depositing Taxes. Separate accounting when deposits are not made or withheld taxes are not paid. Caution! Page 29/ (c) charged with criminal penalties

Section 11. Depositing Taxes. "Averaged" failure-to-deposit penalty.

11. Depositing Taxes. "Averaged" failure-to-deposit penalty.
7. The IRS may assess an "averaged" failure-to-deposit (FDT) penalty of ___% to ___% if you are a monthly schedule depositor and did not properly complete **Form** ___, line ___, when
   (a) 2, 7, 940, 12
   (b) 2, 10, 941, 16
   (c) 2½, 10, 941, 16
   (d) 5, 10, 944, 18
   Answer: See section 11. Depositing Taxes. "Averaged" failure-to-deposit penalty. Page 29/ (b) 2, 10, 941, 16

11. Depositing Taxes. "Averaged" failure-to-deposit penalty.
8. The IRS may assess an "averaged" failure-to-deposit (FDT) penalty of 2% to 10% if you are a monthly schedule depositor and did not properly complete **Form 941**, line 16, when your tax liability shown on **Form 941**, line 10, equaled or exceeded $___.
   (a) 1,000
   (b) 1,500
   (c) 2,000
   (d) 2,500
   Answer: See section 11. Depositing Taxes. "Averaged" failure-to-deposit penalty. Page 29/ (d) 2,500

11. Depositing Taxes. "Averaged" failure-to-deposit penalty.
9. The IRS may also assess an "averaged" failure-to-deposit (FDT) penalty of 2% to 10% if you are a semiweekly schedule depositor and did not properly complete **Form 941**, line 16, when your tax liability shown on **Form 941**, line ___, equaled or exceeded $2,500 and you:
   (a) 5
   (b) 7
   (c) 10
   (d) 12
   Answer: See section 11. Depositing Taxes. "Averaged" failure-to-deposit penalty. Page 29/ (c) 10

© Copyright 2013. All rights reserved. Notice: United States Copyright Laws and International Treaties prohibit unauthorized publication, reproduction, distribution of this Work. Unauthorized use of this copyright in any form, format, publication or document may result in severe civil and criminal penalties. Violations of this copyright are investigated by the United States Department of Justice and carry, upon conviction of fines up to $250,000 and five years confinement. This Work is protected by United States Copyright Laws and International Treaties. Do not Copy, do not reproduce, do not distribute.

Section 11. Depositing Taxes. "Averaged" failure-to-deposit penalty.

11. Depositing Taxes. "Averaged" failure-to-deposit penalty.
10. The IRS <u>may also</u> assess an "averaged" failure-to-deposit (FDT) penalty of 2% to 10% if you are a semiweekly schedule depositor and did not properly complete **Form 941**, line 16, when your tax liability shown on **Form 941**, line 10, equaled or exceeded $2,500 and you:
   • Completed Form 941, line 16, instead of Schedule ___ (Form 941).
   (a)   A
   (b)   B
   (c)   C
   (d)   D
   Answer: See section 11. Depositing Taxes. "Averaged" failure-to-deposit penalty. Page 29/ (b) B

11. Depositing Taxes. "Averaged" failure-to-deposit penalty.
11. The IRS <u>may also</u> assess an "averaged" failure-to-deposit (FDT) penalty of 2% to 10% if you are a semiweekly schedule depositor and did not properly complete **Form 941**, line 16, when your tax liability shown on **Form 941**, line 10, equaled or exceeded $2.500 and you:
   • Completed Form 941, line 16, instead of Schedule ___ (Form 941),
   • Failed to ___ a properly completed Schedule B (Form 941),
   (a)   A, include
   (b)   B, attach
   (c)   C, enclose
   (d)   D, provide
   Answer: See section 11. Depositing Taxes. "Averaged" failure-to-deposit penalty. Page 29/ (b) B, attach

11. Depositing Taxes. "Averaged" failure-to-deposit penalty.
12. The IRS <u>may also</u> assess an "averaged" failure-to-deposit (FDT) penalty of 2% to 10% if you are a semiweekly schedule depositor and did not properly complete **Form 941**, line 16, when your tax liability shown on **Form 941**, line 10, equaled or exceeded $2.500 and you:
   • Completed Form 941, line 16, instead of Schedule ___ (Form 941),
   • Failed to ___ a properly completed Schedule B (Form 941),
   • Improperly completed Schedule B (Form 941) by, **for example**, entering tax deposits instead of tax ___ in the numbered spaces.
   (a)   A, include, liabilities
   (b)   B, attach, liabilities
   (c)   C, enclose, withheld
   (d)   D, provide, withheld
   Answer: See section 11. Depositing Taxes. "Averaged" failure-to-deposit penalty. Page 29/ (b) B, attach, liabilities

Section 11. Depositing Taxes. "Averaged" failure-to-deposit penalty.

11. Depositing Taxes. "Averaged" failure-to-deposit penalty.
13. The FTD penalty is figured by ___ your total tax liability shown on Form 941, line 10, equally throughout the tax period.
    (a) averaging
    (b) combining
    (c) distributing
    (d) disseminating
    Answer: See section 11. Depositing Taxes. "Averaged" failure-to-deposit penalty. Page 29/ (c) distributing

11. Depositing Taxes. "Averaged" failure-to-deposit penalty.
14. The FTD penalty is figured by ___ your total tax liability shown on Form 941, line 10, equally throughout the tax period.
    (a) averaging
    (b) combining
    (c) distributing
    (d) disseminating
    Answer: See section 11. Depositing Taxes. "Averaged" failure-to-deposit penalty. Page 29/ (c) distributing

11. Depositing Taxes. "Averaged" failure-to-deposit penalty.
15. The FTD penalty is figured by ___ your total tax liability shown on Form 941, line 10, equally throughout the tax period. As a result, your deposits and payments ___ as timely because the actual dates of your tax liabilities cannot be accurately determined.
    (a) averaging, may not be accurate
    (b) combining, will not be determined
    (c) distributing, may not be counted
    (d) disseminating, will not be accepted
    Answer: See section 11. Depositing Taxes. "Averaged" failure-to-deposit penalty. Page 29/ (c) distributing, may not be counted

11. Depositing Taxes. "Averaged" failure-to-deposit penalty.
16. You can avoid an "averaged" FTD penalty by ___ your return before you file it. Follow these steps before submitting your Form 941.
    (a) averaging
    (b) reviewing
    (c) checking
    (d) examining
    Answer: See section 11. Depositing Taxes. "Averaged" failure-to-deposit penalty. Page 30/ (b) reviewing

11. Depositing Taxes. "Averaged" failure-to-deposit penalty. Page 29.

11. Depositing Taxes. "Averaged" failure-to-deposit penalty.

17. You can avoid an "averaged" FTD penalty by ___ your return before you file it. Follow these steps before submitting your Form 941.
 • If you are a monthly schedule depositor, report your ___ (not your deposits) in the monthly entry spaces on **Form 941**, line **16**.
 (a) averaging, taxes
 (b) reviewing, tax liabilities
 (c) checking, liabilities
 (d) examining, payroll expense
 Answer: See section 11. Depositing Taxes. "Averaged" failure-to-deposit penalty. Page 30/ (b) reviewing, tax liabilities

11. Depositing Taxes. "Averaged" failure-to-deposit penalty.

18. You can avoid an "averaged" FTD penalty by ___ your return before you file it. Follow these steps before submitting your Form 941.
 • If you are a monthly schedule depositor, report your ___ (not your deposits) in the monthly entry spaces on **Form 941**, line **16**.
 • If you area semiweekly schedule depositor, report your ___ (not your deposits) on Schedule ___ (Form 941) in the lines that represent the dates your employees were paid.
 (a) averaging, taxes, taxes, A
 (b) reviewing, tax liabilities, tax liabilities, B
 (c) checking, liabilities, liabilities, C
 (d) examining, payroll expense, payroll expense, D
 Answer: See section 11. Depositing Taxes. "Averaged" failure-to-deposit penalty. Page 30/ (b) reviewing, tax liabilities, tax liabilities, B

11. Depositing Taxes. "Averaged" failure-to-deposit penalty.

19. You can avoid an "averaged" FTD penalty by ___ your return before you file it. Follow these steps before submitting your Form 941.
 • If you are a monthly schedule depositor, report your ___ (not your deposits) in the monthly entry spaces on **Form 941**, line **16**.
 • If you area semiweekly schedule depositor, report your ___ (not your deposits) on Schedule ___ (Form 941) in the lines that represent the dates your employees were paid.
 • Verify your ___ shown on Form 941, line 16, or the bottom of Schedule B (Form 941) equals your tax liability Shown on Form 941, line 10.
 (a) averaging, taxes, taxes, A, total liability
 (b) reviewing, tax liabilities, tax liabilities, B, total liability
 (c) checking, liabilities, liabilities, C, total required deposit
 (d) examining, payroll expense, payroll expense, D, total tax due
 Answer: See section 11. Depositing Taxes. "Averaged" failure-to-deposit penalty. Page 30/ (b) reviewing, tax liabilities, tax liabilities, B, total liability

Section 11. Depositing Taxes. "Averaged" failure-to-deposit penalty.

11. Depositing Taxes. "Averaged" failure-to-deposit penalty.
20. You can avoid an "averaged" FTD penalty by ___ your return before you file it. Follow these steps before submitting your Form 941.
 • If you are a monthly schedule depositor, report your ___ (not your deposits) in the monthly entry spaces on **Form 941**, line **16**.
 • If you area semiweekly schedule depositor, report your ___ (not your deposits) on Schedule ___ (Form 941) in the lines that represent the dates your employees were paid.
 • Verify your ___ shown on Form 941, line 16, or the bottom of Schedule B (Form 941) equals your tax liability Shown on Form 941, line 10.
 • Do not show ___ amounts on Form 941, line 16, or Schedule B (Form 941).
 (a) averaging, taxes, taxes, A, total liability, estimated
 (b) reviewing, tax liabilities, tax liabilities, B, total liability, negative
 (c) checking, liabilities, liabilities, C, total required deposit, neutral
 (d) examining, payroll expense, payroll expense, D, total tax due, positive
 Answer: See section 11. Depositing Taxes. "Averaged" failure-to-deposit penalty. Page 30/ (b) reviewing, tax liabilities, tax liabilities, B, total liability, negative

11. Depositing Taxes. "Averaged" failure-to-deposit penalty.
21. You can avoid an "averaged" FTD penalty by reviewing your return before you file it. Follow these steps before submitting your Form 941.
 • If you are a monthly schedule depositor, report your tax liabilities (not your deposits) in the monthly entry spaces on **Form 941**, line **16**.
 • If you area semiweekly schedule depositor, report your tax liabilities (not your deposits) on Schedule B (Form 941) in the lines that represent the dates your employees were paid.
 • Verify your total liability shown on Form 941, line 16, or the bottom of Schedule B (Form 941) equals your tax liability Shown on Form 941, line 10.
 • Do not show negative amounts on Form 941, line 16, or Schedule B (Form 941).
 • For prior period errors **do not** ___ your tax liabilities reported on Form 942, line 16, or on Schedule B (Form 941).
 (a) adjust
 (b) alter
 (c) change
 (d) modify
 Answer: See section 11. Depositing Taxes. "Averaged" failure-to-deposit penalty. Page 30/ (a) adjust

Section 11. Depositing Taxes. "Averaged" failure-to-deposit penalty.

11. Depositing Taxes. "Averaged" failure-to-deposit penalty.
22. You can avoid an "averaged" FTD penalty by reviewing your return before you file it. Follow these steps before submitting your Form 941.
    • If you are a monthly schedule depositor, report your tax liabilities (not your deposits) in the monthly entry spaces on **Form 941**, line **16**.
    • If you area semiweekly schedule depositor, report your tax liabilities (not your deposits) on Schedule B (Form 941) in the lines that represent the dates your employees were paid.
    • Verify your total liability shown on Form 941, line 16, or the bottom of Schedule B (Form 941) equals your tax liability Shown on Form 941, line 10.
    • Do not show negative amounts on Form 941, line 16, or Schedule B (Form 941).
    • For prior period errors **do not** ___ your tax liabilities reported on Form 942, line 16, or on Schedule B (Form 941). Instead, file an adjusted return (Form 941-___, 944- ___, or 945- ___) if you are also adjusting your tax liability.
    (a)   adjust, X,X, X
    (b)   alter, A, B, C
    (c)   change, R, R, R
    (d)   modify, S, S, S
    Answer: See section 11. Depositing Taxes. "Averaged" failure-to-deposit penalty. Page 30/ (a) adjust, X, X, X

11. Depositing Taxes. "Averaged" failure-to-deposit penalty.
23. You can avoid an "averaged" FTD penalty by reviewing your return before you file it. Follow these steps before submitting your Form 941.
    • If you are a monthly schedule depositor, report your tax liabilities (not your deposits) in the monthly entry spaces on **Form 941**, line **16**.
    • If you area semiweekly schedule depositor, report your tax liabilities (not your deposits) on Schedule B (Form 941) in the lines that represent the dates your employees were paid.
    • Verify your total liability shown on Form 941, line 16, or the bottom of Schedule B (Form 941) equals your tax liability Shown on Form 941, line 10.
    • Do not show negative amounts on Form 941, line 16, or Schedule B (Form 941).
    • For prior period errors **do not** adjust your tax liabilities reported on Form 942, line 16, or on Schedule B (Form 941). Instead, file an adjusted return (Form 941-X, 944-X, or 945- X) if you are also adjusting your tax liability. If you are only adjusting your deposits in response to a failure-to-deposit penalty notice, see the Instructions for Schedule B (Form 941) or the instructions for Form ___ (for Forms ___ and ___).
    (a)   941-X, 941, 943
    (b)   943-X, 942, 944
    (c)   944-X, 943, 945
    (d)   945-X, 944, 945
    Answer: See section 11. Depositing Taxes. "Averaged" failure-to-deposit penalty. Page 30/ (d) 945-X, 944, 945

The International Leader in Construction Technology Home Study

Instructor's Manual for Tax Test 15E-S12-1 Section 12.Filing Forms 941 or Forms 944

15E-12. General Description. Section 12 Filing Form 941 or Form 944.

Tax Test 15E-S12. Tax Tests for Section 12, 15E-S12 of Section 12. Filing Form 941 or Form 944 continue to be provided in multiple-choice test type question format. Material and information provided in Tax Test 15E-S12-1 includes the following: **Form 941** filing requirements for employers. **Form 944** filing requirements. Form 941 and Form 944 Filing requirements **Exceptions**; Seasonal employers who no longer file for quarters when they regularly have no tax liability because they have paid no wages and the additional listed **Exceptions**; Filing Form 941 or Form 944. Form 941 e-file; Filing Form 941 or Form 944. Electronic filing by reporting agents; Filing Form 941 or Form 944. Penalties(**be aware the use of a reporting agent or other third-party payroll service does not relieve the employer of the tax liability responsibility**-*carefully read this section*); Do not file more than one form 941 per quarter or Form 944 per year; Reminders about filing; Final return.

15E-12. Key Words. Section 12. Filing Form 941 or Form 944.

Tax Test 15E-S12. Form 941. Form 944. Exceptions. Seasonal employers who no longer file for quarters when they regularly have no tax liability because they have paid no wages. Household employers reporting social security and Medicare taxes and/or withheld income tax. Employers reporting wages for employees in American Samoa, Guam, The Commonwealth of the Northern Mariana Islands and the U.S. Virgin Islands or Puerto Rico. Agricultural employers reporting social security, Medicare, and withheld income taxes. Form 941 e-file. Electronic filing by reporting agents. Penalties. Use of a reporting agent or third-party payroll service provider. Do not file more than one Form 941 per quarter. Do not file more tha one Form 944 per year. reminders about filing. Final return. Filing late returns for previous years. Table 3. Reconciling Forms W-2, W-3, and 941 or 944. do not report those prior year adjustments or current-year Forms W-2 and W-3.

© Copyright 2013. All rights reserved. Notice: United States Copyright Laws and International Treaties prohibit unauthorized publication, reproduction, distribution of this Work. Unauthorized use of this copyright in any form, format, publication or document may result in severe civil and criminal penalties. Violations of this copyright are investigated by the United States Department of Justice and carry, upon conviction of fines up to $250,000 and five years confinement. This Work is protected by United States Copyright Laws and International Treaties. Do not Copy, do not reproduce, do not distribute.

A Ficus Tree Publishing Educational-Technical Publications

A Ficus Tree Publishing Quick Notes Page

DU VALL'S TEST'S™
Instructor's Manual Study Guide Series United States Tax Code
IRS Publication 15 Circular E, Employer's Tax Guide Tax Year 2013
Tax Test 15E-S12-1 [Multiple-Choice Questions With Answers]

Section 12. Filing Form 941 or Form 944. Page 30.

12. Filing Form 941 or Form 944.
1. **Form 941**. Each quarter, all employers who pay wages subject to tax withholding (including withholding on sick pay and supplemental unemployment ___) or social security and Medicare taxes must file Form 941 unless the employer is required to file Form 944 or the following exceptions apply.
    (a) benefits
    (b) wages
    (c) income
    (d) compensation
    Answer: See section 12. Filing Form 941 or Form 944. Page 30/ (a) benefits

12. Filing Form 941 or Form 944.
2. **Form 941**. Each quarter, all employers who pay wages subject to tax withholding (including withholding on sick pay and supplemental unemployment benefits) or social security and Medicare taxes must file Form 941 unless the employer is required to file Form 944 or the following exceptions apply. Form 941 must be filed by the ___ of the month that follows the end of the quarter. See the *Calendar*, earlier.
    (a) first day
    (b) 15th
    (c) 20th
    (d) last day
    Answer: See section 12. Filing Form 941 or Form 944. Page 30/ (d) last day

12. Filing Form 941 or Form 944.
3. **Form 944**. If you receive ___ you qualify for the Form 944 program, you must file Form 944 instead of Form 941.
    (a) notice
    (b) written notice
    (c) notification
    (d) written notification
    Answer: See section 12. Filing Form 941 or Form 944. Page 30/ (d) written notification

Section 12. Filing Form 941 or Form 944

12. Filing Form 941 or Form 944
4. **Form 944**. If you receive ___ you qualify for the Form 944 program, you must file Form 944 instead of Form 941. If you received this notification, but prefer to file Form 941, you can request to have your filing requirement changed to Form 941 if ___.
    (a)　notice, you can meet certain requirements
    (b)　written notice, you meet certain conditions
    (c)　notification, you meet certain requirements
    (d)　written notification, you satisfy certain requirements
    Answer: See section 12. Filing Form 941 or Form 944. Page 30/ (d) written notification, you satisfy certain requirements

12. Filing Form 941 or Form 944.
5. **Form 944**. If you receive ___ you qualify for the Form 944 program, you must file Form 944 instead of Form 941. If you received this notification, but prefer to file Form 941, you can request to have your filing requirement changed to Form 941 if ___. See the instructions for Form ___ for details.
    (a)　notice, you can meet certain requirements, 941
    (b)　written notice, you meet certain conditions, 942
    (c)　notification, you meet certain requirements, 943
    (d)　written notification, you satisfy certain requirements, 944
    Answer: See section 12. Filing Form 941 or Form 944. Page 30/ (d) written notification, you satisfy certain requirements, 944

12. Filing Form 941 or Form 944.
6. Employers who must file Form 944 have until the last day of the month that follows the end of the ___ to file Form 944.
    (a)　scheduled deposit
    (b)　each quarter
    (c)　quarter
    (d)　year
    Answer: See section 12. Filing Form 941 or Form 944. Page 30/ (d) year

Section 12. Filing Form 941 or Form 944. Exceptions.

12. Filing Form 941 or Form 944. Exceptions
7. Filing Form 941 or Form 944. **Exceptions**. The following exceptions apply to the filing requirements for Forms 941 and 944.
    • **Seasonal employers who no longer file for quarters when they regularly have no tax liability because they have paid no wages**. To alert the IRS you will not have to file a return for one or more quarters during the year, check the "Seasonal employer" box on Form 941, line ___.
    (a) 14
    (b) 16
    (c) 18
    (d) 20
    Answer: See section 12. Filing Form 941 or Form 944. Page 30/ (c) 18
    Section 12. Filing Form 941 or Form 944. Exceptions. Page 30.

12. Filing Form 941 or Form 944. Exceptions.
8. Filing Form 941 or Form 944. **Exceptions**. The following exceptions apply to the filing requirements for Forms 941 and 944.
    • **Seasonal employers who no longer file for quarters when they regularly have no tax liability because they have paid no wages**. To alert the IRS you will not have to file a return for one or more quarters during the year, check the "Seasonal employer" box on Form 941, line ___. When you fill out Form 941, be sure to check the box on the top of the form that ___ to the quarter reported.
    (a) 14, references
    (b) 16, relates
    (c) 18, corresponds
    (d) 20, matches
    Answer: See section 12. Filing Form 941 or Form 944. Page 30/ (c) 18, corresponds

12. Filing Form 941 or Form 944. Exceptions.
9. Filing Form 941 or Form 944. **Exceptions**. The following exceptions apply to the filing requirements for Forms 941 and 944.
    • **Seasonal employers who no longer file for quarters when they regularly have no tax liability because they have paid no wages**. To alert the IRS you will not have to file a return for one or more quarters during the year, check the "Seasonal employer" box on Form 941, line ___. When you fill out Form 941, be sure to check the box on the top of the form that ___ to the quarter reported. Generally, the IRS will not inquire about unfiled returns if at least one taxable return is filed ___.
    (a) 14, references, semiweekly
    (b) 16, relates, monthly
    (c) 18, corresponds, each year
    (d) 20, matches, each quarter
    Answer: See section 12. Filing Form 941 or Form 944. Page 30/ (c) 18, corresponds, each year

© Copyright 2013. All rights reserved. Notice: United States Copyright Laws and International Treaties prohibit unauthorized publication, reproduction, distribution of this Work. Unauthorized use of this copyright in any form, format, publication or document may result in severe civil and criminal penalties. Violations of this copyright are investigated by the United States Department of Justice and carry, upon conviction of fines up to $250,000 and five years confinement. This Work is protected by United States Copyright Laws and International Treaties. Do not Copy, do not reproduce, do not distribute.

12. Filing Form 941 or Form 944. Exceptions.

12. Filing Form 941 or Form 944. Exceptions.
10. Filing Form 941 or Form 944. **Exceptions**. The following exceptions apply to the filing requirements for Forms 941 and 944.
• **Seasonal employers who no longer file for quarters when they regularly have no tax liability because they have paid no wages**. To alert the IRS you will not have to file a return for one or more quarters during the year, check the "Seasonal employer" box on Form 941, line ___. When you fill out Form 941, be sure to check the box on the top of the form that ___ to the quarter reported. Generally, the IRS will not inquire about unfiled returns if at least one taxable ___ return is filed ___. However, you must check the "Seasonal employer" box on **every** Form ___ you file. Otherwise the IRS will expect a return to be filed for each ___.
(a) 14, references, semiweekly, 944, deposit
(b) 16, relates, monthly, 941, month
(c) 18, corresponds, each year, 941, quarter
(d) 20, matches, each quarter, 944, year
Answer: See section 12. Filing Form 941 or Form 944. Page 30/ (c) 18, corresponds, each year, 941, quarter

12. Filing Form 941 or Form 944. Exceptions.
11. Filing Form 941 or Form 944. **Exceptions**. The following exceptions apply to the filing requirements for Forms 941 and 944.
• **Household employers reporting social security and Medicare taxes and/or withheld income tax**. If you are a sole proprietor and file the Form 941 or Form 944 for ___ employees, you may include taxes for household employees on your Form 941 or Form 944.
(a) business
(b) your business
(c) any
(d) your
Answer: See section 12. Filing Form 941 or Form 944. Page 30/ (a) business

Section 12. Filing Form 941 or Form 944. Exceptions.

12. Filing Form 941 or Form 944. Exceptions.
12. Filing Form 941 or Form 944. **Exceptions**. The following exceptions apply to the filing requirements for Forms 941 and 944.
   • **Household employers reporting social security and Medicare taxes and/or withheld income tax.** If you are a sole proprietor and file the Form 941 or Form 944 for ___ employees, you may include taxes for household employees on your Form 941 or Form 944. Otherwise, report social security and Medicare taxes and income tax withholding for household employees on Schedule ___ (Form 1040), Household Employment Taxes.
   (a) business, H
   (b) your business, H
   (c) any, J
   (d) your, J
   Answer: See section 12. Filing Form 941 or Form 944. Page 30/ (a) business, H

12. Filing Form 941 or Form 944. Exceptions.
13. Filing Form 941 or Form 944. **Exceptions**. The following exceptions apply to the filing requirements for Forms 941 and 944.
   • **Household employers reporting social security and Medicare taxes and/or withheld income tax.** If you are a sole proprietor and file the Form 941 or Form 944 for ___ employees, you may include taxes for household employees on your Form 941 or Form 944. Otherwise, report social security and Medicare taxes and income tax withholding for household employees on Schedule ___ (Form 1040), Household Employment Taxes. See Publication ___, Household Employer's Tax Guide, for more information.
   (a) business, H, 926
   (b) your business, H, 926
   (c) any, J, 927
   (d) your, J, 927
   Answer: See section 12. Filing Form 941 or Form 944. Page 30/ (a) business, H, 926

12. Filing Form 941 or Form 944. Exceptions.
14. Filing Form 941 or Form 944. **Exceptions**. The following exceptions apply to the filing requirements for Forms 941 and 944.
   • **Employers reporting wages for employees in American Samoa, Guam, the Commonwealth of the Northern Mariana Islands, the U.S. Virgin Islands, or Puerto Rico**. If your employees are not subject to U.S. income tax withholding, use Forms ___, ___ or ___,
   (a) 941-SS, 945, Formulario 945(SP)
   (b) 941-SS, 944, Formulario 944(SP)
   (c) 941-SS, 943, Formulario 943(SP)
   (d) 941-SS, 942, Formulario 942(SP)
   Answer: See section 12. Filing Form 941 or Form 944. Page 30/ (b) 941-SS, 944, Formulario 944(SP)

Section 12. Filing Form 941 or Form 944. Exceptions. Page 30.

12. Filing Form 941 or Form 944. Exceptions.
15. Filing Form 941 or Form 944. **Exceptions**. The following exceptions apply to the filing requirements for Forms 941 and 944.
    • **Employers reporting wages for employees in American Samoa, Guam, the Commonwealth of the Northern Mariana Islands, the U.S. Virgin Islands, or Puerto Rico**. If your employees are not subject to U.S. income tax withholding, use Forms 941-SS, 944 or Formulario 944(SP). Employers in Puerto Rico use Formularious 941-PR, 944-SP, or Form ___.
    (a) 943
    (b) 944
    (c) 945
    (d) 946
    Answer: See section 12. Filing Form 941 or Form 944. Page 30/ (b) 944

12. Filing Form 941 or Form 944. Exceptions.
16. Filing Form 941 or Form 944. **Exceptions**. The following exceptions apply to the filing requirements for Forms 941 and 944.
    • **Employers reporting wages for employees in American Samoa, Guam, the Commonwealth of the Northern Mariana Islands, the U.S. Virgin Islands, or Puerto Rico**. If you have both employees who are subject to U.S. income tax withholding and employees who are not subject to U.S. income tax withholding, you must file only Form ___ (or Form 944 or Formulario 944-SP) and include all your employees' wages on that form.
    (a) 941
    (b) 942
    (c) 943
    (d) 944
    Answer: See section 12. Filing Form 941 or Form 944. Page 30/ (a) 941

12. Filing Form 941 or Form 944. Exceptions.
17. Filing Form 941 or Form 944. **Exceptions**. The following exceptions apply to the filing requirements for Forms 941 and 944.
    • **Employers reporting wages for employees in American Samoa, Guam, the Commonwealth of the Northern Mariana Islands, the U.S. Virgin Islands, or Puerto Rico**. If you have both employees who are subject to U.S. income tax withholding and employees who are not subject to U.S. income tax withholding, you must file only Form ___ (or Form 944 or Formulario 944-SP) and include all your employees' wages on that form. For more information, see Publication ___ (Circular SS) Federal Tax Guide for Employers in US Virgin Islands, Guam, American Samoa, and the Commonwealth of the Northern Mariana Islands, or
    (a) 941, 80
    (b) 942, 81
    (c) 943, 82
    (d) 944, 83
    Answer: See section 12. Filing Form 941 or Form 944. Page 30/ (a) 941, 80

Section 12. Filing Form 941 or Form 944. Exceptions. Page 30.

12. Filing Form 941 or Form 944. Exceptions.
18. Filing Form 941 or Form 944. **Exceptions**. The following exceptions apply to the filing requirements for Forms 941 and 944.
    • **Employers reporting wages for employees in American Samoa, Guam, the Commonwealth of the Northern Mariana Islands, the U.S. Virgin Islands, or Puerto Rico**. If you have both employees who are subject to U.S. income tax withholding and employees who are not subject to U.S. income tax withholding, you must file only Form ___ (or Form 944 or Formulario 944-SP) and include all your employees' wages on that form. For more information, see Publication ___ (Circular SS) Federal Tax Guide for Employers in US Virgin Islands, Guam, American Samoa, and the Commonwealth of the Northern Mariana Islands, or Publicacion ___ (Circular PR), Guia Contributiva Federal para Patronos Puertorriquenos.
    (a) 941, 80, 179
    (b) 942, 81, 180
    (c) 943, 82, 181
    (d) 944, 83, 183
    Answer: See section 12. Filing Form 941 or Form 944. Page 30/ (a) 941, 80, 179

12. Filing Form 941 or Form 944. Exceptions.
19. Filing Form 941 or Form 944. **Exceptions**. The following exceptions apply to the filing requirements for Forms 941 and 944.
    • **Agricultural employers reporting social security, Medicare, and withheld income taxes**. Report these taxes on Form ___, Employer's Annual Federal Tax return for Agricultural Employees.
    (a) 941
    (b) 942
    (c) 943
    (d) 944
    Answer: See section 12. Filing Form 941 or Form 944. Page 30/ (c) 943

12. Filing Form 941 or Form 944. Exceptions.
20. Filing Form 941 or Form 944. **Exceptions**. The following exceptions apply to the filing requirements for Forms 941 and 944.
    • **Agricultural employers reporting social security, Medicare, and withheld income taxes**. Report these taxes on Form ___, Employer's Annual Federal Tax return for Agricultural Employees. For more information, see Publication 51 (Circular ___).
    (a) 941, C
    (b) 942, B
    (c) 943, A
    (d) 944, D
    Answer: See section 12. Filing Form 941 or Form 944. Page 30/ (c) 943, A

© Copyright 2013. All rights reserved. Notice: United States Copyright Laws and International Treaties prohibit unauthorized publication, reproduction, distribution of this Work. Unauthorized use of this copyright in any form, format, publication or document may result in severe civil and criminal penalties. Violations of this copyright are investigated by the United States Department of Justice and carry, upon conviction of fines up to $250,000 and five years confinement. This Work is protected by United States Copyright Laws and International Treaties. Do not Copy, do not reproduce, do not distribute.

A Ficus Tree Publishing Educational-Technical Publications

Section 12. Filing Form 941 or Form 944. Form 941 e-file. Page 30.

12. Filing Form 941 or Form 944. Form 941 e-file.
21. The Form 941 e-file program allows a taxpayer to electronically file Form ___ or Form ___ using a computer with an internet connection and commercial tax preparation software.
    (a) 942, 945
    (b) 941, 946
    (c) 944, 945
    (d) 941, 944
    Answer: See section 12. Filing Form 941 or Form 944. Page 30/ (d) 941, 944

12. Filing Form 941 or Form 944. Form 941 e-file.
22. The Form 941 e-file program allows a taxpayer to electronically file Form ___ or Form ___ using a computer with an internet connection and commercial tax preparation software. For more information, visit the IRS website at *www.irs.gov/efile*. or call 1-___-255-0654.
    (a) 942, 945, 800
    (b) 941, 946, 866
    (c) 944, 945, 800
    (d) 941, 944, 866
    Answer: See section 12. Filing Form 941 or Form 944. Page 30/ (d) 941, 944, 866

Filing Form 941 or Form 944. Electronic filing by reporting agents.

12. Filing Form 941 or Form 944. Electronic filing by reporting agents.
23. Reporting agents filing Form 941 or Form 944 for groups of taxpayers can file them electronically. See *Reporting Agents* in section ___ of Publication ___.
    (a) 7, 15
    (b) 7, 15-A
    (c) 8, 15-B
    (d) 8, 15-C
    Answer: See section 12. Filing Form 941 or Form 944. Page 30/ (b) 7, 15-A

Section 12. Filing Form 941 or Form 944. Penalties. Page 30.

12. Filing Form 941 or Form 944. Penalties
24. For each ___ or ___ month a return is not filed when required (disregarding any extensions of the filing deadline), there is a failure-to-file penalty of ___% of the unpaid tax due with that return.
    (a) part, whole, 5
    (b) week, day, 7½
    (c) whole, part, 5
    (d) day, week, 7½
    Answer: See section 12. Filing Form 941 or Form 944. Penalties. Page 30/ (c) whole, part, 5

© Copyright 2013. All rights reserved. Notice: United States Copyright Laws and International Treaties prohibit unauthorized publication, reproduction, distribution of this Work. Unauthorized use of this copyright in any form, format, publication or document may result in severe civil and criminal penalties. Violations of this copyright are investigated by the United States Department of Justice and carry, upon conviction of fines up to $250,000 and five years confinement. This Work is protected by United States Copyright Laws and International Treaties. Do not Copy, do not reproduce, do not distribute.

Section 12. Filing Form 941 or Form 944. Penalties. Page 30.

12. Filing Form 941 or Form 944. Penalties
25. For each whole or part month a return is not filed when required (disregarding any extensions of the filing deadline), there is a failure-to-file penalty of 5% of the unpaid tax due with that return. The maximum penalty is generally ___% of the tax due. Also, for each whole or part month the tax is paid late (disregarding any extensions of the payment deadline). there is a failure-to-pay penalty of ___% per month of the amount of the tax due.
    (a)　7½, 0.3
    (b)　10, 0.3
    (c)　18, 0.5
    (d)　25, 0.5
    Answer: See section 12. Filing Form 941 or Form 944. Penalties. Page 30/ (d) 25, 0.5

12. Filing Form 941 or Form 944. Penalties
26. For each whole or part month a return is not filed when required (disregarding any extensions of the filing deadline), there is a failure-to-file penalty of 5% of the unpaid tax due with that return. The maximum penalty is generally ___% of the tax due. Also, for each whole or part month the tax is paid late (disregarding any extensions of the payment deadline). there is a failure-to-pay penalty of ___% per month of the amount of the tax due. For individual filers only, the failure-to-pay penalty is reduced from ___ per month to ___ per month if an installment agreement is in effect.
    (a)　7½, 0.3, 0.5, 0.25
    (b)　10, 0.3, 0.5, 0.25
    (c)　18, 0.5, 0.5, 0.25
    (d)　25, 0.5, 0.5, 0.25
    Answer: See section 12. Filing Form 941 or Form 944. Penalties. Page 30/ (d) 25, 0.5, 0.5, 0.25

12. Filing Form 941 or Form 944. Penalties
27. For each whole or part month a return is not filed when required (disregarding any extensions of the filing deadline), there is a failure-to-file penalty of 5% of the unpaid tax due with that return. The maximum penalty is generally ___% of the tax due. Also, for each whole or part month the tax is paid late (disregarding any extensions of the payment deadline). there is a failure-to-pay penalty of ___% per month of the amount of the tax due. For individual filers only, the failure-to-pay penalty is reduced from ___ per month to ___ per month if an installment agreement is in effect. You must have filed your ___ on or before the due date of the return to qualify for the reduced penalty.
    (a)　7½, 0.3, 0.5, 0.25, return
    (b)　10, 0.3, 0.5, 0.25, tax report
    (c)　18, 0.5, 0.5, 0.25, tax return
    (d)　25, 0.5, 0.5, 0.25, return
    Answer: See section 12. Filing Form 941 or Form 944. Penalties. Page 30/ (d) 25, 0.5, 0.5, 0.25, return

© Copyright 2013. All rights reserved. Notice: United States Copyright Laws and International Treaties prohibit unauthorized publication, reproduction, distribution of this Work. Unauthorized use of this copyright in any form, format, publication or document may result in severe civil and criminal penalties. Violations of this copyright are investigated by the United States Department of Justice and carry, upon conviction of fines up to $250,000 and five years confinement. This Work is protected by United States Copyright Laws and International Treaties. Do not Copy, do not reproduce, do not distribute.

Section 12. Filing Form 941 or Form 944. Penalties. Page 30.

12. Filing Form 941 or Form 944. Penalties
28. For each whole or part month a return is not filed when required (disregarding any extensions of the filing deadline), there is a failure-to-file penalty of 5% of the unpaid tax due with that return. The maximum penalty is generally 25% of the tax due. Also, for each whole or part month the tax is paid late (disregarding any extensions of the payment deadline). there is a failure-to-pay penalty of 0.5% per month of the amount of the tax due. For individual filers only, the failure-to-pay penalty is reduced from 0.5 per month to 0.25 per month if an installment agreement is in effect. You must have filed your return on or before the due date of the return to qualify for the reduced penalty. The maximum amount of the failure-to-pay penalty is ___ of the tax due.
   (a)   the full amount
   (b)   one-half of the amount
   (c)   25%
   (d)   33%
Answer: See section 12. Filing Form 941 or Form 944. Penalties. Pages 30 and 31/ (c) 25

12. Filing Form 941 or Form 944. Penalties
29. For each whole or part month a return is not filed when required (disregarding any extensions of the filing deadline), there is a failure-to-file penalty of 5% of the unpaid tax due with that return. The maximum penalty is generally 25% of the tax due. Also, for each whole or part month the tax is paid late (disregarding any extensions of the payment deadline). there is a failure-to-pay penalty of 0.5% per month of the amount of the tax due. For individual filers only, the failure-to-pay penalty is reduced from 0.5 per month to 0.25 per month if an installment agreement is in effect. You must have filed your return on or before the due date of the return to qualify for the reduced penalty. The maximum amount of the failure-to-pay penalty is ___ of the tax due. If both penalties apply in any month, the failure-to-file penalty is ___ by the amount of the failure-to-pay penalty.
   (a)   the full amount, reduced
   (b)   one-half of the amount, added
   (c)   25%, reduced
   (d)   33%, added
Answer: See section 12. Filing Form 941 or Form 944. Penalties. Pages 30 and 31/ (c) 25, reduced

12. Filing Form 941 or Form 944. Penalties
30. The penalties will not be charged if you ___ for failing to file or pay.
   (a)   have due cause
   (b)   have reasonable cause
   (c)   have a reasonable cause
   (d)   have an unchallengeable cause
Answer: See section 12. Filing Form 941 or Form 944. Penalties. Pages 30 and 31/ (c) have a reasonable cause

Section 12. Filing Form 941 or Form 944. Penalties. Page 30/31.

12. Filing Form 941 or Form 944. Penalties

31. The penalties will not be charged if you ___ for failing to file or pay. If you receive a penalty notice, you can ___ of why you believe reasonable cause exists.
    (a) have due cause, schedule a meeting with the IRS representative
    (b) have reasonable cause, provide an explanation
    (c) have a reasonable cause, schedule a meeting with the IRS
    (d) have an unchallengeable cause, provide an adequate explanation
    Answer: See section 12. Filing Form 941 or Form 944. Penalties. Pages 30 and 31/ (c) have a reasonable cause, provide an explanation

12. Filing Form 941 or Form 944. Note.

32. In addition to any penalties, interest ___ from the due date of the tax on any unpaid balance.
    (a) accrues
    (b) compounds
    (c) increases
    (d) continues to increase
    Answer: See section 12. Filing Form 941 or Form 944. Note. Page 31/(a) accrues

12. Filing Form 941 or Form 944. Note.

33. In addition to any penalties, interest ___ from the due date of the tax on any unpaid balance. If any income, social security, or Medicare taxes that must be withheld are not withheld or are not paid, you ___ for the trust fund recovery penalty.
    (a) accrues, may be personally liable
    (b) compounds, will be personally liable
    (c) increases, shall be personally liable
    (d) continues to increase, can be held personally liable
    Answer: See section 12. Filing Form 941 or Form 944. Note. Page 31/(a) accrues, may be personally liable

12. Filing Form 941 or Form 944. Note.

34. In addition to any penalties, interest ___ from the due date of the tax on any unpaid balance. If any income, social security, or Medicare taxes that must be withheld are not withheld or are not paid, you ___ for the trust fund recovery penalty. See ***Trust fund recovery penalty*** in section ___.
    (a) accrues, may be personally liable, 11
    (b) compounds, will be personally liable, 12
    (c) increases, shall be personally liable, 13
    (d) continues to increase, can be held personally liable, 11
    Answer: See section 12. Filing Form 941 or Form 944. Note. Page 31/(a) accrues, may be personally liable, 11

Section 12. Filing Form 941 or Form 944. Penalties. Note. Page 31.

12. Filing Form 941 or Form 944. Note.
35. Use of a reporting agent or other third-party payroll service provider does not relieve an employer of the responsibility to ___ tax returns are filed and all taxes are paid or deposited correctly and on time.
    (a) provide correct
    (b) deposit required
    (c) defer responsibility
    (d) ensure
    Answer: See section 12. Filing Form 941 or Form 944. Note. Page 31/(d) ensure

12. Filing Form 941 or Form 944. Do not file more than one Form 941 per quarter or more than one Form 944 per year. Page 31.

12. Filing Form 941 or Form 944. Do not file more than one Form 941 per quarter or more than one Form 944 per year.
36. Employers with multiple locations or ___ must file only one Form 941 per quarter or one Form 941 per year.
    (a) stores
    (b) outlets
    (c) divisions
    (d) businesses
    Answer: See section 12. Filing Form 941 or Form 944. Page 31/(c) divisions

12. Filing Form 941 or Form 944. Do not file more than one Form 941 per quarter or more than one Form 944 per year.
37. Employers with multiple locations or ___ must file only one Form 941 per quarter or one Form 941 per year. Filing more than one return may result in processing delays and may require ___ between you and the IRS.
    (a) stores, resolution
    (b) outlets, meetings
    (c) divisions, correspondence
    (d) businesses, communication
    Answer: See section 12. Filing Form 941 or Form 944. Page 31/(c) divisions, correspondence

Section 12. Filing Form 941 or Form 944. Do not file more than one Form 941 per quarter or more than one Form 944 per year. Page 31.

12. Filing Form 941 or Form 944. Do not file more than one Form 941 per quarter or more than one Form 944 per year. Page 31.

38. Employers with multiple locations or ___ must file only one Form 941 per quarter or one Form 941 per year. Filing more than one return may result in processing delays and may require ___ between you and the IRS. For information on making adjustments to previously filed returns, see ***section*** ___.
    (a) stores, resolution, 10
    (b) outlets, meetings, 12
    (c) divisions, correspondence, 13
    (d) businesses, communication, 14
    Answer: See section 12. Filing Form 941 or Form 944. Page 31/(c) divisions, correspondence, 13

12. Filing Form 941 or Form 944. Reminders about filing

12. Filing Form 941 or Form 944. Reminders about filing.
39. • Do not report more than ___ on a Form 941.
    (a) one quarter
    (b) 1 calendar quarter
    (c) one deposit
    (d) a single tax report
    Answer: See section 12. Filing Form 941 or Form 944. Page 31/(b) 1 calendar quarter

12. Filing Form 941 or Form 944. Reminders about filing.
40. • If you need Form 941 or Form 944, get on from the IRS in time to ___ the return when due. See ***Ordering Employer Tax Products***, earlier.
    (a) file
    (b) send
    (c) submit
    (d) report
    Answer: See section 12. Filing Form 941 or Form 944. Page 31/(a) file

12. Filing Form 941 or Form 944. Reminders about filing.
41. • Enter you ___ and ___ on Form 941 or Form 944.
    (a) name, address
    (b) name, telephone number
    (c) name, e-mail address
    (d) name, EIN
    Answer: See section 12. Filing Form 941 or Form 944. Page 31/(d) name, EIN

12. Filing Form 941 or Form 944. Reminders about filing.

12. Filing Form 941 or Form 944. Reminders about filing.
42. • Enter you ___ and ___ on Form 941 or Form 944. Be sure they are ___ as they appeared on earlier returns.
    (a)   name, address, exactly
    (b)   name, telephone number, identical
    (c)   name, e-mail address, identical
    (d)   name, EIN, exactly
    Answer: See section 12. Filing Form 941 or Form 944. Page 31/(d) name, EIN, exactly

12. Filing Form 941 or Form 944. Reminders about filing.
43. • See the Instructions for Form 941 or the Instructions for Form 944 for information on ___ the form.
    (a)   preparing
    (b)   correctly preparing
    (c)   submitting
    (d)   correctly submitting
    Answer: See section 12. Filing Form 941 or Form 944. Page 31/(a) preparing

Section 12. Filing Form 941 or Form 944. Final return. Page 31.

12. Filing Form 941 or Form 944. Final return.
44. If you go out of business, you must file a ___ for the last quarter (last year for Form 944) in which wages are paid.
    (a)   loss report
    (b)   profit or loss report
    (c)   final return
    (d)   closing return
    Answer: See section 12. Filing Form 941 or Form 944. Page 31/(c) final return

12. Filing Form 941 or Form 944. Final return.
45. If you go out of business, you must file a ___ for the last quarter (last year for Form 944) in which wages are paid. If you continue to pay wages or other compensation for periods following ___ of your business, you must file returns for those periods.
    (a)   loss report, the closure
    (b)   profit or loss report, conclusion
    (c)   final return, termination
    (d)   closing return, closure
    Answer: See section 12. Filing Form 941 or Form 944. Page 31/(c) final return, termination

12. Filing Form 941 or Form 944. Final return.

12. Filing Form 941 or Form 944. Final return.
46. If you go out of business, you must file a ___ for the last quarter (last year for Form 944) in which wages are paid. If you continue to pay wages or other compensation for periods following ___ of your business, you must file returns for those periods. See the Instructions for Form 941 or the Instructions for Form 944 for details on how to file a ___.
   (a) loss report, the closure, closing return
   (b) profit or loss report, conclusion, closing report
   (c) final return, termination, final return
   (d) closing return, closure, closing statement
   Answer: See section 12. Filing Form 941 or Form 944. Page 31/(c) final return, termination, final return

12. Filing Form 941 or Form 944. Final return.
47. If you are required to file a final return, you are also required to furnish Forms ___ to your employees by the due date of your final return.
   (a) W-2
   (b) W-3
   (c) 1088
   (d) 1099
   Answer: See section 12. Filing Form 941 or Form 944. Page 31/(a) W-2

12. Filing Form 941 or Form 944. Final return.
48. If you are required to file a final return, you are also required to furnish Forms ___ to your employees by the due date of your final return. File Forms ___ and ___ with the SSA by the last day of the month that follows the due date of your final return.
   (a) W-2, W-2, W-3
   (b) W-3, W-3, W-4
   (c) 1088, 1088, 1099
   (d) 1099, 1099, W-2
   Answer: See section 12. Filing Form 941 or Form 944. Page 31/(a) W-2, W-2, W-3

12. Filing Form 941 or Form 944. Final return.
49. If you are required to file a final return, you are also required to furnish Forms W-2 to your employees by the due date of your final return. File Forms W-2 and W-3 with the SSA by the last day of the month that follows the due date of your final return. Do not send an original copy of your Form ___ or form ___ to the SSA.
   (a) 440, 489
   (b) 941, 944
   (c) 1088, 1089
   (d) 1098, 1099
   Answer: See section 12. Filing Form 941 or Form 944. Page 31/(b) 941, 944

Section 12. Filing Form 941 or Form 944. Final return.

12. Filing Form 941 or Form 944. Final return.
50. See the General Instructions for Forms ___ and ___ for more information.
    (a)   440, 489
    (b)   941, 944
    (c)   W-2, W-3
    (d)   W-3, W-4
Answer: See section 12. Filing Form 941 or Form 944. Page 31/(c) W-2, W-3

Section 12. Filing Form 941 or Form 944.
Filing late returns for previous years. Page 31.

12. Filing Form 941 or Form 944. Filing late returns for previous years.
51. If possible, get a copy of Form 941 or Form 944 (and separate instructions) with a ___ date showing the year for which your delinquent return is begin filed.
    (a)   current
    (b)   legible
    (c)   post office stamped
    (d)   revision
Answer: See section 12. Filing Form 941 or Form 944. Page 31/(d) revision

12. Filing Form 941 or Form 944. Filing late returns for previous years.
52. If possible, get a copy of Form 941 or Form 944 (and separate instructions) with a ___ date showing the year for which your delinquent return is begin filed. See ***Quick and Easy Access to IRS Tax Help and Products***, located at the end of ___, for various ways to secure any necessary forms and instructions.
    (a)   current, this publication
    (b)   legible, Circular E
    (c)   post office stamped, Circular 15A
    (d)   revision, Circular 15B
Answer: See section 12. Filing Form 941 or Form 944. Page 31/(d) revision, this publication

12. Filing Form 941 or Form 944. Filing late returns for previous years.
53. If possible, get a copy of Form 941 or Form 944 (and separate instructions) with a ___ date showing the year for which your delinquent return is begin filed. See ***Quick and Easy Access to IRS Tax Help and Products***, located at the end of ___, for various ways to secure any necessary forms and instructions. Contact the IRS at 1-___-829-4933
    (a)   current, this publication, 800
    (b)   legible, Circular E, 866
    (c)   post office stamped, Circular 15A, 800
    (d)   revision, Circular 15B, 866
Answer: See section 12. Filing Form 941 or Form 944. Page 31/(d) revision, this publication, 800

Section 12. Filing Form 941 or Form 944. Table 3.
Social Security and Medicare Tax Rates (for 3 prior years). Page 31.

12. Filing Form 941 or Form 944. Table 3. Social Security and Medicare Tax Rates (for 3 prior years)

54. **Table 3 Social Security and Medicare Tax Rates**

Calendar Year	Wage Base Limit (each employee)	Tax Rate Taxable Wages and Tips
2012- Social Security	$110,100	____%

    (a)   5.3
    (b)   8.5
    (c)   10.4
    (d)   15.0
Answer: See section 12. Filing Form 941 or Form 944. Table 3. Page 31/(c) 10.4

12. Filing Form 941 or Form 944. Table 3. Social Security and Medicare Tax Rates (for 3 prior years)

55. **Table 3 Social Security and Medicare Tax Rates**

Calendar Year	Wage Base Limit (each employee)	Tax Rate Taxable Wages and Tips
2012- Medicare	All Wages	____%

    (a)   2.9
    (b)   5.3
    (c)   8.1
    (d)   10.3
Answer: See section 12. Filing Form 941 or Form 944. Table 3. Page 31/(a) 2.9

12. Filing Form 941 or Form 944. Table 3

12. Filing Form 941 or Form 944. Table 3. Social Security and Medicare Tax Rates (for 3 prior years)

56.   **Table 3 Social Security and Medicare Tax Rates**

Calendar Year	Wage Base Limit (each employee)	Tax Rate Taxable Wages and Tips
2011- Social Security	$106, 800	____%

- (a) 2.9
- (b) 5.3
- (c) 8.1
- (d) 10.4

Answer: See section 12. Filing Form 941 or Form 944. Table 3. Page 31/(d) 10.4

12. Filing Form 941 or Form 944. Table 3. Social Security and Medicare Tax Rates (for 3 prior years)

57.   **Table 3 Social Security and Medicare Tax Rates**

Calendar Year	Wage Base Limit (each employee)	Tax Rate Taxable Wages and Tips
2011- Medicare	All Wages	____%

- (a) 2.9
- (b) 5.3
- (c) 8.1
- (d) 10.4

Answer: See section 12. Filing Form 941 or Form 944. Table 3. Page 31/(a) 2.9

12. Filing Form 941 or Form 944. Table 3.

12. Filing Form 941 or Form 944. Table 3. Social Security and Medicare Tax Rates (for 3 prior years)

58.   **Table 3 Social Security and Medicare Tax Rates**

Calendar Year	Wage Base Limit (each employee)	Tax Rate Taxable Wages and Tips
2010- Social Security	$106, 800	____%

    (a)   2.9
    (b)   5.3
    (c)   10.4
    (d)   12.4
Answer: See section 12. Filing Form 941 or Form 944. Table 3. Page 31/(d) 12.4

12. Filing Form 941 or Form 944. Table 3. Social Security and Medicare Tax Rates (for 3 prior years)

59.   **Table 3 Social Security and Medicare Tax Rates**

Calendar Year	Wage Base Limit (each employee)	Tax Rate Taxable Wages and Tips
2010- Medicare	All Wages	____%

    (a)   2.9
    (b)   5.3
    (c)   10.4
    (d)   12.4
Answer: See section 12. Filing Form 941 or Form 944. Table 3. Page 31/(a) 2.9

A Ficus Tree Publishing Quick Notes Page

DU VALL'S TEST'S™
Instructor's Manual Study Guide Series United States Tax Code
IRS Publication 15 Circular E, Employer's Tax Guide Tax Year 2013
Tax Test 15E-S12-2 [Multiple-Choice Questions With Answers]

Section 12. Filing Form 941 or Form 944. Reconciling Forms W-2, W-3, and 941 or 944. Page 31.

12. Filing Form 941 or Form 944. Reconciling Forms W-2, W-3, and 941 or 944.
1. When there are ___ between Forms 941 or 944 filed with the IRS and Forms W-2 and W-3 filed with the SSA, the IRS must contact you to resolve the ___.
   (a) differences, errors
   (b) discrepancies, discrepancies
   (c) differences, differences
   (d) errors, differences
   Answer: See section 12. Filing Form 941 or Form 944. Page 31/(b) discrepancies, discrepancies

12. Filing Form 941 or Form 944. Reconciling Forms W-2, W-3, and 941 or 944.
2. When there are discrepancies between Forms 941 or 944 filed with the IRS and Forms W-2 and W-3 filed with the SSA, the IRS must contact you to resolve the discrepancies. Take the following steps to help reduce discrepancies.
   1. Report ___ as wages and as social security and Medicare wages on Forms W-2 and Form 941 or Form 944.
   (a) bonuses
   (b) bonus payments
   (c) supplementary wages
   (d) payments in kind
   Answer: See section 12. Filing Form 941 or Form 944. Page 31/(a) bonuses

12. Filing Form 941 or Form 944. Reconciling Forms W-2, W-3, and 941 or 944.
3. When there are discrepancies between Forms 941 or 944 filed with the IRS and Forms W-2 and W-3 filed with the SSA, the IRS must contact you to resolve the discrepancies. Take the following steps to help reduce discrepancies.
   2. Report both social security and Medicare wages and taxes ___ on Forms W-2, W-3, 941, and 944.
   (a) combined
   (b) separately
   (c) together
   (d) as distinct and separate
   Answer: See section 12. Filing Form 941 or Form 944. Page 31/(b) separately

© Copyright 2013. All rights reserved. Notice: United States Copyright Laws and International Treaties prohibit unauthorized publication, reproduction, distribution of this Work. Unauthorized use of this copyright in any form, format, publication or document may result in severe civil and criminal penalties. Violations of this copyright are investigated by the United States Department of Justice and carry, upon conviction of fines up to $250,000 and five years confinement. This Work is protected by United States Copyright Laws and International Treaties. Do not Copy, do not reproduce, do not distribute.

Section 12. Filing Form 941 or Form 944.
Reconciling Forms W-2, W-3, and 941 or 944. Page 31.

12. Filing Form 941 or Form 944. Reconciling Forms W-2, W-3, and 941 or 944.
4. When there are discrepancies between Forms 941 or 944 filed with the IRS and Forms W-2 and W-3 filed with the SSA, the IRS must contact you to resolve the discrepancies. Take the following steps to help reduce discrepancies.
3. Report employee share of social security taxes on Form W-2 in the box for social security ___ (box 4), not as social security ___.
(a) wages, income
(b) income, wages
(c) withheld, wages
(d) wages, withheld
Answer: See section 12. Filing Form 941 or Form 944. Page 31/(c) withheld, wages

12. Filing Form 941 or Form 944. Reconciling Forms W-2, W-3, and 941 or 944.
5. When there are discrepancies between Forms 941 or 944 filed with the IRS and Forms W-2 and W-3 filed with the SSA, the IRS must contact you to resolve the discrepancies. Take the following steps to help reduce discrepancies.
4. Report employee share of Medicare taxes on Form W-2 in the box for Medicare Tax withheld (box ___), not as Medicare wages.
(a) 3
(b) 4
(c) 5
(d) 6
Answer: See section 12. Filing Form 941 or Form 944. Page 31/(d) 6

12. Filing Form 941 or Form 944. Reconciling Forms W-2, W-3, and 941 or 944.
6. When there are discrepancies between Forms 941 or 944 filed with the IRS and Forms W-2 and W-3 filed with the SSA, the IRS must contact you to resolve the discrepancies. Take the following steps to help reduce discrepancies.
5. Make sure the social security wage amount for each employee does not exceed the annual wage base limit (for example, $___ for 2013).
(a) 113,500
(b) 113,700
(c) 113,750
(d) 113,825
Answer: See section 12. Filing Form 941 or Form 944. Page 31/(b) 113,700

Section 12. Filing Form 941 or Form 944. Reconciling Forms W-2, W-3, and 941 or 944.

12. Filing Form 941 or Form 944. Reconciling Forms W-2, W-3, and 941 or 944.

7. When there are discrepancies between Forms 941 or 944 filed with the IRS and Forms W-2 and W-3 filed with the SSA, the IRS must contact you to resolve the discrepancies. Take the following steps to help reduce discrepancies.
6. Do not report ___ wages that are not subject to social security or Medicare Taxes as social security or Medicare wages.
   (a) noncash
   (b) in kind
   (c) supplementary
   (d) bonus
   Answer: See section 12. Filing Form 941 or Form 944. Page 31/(a) noncash

12. Filing Form 941 or Form 944. Reconciling Forms W-2, W-3, and 941 or 944.

8. When there are discrepancies between Forms 941 or 944 filed with the IRS and Forms W-2 and W-3 filed with the SSA, the IRS must contact you to resolve the discrepancies. Take the following steps to help reduce discrepancies.
7. If you used an EIN on any Form 941 or Form 944 for the year that is different from the EIN reported on Form W-3, enter the other EIN on Form W-3 in the box for "___."
   (a) Supplemental EIN numbers
   (b) SSN EIN
   (c) Other EIN used this year
   (d) SSN EIN number only
   Answer: See section 12. Filing Form 941 or Form 944. Page 31/(c) Other EIN used this year

12. Filing Form 941 or Form 944. Reconciling Forms W-2, W-3, and 941 or 944.

9. When there are discrepancies between Forms 941 or 944 filed with the IRS and Forms W-2 and W-3 filed with the SSA, the IRS must contact you to resolve the discrepancies. Take the following steps to help reduce discrepancies.
8. Be sure the ___ on Form W-3 are the total of amounts from Forms W-2.
   (a) figures
   (b) numbers
   (c) amounts
   (d) information provided
   Answer: See section 12. Filing Form 941 or Form 944. Page 31/(c) amounts

Section 12. Filing Form 941 or Form 944.
Reconciling Forms W-2, W-3, and 941 or 944.

12. Filing Form 941 or Form 944. Reconciling Forms W-2, W-3, and 941 or 944.
10. When there are discrepancies between Forms 941 or 944 filed with the IRS and Forms W-2 and W-3 filed with the SSA, the IRS must contact you to resolve the discrepancies. Take the following steps to help reduce discrepancies.
   9. Reconcile Form W-3 with your four quarterly Forms 941 or annual Form 944 by comparing ___ reported for:
   (a)   figures
   (b)   numbers
   (c)   amounts
   (d)   information provided
   Answer: See section 12. Filing Form 941 or Form 944. Page 31/(c) amounts

12. Filing Form 941 or Form 944. Reconciling Forms W-2, W-3, and 941 or 944.
11. When there are discrepancies between Forms 941 or 944 filed with the IRS and Forms W-2 and W-3 filed with the SSA, the IRS must contact you to resolve the discrepancies. Take the following steps to help reduce discrepancies.
   9. Reconcile Form W-3 with your four quarterly Forms 941 or annual Form 944 by comparing amounts reported for:
   a. Income tax withholding;
   b. Social security wages, social security tips, and Medicare wages and ___.
   (a)   noncash income
   (b)   noncash bonuses
   (c)   correct income amounts
   (d)   tips
   Answer: See section 12. Filing Form 941 or Form 944. Page 31/(d) tips

12. Filing Form 941 or Form 944. Reconciling Forms W-2, W-3, and 941 or 944.
12. When there are discrepancies between Forms 941 or 944 filed with the IRS and Forms W-2 and W-3 filed with the SSA, the IRS must contact you to resolve the discrepancies. Take the following steps to help reduce discrepancies.
   9. Reconcile Form W-3 with your four quarterly Forms 941 or annual Form 944 by comparing amounts reported for:
   a. Income tax withholding;
   b. Social security wages, social security tips, and Medicare wages and ___. Form W-3 should include Forms 941 or Form 944 ___ for the current year (that is, if the Form 941 or Form 955 adjustments include amounts for a prior year, do not
   (a)   noncash income, adjustments
   (b)   noncash bonuses, corrections
   (c)   correct income amounts, corrections
   (d)   tips, adjustments
   Answer: See section 12. Filing Form 941 or Form 944. Page 31/(d) tips, adjustments

Section 12. Filing Form 941 or Form 944.
Reconciling Forms W-2, W-3, and 941 or 944.

12. Filing Form 941 or Form 944. Reconciling Forms W-2, W-3, and 941 or 944.
13. When there are discrepancies between Forms 941 or 944 filed with the IRS and Forms W-2 and W-3 filed with the SSA, the IRS must contact you to resolve the discrepancies. Take the following steps to help reduce discrepancies.
   9. Reconcile Form W-3 with your four quarterly Forms 941 or annual Form 944 by comparing amounts reported for:
   a. Income tax withholding;
   b. Social security wages, social security tips, and Medicare wages and ___. Form W-3 should include Forms 941 or Form 944 ___ for the current year (that is, if the Form 941 or Form 955 adjustments include amounts for a prior year, do not ___ those prior year adjustments on the current-year Forms W-2 and W-3; and
   (a) noncash income, adjustments, include
   (b) noncash bonuses, corrections, include
   (c) correct income amounts, corrections, add
   (d) tips, adjustments, report
   Answer: See section 12. Filing Form 941 or Form 944. Pages 31 and 32/(d) tips, adjustments, report

12. Filing Form 941 or Form 944. Reconciling Forms W-2, W-3, and 941 or 944.
14. When there are discrepancies between Forms 941 or 944 filed with the IRS and Forms W-2 and W-3 filed with the SSA, the IRS must contact you to resolve the discrepancies. Take the following steps to help reduce discrepancies.
   9. Reconcile Form W-3 with your four quarterly Forms 941 or annual Form 944 by comparing amounts reported for:
   c. Social security and Medicare taxes. Generally, the amounts shown on the four quarterly Forms 941 or the annual Form 944, including current-year adjustments, should be ___ the amounts shown on Form W-3.
   (a) approximately twice
   (b) approximately double
   (c) approximately trice
   (d) approximately equal
   Answer: See section 12. Filing Form 941 or Form 944. Page 32/(a) approximately twice

Section 12. Filing Form 941 or Form 944. Reconciling Forms W-2, W-3, and 941 or 944. Page 32.

12. Filing Form 941 or Form 944. Reconciling Forms W-2, W-3, and 941 or 944.

15. When there are discrepancies between Forms 941 or 944 filed with the IRS and Forms W-2 and W-3 filed with the SSA, the IRS must contact you to resolve the discrepancies. Take the following steps to help reduce discrepancies.
   9. Reconcile Form W-3 with your four quarterly Forms 941 or annual Form 944 by comparing amounts reported for:
   c. Social security and Medicare taxes. Generally, the amounts shown on the four quarterly Forms 941 or the annual Form 944, including current-year adjustments, should be ___ the amounts shown on Form W-3. This is because Form 941 and Form 944 include ___ the employer and employee shares of social security and Medicare taxes.
   - (a) approximately twice, both
   - (b) approximately double, each
   - (c) approximately triple, all
   - (d) approximately equal, both

   Answer: See section 12. Filing Form 941 or Form 944. Page 32/(a) approximately twice, both

12. Filing Form 941 or Form 944. Reconciling Forms W-2, W-3, and 941 or 944.

16. Do not report on Form 941 or Form 944 ___ withholding or income tax withholding on nonpayroll payments such as pensions, annuities, and gambling winnings.
   - (a) special
   - (b) backup
   - (c) additional
   - (d) supplemental

   Answer: See section 12. Filing Form 941 or Form 944. Page 32/(b) backup

12. Filing Form 941 or Form 944. Reconciling Forms W-2, W-3, and 941 or 944.

17. Do not report on Form 941 or Form 944 ___ withholding or income tax withholding on nonpayroll payments such as pensions, annuities, and gambling winnings. Nonpayroll withholding must be reported on Form ___.
   - (a) special, 944
   - (b) backup, 945
   - (c) additional, 946
   - (d) supplemental, 947

   Answer: See section 12. Filing Form 941 or Form 944. Page 32/(b) backup, 945

Section 12. Filing Form 941 or Form 944.
Reconciling Forms W-2, W-3, and 941 or 944. Page 32.

12. Filing Form 941 or Form 944. Reconciling Forms W-2, W-3, and 941 or 944.
18. Do not report on Form 941 or Form 944 ___ withholding or income tax withholding on nonpayroll payments such as pensions, annuities, and gambling winnings. Nonpayroll withholding must be reported on Form ___. See the Instructions for Form ___ for details.
   (a) special, 944, 944
   (b) backup, 945, 945
   (c) additional, 946, 946
   (d) supplemental, 947, 947
   Answer: See section 12. Filing Form 941 or Form 944. Page 32/(b) backup, 945, 945

12. Filing Form 941 or Form 944. Reconciling Forms W-2, W-3, and 941 or 944.
19. Income tax withholding required to be reported on Forms 1099 or W-2G must be reported on Form ___.
   (a) 942
   (b) 943
   (c) 944
   (d) 945
   Answer: See section 12. Filing Form 941 or Form 944. Page 32/(d) 945

12. Filing Form 941 or Form 944. Reconciling Forms W-2, W-3, and 941 or 944.
20. Only taxes and withholding ___ on Form W-2 should be reported on Form 941 or Form 944.
   (a) reported
   (b) posted
   (c) properly reported
   (d) Properly deposited
   Answer: See section 12. Filing Form 941 or Form 944. Page 32/(c) properly reported

12. Filing Form 941 or Form 944. Reconciling Forms W-2, W-3, and 941 or 944.
21. Amounts reported on Forms W-2, W-3, and forms 941 or Form 944 may not match for ___ reasons.
   (a) valid
   (b) a number of
   (c) a variety of
   (d) countless
   Answer: See section 12. Filing Form 941 or Form 944. Page 32/(a) valid

Section 12. Filing Form 941 or Form 944. Reconciling Forms W-2, W-3, and 941 or 944.

12. Filing Form 941 or Form 944. Reconciling Forms W-2, W-3, and 941 or 944.

22. Amounts reported on Forms W-2, W-3, and forms 941 or Form 944 may not match for valid reasons. If they do not match, you should ___ the reasons they are valid.
    (a) examine
    (b) determine
    (c) research
    (d) be able to substantiate
    Answer: See section 12. Filing Form 941 or Form 944. Page 32/(b) determine

12. Filing Form 941 or Form 944. Reconciling Forms W-2, W-3, and 941 or 944.

23. Amounts reported on Forms W-2, W-3, and forms 941 or Form 944 may not match for valid reasons. If they do not match, you should ___ the reasons they are valid. Keep your ___ so you will have a record of why the amounts did not match in case there are inquiries from the IRS or the SSA.
    (a) examine, documents in order
    (b) determine, reconciliation
    (c) research, documents
    (d) be able to substantiate, audit
    Answer: See section 12. Filing Form 941 or Form 944. Page 32/(b) determine, reconciliation

12. Filing Form 941 or Form 944. Reconciling Forms W-2, W-3, and 941 or 944.

24. Amounts reported on Forms W-2, W-3, and forms 941 or Form 944 may not match for valid reasons. If they do not match, you should ___ the reasons they are valid. Keep your ___ so you will have a record of why the amounts did not match in case there are inquiries from the IRS or the SSA. See the Instructions for Schedule D (Form 941) if you need to explain any discrepancies that
    (a) examine, documents in order
    (b) determine, reconciliation
    (c) research, documents
    (d) be able to substantiate, audit
    Answer: See section 12. Filing Form 941 or Form 944. Page 32/(b) determine, reconciliation

Section 12. Filing Form 941 or Form 944. Reconciling Forms W-2, W-3, and 941 or 944.

12. Filing Form 941 or Form 944. Reconciling Forms W-2, W-3, and 941 or 944.

25. Amounts reported on Forms W-2, W-3, and forms 941 or Form 944 may not match for valid reasons. If they do not match, you should ___ the reasons they are valid. Keep your ___ so you will have a record of why the amounts did not match in case there are inquiries from the IRS or the SSA. See the Instructions for Schedule D (Form 941) if you need to explain any discrepancies that were caused by an acquisition, statutory merger, or ___.

   (a) examine, documents in order, consolidation
   (b) determine, reconciliation, consolidation
   (c) research, documents, sales
   (d) be able to substantiate, audit, sales

   Answer: See section 12. Filing Form 941 or Form 944. Page 32/(b) determine, reconciliation, consolidation

A Ficus Tree Publishing LLC., Quick Notes Page.

Instructor's Manual for Tax Test 15E-S13
Section 13
Reporting Adjustments To Form 941 Or Form 944

General Description. Section 13. 15E-13.

Tax Test 15E-S13. Tax Test 15E-S13, Section 13. Introduces Reporting Adjustments to Form 941 or Form 944; Reporting Adjustments to Form 941 or 944. Current Period Adjustments; Reporting Adjustments to Form 941 or Form 944. Fractions-of-cents adjustment; Reporting Adjustments to Form 941 or Form 944. Fractions-of-cents adjustments. TIP; Reporting Adjustments to Form 941 or Form 944. Third-party sick pay. A word of caution. Study and know the information provided in Circular E regarding Fractions-of-cents Adjustment.

Key Words. Section 13. 15E-13.

Tax Test 15E-S13. Reporting Adjustments to Form 941 or Form 944 - Life Insurance Premiums. Adjustment of tax on group-term life insurance paid for former employees. No change to record of federal tax liability. Fractions-of-cents adjustment. Forms For Prior Period Adjustments. **Administrative Error**. Income Tax Withholding Adjustments. Additional Medicare Tax Withholding Adjustments. Collecting Underwithheld Taxes From Employees. Refunding Amounts Incorrectly Withheld From Employees. Correcting filed Forms W-2 and W-3. Third-party sick pay. Life insurance premiums. Adjustment of tax on third-party sick pay. Adjustment of tax on tips. Adjustment of tax on group-term life insurance premium paid for former employees. No change to record of federal tax liability. Prior Period Adjustments. Background. Correcting employment taxes. Income tax withholding adjustments. Wage Repayments. Repayment of current year wages. Repayment of prior year wages. Employee reporting of repayment.

© Copyright 2013. All rights reserved. Notice: United States Copyright Laws and International Treaties prohibit unauthorized publication, reproduction, distribution of this Work. Unauthorized use of this copyright in any form, format, publication or document may result in severe civil and criminal penalties. Violations of this copyright are investigated by the United States Department of Justice and carry, upon conviction of fines up to $250,000 and five years confinement. This Work is protected by United States Copyright Laws and International Treaties. Do not Copy, do not reproduce, do not distribute.

A Ficus Tree Publishing Educational-Technical Publications

A Ficus Tree Publishing Quick Notes Page

DU VALL'S TEST'S™
Instructor's Manual Study Guide Series United States Tax Code
IRS Publication 15 Circular E, Employer's Tax Guide Tax Year 2013
Tax Test 15E-S13-1 [Multiple-Choice Questions With Answers]

Section 13. Reporting Adjustments to Form 941 or Form 944. Current Period Adjustments. Page 32.

13. Reporting Adjustments to Form 941 or Form 944. Current Period Adjustments

1. In certain cases, amounts reported as social security and Medicare taxes on Form 941, lines __-__, column 2(Form 944, lines __-__, column 2), must be adjusted to
   - (a) 2a, 2d, 3a, 3c
   - (b) 3a, 3d, 4a, 4d
   - (c) 4a, 4d, 5a, 5c
   - (d) 5a, 5d, 4a, 4c

   Answer: See section 13. Reporting Adjustments to Form 941 or Form 944, Current Period Adjustment. Page 32/(d) 5a, 5d, 4a, 4c

13. Reporting Adjustments to Form 941 or Form 944. Current Period Adjustments

2. In certain cases, amounts reported as social security and Medicare taxes on Form 941, lines __-__, column 2(Form 944, lines __-__, column 2), must be adjusted to ___ at your correct tax liability.
   - (a) 2a, 2d, 3a, 3c, ascertain
   - (b) 3a, 3d, 4a, 4d, develop
   - (c) 4a, 4d, 5a, 5c, determine
   - (d) 5a, 5d, 4a, 4c, arrive

   Answer: See section 13. Reporting Adjustments to Form 941 or Form 944, Current Period Adjustment. Page 32/(d) 5a, 5d, 4a, 4c, arrive

13. Reporting Adjustments to Form 941 or Form 944. Current Period Adjustments

3. In certain cases, amounts reported as social security and Medicare taxes on Form 941, lines __-__, column 2(Form 944, lines __-__, column 2), must be adjusted to ___ at your correct tax liability (for example, excluding withheld by a third-party payor or amounts you were not required to withhold).
   - (a) 2a, 2d, 3a, 3c, ascertain, adding
   - (b) 3a, 3d, 4a, 4d, develop, removing
   - (c) 4a, 4d, 5a, 5c, determine, including
   - (d) 5a, 5d, 4a, 4c, arrive, excluding

   Answer: See section 13. Reporting Adjustments to Form 941 or Form 944, Current Period Adjustment. Page 32/(d) 5a, 5d, 4a, 4c, arrive, excluding

Section 13. Reporting Adjustments to Form 941 or Form 944. Current Period Adjustments

13. Reporting Adjustments to Form 941 or Form 944. Current Period Adjustments

4. In certain cases, amounts reported as social security and Medicare taxes on Form 941, lines __-__, column 2(Form 944, lines __-__, column 2), must be adjusted to ___ at your correct tax liability (for example, excluding withheld by a third-party payor or amounts you were not required to withhold). Current period adjustments are reported on Form 941, lines ___, or Form 944, line ___, and include the following types of adjustments.
   (a) 2a, 2d, 3a, 3c, ascertain, adding, 4-6, 3
   (b) 3a, 3d, 4a, 4d, develop, removing, 5-7, 4
   (c) 4a, 4d, 5a, 5c, determine, including, 6-8, 5
   (d) 5a, 5d, 4a, 4c, arrive, excluding, 7-9, 6
   Answer: See section 13. Reporting Adjustments to Form 941 or Form 944, Current Period Adjustment. Page 32/(d) 5a, 5d, 4a, 4c, arrive, excluding, 7-9, 6

Section 13. Reporting Adjustments to Form 941 or Form 944. Fractions-of-cents Adjustment. Page 32

13. Reporting Adjustments to Form 941 or Form 944. Fractions-of-cents adjustment.

5. If there is a small difference between total taxes after adjustments (Form 941, line ___; Form 944, line ___) and total deposits (Form 94, line ___; Form 944, line ___), it may be caused, all
   (a) 11, 8, 14, 11
   (b) 10, 7, 13, 10
   (c) 10, 7, 13, 10
   (d) 10, 8, 13, 10
   Answer: See section 13. Reporting Adjustments to Form 941 or Form 944, Fraction-of-cents adjustment. Page 32/(c) 10, 7, 13, 10

13. Reporting Adjustments to Form 941 or Form 944. Fractions-of-cents adjustment.

6. If there is a small difference between total taxes after adjustments (Form 941, line ___; Form 944, line ___) and total deposits (Form 94, line ___; Form 944, line ___), it may be caused, all or in part, by ___ to the nearest cent each time you computed payroll.
   (a) 11, 8, 14, 11, not rounding
   (b) 10, 7, 13, 10, rounding down
   (c) 10, 7, 13, 10, rounding up
   (d) 10, 8, 13, 10, rounding
   Answer: See section 13. Reporting Adjustments to Form 941 or Form 944, Fraction-of-cents adjustment. Page 32/(c) 10, 7, 13, 10, rounding

Section 13. Reporting Adjustments to Form 941 or Form 944. Fractions-of-cents Adjustment. Page 32

13. Reporting Adjustments to Form 941 or Form 944. Fractions-of-cents adjustment.

7. This rounding occurs when you ___ the amount of social security and medicare tax to be withheld and deposited from each employee's wages.
   (a) figure
   (b) compute
   (c) calculate
   (d) estimate
   Answer: See section 13. Reporting Adjustments to Form 941 or Form 944, Fraction-of-cents adjustment. Page 32/(a) figure

13. Reporting Adjustments to Form 941 or Form 944. Fractions-of-cents adjustment.

8. The IRS refers rounding ___ relating to employee withholding of social security and Medicare taxes as "fractions-of-cents adjustments.
   (a) fractions
   (b) cents
   (c) differences
   (d) decimals
   Answer: See section 13. Reporting Adjustments to Form 941 or Form 944, Fraction-of-cents adjustment. Page 32/(c) differences

13. Reporting Adjustments to Form 941 or Form 944. Fractions-of-cents adjustment.

9. The IRS refers rounding ___ relating to employee withholding of social security and Medicare taxes as "fractions-of-cents adjustments. If you pay your taxes with Form 941 (or form 944) instead of making deposits because your total taxes for the quarter (year for Form 944) are less than $___, you may also report a fractions-of-cents adjustment.
   (a) fractions, 1,500
   (b) cents, 2,000
   (c) differences, 2,500
   (d) decimals, 3,000
   Answer: See section 13. Reporting Adjustments to Form 941 or Form 944, Fraction-of-cents adjustment. Page 32/(c) differences, 2,500

13. Reporting Adjustments to Form 941 or Form 944. Fractions-of-cents adjustment.

10. To determine if you have a fractions-of-cents adjustment for 2013, ___ the total wages and tips for the quarter subject to:
    (a) multiply
    (b) divide
    (c) add
    (d) subtract
    Answer: See section 13. Reporting Adjustments to Form 941 or Form 944, Fraction-of-cents adjustment. Page 32/(a) multiply

© Copyright 2013. All rights reserved. Notice: United States Copyright Laws and International Treaties prohibit unauthorized publication, reproduction, distribution of this Work. Unauthorized use of this copyright in any form, format, publication or document may result in severe civil and criminal penalties. Violations of this copyright are investigated by the United States Department of Justice and carry, upon conviction of fines up to $250,000 and five years confinement. This Work is protected by United States Copyright Laws and International Treaties. Do not Copy, do not reproduce, do not distribute.

A Ficus Tree Publishing Educational-Technical Publications

Section 13. Reporting Adjustments to Form 941 or Form 944. Fractions-of-cents Adjustment. Page 32

13. Reporting Adjustments to Form 941 or Form 944. Fractions-of-cents adjustment.

11. To determine if you have a fractions-of-cents adjustment for 2013, ___ the total wages and tips for the quarter subject to:
    • Social security tax ___ on Form 941 or Form 944 by employee's tax rate for social security.
    (a) multiply, reported
    (b) divide, recorded
    (c) add, computed
    (d) subtract, totaled
    Answer: See section 13. Reporting Adjustments to Form 941 or Form 944, Fraction-of-cents adjustment. Page 32/(a) multiply, reported

13. Reporting Adjustments to Form 941 or Form 944. Fractions-of-cents adjustment.

12. To determine if you have a fractions-of-cents adjustment for 2013, ___ the total wages and tips for the quarter subject to:
    • Social security tax ___ on Form 941 or Form 944 by employee's tax rate for social security.
    • Medicare tax reported on Form 941 or Form 944 by ___% (___), and
    (a) multiply, reported, 1.45, .0145
    (b) divide, recorded, 1.35, .0135
    (c) add, computed, 1.25, .0125
    (d) subtract, totaled, 1.15, .0115
    Answer: See section 13. Reporting Adjustments to Form 941 or Form 944, Fraction-of-cents adjustment. Page 32/(a) multiply, reported, 1.45, .0145

13. Reporting Adjustments to Form 941 or Form 944. Fractions-of-cents adjustment.

13. To determine if you have a fractions-of-cents adjustment for 2013, ___ the total wages and tips for the quarter subject to:
    • Social security tax ___ on Form 941 or Form 944 by employee's tax rate for social security.
    • Medicare tax reported on Form 941 or Form 944 by ___% (___), and
    • Additional Medicare Tax reported on Form 941 or 944 by ___% (___).
    (a) multiply, reported, 1.45, .0145, 0.9, .009
    (b) divide, recorded, 1.35, .0135, 0.9, .009
    (c) add, computed, 1.25, .0125, 0.7, .007
    (d) subtract, totaled, 1.15, .0115, 0.7, .007
    Answer: See section 13. Reporting Adjustments to Form 941 or Form 944, Fraction-of-cents adjustment. Page 32/(a) multiply, reported, 1.45, .0145, 0.9, .009

Section 13. Reporting Adjustments to Form 941 or Form 944. Fractions-of-cents adjustment. Page 32

13. Reporting Adjustments to Form 941 or Form 944. Fractions-of-cents adjustment.

14. Compare these amounts (the employee share of social security and Medicare taxes) with the ___ social security and Medicare taxes actually withheld from employees for the quarter (from your payroll records).
    (a) employee
    (b) total
    (c) employer
    (d) combined
    Answer: See section 13. Reporting Adjustments to Form 941 or Form 944, Fraction-of-cents adjustment. Page 32/(b) total

13. Reporting Adjustments to Form 941 or Form 944. Fractions-of-cents adjustment.

15. Compare these amounts (the employee share of social security and Medicare taxes) with the ___ social security and Medicare taxes actually withheld from employees for the quarter (from your payroll records). The difference, positive or negative, is ___ fractions-of-cents adjustment to be reported on Form 941,
    (a) employee, the
    (b) total, your
    (c) employer, the
    (d) combined, your
    Answer: See section 13. Reporting Adjustments to Form 941 or Form 944, Fraction-of-cents adjustment. Page 32/(b) total, your

13. Reporting Adjustments to Form 941 or Form 944. Fractions-of-cents adjustment.

16. Compare these amounts (the employee share of social security and Medicare taxes) with the total social security and Medicare taxes actually withheld from employees for the quarter (from your payroll records). The difference, positive or negative, is your fractions-of-cents adjustment to be reported on Form 941, line ___, or Form 944, line ___.
    (a) 5, 4
    (b) 6, 5
    (c) 7, 6
    (d) 8, 7
    Answer: See section 13. Reporting Adjustments to Form 941 or Form 944, Fraction-of-cents adjustment. Page 32/(c) 7, 6

Section 13. Reporting Adjustments to Form 941 or Form 944. Fractions-of-cents Adjustment. Page 32

13. Reporting Adjustments to Form 941 or Form 944. Fractions-of-cents adjustment.

17. Compare these amounts (the employee share of social security and Medicare taxes) with the total social security and Medicare taxes actually withheld from employees for the quarter (from your payroll records). The difference, positive or negative, is your fractions-of-cents adjustment to be reported on Form 941, line ___, or Form 944, line ___. If the actual amount withheld is less, report a negative adjustment using a minus sign (if possible, other wise use ___) in the entry space.
    - (a) 5, 4, quotation
    - (b) 6, 5, quotation
    - (c) 7, 6, parentheses
    - (d) 8, 7, parental

    Answer: See section 13. Reporting Adjustments to Form 941 or Form 944, Fraction-of-cents adjustment. Page 32/(c) 7, 6, parentheses

13. Reporting Adjustments to Form 941 or Form 944. Fractions-of-cents adjustment.

18. Compare these amounts (the employee share of social security and Medicare taxes) with the total social security and Medicare taxes actually withheld from employees for the quarter (from your payroll records). The difference, positive or negative, is your fractions-of-cents adjustment to be reported on Form 941, line ___, or Form 944, line ___. If the actual amount withheld is less, report a negative adjustment using a minus sign (if possible, other wise use ___) in the entry space. If the actual amount is more, report a ___ adjustment.
    - (a) 5, 4, quotation, increased
    - (b) 6, 5, quotation, plus
    - (c) 7, 6, parentheses, positive
    - (d) 8, 7, parental, positive

    Answer: See section 13. Reporting Adjustments to Form 941 or Form 944, Fraction-of-cents adjustment. Page 32/(c) 7, 6, parentheses, positive

13. Reporting Adjustments to Form 941 or Form 944. Fractions-of-cents adjustment. TIP

19. *For the above adjustments, prepare and retain a brief ___ statement explaining the nature and amount of each. Do not attach the statement to Form 941 or Form 944.*
    - (a) summary
    - (b) outline
    - (c) detailed
    - (d) supporting

    Answer: See section 13. Reporting Adjustments to Form 941 or Form 944, Fraction-of-cents adjustment. TIP. Page 32/(d) supporting

Section 13. Reporting Adjustments to Form 941 or Form 944. Fractions-of-cents Adjustment. Page 32

13. Reporting Adjustments to Form 941 or Form 944. Fractions-of-cents adjustment. Example

20. *For the above adjustments, prepare and retain a brief supporting statement explaining the nature and amount of each. Do not attach the statement to Form 941 or Form 944.*
    Example. Cedar, Inc. was entitled to the following current period adjustments.
    • **Fractions of Cents**. Cedar, Inc. determined the amounts withheld and deposited for social security and Medicare taxes during the quarter were a net $___ more than the employee share of the amount figured on Form 941, lines
    (a)   1.44
    (b)   1.45
    (c)   1.46
    (d)   1.47
    Answer: See section 13. Reporting Adjustments to Form 941 or Form 944, Fraction-of-cents adjustment. Example. Page 32/(a) 1.44

13. Reporting Adjustments to Form 941 or Form 944. Fractions-of-cents adjustment. Example

21. *For the above adjustments, prepare and retain a brief supporting statement explaining the nature and amount of each. Do not attach the statement to Form 941 or Form 944.*
    Example. Cedar, Inc. was entitled to the following current period adjustments.
    • **Fractions of Cents**. Cedar, Inc. determined the amounts withheld and deposited for social security and Medicare taxes during the quarter were a net $___ more than the employee share of the amount figured on Form 941, lines ___, column 2 (social security and Medicare taxes).
    (a)   1.44, 5a-5d
    (b)   1.45, 5a-5e
    (c)   1.46, 5b-5d
    (d)   1.47, 5b-5e
    Answer: See section 13. Reporting Adjustments to Form 941 or Form 944, Fraction-of-cents adjustment. Example. Page 32/(a) 1.44, 5a-5d

Section 13. Reporting Adjustments to Form 941 or Form 944. Fractions-of-cents Adjustment. Page 32

13. Reporting Adjustments to Form 941 or Form 944. Fractions-of-cents adjustment. Example

22. *For the above adjustments, prepare and retain a brief supporting statement explaining the nature and amount of each. Do not attach the statement to Form 941 or Form 944. **Example**. Cedar, Inc. was entitled to the following current period adjustments.*
    *• **Fractions of Cents**. Cedar, Inc. determined the amounts withheld and deposited for social security and Medicare taxes during the quarter were a net $___ more than the employee share of the amount figured on Form 941, lines ___ , column 2 (social security and Medicare taxes). This difference was ___ by adding or dropping fractions of cents when figuring social security and Medicare taxes for each wage payment.*
    (a)   1.44, 5a-5d, caused
    (b)   1.45, 5a-5e, created
    (c)   1.46, 5b-5d, developed
    (d)   1.47, 5b-5e, created
    Answer: See section 13. Reporting Adjustments to Form 941 or Form 944, Fraction-of-cents adjustment. Example. Page 32/(a) 1.44, 5a-5d, caused

13. Reporting Adjustments to Form 941 or Form 944. Fractions-of-cents adjustment. Example

23. *For the above adjustments, prepare and retain a brief supporting statement explaining the nature and amount of each. Do not attach the statement to Form 941 or Form 944. **Example**. Cedar, Inc. was entitled to the following current period adjustments.*
    *• **Fractions of Cents**. Cedar, Inc. determined the amounts withheld and deposited for social security and Medicare taxes during the quarter were a net $___ more than the employee share of the amount figured on Form 941, lines ___ , column 2 (social security and Medicare taxes). This difference was ___ by adding or dropping fractions of cents when figuring social security and Medicare taxes for each wage payment. Cedar, Inc. must report a positive $1.44 fractions-of-cents adjustment on Form 941, line ___ .*
    (a)   1.44, 5a-5d, caused, 7
    (b)   1.45, 5a-5e, created, 8
    (c)   1.46, 5b-5d, developed, 9
    (d)   1.47, 5b-5e, created, 10
    Answer: See section 13. Reporting Adjustments to Form 941 or Form 944, Fraction-of-cents adjustment. Example. Page 32/(a) 1.44, 5a-5d, caused, 7

13. Reporting Adjustments to Form 941 or Form 944. Third-party sick pay. Example

13. Reporting Adjustments to Form 941 or Form 944. Third-party sick pay. Example

24. *For the above adjustments, prepare and retain a brief supporting statement explaining the nature and amount of each. Do not attach the statement to Form 941 or Form 944. **Example**. Cedar, Inc. was entitled to the following current period adjustments.*
    • **Third-party sick pay**. Cedar, Inc. included taxes of $2,000 for sick pay on Form 941, lines ___ and ___, column 2, for social security and Medicare taxes. However,
    (a) 5a, 5b
    (b) 5a, 5c
    (c) 5b, 5d
    (d) 5c, 5e
    Answer: See section 13. Reporting Adjustments to Form 941 or Form 944, Third-party sick pay. Example. Page 32/(a) 5a, 5c

13. Reporting Adjustments to Form 941 or Form 944. Third-party sick pay. Example

25. *For the above adjustments, prepare and retain a brief supporting statement explaining the nature and amount of each. Do not attach the statement to Form 941 or Form 944. **Example**. Cedar, Inc. was entitled to the following current period adjustments.*
    • **Third-party sick pay**. Cedar, Inc. included taxes of $2,000 for sick pay on Form 941, lines ___ and ___, column 2, for social security and Medicare taxes. However, the third-part payor of the
      sick pay withheld and paid the employee share of ($___ of these taxes.
    (a) 5a, 5b, 1,000
    (b) 5a, 5c, 1,000
    (c) 5b, 5d, 1,500
    (d) 5c, 5e, 1,500
    Answer: See section 13. Reporting Adjustments to Form 941 or Form 944, Third-party sick pay. Example. Page 32/(a) 5a, 5c, 1,000

13. Reporting Adjustments to Form 941 or Form 944. Third-party sick pay. Example

26. *For the above adjustments, prepare and retain a brief supporting statement explaining the nature and amount of each. Do not attach the statement to Form 941 or Form 944. **Example**. Cedar, Inc. was entitled to the following current period adjustments.*
    • **Third-party sick pay**. Cedar, Inc. included taxes of $2,000 for sick pay on Form 941, lines ___ and ___, column 2, for social security and Medicare taxes. However, the third-part payor of the
      sick pay withheld and paid the employee share of ($___ of these taxes. Cedar, Inc. is entitled to a $___ sick pay adjustment (negative) on Form 941, line ___.
    (a) 5a, 5b, 1,000, 1,000, 8
    (b) 5a, 5c, 1,000, 1,000, 9
    (c) 5b, 5d, 1,500, 1,500, 10
    (d) 5c, 5e, 1,500, 1,500, 11
    Answer: See section 13. Reporting Adjustments to Form 941 or Form 944, Third-party sick pay. Example. Page 32/(a) 5a, 5c, 1,000, 1,000, 8

Section 13. Reporting Adjustments to Form 941 or Form 944. Life Insurance premiums. Example.

13. Reporting Adjustments to Form 941 or Form 944. Life insurance premiums. Example

27. *For the above adjustments, prepare and retain a brief supporting statement explaining the nature and amount of each. Do not attach the statement to Form 941 or Form 944. Example. Cedar, Inc. was entitled to the following current period adjustments.*
    • **Life insurance premiums**. Cedar, Inc. paid group-term life insurance premiums for policies in excess of $___ for former employees.
    (a) 10,000
    (b) 25,000
    (c) 50,000
    (d) 100,000
    Answer: See section 13. Reporting Adjustments to Form 941 or Form 944, Life insurance premiums. Example. Page 32/(c) 50,000

13. Reporting Adjustments to Form 941 or Form 944. Life insurance premiums. Example

28. *For the above adjustments, prepare and retain a brief supporting statement explaining the nature and amount of each. Do not attach the statement to Form 941 or Form 944. Example. Cedar, Inc. was entitled to the following current period adjustments.*
    • **Life insurance premiums**. Cedar, Inc. paid group-term life insurance premiums for policies in excess of $___ for former employees. The former employees must pay the employee share of social security and Medicare taxes ($___) on the policies.
    (a) 10,000, 100
    (b) 25,000, 150
    (c) 50,000, 200
    (d) 100,000, 300
    Answer: See section 13. Reporting Adjustments to Form 941 or Form 944, Life insurance premiums. Example. Page 32/(c) 50,000, 200

13. Reporting Adjustments to Form 941 or Form 944. Life insurance premiums. Example

29. *For the above adjustments, prepare and retain a brief supporting statement explaining the nature and amount of each. Do not attach the statement to Form 941 or Form 944. Example. Cedar, Inc. was entitled to the following current period adjustments.*
    • **Life insurance premiums**. Cedar, Inc. paid group-term life insurance premiums for policies in excess of $___ for former employees. The former employees must pay the employee share of social security and Medicare taxes ($___) on the policies. However, Cedar, Inc. must include the employee share of these taxes with the social security and Medicare taxes reported on Form 941, lines ___ and ___, column 2. Therefore, cedar, ,Inc. is entitled to a negative $200 adjustment on Form 941, line___.
    (a) 10,000, 100, 3a, 3c, 7
    (b) 25,000, 150, 4a, 4c, 8
    (c) 50,000, 200, 5a, 5c, 9
    (d) 100,000, 300, 6a, 6c, 10
    Answer: See section 13. Reporting Adjustments to Form 941 or Form 944, Life insurance premiums. Example. Page 32/(c) 50,000, 200, 5a, 5c, 9

Section 13. Reporting Adjustments to Form 941 or Form 944. Adjustment of tax on third-party sick pay. Page 32/33

13. Reporting Adjustments to Form 941 or Form 944. Adjustment of tax on third-party sick pay.
30. Report both the employer and employee shares of social security and Medicare taxes for sick pay on Form 941, lines ___ and ___ (Form 944, lines ___ and ___).
    (a) 3a, 3c, 2a, 2c
    (b) 4a, 4c, 3a, 3c
    (c) 5a, 5c, 4a, 4c
    (d) 6a, 6c, 5a, 5c
    Answer: See section 13. Reporting Adjustments to Form 941 or Form 944, Adjustment of tax on third-party sick pay. Pages 32 and 33/(c) 5a, 5c, 4a, 4c

13. Reporting Adjustments to Form 941 or Form 944. Adjustment of tax on third-party sick pay.
31. If the aggregate wages paid for an employee by the employer and third-party payor exceed $200,000 for the calendar year, report the Additional Medicare Tax on Form 941, line ___.
    (a) 5d
    (b) 6d
    (c) 7d
    (d) 8d
    Answer: See section 13. Reporting Adjustments to Form 941 or Form 944, Adjustment of tax on third-party sick pay. Example. Pages 32 and 33/(a) 5d

13. Reporting Adjustments to Form 941 or Form 944. Adjustment of tax on third-party sick pay.
32. If the aggregate wages paid for an employee by the employer and third-party payor exceed $200,000 for the calendar year, report the Additional Medicare Tax on Form 941, line ___. Show as a negative adjustment on Form 941, line___ (Form 944, line ___), the social security and Medicare taxes withheld on sick pay by a third-party payor.
    (a) 5d, 8, 6
    (b) 6d, 8, 7
    (c) 7d, 9, 6
    (d) 8d, 9, 7
    Answer: See section 13. Reporting Adjustments to Form 941 or Form 944, Adjustment of tax on third-party sick pay. Pages 32 and 33/(a) 5d, 8, 6

Section 13. Reporting Adjustments to Form 941 or Form 944. Adjustment of tax on third-party sick pay. Page 32/33

13. Reporting Adjustments to Form 941 or Form 944. Adjustment of tax on third-party sick pay.

33. If the aggregate wages paid for an employee by the employer and third-party payor exceed $200,000 for the calendar year, report the Additional Medicare Tax on Form 941, line ___. Show as a negative adjustment on Form 941, line___ (Form 944, line ___), the social security and Medicare taxes withheld on sick pay by a third-party payor. See section ___ of Publication ___ for more information.
    (a) 5d, 8, 6, 6, 15-A
    (b) 6d, 8, 7, 6, 15-A
    (c) 7d, 9, 6, 7, 15-B
    (d) 8d, 9, 7, 7, 15-C
    Answer: See section 13. Reporting Adjustments to Form 941 or Form 944, Adjustment of tax on third-party sick pay. Pages 32 and 33/(a) 5d, 8, 6, 6, 15-A

Section 13. Reporting Adjustments to Form 941 or Form 944. Adjustment of tax on tips. Page 33.

13. Reporting Adjustments to Form 941 or Form 944. Adjustment of tax on tips.

34. If by the 10th of the month after the month you received an employee's report on tips, you do not have enough employee funds available to withhold the employee's share of social security and Medicare taxes, you ___.
    (a) you must contact the employee regarding the shortage
    (b) no longer have to collect it
    (c) must contact the IRS
    (d) place the collected funds in the IRS trust fund account
    Answer: See section 13. Reporting Adjustments to Form 941 or Form 944, Adjustment of tax on tips. Page 33 /(b) no longer have to collect it

13. Reporting Adjustments to Form 941 or Form 944. Adjustment of tax on tips.

35. If by the 10th of the month after the month you received an employee's report on tips, you do not have enough employee funds available to withhold the employee's share of social security and Medicare taxes, you ___. However, report the entire amount of these tips on Form 941, lines ___, and ___ (Form 944, line ___ and ___). 5a, 5b, 4a, 4b
    (a) you must contact the employee regarding the shortage
    (b) no longer have to collect it, 5b, 5c, 4b, 4c
    (c) must contact the IRS, 6a, 6b, 5a, 5b
    (d) place the collected funds in the IRS trust fund account, 7a, 7b, 6a, 6b
    Answer: See section 13. Reporting Adjustments to Form 941 or Form 944, Adjustment of tax on tips. Page 33 /(b) no longer have to collect it, 5b, 5c, 4b, 4c

Section 13. Reporting Adjustments to Form 941 or Form 944. Adjustment of tax on tips. Page 33.

13. Reporting Adjustments to Form 941 or Form 944. Adjustment of tax on tips.
36. If by the 10th of the month after the month you received an employee's report on tips, you do not have enough employee funds available to withhold the employee's share of social security and Medicare taxes, you ___. However, report the entire amount of these tips on Form 941, lines ___, and ___ (Form 944, line ___ and ___). If the aggregate wages and tips paid for an employee exceed $200,000 for the calendar year, report the Additional Medicare Tax on Form 941, line ___.
   (a)   you must contact the employee regarding the shortage, 5a, 5b, 4a, 4b, 4d
   (b)   no longer have to collect it, 5b, 5c, 4b, 4c, 5d
   (c)   must contact the IRS, 6a, 6b, 5a, 5b, 6d
   (d)   place the collected funds in the IRS trust fund account, 7a, 7b, 6a, 6b, 7d
   Answer: See section 13. Reporting Adjustments to Form 941 or Form 944, Adjustment of tax on tips. Page 33 /(b) no longer have to collect it, 5b, 5c, 4b, 4c, 5d

13. Reporting Adjustments to Form 941 or Form 944. Adjustment of tax on tips.
37. If by the 10th of the month after the month you received an employee's report on tips, you do not have enough employee funds available to withhold the employee's share of social security and Medicare taxes, you no longer have to collect it. However, report the entire amount of these tips on Form 941, lines 5b, and 5c (Form 944, line 4b and 4c). If the aggregate wages and tips paid for an employee exceed $200,000 for the calendar year, report the Additional Medicare Tax on Form 941, line 5d. Include as a negative adjustment on Form 941, line ___ (Form 944, line ___), the total uncollected employee share of the social security and Medicare taxes.
   (a)   7, 4
   (b)   8, 5
   (c)   9, 6
   (d)   10, 7
   Answer: See section 13. Reporting Adjustments to Form 941 or Form 944, Adjustment of tax on tips. Page 33 /(c) 9, 6

Section 13. Reporting Adjustments to Form 941 or Form 944. Adjustment of tax on group-term life insurance premiums paid for former employees. Page 33.

13. Reporting Adjustments to Form 941 or Form 944. Adjustment of tax on group-term life insurance premiums paid for former employees.

38. The employee share of social security and Medicare taxes for premiums over $50,000 for a former employee is paid by the former employee with ___ and is not collected by the employer.
    (a) deposits made by the employee to the general tax fund
    (b) previous collected funds
    (c) previously collected funds
    (d) his or her tax return

    Answer: See section 13. Reporting Adjustments to Form 941 or Form 944, Adjustment of tax on group-term life insurance premiums paid for former employees. Page 33 /(d) his or her tax return

13. Reporting Adjustments to Form 941 or Form 944. Adjustment of tax on group-term life insurance premiums paid for former employees.

39. The employee share of social security and Medicare taxes for premiums over $50,000 for a former employee is paid by the former employee with ___ and is not collected by the employer. However, include all social security and Medicare taxes for such coverage on Form 941, line ___ and ___ (Form 944, lines ___ and ___).
    (a) deposits made by the employee to the general tax fund, 2a, 2c, 1a, 1c,
    (b) previous collected funds, 3a, 3c, 2a, 2c
    (c) previously collected funds, 4a, 4c, 3a, 3c
    (d) his or her tax return, 5a, 5c, 4a, 4c

    Answer: See section 13. Reporting Adjustments to Form 941 or Form 944, Adjustment of tax on group-term life insurance premiums paid for former employees. Page 33 /(d) his or her tax return, 5a, 5c, 4a, 4c

Section 13. Reporting Adjustments to Form 941 or Form 944. Adjustment of tax on group-term life insurance premiums paid for former employees. Page 33.

13. Reporting Adjustments to Form 941 or Form 944. Adjustment of tax on group-term life insurance premiums paid for former employees.

40. The employee share of social security and Medicare taxes for premiums over $50,000 for a former employee is paid by the former employee with ___ and is not collected by the employer. However, include all social security and Medicare taxes for such coverage on Form 941, line ___ and ___ (Form 944, lines ___ and ___). If the amount paid for an employee for premiums on group-term life insurance combined with other wages exceeds $200,000 for the calendar year, report the Additional Medicare Tax on Form 941, line ___.

   (a)   deposits made by the employee to the general tax fund, 2a, 2c, 1a, 1c, 2d
   (b)   previous collected funds, 3a, 3c, 2a, 2c, 3d
   (c)   previously collected funds, 4a, 4c, 3a, 3c, 4d
   (d)   his or her tax return, 5a, 5c, 4a, 4c, 5d

Answer: See section 13. Reporting Adjustments to Form 941 or Form 944, Adjustment of tax on group-term life insurance premiums paid for former employees. Page 33 /(d) his or her tax return, 5a, 5c, 4a, 4c, 5d

13. Reporting Adjustments to Form 941 or Form 944. Adjustment of tax on group-term life insurance premiums paid for former employees.

41. The employee share of social security and Medicare taxes for premiums over $50,000 for a former employee is paid by the former employee with his or her tax return and is not collected by the employer. However, include all social security and Medicare taxes for such coverage on Form 941, line 5a and 5b (Form 944, lines 4a and 4c). If the amount paid for an employee for premiums on group-term life insurance combined with other wages exceeds $200,000 for the calendar year, report the Additional Medicare Tax on Form 941, line 5d. Back out the amount of the employee share of these taxes as a negative adjustment on Form 941, line ___ (Form 944, line ___).

   (a)   9, 6
   (b)   10, 7
   (c)   11, 8
   (d)   12, 9

Answer: See section 13. Reporting Adjustments to Form 941 or Form 944, Adjustment of tax on group-term life insurance premiums paid for former employees. Page 33 /(a) 9. 6

© Copyright 2013. All rights reserved. Notice: United States Copyright Laws and International Treaties prohibit unauthorized publication, reproduction, distribution of this Work. Unauthorized use of this copyright in any form, format, publication or document may result in severe civil and criminal penalties. Violations of this copyright are investigated by the United States Department of Justice and carry, upon conviction of fines up to $250,000 and five years confinement. This Work is protected by United States Copyright Laws and International Treaties. Do not Copy, do not reproduce, do not distribute.

Section 13. Reporting Adjustments to Form 941 or Form 944. Adjustment of tax on group-term life insurance premiums paid for former employees. Page 33.

13. Reporting Adjustments to Form 941 or Form 944. Adjustment of tax on group-term life insurance premiums paid for former employees.

42. The employee share of social security and Medicare taxes for premiums over $50,000 for a former employee is paid by the former employee with his or her tax return and is not collected by the employer. However, include all social security and Medicare taxes for such coverage on Form 941, line 5a and 5b (Form 944, lines 4a and 4c). If the amount paid for an employee for premiums on group-term life insurance combined with other wages exceeds $200,000 for the calendar year, report the Additional Medicare Tax on Form 941, line 5d. Back out the amount of the employee share of these taxes as a negative adjustment on Form 941, line ___ (Form 944, line ___). See Publication ___ for more information on group-term life insurance.
    (a) 9, 6, 15-B
    (b) 10, 7, 15-A
    (c) 11, 8, 15
    (d) 12, 9, 15-C
    Answer: See section 13. Reporting Adjustments to Form 941 or Form 944, Adjustment of tax on group-term life insurance premiums paid for former employees. Page 33 /(a) 9. 6, 15-B

Section 13. Reporting Adjustments to Form 941 or Form 944. No change to record of federal tax liability. Page 33.

13. Reporting Adjustments to Form 941 or Form 944. No change to record of federal tax liability.

43. Do not make any changes to your record of federal tax liability reported on Form 941, line ___, or Schedule ___ (Form 941) (Form 945-A for Form 944 filers) for current period adjustments.
    (a) 15, B
    (b) 16, B
    (c) 15, A
    (d) 16, C
    Answer: See section 13. Reporting Adjustments to Form 941 or Form 944, No change to record of federal tax liability. Page 33 /(b) 16, B

Section 13. Reporting Adjustments to Form 941 or Form 944. No change to record of federal tax liability. Page 33.

13. Reporting Adjustments to Form 941 or Form 944. No change to record of federal tax liability.

44. The amounts reported on the record ___ the actual amounts you withheld from employees' wages for social security and Medicare taxes.
    (a) are
    (b) will be
    (c) reflect
    (d) shall be
    Answer: See section 13. Reporting Adjustments to Form 941 or Form 944, No change to record of federal tax liability. Page 33 /(c) reflect

13. Reporting Adjustments to Form 941 or Form 944. No change to record of federal tax liability.

45. Because the current period adjustments make the amounts reported on Form 941, lines 5a-5d. column 2 (Form 944, lines 4a-4c, column 2), ___ the actual amounts you withheld (the amounts reported on the record), no additional ___ to the record of federal tax liability are necessary for these adjustments.
    (a) represent, changes
    (b) equal, adjustments
    (c) equal, changes
    (d) approximate, adjustments
    Answer: See section 13. Reporting Adjustments to Form 941 or Form 944, No change to record of federal tax liability. Page 33 /(c) equal, changes

Section 13. Reporting Adjustments to Form 941 or Form 944. Prior Period Adjustments. Page 33.

13. Reporting Adjustments to Form 941 or Form 944. Prior Period Adjustments. Forms for prior period adjustments.

46. **Forms for prior period adjustments.** The Internal Revenue Service has developed Form ___ and Form ___ to replace Form 941c, Supporting Statement to Correct Information.
    (a) 941-W, 944-W
    (b) 941-X, 944-X
    (c) 941-Y, 944-Y
    (d) 941-Z, 944-Z
    Answer: See section 13. Reporting Adjustments to Form 941 or Form 944, Prior period adjustments. Page 33./ (b) 941-X, 944-X

Section 13. Reporting Adjustments to Form 941 or Form 944. Prior Period Adjustments. Page 33.

13. Reporting Adjustments to Form 941 or Form 944. Forms for prior period adjustments.
47. **Forms for prior period adjustments.** The Internal Revenue Service has developed Form ___ and Form ___ to replace Form 941c, Supporting Statement to Correct Information. There are also Forms 943-X, 954-X, and ___ to report corrections on corresponding returns.
   - (a) 941-W, 944-W, MR-1W
   - (b) 941-X, 944-X, CT-1X
   - (c) 941-Y, 944-Y, DR-2Y
   - (d) 941-Z, 944-Z, DR-3Z

   Answer: See section 13. Reporting Adjustments to Form 941 or Form 944, Prior period adjustments. Page 33./ (b) 941-X, 944-X, CT-1X

13. Reporting Adjustments to Form 941 or Form 944. Forms for prior period adjustments.
48. **Forms for prior period adjustments.** Form 941-X and Form 944-X also replace Form ___ Claim for Refund or Request for Abatement, for employers to request a refund or abatement of overreported employment taxes.
   - (a) 841
   - (b) 842
   - (c) 843
   - (d) 844

   Answer: See section 13. Reporting Adjustments to Form 941 or Form 944, Prior period adjustments. Page 33./ (c) 843

13. Reporting Adjustments to Form 941 or Form 944. Forms for prior period adjustments.
49. **Forms for prior period adjustments.** Form 941-X and Form 944-X also replace Form ___ Claim for Refund or Request for Abatement, for employers to request a refund or abatement of overreported employment taxes. Continue to use Form ___ when requesting a refund or abatement of assessed interest or penalties.
   - (a) 841, 841
   - (b) 842, 842
   - (c) 843, 843
   - (d) 844, 844

   Answer: See section 13. Reporting Adjustments to Form 941 or Form 944, Prior period adjustments. Page 33./ (c) 843, 843

© Copyright 2013. All rights reserved. Notice: United States Copyright Laws and International Treaties prohibit unauthorized publication, reproduction, distribution of this Work. Unauthorized use of this copyright in any form, format, publication or document may result in severe civil and criminal penalties. Violations of this copyright are investigated by the United States Department of Justice and carry, upon conviction of fines up to $250,000 and five years confinement. This Work is protected by United States Copyright Laws and International Treaties. Do not Copy, do not reproduce, do not distribute.

Reporting Adjustments to Form 941 or Form 944.
Forms for prior period adjustments. TIP

Reporting Adjustments to Form 941 or Form 944. Forms for prior period adjustments. TIP

50. TIP. See *Revenue Ruling 2009-39, 2009-52 I.R.B.___*, for examples of how the interest-free adjustment and claim refund rules apply in ___ different situations.
  (a) 948, 7
  (b) 949, 8
  (c) 950, 9
  (d) 951, 10
  Answer: See section 13. Reporting Adjustments to Form 941 or Form 944, Prior period adjustments. **TIP**. Page 33./ (d) 951, 10

13. Reporting Adjustments to Form 941 or Form 944. Prior Period Adjustments. Forms for prior period adjustments. TIP

51. TIP. See Revenue Ruling 2009-39, 2009-52 I.R.B.___, for examples of how the interest-free adjustment and claim refund rules apply in ___ different situations. You can find Revenue Ruling 2009-___, at *www.irs.gov/irb/2009-52.IRB/ar14.html*.
  (a) 948, 7, 36
  (b) 949, 8, 37
  (c) 950, 9, 38
  (d) 951, 10, 39
  Answer: See section 13. Reporting Adjustments to Form 941 or Form 944, Prior period adjustments. **TIP**. Page 33./ (d) 951, 10, 39

Section 13. Reporting Adjustments to Form 941 or Form 944.
Prior Period Adjustments. Background. Page 33.

13. Reporting Adjustments to Form 941 or Form 944. Prior Period Adjustments. Background

52. Treasury Decision ___ changed the procedure for making interest-free adjustments to employment taxes reported on Form 941 and Form 944 and for filing a claim for refund of employment taxes.
  (a) 9405
  (b) 9406
  (c) 9407
  (d) 9408
  Answer: See section 13. Reporting Adjustments to Form 941 or Form 944, Background. Page 33./ (a) 9405

Section 13. Reporting Adjustments to Form 941 or Form 944. Prior Period Adjustments. Background

13. Reporting Adjustments to Form 941 or Form 944. Prior Period Adjustments. Background

53. Treasury Decision ___ changed the procedure for making interest-free adjustments to employment taxes reported on Form 941 and Form 94 for filing a claim for refund of employment taxes. Treasury Decision 9405, 2008-32 I.R.B. ___, is available at ***www.irs.gov/irb/2008-32.irb/ar13.html***.
    (a) 9405, 293
    (b) 9406, 294
    (c) 9407, 295
    (d) 9408, 296
    Answer: See section 13. Reporting Adjustments to Form 941 or Form 944, Background. Page 33./(a) 9405, 293

13. Reporting Adjustments to Form 941 or Form 944. Prior Period Adjustments. Background

54. You will use the adjustment process if you underreported employment taxes and are making a payment, or if you overreported employment taxes and are making a payment, of if you overreported employment taxes and will be applying the ___ to the Form 941 or Form 944 period during which you file Form 941-X or Form 944-X.
    (a) correction
    (b) credit
    (c) change
    (d) revision
    Answer: See section 13. Reporting Adjustments to Form 941 or Form 944, Background. Page 33./ (b) credit

13. Reporting Adjustments to Form 941 or Form 944. Prior Period Adjustments. Background

55. You will use the adjustment process if you underreported employment taxes and are making a payment, or if you overreported employment taxes and are making a payment, of if you overreported employment taxes and will be applying the ___ to the Form 941 or Form 944 period during which you file Form 941-X or Form 944-X. You will use the claim process if you overreported employment taxes and are requesting a refund or abatement of the overreported ___.
    (a) correction, payment
    (b) credit, amount
    (c) change, deposit
    (d) revision, funds
    Answer: See section 13. Reporting Adjustments to Form 941 or Form 944, Background. Page 33./(b) credit, amount

Section 13. Reporting Adjustments to Form 941 or Form 944. Prior Period Adjustments. Background. Page 33.

13. Reporting Adjustments to Form 941 or Form 944. Prior Period Adjustments. Background

56. You will use the adjustment process if you underreported employment taxes and are making a payment, or if you overreported employment taxes and are making a payment, of if you overreported employment taxes and will be applying the ___ to the Form 941 or Form 944 period during which you file Form 941-X or Form 944-X. You will use the claim process if you overreported employment taxes and are requesting a refund or abatement of the overreported ___. We use the terms "correct" and "corrections" to include interest-free adjustments under sections 6205 and ___, and
    (a) correction, payment, 6412
    (b) credit, amount, 6413
    (c) change, deposit, 6414
    (d) revision, funds, 6115
    Answer: See section 13. Reporting Adjustments to Form 941 or Form 944, Background. Page 33./(b) credit, amount, 6413

13. Reporting Adjustments to Form 941 or Form 944. Prior Period Adjustments. Background

57. You will use the adjustment process if you underreported employment taxes and are making a payment, or if you overreported employment taxes and are making a payment, of if you overreported employment taxes and will be applying the ___ to the Form 941 or Form 944 period during which you file Form 941-X or Form 944-X. You will use the claim process if you overreported employment taxes and are requesting a refund or abatement of the overreported ___. We use the terms "correct" and "corrections" to include interest-free adjustments under sections 6205 and ___, and claims for abatement under sections 6402, 6414, and ___ of the Internal Revenue Code.
    (a) correction, payment, 6412, 6403
    (b) credit, amount, 6413, 6404
    (c) change, deposit, 6414, 6405
    (d) revision, funds, 6115, 6406
    Answer: See section 13. Reporting Adjustments to Form 941 or Form 944, Background. Page 33./(b) credit, amount, 6413, 6404

DU VALL'S TEST'S™
Instructor's Manual Study Guide Series United States Tax Code
IRS Publication 15 Circular E, Employer's Tax Guide Tax Year 2013
Tax Test 15E-S13-2 [Multiple-Choice Questions With Answers]

Section 13. Reporting Adjustments to Form 941 or Form 944. Prior Period Adjustments. Correcting employment taxes. Page 33.

13. Reporting Adjustments to Form 941 or Form 944. Prior Period Adjustments. Correcting employment taxes

1. **Correcting employment taxes**. When you discover an error on a previously filed Form 941 or Form 944, you **must**:
   • Correct that error using Form 941-X or Form 944-X,
   • File a separate Form 942-X or Form 944-X for each Form 941 or Form 944 you are correcting,
   and
   • File Form 941-X or Form 944-X ___. **Do not** file with Form 941 or Form 944.
   (a) singularly
   (b) independently
   (c) separately
   (d) uniformly
   Answer: See section 13. Reporting Adjustments to Form 941 or Form 944, Correcting employment taxes. Page 33./ (c) separately

13. Reporting Adjustments to Form 941 or Form 944. Prior Period Adjustments. Correcting employment taxes

2. **Correcting employment taxes**. Continue to report current quarterly adjustments for fractions of cents, third-party sick pay, tips and group-term life insurance on Form 941 using lines ___, and on Form 944 using line ___.
   (a) 1-4, 4
   (b) 1- 5, 5
   (c) 7 and 8, 6
   (d) 7-9, 6
   Answer: See section 13. Reporting Adjustments to Form 941 or Form 944, Correcting employment taxes. Page 33./ (d) 7-9, 6

Section 13. Reporting Adjustments to Form 941 or Form 944. Prior Period Adjustments. Correcting employment taxes. Page 33.

13. Reporting Adjustments to Form 941 or Form 944. Prior Period Adjustments. Correcting employment taxes

3. **Correcting employment taxes**. Report the correction of underreported and overreported amounts for the same tax period on a single Form 941-X or 944-X unless you are ___.
   (a) requesting a refund
   (b) submitting a payment
   (c) submitting a deposit
   (d) requesting a credit
   Answer: See section 13. Reporting Adjustments to Form 941 or Form 944, Correcting employment taxes. Page 33./ (a) requesting a refund

13. Reporting Adjustments to Form 941 or Form 944. Prior Period Adjustments. Correcting employment taxes

4. **Correcting employment taxes**. If you are requesting a refund and are correcting both underreported and overreported amounts, file ___ Form 941-X or Form 944 unless
   (a) a single
   (b) one
   (c) only one
   (d) a backup
   Answer: See section 13. Reporting Adjustments to Form 941 or Form 944, Correcting employment taxes. Page 33./ (b) one

13. Reporting Adjustments to Form 941 or Form 944. Prior Period Adjustments. Correcting employment taxes

5. **Correcting employment taxes**. If you are requesting a refund and are correcting both underreported and overreported amounts, file ___ Form 941-X or Form 944 correcting the underreported amounts only and a ___ Form 941-X or Form 944-X correcting the overreported amounts.
   (a) a single, another
   (b) one, second
   (c) only one additional
   (d) a backup, another
   Answer: See section 13. Reporting Adjustments to Form 941 or Form 944, Correcting employment taxes. Page 33./ (b) one, second

Section 13. Reporting Adjustments to Form 941 or Form 944. Prior Period Adjustments. Correcting employment taxes. Page 33

13. Reporting Adjustments to Form 941 or Form 944. Prior Period Adjustments. Correcting employment taxes

6. **Correcting employment taxes**. See the chart on the back of Form 941-X or Form 944-X for help in choosing whether to use the ___ process or the ___ process.
   (a) due, adjustment
   (b) claim, due
   (c) adjustment, claim
   (d) claim, adjustment
   Answer: See section 13. Reporting Adjustments to Form 941 or Form 944, Correcting employment taxes. Page 33./ (c) adjustment, claim

13. Reporting Adjustments to Form 941 or Form 944. Prior Period Adjustments. Correcting employment taxes

7. **Correcting employment taxes**. See the chart on the back of Form 941-X or Form 944-X for help in choosing whether to use the ___ process or the ___ process. See the Instructions for Form 941-X or the Instructions for Form 944-X for ___ on how to make the adjustment or claim for refund or abatement.
   (a) due, adjustment, instructions
   (b) claim, due, directions
   (c) adjustment, claim, details
   (d) claim, adjustment, instructions
   Answer: See section 13. Reporting Adjustments to Form 941 or Form 944, Correcting employment taxes. Page 33./ (c) adjustment, claim, details

13. Reporting Adjustments to Form 941 or Form 944. Income tax withholding adjustments. Page 33.

13. Reporting Adjustments to Form 941 or Form 944. Prior Period Adjustments. Income tax withholding adjustments.

8. **Income tax withholding adjustments**. In the current calendar year, correct prior quarter income tax withholding errors by making the correction on Form ___ when you discover the error.
   (a) 941
   (b) 941-X
   (c) 944
   (d) 944-X
   Answer: See section 13. Reporting Adjustments to Form 941 or Form 944, Income tax withholding adjustments. Page 33./ (b) 941-X

13. Reporting Adjustments to Form 941 or Form 944.
Income tax withholding adjustments. Page 33.

13. Reporting Adjustments to Form 941 or Form 944. Income tax withholding adjustments.
9. **Income tax withholding adjustments.** You may make an adjustment ___ to correct income tax withholding errors discovered during the same calendar year in which you paid the wages.
   (a) when
   (b) when necessary
   (c) only
   (d) when required
   Answer: See section 13. Reporting Adjustments to Form 941 or Form 944, Income tax withholding adjustments. Page 34./ (c) only

13. Reporting Adjustments to Form 941 or Form 944. Income tax withholding adjustments.
10. **Income tax withholding adjustments.** You may make an adjustment ___ to correct income tax withholding errors discovered during the same calendar year in which you paid the wages. This is because the employee uses the amount shown of Form ___ as a credit when filing his or her income tax return (Form 1040, etc.)
    (a) when, SSA-W-1
    (b) when necessary, W-1
    (c) only, W-2
    (d) when required, W-3
    Answer: See section 13. Reporting Adjustments to Form 941 or Form 944, Income tax withholding adjustments. Page 34./ (c) only, W-2

13. Reporting Adjustments to Form 941 or Form 944. Income tax withholding adjustments (administrative error).
11. **Income tax withholding adjustments.** You cannot adjust amounts reported as income tax withheld in a prior calendar year unless it is to correct ___ or section 3509 applies.
    (a) administrative error
    (b) administration error
    (c) administrator error
    (d) accounting error
    Answer: See section 13. Reporting Adjustments to Form 941 or Form 944, Income tax withholding adjustments. Page 34./ (a) administrative error

13. Reporting Adjustments to Form 941 or Form 944. Prior Period Adjustments. Income tax withholding adjustments. Page 34.

13. Reporting Adjustments to Form 941 or Form 944. Prior Period Adjustments. Income tax withholding adjustments (administrative error).

12. **Income tax withholding adjustments.** An <u>administrative error</u> occurs if ___ on Form 941 or Form 944 is not the amount you actually withheld.
    - (a) the amount you entered
    - (b) the amount entered
    - (c) amounts entered
    - (d) the tax amounts entered

    Answer: See section 13. Reporting Adjustments to Form 941 or Form 944, Income tax withholding adjustments. Page 34./ (a) the amount you entered

13. Reporting Adjustments to Form 941 or Form 944. Prior Period Adjustments. Income tax withholding adjustments (administrative error).

13. **Income tax withholding adjustments.** For example, if the total income tax actually withheld was incorrectly reported on Form 941 or Form 944 due to a ___ or ___ error, **this would be an <u>administrative error</u>**.
    - (a) mathematical, bookkeeping
    - (b) mathematical, transposition
    - (c) transposition, mathematical
    - (d) bookkeeping, transposition

    Answer: See section 13. Reporting Adjustments to Form 941 or Form 944, Income tax withholding adjustments. Page 34./ (b) mathematical, transposition

13. Reporting Adjustments to Form 941 or Form 944. Prior Period Adjustments. Income tax withholding adjustments (administrative error).

14. **Income tax withholding adjustments.** For example, if the total income tax actually withheld was incorrectly reported on Form 941 or Form 944 due to a ___ or ___ error, **this would be an <u>administrative error</u>**. The <u>administrative error</u> adjustment ___ the amount reported on Form 941 or Form 944 to agree with the amount actually withheld from employees and reported on their Forms___.
    - (a) mathematical, bookkeeping, changes, 1040
    - (b) mathematical, transposition, corrects, W-2
    - (c) transposition, mathematical, W-3, changes
    - (d) bookkeeping, transposition, corrects, 1089

    Answer: See section 13. Reporting Adjustments to Form 941 or Form 944, Income tax withholding adjustments. Page 34./ (b) mathematical, transposition, corrects, W-2

Section 13. Reporting Adjustments to Form 941 or Form 944. Additional Medicare Tax withholding adjustments. Page 34.

13. Reporting Adjustments to Form 941 or Form 944. Prior Period Adjustments. Additional Medicare Tax withholding adjustments.

15. **Additional Medicare Tax withholding adjustments.** Generally, The ___ discussed above under *Income tax withholding adjustments* apply to Additional Medicare Tax withholding adjustments.
    - (a) regulations
    - (b) IRS rules
    - (c) rules
    - (d) requirements

    Answer: See section 13. Reporting Adjustments to Form 941 or Form 944, Additional Medicare Tax withholding adjustments. Page 34./ (c) rules

13. Reporting Adjustments to Form 941 or Form 944. Prior Period Adjustments. Additional Medicare Tax withholding adjustments.

16. **Additional Medicare Tax withholding adjustments.** Generally, The ___ discussed above under *Income tax withholding adjustments* apply to Additional Medicare Tax withholding adjustments. That is, you may make an adjustment only to correct Additional Medicare tax withholding ___ discovered during the same calendar year you paid wages.
    - (a) regulations, taxes
    - (b) IRS rules, adjustments
    - (c) rules, errors
    - (d) requirements, adjustments

    Answer: See section 13. Reporting Adjustments to Form 941 or Form 944, Additional Medicare Tax withholding adjustments. Page 34./ (c) rules, errors

13. Reporting Adjustments to Form 941 or Form 944. Prior Period Adjustments. Additional Medicare Tax withholding adjustments.

17. **Additional Medicare Tax withholding adjustments.** Generally, The ___ discussed above under *Income tax withholding adjustments* apply to Additional Medicare Tax withholding adjustments. That is, you may make an adjustment only to correct Additional Medicare tax withholding ___ discovered during the same calendar year you paid wages. You should not adjust amounts reported in a prior calendar year unless it is to correct an administrative error or section ___ applies.
    - (a) regulations, taxes, 3507
    - (b) IRS rules, adjustments, 3508
    - (c) rules, errors, 3509
    - (d) requirements, adjustments, 3510

    Answer: See section 13. Reporting Adjustments to Form 941 or Form 944, Additional Medicare Tax withholding adjustments. Page 34./ (c) rules, errors, 3509

Section 13. Reporting Adjustments to Form 941 or Form 944. Additional Medicare Tax withholding adjustments. Page 34.

13. Reporting Adjustments to Form 941 or Form 944. Prior Period Adjustments. Additional Medicare Tax withholding adjustments.

18. **Additional Medicare Tax withholding adjustments.** If you have overpaid Additional Medicare Tax, you should not file a claim for refund for the amount of the overpayment unless the amount ___ from the employee's wages.
    (a) was withheld
    (b) was not withheld
    (c) is not withheld
    (d) was not actually withheld
    Answer: See section 13. Reporting Adjustments to Form 941 or Form 944, Additional Medicare Tax withholding adjustments. Page 34./ (d) was not actually withheld

13. Reporting Adjustments to Form 941 or Form 944. Collecting underwithheld taxes from employees. Page 34.

13. Reporting Adjustments to Form 941 or Form 944. Prior Period Adjustments. Collecting underwithheld taxes from employees.

19. **Collecting underwithheld taxes from employees.** If you withheld no income, social security, or Medicare taxes or less that the correct amount from an employee's wages, you can make it up from ___ to that employee.
    (a) later pay
    (b) later wages
    (c) later deductions
    (d) taxes
    Answer: See section 13. Reporting Adjustments to Form 941 or Form 944, Collecting underwithheld taxes from employees. Page 34./ (a) later pay

13. Reporting Adjustments to Form 941 or Form 944. Prior Period Adjustments. Collecting underwithheld taxes from employees.

20. **Collecting underwithheld taxes from employees.** If you withheld no income, social security, or Medicare taxes or less that the correct amount from an employee's wages, you can make it up from ___ to that employee. But ___ who owes the underpayment.
    (a) later pay, you are the one
    (b) later wages, you and the employee are the ones
    (c) later deductions, both the employer and employee are the ones
    (d) taxes, it is the employer
    Answer: See section 13. Reporting Adjustments to Form 941 or Form 944, Collecting underwithheld taxes from employees. Page 34./ (a) later pay, you are the one

13. Reporting Adjustments to Form 941 or Form 944. Collecting underwithheld taxes from employees. Page 34.

13. Reporting Adjustments to Form 941 or Form 944. Prior Period Adjustments. Collecting underwithheld taxes from employees.

21. **Collecting underwithheld taxes from employees.** Reimbursement is a matter for ___ between you and the employee.
    (a) to be resolved
    (b) settlement
    (c) resolution
    (d) discussion and settlement
    Answer: See section 13. Reporting Adjustments to Form 941 or Form 944, Collecting underwithheld taxes from employees. Page 34./ (b) settlement

13. Reporting Adjustments to Form 941 or Form 944. Prior Period Adjustments. Collecting underwithheld taxes from employees.

22. **Collecting underwithheld taxes from employees.** Underwithheld income tax must be recovered from the employee on or before the ___.
    (a) last day of the year
    (b) last day of the fiscal year
    (c) last day of the calendar year
    (d) last day of the current calendar year
    Answer: See section 13. Reporting Adjustments to Form 941 or Form 944, Collecting underwithheld taxes from employees. Page 34./ (c) last day of the calendar year

13. Reporting Adjustments to Form 941 or Form 944. Prior Period Adjustments. Collecting underwithheld taxes from employees.

23. **Collecting underwithheld taxes from employees.** Underwithheld income tax must be recovered from the employee on or before the ___.
    (a) last day of the year
    (b) last day of the fiscal year
    (c) last day of the calendar year
    (d) last day of the current calendar year
    Answer: See section 13. Reporting Adjustments to Form 941 or Form 944, Collecting underwithheld taxes from employees. Page 34./ (c) last day of the calendar year

13. Reporting Adjustments to Form 941 or Form 944.
Collecting underwithheld taxes from employees. Page 34.

13. Reporting Adjustments to Form 941 or Form 944. Prior Period Adjustments. Collecting underwithheld taxes from employees.

24. **Collecting underwithheld taxes from employees.** Underwithheld income tax must be recovered from the employee on or before the ___. There are special rules for tax on tips (see section ___) and fringe benefits (see section ___).
    (a) last day of the year, 4, 3
    (b) last day of the fiscal year, 3, 4
    (c) last day of the calendar year, 6, 5
    (d) last day of the current calendar year, 5, 6
    Answer: See section 13. Reporting Adjustments to Form 941 or Form 944, Collecting underwithheld taxes from employees. Page 34./ (c) last day of the calendar year, 6, 5

13. Reporting Adjustments to Form 941 or Form 944.
Refunding amounts incorrectly withheld from employees. Page 34.

13. Reporting Adjustments to Form 941 or Form 944. Prior Period Adjustments. Refunding amounts incorrectly withheld from employees.

25. **Refunding amounts incorrectly withheld from employees.** If you withheld more than the correct amount of income, social security, or Medicare Taxes from wages paid, ___ or reimburse the employee the excess.
    (a) refund
    (b) restore
    (c) pay
    (d) repay
    Answer: See section 13. Reporting Adjustments to Form 941 or Form 944, Refunding amounts incorrectly withheld from employees. Page 34./ (d) repay

13. Reporting Adjustments to Form 941 or Form 944. Prior Period Adjustments. Refunding amounts incorrectly withheld from employees.

26. **Refunding amounts incorrectly withheld from employees.** Any excess income tax or Additional Medicare Tax withholding ___ be repaid or reimbursed to the employee before the end of the calendar year in which it was withheld.
    (a) should
    (b) must
    (c) shall
    (d) is to
    Answer: See section 13. Reporting Adjustments to Form 941 or Form 944, Refunding amounts incorrectly withheld from employees. Page 34./ (a) should

13. Reporting Adjustments to Form 941 or Form 944.
Refunding amounts incorrectly withheld from employees. Page 34.

13. Reporting Adjustments to Form 941 or Form 944. Prior Period Adjustments. Refunding amounts incorrectly withheld from employees.

27. **Refunding amounts incorrectly withheld from employees.** Keep in your records the employees written ___ showing the date and amount of repayment or record of reimbursement.
    (a) record
    (b) receipt
    (c) statement
    (d) pay stub
    Answer: See section 13. Reporting Adjustments to Form 941 or Form 944, Refunding amounts incorrectly withheld from employees. Page 34./ (b) receipt

13. Reporting Adjustments to Form 941 or Form 944. Prior Period Adjustments. Refunding amounts incorrectly withheld from employees.

28. **Refunding amounts incorrectly withheld from employees.** Keep in your records the employees written ___ showing the date and amount of repayment or record of reimbursement. If you did not repay or reimburse the employee, you must report and pay___ excess amount when you file Form 941 for the quarter (of Form 944 for the year) in which you withheld too much tax.
    (a) record, every
    (b) receipt, each
    (c) statement, all
    (d) pay stub, each
    Answer: See section 13. Reporting Adjustments to Form 941 or Form 944, Refunding amounts incorrectly withheld from employees. Page 34./ (b) receipt, each

Section 13. Reporting Adjustments to Form 941 or Form 944.
Correcting filed Forms W-2 and W-3. Page 34.

13. Reporting Adjustments to Form 941 or Form 944. Prior Period Adjustments. Correcting filed Forms W-2 and W-3.

29. **Correcting files Forms W-2 and W-3.** When adjustments are made to correct wages and social security and Medicare taxes because of a change in the wage totals reported for a previous year, you also need to file Form W-2___ and Form W-3___ with the SSA.
    (a) a, a
    (b) b, b
    (c) c, c
    (d) d, d
    Answer: See section 13. Reporting Adjustments to Form 941 or Form 944, Correcting filled Forms W-2 and W-3. Page 34./ (c) c, c

Section 13. Reporting Adjustments to Form 941 or Form 944. Correcting filed Forms W-2 and W-3. Page 34.

13. Reporting Adjustments to Form 941 or Form 944. Prior Period Adjustments. Correcting filed Forms W-2 and W-3.

30. **Correcting filed Forms W-2 and W-3.** When adjustments are made to correct wages and social security and Medicare taxes because of a change in the wage totals reported for a previous year, you also need to file Form W-2___ and Form W-3___ with the SSA. Up to ___ Forms W-2c per Form W-3c may now be filed per session over the internet, with no limit on the number of sessions. For more information, Visit the Social Security Administration's Employer W-2 Filing Instructions & Information webpage at *www.socialsecurity.gov/employer*.
    - (a) a, a, three
    - (b) b, b, four
    - (c) c, c, five
    - (d) d, d, six

    Answer: See section 13. Reporting Adjustments to Form 941 or Form 944, Correcting filled Forms W-2 and W-3. Page 34./ (c) c, c, five

13. Reporting Adjustments to Form 941 or Form 944. Exceptions to interest-free corrections of employment taxes. Page 34.

13. Reporting Adjustments to Form 941 or Form 944. Prior Period Adjustments. Exceptions to interest-free corrections of employment taxes.

31. **Exceptions to interest-free corrections of employment taxes.** A correction will **not** be eligible for interest-free treatment if:
    • The failure to report to an issue ___ in an IRS examination of a prior return, or
    - (a) discovered
    - (b) discussed
    - (c) challenged
    - (d) raised

    Answer: See section 13. Reporting Adjustments to Form 941 or Form 944, Exceptions to interest-free corrections of employment taxes. Page 34./ (d) raised

13. Reporting Adjustments to Form 941 or Form 944.
Exceptions to interest-free corrections of employment taxes. Page 34.

13. Reporting Adjustments to Form 941 or Form 944. Prior Period Adjustments.
Exceptions to interest-free corrections of employment taxes.

32. **Exceptions to interest-free corrections of employment taxes.** A correction will **not** be eligible for interest-free treatment if:
    • The failure to report to an issue ___ in an IRS examination of a prior return, or
    • The employer ___ underreported its employment tax liability.
    (a)   discovered, deceitfully
    (b)   discussed, intentionally
    (c)   challenged, willfully
    (d)   raised, knowingly
    Answer: See section 13. Reporting Adjustments to Form 941 or Form 944, Exceptions to interest-free corrections of employment taxes. Page 34./ (d) raised, knowingly

13. Reporting Adjustments to Form 941 or Form 944. Prior Period Adjustments.
Exceptions to interest-free corrections of employment taxes.

33. **Exceptions to interest-free corrections of employment taxes.** A correction will **not** be eligible for interest-free treatment after the **earlier** of the following:
    • Receipt of an IRS notice and demand for payment ___ or
    (a)   following assessment
    (b)   after assessment
    (c)   requiring assessment
    (d)   assessment
    Answer: See section 13. Reporting Adjustments to Form 941 or Form 944, Exceptions to interest-free corrections of employment taxes. Page 34./ (b) after assessment

13. Reporting Adjustments to Form 941 or Form 944. Prior Period Adjustments.
Exceptions to interest-free corrections of employment taxes.

34. **Exceptions to interest-free corrections of employment taxes.** A correction will **not** be eligible for interest-free treatment after the **earlier** of the following:
    • Receipt of an IRS notice and demand for payment ___ or
    • Receipt of an IRS Notice of determination of Worker Classification. (Letter ___).
    (a)   following assessment, 3521
    (b)   after assessment, 3522
    (c)   requiring assessment, 3523
    (d)   assessment, 3524
    Answer: See section 13. Reporting Adjustments to Form 941 or Form 944, Exceptions to interest-free corrections of employment taxes. Page 34./ (b) after assessment, 3523

Section 13. Reporting Adjustments to Form 941 or Form 944. Wage Repayments. Page 34.

13. Reporting Adjustments to Form 941 or Form 944. Wage Repayments

35. **Wage Repayments**. If an employee repays you for wages received in error, do not ___ the repayments against current-year wages unless the repayments are for amounts received in error in the current year.
    - (a) charge
    - (b) credit
    - (c) offset
    - (d) include

    Answer: See section 13. Reporting Adjustments to Form 941 or Form 944. Wage Repayments Page 34./ (c) offset

13. Reporting Adjustments to Form 941 or Form 944. Wage Repayments. Repayments of current year wages.

36. **Wage Repayments**. If you receive repayments for wages paid during a prior quarter in the current year, report adjustments on Form ___ to recover income tax withholding and social security and Medicare taxes for the repaid wages.
    - (a) 941
    - (b) 941-X
    - (c) 944
    - (d) 944-X

    Answer: See section 13. Reporting Adjustments to Form 941 or Form 944. Wage Repayments Page 34./ (b) 941-X

13. Reporting Adjustments to Form 941 or Form 944. Wage Repayments. Repayments of current year wages.

37. **Wage Repayments**. If you receive repayments for wages paid during a prior year, report adjustments on Form ___ or Form ___ to recover income tax withholding and social security and Medicare taxes for the repaid wages.
    - (a) 941, 944
    - (b) 941-X, 944-X
    - (c) 944, 945
    - (d) 944-X, 945-X

    Answer: See section 13. Reporting Adjustments to Form 941 or Form 944. Wage Repayments Page 34./ (b) 941-X, 944-X

Section 13. Reporting Adjustments to Form 941 or Form 944. Wage Repayments. Page 34.

13. Reporting Adjustments to Form 941 or Form 944. Wage Repayments. Repayments of prior year wages.

38. **Wage Repayments**. If you receive repayments for wages paid during a prior year, report adjustments on Form 941-X or Form 944-X to recover income tax withholding and social security and Medicare taxes for the repaid wages. You should not make an adjustment for income tax or Additional Medicare Tax withholding because the wages were wages and income to the employee for the ___.
   (a) prior quarter
   (b) previous quarter
   (c) previous year
   (d) prior year
   Answer: See section 13. Reporting Adjustments to Form 941 or Form 944. Wage Repayments Page 34./ (d) prior year

13. Reporting Adjustments to Form 941 or Form 944. Wage Repayments. Repayments of prior year wages.

39. **Wage Repayments**. You must also file Forms ___ and ___ with the SSA to correct social security and Medicare wages and taxes.
   (a) W-2a, W-3a
   (b) W-2b, W-3b
   (c) W-2c, W-3c
   (d) W-2d, W-3d
   Answer: See section 13. Reporting Adjustments to Form 941 or Form 944. Wage Repayments Page 34./ (c) W-2c, W-3c

13. Reporting Adjustments to Form 941 or Form 944. Wage Repayments. Repayments of prior year wages.

40. **Wage Repayments**. Do not correct wages (box___) on Form ___ for the amount paid in error.
   (a) 1, W-2c
   (b) 2, W-2d
   (c) 3, W-3c
   (d) 4, W-3d
   Answer: See section 13. Reporting Adjustments to Form 941 or Form 944. Wage Repayments Page 34./ (a) 1, W-2c

13. Reporting Adjustments to Form 941 or Form 944. Wage Repayments. Repayments of prior year wages.

13. Reporting Adjustments to Form 941 or Form 944. Wage Repayments. Repayments of prior year wages.

41. **Wage Repayments**. Do not correct wages (box___) on Form ___ for the amount paid in error. Give a copy of Form ___ to the employee.
    (a) 1, W-2c, W-2c
    (b) 2, W-2d, W-2d
    (c) 3, W-3c, W-3c
    (d) 4, W-3d, W-3d
    Answer: See section 13. Reporting Adjustments to Form 941 or Form 944. Wage Repayments Page 34./ (a) 1, W-2c, W-2c

Section 13. Reporting Adjustments to Form 941 or Form 944. Wage Repayments. Employee reporting of repayment. Page 34.

13. Reporting Adjustments to Form 941 or Form 944. Wage Repayments. Employee reporting of repayment.

42. **Wage Repayments. Employee reporting of repayment.** The wages paid in error in the prior year ___ to the employee for that year.
    (a) are not taxable
    (b) remain taxable
    (c) shall not be taxable
    (d) will be taxable
    Answer: See section 13. Reporting Adjustments to Form 941 or Form 944. Wage Repayments Page 34./ (b) remain taxable

13. Reporting Adjustments to Form 941 or Form 944. Wage Repayments. Employee reporting of repayment.

43. **Wage Repayments. Employee reporting of repayment.** The wages paid in error in the prior year ___ to the employee for that year. This is because the employee received and ___ during that year.
    (a) are not taxable, used those funds
    (b) remain taxable, had use of those funds
    (c) shall not be taxable, used the funds
    (d) will be taxable, used the funds as income
    Answer: See section 13. Reporting Adjustments to Form 941 or Form 944. Wage Repayments Page 34./ (b) remain taxable, had use of those funds

Section 13. Reporting Adjustments to Form 941 or Form 944. Wage Repayments. Employee reporting of repayment. Page 34.

13. Reporting Adjustments to Form 941 or Form 944. Wage Repayments. Employee reporting of repayment.

44. **Wage Repayments. Employee reporting of repayment.** The wages paid in error in the prior year ___ to the employee for that year. This is because the employee received and ___ during that year. The employee is not entitled to file an amended return (Form ___) to recover the income tax on those wages.
    (a) are not taxable, used those funds, 1018W
    (b) remain taxable, had use of those funds, 1040X
    (c) shall not be taxable, used the funds, 1043-X
    (d) will be taxable, used the funds as income, 1044X
    Answer: See section 13. Reporting Adjustments to Form 941 or Form 944. Wage Repayments Page 34./ (b) remain taxable, had use of those funds, 1040X

13. Reporting Adjustments to Form 941 or Form 944. Wage Repayments. Employee reporting of repayment.

45. **Wage Repayments. Employee reporting of repayment.** The wages paid in error in the prior year ___ to the employee for that year. This is because the employee received and ___ during that year. The employee is not entitled to file an amended return (Form ___) to recover the income tax on those wages. Instead, the employee is entitled to a ___ (or credit in some cases) for the repaid wages on his or her income tax return for the year of repayment.
    (a) are not taxable, used those funds, 1018W, rebate
    (b) remain taxable, had use of those funds, 1040X, deduction

    (c) shall not be taxable, used the funds, 1043-X, refund
    (d) will be taxable, used the funds as income, 1044X, adjustment
    Answer: See section 13. Reporting Adjustments to Form 941 or Form 944. Wage Repayments Page 34./ (b) remain taxable, had use of those funds, 1040X, deduction

A Ficus Tree Publishing Quick Notes Page.

© Copyright 2013. All rights reserved. Notice: United States Copyright Laws and International Treaties prohibit unauthorized publication, reproduction, distribution of this Work. Unauthorized use of this copyright in any form, format, publication or document may result in severe civil and criminal penalties. Violations of this copyright are investigated by the United States Department of Justice and carry, upon conviction of fines up to $250,000 and five years confinement. This Work is protected by United States Copyright Laws and International Treaties. Do not Copy, do not reproduce, do not distribute.

A Ficus Tree Publishing Educational-Technical Publications

The International Leader in Construction Technology Home Study

Instructor's Manual for Tax Test 15E-S14 (FUTA) Tax Federal Unemployment Tax

General Description.
Section 14. Federal Unemployment Tax (FUTA). Page 35.

Tax Test 15E-S14. Tax Test 15E-S14 is the study of IRS Circular E, Employer's Tax Guide, Section 14. Federal Unemployment (FUTA) Tax (The complete title of the federal unemployment tax is The Federal Unemployment Tax Act). Federal Unemployment (FUTA) Tax. TIP; Federal Unemployment Tax (FUTA) Tax. Who must pay? Federal Unemployment (FUTA) Tax. Computing FUTA Tax; Federal Unemployment (FUTA) Tax. Successor Employer; Federal Unemployment (FUTA) Tax. Depositing FUTA tax; Federal Unemployment (FUTA) Tax. When to deposit.

Key Words.
Section 14. Federal Unemployment Tax (FUTA) Tax. Page 35.

Tax Test 15E-S14. The title of Section 14. Federal Unemployment (FUTA) Tax in the initial key word, sentence, or phrase. In Circular E, Employer's Tax Guide the key words are set in bold print. The words in bold print identifying the subpart of the section will generally appear in the subject index at the conclusion of a text. The Title of the Section will generally appear as a part of the Contents at the beginning of each textbook. From the bold print identifying the parts and subparts of IRS Publication 15, Employers Tax Guide for the current year. Thus, additional important information is obtained from the primary, secondary and minor headings of the basic text. From **page 35**, as follows below:

Federal Unemployment (FUTA) Tax. TIP. Who must pay? General test. Household employees test. Farmworkers test. Computing FUTA Tax. TIP. Successor employer. Depositing FUTA Tax. Household employees. When to deposit. Table 4. When to Deposit FUTA Taxes. Reporting FUTA Taxes. Household employees. Electronic filing by reporting agents.

© Copyright 2013. All rights reserved. Notice: United States Copyright Laws and International Treaties prohibit unauthorized publication, reproduction, distribution of this Work. Unauthorized use of this copyright in any form, format, publication or document may result in severe civil and criminal penalties. Violations of this copyright are investigated by the United States Department of Justice and carry, upon conviction of fines up to $250,000 and five years confinement. This Work is protected by United States Copyright Laws and International Treaties. Do not Copy, do not reproduce, do not distribute.

A Ficus Tree Publishing Educational-Technical Publications

A Ficus Tree Publishing Quick Notes Page

DU VALL'S TEST'S™
Instructors Manual Study Guide Series United States Tax Code
IRS Publication 15 Circular E, Employer's Tax Guide Tax Year 2013
Tax Test 15E-S14 [Multiple-Choice Questions With Answers]

Section 14. Federal Unemployment (FUTA) Tax. Page 35.

14. Federal Unemployment (FUTA) Tax.
1. Federal Unemployment (FUTA) Tax. The **Federal Unemployment Tax Act**, with ___ systems, provides for payments of unemployment compensation to workers who have lost their jobs.
   (a) state unemployment
   (b) supplementary
   (c) local
   (d) locally sponsored
   Answer: See section 14. Federal Unemployment (FUTA) Tax. Page 35./ (a) state unemployment

14. Federal Unemployment (FUTA) Tax.
2. Federal Unemployment (FUTA) Tax. The **Federal Unemployment Tax Act**, with ___ systems, provides for payments of unemployment compensation to workers who have lost their jobs. Most employers pay ___ a federal and a state unemployment tax.
   (a) state unemployment, both
   (b) supplementary, additionally
   (c) local, both
   (d) locally sponsored, additionally
   Answer: See section 14. Federal Unemployment (FUTA) Tax. Page 35./ (a) state unemployment, both

14. Federal Unemployment (FUTA) Tax.
3. Federal Unemployment (FUTA) Tax. The **Federal Unemployment Tax Act**, with ___ systems, provides for payments of unemployment compensation to workers who have lost their jobs. Most employers pay ___ a federal and a state unemployment tax. For a list of ___ unemployment agencies, visit the U.S. Department of Labor's website at *www.workforcesecurity.doleta.gov/unemployment/agencies.asp*.
   (a) state unemployment, both, state
   (b) supplementary, additionally, all
   (c) local, both, state and federal
   (d) locally sponsored, additionally, state
   Answer: See section 14. Federal Unemployment (FUTA) Tax. Page 35./ (a) state unemployment, both, state

Section 14. Federal Unemployment (FUTA) Tax

14. Federal Unemployment (FUTA) Tax.
4. Federal Unemployment (FUTA) Tax. Only the ___ pays FUTA tax;
    (a)   employee
    (b)   employer
    (c)   state
    (d)   federal government
Answer: See section 14. Federal Unemployment (FUTA) Tax. Page 35./ (b) employer

14. Federal Unemployment (FUTA) Tax.
5. Federal Unemployment (FUTA) Tax. Only the ___ pays FUTA tax; it is not withheld from the employee's wages. For more information, see the Instructions for Form ___.
    (a)   employee, 940
    (b)   employer, 940
    (c)   state, 941
    (d)   federal government, 944
Answer: See section 14. Federal Unemployment (FUTA) Tax. Page 35./ (b) employer, 940

14. Federal Unemployment (FUTA) Tax. TIP
6. Federal Unemployment (FUTA) Tax. TIP. Services rendered by a federally recognized Indian tribal government (or any subdivision, subsidiary, or business wholly owned by such an Indian tribe) are exempt from FUTA tax, subject to the tribe's compliance with ___.
    (a)   federal regulations
    (b)   federal laws
    (c)   state law
    (d)   state statutes
Answer: See section 14. Federal Unemployment (FUTA) Tax. TIP. Page 35./ (c) state law

14. Federal Unemployment (FUTA) Tax. TIP
7. Federal Unemployment (FUTA) Tax. TIP. Services rendered by a federally recognized Indian tribal government (or any subdivision, subsidiary, or business wholly owned by such an Indian tribe) are exempt from FUTA tax, subject to the tribe's compliance with ___. For more information, see Internal Revenue Code section ____(__).
    (a)   federal regulations, 3307, c
    (b)   federal laws, 3308, d
    (c)   state law, 3309, d
    (d)   state statutes, 3309, e
Answer: See section 14. Federal Unemployment (FUTA) Tax. TIP. Page 35./ (c) state law, 3309, d

Section 14. Federal Unemployment (FUTA) Tax. Who must pay?

14. Federal Unemployment (FUTA) Tax. Who must pay?
8. Federal Unemployment (FUTA) Tax. Use the following ___ tests to determine whether you must pay FUTA tax.
   (a)   two
   (b)   three
   (c)   four
   (d)   five
   Answer: See section 14. Federal Unemployment (FUTA) Tax. Page 35./ (b) three

14. Federal Unemployment (FUTA) Tax. Who must pay?
9. Federal Unemployment (FUTA) Tax. Use the following ___ tests to determine whether you must pay FUTA tax. Each test applies to a different ___ of employee, and
   (a)   two, type
   (b)   three, category
   (c)   four, class
   (d)   five, classification
   Answer: See section 14. Federal Unemployment (FUTA) Tax. Page 35./ (b) three, category

14. Federal Unemployment (FUTA) Tax. Who must pay?
10. Federal Unemployment (FUTA) Tax. Use the following ___ tests to determine whether you must pay FUTA tax. Each test applies to a different ___ of employee, and each is ___ of the others.
    (a)   two, type, unique
    (b)   three, category, independent
    (c)   four, class, unrelated
    (d)   five, classification, unique
    Answer: See section 14. Federal Unemployment (FUTA) Tax.   Page 35./ (b) three, category, independent

14. Federal Unemployment (FUTA) Tax. Who must pay?
11. Federal Unemployment (FUTA) Tax. Use the following ___ tests to determine whether you must pay FUTA tax. Each test applies to a different ___ of employee, and each is ___ of the others. If a test ___ your situation, you are subject to FUTA tax on the wages you pay to employees in that category during the current calendar year.
    (a)   two, type, unique, relates
    (b)   three, category, independent, describes
    (c)   four, class, unrelated, defines
    (d)   five, classification, unique, is similar to
    Answer: See section 14. Federal Unemployment (FUTA) Tax. Page 35./ (b) three, category, independent, describes

Section 14. Federal Unemployment (FUTA) Tax. Who must pay?

14. Federal Unemployment (FUTA) Tax. Who must pay?
12. Federal Unemployment (FUTA) Tax. Use the following three tests to determine whether you must pay FUTA tax. Each test applies to a different category of employee, and each is independent of the others. If a test describes your situation, you are subject to FUTA tax on the wages you pay to employees in that category during the current calendar year.
    1. **General test**. You are subject to FUTA tax in 2013 on wages you pay employees who are not ___ or household workers if:
    (a) office workers
    (b) industrial workers
    (c) farmworkers
    (d) construction workers
    Answer: See section 14. Federal Unemployment (FUTA) Tax. Page 35./ (c) farmworkers

14. Federal Unemployment (FUTA) Tax. Who must pay?
13. Federal Unemployment (FUTA) Tax. Use the following three tests to determine whether you must pay FUTA tax. Each test applies to a different category of employee, and each is independent of the others. If a test describes your situation, you are subject to FUTA tax on the wages you pay to employees in that category during the current calendar year.
    1. **General test**. You are subject to FUTA tax in 2013 on wages you pay employees who are not ___ or household workers if:
    a. You paid wages of $___ or more in any calendar quarter in 2012 or 2013, or
    (a) office workers, 1,000
    (b) industrial workers, 1, 250
    (c) farmworkers, 1,500
    (d) construction workers, 1,800
    Answer: See section 14. Federal Unemployment (FUTA) Tax. Page 35./ (c) farmworkers, 1,500

14. Federal Unemployment (FUTA) Tax. Who must pay?
14. Federal Unemployment (FUTA) Tax. Use the following three tests to determine whether you must pay FUTA tax. Each test applies to a different category of employee, and each is independent of the others. If a test describes your situation, you are subject to FUTA tax on the wages you pay to employees in that category during the current calendar year.
    1. **General test**. You are subject to FUTA tax in 2013 on wages you pay employees who are not ___ or household workers if:
    a. You paid wages of $___ or more in any calendar quarter in 2012 or 2013, or
    b. You had one or more employees for at least some part of a day in any___ or more different weeks in 2012 or ___ or more different weeks in 2013.
    (a) office workers, 1,000, 8, 8
    (b) industrial workers, 1, 250, 12, 12
    (c) farmworkers, 1,500, 20, 20
    (d) construction workers, 1,800, 26, 26
    Answer: See section 14. Federal Unemployment (FUTA) Tax. Page 35./ (c) farmworkers, 1,500, 20, 20

Section 14. Federal Unemployment (FUTA) Tax. Who must pay?

14. Federal Unemployment (FUTA) Tax. Who must pay?
15. Federal Unemployment (FUTA) Tax. Use the following three tests to determine whether you must pay FUTA tax. Each test applies to a different category of employee, and each is independent of the others. If a test describes your situation, you are subject to FUTA tax on the wages you pay to employees in that category during the current calendar year.
2. **Household employees test**. You are subject to FUTA tax if you paid total cash wages of $___ or more to household employees in any calendar quarter in 2012 or 2013.
(a)   1,000
(b)   1,250
(c)   1,500
(d)   1,850
Answer: See section 14. Federal Unemployment (FUTA) Tax. Page 35./ (a) 1,000

14. Federal Unemployment (FUTA) Tax. Who must pay?
16. Federal Unemployment (FUTA) Tax. Use the following three tests to determine whether you must pay FUTA tax. Each test applies to a different category of employee, and each is independent of the others. If a test describes your situation, you are subject to FUTA tax on the wages you pay to employees in that category during the current calendar year.
2. **Household employees test**. You are subject to FUTA tax if you paid total cash wages of $___
or more to household employees in any calendar quarter in 2012 or 2013. A household employee is an employee who performs work in a private home, local ___, or local fraternity or
sorority chapter.
(a)   1,000, college club
(b)   1,250, supper club
(c)   1,500, charitable club
(d)   1,850, charitable club organization
Answer: See section 14. Federal Unemployment (FUTA) Tax. Page 35./ (a) 1,000, college club

Section 14. Federal Unemployment (FUTA) Tax. Who must pay?

14. Federal Unemployment (FUTA) Tax. Who must pay?
17. Federal Unemployment (FUTA) Tax. Use the following three tests to determine whether you must pay FUTA tax. Each test applies to a different category of employee, and each is independent of the others. If a test describes your situation, you are subject to FUTA tax on the wages you pay to employees in that category during the current calendar year.
3. **Farmworkers test**. You are subject to FUTA tax on the wages you pay to farmworkers if:
a. You paid cash wages of $___ or more during any calendar quarter in 2012 or 2013, or
b. You employed ___ or more farmworkers during at least part of a day (whether or not at the same time) during ___ or more different weeks in 2012 or ___ or more different weeks in 2013.
   (a) 10,000, 10, 10, 20
   (b) 15,000, 10, 20, 10
   (c) 20,000, 10, 20, 20
   (d) 25,000, 10, 26, 20
   Answer: See section 14. Federal Unemployment (FUTA) Tax. Page 35./ (c) 20,000, 10, 20, 20

Section 14. Federal Unemployment (FUTA) Tax. Computing FUTA Tax. Page 35.

14. Federal Unemployment (FUTA) Tax. Computing FUTA tax.
18. Federal Unemployment (FUTA) Tax. For 2013, the tax rate is ___%.
   (a) 3
   (b) 3.5
   (c) 5.2
   (d) 6.0
   Answer: See section 14. Federal Unemployment (FUTA) Tax. Page 35./ (d) 6.0

14. Federal Unemployment (FUTA) Tax. Computing FUTA tax.
19. Federal Unemployment (FUTA) Tax. For 2013, the tax rate is ___%. The tax applies to the first $___ you pay to each employee as wages during the year.
   (a) 3, 5,000
   (b) 3.5, 5,000
   (c) 5.2, 6,500
   (d) 6.0, 7,000
   Answer: See section 14. Federal Unemployment (FUTA) Tax. Page 35./ (d) 6.0, 7,000

Section 14. Federal Unemployment (FUTA) Tax. Computing FUTA Tax. Page 35.

14. Federal Unemployment (FUTA) Tax. Computing FUTA tax.
20. Federal Unemployment (FUTA) Tax. For 2013, the tax rate is ___%. The tax applies to the first $___ you pay to each employee as wages during the year. The $___ is the federal wage base. Your state wage base may differ.
   (a)   3, 5,000, 5,000
   (b)   3.5, 5,000, 5,000
   (c)   5.2, 6,500, 6,500
   (d)   6.0, 7,000, 7,000
   Answer: See section 14. Federal Unemployment (FUTA) Tax. Page 35./ (d) 6.0, 7,000, 7,000

14. Federal Unemployment (FUTA) Tax. Computing FUTA tax.
21. Generally, you can take a credit against your FUTA tax for amounts you paid into ___ unemployment funds.
   (a)   state
   (b)   federal
   (c)   other
   (d)   special
   Answer: See section 14. Federal Unemployment (FUTA) Tax.   Page 35./ (a) state

14. Federal Unemployment (FUTA) Tax. Computing FUTA tax.
22. Generally, you can take a credit against your FUTA tax for amounts you paid into ___ unemployment funds. The credit may be a much as ___% of FUTA taxable wages.
   (a)   state, 5.4
   (b)   federal, 5.5
   (c)   other, 5.6
   (d)   special, 5.7
   Answer: See section 14. Federal Unemployment (FUTA) Tax. Page 35./ (a) state, 5.4

14. Federal Unemployment (FUTA) Tax. Computing FUTA tax.
23. Generally, you can take a credit against your FUTA tax for amounts you paid into ___ unemployment funds. The credit may be a much as ___% of FUTA taxable wages. If you are entitled to the ___% credit, the FUTA tax rate after credit is ___%.
   (a)   state, 5.4, maximum 5.4, 0.6
   (b)   federal, 5.5, maximum 5.5, 0.5
   (c)   other, 5.6, minimum, 5.3, 0.5
   (d)   special, 5.7, minimum, 5.2, 0.5
   Answer: See section 14. Federal Unemployment (FUTA) Tax. Page 35./ (a) state, 5.4, maximum, 5.4, 0.6

Section 14. Federal Unemployment (FUTA) Tax. Computing FUTA Tax. Page 35.

14. Federal Unemployment (FUTA) Tax. Computing FUTA tax.
24.   Generally, you can take a credit against your FUTA tax for amounts you paid into state unemployment funds. The credit may be a much as 5.4 % of FUTA taxable wages. If you are entitled to the 5.4% credit, the FUTA tax rate after credit is 0.6%. You are entitled to the maximum credit if you paid your state unemployment taxes ___, on time, and on all the same wages as are subject to FUTA tax, and as long as
   (a)   in a timely manner
   (b)   in full
   (c)   when due
   (d)   when required
   Answer: See section 14. Federal Unemployment (FUTA) Tax. Page 35./ (b) in full

14. Federal Unemployment (FUTA) Tax. Computing FUTA tax.
25.   Generally, you can take a credit against your FUTA tax for amounts you paid into state unemployment funds. The credit may be a much as 5.4 % of FUTA taxable wages. If you are entitled to the 5.4% credit, the FUTA tax rate after credit is 0.6%. You are entitled to the maximum credit if you paid your state unemployment taxes ___, on time, and on all the same wages as are subject to FUTA tax, and as long as the state is not determined to be a ___.
   (a)   in a timely manner, tax reduction state
   (b)   in full, credit reduction state
   (c)   when due, state not included in this tax program
   (d)   when required, a superimposed tax state
   Answer: See section 14. Federal Unemployment (FUTA) Tax. Page 35./ (b) in full, credit reduction state

14. Federal Unemployment (FUTA) Tax. Computing FUTA tax.
26.   Generally, you can take a credit against your FUTA tax for amounts you paid into state unemployment funds. The credit may be a much as 5.4 % of FUTA taxable wages. If you are entitled to the 5.4% credit, the FUTA tax rate after credit is 0.6%. You are entitled to the maximum credit if you paid your state unemployment taxes ___, on time, and on all the same wages as are subject to FUTA tax, and as long as the state is not determined to be a ___. See the Instructions for Form ___ to determine the credit.
   (a)   in a timely manner, tax reduction state, 940
   (b)   in full, credit reduction state, 940
   (c)   when due, state not included in this tax program, 941
   (d)   when required, a superimposed tax state, 941
   Answer: See section 14. Federal Unemployment (FUTA) Tax. Page 35./ (b) in full, credit reduction state, 940

Section 14. Federal Unemployment (FUTA) Tax. Computing FUTA Tax. Page 35.

14. Federal Unemployment (FUTA) Tax. Computing FUTA tax.
27. In some states, the wages subject to state unemployment tax are the same as wages to ___.
    (a) social security
    (b) Medicare
    (c) FUTA tax
    (d) COBRA
    Answer: See section 14. Federal Unemployment (FUTA) Tax. Page 35./ (c) FUTA tax

14. Federal Unemployment (FUTA) Tax. Computing FUTA tax.
28. In some states, the wages subject to state unemployment tax are the same as wages to ___. However, certain states ___ some types of wages from state unemployment tax, even though they are subject to FUTA tax (for example, wages paid to corporate officers, certain payments of sick pay by unions, and certain fringe benefits).
    (a) social security, include
    (b) Medicare, include
    (c) FUTA tax, exclude
    (d) COBRA, exclude
    Answer: See section 14. Federal Unemployment (FUTA) Tax. Page 35./ (c) FUTA tax, exclude

14. Federal Unemployment (FUTA) Tax. Computing FUTA tax.
29. In some states, the wages subject to state unemployment tax are the same as wages to ___. However, certain states ___ some types of wages from state unemployment tax, even though they are subject to FUTA tax (for example, wages paid to corporate officers, certain payments of sick pay by unions, and certain fringe benefits). In such a case, you may be required to deposit more than ___% FUTA tax on those wages.
    (a) social security, include, 0.5
    (b) Medicare, include, 0.5
    (c) FUTA tax, exclude, 0.6
    (d) COBRA, exclude, 0.6
    Answer: See section 14. Federal Unemployment (FUTA) Tax. Page 35./ (c) FUTA tax, exclude, 0.6

Section 14. Federal Unemployment (FUTA) Tax. Computing FUTA Tax. Page 35.

14. Federal Unemployment (FUTA) Tax. Computing FUTA tax.
30. In some states, the wages subject to state unemployment tax are the same as wages to ___. However, certain states ___ some types of wages from state unemployment tax, even though they are subject to FUTA tax (for example, wages paid to corporate officers, certain payments of sick pay by unions, and certain fringe benefits). In such a case, you may be required to deposit more than ___% FUTA tax on those wages. See the Instructions for Form ___ for more information.
   (a) social security, include, 0.5, 942
   (b) Medicare, include, 0.5, 942
   (c) FUTA tax, exclude, 0.6, 940
   (d) COBRA, exclude, 0.6, 940
   Answer: See section 14. Federal Unemployment (FUTA) Tax. Page 35./ (c) FUTA tax, exclude, 0.6, 940

14. Federal Unemployment (FUTA) Tax. Computing FUTA tax. TIP
31. In years when there are credit reduction states, you must include ___ for credit reduction with your ___ quarter deposit.
   (a) all credits, last
   (b) the credits, second
   (c) liabilities, third
   (d) liabilities owed, fourth
   Answer: See section 14. Federal Unemployment (FUTA) Tax. TIP. Page 35./ (d) liabilities owed, fourth

14. Federal Unemployment (FUTA) Tax. Computing FUTA tax. TIP
32. In years when there are credit reduction states, you must include ___ for credit ___ with your ___ quarter deposit.
   (a) all credits, last
   (b) the credits, second
   (c) liabilities, third
   (d) liabilities owed, reduction, fourth
   Answer: See section 14. Federal Unemployment (FUTA) Tax. TIP. Page 35./ (d) liabilities owed, reduction, fourth

Section 14. Federal Unemployment (FUTA) Tax. Computing FUTA Tax. TIP Page 35.

14. Federal Unemployment (FUTA) Tax. Computing FUTA tax. TIP

33. In years when there are credit reduction states, you must include ___ for credit reduction with your ___ quarter deposit. you may deposit the ___ extra liability throughout the year, but it is not due until the due date in the ___ quarter, and the associated liability should be recorded as being incurred in the ___.
    (a) all credits, last, increased, last, last
    (b) the credits, second, expected, second, second
    (c) liabilities, third, expected, third, third
    (d) liabilities owed, fourth, anticipated, fourth, fourth
    Answer: See section 14. Federal Unemployment (FUTA) Tax. TIP. Page 35./ (d) liabilities owed, fourth, anticipated, fourth, fourth

14. Federal Unemployment (FUTA) Tax. Computing FUTA tax. TIP

34. In years when there are credit reduction states, you must include ___ for credit reduction with your ___ quarter deposit. you may deposit the ___ extra liability throughout the year, but it is not due until the due date in the ___ quarter, and the associated liability should be recorded as being incurred in the ___. See the Instructions for Form 940 for more information.
    (a) all credits, last, increased, last, last
    (b) the credits, second, expected, second, second
    (c) liabilities, third, expected, third, third
    (d) liabilities owed, fourth, anticipated, fourth, fourth
    Answer: See section 14. Federal Unemployment (FUTA) Tax. TIP. Page 35./ (d) liabilities owed, fourth, anticipated, fourth, fourth

Section 14. Federal Unemployment (FUTA) Tax. Successor employer.

14. Federal Unemployment (FUTA) Tax. Computing FUTA tax. Successor employer.

35. If you acquired a business from an employer who was liable for FUTA tax, you may be able to ___ the wages that employer paid to the employees who continue to work for you when
    (a) count
    (b) assume
    (c) compute
    (d) factor in
    Answer: See section 14. Federal Unemployment (FUTA) Tax. Successor employer. Page 35./ (a) count

Section 14. Federal Unemployment (FUTA) Tax.

Federal Unemployment (FUTA) Tax. Successor employer.
36. If you acquired a business from an employer who was liable for FUTA tax, you may be able to ___ the wages that employer paid to the employees who continue to work for you when you figure the $___ FUTA tax wage base. See the Instructions for Form 940.
   (a) count, 7,000
   (b) assume, 7.500
   (c) compute, 8,000
   (d) factor in, 8,500
   Answer: See section 14. Federal Unemployment (FUTA) Tax. Successor employer. Page 35./ (a) count, 7,000

Section 14. Federal Unemployment (FUTA) Tax. Depositing FUTA Tax

14. Federal Unemployment (FUTA) Tax. Depositing FUTA tax.
37. Depositing FUTA tax. For deposit purposes, figure FUTA tax ___.
   (a) semiweekly
   (b) monthly
   (c) quarterly
   (d) annually
   Answer: See section 14. Federal Unemployment (FUTA) Tax. Depositing FUTA tax. Page 35./ (c) quarterly

14. Federal Unemployment (FUTA) Tax. Depositing FUTA tax.
38. Determine your FUTA tax liability by ___ the amount of taxable wages paid during the quarter by ___%.
   (a) adding, 0.6
   (b) multiplying, 0.6
   (c) subtracting, 0.5
   (d) dividing, 0.5
   Answer: See section 14. Federal Unemployment (FUTA) Tax. Depositing FUTA tax. Page 35./ (b) multiplying, 0.6

14. Federal Unemployment (FUTA) Tax. Depositing FUTA tax.
39. Determine your FUTA tax liability by ___ the amount of taxable wages paid during the quarter by ___%. Stop depositing FUTA tax on an employee's wages when he or she reaches $___ in taxable wages for the calendar year.
   (a) adding, 0.6, 6,500
   (b) multiplying, 0.6, 7,000
   (c) subtracting, 0.5, 7,500
   (d) dividing, 0.5, 8,000
   Answer: See section 14. Federal Unemployment (FUTA) Tax. Depositing FUTA tax. Page 35./ (b) multiplying, 0.6, 7,000

© Copyright 2013. All rights reserved. Notice: United States Copyright Laws and International Treaties prohibit unauthorized publication, reproduction, distribution of this Work. Unauthorized use of this copyright in any form, format, publication or document may result in severe civil and criminal penalties. Violations of this copyright are investigated by the United States Department of Justice and carry, upon conviction of fines up to $250,000 and five years confinement. This Work is protected by United States Copyright Laws and International Treaties. Do not Copy, do not reproduce, do not distribute.

Section 14. Federal Unemployment (FUTA) Tax. Depositing FUTA Tax.

14. Federal Unemployment (FUTA) Tax. Depositing FUTA tax.
40. If your FUTA tax liability for any calendar quarter is $___ or less, you do not have to deposit the tax.
    (a) 500
    (b) 1,000
    (c) 1,500
    (d) 1,850
    Answer: See section 14. Federal Unemployment (FUTA) Tax. Depositing FUTA tax. Page 35./ (a) 500

14. Federal Unemployment (FUTA) Tax. Depositing FUTA tax.
41. If your FUTA tax liability for any calendar quarter is $___ or less, you do not have to deposit the tax. Instead, you may carry it forward and add it to the ___ figured in the next quarter to see if you must make a deposit.
    (a) 500, liability
    (b) 1,000, amount
    (c) 1,500, total amount
    (d) 1,850, tax
    Answer: See section 14. Federal Unemployment (FUTA) Tax. Depositing FUTA tax. Page 35./ (a) 500, liability

14. Federal Unemployment (FUTA) Tax. Depositing FUTA tax.
42. If your FUTA tax liability for any calendar quarter is over $___ (including any FUTA tax carried forward from an earlier quarter), you must deposit the tax by electronic funds transfer. See section 11 for more information on electronic funds transfer.
    (a) 500
    (b) 1,000
    (c) 1,500
    (d) 1,850
    Answer: See section 14. Federal Unemployment (FUTA) Tax. Depositing FUTA tax. Page 35./ (a) 500

Section 14. Federal Unemployment (FUTA) Tax. Household employees.

14. Federal Unemployment (FUTA) Tax. Household employees.
43. Household employees. You are not required to deposit FUTA taxes for household employees unless you report their wages of Form ___, ___, or ___. See Publication 926 for more information.
    (a) 940, 941, 942
    (b) 941, 942, 943
    (c) 941, 942, 944
    (d) 941, 943, 944
    Answer: See section 14. Federal Unemployment (FUTA) Tax. Household employees. Page 35./ (d) 941, 943, 944

© Copyright 2013. All rights reserved. Notice: United States Copyright Laws and International Treaties prohibit unauthorized publication, reproduction, distribution of this Work. Unauthorized use of this copyright in any form, format, publication or document may result in severe civil and criminal penalties. Violations of this copyright are investigated by the United States Department of Justice and carry, upon conviction of fines up to $250,000 and five years confinement. This Work is protected by United States Copyright Laws and International Treaties. Do not Copy, do not reproduce, do not distribute.

Section 14. Federal Unemployment (FUTA) Tax. When to deposit.

14. Federal Unemployment (FUTA) Tax. When to deposit.
44. When to deposit. Deposit the FUTA tax by the ___ of the first month that follows the end of the quarter.
    (a)   first day
    (b)   first Monday
    (c)   first Wednesday
    (d)   last day
    Answer: See section 14. Federal Unemployment (FUTA) Tax. When to deposit. Page 35./ (d) last day

14. Federal Unemployment (FUTA) Tax. When to deposit.
45. When to deposit. If the due date for making your deposit falls on a Saturday, Sunday or legal holiday, you may make your deposit on the next ___.
    (a)   Tuesday
    (b)   Wednesday
    (c)   banking day
    (d)   business day
    Answer: See section 14. Federal Unemployment (FUTA) Tax. When to deposit. Pages 35 and 36./ (d) business day

14. Federal Unemployment (FUTA) Tax. When to deposit.
46. If your liability for the fourth quarter (plus any undeposited amount from any earlier quarter is over $___, deposit the entire amount by the due date of Form 940 (____).
    (a)   500, January 31
    (b)   1,000, January 31
    (c)   1,500, March 15
    (d)   2,500, March 15
    Answer: See section 14. Federal Unemployment (FUTA) Tax. When to deposit. Page 36/ (a) 500, January 31

14. Federal Unemployment (FUTA) Tax. When to deposit.
47. If your liability for the fourth quarter (plus any undeposited amount from any earlier quarter is over $___, deposit the entire amount by the due date of Form 940 (____). If it is $___ or less, you can make a deposit, pay the tax with a credit or debit card, or pay the tax with your 2012 Form 940 by January 31. For information on paying your taxes with a credit or debit card, visit the IRS website at *www.irs.gov/e-pay*.
    (a)   500, January 31, 500
    (b)   1,000, January 31, 1,000
    (c)   1,500, March 15, 1,500
    (d)   2,500, March 15, 2,500
    Answer: See section 14. Federal Unemployment (FUTA) Tax. When to deposit. Page 36/ (a) 500, January 31, 500

Section 14. Table 4. When to Deposit FUTA Taxes. Page 36.

14. Federal Unemployment (FUTA) Tax. When to deposit. Table 4
48. The first quarter consisting of January, February, and March ending March 31 requires FUTA tax
    to be deposited by the due date of ___.
    (a) Apr. 30
    (b) July 31
    (c) Oct. 31
    (d) Jan. 31
    Answer: See section 14. Federal Unemployment (FUTA) Tax. When to deposit. Table 4. Page 36/ (a) Apr. 30

14. Federal Unemployment (FUTA) Tax. When to deposit. Table 4
49. The second quarter consisting of April, May, June, and ending June 30 requires FUTA tax
    to be deposited by the due date of ___.
    (a) Apr. 30
    (b) July 31
    (c) Oct. 31
    (d) Jan. 31
    Answer: See section 14. Federal Unemployment (FUTA) Tax. When to deposit. Table 4. Page 36/ (b) July 31

14. Federal Unemployment (FUTA) Tax. When to deposit. Table 4
50. The third quarter consisting of July, August, September, and ending Sept. 30 requires FUTA tax
    to be deposited by the due date of ___.
    (a) Apr. 30
    (b) July 31
    (c) Oct. 31
    (d) Jan. 31
    Answer: See section 14. Federal Unemployment (FUTA) Tax. When to deposit. Table 4. Page 36/ (c) Oct. 31

14. Federal Unemployment (FUTA) Tax. When to deposit. Table 4
51. The fourth quarter consisting of Oct, Nov, Dec, and ending Dec. 31 requires FUTA tax
    to be deposited by the due date of ___.
    (a) Apr. 30
    (b) July 31
    (c) Oct. 31
    (d) Jan. 31
    Answer: See section 14. Federal Unemployment (FUTA) Tax. When to deposit. Table 4. Page 36/(d) Jan. 31

Section 14. Table 4. When to Deposit FUTA Taxes. Reporting FUTA Tax. Page 36.

14. Federal Unemployment (FUTA) Tax. Reporting FUTA tax.
52. Use Form ___ to report FUTA tax.
   (a) 940
   (b) 941
   (c) 942
   (d) 943

   Answer: See section 14. Federal Unemployment (FUTA) Tax. When to deposit. Page 36/
   (a) 940

14. Federal Unemployment (FUTA) Tax. Reporting FUTA tax.
53. Use Form 940 to report FUTA tax. File your 2012 Form 940 by January ___, 2013.
   (a) 2
   (b) 10
   (c) 15
   (d) 31

   Answer: See section 14. Federal Unemployment (FUTA) Tax. When to deposit. Page 36/
   (d) 31

14. Federal Unemployment (FUTA) Tax. Reporting FUTA tax.
54. Use Form 940 to report FUTA tax. File your 2012 Form 940 by January 31, 2013. However, if you deposited all FUTA tax when due, you may file on or before ___, 2013.
   (a) January 31
   (b) February 1,
   (c) February 11
   (d) February 15

   Answer: See section 14. Federal Unemployment (FUTA) Tax. When to deposit. Page 36/
   (c) February 11

14. Federal Unemployment (FUTA) Tax. Reporting FUTA tax.
55. Use Form 940 to report FUTA tax. File your 2012 Form 940 by January 31, 2013. However, if you deposited all FUTA tax when due, you may file on or before ___, 2013. If you do not receive Form 940, you can get a form by calling 1-800-TAX-FORM (1-800-___-___).
   (a) January 31, 827, 3676
   (b) February 1, 829, 3677
   (c) February 11, 829, 3676
   (d) February 15, 830, 3678

   Answer: See section 14. Federal Unemployment (FUTA) Tax. When to deposit. Page 36/
   (c) February 11, 929, 3676

14. Federal Unemployment (FUTA) Tax.
Reporting FUTA Tax. Household employees. Page 36.

14. Federal Unemployment (FUTA) Tax. Household employees.
56. **Household employees**. If you did not report employment taxes for household employees on forms 941, 943, or 944, report FUTA tax for these employees on Schedule ___ (Form 1040).
 (a) A
 (b) D
 (c) F
 (d) H
 Answer: See section 14. Federal Unemployment (FUTA) Tax. When to deposit. Household employees. Page 36/ (d) H

14. Federal Unemployment (FUTA) Tax. Household employees.
57. **Household employees**. If you did not report employment taxes for household employees on forms 941, 943, or 944, report FUTA tax for these employees on Schedule ___ (Form 1040). See Publication ___ for more information.
 (a) A, 923
 (b) D, 924
 (c) F, 925
 (d) H, 926
 Answer: See section 14. Federal Unemployment (FUTA) Tax. When to deposit. Household employees. Page 36/ (d) H, 926

14. Federal Unemployment (FUTA) Tax. Household employees.
58. **Household employees**. If you did not report employment taxes for household employees on forms 941, 943, or 944, report FUTA tax for these employees on Schedule ___ (Form 1040). See Publication ___ for more information. You must have an ___ to file Schedule ___ (Form 1040)
 (a) A, 923, SSN, A
 (b) D, 924, SSN, D
 (c) F, 925, EIN, F
 (d) H, 926, EIN, H
 Answer: See section 14. Federal Unemployment (FUTA) Tax. When to deposit. Household employees. Page 36/ (d) H, 926, EIN, H

Section 14. Federal Unemployment (FUTA) Tax. Reporting FUTA Tax. Electronic filing by reporting agents. Page 36.

14. Federal Unemployment (FUTA) Tax. Electronic filing by reporting agents.

59. **Electronic filing by reporting agents**. Reporting agents filing Forms 940 for groups of taxpayers can file them electronically. See the Reporting Agent discussion in section___ of Publication 15-A
    (a) 6
    (b) 7
    (c) 8
    (d) 9

    Answer: See section 14. Federal Unemployment (FUTA) Tax. When to deposit. Electronic filing by reporting agents. Page 36/ (b) 7

Instructor's Manual for Tax Test 15E-S15-1
Section 15.
Special Rules For Various Types Of Services And Payments

General Description. Section 15.

Tax Test 15E-S15. Commencing at Page 37 of IRS Publication 15, Employers Tax Guide for the current year the section continuing through and includes all of page 41. Tax Test 15E-S15 Page 37, addresses the following: Treatment Under Employment Taxes. Section 15. Special Rules for Various Types of Services and Payments; Alien nonresident; Alien resident; Cafeteria Plan benefits under section 125; Deceased worker; Dependent care assistance program; Disabled worker's wages; Employee business expense reimbursement; Fishing and related activities; Foreign governments and international organizations; Foreign service by U.S. citizens.

Key Words. Section 15
Special Rules for Various Types of Services and Payments

Tax Test 15E-S15. The title of Section 15. Special Rules for Various Types of Services and Payments is the initial key word, sentence, or phrase. In Circular E, Employer's Tax Guide the key words are set in bold print. The words in bold print identifying the subpart of the section will generally appear in the subject index at the conclusion of a text. The Title of the Section will generally appear as a part of the Contents at the beginning of each textbook. From the bold print identifying the parts and subparts of IRS Publication 15, Employers Tax Guide for the current year. Thus, additional important information is obtained from the primary, secondary and minor headings of the basic text. From **page 37**, as follows below:

Special Classes of Employment and Special Types of Payments. Treatment Under Employment Taxes. Income Tax Withholding. Social Security and Medicare (including Additional Medicare Tax when wages are paid in excess of $200,000). FUTA. Aliens, nonresident: 1. service performed in the U.S. 2. Service performed outside U.S. Cafeteria plan benefits under section 125. Deceased worker: 1. Wages paid to beneficiary or estate in same calendar year as worker's death. See the instructions for Forms W-2 and W-3 for details. 2. Wages paid to beneficiary or estate after calendar year of worker's death. Dependent care assistance programs. Disabled worker's wages paid after year in which worker became entitled to disability insurance benefits under the Social Security Act. Employee business expense reimbursement: 1. Accountable plan. 2. Nonaccountable plan. Family employees. 1. Child employed by parent for partnership in which each partner is a parent of the child. 2. Parent employed by child. 3. Spouse employed by spouse. Fishing and related activity. Foreign governments and international organizations.

Key Words. Section 15
Special Rules for Various Types of Services and Payments
Key Word page numbers provided for this section reference to IRS Publication 15 only.

Examine Section 15. Special Rules for Various Types of Services and Payments. Page 37. Note that the standard sequence of Section 15 is alphabetical throughout the section. The special classes are identified in the left column whereas the Treatment Under Employment Taxes basic categories of Income Tax Withholding. Social Security and Medicare (including Additional Medicare Tax when wages are paid in excess of $200,000). and FUTA are carried in the three right columns.

The purpose of this section is to identify the tax to **Withhold**. to **Exempt**, and/or **Taxable,** or treated the same as **U.S. Citizen.** Each page of Section 15 follows a similar structure. Section 15 is very important but often overlooked or ignored because it is assumed that it is easily read and mastered. This is about knowing where to locate correct important information quickly for study, research and testing.

DU VALL'S TEST'S™
Instructor's Manual Study Guide Series United States Tax Code
IRS Publication 15 Circular E, Employer's Tax Guide Tax Year 2013
Tax Test 15E-S15-1 [Multiple-Choice Questions With Answers]

Section 15. Special Rules for Various Types of Services and Payments.
15. Special Rules for Various Types of Services and Payments. Page 37.
Section references are to the Internal Revenue Code unless otherwise noted.

15. Aliens, nonresident:
1. Under Section 15. Special Rules for Various Types of Services and Payments **Nonresident Aliens** and Foreign Entities, and IRS Publication ___ and Publication ___, U.S. Tax Guide for Aliens.
   (a) 489, 440
   (b) 515, 519
   (c) 535, 545
   (d) 550, 551
   Answer: See Section 15. Special Rules for Various Types of Services and Payments, Special Classes of Employment and Special Types of Payments, Aliens, nonresident, page 37/ (b) 515, 519

15. Aliens, resident:
2. Under Section 15. Special Rules for Various Types of Services and Payments, Special Classes of Employment and Special Types of Payments for **Aliens, resident:**
   1. Service performed in the U.S. the withholding of Income Tax and Federal Unemployment tax is the same as U. S. citizen while Social Security and Medicare taxes are the same as a U.S. citizen but Exempt if any part of service as crew member of ___ or ___ is performed outside the U.S.
   (a) ship, airplane
   (b) vessel, airplane
   (c) foreign vessel, aircraft
   (d) foreign flag vessel, commercial carrier
   Answer: See Section 15. Special Rules for Various Types of Services and Payments, Special Classes of Employment and Special Types of Payments, Aliens, resident, 1. Service performed in the U.S. Page 37/ (c) foreign vessel, aircraft

Section 15. Special Rules for Various Types of Services and Payments.

15. Aliens, resident:
3. Under Section 15. Special Rules for Various Types of Services and Payments, Special Classes of Employment and Special Types of Payments for **Aliens, resident:**
2. <u>Service performed outside U.S.</u> by a nonresident alien the income tax withhold requirement is ___.
   (a) Withhold
   (b) Not withheld
   (c) Under special circumstances may be withheld
   (d) Cannot be withheld
   Answer: See Section 15. Special Rules for Various Types of Services and Payments, Treatment Under Employment Taxes. Page 37/ (a) Withhold

15. Aliens, resident:
4. Under Section 15. Special Rules for Various Types of Services and Payments, Treatment Under Employment Taxes, for resident aliens <u>services performed outside</u> the U. S. Social Security and Medicare tax is___ if (1) working for an American employer or
   (a) Not taxable
   (b) Not and cannot be withheld
   (c) Shall be withheld
   (d) Taxable
   Answer: See Section 15. Special Rules for various Types of Services and Payments. (1) Social Security and Medicare. Page 37/ (d) Taxable

15. Aliens, resident:
5. Under Section 15. Special Rules for Various Types of Services and Payments, Treatment Under Employment Taxes, for resident aliens <u>services performed outside</u> the U. S. Social Security and Medicare tax is___ if (1) working for an American employer or (2) an American employer by agreement ___ U.S. citizens and residents employed by its foreign affiliates.
   (a) Not taxable, does not cover
   (b) Not and cannot be withheld, is required to cover
   (c) Shall be withheld, agrees
   (d) Taxable, covers
   Answer: See Section 15. Special Rules for various Types of Services and Payments. (1) Social Security and Medicare. Page 37/ (d) Taxable, covers

Section 15. Special Rules for Various Types of Services and Payments.

15. Aliens, resident:
6. Section 15. The statement "Exempt unless on or in connections with an American vessel or aircraft and either <u>performed under contract</u> made in U. S., or alien is employed on such vessel or aircraft when it touches U. S. port." pertains to ___.
   - (a) corporations
   - (b) Medicare
   - (c) FUTA
   - (d) Income Tax Withholding

   Answer: See Section 15. Special Rules for Various Types of Services and Payments, Treatment Under Employment Taxes, Aliens, resident, 2. Service performed outside U. S. Page 37/ (c) FUTA

15. Cafeteria plan benefits under section 125.
7. Section 15. The statement. If employee chooses cash, subject to all employment taxes. If employee chooses another benefit, the treatment is the same as if the benefit was provided outside the plan. See Publication 15-B for more information." Discusses ___.
   - (a) Retirement plans under 401K
   - (b) the Archer plan benefits under section 122
   - (c) the Cafeteria plan benefits under section 125
   - (d) Workers' Compensation plans under Chapter 440

   Answer: See Section 15. Special Rules for Various Types of Services and Payments, Special Classes of Employment and Special Types of Payments, Cafeteria plan benefits under section 125, page 37/ the Cafeteria plan benefits under section 125

15. Deceased worker:
8. The wages paid to a beneficiary or estate of a deceased worker in the same calendar year as the worker's death under Income Tax Withholding rules are ___. See instructions for Forms W-2 and W-3 for details.
   - (a) Taxable
   - (b) Cannot be taxed
   - (c) Shall be taxed
   - (d) Exempt

   Answer: See Section 15. Special Rules for Various Types of Services and Payments, 1. Deceased Worker, Income Tax Withholding. Page 37/(d) Exempt

Section 15. Special Rules for Various Types of Services and Payments.

15. Deceased worker:
9. The wages paid to a beneficiary or estate of a deceased worker in the same calendar year as the worker's death under Treatment Under Employment Taxes, Social Security and Medicare taxes are ___.
   (a) Not taxable
   (b) Nontaxable
   (c) Taxable
   (d) Exempt
   Answer: See Section 15. Special Rules for Various Types of Services and Payments, Special Classes of Employment and Special Types of Payments, Treatment Under Employment Taxes, Social Security and Medicare. Page 37/ (c) Taxable

15. Deceased worker:
10. The wages paid to a beneficiary or estate of a deceased worker in the same calendar year as the worker's death, Special Classes of Employment and Special Types of Payments, Treatment Under Employment Taxes, Federal Unemployment are ___.
    (a) Exempt
    (b) Taxable
    (c) Not taxable
    (d) Nontaxable
    Answer: See Section 15. Special Rules for Various Types of Services and Payments, Special Classes of Employment and Special Types of Payments, Treatment Under Unemployment Taxes, Federal Unemployment. Page 37/ (b) Taxable

15. Deceased worker:
11. The wages paid to a beneficiary or estate of a deceased worker after the calendar year of the worker's death, Special Classes of Employment and Special Types of Payments, Treatment Under Employment Taxes, Income Tax Withholding shall be ___.
    (a) Considered taxable
    (b) Exempt
    (c) Non-exempt
    (d) Taxable
    Answer: See Section 15. Special Rules for Various Types of Services and Payments, Special Classes of Employment and Special Types of Payments, Treatment Under Employment Taxes, 2. Wages paid to beneficiary or estate after calendar year of worker's death. Page 37/ (b) Exempt

Section 15. Special Rules for Various Types of Services and Payments.

15. Deceased worker:
12. The wages paid to a beneficiary or estate of a deceased worker after the calendar year of the worker's death, Special Classes of Employment and Special Types of Payments, Treatment Under Employment Taxes, Social Security and Medicare tax withholding shall be ___.
    (a) Considered taxable
    (b) Exempt
    (c) Non-exempt
    (d) Taxable
    Answer: See Section 15. Special Rules for Various Types of Services and Payments, Special Classes of Employment and Special Types of Payments, Treatment Under Employment Taxes, Deceased Worker: 2. Wages paid to beneficiary or estate after calendar year of worker's death, Social Security and Medicare. Page 37/ (b) Exempt

15. Deceased worker:
13. The wages paid to a beneficiary or estate of a deceased worker after the calendar year of the worker's death, Special Classes of Employment and Special Types of Payments, Treatment Under Employment Taxes, Federal Unemployment Tax (FUTA) withholding shall be ___.
    (a) Considered taxable
    (b) Exempt
    (c) Non-exempt
    (d) Taxable
    Answer: See Section 15. Special Rules for Various Types of Services and Payments, Special Classes of Employment and Special Types of Payments, Treatment Under Employment Taxes, Federal Unemployment. Page 37/ (b) Exempt

15. Dependent care assistance program.
14. Dependent care assistant programs are exempt to the extent it is reasonable to believe amounts are excludable from gross income under section ___.
    (a) 125
    (b) 126
    (c) 128
    (d) 129
    Answer: See Section 15. Special Rules for Various Types of Services and Payments, Dependent care assistance programs. Page 37/ (d) 129

Section 15. Special Rules for Various Types of Services and Payments.

15. Disabled worker's wages

15. According to Section 15. Special Rules for Various Types of Services and Payments, Special Classes of Employment and Special Types of Payments, Treatment Under Employment Taxes, Income Tax Withholding of a disabled worker's wages paid after year in which worker became entitled to disability insurance benefits under the Social Security Act, ___ Income tax.
    (a) Exempt
    (b) Withhold
    (c) Do not withhold
    (d) Shall not withhold
    Answer: See Section 15. Special Rules for Various Types of Services and Payments, Special Classes of Employment and Special Types of Payments, Treatment Under Employment Taxes, Disabled worker's wages. Page 37/ (b) Withhold

15. Disabled worker's wages

16. According to Section 15. Special Rules for Various Types of Services and Payments, Special Classes of Employment and Special Types of Payments, Treatment Under Employment Taxes, Social Security and Medicare taxes are ___, if worker did not perform any service during the period for which payment is made.
    (a) Taxable
    (b) Nontaxable
    (c) Exempt
    (d) Not exempt
    Answer: See Section 15. Special Rules for Various Types of Services and Payments, Special Classes of Employment and Special Types of Payments, Treatments Under Employment Taxes, Social Security and Medicare, Disabled worker's wages. Page 37/ (c) Exempt

15. Disabled worker's wages

17. According to Section 15. Special Rules for Various Types of Services and Payments, a disabled worker's wages paid after year in which worker became entitled to disability benefits under FUTA are ___.
    (a) Taxable
    (b) Exempt
    (c) Nontaxable
    (d) Not exempt
    Answer: See Section 15. Special Rules for Various Services and Payments, Special Classes of Employment and Special Types of Payments, Treatment Under Employment Taxes, Disabled worker's wages. Page 37/ (a) Taxable

Section 15. Special Rules for Various Types of Services and Payments.

15. Employee business expense reimbursement.
18. According to Section 15. Special Rules for Various Types of Services and Payments, there are ___ plans available to obtain employee business expense reimbursement.
    (a) 2
    (b) 3
    (c) 4
    (d) 5
    Answer: See Section 15. Special Rules for Various Types of Services and Payments, Special Classes of Employment and Special Types of Payments, Employee business expense reimbursement. Page 37/ (a) 2

15. Employee business expense reimbursement.
19. According to Section 15. Special Rules for Various Types of Services and Payments, the employee business expense reimbursement plans are the: ___
    (a) Nonaccountable plan, Accountable plan
    (b) Accountable plan, Nonaccountable plan
    (c) Accounting plan, Non-accounting plan. Audit plan
    (d) Accounting plan, Non-accounting plan, Audit plan, Expense account plan
    Answer: See Section 15. Special Rules for Various Types of Services and Payments, Special Classes of Employment and Special Types of Payments, Employee business expense reimbursement. Page 37/ (b) Accountable plan, Nonaccountable plan

15. Employee business expense reimbursement.
20. According to Section 15. Special Rules for Various Types of Services and Payments an accountable plan has ___ parts.
    (a) 2
    (b) 3
    (c) 4
    (d) 5
    Answer: See Section 15. Special Rules for Various Types of Services and Payments. Special Classes of Employment and Special Types of Payments, Employee business reimbursement. Page 37/ (a) 2. (a. Amounts not exceeding specified government rate for per diem or standard mileage, and b. Amounts in excess of specified government rate for per diem or standard mileage).

Section 15. Special Rules for Various Types of Services and Payments.

15. Employee business expense reimbursement.
21. Employee business expense reimbursement under 1. Accountability plan for amounts not exceeding specified government rate for per diem or standard mileage, the Income Tax Withholding is ___.
    (a) Exempt
    (b) Taxable
    (c) Not exempt
    (d) Nontaxable
    Answer: See Section 15. Special Rules for Various Types of Services and Payments, Special Classes of Employment and Special Types of Payments, Treatment Under Employment Taxes, Employee business expense reimbursement, 1a. Accountable plan. Page 37/ Exempt

15. Employee business expense reimbursement.
22. Employee business expense reimbursement under 1. Accountable plan. a. Amounts not exceeding specified government rate for per diem or standard mileage, the Social Security and Medicare tax is ___.
    (a) Exempt
    (b) Taxable
    (c) Not exempt
    (d) Nontaxable
    Answer: See Section 15. Special Rules for Various Types of Services and Payments, Special Classes of Employment and Special Types of Payments, Treatment Under Employment Taxes, Employee business expense reimbursement, 1a. Accountable plan. Page 37/Exempt

15. Employee business expense reimbursement.
23. Employee business expense reimbursement under 1. Accountable plan. a. Amounts not exceeding specified government rate for per diem or standard mileage, the Federal Unemployment Tax (FUTA) is ___.
    (a) Nontaxable
    (b) Not exempt
    (c) Taxable
    (d) Exempt
    Answer: See Section 15. Special Rules for Various Types of Services and Payments, Special Classes of Employment and Special Types of Payments, Treatment Under Employment Taxes, Employee business expense reimbursement, 1a. Accountability plan. Page 37/ Exempt

Section 15. Special Rules for Various Types of Services and Payments.

15. Employee business expense reimbursement.
24. Employee business expense reimbursement 1. b. Amounts in excess of specified government rate for per diem or standard mileage, for Income Tax Withholding you ___.
    (a) Nontaxable
    (b) Withhold
    (c) Exempt
    (d) Taxable

    Answer: See Section 15. Special Rules for Various Types of Services and Payments, Special Classes of Employment and Special Types of Payments, Treatment Under Employment Taxes, Employee business expense reimbursement. 1b. Amounts in excess of specified government rate for per diem or standard mileage. Page 37/ (b) Withhold

15. Employee business expense reimbursement.
25. Employee business expense reimbursement 1b. Amounts is excess of specified government rate for per diem or standard mileage, Social Security and Medicare is ___.
    (a) Exempt
    (b) Nontaxable
    (c) Taxable
    (d) Shall not be taxed

    Answer: See Section 15. Special Rules for Various Types of Services and Payments, Special Classes of Employment and Special Types of Payments, Treatment Under Employment Taxes, Employee business expense reimbursement, b. Amounts in excess of specified government rate for per diem or standard mileage. Page 37/ (c) Taxable

15. Employee business expense reimbursement.
26. Employee business expense reimbursement 1.b. Amounts in excess of specified government rate for per diem or standard mileage, FUTA is ___.
    (a) Non-taxable
    (b) Exempt
    (c) Not to be taxed
    (d) Taxable

    Answer: See Section 15. Special Rules for Various Types of Services and Payments, Special Classes of Employment and Special Types of Payments, Treatment Under Employment Terms, Employee business expense reimbursement, 1. Accountable plan. 1b. Amounts in excess of specified government rate for per diem or standard mileage. Page 37/ (d) Taxable

Section 15. Special Rules for Various Types of Services and Payments.

15. Employee business expense reimbursement.
27.   Employee business expense reimbursement 2. Nonaccountable plan. Special Classes of Employment and Special Types of Payments, Treatment Under Employment Taxes, for Income Tax Withholding you ___.
   (a)   Exempt
   (b)   Do not withhold
   (c)   Withhold
   (d)   Must justify your decision
   Answer: See Section 15. Special Rules for Various Types of Services and Payments, Special Classes of Employment and Special Types of Payments, Treatment Under Employment Taxes, 2. Nonaccountable plan. See Section 5 for details. Page 37/ (c) Withhold

15. Employee business expense reimbursement.
28.   Employee business expense reimbursement 2. Nonaccountable plan. Special Classes of Employment and Special Types of Payments, Treatment Under Employment Taxes, Social Security and Medicare taxes are ___.
   (a)   Exempt
   (b)   Nontaxable
   (c)   Not to be taxed
   (d)   Taxable
   Answer: See Section 15. Special Rules for Various Types of Services and Payments, Special Classes of Employment and Special Types of Payments, Treatment Under Employment Taxes, 2. Nonaccountable plan. See section 5 for details. Page 37/ (d) Taxable

15. Employee business expense reimbursement.
29.   Employee business expense reimbursement 2. Nonaccountable plan. Special Classes of Employment and Special Types of Payments, Treatment Under Employment Taxes, Federal Unemployment (FUTA) is ___.
   (a)   Taxable
   (b)   Nontaxable
   (c)   Shall not be taxed
   (d)   Shall be taxed
   Answer: See Section 15. Special Rules for Various Types of Services and Payments, Special Classes of Employment and Special Types of Payments, Treatment Under Employment Taxes, Federal Unemployment Tax. Page 37/ (a) Taxable

Section 15. Special Rules for Various Types of Services and Payments.

15. Employee business expense reimbursement.
30. **Family employees**: 1. Child employed by parent (or partnership in which each partner is a parent of the child). Income Tax Withholding is ___.
    (a) Not withheld
    (b) Withhold
    (c) Exempt
    (d) Not exempt
    Answer: See Section 15. Special Rules for Various Types of Services and Payments, Special Classes of Employment and Special Types of Payments, Treatment Under Employment Taxes, Family employees, 1. Child employed by parent. Page 37/ (b) Withhold

15. Employee business expense reimbursement.
31. **Family employees**: 1. Child employed by parent (or partnership in which each partner is a parent of the child). Social Security and Medicare taxes are exempt until age ___; age ___ for domestic service.
    (a) 15, 18
    (b) 16, 18
    (c) 17, 20
    (d) 18, 21
    Answer: See Section 15. Special Rules for Various Types of Services and Payments, Special Classes of Employment and Special Types of Payments, Treatment Under Employment Taxes, Family Employees, Social Security and Medicare. Page 37/(d) 18, 21

15. Employee business expense reimbursement.
32. **Family Employees**: 1. Child employed by parent (or partnership in which each partner is a parent of the child). Federal Unemployment Tax (FUTA) is exempt until age of ___.
    (a) 15
    (b) 17
    (c) 18
    (d) 21
    Answer: See Section 15. Special Rules for Various Types of Services and Payments, Special Classes of Employment and Types of Payments, Treatment Under Employment Taxes, Family employees, Federal Unemployment Tax (FUTA). Page 37/ (d) 21

Section 15. Special Rules for Various Types of Services and Payments.

15. Employee business expense reimbursement.

33. **Family employees**: 2. Parent employed by child. Section 15. Special Rules for Various Types of Services and Payments. Special Classes of Employment and Special Types of Payments, Treatment Under Employment Taxes, Income Tax Withholding is required to ___.
    - (a) Taxed
    - (b) Withhold
    - (c) Nontaxable
    - (d) Exempt

    Answer: See Section 15. Special Rules for Various Types of Services and Payments, Special Classes of Employment and Special Types of Payments, Treatment Under Employment Taxes, Family employees, 2. Parent employed by child. Page 37/ (b) Withhold

15. Employee business expense reimbursement.

34. **Family employees**: 2. Parent employed by child. Section 15. Special Rules for Various Types of Services and Payments. Special Classes of Employment and Special Types of Payments, Treatment Under Employment Taxes, Social Security and Medicare are taxable if in the ___ of the son's or daughter's business.
    - (a) activities
    - (b) operations
    - (c) course
    - (d) business

    Answer: See Section 15. Special Rules for Various Types of Services and Payments, Special Classes of Employment and Special Types of Payments, Treatments Under Employment Taxes, Family employees, 2. Parent employed by child, Social Security. Page 37/ (c) course

15. Employee business expense reimbursement.

35. Family employees: 2. Parent employed by child. Section 15. Special Rules for Various Types of Services and Payments, Special Classes of Employment and Special Types of Payments, Treatment Under Employment Taxes, Social Security and Medicare are taxable if in the ___ of the son's or daughter's business. For domestic services, see Section ___.
    - (a) activities, 1
    - (b) operations, 2
    - (c) course, 3
    - (d) business, 4

    Answer: See Section 15. Special Rules for Various Types of Services and Payments, Special Types of Services and Payments, Treatment Under Employment Taxes, Family employees, 2. Parent employed by child, Social Security and Medicare. Page 37/ (c) course, 3

Section 15. Special Rules for Various Types of Services and Payments.

15. Employee business expense reimbursement.

36. **Family employees**: 2. Parent employed by child. Section 15. Special Rules for Various Types of Services and Payments, Special Classes of Employment and Special Types of Payments, Treatment Under Employment Taxes, Federal Unemployment Tax (FUTA) is ___.

    (a) Taxable
    (b) Exempt
    (c) Nonexempt
    (d) Nontaxable

    Answer: See Section 15. Special Rules for Various Types of Services and Payments, Special Classes of Employment and Special Types of Payments, Treatment Under Employment Taxes, Family employees, 2. Parent employed by child, Federal Unemployment Tax. Page 37/ (b) Exempt

15. Employee business expense reimbursement.

37. Family employees: 3. Spouse employed by spouse. Employer shall ___ according to Circular E, Treatment Under Employment Taxes, Income Tax Withholding.

    (a) Be withheld
    (b) Withhold
    (c) Not be withheld
    (d) Be exempt

    Answer: See Section 15. Special Rules for Various Types of Services and Payments, Special Classes of Employment and Special Types of Payments, Treatment Under Employment Taxes, Family employees, 3. Spouse employed by spouse. Page 37/ (b) Withhold

15. Employee business expense reimbursement.

38. Family employees: 3. Spouse employed by spouse. Social Security and Medicare are taxable in the ___ of the spouse's business.

    (a) course
    (b) operations
    (c) business
    (d) activities

    Answer: See Section 15. Special Rules for Various Types of Services and Payments, Special Classes of Employment and Special Types of Payments, Treatment Under Employment Taxes, 3. Spouse employed by spouse, Social Security and Medicare. Page 37/(a) course

Section 15. Special Rules for Various Types of Services and Payments.

15. Employee business expense reimbursement.

39. Family employees: 3. Spouse employed by spouse. Federal Unemployment Tax (FUTA) is ___.
    (a) Exempt
    (b) Withheld
    (c) To be withheld
    (d) Shall be exempt

    Answer: See Section 15. Special Rules for Various Types of Services and Payments, Special Classes of Employment and Special Types of Payments, Treatment Under Employment Taxes, 3. Spouse employed by spouse, Federal Unemployment Tax (FUTA). See section 3 for more information. Page 37/ (a) Exempt

15. Fishing and related activities.

40. For IRS information related to Fishing and related activities. See Publication ___, Tax Guide for Small Businesses.
    (a) 324
    (b) 334
    (c) 434
    (d) 534

    Answer: See Section 15. Special Rules for Various Types of Services and Payments, Special Classes of Employment and Special Types of Payments, Treatment Under Employment Taxes, Fishing and related activities. Page 37/ (b) 334

15. Foreign governments and international organizations.

41. As provided by Section 15. Special Rules for Various Types of Services and Payments, Special Classes of Employment and Special Types of Payments. Foreign governments and international organizations are exempt from Income Tax Withholding, Social Security and ___.
    (a) Worker's Compensation
    (b) FUTA
    (c) Federal Unemployment
    (d) FICA

    Answer: See Section 15. Special Rules for Various Services and Payments, Special Classes of Employment and Special Types of Payments, Treatment Under Unemployment Taxes, Foreign governments and international organizations. Page 37/ (b) FUTA

Section 15. Special Rules for Various Types of Services and Payments.

15. Foreign service by U.S. citizens:
42.   Section 15. Special Rules for Various Types of Services and Payments, Special Classes of Employment and Special Types of Payments, Treatment Under Employment Taxes, Foreign service by U.S. citizens: 1. As U.S. government employees. Section 15. states in Treatment Under Employment Taxes - The tax rules of the IRS require that the federal government ___ income tax.
   (a)   Withheld
   (b)   Withhold
   (c)   are Exempt
   (d)   are collected
Answer: See Section 15. Special Rules for Various Types of Services and Payments, Special Classes of Employment and Special Types of Payments, Treatment Under Employment Taxes. Page 38/ (b) Withhold

15. Foreign service by U.S. citizens:
43.   Section 15. Special Rules for Various Types of Services and Payments, Special Classes of Employment and Special Types of Payments, Treatment Under Employment Taxes, Foreign service by U.S. citizens the Social Security and Medicare taxes 1. As U.S. government employees, are ___.
   (a)   Withheld
   (b)   Exempt
   (c)   Same as within U.S.
   (d)   The same as within the U.S.
Answer: See Section 15. Special Rules for Various Types of Services and Payments, Special Classes of Employment and Special Types of Payments, Treatment Under Employment Taxes. Page 38/ (c) Same as within U.S.

Section 15. Special Rules for Various Types of Services and Payments. Page 38.

15. Foreign service by U.S. citizens:
44.   Section 15. Special Rules for Various Types of Services and Payments, Special Classes of Employment and Special Types of Payments, Treatment Under Employment Taxes, Foreign service by United States citizens employed by the United States government under Foreign service by U.S. citizens: 1. As U.S. government employees, Federal Unemployment Tax (FUTA) is ___.
   (a)   Withheld
   (b)   Exempt
   (c)   Taxable
   (d)   Nontaxable
Answer: See Section 15. Special Rules for Various Types of Services and Payments, Special Classes of Employment and Special Types of Payments, Treatment Under Employment Taxes, Foreign service by U.S. citizens: 1. As U.S. government employees, Federal Unemployment. Page 38/ (b) Exempt

© Copyright 2013. All rights reserved. Notice: United States Copyright Laws and International Treaties prohibit unauthorized publication, reproduction, distribution of this Work. Unauthorized use of this copyright in any form, format, publication or document may result in severe civil and criminal penalties. Violations of this copyright are investigated by the United States Department of Justice and carry, upon conviction of fines up to $250,000 and five years confinement. This Work is protected by United States Copyright Laws and International Treaties. Do not Copy, do not reproduce, do not distribute.

Section 15. Special Rules for Various Types of Services and Payments.

15. Foreign service by U.S. citizens:

45. Section 15. Special Rules for Various Types of Services and Payments, Special Classes of Employment and Special Types of Payments, Treatment Under Employment Taxes. Foreign service by U.S. citizens: 2. For foreign affiliates of American employer's and other private employers. IRS rules for Income Tax Withholding. Exempt if at the time of payment (1) it is reasonable to believe employee is entitled to exclusion from income under section ___ or
 (a) 946
 (b) 731
 (c) 911
 (d) 1099

Answer: See Section 15. Special Rules for Various Types of Services and Payments, Special Classes of Employment and Special Types of Payments, Treatment Under Employment Taxes. Foreign Service by U.S. citizens: 2. For foreign affiliates of American Employers and other private employers. Income Tax Withholding. Page 38/ (c) 911

DU VALL'S TEST'S™
Instructor's Manual Study Guide Series United States Tax Code
IRS Publication 15 Circular E, Employer's Tax Guide Tax Year 2013
Tax Test 15E-S15-2 [Multiple-Choice Questions With Answers]

Section 15. Special Rules for Various Types of Services and Payments.

15. Foreign service by U.S. citizens:
1. Section 15. Special Rules for Various Types of Services and Payments, Special Classes of Employment and Special Types of Payments, Treatment Under Employment Taxes. Foreign service by U.S. citizens: 2. For foreign affiliates of American employer's and other private employers. IRS rules for Income Tax Withholding. Exempt if at the time of payment (1) it is reasonable to believe employee is entitled to exclusion from income under section ___ or (2) the employer is required by law of the foreign country to ___ on such payment.
   (a)   946, withhold tax
   (b)   731, withhold extra tax
   (c)   911, withhold income tax
   (d)   1099, withhold all additional taxes
   Answer: See Section 15. Special Rules for Various Types of Services and Payments, Special Classes of Employment and Special Types of Payments, Treatment Under Employment Taxes. Foreign Service by U.S. citizens: 2. For foreign affiliates of American Employers and other private employers. Income Tax Withholding. Page 38/ (c) 911, withhold income tax

15. Foreign service by U.S. citizens:
2. Section 15. Special Rules for Various Types of Services and Payments, Special Classes of Employment and Special Types of Payments, Treatment Under Employment Taxes. Social Security and Medicare: Exempt unless (1) an American employer by agreement ____U.S. citizens employed by its foreign affiliates.
   (a)   requires
   (b)   mandates
   (c)   a mandatory agreement
   (d)   covers
   Answer: See Section 15. Special Rules for Various Types of Services and Payments, Special Classes of Employment and Special Types of Payments, Treatment Under Employment Taxes, Foreign service by U.S. citizen. 2. For foreign affiliates of American employers and other private employers. Social Security and Medicare. Page 38/(d) covers

Section 15. Special Rules for Various Types of Services and Payments.

15. Foreign service by U.S. citizens:

3. Section 15. Special Rules for Various Types of Services and Payments, Special Classes of Employment and Special Types of Payments, Treatment Under Employment Taxes. Foreign service by U.S. citizens: 2. For foreign affiliates of American employers and other private employers. Under IRS rules Federal Unemployment Taxes (FUTA) are exempt unless (1) on an American vessel or aircraft and work is performed under contract ___ or worker is employed on a vessel when it touches U.S. port or.
   - (a) made in U.S.
   - (b) signed in the United States
   - (c) valid in the United States
   - (d) and included by the agreement

   Answer: See Section 15. Special Rules for Various Types of Services and Payments, Special Classes of Employment and Special Types of Payments, Treatment Under Employment Taxes, Foreign service by U.S. citizens: 2. For foreign affiliates of American employers and other private employers. Page 38/ (a) made in U.S.

15. Foreign service by U.S. citizens:

4. Section 15. Special Rules for Various Types of Services and Payments, Special Classes of Employment and Special Types of Payments, Treatment Under Employment Taxes. Foreign service by U.S. citizens: 2. For foreign affiliates of American employers and other private employers. Under IRS rules Federal Unemployment Taxes (FUTA) are exempt unless (1) on an American vessel or aircraft and work is performed under contract ___ or worker is employed on a vessel when it touches U.S. port or (2) U.S. citizen works for American employer (except in a ___ country with which the U.S. has an agreement for unemployment compensation) or in the U.S. Virgin Islands.
   - (a) made in U.S., contiguous
   - (b) signed in the United States, cooperating
   - (c) valid in the United States, trade
   - (d) and included by the agreement, friendly

   Answer: See Section 15. Special Rules for Various Types of Services and Payments, Special Classes of Employment and Special Types of Payments, Treatment Under Employment Taxes, Foreign service by U.S. citizens: 2. For foreign affiliates of American employers and other private employers. Page 38/ (a) made in U.S., contiguous

Section 15. Special Rules for Various Types of Services and Payments.

15. Fringe benefits.

5. Section 15. Special Rules for Various Types of Services and Payments. Special Classes of Employment and Special Types of Payments, Treatment Under Employment Taxes. Fringe Benefits. Taxable on excess of fair market value of the benefit over the ___ paid for it by an employee and any amount ___ by law.
   (a) minimum amount, deemed excessive
   (b) sum of an amount, excludable
   (c) sum of the amount, excludable
   (d) value of the amount, deemed excessive
   Answer: See Section 15. Special Rules for Various Types of Services and Payments, Special Classes of Employment and Special Types of Payments, Treatment Under Employment Taxes. Fringe benefits. Page 38/(b) sum of an amount, excludable

15. Fringe benefits.

6. Section 15. Special Rules for Various Types of Services and Payments, Special Classes of Employment and Special Types of Payments, Treatment Under Employment Taxes, Fringe benefits. Taxable on excess of fair market value of the benefit sum of an amount paid by the employee and any amount deemed excessive by law. However, special ___ rules may apply.
   (a) taxes
   (b) income tax
   (c) valuation
   (d) amount
   Answer: See Section 15 Special Rules for Various Types of Services and Payments, Special Classes of Employment and Special Types of Payments, Treatment Under Employment Taxes, Fringe benefits. Benefits provided under cafeteria plans. Page 38/ (c) valuation

15. Fringe benefits.

7. Section 15. Special Rules for Various Types of Services and Payments, Special Classes of Employment and Special Types of Payments, Treatment Under Employment Taxes, Fringe benefits. Taxable on excess of fair market value of the benefit sum of an amount paid by the employee and any amount deemed excessive by law. However, special valuation rules may apply. Benefits provided under ___ plans may qualify for exclusion from wages for social security, Medicate, and FUTA taxes.
   (a) medical
   (b) cafeteria
   (c) Medical Savings Plan
   (d) Archer
   Answer: See Section 15 Special Rules for Various Types of Services and Payments, Special Classes of Employment and Special Types of Payments, Treatment Under Employment Taxes, Fringe benefits. Benefits provided under cafeteria plans. Page 38/ (b) cafeteria

Section 15. Special Rules for Various Types of Services and Payments.

15. Fringe benefits.

8. Section 15. Special Rules for Various Types of Services and Payments, Special Classes of Employment and Special Types of Payments, Treatment Under Employment Taxes, Fringe benefits. Taxable on excess of fair market value of the benefit sum of an amount paid by the employee and any amount deemed excessive by law. However, special valuation rules may apply. Benefits provided under cafeteria plans may qualify for exclusion from wages for social security, Medicate, and FUTA taxes, See Publication ___ for details.
   - (a) 14-A
   - (b) 14-B
   - (c) 15-A
   - (d) 15-B

   Answer: See Section 15 Special Rules for Various Types of Services and Payments, Special Classes of Employment and Special Types of Payments, Treatment Under Employment Taxes, Fringe benefits. Benefits provided under cafeteria plans. Page 38. (d) 15-B

15. Government Employment.

9. Section 15. Special Rules for Various Types of Services and Payments, Special Classes of Employment and Special Types of Payments, Treatment Under Employment Taxes, Government employment: State/local governments and political subdivisions, employees of: 1. Salaries and wages (includes payments to most elected and appointed officials). See chapter ___ of Publication ___, Federal-State reference Guide.
   - (a) 1, 961
   - (b) 2, 962
   - (c) 3, 963
   - (d) 4, 964

   Answer: See Section 15. Special Rules for Various Types of Services and Payments, Special Classes of Employment and Special Types of Payments, Treatment Under Employment Taxes, Income Tax Withholding, Government employment. Page 38/ (c) 3, 963

Section 15. Special Rules for Various Types of Services and Payments.

15. Government Employment.
10. Section 15. Special Rules for Various Types of Services and Payments, Special Classes of Employment and Special Types of Payments, Treatment Under Employment Taxes, Government employment: State/local governments and political subdivisions, employees of: 1. Salaries and wages (includes payments to most elected and appointed officials.) Treatment Under Employment Taxes, Income Tax Withholding ___.
    (a) Withhold
    (b) Withheld
    (c) Shall withhold
    (d) Shall be withheld
    Answer: See Section 15. Special Rules for Various Types of Services and Payments, Special Classes of Employment and Special Types of Payments, Treatment Under Employment Taxes, Income Tax Withholding, Government employment. Page 38/ (a) Withhold

15. Government Employment.
11. Section 15. Special Rules for Various Types of Services and Payments. Special Classes of Employment and Special Types of Payments. Treatment Under Employment Taxes. Social Security and Medicare. Generally, taxable for (1) services performed by employees who are either (a) covered under a section ___ agreement or.
    (a) DD 214
    (b) SS 215
    (c) 218
    (d) 1019
    Answer: See Section 15. Special Rules for Various Types of Services and Payments, Special Classes of Employment and Special Types of Payments, Treatment Under Employment Taxes, Social Security and Medicare, Government employment: State/local governments and political subdivisions, employees of: 1. Social Security and Medicare. Page 38/(c) 218

15. Government Employment.
12. Section 15. Special Rules for Various Types of Services and Payments, Special Classes of Employment and Special Types of Payments, Treatment Under Employment Taxes, Government employment: Federal Unemployment Tax (FUTA), ___.
    (a) Exempt
    (b) Withhold
    (c) Withheld
    (d) Not Exempt
    Answer: See Section 15. Special Rules for Various Types of Services and Payments, Special Classes of Employment and Special Types of Payments, Treatment Under Employment Taxes, Federal Unemployment, Government Employment, 1. Page 38/ (a) Exempt

Section 15. Special Rules for Various Types of Services and Payments.

15. Government Employment.
13. Section 15. Special Rules for Various Types of Services and Payments, Special Classes of Employment and Special Types of Payments, Treatment Under Employment Taxes, Government employment: Social Security and Medicare Generally, taxable for (1) services performed by employees who are either (a) covered under a section___ agreement or (b) not a member of a ___ system (mandatory social security and Medicare coverage) and
    (a) DD 214, government retirement system
    (b) SS 215, governmental retirement system
    (c) 218, public retirement system
    (d) 1019, union retirement system
    Answer: See Section 15. Special Rules for Various Types of Services and Payments, Special Classes of Employment and Special Types of Payments, Treatment Under Employment Taxes, Government employment: Social Security and Medicare. Page 38/ (c) 218, public retirement system

15. Government Employment.
14. Section 15. Special Rules for Various Types of Services and Payments, Special Classes of Employment and Special Types of Payments, Treatment Under Employment Taxes, Government employment: Social Security and Medicare Generally, taxable for (1) services performed by employees who are either (a) covered under a section___ agreement or (b) not a member of a ___ system (mandatory social security and Medicare coverage) and (2) (for Medicare tax only) for services performed by employees hired or rehired after ___ who are not covered under a section 218 agreement or the mandatory social security provisions, unless
    (a) DD 214, government retirement system, 12/31/85
    (b) SS 215, governmental retirement system, 1/31/86
    (c) 218, public retirement system, 3/31/86
    (d) 1019, union retirement system, 6/30/86
    Answer: See Section 15. Special Rules for Various Types of Services and Payments, Special Classes of Employment and Special Types of Payments, Treatment Under Employment Taxes, Government employment: Social Security and Medicare. Page 38/ (c) 218, public retirement system, 3/31/86

Section 15. Special Rules for Various Types of Services and Payments.

15. Government Employment.

15. Section 15. Special Rules for Various Types of Services and Payments, Special Classes of Employment and Special Types of Payments, Treatment Under Employment Taxes, Government employment: Social Security and Medicare Generally, taxable for (1) services performed by employees who are either (a) covered under a section___ agreement or (b) not a member of a ___ system (mandatory social security and Medicare coverage) and (2) (for Medicare tax only) for services performed by employees hired or rehired after ___ who are not covered under a section 218 agreement or the mandatory social security provisions, unless specifically excluded by law. See Publication ___.
   (a) DD 214, government retirement system, 12/31/85, 961
   (b) SS 215, governmental retirement system, 1/31/86, 962
   (c) 218, public retirement system, 3/31/86, 963
   (d) 1019, union retirement system, 6/30/86, 964
   Answer: See Section 15. Special Rules for Various Types of Services and Payments, Special Classes of Employment and Special Types of Payments, Treatment Under Employment Taxes, Government employment: Social Security and Medicare. Page 38/ (c) 218, public retirement system, 3/31/86, 963

15. Government Employment. 2. Election workers.

16. Section 15. Special Rules for Various Types of Services and Payments, Special Classes of Employment and Special Types of Payments, Treatment Under Employment Taxes, Government employment: 2. Election workers. Income Tax Withholding. ___.
   (a) Withhold
   (b) Exempt
   (c) Exception
   (d) Exempt if less than $2000
   Answer: See Section 15. Special Rules for Various Types of Services and Payments, Special Classes of Employment and Special Types of Payments, Treatment Under Employment Taxes, Election workers. Page 38/ (b) Exempt

15. Government Employment. 2. Election workers.

17. Election individuals are workers who are employed to ___ for state or local governments at election booths in connection with national, state, or local elections.
   (a) supervise
   (b) assist with the election process
   (c) perform services
   (d) observe and assist with the election process
   Answer: See Section 15. Special Rules for Various Types of Services and Payments, Government employment: 2. Election workers. Page 38/ (c) perform services

Section 15. Special Rules for Various Types of Services and Payments.

15. Government Employment. 2. Election workers.

18. Government employment: 2. Election workers. Election individuals are workers who are employed to perform services for state or local governments at election booths in connection with national, state, or local elections. Note. File Form ___ for payments of $___ or more even if no social security or Medicare taxes were withheld.
    (a)   W-1, 500
    (b)   W-2, 600
    (c)   W-3, 1,000
    (d)   W-4, 1,200
    Answer: See Section 15. Special Rules for Various Types of Services and Payments, Special Classes of Employment and Special Types of Payments, Government employment: 2. Election workers. Note. Page 38/ (b) W-2, 600

15. Government Employment. 2. Election workers.

19. Section 15. Special Rules for Various Types of Services and Payments. Special Classes of Employment and Special Types of Payments, <u>Treatment under Employment Taxes</u>. Election workers. Election individuals are workers who are employed to perform services for state and local governments at election booths in connection with national, state, or local elections. In the column heading "Treatment Under Employment Taxes" Social Security and Medicare are taxable if paid $___ or more in 2013 (Lesser amount if specified as a section ___ social security agreement). See Revenue Ruling 2000-6.
    (a)   850, 218
    (b)   1,000, 219
    (c)   1,600, 218
    (d)   2,500, 219
    Answer: See Section 15. Special Rules Various Types of Services and Payments, Special Classes of Employment and Special Types of Payments, Treatment Under Employment Taxes, Government workers. Page 38/ (c) 1,600, 218

15. Government Employment. 2. Election workers.

20. Federal unemployment taxes (FUTA) for wages paid to Government workers employed as election workers are ___.
    (a)   Taxable
    (b)   Exempt
    (c)   non taxable
    (d)   subject to special tax provisions
    Answer: See Section 15. Special Rules for Various Types of Services and Payments Special Types of Services and Payments, Special Classes of Employment and Special Types of Payments, Treatment Under Employment Taxes, Government workers. Page 38/ (b) Exempt

Section 15. Special Rules for Various Types of Services and Payments.

15. Government Employment. 3. Emergency workers.

21. IRS rules regarding taxes on wages of <u>Emergency workers</u> who were hired on a temporary basis in response to a specific unforeseen emergency and are not intended to become permanent employees require Government employers to ___ Federal Income Tax.
    (a) Withhold
    (b) Withheld
    (c) Must be withheld
    (d) Exempt
    Answer: See Section 15. Special Rules for Various Types of Services and Payments, Special Classes of Employment and Special Types of Payments, Treatment Under Employment Taxes, Government employment, 3. Emergency workers, Income Tax Withholding. Page 38/ (a) Withhold

15. Government Employment. 3. Emergency workers.

22. The Social Security and Medicare tax payments of emergency workers serving on a temporary basis in case of fire, storm, snow, earthquake, flood, or similar emergency are ___.
    (a) Taxable
    (b) nontaxable
    (c) Exempt
    (d) not exempt
    Answer: See Section 15. Special Rules for Various Types of Services and Payments, Special Classes of Employment and Special Types of Payments, Treatment Under Employment Taxes, Government employment, 3. Emergency workers. Page 38/ (c) Exempt

15. Government Employment. 3. Emergency workers.

23. Federal Unemployment Tax (FUTA) of emergency workers serving on a temporary basis in case of fire, storm, snow, earthquake, flood or similar emergency are ___.
    (a) Exempt
    (b) Withhold
    (c) Withheld
    (d) Taxable
    Answer: See Section 15. Special Rules for Various Types of Services and Payments, Special Classes of Employment and Special Types of Payments, Treatment Under Employment Taxes, Government employment, 3. Emergency workers. Page 38/(a) Exempt

Section 15. Special Rules for Various Types of Services and Payments.

15. Government Employment. 3. Emergency workers.

24. According to Section 15. Special Rules for Various Types of Services and Payments. Special Classes of Employment and Special Types of Payments: Treatment Under Employment Taxes, Government employment: <u>U.S. federal government employees</u>, the Income Tax Withhold is listed as Withhold and the Federal Unemployment tax is listed as Exempt. However, Social Security and Medicare are listed as **Taxable for Medicare** but qualified as Taxable for social security unless hired before ___. See section 3121(b)(5).
    (a) 1934
    (b) 1944
    (c) 1984
    (d) 1994
    Answer: See Section 15. Special Rules for Various Types of Services and Payments, Special Classes of Employment and Special Types of Payments, Treatment Under Employment Taxes, Government employment, U.S. federal government employees, Social Security and Medicare. Page 38/ (c) 1984

15. Homeworkers (industrial, cottage industry):

25. Section 15. Special Rules for Various Types of Services and Payments. Special Classes of Employment and Special Types of Payments, Treatment Under Employment Taxes. Homeworkers (industrial, cottage industry): 1. Common law employees. Treatment Under Employment Taxes, Income Tax Withholding to ___.
    (a) Be exempt
    (b) Withhold
    (c) Exempt
    (d) Not be withheld
    Answer: See Section 15. Special Rules for Various Types of Services and Payments, Special Classes of Employment and Special Types of Payments, Treatment Under Employment Taxes, Homeworkers (industrial, cottage industry), 1. Common law employees. Page 39/ Withhold

15. Homeworkers (industrial, cottage industry):

26. Section 15. Special Rules for Various Types of Services and Payments. Special Classes of Employment and Special Types of Payments, Treatment Under Employment Taxes. Homeworkers (Industrial, cottage industry): 1. Common law employees. The Income tax Withholding, Social Security and Federal Unemployment taxes listed under Treatment Under Employment Taxes are ___, ___, and ___.
    (a) Withheld, Taxable, Taxable
    (b) Withhold, Taxable, Taxable
    (c) Withheld, Taxable, Exempt
    (d) Withheld, Exempt, Taxable
    Answer: See Section 15. Special Rules for Various Types of Services and Payments, Special Classes of Employment and Special Types of Payments, Treatment Under Employment Taxes Homeworkers (industrial, cottage industry): 1. Common law employees. Page 39/ (b) Withhold, Taxable, Taxable

Section 15. Special Rules for Various Types of Services and Payments.

15. Homeworkers (industrial, cottage industry):
27. Section 15. Special Rules for Various Types of Services and Payments, Special Classes of Employment and Special Types of Payments, Treatment Under Employment Taxes, Homeworkers (industrial, cottage industry): 2. Statutory employees are exempt from Income tax withholding and exempt from Federal Unemployment Tax (FUTA). However, the social security and Medicare taxes are taxable if paid $___ or more in cash in a year.
    (a) 100
    (b) 1,000
    (c) 1,500
    (d) 2,500
    Answer: See Section 15. Special Rules for Various Types of Services and Payments, Special Classes of Employment and Special Types of Payments, Treatment Under Employment Taxes, Homeworkers (industrial, cottage industry): 2. Statutory employees, See section 2 for details. Page 39/ (a) 100

15. Hospital employees:
28. Section 15. Special Rules for Various Types of Services and Payments, Special Classes of Employment and Special Types of Payments, Treatment Under Employment Taxes, Hospital employees: **1. Interns** - Income Tax Withholding is withheld, Social Security and Medicare are Taxable and Federal Unemployment Tax (FUTA) is ___.
    (a) not taxable
    (b) exempt
    (c) Taxable
    (d) Exempt
    Answer: See Section 15. Special Rules for Various Types of Services and Payments. Special Classes of Employment and Special Types of Payments. Treatment Under Employment Taxes. Hospital employees: 1. Interns. Page 39/ (d) Exempt

15. Hospital employees:
29. Section 15. Special Rules for Various Types of Services and Payments. Special Classes of Employment and Special Types of Payments. Treatment Under Employment Taxes. Hospital employees: **2. Patients**. The Special Classes of Employment and Special Types of Payment. Treatment Under Employment Taxes. Income Tax Withholding states "Withhold" with Federal Unemployment Tax (FUTA) "Exempt". However, Social Security are "Taxable" but (Exempt for ___.
    (a) charity hospitals
    (b) religious and non-profit hospitals
    (c) local government hospitals
    (d) state or local government hospitals
    Answer: See Section 15. Special Rules for Various Types of Services and Payments, Special Classes of Employment and Special Types of Payments, Treatment Under Employment Taxes, 2. Patients. Page 39/ (d) state or local hospitals

Section 15. Special Rules for Various Types of Services and Payments.

15. Household employees:
30. For the Special Classes of Employment and Special Types of Payments, Household employee: 1. Domestic service in private homes. Income Tax Withholding is Exempt (___ if both employer and employee agree).
    (a) withheld
    (b) withhold
    (c) only
    (d) unless
    Answer: See Section 15. Special Rules for Various Types of Services and Payments. Treatment Under Employment Taxes, Household employees, 1. Domestic service. Page 39/ (b) withhold

15. Household employees:
31. Section 15. Special Rules for Various Types of Services and Payments. Special Classes of Employment and Special Types of Payments. Treatments Under Employment Taxes. Social Security and Medicate. Household employees. <u>1. Domestic service in private homes</u>. Social Security and Medicare taxes are taxable if paid $___ or more in cash in 2013. Exempt if performed by an individual under age ___ during any portion of the calendar year and is not the principal occupation of the employee.
    (a) 1,000, 16
    (b) 1,500, 16
    (c) 1,800, 18
    (d) 2,000, 18
    Answer: See Section 15. Special Rules for Various Types of Services and Payments. Special Classes of Employment and Special Types of Payments, Treatment Under Employment Taxes. Household employees. 1. Domestic service in private homes. Page 39/ (c) 1,800, 18

15. Household employees:
32. Household employees, 1. Domestic service in private homes. Federal Unemployment Taxes (FUTA) are ___ if the employer paid total cash wages of $___ or more in any quarter in the current or preceding calendar year.
    (a) Taxable, 1,000
    (b) Taxable, 1,200
    (c) taxed, 1,200
    (d) taxes, 1,500
    Answer: See Section 15. Special Rules for Various Types of Services and Payments. Special Classes of Employment and Special Types of Payments, Treatment Under Employment Taxes, Household employees. 1. Domestic service in private homes, Federal Unemployment Taxes. Page 39/ (a) Taxable, 1,000

Section 15. Special Rules for Various Types of Services and Payments

15. Household employees:
33. Household employees 2. Domestic service in college clubs, fraternities, and sororities. Income Tax Withholding. Exempt (withhold if employer and employee _____).
    (a) agree
    (b) are under statute law
    (c) are under common law
    (d) are under college or university employment

    Answer: See Section 15. Special Rules for Various Types of Services and Payments. Special Classes of Employment and Special Types of Payments. Treatment Under Employment Taxes. Household employees: 2. Domestic service in college clubs, fraternities, and sororities. Page 39/(a) agree

15. Household employees:
34. Household employees 2. Domestic service in college clubs, fraternities, and sororities. Social Security and Medicare. Exempt if paid to a regular student; also exempt if the employee is paid less than $___ in a year by an income-tax-exempt employer.
    (a) 100
    (b) 1,000
    (c) 1,200
    (d) 1,500

    Answer: See Section 15. Special Rules for Various Types of Services and Payments. Special Classes of Employment and Special Types of Payments. Treatment Under Employment Taxes. Household employees: 2. Domestic service in college clubs, fraternities, and sororities, Social Security and Medicare. Page 39/

15. Household employees:
35. Household employees 2. Domestic service in college clubs, fraternities, and sororities. Federal Unemployment Taxes (FUTA) are ___ if employer paid total cash wages of $1,000 or more in any quarter in the current or preceding calendar year.
    (a) Collected
    (b) Taxable
    (c) Nontaxable
    (d) Exempt

    Answer: See Section 15. Special Rules for Various Types of Services and Payments. Special Classes of Employment and Special Types of Payments. Treatment Under Employment Taxes. Household employees: 2. Domestic service in college clubs, fraternities, and sororities. Federal Unemployment. Page 39/(b) 1,000

Section 15. Special Rules for Various Types of Services and Payments

15. Insurance for employees:
36. Insurance for employees: 1. Accident and health insurance premiums under a plan or system for employees and their dependents generally or for a class or classes of employees and their dependents. Income Tax Withholding. Exempt (except ___).
    (a) 2% shareholder-employees of S corporations
    (b) 3% shareholder-employees of S corporations
    (c) partners of incorporated limited partnerships
    (d) partners of incorporated S corporations or partnerships
    Answer: See Section 15. Special Rules for Various Types of Services and Payments. Special Classes of Employment and Special Types of Payments. Treatment Under Employment Taxes. Insurance for employees. 1. Page 39/(a) 2% shareholder-employees of S corporations

15. Insurance for employees:
37. Section 15. Insurance for employees: Social Security and Medicare Taxes are ___.
    (a) Taxable
    (b) Withhold
    (c) Expendable
    (d) Exempt
    Answer: See Section 15. Special Rules for Various Types of Services and Payments. Special Classes of Employment and Special Types of Payments. Treatment Under Employment Taxes. Page 39/(d) Exempt

15. Insurance for employees:
38. Section 15. Special Classes of Employment and Special Types of Payments. Treatment Under Employment Taxes. Federal Unemployment Insurance (FUTA). Insurance for employees.
    1. Accident and health insurance premiums under a plan or system for employees and their dependents generally or for a class or classes of employees and their dependents are ___.
    (a) Exempt
    (b) Taxable
    (c) Nontaxable
    (d) Withheld
    Answer: See Section 15. Special Rules for Various Types of Services and Payments. Page 39/(a) Exempt

Section 15. Special Rules for Various Types of Services and Payments

15. Insurance for employees:
39. Group-term life insurance costs under Section 15. Special Rules for Various Types of Services and Payments. Special Classes of Employment and Special Types of Payments. Treatment Under Employment Taxes Income Tax Withholding are ___.
   (a) Withheld
   (b) Taxable
   (c) Exempt
   (d) Not exempt
   Answer: See Section 15. Income Tax Withholding. Insurance for employees: 2. Group-term life insurance costs. Page 39/(c) Exempt

15. Insurance for employees:
40. Social Security and Medicare as addressed in Section 15. Special Rules for Various Types of Services and Payments for Group-term life insurance costs are Exempt, except for the cost of group-term life insurance ___ in the employee's gross income. Special rules apply for former employees.
   (a) excludable
   (b) includible
   (c) taxable
   (d) accessed
   Answer: See Section 15. Special Rules for Various Types of Services and Payments. Special Classes of Employment and Special Types of Payments. Treatment Under Employment Taxes Insurance for employees: 2. Group-term life insurance costs. Social Security and Medicare. Page 39/ (b) includable

15. Insurance for employees:
41. Section 15. Special Rules for Various Types of Services and Payments. Treatment Under Employment Taxes. Insurance for employees: 2. Group-term life insurance costs. Federal Unemployment Tax (FUTA) is ___.
   (a) Not taxable
   (b) Taxable
   (c) Required
   (d) Exempt
   Answer: See Section 15. Special Rules for Various Types of Services and Payments. Special Classes of Employment and Special Types of Payments. Treatment Under Employment Taxes. 2. Group-term life insurance costs. Federal Unemployment Tax. page 39/(d) Exempt

Section 15. Special Rules for Various Types of Services and Payments

15. Insurance agent or solicitors:
42. Insurance agents or solicitors:
    1. Full-time life insurance salesperson. Income Tax Withholding. Withhold only if employee under ___. See <u>section 2</u>.
    (a) charges
    (b) statute law
    (c) common law
    (d) civil law
    Answer: See Section 15 Special Rules for Various Types of Services and Payments. Special Classes of Employment and Special Types of Payments. Treatment Under Employment Taxes. Income Tax Withholding. Page 39/(c) common law

15. Insurance agent or solicitors:
43. Insurance agents or solicitors: 1. Full-time life insurance salesperson. Treatments Under Employment Taxes. Social Security and Medicare is Taxable, however, Federal Unemployment is Taxable (FUTA) if (1) employee ___ and (2) not paid solely by ___.
    (a) is under civil law, the employer
    (b) common law, commissions
    (c) statute law, payroll
    (d) statute law, certified payroll
    Answer: See Section 15. Special Rules for Various Types of Services and Payments. Special Classes of Employment and Special Types of Payments. Treatment Under Employment Taxes, Insurance agents or solicitors: 1. Full-time life insurances salesperson, Federal Unemployment Tax. Page 39/(b) common law, commissions

15. Insurance agent or solicitors:
44. 15 Special Rules for Various Types of Services and Payments. Special Classes of Employment and Special Types of Payments, Treatment Under Employment Taxes. Insurance agents or solicitors: <u>2. Other salesperson of life, causality</u>, etc., insurance. Income Tax Withholding - Treatment Under Employment Taxes. Withhold only if employee under ___. See <u>section 2</u>.
    (a) civil law
    (b) common law
    (c) statute law
    (d) federal law
    Answer: See Section 15. Special Rules for Various Types of Services and Payments. Special Classes of Employment and Special Types of Payments. Treatment Under Employment Taxes. Insurance agents or solicitors: 2. Other salesperson of life, casualty, etc., insurance. Withhold only if employee under common law. Page 39/(b) common law

Section 15. Special Rules for Various Types of Services and Payments

15. Insurance agent or solicitors:
45. Social security and Medicare taxes of other salesperson of life, casualty, etc., insurance are taxable only if employee under ___.
    (a) civil law
    (b) common law
    (c) statute law
    (d) federal law
    Answer: See Section 15. Special Rules for Various Types of Services and Payments. Special Classes of Employment and Special Types of Payments. Treatment Under Employment Taxes. Insurance agents or solicitors: 2. Other salesperson of life, casualty, etc., insurance. Social Security and Medicare. Page 39/ common law

15. Insurance agent or solicitors:
46. The Federal Unemployment taxes (FUTA) of Insurance agents or solicitors, the salesperson of life, casualty, etc., insurances are taxable if (1) employee under common law and (2) not paid ___ by commissions.
    (a) weekly
    (b) bi-weekly
    (c) only
    (d) solely
    Answer: See Section 15. Special Rules for Various Types of Services and Payments. Special Classes of Employment and Special Types of Payments. Treatment Under Employment Taxes. Federal Unemployment Tax (FUTA). 2. Taxable if (1) employee under common law and (2) not paid solely by commission. Page 39/(d) solely

15. Interest on loans with below-market interest rates:
47. Section 15. Special Rules for Various Types of Services and Payments. Special Classes of Employment and Special Types of Payments. Treatment Under Employment Taxes. Interest on loans with below-market interest (foregone interest and deemed original issue discount). Under Income Tax Withholding, Social Security and Medicare and Federal Unemployment Tax (FUTA) See ___.
    (a) Publication 15-A
    (b) Publication 15-B
    (c) Publication 15-C
    (d) Publication 15-D
    Answer: See Section 15. Special Rules for Various Types of Services and Payments. Special Classes of Employment and Special Types of Payments. Interest on loans with below-market interest rates. Page 39/ (a) Publication 15-A

Section 15. Special Rules for Various Types of Services and Payments

15. Leave-sharing plans:

48. Section 15. Special Rules for Various Types of Services and Payments. Special Classes of Employment and Special Types of Payments. Treatment under Employment Taxes. Leave-sharing plans: Income Tax Withholding, Social Security and Medicare and Federal Unemployment are ___, ___, ___.
    (a) Withhold, Exempt, Exempt
    (b) Withhold, Taxable, Taxable
    (c) Exempt, Exempt, Withhold
    (d) Taxable, Exempt, Exempt
    Answer: See Section 15. Special Rules for Various Types of Services and Payments. Special Classes of Employment and Special Types of Payments. Treatment Under Employment Taxes. Leave-sharing plans: Page 39/ (b) Withhold, Taxable, Taxable

15. Newspaper carriers and vendors:

49. <u>Newspaper carriers and vendors</u>: Newspaper carriers under age 18; newspaper and vendors buying at fixed price and retaining receipts from sales to customers. See Publication 15-A for information on statutory nonemployee status. Treatment Under Employment Taxes. Social Security and Medicare - Exempt, Federal Unemployment Tax (FUTA) - Exempt, Income Tax Withholding - Exempt (withhold if ___).
    (a) both parties agree
    (b) withhold if both employer and employee agree
    (c) withhold if both employee and employer agree
    (d) withhold if both employer and employee voluntarily agree
    Answer: See Section 15. Special Rules for Various Types of Services and Payments. Special Classes of Employment and Special Types of Payments. Treatment Under Employment Taxes. Income Tax Withholding. Newspaper carriers and vendors: Page 39/ (d) withhold if both employer and employee voluntarily agree

15. Noncash payments:

50. For household work, agricultural labor, and service not in the of the employer's trade or business income tax withholding is exempt unless both the employer and employee ___.
    (a) agree
    (b) voluntarily agree
    (c) agree voluntarily
    (d) agree in writing to the IRS
    Answer: See Section 15. Special Rules for Various Types of Services and Payments. Special Classes of Employment and Special Types of Payments. Treatment Under Employment Taxes. Noncash payments. Income Tax Withholding. 1. For household work, agricultural labor, and service not in the course of the employer's trade or business. Page 40/ (b) voluntarily agree

Section 15. Special Rules for Various Types of Services and Payments

15. Noncash payments:
51. For household work, agricultural labor, and service not in the employer's trade or business social security and Medicare and Federal Unemployment Taxes (FUTA) are ___.
    - (a) Taxable
    - (b) Withheld
    - (c) Withhold
    - (d) Exempt

    Answer: See Section 15. Special Rules for Various Types of Services and Payments. Special Classes of Employment and Special Types of Payments. Treatment Under Employment Taxes. Treatment Under Employment Taxes. Social Security and Medicare, Federal Unemployment Tax (FUTA). Page 40/ Exempt

15. Noncash payments:
52. To certain retail commission salespersons ordinarily paid solely on a cash commission basis. Income Tax Withholding is___ with employer, except to the extent employee's supplemental wages during the year exceed $___.
    - (a) Required, 10,000
    - (b) Mandatory, 100,000
    - (c) Optional, 1,000,000
    - (d) Required, 1,500,000

    Answer: See Section 15. Special Rules for Various Types of Services and Payments. Special Classes of Employment and Special Types of Payments. Treatment Under Employment Taxes. Income Tax Withholding. 2. To certain retail commission salespersons ordinarily paid solely on a cash commission basis. Page 40/ (c) Optional, $1,000,000

15. Noncash payments:
53. To certain retail commission salespersons ordinarily paid solely on a cash commission basis Social Security and Medicare and Federal Unemployment are ___.
    - (a) Exempt
    - (b) Taxable
    - (c) Not taxable
    - (d) Not exempt

    Answer: See Section 15. Special Rules for Various Types of Services and Payments. Special Classes of Employment and Special Types of Payments. Treatment Under Employment Taxes. Noncash payments: 2. To certain retail commission salespersons ordinarily paid solely on a cash commission basis. Page 40/(b) Taxable

Section 15. Special Rules for Various Types of Services and Payments

15. Nonprofit organizations.

54. Section 15 directs information about Treatment Under Employment Taxes of Nonprofit organizations to IRS Publication ___.
    - (a) 15-A
    - (b) 15-B
    - (c) 15-C
    - (d) 15-D

    Answer: See Section 15. Special Rules for Various Types of Services and Payments. Special Classes of Employment and Special Types of Payments. Treatment Under Employment Taxes. Nonprofit organizations. Page 40/(a) 15-A

15. Officers or shareholders of an S Corporation.

55. Officers or shareholders of an S Corporation. Distributions and other payments by an S corporation to a corporate officer or shareholder must be treated as wages to the extent the amounts are reasonable compensation for services to the corporation by an employee. See the instructions for Form _____.
    - (a) 941s
    - (b) 944g
    - (c) 1019S
    - (d) 1120S

    Answer: See Section 15. Special Rules for Various Types of Services and Payments. Page 40/ (d) 1120S

15. Officers or shareholders of an S Corporation.

56. Under the requirements of IRS rules for Officers or shareholders of an S Corporation the Income Tax Withholding, Social Security and Medicare and Federal Unemployment Taxes (FUTA) are ___, ___ and ___.
    - (a) Withheld, Exempt, Taxable
    - (b) Withhold, Taxable, Taxable
    - (c) Exempt, Exempt, Exempt
    - (d) Taxable, Taxable, Taxable

    Answer: See Section 15. Special Rules for Various Types of Services and Payments. Special Classes of Employment and Special types of Payments. Treatment Under Employment Taxes. Officers or shareholders of an S Corporation. Page 40/ (b) Withhold, Taxable, Taxable

Section 15. Special Rules for Various Types of Services and Payments

15. Partners:

57. Partners: Payments to general or limited partners of a partnership. See Publication ___, Partnerships, for reporting rules.
    (a) 541
    (b) 641
    (c) 741
    (d) 915
    Answer: See Section 15. Special Rules for Various Types of Services and Payments. Special Classes of Employment and Special Types of Payments. Treatment Under Employment Taxes. Partners. Page 40/(a) 541

15. Partners:

58. Under the requirements of IRS rules for Partners: Payments to general or limited partners of a partnership Income Tax Withholding, Social Security and Medicare and Federal Unemployment taxes are ___, ___, ___.
    (a) Exempt, Exempt, Exempt
    (b) Withhold, Taxable, Taxable
    (c) Exempt, Taxable, Taxable
    (d) Withhold, Exempt, Exempt
    Answer: See Section 15. Special Rules for Various Types of Services and Payments. Special Classes of Employment and Special Types of Payments. Treatment Under Employment Taxes. Partners. Page 40/ Exempt, Exempt, Exempt

15. Railroads:

59. Railroads: Payments subject to the Railroad Retirement Act. See Publication ___. Social Security and Equivalent Railroad Retirement Benefit, for more details.
    (a) 715
    (b) 815
    (c) 915
    (d) 1015
    Answer: See Section 15. Special Rules for Various Types of Services and Payments. Special Classes of Employment and Special Types of Payments. Treatment Under Employment Taxes. Railroads: Page 40/ (c) 915

15. Railroads:

60. Under the requirements of IRS rules for Railroads. Special Classes of Employment and Special Types of Payments. Treatment Under Employment Taxes. Income Tax Withholding, Social Security and Medicare and Federal Unemployment Taxes (FUTA) are ___, ___, ___.
    (a) Withhold, Exempt, Exempt
    (b) Withheld, Taxable, Taxable
    (c) Withhold, Exempt, Taxable
    (d) Withheld, Exempt, Exempt
    Answer: See Section 15. Special Rules for Various Types of Services and Payments. Railroads: Page 40/ (a) Withhold, Exempt, Exempt

© Copyright 2013. All rights reserved. Notice: United States Copyright Laws and International Treaties prohibit unauthorized publication, reproduction, distribution of this Work. Unauthorized use of this copyright in any form, format, publication or document may result in severe civil and criminal penalties. Violations of this copyright are investigated by the United States Department of Justice and carry, upon conviction of fines up to $250,000 and five years confinement. This Work is protected by United States Copyright Laws and International Treaties. Do not Copy, do not reproduce, do not distribute.

Section 15. Special Rules for Various Types of Services and Payments

A Ficus Tree Publishing Quick Notes Page

DU VALL'S TEST'S™
Instructor's Manual Study Guide Series United States Tax Code
IRS Publication 15 Circular E, Employer's Tax Guide Tax Year 2013
Tax Test 15E-S15-3 [Multiple-Choice Questions With Answers]

Section 15. Special Rules for Various Types of Services and Payments.

15. Religious exemptions:

1. Special Classes of Employment and Special Types of Payments. Religious exemptions. Treatment Under Employment Taxes. See Publication ___ and Publication ___, Social Security and Other information for Members of the Clergy and Religious Workers.
   - (a)   15-A, 517
   - (b)   15-A, 915
   - (c)   941, 945
   - (d)   1099, 1010

   Answer: See Section 15. Special Rules for Various Types of Services and Payments. Special Classes of Employment and Special Types of Payments. Treatment Under Employment Taxes. Religious Exemptions. Page 40/(a) 15-A, 517

15. Retirement and pension plans:

2. Section 15. Special Rules for Various Types of Services and Payments. Special Classes of Employment and Special Types of Payments. Treatment Under Employment Taxes. Retirement and pension plans: 1. Employer contributions to a qualified plan. Income Tax Withholding is ___.
   - (a)   Not exempt
   - (b)   Taxable
   - (c)   Exempt
   - (d)   Withheld

   Answer: See Section 15. Special Rules for Various Types of Services and Payments. Special Classes of Employment and Special Types of Payments. Page 40/ (c) Exempt

15. Retirement and pension plans:

3. Section 15. Special Rules for Various Types of Services and Payments. Special Classes of Employment and Special Types of Payments. Retirement and pension plans: 1. Employer contributions to a qualified plan. Social Security and Medicare taxes are ___.
   - (a)   Not exempt
   - (b)   Taxable
   - (c)   Exempt
   - (d)   Withhold

   Answer: See Section 15. Special Rules for Various Types of Services and Payments. Special Classes of Employment and Special Types of Payments. Treatment Under Employment Taxes. Retirement and pension plans: 1. Employer contributions to a qualified plan. Page 40/ (c) Exempt

Section 15. Special Rules for Various Types of Services and Payments.

15. Retirement and pension plans:

4. Section 15. Special Rules for Various Types of Services and Payments. Special Classes of Employment and Special Types of Payments. Treatment Under Employment Taxes. Retirement and pension plans: Employer contributions to a qualified plan. Federal Unemployment Taxes (FUTA) are ___.
   - (a) Not exempt
   - (b) Taxable
   - (c) Exempt
   - (d) Withhold

   Answer: See Section 15. Special Rules for Various Types of Services and Payments. Special Classes of Employment and Special Types of Payments. Treatment Under Employment Taxes. Federal Unemployment Tax (FUTA). Retirement and pension plans. 1. Employer contributions to a qualified plan. Page 40/ (c) Exempt

15. Retirement and pension plans:

5. Elective employee contributions and deferrals to a plan containing a qualified cash or deferred compensation arrangement Income Tax Withholding is ___, but
   - (a) Exempt
   - (b) Generally exempt
   - (c) Taxable
   - (d) Withhold

   Answer: See Section 15. Retirement and pension plans: 2. Page 40/ (b) Generally exempt

15. Retirement and pension plans:

6. Elective employee contributions and deferrals to a plan containing a qualified cash or deferred compensation arrangement (for example, 401(k)) are generally exempt but see section 402(g) for ___ SEP limitation.
   - (a) reduction
   - (b) income reduction
   - (c) wage reduction
   - (d) salary reduction

   Answer: See Section 15. Special Rules for Various Types of Services and Payments. Special Classes of Employment and Special Types of Payments. Treatment Under Employment Taxes. Retirement and pension plans: 2. Page 40/ (d) salary reduction

Section 15. Special Rules for Various Types of Services and Payments.

15. Retirement and pension plans:
7. Elective employee contributions and deferrals to a plan containing a qualified cash or deferred compensation arrangement (for example, 401(k)). <u>Social Security</u> and <u>Medicare</u> are ___.
   (a) Deferred
   (b) Exempt
   (c) Taxable
   (d) Withhold

   Answer: See Section 15. Special Rules for Various Types of Services and Payments. Special Classes of Employment and Special Types of Payments. Treatment Under Employment Taxes. Retirement and pension plans: 2. Elective employee contributions and deferrals to a plan containing a qualified cash or deferred compensation. Page 40/ (c) Taxable

15. Retirement and pension plans:
8. Elective employee contributions and deferrals to a plan containing a qualified cash or deferred compensation arrangement (for example, 401(k)). <u>Federal Unemployment Tax (FUTA)</u> is ___.
   (a) Exempt
   (b) Withhold
   (c) Withheld
   (d) Taxable

   Answer: See Section 15. Special Rules for Various Types of Services and Payments. Special Classes of Employment and Special Types of Payments. Treatment Under Employment Taxes. Federal Unemployment Tax. Retirement and pension plans. Page 40/ (d) Taxable

15. Retirement and pension plans:
9. As described in the IRS Employer's Tax Guide the letters SEP defined mean ___.
   (a) the abbreviation for the month of September
   (b) Standard Electronic Processing
   (c) Standard Electronically Processed
   (d) simplified employee pension plan

   Answer: See Section 15. Special Classes of Employment and Special Types of Payments. Retirement and pension plans: 3. Employer contributions to individual retirement accounts under simplified employee pension plan (SEP). Page 40/ (d) simplified employee pension plan

Section 15. Special Rules for Various Types of Services and Payments.

15. Retirement and pension plans:
10. 3. Employer contributions to individual retirement under simplified employee pension plan (SEP) treatment under employment taxes are generally exempt, but see section ___ for salary reduction SEP limitation.
    - (a) 400(a)
    - (b) 401(d)
    - (c) 402(g)
    - (d) 403(h)

    Answer: See Section 15. Special Rules for Various Types of Services and Payments. Special Classes of Employment and Special Types of Payments. Income Tax Withholding. Retirement and pension plans. Page 40/ (c) 402(g)

15. Retirement and pension plans:
11. Section 15. Special Rules for various Types of Services and Payments. Special Classes of Employment and Special Types of Payments. Treatment Under Employment Taxes. Retirement and pension plans: 3. Employer contributions to individual retirement accounts under simplified employee plan (SEP). Social Security and Medicare and Federal Unemployment Tax (FUTA) are Exempt, except for ___.
    - (a) income deductions/reductions under SEP agreement
    - (b) amounts contributed under a salary reduction SEP agreement
    - (c) income amounts contributed to SEP agreement for salary reductions
    - (d) income amounts contributed to SEP agreement for wage reduction.

    Answer: See Section 15. Special Rules for Various Types of Services and Payments. Special Classes of Employment and Special Types of Payments. Treatment Under Employment Taxes. Social Security and Medicare and Federal Unemployment. 3. Employer contributions to individual retirement accounts under simplified employee pension plan. Page 40/ (b) amounts contributed under a salary reduction SEP agreement

15. Retirement and pension plans:
12. Employer contributions to section ___ annuities are <u>Generally exempt</u>, but see section 402(g) for limitation.
    - (a) 401(a)
    - (b) 402(g)
    - (c) 403(b)
    - (d) 404(c)

    Answer: See Section 15. Special Rules for Various Types of Services and Payments. Special Classes of Employment and Special Types of Payments. Treatment Under Employment Taxes. Retirement and pension plans: <u>4. Employer contributions to section 403(b) annuities</u>. Page 40/ (c) 403(b)

Section 15. Special Rules for Various Types of Services and Payments.

15. Retirement and pension plans:
13. Employer contributions to section 403(b) annuities are generally exempt and are taxable if paid through a salary reduction agreement (___ or otherwise).
    (a) approved
    (b) IRS approved program
    (c) IRS approved retirement plan
    (d) written

    Answer: See Section 15. Special Rules for Various Types of Services and Payments. Special Classes of Employment and Special Types of Payments. Treatment Under Employment Taxes. Retirement and pension plans: 4. Employer contributions to section 403(b) annuities. Page 40/ (d) written

15. Retirement and pension plans:
14. Under IRS rules Employee salary reduction contributions to a ___ retirement account under Income Tax Withholding are ___.
    (a) SIMPLE, Exempt
    (b) 402(k), Exempt
    (c) Railroad, Taxable
    (d) Keogh, Taxable

    Answer: See Section 15. Special Rules for Various Types of Services and Payments. Special Classes of Employment and Special Types of Payments. Retirement and pension plans: 5. Employee salary reduction contributions to a SIMPLE retirement account. Page 40/ (a) SIMPLE, Exempt

15. Retirement and pension plans:
15. See Publication 15-A for information on pensions, ___, and employer contributions to nonqualified deferred compensation arrangements.
    (a) funds
    (b) medical savings
    (c) annuities
    (d) archer

    Answer: See Section 15. Special Rules for Various Types of Services and Payments. Page 40/ (c) annuities

Section 15. Special Rules for Various Types of Services and Payments.

15. Retirement and pension plans:
16. Employee salary reduction contributions to a SIMPLE retirement account. Treatment Under Employment Taxes <u>Social Security</u> and <u>Medicare</u> are ___.
    (a) Taxable
    (b) Exempt
    (c) Withhold
    (d) Nontaxable

    Answer: See Section 15 Special Rules for Various Types of Services and Payments. Special Classes of Employment and Special Types of Payments. Treatment Under Employment Taxes. Retirement and pension plans. 5. Employee salary reduction contributions to a SIMPLE retirement account. Social Security and Medicare. Page 40/ (a) Taxable

15. Retirement and pension plans:
17. Employee salary reduction contributions to a SIMPLE retirement account Treatment under Employment Taxes Federal Unemployment Tax (FUTA) is ___.
    (a) Taxable
    (b) Exempt
    (c) Withhold
    (d) Nontaxable

    Answer: See Section 15. Special Rules for Various Types of Services and Payments. Special Classes of Employment and Special Types of Payments. Treatment Under Employment Taxes. Retirement and pension plans: 5. Employee salary reduction contributions to a SIMPLE retirement account. Page 40/ (a) Taxable

15. Retirement and pension plans:
18. Section 15. Special Rules for Various Types of Services and Payments, Special Classes of Employment and Special Types of Payments, Treatment Under Employment Taxes. Retirement and pension plans: 6. Distribution from qualified retirement and pension plans and section 403(b) annuities. Income Tax Withholding. Withhold, but recipient may elect exemption on Form ___ in certain cases;
    (a) 941
    (b) 944
    (c) W-4
    (d) W-4P

    Answer: See Section 15. Special Rules for Various Types of Services and Payments. Treatment Under Employment Taxes. 6. Distributions from qualified retirement and pension plans under section 403(b) annuities. Page 40/ (d) W-4P

Section 15. Special Rules for Various Types of Services and Payments.

15. Retirement and pension plans:
19. Distributions from qualified retirements and pension plans and section 403(b) annuities. Income Tax Withholding. Withhold, but recipient may elect exemption on Form W-4P in certain cases; mandatory ___% withholding applies to an eligible rollover distribution that is not a direct rollover;
   (a) 20
   (b) 10
   (c) 15
   (d) 25

   Answer: See Section 15. Special Rules for Various Types of Services and Payments. Special Classes of Employment and Special Types of Payments. Treatment Under Employment Taxes. Income Tax Withholding. 6. Distributions from qualified retirement and pension plans and section 403(b) annuities. Page 40/ (a) 20

15. Retirement and pension plans:
20. Distributions from qualified retirements and pension plans and section 403(b) annuities. Income Tax Withholding. Withhold, but recipient may elect exemption on Form W-4P in certain cases; mandatory ___% withholding applies to an eligible rollover distribution that is not a direct rollover; exempt for ___. See Publication 15-A.
   (a) 20, direct rollover
   (b) 10, rollover
   (c) 15, direct rollover
   (d) 25, rollover

   Answer: See Section 15. Special Rules for Various Types of Services and Payments. Special Classes of Employment and Special Types of Payments. Treatment Under Employment Taxes. Income Tax Withholding. 6. Distributions from qualified retirement and pension plans and section 403(b) annuities. page 40/ (a) 20, direct rollover

15. Retirement and pension plans:
21. Social Security and Medicare and Federal Unemployment Taxes, Retirement and pension plans. 6. Distributions from qualified retirement and pension plans and section 403(b) annuities are ___.
   (a) Taxable
   (b) Exempt
   (c) Withhold
   (d) Withheld

   Answer: See Section 15. Special Rules for Various Types of Services and Payments. Special Classes of Employment and Special Types of Payments. Treatment Under Employment Taxes. 6. Distribution from qualified retirement and pension plans and section 403(b) annuities. Page 40/ (b) Exempt

Section 15. Special Rules for Various Types of Services and Payments.

15. Salespersons:
22. Section 15. Special Rules for Various Types of Services and Payments. Special Classes of Employment and Special Types of Payments. Treatment Under Employment Taxes. Salespersons:
1. Common law employees. Income Tax Withholding ___,
   (a) Withhold
   (b) Withheld
   (c) Exempt
   (d) Taxable
   Answer: See 15. Special Rules for Various Types of Services and Payments. Salespersons: 1. Common law employees. Page 40/ (a) Withhold

15. Salespersons:
23. Section 15. Special Rules for Various Type of Services and Payments. Special Classes of Employment and Special Types of Payments. Treatment Under Employment Taxes. Salespersons:
1. Common law employees. Social Security and Medicare (including Additional Medicare Tax when wages are paid in excess of $200,000) are ___.
   (a) Withhold
   (b) Withheld
   (c) Exempt
   (d) Taxable
   Answer: See Section 15. Special Rules for Various Types of Services and Payments. Treatment Under Employment Taxes. Salespersons. 1. Common law employees. page 40/ (d) Taxable

15. Salespersons:
24. Salespersons:
1. Common law employees. Treatment Under Employment Taxes. Federal Unemployment Tax (FUTA) is ___.
   (a) Withhold
   (b) Withheld
   (c) Exempt
   (d) Taxable
   Answer: See Section 15. Special Rules for Various Services and Payments. Social Security and Medicare. Page 40/ (d) Taxable

Section 15. Special Rules for Various Types of Services and Payments.

15. Salespersons:

25. Salespersons:
    2. Statutory employees, Treatment Under Employment Taxes. Federal Unemployment Tax (FUTA) is ___, except for full-time life insurance sales agents.
    (a) Withhold
    (b) Withheld
    (c) Exempt
    (d) Taxable
    Answer: See Section 15. Special Rules for Various Types of Services and Payments. Treatment Under Employment Taxes. Salespersons: 2. Statutory employees Federal Unemployment (FUTA). Page 40/(d) Taxable

15. Salespersons:

26. Salespersons: 2. Statutory employees, Treatment Under Employment Taxes. Income Tax Withholding is ___,
    (a) Withhold
    (b) Withheld
    (c) Exempt
    (d) Taxable
    Answer: See Section 15. Special Rules for Various Types of Services and Payments. Treatment Under Employment Taxes. Salespersons: 2. Statutory employees. Income Tax Withholding. Page 40/(c) Exempt

15. Salespersons:

27. Salespersons: 2. Statutory employees, Treatment Under Employment Taxes. Social Security and Medicare (including Additional Medicare Tax when wages are paid in excess of $200,000) is ___,
    (a) Withhold
    (b) Withheld
    (c) Exempt
    (d) Taxable
    Answer: See Section 15. Special Rules for Various Types of Services and Payments. Treatment Under Employment Taxes. Salespersons: 2. Statutory employees. Income Tax Withholding. Page 40/(d) Taxable

Section 15. Special Rules for Various Types of Services and Payments.

15. Salespersons:
28. 3. Statutory nonemployees (qualified real estate agents, direct sellers, and certain companion sitters) per Section 15. Special Rules for Various Services and Payments. Special Classes of Employment and Special Types of Payments. Treatment Under Employment Taxes. Income Tax Withholding is ___.
    (a) Withhold
    (b) Withheld
    (c) Exempt
    (d) Taxable
    Answer: See Section 15. Special Rules for Various Types of Services and Payments. 3. Statutory nonemployees. Treatment Under Employment Taxes. Page 40/ (c) Exempt

15. Salespersons:
29. 3. Statutory nonemployees (qualified real estate agents, direct sellers, and certain companion sitters) per Section 15. Special Rules for Various Services and Payments. Special Classes of Employment and Special Types of Payments. Treatment Under Employment Taxes. Social Security and Medicare (including Additional Medicare Tax when wages are paid in excess of $200,000) are ___.
    (a) Withhold
    (b) Withheld
    (c) Exempt
    (d) Taxable
    Answer: See Section 15. Special Rules for Various Types of Services and Payments. 3. Statutory nonemployees. Treatment Under Employment Taxes. Page 40/ (c) Exempt

15. Salespersons:
30. 3. Statutory nonemployees (qualified real estate agents, direct sellers, and certain companion sitters) per Section 15. Special Rules for Various Services and Payments. Special Classes of Employment and Special Types of Payments. Treatment Under Employment Taxes. Federal Unemployment Tax (FUTA) is ___.
    (a) Withhold
    (b) Withheld
    (c) Exempt
    (d) Taxable
    Answer: See Section 15. Special Rules for Various Types of Services and Payments. 3. Statutory nonemployees. Treatment Under Employment Taxes. Page 40/ (c) Exempt

Section 15. Special Rules for Various Types of Services and Payments.

15. Scholarships and fellowship grants:
31. Scholarships and fellowship grants (includible in income under section ___).
    (a) 115(a)
    (b) 116(b)
    (c) 117(c)
    (d) 118(d)
    Answer: See Section 15. Special Rules for Various Types of Services and Payments. Special Classes of Employment and Special Types of Payments. Scholarships and fellowship grants. Page 40/ (c) 117(c)

15. Scholarships and fellowship grants:
32. Scholarships and fellowship grants (includible in income under section ___). Income tax ___.
    (a) 115(a), Taxable
    (b) 116(b), Withheld
    (c) 117(c), Withhold
    (d) 118(d), Exempt
    Answer: See Section 15. Special Rules for Various Types of Services and Payments. Special Classes of Employment and Special Types of Payments. Scholarships and fellowship grants. Page 40/ (c) 117(c), Withhold

15. Scholarships and fellowship grants:
33. Scholarships and fellowship grants (includible in income under section 117(c)). Social Security and Medicare (including Additional Medicate Tax when wages are paid in excess of $200,000. Taxability depends on the ___ of the employment and the status of the organization, See Students, scholars, trainees, teachers, etc. on the next page.
    (a) type
    (b) method
    (c) means
    (d) nature
    Answer: See Section 15. Special Rules for Various Types of Services and Payments. Special Classes of Employment and Special Types of Payments. Scholarships and fellowship grants. Page 40/ (d) nature

15. Scholarships and fellowship grants:
34. Scholarships and fellowship grants (includible in income under section 117(c)). Federal Unemployment Tax (FUTA). Taxability depends on the ___ of the employment and the status of the organization, See Students, scholars, trainees, teachers, etc. on the next page.
    (a) type
    (b) method
    (c) means
    (d) nature
    Answer: See Section 15. Special Rules for Various Types of Services and Payments. Special Classes of Employment and Special Types of Payments. Scholarships and fellowship grants. Page 40/ (d) nature

Section 15. Special Rules for Various Types of Services and Payments.

15. Severance or dismissal pay.
35. Treatment Under Employment Taxes. Income Tax Withholding ___.
    (a) Withheld
    (b) Withhold
    (c) Taxable
    (d) Exempt
    Answer: See Section 15. Special Rules for Various Types of Services and Payments. Treatment Under Employment Taxes, Severance or dismissal pay. Income Tax Withholding. Page 40/ (b) Withhold

15. Severance or dismissal pay.
36. Treatment under Employment Taxes. Social Security and Medicare Tax (including Additional Medicare Tax when wages are paid in excess of $200,000) ___.
    (a) Withheld
    (b) Withhold
    (c) Taxable
    (d) Exempt
    Answer: See Section 15. Special Rules for Various Types of Services and Payments. Treatment Under Employment Taxes, Severance or dismissal pay. Social Security and Medicare Tax. Page 40/ (c) Taxable

15. Severance or dismissal pay.
37. Treatment under Employment Taxes. Federal Unemployment Tax (FUTA) ___.
    (a) Withheld
    (b) Withhold
    (c) Taxable
    (d) Exempt
    Answer: See Section 15. Special Rules for Various Types of Services and Payments. Treatment Under Employment Taxes, Severance or dismissal pay. Social Security and Medicare Tax. Page 40/ (c) Taxable

15. Service not in the course of the employer's trade or business:
38. Service not in the course of the employer's trade or business (other than on a farm operated for profit or for household employment in ___).
    (a) a private home
    (b) a nursing home
    (c) nursing homes
    (d) private homes
    Answer: See Section 15. Special Rules for Various Types of Services and Payments. Special Classes of Employment and Special Types of Payments. Service not in the course of the employer's trade or business. Page 41/ (a) in a private home

Section 15. Special Rules for Various Types of Services and Payments.

15. Service not in the course of the employer's trade or business:
39. Service not in the course of the employer's trade or business. Income Tax Withholding. Withhold only if employee earns $___ or more in cash in a quarter and works on ___ or more different days in that quarter or in the preceding quarter.
    - (a) 25, 30
    - (b) 50, 24
    - (c) 100, 30
    - (d) 1,000, 24

    Answer: See Section 15. Special Rules for Various Types of Services and Payments. Treatment Under Employment Taxes. Income Tax Withholding. Page 41/(b) 50, 24

15. Service not in the course of the employer's trade or business:
40. Service not in the course of the employer's trade or business. <u>Social Security</u> and <u>Medicare</u> are <u>Taxable</u> if employee receives $___ or more in cash in a calendar year.
    - (a) 50
    - (b) 100
    - (c) 500
    - (d) 1,000

    Answer: See Section 15. Special Rules for Various Types of Services and Payments. Treatment Under Employment Taxes. Social Security and Medicare. Page 41/ (b) 100

15. Service not in the course of the employer's trade or business:
41. Service not in the course of the employer's trade or business. Federal Unemployment Tax (FUTA). Taxable only if employee earns $___ or more in cash in a quarter and works on ___ or more different days in that quarter or in the preceding quarter.
    - (a) 50, 24
    - (d) 100, 30
    - (c) 500, 60
    - (d) 1,000, 90

    Answer: See Section 15. Special Rules for Various Types of Services and Payments. Treatment Under Employment Taxes. Service not in the course of the employer's trade or business. Federal Unemployment. Page 41/ (a) 50, 24

15. Sick pay:
42. Section 15. Special Rules for Various Types of Services and Payments. Treatment Under Employment Taxes. Sick pay. See Publication ___.
    - (a) 15
    - (b) 15-A
    - (c) 15-B
    - (d) 15-C

    Answer: See Section 15. Special Rules for Various Types of Services and Payments. Treatment Under Employment Taxes. Sick pay. Page 41/(b) 15-A

Section 15. Special Rules for Various Types of Services and Payments.

15. Sick pay:
43. Section 15. Special Rules for Various Types of Services and Payments. Treatment Under Employment Taxes. Sick pay. Income Tax Withholding. ___.
   (a) Withhold
   (b) Withheld
   (c) Taxable
   (d) Exempt
   Answer: See Section 15. Special Rules for Various Types of Services and Payments. Treatment Under Employment Taxes. Sick pay. Page 41/(a) Withhold

15. Sick pay:
44. Section 15. Special Rules for Various Types of Services and Payments. Treatment Under Employment Taxes. Sick pay. Social Security and Medicare (Including Additional Medicare Tax when wages are paid in excess of $200,000). Exempt after end of ___ calendar months after the calendar month employee last worked for employer.
   (a) one
   (b) 3
   (c) 6
   (d) 12
   Answer: See Section 15. Special Rules for Various Types of Services and Payments. Treatment Under Employment Taxes. Sick pay. Page 41/(c) 6

15. Sick pay:
45. Section 15. Special Rules for Various Types of Services and Payments. Treatment Under Employment Taxes. Sick pay. Federal Unemployment Tax (FUTA). Exempt after end of ___ calendar months after the calendar month employee last worked for employer.
   (a) 3ne
   (b) 6
   (c) 12
   (d) 18
   Answer: See Section 15. Special Rules for Various Types of Services and Payments. Treatment Under Employment Taxes. Sick pay. Page 41/(b) 6

Section 15. Special Rules for Various Types of Services and Payments.

15. Students, scholars, trainees, teachers, etc.:
46. Section 15. Students, scholars, trainees, teachers, etc.: 1. Student enrolled and regularly attending classes, performing services for:
a. Private school, college or university. Treatment Under Employment Taxes. Income Tax Withholding. ___.
   - (a) Withhold
   - (b) Withheld
   - (c) Taxable
   - (d) Exempt

   Answer: See Section 15. Special Rules for Various Types of Services and Payments. Treatment Under Employment Taxes. Income Tax Withholding. Students, scholars, trainees, teachers, etc.: 1. Students enrolled and regularly attending classes, performing services for: Page 41/ (a) Withhold

15. Students, scholars, trainees, teachers, etc.:
47. Section 15. Students, scholars, trainees, teachers, etc.: 1. Student enrolled and regularly attending classes, performing services for: a. Private school, college or university. Treatment Under Employment Taxes. Social Security and Medicare (including Additional Medicare Tax when wages are paid in excess of $200,000) ___.
   - (a) Withhold
   - (b) Withheld
   - (c) Taxable
   - (d) Exempt

   Answer: See Section 15. Special ,Rules for Various Types of Services and Payments. Treatment Under Employment Taxes. Page 41/ (d) Exempt

15. Students, scholars, trainees, teachers, etc.:
48. Section 15. Students, scholars, trainees, teachers, etc.: 1. Student enrolled and regularly attending classes, performing services for: a. Private school, college or university. Treatment Under Employment Taxes. Federal Unemployment Tax (FUTA)___.
   - (a) Withhold
   - (b) Withheld
   - (c) Taxable
   - (d) Exempt

   Answer: See Section 15. Special ,Rules for Various Types of Services and Payments. Treatment Under Employment Taxes. Page 41/ (d) Exempt

Section 15. Special Rules for Various Types of Services and Payments.

15. Students, scholars, trainees, teachers, etc.:
49. Special Classes of Employment and Special Types of Payments. Students, scholars, trainees, teachers, etc.: b. Auxiliary nonprofit organization operated for and controlled by school, college, or university. Treatment Under Employment Taxes. Income Tax Withholding. ___.
   (a) Withhold
   (b) Withheld
   (c) Taxable
   (d) Exempt
   Answer: See Section 15. Special Rules for Various Types of Services and Payments. Income Tax Withholding. Page 41/ (a) Withhold

15. Students, scholars, trainees, teachers, etc.:
50. Special Classes of Employment and Special Types of Payments. Students, scholars, trainees, teachers, etc.: b. Auxiliary nonprofit organization operated for and controlled by school, college, or university. Treatment Under Employment Taxes. Social Security and Medicare (including Additional Medicare Tax when wages are paid in excess of $200,000). Exempt unless services are covered by a section ___ (Social Security Act) agreement.
   (a) 118
   (b) 119
   (c) 218
   (d) 219
   Answer: See Section 15. Special Rules for Various Types of Services and Payments. Treatment Under Employment Taxes. Social Security and Medicare. Students, scholars, trainees, teachers, etc.: Page 41/ (c) 218

15. Students, scholars, trainees, teachers, etc.:
51. Special Classes of Employment and Special Types of Payments. Students, scholars, trainees, teachers, etc.: b. Auxiliary nonprofit organization operated for and controlled by school, college, or university. Treatment Under Employment Taxes. Federal Unemployment Tax (FUTA) ___.
   (a) Exempt
   (b) Withhold
   (c) Taxable
   (d) Not applicable
   Answer: See Section 15. Special Rules for Various Types of Services and Payments. Treatment Under Employment Taxes. Social Security and Medicare. Students, scholars, trainees, teachers, etc.: Page 41/ (a) Exempt

Section 15. Special Rules for Various Types of Services and Payments.

15. Students, scholars, trainees, teachers, etc.:
52. Section 15. Special Classes of Employment and Special Types of Payments. Students, scholars, trainees, teachers, etc.: c. Public school, college, or university. Treatment Under Employment Taxes. Income Tax Withholding. _____.
    (a) Withhold
    (b) Withheld
    (c) Taxable
    (d) Exempt
    Answer: See Section 15. Special Rules for Various Types of Services and Payments. Students, scholars, trainees, teachers, etc.: c. Treatment Under Employment Taxes. Page 41/ (a) Withhold

15. Students, scholars, trainees, teachers, etc.:
53. Students, scholars, trainees, teachers, etc.: Public school, college, or university. Social Security and Medicare Treatment Under Employment Taxes. Exempt unless services are covered by a section ___ (Social Security Act) agreement.
    (a) 215
    (b) 216
    (c) 217
    (d) 218
    Answer: See Section 15. Special Rules for Various Types of Services and Payments. Exempt unless services are covered by a section 218 (Social Security Act) agreement. Page 41/ (d) 218

15. Students, scholars, trainees, teachers, etc.:
54. Section 15. Special Rules for Various Types of Services and Payments. Special Classes of Employment and Special Types of Payments. Treatment Under Employment Taxes. Students, scholars, trainees, teachers, etc.: c. Public schools, college, or university. Federal Unemployment Tax (FUTA) ___.
    (a) Withhold
    (b) Exempt
    (c) Taxable
    (d) Withheld
    Answer: See Section 15. Special Rules for Various Types of Services and Payments. Treatment Under Employment Taxes. Federal Unemployment tax (FUTA). Page 41/(b) Exempt

Section 15. Special Rules for Various Types of Services and Payments.

15. Students, scholars, trainees, teachers, etc.:
55. Section 15. Special Classes of Employment and Special Types of Payments. Students, scholars, trainees, teachers, etc.: 2. Full-time student performing service for academic credit, combining instruction with work experience as an integral part of the program. Treatment Under Employment Taxes. Income Tax Withholding.____.
- (a) Withhold
- (b) Withheld
- (c) Taxable
- (d) Exempt

Answer: See Section 15. Special Rules for Various Types of Services and Payments. Special Classes of Employment and Special Types of Payments. Treatment Under Employment Taxes. Page 41/ (a) Withhold

15. Students, scholars, trainees, teachers, etc.:
56. Section 15. Special Classes of Employment and Special Types of Payments. Treatment Under Employment Taxes. Students, scholars, trainees, teachers, etc.: 2. Full-time student performing service for academic credit, combining instruction with work experience as an integral part of the program. Treatment Under Employment Taxes. Social Security and Medicare ____.
- (a) Withhold
- (b) Withheld
- (c) Taxable
- (d) Exempt

Answer: See Section 15. Special Rules for Various Types of Services and Payments. Special Classes of Employment and Special Types of Payments. Social Security and Medicare. Page 41/ (c) Taxable

Section 15. Special Rules for Various Types of Services and Payments.

15. Students, scholars, trainees, teachers, etc.:

57. Section 15. Special Classes of Employment and Special Types of Payments. Treatment Under Employment Taxes. Students, scholars, trainees, teachers, etc.: 2. Full-time student performing service for academic credit, combining instruction with work experience as an integral part of the program. Treatment Under Employment Taxes. Federal Unemployment Tax (FUTA) ___.
    - (a) Taxable, unless program was established for or on behalf of an employer or group of employers
    - (b) Exempt, unless program was established for or on behalf of an employer or group of employers
    - (c) Withheld, unless program was established for or on behalf of an employer or group of employers
    - (d) Withhold, if program was not established for or on behalf of a college or university group

    Answer: See Section 15. Special Rules for Various Types of Services and Payments. Treatment Under Employment Taxes. Students, scholars, trainees, teachers, etc.: 2. Full-time student performing service for academic credit, combining instruction with work experience as an integral part of the program. Page 41/ Exempt, unless program was established for or on behalf of an employer or group of employers

15. Students, scholars, trainees, teachers, etc.:

58. Section 15. Special Classes of Employment and Special Types of Payments. Treatment Under Employment Taxes. Students, scholars, trainees, teachers, etc.: 3. Student nurse performing part-time services for nominal earnings at hospital as incidental part of training. Income Tax Withholding. _____.
    - (a) Withheld
    - (b) Withhold
    - (c) Taxable
    - (d) Exempt

    Answer: See Section 15. Special Rules for Various Types of Services and Payments. Special Classes of Employment and Special Types of Payments. Treatment Under Employment Taxes. Page 41/ Withhold

Section 15. Special Rules for Various Types of Services and Payments.

15. Students, scholars, trainees, teachers, etc.:
59. Section 15. Special Rules for Various Types of Services and Payments. Special Classes of Employment and Special Types of Payments. Treatment Under Employment Taxes. Students, scholars, trainees, teachers, etc.: 3. Student nurse performing part-time services for nominal earnings at hospital as incidental part of training. Social Security and Medicare (including Additional Medicare Tax when wages are paid in excess of $200,000)___.
   - (a) Withheld
   - (b) Withhold
   - (c) Taxable
   - (d) Exempt

   Answer: See Section 15. Special Classes of Employment and Special Types of Payments. Page 41/(d) Exempt

15. Students, scholars, trainees, teachers, etc.:
60. Section 15. Special Rules for Various Types of Services and Payments. Special Classes of Employment and Special Types of Payments. Treatment Under Employment Taxes. Students, scholars, trainees, teachers, etc.: 3. Student nurse performing part-time services for nominal earnings at hospital as incidental part of training. Federal Unemployment Tax (FUTA) ___.
   - (a) Withheld
   - (b) Withhold
   - (c) Taxable
   - (d) Exempt

   Answer: See Section 15. Special Classes of Employment and Special Types of Payments. Page 41/ (d) Exempt

DU VALL'S TEST'S™
Instructor's Manual For Study Guide Series United States Tax Code
IRS Publication 15 Circular E, Employer's Tax Guide Tax Year 2013
Tax Test 15E-S15-4 [Multiple-Choice Questions With Answers]

Section 15. Special Rules for Various Types of Services and Payments. .

15. Students, scholars, trainees, teachers, etc.:
1. Section 15. Students, scholars, trainees, teachers, etc,: 4. Student employed by organized camps. Treatment Under Employment Taxes. Income Tax Withholding.___.
   - (a) Withheld
   - (b) Withhold
   - (c) Taxable
   - (d) Exempt

   Answer: See Section 15. Special Rules for Various Types of Services and Payments. Page 41/ (b) Withhold

15. Students, scholars, trainees, teachers, etc.:
2. Section 15. Students, scholars, trainees, teachers, etc.: 4. Student employed by organized camps, Treatment Under Employment Taxes. Social Security and Medicare (Including Additional Medicare Tax when wages are paid in excess of $200,000)___.
   - (a) Withheld
   - (b) Withhold
   - (c) Taxable
   - (d) Exempt

   Answer: See Section 15. Special Rules for Various Types of Services and Payments. Page 41/(c) Taxable

15. Students, scholars, trainees, teachers, etc.:
3. Section 15. Students scholars, trainees, teachers, etc.: 4. Student employed by organized camps, Treatment Under Employment Taxes. Federal Unemployment Tax (FUTA)___.
   - (a) Withheld
   - (b) Withhold
   - (c) Taxable
   - (d) Exempt

   Answer: See Section 15. Special Rules for Various Types of Services and Payments. Page 41/ (d) Exempt

© Copyright 2013. All rights reserved. Notice: United States Copyright Laws and International Treaties prohibit unauthorized publication, reproduction, distribution of this Work. Unauthorized use of this copyright in any form, format, publication or document may result in severe civil and criminal penalties. Violations of this copyright are investigated by the United States Department of Justice and carry, upon conviction of fines up to $250,000 and five years confinement. This Work is protected by United States Copyright Laws and International Treaties. Do not Copy, do not reproduce, do not distribute.

A Ficus Tree Publishing Educational-Technical Publications

Section 15. Special Rules for Various Types of Services and Payments.

15. Students, scholars, trainees, teachers, etc.:

4. Section 15. Students, scholars, trainees, teachers, etc.: 5. Student, scholar, trainee, teacher, etc., as nonimmigrant under section 101(a)(15)(F), (J), (M), or Q of the Immigration and Nationality Act (that is, aliens holding F-1, J-1, M-1, or Q-1 ___).
    (a) Forms
    (b) rules
    (c) visas
    (d) agreements
   Answer: See Section 15. Special Rules for Various Types of Services and Payments. Special Classes of Employment and Special Types of Payments. Page 41/(c) visas

15. Students, scholars, trainees, teachers, etc.:

5. Section 15. Students, scholars, trainees, teachers, etc.: Treatment Under Employment Taxes. Income Tax Withholding. ___ .
    (a) Withhold unless excepted by regulations
    (b) Withheld unless excepted by regulations
    (c) Taxable unless excepted by regulations
    (d) Exempt unless required by regulations
   Answer: See Section 15. Special Rules for Various Types of Services and Payments. Special Classes of Employment and Special Types of Payments. Treatment Under Employment Taxes. Income Tax Withholding. Page 41/ (a) Withhold unless excepted by regulations

15. Students, scholars, trainees, teachers, etc.:

6. Section 15. Students, scholars, trainees, teachers, etc.: Treatment Under Employment Taxes. Social Security and Medicare (including Additional Medicare tax when wages are paid in excess of $200,000). Exempt if service is performed for purpose specified in section 101(a)(15)(F), (J), (M), or (Q) of ___ and ___ Act.
    (a) Alien, Residency
    (b) Immigration, Nationality
    (c) Nationality, Immigration
    (d) Nationality, Alien Immigration
   Answer: See Section 15. Special Rules for Various Types of Services and Payments. Special Rules for Various Types of Services and Payments. Special Classes of Employment and Special Types of Payments. Treatment Under Employment Taxes. Students, scholars, trainees, teachers, etc.: 5. Student, scholar, trainee, teacher, etc.: Page 41/ (b) Immigration, Nationality

Section 15. Special Rules for Various Types of Services and Payments.

15. Students, scholars, trainees, teachers, etc.:

7. Section 15. Students, scholars, trainees, teachers, etc.: Treatment Under Employment Taxes. Federal Unemployment Tax (FUTA). Exempt if service is performed for purpose specified in section 101(a)(15)(F), (J), (M), or (Q) of ___ and ___ Act. However, these taxes may apply if the employee becomes a resident alien. See the special residency tests for exempt individuals in chapter 1 of Publication ____.
   - (a) Alien, Residency, 515
   - (b) Immigration, Nationality, 519
   - (c) Nationality, Immigration, 520
   - (d) Nationality, Alien Immigration, 521

   Answer: See Section 15. Special Rules for Various Types of Services and Payments. Special Rules for Various Types of Services and Payments. Special Classes of Employment and Special Types of Payments. Treatment Under Employment Taxes. Students, scholars, trainees, teachers, etc.: 5. Student, scholar, trainee, teacher, etc.: Page 41/ (b) Immigration, Nationality, 519

15. Supplemental unemployment compensation plan benefits.

8. Section 15. Special Classes of Employment and Special Types of Payments. Treatment Under Employment Taxes. Supplemental unemployment compensation plan benefits Income Tax Withholding. ___.
   - (a) Withhold
   - (b) Withheld
   - (c) Exempt
   - (d) Taxable

   Answer: See Section 15. Supplemental unemployment compensation plan benefits. Page 41/ (a) Withhold

15. Supplemental unemployment compensation plan benefits.

9. Section 15. Special Rules for Various Types of Services and Payments. Special Classes of Employment and Special Types of Payments. Treatment Under Employment Taxes. Supplemental unemployment compensation plan benefits. Social Security and Medicare (including Additional Medicare Tax when wages are paid in excess of $200,000). Exempt under certain conditions. See Publication ___.
   - (a) 15-A
   - (b) 15-B
   - (c) 15-C
   - (d) 15-D

   Answer: See Section 15. Special Rules for Various Types of Services and Payments. Page 41/ (a) 15-A

Section 15. Special Rules for Various Types of Services and Payments.

15. Supplemental unemployment compensation plan benefits.
10.   Section 15. Special Rules for Various Types of Services and Payments. Special Classes of Employment and Special Types of Payments. Treatment Under Employment Taxes. Supplemental unemployment compensation plan benefits. Federal Unemployment Tax. ___ under certain conditions See Publication 15-A.
    (a)   Withhold
    (b)   Withheld
    (c)   Exempt
    (d)   Taxable
    Answer: See Section 15. Special Rules for Various Types of Services and Payments. Page 41/ (c) Exempt

15. Tips
11.   Special Classes of Employment and Special Types of Payments. Treatment Under Employment Taxes. Tips: 1. If $___ or more in a month. Income Tax Withholding. ___.
    (a)   20, Withheld
    (b)   20, Withhold
    (c)   50, Taxable
    (d)   50, Exempt
    Answer: See Section 15. Special Rules for Various Types of Services and Payments. Page 41/ (b) 20, Withhold

15. Tips:
12.   15. Special Rules for Various Types of Services and Payments. Special Classes of Employment and Special Types of Payments. Treatment Under Employment Taxes. Tips: 1. If $___ or more a month, Social Security and Medicare (including Additional Medicare Tax when wages are paid in excess of $200,000). ___ under certain conditions.
    (a)   20, Taxable
    (b)   20, Exempt
    (c)   50, Withhold
    (d)   50, Withheld
    Answer: See Section 15. Special Rules for Various Types of Services and Payments. Page 41/(a) 20, Taxable

Section 15. Special Rules for Various Types of Services and Payments.

15 Tips:
13. 15. Special Rules for Various Types of Services and Payments. Special Classes of Employment and Special Types of Payments. Treatment Under Employment Taxes. Tips 1. if $___ or more in a month. Federal Unemployment Tax (FUTA). Taxable for all tips ___ in writing to employer.
    (a) 20, recorded
    (b) 20, reported
    (c) 50, documented
    (d) 50, listed
    Answer: See Section 15. Special Rules for Various Types of Services and Payments.
    (b) 20, reported

15 Tips:
14. 15. Special Rules for Various Types of Services and Payments. Special Classes of Employment and Special Types of Payments. Treatment Under Employment Taxes. Tips: 2. If less than $___ in a month.
    (a) 20
    (b) 25
    (c) 50
    (d) 100
    Answer: See Section 15. Special Classes of Employment and Special Types of Payments, Treatment Under Employment Taxes. Page 41/ (a) 20

15 Tips:
15. 15. Special Rules for Various Types of Services and Payments. Special Classes of Employment and Special Types of Payments. Treatment Under Employment Taxes. Tips: 2. If less than $___ in a month. See section ___ for more information.
    (a) 20, 6
    (b) 25, 7
    (c) 50, 8
    (d) 100, 9
    Answer: See Section 15. Special Classes of Employment and Special Types of Payments, Treatment Under Employment Taxes. Page 41/ (a) 20, 6

15 Tips:
16. Section 15. Special Rules for Various Types of Services and Payments. Special Classes of Employment and Special Types of Payments. Treatment Under Employment Taxes. Tips: 2. Income Tax Withholding. ___,
    (a) Withheld
    (b) Withhold
    (c) Taxable
    (d) Exempt
    Answer: See Section 15. Special Rules for Various Types of Services and Payments. Page 41/(d) Exempt

Section 15. Special Rules for Various Types of Services and Payments.

15 Tips:

17. Section 15. Special Rules for Various Types of Services and Payments. Special Classes of Employment and Special Types of Payments. Treatment Under Employment Taxes. Tips: 2. Social Security and Medicare (including Additional Medicare Tax when wages are paid exceeding $200,000). ___,
    - (a) Withheld
    - (b) Withhold
    - (c) Taxable
    - (d) Exempt

    Answer: See Section 15. Special Rules for Various Types of Services and Payments. Page 41/(d) Exempt

15 Worker's Compensation:

18. Section 15. Special Rules for Various Types of Services and Payments. Special Classes of Employment and Special Types of Payments. Treatment Under Employment Taxes. Workers Compensation. Federal Unemployment Tax (FUTA) ___,
    - (a) Withheld
    - (b) Withhold
    - (c) Taxable
    - (d) Exempt

    Answer: See Section 15. Special Rules for Various Types of Services and Payments. Page 41/(d) Exempt

15 Worker's Compensation:

19. Section 15. Special Rules for Various Types of Services and Payments. Special Classes of Employment and Special Types of Payments. Treatment Under Employment Taxes. Workers Compensation. Income Tax Withholding. ___,
    - (a) Withheld
    - (b) Withhold
    - (c) Taxable
    - (d) Exempt

    Answer: See Section 15. Special Rules for Various Types of Services and Payments. Page 41/(d) Exempt

15 Worker's Compensation:

20. Section 15. Special Rules for Various Types of Services and Payments. Special Classes of Employment and Special Types of Payments. Treatment Under Employment Taxes. Workers Compensation. Social Security and Medicare (including Additional Medicare Tax when wages are paid in excess of $200,000). ___,
    - (a) Withheld
    - (b) Withhold
    - (c) Taxable
    - (d) Exempt

    Answer: See Section 15. Special Rules for Various Types of Services and Payments. Page 41/(d) Exempt

The International Leader in Construction Technology Home Study

Instructor's Manual for Tax Test 15E-S16 Section 16.
How To Use The Income Tax Withholding Tables

General Description. Section 16. Tax Test 15E-S16

Tax Test 15E-S16-1. Tax Test 15E-S16-1 introduces Section 16. How To Use Income Tax Withholding Tables. Study material, information and multiple-choice questions provided from Tax Test 15E-28 include the following: Section 15. Special Rules for Various Types of Services and Payments; Students, scholars, trainees, teachers, etc.; Supplemental unemployment compensation plan benefits; Tips; Worker's compensation; Section 16. How To Use Income tax Withholding Tables; Wage Bracket Method; Percentage Method; How to Use Income Tax Withholding Tables. Table 5; Section 16. Adjusting wage bracket withholding for employees claiming more than 10 withholding allowances; Section 16. Percentage Method; Table 5. Percentage method Amount for One Withholding Allowance.

Key Words. Section 16. Tax Test 15E-S16
How To Use The Income Tax Withholding Tables

Key Word page numbers provided for this section reference to IRS Publication 15 only.

Tax Test 15E-S16-1. The title of Section 16. How To Use The Income Tax Withholding Tables is the initial key word, sentence, or phrase. In Circular E, Employer's Tax Guide the key words are set in bold print. The words in bold print identifying the subpart of the section will generally appear in the subject index at the conclusion of a text. The Title of the Section will generally appear as a part of the Contents at the beginning of each textbook. From the bold print identifying the parts and subparts of IRS Publication 15, Employers Tax Guide for the current year. Thus, additional important information is obtained from the primary, secondary and minor headings of the basic text. From **page 42, 43, and 44** as follow below:

Section 16. How to Use the Income tax Withholding Tables. TIP. Wage Bracket Method. Adjusting wage bracket withholding for employees claiming more than 10 withholding allowances. Percentage Method. Table 5. Percentage Method -Amount of One Withholding Allowance. Annual income tax withholding. Alternative Methods of Income Tax Withholding. Formula tables for percentage method. Wage bracket percentage method tables. Combined income, social security, and Medicare Withholding tables. Publication 15-A.

© Copyright 2013. All rights reserved. Notice: United States Copyright Laws and International Treaties prohibit unauthorized publication, reproduction, distribution of this Work. Unauthorized use of this copyright in any form, format, publication or document may result in severe civil and criminal penalties. Violations of this copyright are investigated by the United States Department of Justice and carry, upon conviction of fines up to $250,000 and five years confinement. This Work is protected by United States Copyright Laws and International Treaties. Do not Copy, do not reproduce, do not distribute.

A Ficus Tree Publishing Educational-Technical Publications

How To Use The Income Tax Withholding Tables

A Ficus Tree Publishing LLC., Quick Notes Page.

DU VALL'S TEST'S™
Instructor's Manual Study Guide Series United States Tax Code
IRS Publication 15 Circular E, Employer's Tax Guide Tax Year 2013
Tax Test 15E-S16-1 [Multiple-Choice Questions With Answers]

Section 16. How To Use Income Tax Withholding Tables. Page 42

Section 16.
1. There are ___ ways to figure income tax withholding.
   (a) four
   (b) several
   (c) five
   (d) many
   Answer: See Section 16. How To Use the Income Tax Withholding Tables. Page 42/ (b) several

Section 16.
2. The following methods of withholding are based on the information you get from your employees based on Form ___.
   (a) W-2
   (b) W-3
   (c) W-4
   (d) 944
   Answer: See Section 16. How To Use the Income Tax Withholding Tables. Page 42/ (c) W-4

Section 16.
3. The following methods of withholding are based on the information you get from your employees based on ___. See section___ for more information on Form ___.
   (a) W-2, 6, W-2
   (b) W-3, 7, W-3
   (c) W-4, 8, W-3
   (d) W-4, 9, W-4,
   Answer: See Section 16. How To Use the Income Tax Withholding Tables. Page 42/(d) W-4, 9, W-4

Section 16. TIP
4. *Adjustments are not required when there will be ___ number of pay periods,*
   (a) *more than the usual*
   (b) *less than the usual*
   (c) *no change in the*
   (d) *fewer than the usual*
   Answer: See Section 16. How To Use the Income Tax Withholding Tables. TIP. Page 42/ (a) *more than the usual*

How To Use The Income Tax Withholding Tables

Section 16. TIP

5. Adjustments are not required when there will be ___ number of pay periods, for example, ___ biweekly pay dates instead of ___.
   (a) more than the usual, 27, 26
   (b) less than the usual, 26, 27
   (c) more than the usual, 27, 28 as in February
   (d) less than the usual, 26, 27 as in February
   Answer: See Section 16. How To Use the Income Tax Withholding Tables. TIP. Page 42/ (a) more than the usual, 27, 26

Section 16.

6. **Wage Bracket Method**: Under the wage bracket method, find the proper table (on pages ___) for your payroll period and
   (a) 44-63
   (b) 45-64
   (c) 46-65
   (d) 47-66
   Answer: See Section 16. How To Use the Income Tax Withholding Tables. Wage Bracket Method. Page 42/ (c) 46-65

Section 16.

7. **Wage Bracket Method**: Under the wage bracket method, find the proper table (on pages 46-65) for your payroll period and the employee's ___ status as shown on his or her Form ___.
   (a) marshal, W-2
   (b) martial, W-4
   (c) marital, W-4
   (d) marshaling, W-3
   Answer: See Section 16. How To Use the Income Tax Withholding Tables. Wage Bracket Method. Page 42/(c) marital, W-4

Section 16.

8. Under the wage bracket method, find the proper table for your payroll period and the employee's ___ status as shown or his or her Form ___. Then, based on the number of withholding allowances claimed on the Form ___ and the amount of wages, find the amount of ___ tax to withhold.
   (a) marshal, W-2, W-2, federal
   (b) martial, W-3, W-3, FUTA
   (c) marital, W-4, W-4, income
   (d) marshaling, W-3, W-4,
   Answer: See Section 16. How To Use the Income Tax Withholding Tables, Wage Bracket Method. Page 42/ (c) marital, W-4, W-4, income

How To Use The Income Tax Withholding Tables
Section 16. How To Use Income Tax Withholding Tables. Wage Bracket Method. Page 42.

Section 16.
9. If your employee is claiming more than ___ withholding allowances, see below.
   (a) 4
   (b) 6
   (c) 8
   (d) 10
   Answer: See Section 16. How To Use the Income Tax Withholding Tables. Wage Bracket Method. Page 42/ (d) 10

Section 16.
10. If you cannot use the wage bracket tables because wages ___ shown in the last bracket of the table, use
    (a) exceeded the amount
    (b) exceed the amount
    (c) are more than the amounts
    (d) are more than the combined amounts
    Answer: See Section16. How To Use the Income Tax Withholding Tables. Wage Bracket Method. Page 42/ (b) exceed the amount

Section 16.
11. If you cannot use the wage bracket tables because wages ___ shown in the last bracket of the table, use the ___ method of withholding described below.
    (a) exceeded the amount, percentage
    (b) exceed the amount, percentage
    (c) are more than the amounts, combined
    (d) are more than the amounts, combined tax reduction
    Answer: See Section16. How To Use the Income Tax Withholding Tables. Wage Bracket Method. Page 42/ (b) exceed the amount, percentage

Section 16. How to Use Income Tax Withholding Tables. Table 5.
12. Be sure to ___ wages by the amount of total withholding allowances in **Table 5** on this page before using the percentage method tables (pages ___).
    (a) reduce, 44-45
    (b) increase, 45-46
    (c) correct, 46-47
    (d) verify, 47-48
    Answer: See Section 16. How To Use the Income Tax Withholding Tables. Wage Bracket Method. Page 42/ (a) reduce, 44-45

How To Use The Income Tax Withholding Tables

Section 16. Adjusting wage bracket withholding for employees claiming more than 10 withholding allowances. Page 42.

Section 16.
13. The wage bracket tables can be used if an employee claims up to ___ allowances.
    (a) 4
    (b) 6
    (c) 8
    (d) 10
    Answer: See Section 16. How To Use the Income Tax Withholding Tables Wage Bracket Method. Adjusting wage bracket withholding for employees claiming more than **10** withholding allowances. Page 42/ (d) 10

Section 16.
14. More than **10** allowances may be claimed because of the ___ allowance, additional allowances for deductions and credits, and the ___ itself.
    (a) withholding, tax
    (b) deductable, tax base
    (c) total, tax base
    (d) special withholding, system,
    Answer: See Section 16. How To Use the Income Tax Withholding Tables. Wage Bracket Method. Adjusting wage bracket withholding for employees claiming more than 10 withholding allowances. Page 42/ (d) special withholding, system

Section 16.
15. More than **10** allowances may be claimed because of the ___ allowance, additional allowances for deductions and credits, and the ___ itself.
    (a) withholding, tax
    (b) deductable, tax base
    (c) total, tax base
    (d) special withholding, system,
    Answer: See Section 16. How To Use the Income Tax Withholding Tables. Wage Bracket Method. Adjusting wage bracket withholding for employees claiming more than 10 withholding allowances. Page 42/ (d) special withholding, system

© Copyright 2013. All rights reserved. Notice: United States Copyright Laws and International Treaties prohibit unauthorized publication, reproduction, distribution of this Work. Unauthorized use of this copyright in any form, format, publication or document may result in severe civil and criminal penalties. Violations of this copyright are investigated by the United States Department of Justice and carry, upon conviction of fines up to $250,000 and five years confinement. This Work is protected by United States Copyright Laws and International Treaties. Do not Copy, do not reproduce, do not distribute.

How To Use The Income Tax Withholding Tables

Section 16.
16. Adapt the tables to more than 10 allowances as follows: 1. Multiply the number of withholding allowances over 10 by the allowance ___ for the payroll period. .
(a) credit
(b) debit
(c) value
(d) taxes
Answer: See Section 16. How To Use the Income Tax Withholding Tables. Wage Bracket Method. Adjusting wage bracket withholding for employees claiming more than 10 withholding allowances. Page 42/ (c) value

Section 16. Adjusting wage bracket withholding for employees claiming more than 10 withholding allowances. Page 42.

Section 16.
17. Adapt the tables to more than 10 allowances as follows: 1. Multiply the number of withholding allowances over 10 by the allowance ___ for the payroll period. The allowance ___ are in *Table 5* below.
(a) credit, credits
(b) debit, debits
(c) value, values
(d) tax, taxes
Answer: See Section 16. How To Use the Income Tax Withholding Tables. Wage Bracket Method. Adjusting wage bracket withholding for employees claiming more than 10 withholding allowances. Page 42/(c) value, values

Section 16.
18. Adapt the tables to more than 10 allowances as follows: 2. ___ the result from the employee's wages.
(a) Add
(b) Subtract
(c) Multiply
(d) Divide
Answer: See Section 16. How To Use the Income Tax Withholding Tables. Wage Bracket Method. Adjusting wage bracket withholding for employees claiming more than 10 withholding allowances. Page 42/(b) Subtract

How To Use The Income Tax Withholding Tables

Section 16.
19. Adapt the tables to more than 10 allowances as follows: 2. Subtract the result from the employee's wages. 3. On this amount, find and withhold the tax in the ___ for 10 allowances.
    (a) column
    (b) table
    (c) section
    (d) chart
    Answer: See Section 16. How To Use the Income Tax Withholding Tables. Wage Bracket Method. Adjusting wage bracket withholding for employees claiming more than 10 withholding allowances. Page 42/(a) column

Section 16.
20. This is a ___ method. If you use the wage bracket tables, you may continue to withhold the amount in the "10" column when your employee has more than 10 allowances, using the method above. You can also use any other method described below.
    (a) standard
    (b) typical
    (c) voluntary
    (d) practical
    Answer: See Section 16. How To Use the Income Tax Withholding Tables. Wage Bracket Method. Adjusting wage bracket withholding for employees claiming more than 10 withholding allowances. Page 42/(c) voluntary

How To Use The Income Tax Withholding Tables
Section 16. Percentage Method. Page 42.

Section 16. Percentage Method
21. If you do not want to use the wage bracket tables on pages ___ to figure how much income tax to withhold, you can
    (a) 43-61
    (b) 46-65
    (c) 48-65
    (d) 49-67
    Answer: See Section 16. How To use the Income Tax Withholding Tables. Percentage Method. Page 42/ (b) 46-65

The International Leader in Construction Technology Home Study

How To Use The Income Tax Withholding Tables
Section 16. Percentage Method

Section 16.
22. If you do not want to use the wage bracket tables on pages 46-65 to figure how much income tax to withhold, you can use a percentage ___ based on Table 5 on this page and the ___ rate table.
    (a) computation, wage
    (b) amount, appropriate
    (c) computation, appropriate
    (d) figures, wage
    Answer: See Section 16. How To use the Income Tax Withholding Tables. Percentage Method. Page 42/ (c) computation, appropriate

Section 16.
23. If you do not want to use the wage bracket tables on pages 38-57 to figure how much txt to withhold, you can use a percentage ___ based on Table 5 on this page and the ___ rate table. This method works for any number of withholding allowances the employee claims and any amount of ___.
    (a) computation, appropriate, wages
    (b) computation, appropriate, payroll
    (c) figures, wage, wages
    (d) figures wages, wage
    Answer: See Section 16. How To Use the Income Tax Withholding Tables. Percentage Method. Page 42/ (a) computation, appropriate, wages

Section 16.
24. Use these steps to figure the income tax to withhold under the ___ method.
    (a) percentage
    (b) wage bracket
    (c) alternative method
    (d) alternative method 2
    Answer: See Section 16. How to Use the Income Tax Withholding Tables. Percentage Method. Page 42/ (a) percentage

Section 16.
25. Use these steps to figure the income tax to withhold under the percentage method. 1. Multiply one withholding allowance for your ___ (see *Table 5* below) by the number of allowances the employee claims.
    (a) payroll
    (b) payroll period
    (c) payroll quarter
    (d) tax period
    Answer: See Section 16. How To Use the Income Tax Withholding Tables. Percentage Method. Page 42/(b) payroll period

© Copyright 2013. All rights reserved. Notice: United States Copyright Laws and International Treaties prohibit unauthorized publication, reproduction, distribution of this Work. Unauthorized use of this copyright in any form, format, publication or document may result in severe civil and criminal penalties. Violations of this copyright are investigated by the United States Department of Justice and carry, upon conviction of fines up to $250,000 and five years confinement. This Work is protected by United States Copyright Laws and International Treaties. Do not Copy, do not reproduce, do not distribute.

A Ficus Tree Publishing Educational-Technical Publications

How To Use The Income Tax Withholding Tables
Section 16. Percentage Method

Section 16.

26. Use these steps to figure the income tax to withhold under the percentage method. 1. Multiply one withholding allowance for your ___(see Table 5 below) by the number of allowances the employee claims. 2. Subtract that amount from the employee's wages. 3. Determine the amount to withhold from the appropriate table on pages ___.
    (a) payroll period, 44-45
    (b) payroll, 44-47
    (c) payroll quarter, 44-48
    (d) tax period, 37, 38
    Answer: See Section 16. How To Use the Income Tax Withholding Tables. Percentage Method. Page 42/(a) payroll period, 44-45

Section 16. Table 5. Percentage Method—2013 Amount for One Withholding Allowance.

Percentage Method:

27. Section 16. Table 5 Percentage Method—2013 Amount for One Withholding Allowance. From Table 5—The Weekly payroll period for one withholding allowance is $___.
    (a) 72.23
    (b) 73.76
    (c) 74.98
    (d) 75.00
    Answer: Section 16. How To Use the Income Tax Withholding Tables Percentage Method. Table 5 Percentage Method — 2013 Amount for One Withholding Allowance. Weekly. Page 42/(d) 75.00

Section 16. How To Use the Income tax Withholding Tables - Be aware Social Security and Medicare and Federal Unemployment Tax is not included in the tax computations for this part.

Section 16. Percentage Method:

28. Section 16. Table 5. For Tax Year 2013. The Biweekly payroll period for one withholding allowance is $___.
    (a) 140.31
    (b) 142.00
    (c) 145.05
    (d) 150.00
    Answer: Section 16. How To Use the Income Tax Withholding Tables. Table 6. Percentage Method — 2013 Amount for One Withholding Allowance. Biweekly. Page 42/ (d) 150.00

How To Use The Income Tax Withholding Tables

Section 16. Percentage Method:

29. Section 16. Table 5. For Tax Year 2013. The Semimonthly payroll period for one withholding allowance is $___.
    (a) 155.89
    (b) 159.92
    (c) 159.98
    (d) 162.50
    Answer: Section 16. How To Use the Income Tax Withholding Tables. Table 6. Percentage Method — 2013 Amount for One Withholding Allowance. Semimonthly. Page 42/(d) 162.50

Section 16. Percentage Method:

30. Section 16. Table 5. For Tax Year 2013. The Monthly payroll period for one allowance is $___.
    (a) 510.17
    (b) 515.23
    (c) 518.33
    (d) 525.00
    Answer: Section 16. How To Use the Income Tax Withholding Tables. Percentage Method. Table 5. Percentage Method — 2013 Amount for One Withholding Allowance. Monthly. Page 42/ (d) 525.00

Section 16. Percentage Method:

31. Section 16. Table 5. The Quarterly payroll period for one allowance is $___.
    (a) 955.53
    (b) 965.00
    (c) 970.15
    (d) 975.00
    Answer: Section 16. How To Use the Income Tax Withholding Tables. Percentage Method. Table 5. Percentage Method — 2013 Amount for One Withholding Allowance. Quarterly. Page 42/(d) 975.00

Section 16. Percentage Method:

32. Section 16. Table 5. For tax year 2013. The Semiannually payroll period for one withholding allowance is $___.
    (a) 1,915.00
    (b) 1,925.00
    (c) 1,933.00
    (d) 1,950.00
    Answer: Section 16. How To Use the Income Tax Withholding Tables. Percentage Method. Table 5. Percentage Method — 2013 Amount for One Withholding Allowance. Semiannually. Page 42/ (d) 1,950.00

© Copyright 2013. All rights reserved. Notice: United States Copyright Laws and International Treaties prohibit unauthorized publication, reproduction, distribution of this Work. Unauthorized use of this copyright in any form, format, publication or document may result in severe civil and criminal penalties. Violations of this copyright are investigated by the United States Department of Justice and carry, upon conviction of fines up to $250,000 and five years confinement. This Work is protected by United States Copyright Laws and International Treaties. Do not Copy, do not reproduce, do not distribute.

A Ficus Tree Publishing Educational-Technical Publications

How To Use The Income Tax Withholding Tables

Section 16. Percentage Method:

33. Section 16. Table 5. For tax year 2013. The Annual payroll period for one withholding allowance is $___.
    (a) 3,600.00
    (b) 3,700.00
    (c) 3,800.00
    (d) 3,900.00
    Answer: Section 16. How To Use the Income Tax Withholding Tables. Percentage Method. Table 5. Percentage Method — 2013 Amount for One Withholding Allowance. Annually. Page 42/ (d) 3.900

Section 16. Percentage Method:

34. Section 16. Table 5. The Daily or miscellaneous (each day of the payroll period) for one withholding allowance is $___.
    (a) 14.78
    (b) 14.98
    (c) 15.00
    (d) 15.28
    Answer: Section 16. How To Use the Income Tax Withholding Tables. Percentage Method. Table 5. Percentage Method — 2012 Amount for One Withholding Allowance, Daily. Page 42/ (c) 15.00

16. Percentage Method: Page 42/From 2013 IRS Circular E, Employer's Tax Guide. IRS Example: From Circular E Tax Year 2013 (IRS Example)

An unmarried employee is paid **$600 weekly** ($600.00 divided by 40 hours = $15.00 per hour). This employee has in effect a Form W-4 claiming two withholding allowances. Using the percentage method, figure the income tax to withhold as follows:

1. Total wage payment	$600.00
2. One allowance	$75.00
3. Allowances claimed on Form W-4	2
4. Multiply line 2 by line 3	$150.00
5. Amount subject to withholding (subtract line 4 from line 1)	
Difference =	**$450.00**

6. Tax to be withheld on $450.00 (from Table 1 — single person, page 44, 2013) **$52.60**

But where does the $52.60 come from? How is it derived?

How To Use The Income Tax Withholding Tables

Solution:
But where does the $52.60 come from? How is it derived?
From Table 1 page 44 of 2013 E: Reading Table 1 - page 44, Weekly Payroll Period we have the following: Over $214 but not over $739 the amount of income tax to withhold is $17.20 plus 15% of excess over $214 (we suggest that you carefully read this complete explanation).

7. $450.00 - $214 = $236.00
8. 15% of $236.00 = 236.00 x 0.15
9. 35.40 is the result so $35.40
10. $35.40 + $17.20 = $52.60
11. $52.60 does not need to be rounded up, Thus our answer is $52.60. Our answer matches the answer of the IRS Example of $52.60.
12. Therefore, the correct answer is: $52.60

Note: To figure income tax to withhold, you may reduce the last digit of the wages to zero, or figure the wages to the nearest dollar.

Section 16. Table 5. Percentage Method—2013 Amount for One Withholding Allowance

Section 16. Percentage Method:

35. **Annual income tax withholding.** Figure the income tax to withhold on annual wages under the Percentage Method for an annual payroll period. Then ___ the tax back to the payroll period.
    (a) roll
    (b) compute
    (c) figure
    (d) prorate
    Answer: (d) prorate, Section 16. How To Use the Income Tax Withholding Tables. Percentage Method. Annual income tax withholding. Page 42/ (d) prorate

Section 16. Table 5. Percentage Method—2013 Amount for One Withholding Allowance
Solve the following: Section 16. Percentage Method

36. An unmarried employee is paid $600 weekly ($600 ÷ 40 hours is equal to a wage of $15.00 per hour). This employee has in effect a Form W-4 claiming **three withholding allowances**. Using the percentage method, figure the income tax to withhold as follows. To figure the income tax to withhold, you may reduce the last digit of the wages to zero or figure the wages to the nearest dollar.

    1. Total wage payment   600.00
    2. One allowance $75.00
    3. Allowance claimed on Form W-4   **3**
    4. Multiply line 2 by line 3 $75.00 x 3 = 225) $225.00
    5. Amount subject to withholding
       (subtract line 4 from line 1) ($600.00- $225.00) = $375.00 $375.00
    6. Tax to be withheld on $375.00 from Table 1 — single person, page 44.

       = $?

How To Use The Income Tax Withholding Tables

Hint: Go back to Table I — weekly payroll period
Over $214.00 but not over — $739 (17.20 plus 15%) of the excess over — $214
7. $375.00 - $214.00 = $161.00
8. 15 ÷ 100 = 0.15
9. $161.00 x 0.15 = $24.15
10. $24.15 + $17.20 = $43.35
11. $43.35 rounded off = $43.35

Answer: Tax to be withheld is $___. See answer (d) below.
(a) 39.95
(b) 40.10
(c) 43.35
(d) **$43.35**

Section 16. Table 5. Percentage Method—2013 Amount for One Withholding Allowance

Solve the following:

Section 16. Percentage Method

37. An unmarried employee is paid $500 weekly ($12.50 for a 40 hour work week). This employee has in effect a Form W-4 claiming **two withholding allowances**. Using the percentage method, figure the income tax to withhold as follows. To figure the income tax to withhold, you may reduce the last digit of the wages to zero, or figure the wages to the nearest dollar.

1.	Total wage payment	500.00
2.	One allowance	$75.00
3.	Allowance claimed on Form W-4	2
4.	Multiply line 2 by line 3	$150.00
5.	Amount subject to withholding (subtract line 4 from line 1)	$350.00
6.	Tax to be withheld on $350.00 from Table 1 — single person, page 44.	$____.

Hint: Table I — weekly payroll period
Over $42.00 but not over — $214 ($0.00 plus 10%) of the excess over — $42
7. $350.00 - $42.00 = $308.00
8. 10 ÷ 100 = 0.10
9. $308.00 x 0.10 = $30.80
10. $30.80 + $0.00 = $30.80
11. $30.80 rounded off = $30.80

Answer: Tax to be withheld is $___. See answer (d) below.
(a) 30.80
(b) 40.10
(c) 43.35
(d) **$30.80**

© Copyright 2013. All rights reserved. Notice: United States Copyright Laws and International Treaties prohibit unauthorized publication, reproduction, distribution of this Work. Unauthorized use of this copyright in any form, format, publication or document may result in severe civil and criminal penalties. Violations of this copyright are investigated by the United States Department of Justice and carry, upon conviction of fines up to $250,000 and five years confinement. This Work is protected by United States Copyright Laws and International Treaties. Do not Copy, do not reproduce, do not distribute.

545

The International Leader in Construction Technology Home Study

How To Use The Income Tax Withholding Tables
Section 16. Table 5. Percentage Method—2013 Amount for One Withholding Allowance

Solve the following:

Section 16. Percentage Method

38. An unmarried employee is paid $480 weekly ($12.00 for a 40 hour work week). This employee has in effect a Form W-4 claiming **two withholding allowances**. Using the percentage method, figure the income tax to withhold as follows. To figure the income tax to withhold, you may <u>reduce the last digit of the wages to zero</u>, or figure the wages to the nearest dollar.

   1. Total wage payment   480.00
   2. One allowance $75.00
   3. Allowance claimed on Form W-4   2
   4. Multiply line 2 by line 3 $150.00
   5. Amount subject to withholding
      (subtract line 4 from line 1) $330.00
   6. Tax to be withheld on $330.00 from Table 1 — single
      person, page 44. $_____.

   Hint: Table I — weekly payroll period
   Over $42.00 but not over — $214 ($0.00 plus 10%) of the excess over — $214

   7. $330.00 - $214.00 = $116.00
   8. 10 ÷ 100 = 0.10
   9. $116.00 x 0.10 = $11.60
   10. $11.60 + $0.00 = $11.60
   11. $11.60 rounded off = $11.60

   Answer: Tax to be withheld is $___. See answer (a) below.
   (a) **<u>11.60</u>**
   (b) 25.10
   (c) 30.10
   (d) 38.85

The International Leader in Construction Technology Home Study

How To Use The Income Tax Withholding Tables
Section 16. Table 5. Percentage Method—2013 Amount for One Withholding Allowance

Solve the following:

Section 16. Percentage Method

39. An unmarried (divorced) employee is paid **$800** weekly ($20.00 hour for a 40 hour week). This employee has in effect a Form W-4 claiming **two withholding allowances**. Using the percentage method, figure the income tax to withhold as follows. To figure the income tax to withhold.

    You may <u>reduce the last digit of the wages to zero</u>, or figure the wages to the nearest dollar.

    1. Total wage payment   800.00
    2. One allowance $75.00
    3. Allowance claimed on Form W-4   2
    4. Multiply line 2 by line 3 $150.00
    5. Amount subject to withholding
        (subtract line 4 from line 1) $650.00
    6. Tax to be withheld on $650.00 from Table 1 — single
        person, page 44. $_____.

    Hint: Table I — weekly payroll period
    Over $214.00 but not over — $739 (17.20 plus 15%) of the excess over — $214
    7. $650.00 - $214.00 = $436.00
    8. 15 ÷ 100 = 0.15
    9. $436.00 x 0.15 = $65.40
    10. $65.40 + $17.20 = $84.25
    11. $84.25 rounded off = $84.25

    Answer: Tax to be withheld is $___. See answer (d) below.
    (a) 80.85
    (b) 81.16
    (c) 81.25
    (d) **$84.25**

A Ficus Tree Publishing Educational-Technical Publications

How To Use The Income Tax Withholding Tables
Section 16. Table 5. Percentage Method—2013 Amount for One Withholding Allowance

Solve the following:

Section 16. Percentage Method

40. An unmarried (divorced) employee is paid **$800** weekly ($20.00 hour for a 40 hour week). This employee has in effect a Form W-4 claiming **three withholding allowances**. Using the percentage method, figure the income tax to withhold as follows. To figure the income tax to withhold.

    You may <u>reduce the last digit of the wages to zero</u>, or figure the wages to the nearest dollar.

    1. Total wage payment   800.00
    2. One allowance $75.00
    3. Allowance claimed on Form W-4   <u>3</u>
    4. Multiply line 2 by line 3   <u>$225.00</u>
    5. Amount subject to withholding (subtract line 4 from line 1) $575.00
    6. Tax to be withheld on $650.00 from Table 1 — single person, page 44. $_____.

    Hint: Table I — weekly payroll period
    Over $739.00 but not over — $1,732.00 (95.95 plus 25%) of the excess over — $739

    7. $800.00 - $575.00 = $225.00
    8. 15 ÷ 100 = 0.25
    9. $225.00 x 0.25 = $56.25
    10. $56.25 + $95.95 = $152.20
    11. $152.20 rounded off = $152.20

    Answer: Tax to be withheld is $___. See answer (d) below.
    (a) 110.92
    (b) 110.95
    (c) 110.98
    (d) **152.20**

548
The International Leader in Construction Technology Home Study

How To Use The Income Tax Withholding Tables

A Ficus Tree Publishing Quick Notes Page

© Copyright 2013. All rights reserved. Notice: United States Copyright Laws and International Treaties prohibit unauthorized publication, reproduction, distribution of this Work. Unauthorized use of this copyright in any form, format, publication or document may result in severe civil and criminal penalties. Violations of this copyright are investigated by the United States Department of Justice and carry, upon conviction of fines up to $250,000 and five years confinement. This Work is protected by United States Copyright Laws and International Treaties. Do not Copy, do not reproduce, do not distribute.

A Ficus Tree Publishing Educational-Technical Publications

The International Leader in Construction Technology Home Study

Instructor's Manual Tax Test 15E-S16-2
Section 16.Percentage Method.
Work Problems With Solutions

General Description.

Tax Test 15E-S16-2. Tax Test 15E-S16-2. The primary focus of Tax Test 15E-S16-2 is problem solving by the study and working of tax type problems. Attention is directed to solving **"The Missing Steps."** The systematic exploration of the internal parts of computing and using tax tables. Please be aware that errors, omissions, or oversights may exist in this work. Any errors, omissions, or oversights that may exist are unintentional on the part of the author, staff, publisher or employees, associates or parties associated with the publication of this work. This Work is the Instructor's Manual for the student study guide and workbook only. Further, It is stated again, this Work is not an official United States publication.

Study material and information contained and provided by Tax Test 15E-S16-2 includes the following: Percentage Method; The Missing Steps; Percentage Method. Annual income tax withholding problems; IRS Examples. Test Type question; Alternative Methods of Income tax Withholding; BYWEEKLY Payroll Period Example.

DU VALL'S TEST'S™
Instructor's Manual For Study Guide Series United States Tax Code
IRS Publication 15 Circular E, Employer's Tax Guide Tax Year 2013
Tax Test 15E-S16-2 [Multiple-Choice Questions With Answers]

Percentage Method—2013 Amount for One Withholding Allowance
Percentage Method: Page 42/From 2013 IRS Circular E, Employer's Tax Guide.
IRS Example: From Circular E Tax Year 2013 (Comparison Example-Review)

An unmarried employee is paid **$600 weekly**. This employee has in effect a Form W-4 claiming two withholding allowances. Using the percentage method, figure the income tax to withhold as follows:

1. Total wage payment $600.00
2. One allowance $75.00
3. Allowances claimed on Form W-4   2
4. Multiply line 2 by line 3 $150.00
5. Amount subject to withholding (subtract line 4 from line 1)   **$450.00**

6. Tax to be withheld on $450.00 (from Table 1 — single person, page 44, 2013)
= **$52.60** But where does the $52.60 come from? How is it derived? Table 1 page 44 of 2013 E:

© Copyright 2013. All rights reserved. Notice: United States Copyright Laws and International Treaties prohibit unauthorized publication, reproduction, distribution of this Work. Unauthorized use of this copyright in any form, format, publication or document may result in severe civil and criminal penalties. Violations of this copyright are investigated by the United States Department of Justice and carry, upon conviction of fines up to $250,000 and five years confinement. This Work is protected by United States Copyright Laws and International Treaties. Do not Copy, do not reproduce, do not distribute.

A Ficus Tree Publishing Educational-Technical Publications

How To Use The Income Tax Withholding Tables

Reading Table 1 - page 44, Weekly Payroll Period we have the following: Over $214 but not over $739 the amount of income tax to withhold is $17.20 plus 15% of excess over $214 (we suggest that you carefully read this complete explanation).

7. $450.00 - $214 = $236.00
8. 15% of $236.00 = 236.00 x 0.15
9. 35.40 is the result so $35.40
10. $35.40 + $17.20 = $52.60
11. $52.60 does not need to be rounded up, Thus our answer is $52.60. Our answer matches the answer of the IRS Example of $52.60.
12. The correct answer is: $52.60

To figure income tax to withhold, you may reduce the last digit of the wages to zero, or figure the wages to the nearest dollar.

Section 16. Percentage Method

1. An unmarried (divorced) employee is paid **$800** weekly ($20.00 hour for a 40 hour week). This employee has in effect a Form W-4 claiming **four withholding allowances**. Using the percentage method, figure the income tax to withhold as follows. To figure the income tax to withhold.

   You may reduce the last digit of the wages to zero, or figure the wages to the nearest dollar.

1.	Total wage payment	800.00
2.	One allowance	$75.00
3.	Allowance claimed on Form W-4	4
4.	Multiply line 2 by line 3	$300.00
5.	Amount subject to withholding (subtract line 4 from line 1)	$500.00
6.	Tax to be withheld on $500.00 from Table 1 — single person, page 44.	$_____

   Hint: Table I — weekly payroll period
   Over $739.00 but not over — $1,732.00 (95.95 plus 25%) of the excess over — $739

   7. $800.00 - $500.00 = $300.00
   8. 15 ÷ 100 = 0.25
   9. $300.00 x 0.25 = $75.00
   10. $75.00 + $95.95 = $170.95
   11. $170.95 rounded off = $170.95

   Answer: Tax to be withheld is $____. See answer (d) below.
   (a) 150.95
   (b) 169.25
   (c) 170.85
   (d) **170.95**

© Copyright 2013. All rights reserved. Notice: United States Copyright Laws and International Treaties prohibit unauthorized publication, reproduction, distribution of this Work. Unauthorized use of this copyright in any form, format, publication or document may result in severe civil and criminal penalties. Violations of this copyright are investigated by the United States Department of Justice and carry, upon conviction of fines up to $250,000 and five years confinement. This Work is protected by United States Copyright Laws and International Treaties. Do not Copy, do not reproduce, do not distribute.

The International Leader in Construction Technology Home Study

How To Use The Income Tax Withholding Tables

Section 16. Percentage Method. Annual income tax withholding

2. Figure the income tax to withhold on ___ under the Percentage Method for an annual payroll period (See Table 5. Percentage Method—2013 Amount for One Withholding Allowance). Use the example provided with Table 5.
   - (a) weekly wages
   - (b) monthly wages
   - (c) quarterly wages
   - (d) annual wages

   Answer: See Section 16. How To Use the Income Tax Withholding Tables. Annual income tax withholding. Page 42/ (d) annual wages

Section 16. Percentage Method. Annual income tax withholding

3. Figure the income tax to withhold on ___ under the Percentage Method for an annual payroll period (See Table 5. Percentage Method—2013 Amount for One Withholding Allowance). Use the example provided with Table 5. Then ___ the tax back to the payroll period.
   - (a) weekly wages, adjust
   - (b) monthly wages, figure
   - (c) quarterly wages, compute
   - (d) annual wages, prorate

   Answer: See Section 16. How To Use the Income Tax Withholding Tables. Annual income tax withholding. Page 42/ (d) annual wages, prorate

Section 16. IRS Example.

4. A married person claims four withholding allowances. She is paid $1,000 a week. Multiply the weekly wages by ___ weeks to figure the annual wage of $___.
   - (a) 1, 1,000
   - (b) 12, 1,000
   - (c) 26, 26,000
   - (d) 52, 52,000

   Answer: See Section 16. How To Use the Income Tax Withholding Tables. Annual income tax withholding. Page 42/ (d) 52, 52,000

Section 16. IRS Example.

5. A married person claims four withholding allowances. She is paid $1,000 a week. Multiply the weekly wages by 52 weeks to figure the annual wage of $52,000. Subtract $___ (the value of four withholding allowances for 2013) for a balance of $___.
   - (a) 7,858
   - (b) 12, 500
   - (c) 15, 600
   - (d) 26,000

   Answer: See Section 16. How To Use the Income Tax Withholding Tables. Annual income tax withholding. Page 42/ (c) 15,600

© Copyright 2013. All rights reserved. Notice: United States Copyright Laws and International Treaties prohibit unauthorized publication, reproduction, distribution of this Work. Unauthorized use of this copyright in any form, format, publication or document may result in severe civil and criminal penalties. Violations of this copyright are investigated by the United States Department of Justice and carry, upon conviction of fines up to $250,000 and five years confinement. This Work is protected by United States Copyright Laws and International Treaties. Do not Copy, do not reproduce, do not distribute.

A Ficus Tree Publishing Educational-Technical Publications

How To Use The Income Tax Withholding Tables
Section 16. Percentage Method. Annual income tax withholding

Section 16. IRS Example.
6. Using the Table 7 for the annual payroll period on page ___, $3,322.50 is withheld.
    (a) 44
    (b) 45
    (c) 46
    (d) 47
    Answer: See Section 16. How To Use the Income Tax Withholding Tables. Annual income tax withholding. Page 42/ (b) 45

Section 16. IRS Example. The missing steps.
7. Using the Table 7 (b) **Married person**, for the annual payroll period on page ___, $3,322.50 is withheld.
    (a) 44
    (b) 45
    (c) 46
    (d) 47
    Answer: See Section 16. How To Use the Income Tax Withholding Tables. Annual income tax withholding. Page 42/ (b) 45

THE MISSING STEPS:
a. Multiply the weekly wages by 52 weeks (total number of weeks per year)
b. $1000.00 time 52 weeks = $52,000.00
c. Subtract the withholding allowances. (For tax year 2013 one withholding allowance of $75.00 (Table 5)
is allowed for each dependent.
d. $75.00 times four allowances = $300.00 each week
e. $300.00 times 52 weeks = $15,600.00
f. Subtract $15,600.00 from $52,000.00 = $36,400.00
g. Use **Table 7—ANNUAL Payroll period** (b) Married person— (Over $26,150.00 but not over $80,800.00)
   $1,785.00 plus 15% of the excess over $26,150.00.
   $36,400.00 - $26,150.00 = $10,250
   $10,250 times 15% = 10,250 times 0.15
   $1537.50 plus $1785.00 = **$3322.50**
   $3,322.50 to be withheld.
h. Divide $3,322.50 by 52 (the number of weeks in a calendar year) = **$69.89432**
i. Rounding off the number = $69.89 to be withheld each week. This answer checks with the IRS Example on Page 42.

Warning — carefully read each problem and double check yourself as to the use of the correct table.

How To Use The Income Tax Withholding Tables

Section 16. IRS Example.
8. Using the table for the annual payroll period on page ___, $3,322.50 is withheld. Divide the annual tax by 52. The weekly income tax to withhold is $___.
    (a) 44, 63.75
    (b) 45, 63.89
    (c) 46, 63.93
    (d) 47, 63.97
    Answer: See Section 16. How To Use the Income Tax Withholding Tables. Annual income tax withholding. Page 42/ (b) 45, 63.89

Section 16. Alternative Methods of Income Tax Withholding

Section 16. IRS Example.
9. Rather than the *Wage Bracket Method* or *Percentage Method* described above, you can use an ___ method to withhold income tax.
    (a) alternative
    (b) third
    (c) modified
    (d) new
    Answer: See Section 16. How To Use the Income Tax Withholding Tables. Annual income tax withholding. Pages 42 and 43/ (a) alternative

Section 16. IRS Example.
10. Rather than the *Wage Bracket Method* or *Percentage Method* described above, you can use an ___ method to withhold income tax. Publication ___ describes these alternative methods and contains:
    (a) alternative, 15-A
    (b) third, 15-B
    (c) modified, 15-C
    (d) new, 15-D
    Answer: See Section 16. How To Use the Income Tax Withholding Tables. Annual income tax withholding. Pages 42 and 43/ (a) alternative, 15-A

Section 16. IRS Example.
11. Rather than the *Wage Bracket Method* or *Percentage Method* described above, you can use an alternative method to withhold income tax. Publication 15-A describes these alternative methods and contains:
    • Formula tables for percentage method withholding for ___ systems.
    (a) automatic payroll
    (b) automated payroll
    (c) automated depositing
    (d) automatic deposit
    Answer: See Section 16. How To Use the Income Tax Withholding Tables. Annual income tax withholding. Pages 42 and 43/ (b) automated payroll

How To Use The Income Tax Withholding Tables
Section 16. Alternative Methods of Income Tax Withholding

Section 16. IRS Example.
12. Rather than the *Wage Bracket Method* or *Percentage Method* described above, you can use an alternative method to withhold income tax. Publication 15-A describes these alternative methods and contains:
    • Formula tables for percentage method withholding for ___ systems.
    • Wage bracket ___ method tables (for automated payroll systems).
    (a) automatic payroll, tax
    (b) automated payroll, percentage
    (c) automated depositing,
    (d) automatic deposit, percent
    Answer: See Section 16. How To Use the Income Tax Withholding Tables. Annual income tax withholding. Pages 42 and 43/ (b) automated payroll, percentage

Section 16. IRS Example.
13. Rather than the *Wage Bracket Method* or *Percentage Method* described above, you can use an alternative method to withhold income tax. Publication 15-A describes these alternative methods and contains:
    • Formula tables for percentage method withholding for ___ systems.
    • Wage bracket ___ method tables (for automated payroll systems), and
    • Combined ___, social security and Medicare tax withholding tables.
    (a) automatic payroll, tax
    (b) automated payroll, percentage, income
    (c) automated depositing, depositing
    (d) automatic deposit, percent, tax
    Answer: See Section 16. How To Use the Income Tax Withholding Tables. Annual income tax withholding. Pages 42 and 43/ (b) automated payroll, percentage, income

Section 16. IRS Example.
14. Rather than the *Wage Bracket Method* or *Percentage Method* described above, you can use an alternative method to withhold income tax. Publication 15-A describes these alternative methods and contains:
    • Formula tables for percentage method withholding for ___ systems.
    • Wage bracket ___ method tables (for automated payroll systems), and
    • Combined ___, social security and Medicare tax withholding tables.
    Some of the alternative methods explained in Publication 15-A are ___ wages, average estimated wages, cumulative wages and part-year employment.
    (a) automatic payroll, tax, monthly
    (b) automated payroll, percentage, income, annualized
    (c) automated depositing, depositing, annual
    (d) automatic deposit, percent, tax, quarterly
    Answer: See Section 16. How To Use the Income Tax Withholding Tables. Annual income tax withholding. Pages 42 and 43/ (b) automated payroll, percentage, income, annualized

How To Use The Income Tax Withholding Tables
Section 16. Alternative Methods of Income Tax Withholding

Section 16. IRS Example.
15. Rather than the *Wage Bracket Method* or *Percentage Method* described above, you can use an alternative method to withhold income tax. Publication 15-A describes these alternative methods and contains:
    • Formula tables for percentage method withholding for automated payroll systems.
    • Wage bracket percentage method tables (for automated payroll systems), and
    • Combined income, social security and Medicare tax withholding tables.
    Some of the alternative methods explained in Publication 15-A are annualized wages, average estimated wages, cumulative wages and part-year employment. In addition to the Formula tables, Wage bracket percentage method tables, and Combined income, social security and Medicare tax withholding tables, Publication 15-A provides information for ___ additional, alternative methods.
    (a) 3
    (b) 4
    (c) 5
    (d) 6
    Answer: See Section 16. How To Use the Income Tax Withholding Tables. Annual income tax withholding. Pages 42 and 43/ (b) 4

Section 16. Example.
16. A married person claims four withholding allowances. She is paid $2,000 a week. Multiply the weekly wages by ___ weeks to figure the annual wage of $___.
    (a) 4, 2,000
    (b) 12, 52,000
    (c) 26, 103,000
    (d) 52, 104,000
    Answer: See Section 16. How To Use the Income Tax Withholding Tables. Annual income tax withholding. Page 42/ (d) 52, 104,000

Section 16. Example.
17. A married person claims four withholding allowances. She is paid $2,000 a week. Multiply the weekly wages by 52 weeks to figure the annual wage of $104,000. Subtract $___ (The value of four withholding allowances for 2013).
    (a) 15,250
    (b) 15,300
    (c) 15,400
    (d) 15,600
    Answer: See Section 16. How To Use the Income Tax Withholding Tables. Annual income tax withholding. Page 42/ (d) 15,600

How To Use The Income Tax Withholding Tables
Section 16. Percentage Method. Annual income tax withholding (Examples)

Section 16. Example.
18. A married person claims four withholding allowances. She is paid $2,000 a week. Multiply the weekly wages by 52 weeks to figure the annual wage of $104,000. Subtract $15, 600 (The value of four withholding allowances for 2013) for a balance of ___.
    (a) 88,250
    (b) 88,300
    (c) 88,400
    (d) 88,500
    Answer: See Section 16. How To Use the Income Tax Withholding Tables. Annual income tax withholding. Page 42/ (c) 88,400

Section 16. Example.
19. A married person claims four withholding allowances. She is paid $2,000 a week. Multiply the weekly wages by 52 weeks to figure the annual wage of $104,000. Subtract $15, 600 (The value of four withholding allowances for 2013) for a balance of $88,400. Using the Table (7)(b) for the annual payroll period on page 45, $___ is withheld weekly. Note: This problem is identical to the problem stated for a married person earning $1,000.00 per week. However, the income amount is doubled for this example.
    (a) 228.49
    (b) 228.50
    (c) 228.51
    (d) 228.57
    Answer: See Section 16. How To Use the Income Tax Withholding Tables. Annual income tax withholding. Page 42/ (c) $228.51
    Solution: The Missing Steps.
    Multiply the weekly wages by 52 weeks (the total number of weeks in a calendar year).
      a. $2000.00 times 52 = $104,000.00
      b. Multiply the weekly withholding allowances. For tax year 2013 one withholding allowance of
         $75.00 is allowed for each dependent. Thus $75.00 times 4 = $300.00
      c. $300.00 per week multiplied by 52 weeks is equal to $15,600.00 per year tax allowance.
      d. Subtract $15,600.00 from the annual income of $104,000.00 = $88,400.00
      e. From Table 7(b)—**Annual Payroll Period Married person** read (Over **$80,800** but not over — **$154,700**) $9,982.50 plus 25% over — $80,800).
      f. $88,400.00 - $80,800.00 = $7600.00
      g. $7,600.00 times 0.25 = $1,900.00 + $9,982.50
      h. $9,982.50 plus $1,900.00 = $11,882.50
      i. Divide $11, 882.50 by 52 weeks (calendar year) = $228.50961
      j. Rounding off the numbers = $228.51 to be withheld weekly

The International Leader in Construction Technology Home Study

How To Use The Income Tax Withholding Tables
Section 16. Percentage Method. Annual income tax withholding (Examples)

Section 16. Example.

20. A married person claims four withholding allowances. She is paid $1,100 a week. Solve by multiplying the weekly wages by 52 weeks to figure the annual wage of $57,200.00. Subtract $15, 600 (The value of four withholding allowances for 2013) for a balance of $. Using the Table (7)(b) for the annual payroll period on page 45, $___ is withheld each week. Note: This problem is identical to the problem stated for a married person earning $1,000.00 per week. However, the income amount stated for this example is one-hundred dollars more in income per week.
    (a)   75.55
    (b)   79.55
    (c)   80.04
    (d)   80.05

Answer: See Section 16. How To Use the Income Tax Withholding Tables. Annual income tax withholding. Page 42/ (d) 80.05

Solution: The Missing Steps.

Multiply the weekly wages by 52 weeks (the total number of weeks in a calendar year).
  a. $1,100.00 times 52 = $57,200.00
  b. Multiply the weekly withholding allowances. For tax year 2013 one withholding allowance of $75.00 is allowed for each dependent. Thus $75.00 times 4 = $300.00
  c. $300.00 per week multiplied by 52 weeks is equal to $15,600.00 per year tax allowance.
  d. Subtract $15,600.00 from the annual income of $57,200.00 = $42,000.00
  e. From Table 7(b)—**Annual Payroll Period Married person** read (Over **$26,150** but not over — **$80,800**) the amount to withhold is $1,785.00 plus 15% over — $26,150.00).
  f. $42,000 - $26,150 = $15,850
  g. $15,850 times 15% = 2377.50
  h. $2,377.50 + 1785.00 = 4162.50
  i. Divide $4,162.50 by 52 weeks= $80.0480
  j. Rounding off the numbers = $80.05 is withheld each week

© Copyright 2013. All rights reserved. Notice: United States Copyright Laws and International Treaties prohibit unauthorized publication, reproduction, distribution of this Work. Unauthorized use of this copyright in any form, format, publication or document may result in severe civil and criminal penalties. Violations of this copyright are investigated by the United States Department of Justice and carry, upon conviction of fines up to $250,000 and five years confinement. This Work is protected by United States Copyright Laws and International Treaties. Do not Copy, do not reproduce, do not distribute.

A Ficus Tree Publishing Educational-Technical Publications

How To Use The Income Tax Withholding Tables
Section 16. Percentage Method. Annual income tax withholding (Examples)

Section 16. Example.

21. A married person claims four withholding allowances. She is paid $1,500 a week. Solve by multiplying the weekly wages by 52 weeks to figure the annual wage of $78,000.00. Subtract $15, 600 (The value of four withholding allowances for 2013) for a balance of $62,400. Using the Table (7)(b) for the annual payroll period on page 45, $___ is withheld. Note: This problem is identical to the problem stated for a married person earning $1,000.00 per week. However, the income amount stated for this example is $1,500.00 in income per week.
    (a) 138.85
    (b) 138.89
    (c) 138.91
    (d) 138.95

    Answer: See Section 16. How To Use the Income Tax Withholding Tables. Annual income tax withholding. Page 42/ (b) 138.89

    Solution: The Missing Steps.
    Multiply the weekly wages by 52 weeks (the total number of weeks in a calendar year).
    a. $1,500.00 times 52 = $78,000.00
    b. Multiply the weekly withholding allowances. For tax year 2013 one withholding allowance of $75.00 is allowed for each dependent. Thus $75.00 times 4 = $300.00
    c. $300.00 per week multiplied by 52 weeks is equal to $15,600.00 per year tax allowance.
    d. Subtract $15,600.00 from the annual income of $78,000.00 = $62,400.
    e. From Table 7(b)—**Annual Payroll Period Married person** read (Over **$26,150** but not over — **$80,800**) the amount to withhold is $1,785.00 plus 15% over — $26,150.00).
    f. $62,400 - $26,150 = $36,250
    g. $36,250 times 15% (0.15) = $5,437.50
    h. $5.427.50 + 1785.00 = 7222.50
    i. Divide $7,222.50 by 52 weeks= $138.8942
    j. Rounding off the numbers = $138.89 to be withheld each week

The International Leader in Construction Technology Home Study

How To Use The Income Tax Withholding Tables
Section 16. Percentage Method. Annual income tax withholding (Examples)

Section 16. Example.

22. A married person claims four withholding allowances. She is paid **$1,800** a week. Solve by multiplying the weekly wages by 52 weeks to figure the annual wage of **$93,600.00**. Subtract **$15, 600** (The value of four withholding allowances for 2013) for a balance of **$78,000**. Using the Table (7)(b) for the annual payroll period on page 45, $___ is withheld each week. Note: This problem is identical to the problem stated for a married person earning $1,000.00 per week. However, the income amount stated for this example is **$1,800.00** in income per week.
    (a)   138.99
    (b)   183.85
    (c)   183.89
    (d)   183.91

Answer: See Section 16. How To Use the Income Tax Withholding Tables. Annual income tax withholding. Page 42/ (c) **183.89**

Solution: The Missing Steps.
Multiply the weekly wages by 52 weeks (the total number of weeks in a calendar year).
  a. $1,800.00 times 52 = **$93,600.00**
  b. Multiply the weekly withholding allowances. For tax year 2013 one withholding allowance of $75.00 is allowed for each dependent. Thus $75.00 times 4 = $300.00
  c. $300.00 per week multiplied by 52 weeks is equal to $15,600.00 per year tax allowance.
  d. Subtract **$15,600.00** from the annual income wage of **$93,600.00 = $78,000.00**
  e. From Table 7(b)—**Annual Payroll Period Married person** read (Over **$26,150** but not over — **$80,800**) the amount to withhold is $1,785.00 plus 15% over — $26,150.00).
  f. **$78,000 - $26,150 = $51,850**
  g. **$51,850** times 15% (0.15) = **$7777.50**
  h. **$7,777.50 + 1,785.00 = $9,562.50**
  i. Divide **$9,562.50** by **52 weeks**= **$183.8942**
  j. Rounding off the numbers = **$183.89** to be withheld each week

© Copyright 2013. All rights reserved. Notice: United States Copyright Laws and International Treaties prohibit unauthorized publication, reproduction, distribution of this Work. Unauthorized use of this copyright in any form, format, publication or document may result in severe civil and criminal penalties. Violations of this copyright are investigated by the United States Department of Justice and carry, upon conviction of fines up to $250,000 and five years confinement. This Work is protected by United States Copyright Laws and International Treaties. Do not Copy, do not reproduce, do not distribute.

A Ficus Tree Publishing Educational-Technical Publications

The International Leader in Construction Technology Home Study

How To Use The Income Tax Withholding Tables

Section 16. Percentage Method.
Table 1—Weekly Payroll Period (Examples) (b) Married person

Section 16. Example.
23. A married person claims two withholding allowances. She is paid **$400.00** weekly. Determine the **2013** <u>income tax withholding</u> for this individual.
   (a)   25.00
   (b)   25.55
   (c)   25.75
   (d)   25.95

Answer: See Section 16. How To Use the Income Tax Withholding Tables. Percentage Method Tables for Income Tax Withholding. Page 44/ (a) 25.00

Solution: The Missing Steps.
Go to Table 1-Weekly payroll (b) Married person—If the amount of wages(after subtracting withholding allowances) is: Not over $160 the amount to withhold is $0. If the amount is <u>OVER</u> $160 <u>But Not Over</u> —$503 The amount to withhold is: $0.00 plus 10% of the excess over $160.
Check:
a. $400.00 minus 150.00 = **$250.00**
b. Over $160.00 but not over — $503 = $0.00 plus 10%
c. 10% is 0.10
d. $250.00 times 0.10 = $25.00
The income tax to withhold from each weekly pay is <u>$25.00</u>. **Note this is income tax only. Social Security, Medicare and Federal Unemployment Tax (FUTA) must be computed separately.**

© Copyright 2013. All rights reserved. Notice: United States Copyright Laws and International Treaties prohibit unauthorized publication, reproduction, distribution of this Work. Unauthorized use of this copyright in any form, format, publication or document may result in severe civil and criminal penalties. Violations of this copyright are investigated by the United States Department of Justice and carry, upon conviction of fines up to $250,000 and five years confinement. This Work is protected by United States Copyright Laws and International Treaties. Do not Copy, do not reproduce, do not distribute.

A Ficus Tree Publishing Educational-Technical Publications

How To Use The Income Tax Withholding Tables

Section 16. Example.

24. A married person claims two withholding allowances. She is paid **$500.00** weekly. Determine the **2013** income tax withholding for this individual.

    (a) 35.00
    (b) 35.55
    (c) 35.75
    (d) 35.95

    Answer: See Section 16. How To Use the Income Tax Withholding Tables. Percentage Method Tables for Income Tax Withholding. Page 44/ (a) 35.00

    Solution: The Missing Steps.

    Go to Table 1-Weekly payroll (b) Married person—If the amount of wages(after subtracting withholding allowances) is: Not over $160 the amount to withhold is $0. If the amount is OVER $160 But Not Over —$503 The amount to withhold is: $0.00 plus 10% of the excess over $160.

    Check:

    a. $500.00 minus 150.00 = **$350.00**

    b. Over $160.00 but not over — $503 = $0.00 plus 10%

    c. 10% is 0.10

    d. $350.00 times 0.10 = $35.00

    The income tax to withhold from each weekly pay is $35.00.

Note this is income tax only. Social Security, Medicare and Federal Unemployment Tax (**FUTA**) must be computed separately.

How To Use The Income Tax Withholding Tables

Section 16. Example.

25. A married person claims two withholding allowances. She is paid **$850.00** weekly. Determine the **2013** income tax withholding for this individual.
    (a) $63.65
    (b) $63.75
    (c) $63.85
    (d) $83.95

Answer: See Section 16. How To Use the Income Tax Withholding Tables. Percentage Method Tables for Income Tax Withholding. Page 44/ (c) $63.85

Solution: The Missing Steps.

Wages = $850.00 - $150.00 (the dependent allowance deduction) this equals $700.00
Go to **Table 1-Weekly payroll (b) Married person**—If the amount of wages(after subtracting withholding allowances) is: If the amount is OVER **$503.00** But Not Over —**$1,554.00** The amount to withhold is: **$34.50** plus **15% of the excess over $503**.
Check:
a. $700.00 minus $503.00 = **$197.00**
b. $197.00 times 15% (0.15) = **$29.55**
c. **$29.55 + 34.30 = $63.85**
d. $83.95 exceeds the base value

Thus, **$63.85 is the correct answer**

The income tax to withhold from each weekly pay is $63.85. **Note this is income tax only. Social Security, Medicare and Federal Unemployment Tax (FUTA) must be computed separately.**

How To Use The Income Tax Withholding Tables

Section 16. Example.

26. A married person claims two withholding allowances. She is paid **$1150.00** weekly. Determine the **2013** income tax withholding for this individual.
    (a) $104.85
    (b) $105.85
    (c) $106.85
    (d) $108.85

    Answer: See Section 16. How To Use the Income Tax Withholding Tables. Percentage Method Tables for Income Tax Withholding. Page 44/ (d) $108.85

    Solution: The Missing Steps.
    Wages = $1150.00 - $150.00 (the dependent allowance deduction) this equals $1000.00
    Go to **Table 1-Weekly payroll (b) Married person**—If the amount of wages(after subtracting withholding allowances) is: If the amount is OVER **$503.00** But Not Over —**$1,554.00** The amount to withhold is: **$34.50** plus **15% of the excess over $503**.
    Check:
    a. $1,000.00 minus $503.00 = **$497.00**
    b. $497.00 times 15% (0.15) = **$74.55**
    c. **$74.55 + 34.30 = $108.85**
    d. **$108.85 is the correct answer**
    The income tax to withhold from each weekly pay is $108.85.

Note this is income tax only. Social Security, Medicare and Federal Unemployment Tax (FUTA) must be computed separately.

How To Use The Income Tax Withholding Tables

Section 16. Example.

27. A married person claims two withholding allowances. She is paid **$1550.00** weekly. Determine the **2013** income tax withholding for this individual.
    (a) $134.85
    (b) $145.85
    (c) $156.85
    (d) $168.85

    Answer: See Section 16. How To Use the Income Tax Withholding Tables. Percentage Method Tables for Income Tax Withholding. Page 44/ (d) $168.85
    Solution: The Missing Steps.
    Wages = $1550.00 - $150.00 (the dependent allowance deduction) this equals $1400.00
    Go to **Table 1-Weekly payroll (b) Married person**—If the amount of wages(after subtracting withholding allowances) is: If the amount is OVER **$503.00** But Not Over **—$1,554.00** The amount to withhold is: **$34.50** plus **15% of the excess over $503**.
    Check:
    a. $1,400.00 minus $503.00 = **$897.00**
    b. $897.00 times 15% (0.15) = **$134.55**
    c. **$134.55 + 34.30 = $168.85**
    d. **$168.85 is the correct answer**
    The income tax to withhold from each weekly pay is $168.85. **Note this is income tax only. Social Security, Medicare and Federal Unemployment Tax (FUTA) must be computed separately.**

The International Leader in Construction Technology Home Study

How To Use The Income Tax Withholding Tables

Section 16. Example.

28. A married person claims two withholding allowances. She is paid **$1850.00** weekly. Determine the **2013** <u>income tax withholding</u> for this individual.
    (a) $134.85
    (b) $145.85
    (c) $156.85
    (d) $168.85

    Answer: See Section 16. How To Use the Income Tax Withholding Tables. Percentage Method Tables for Income Tax Withholding. Page 44/ (d) $168.85

    Solution: The Missing Steps.

    Wages = $1850.00 - $150.00 (the dependent allowance deduction) this equals $1700.00

    Go to **Table 1-Weekly payroll (b) Married person**—If the amount of wages(after subtracting withholding allowances) is: If the amount is <u>OVER</u> **$503.00** <u>But Not Over</u> —**$1,554.00** The amount to withhold is: **$34.50** plus **15% of the excess over $503**.

    However, the amount of $1850.00 is over $$1554.00 therefore we must drop down to the next computation where the amount is Over $1,554 but less than $2,975. Therefore we must withhold $191.95 plus 25% (0.25) of the excess over $1,554.00. The example is thus rewritten as follows:

How To Use The Income Tax Withholding Tables

Section 16. Percentage Method. Table 1—Weekly Payroll Period (Examples) (b) Married person

Section 16. Example. 28. continuation.
28.   A married person claims two withholding allowances. She is paid **$1850.00** weekly. Determine the **2013** income tax withholding for this individual.
    - (a) $228.15
    - (b) $228.25
    - (c) $228.35
    - (d) $228.45

    Answer: See Section 16. How To Use the Income Tax Withholding Tables. Percentage Method Tables for Income Tax Withholding. Page 44/ (d) $228.45

    Solution: The Missing Steps.
    Wages = $1850.00 - $150.00 (the dependent allowance deduction) this equals $1,700.00
    Go to **Table 1-Weekly payroll (b) Married person**—If the amount of wages(after subtracting withholding allowances) is: If the amount is OVER **$1,554.00** But Not Over —**$2,975.00** The amount to withhold is: **$191.95 plus 25% (0.25) of the excess over $1,554.00**.

    Check:
    a. $1,850.00 minus $150.00 = **$1,700.00**
    b. $1,700 - $1,554.00 = $146.00
    c. $146.00 **TIMES** 0.25 = ($36.5 + $191.95)
    d. **$228.45**
    Thus **$228.45**
    The income tax to withhold from each weekly pay is $168.85. **Note this is income tax only. Social Security, Medicare and Federal Unemployment Tax (FUTA) must be computed separately.**

The International Leader in Construction Technology Home Study

How To Use The Income Tax Withholding Tables

Section 16. Example.

29. A married person claims two withholding allowances. She is paid **$2,150.00** weekly. Determine the **2013** income tax withholding for this individual.
    - (a) $303.15
    - (b) $303.25
    - (c) $303.35
    - (d) $303.45

    Answer: See Section 16. How To Use the Income Tax Withholding Tables. Percentage Method Tables for Income Tax Withholding. Page 44/ (d) $303.45

    Solution: The Missing Steps.

    Wages = $2,150.00 - $150.00 (the dependent allowance deduction) this equals $2,000.00

    Go to **Table 1-Weekly payroll (b) Married person**—If the amount of wages(after subtracting withholding allowances) is: If the amount is OVER **$1,554.00** But Not Over —**$2,975.00** The amount to withhold is: **$191.95 plus 25% (0.25) of the excess over $1,554.00**.

    Check:

    a. $2,150.00 minus $150.00 = **$2,000.00**

    b. $2,000.00 - $1,554.00 = $446.00

    c. $446.00 **TIMES** 0.25 = ($111.50 + $191.95)

    d. **$303.45**

    Thus **$303.45**

    The income tax to withhold from each weekly pay is $303.45. **Note this is income tax only. Social Security, Medicare and Federal Unemployment Tax (FUTA) must be computed separately.**

How To Use The Income Tax Withholding Tables

Section 16. Example.
30. A married person claims two withholding allowances. She is paid **$2,550.00** weekly. Determine the **2013** income tax withholding for this individual.
    (a) $390.65
    (b) $390.75
    (c) $390.85
    (d) $390.95

Answer: See Section 16. How To Use the Income Tax Withholding Tables. Percentage Method Tables for Income Tax Withholding. Page 44/ (d) $390.95
Solution: The Missing Steps.
Wages = $2,550.00 - $150.00 (the dependent allowance deduction) this equals $2,350.00
Go to **Table 1-Weekly payroll (b) Married person**—If the amount of wages(after subtracting withholding allowances) is: If the amount is OVER **$1,554.00** But Not Over —**$2,975.00** The amount to withhold is: **$191.95 plus 25% (0.25) of the excess over $1,554.00**.
Check:
a. $2,550.00 minus $150.00 = **$2,350.00**
b. $2,350.00 - $1,554.00 = $796.00
c. $796.00 **TIMES** 0.25 = ($199.00 + $191.95)
d. **$390.95**
Thus **$390.95**

The income tax to withhold from each weekly pay is $303.45. **Note this is income tax only. Social Security, Medicare and Federal Unemployment Tax (FUTA) must be computed separately.**

How To Use The Income Tax Withholding Tables

Section 16. Example.
31.   A married person claims two withholding allowances. She is paid **$2,950.00** weekly. Determine the **2013** income tax withholding for this individual.
   (a) $503.15
   (b) $503.25
   (c) $503.35
   (d) $503.45

Answer: See Section 16. How To Use the Income Tax Withholding Tables. Percentage Method Tables for Income Tax Withholding. Page 44/ (d) $503.45

Solution: The Missing Steps.

Wages = $2,950.00 - $150.00 (the dependent allowance deduction) this equals $2,800.00

Go to **Table 1-Weekly payroll (b) Married person**—If the amount of wages(after subtracting withholding allowances) is: If the amount is OVER **$1,554.00** But Not Over —**$2,975.00** The amount to withhold is: **$191.95 plus 25% (0.25) of the excess over $1,554.00**.

Check:
a. $2,950.00 minus $150.00 = **$2,800.00**
b. $2,800.00 - $1,554.00 = $1,246.00
c. $1,246.00 **TIMES** 0.25 = ($311.50 + $191.95)
d. **$503.45**
Thus **$503.45**

The income tax to withhold from each weekly pay is $503.45. **Note this is income tax only. Social Security, Medicare and Federal Unemployment Tax (FUTA) must be computed separately.**

How To Use The Income Tax Withholding Tables

Section 16. Example.

32. A married person claims two withholding allowances. She is paid **$3,250.00** weekly. This employee earns an annual income of $169,000.00 not including bonuses. Determine only, the **2013** weekly income tax withholding for this individual.
    - (a) $578.25
    - (b) $578.35
    - (c) $578.45
    - (d) $578.55

    Answer: See Section 16. How To Use the Income Tax Withholding Tables. Percentage Method Tables for Income Tax Withholding. Page 44/ (c) $578.45

    Solution: The Missing Steps.

    Wages = $2,950.00 - $150.00 (the dependent allowance deduction) this equals $2,800.00

    Go to **Table 1-Weekly payroll (b) Married person**—If the amount of wages(after subtracting withholding allowances) is: If the amount is OVER **$1,554.00** But Not Over —**$2,975.00** The amount to withhold is: **$191.95 plus 25% of the amount over $1,554.00**

    Check:
    a. $3,250.00 minus $150.00 = **$3,100.00**
    b. $3,100.00 - $1,554.00 = $1,546.00
    c. $1,546.00 **TIMES** 0.25 = ($386.50 + $191.95)
    d. **$578.45**

    Thus **$578.45**

    The income tax to withhold from each weekly pay is $578.45. **Note this is income tax only. Social Security, Medicare and Federal Unemployment Tax (FUTA) must be computed separately.**

The International Leader in Construction Technology Home Study

How To Use The Income Tax Withholding Tables

Section 16. Example.

33. A married person claims two withholding allowances. She is paid **$3,550.00** weekly. Determine only, the **2013** weekly income tax withholding for this individual.
    (a) $665.20
    (b) $665.23
    (c) $665.25
    (d) $665.35

    Answer: See Section 16. How To Use the Income Tax Withholding Tables. Percentage Method Tables for Income Tax Withholding. Page 44/ (a) $665.20

    Solution: The Missing Steps.

    Wages = $3,550.00 - $150.00 (the dependent allowance deduction) this equals $3,400.00

    Go to **Table 1-Weekly payroll (b) Married person**—*If the amount of wages(after subtracting withholding allowances) is: If the amount is OVER $2,975.00 But Not Over —$4,449.00 The amount to withhold is: $119.00 +547.20.*

    Check:

    a. $3,550.00 minus $150.00 = **$3,400.00**

    b. $3,400.00 - $2,975.00 = $425.00

    c. $425.00 **TIMES** 0.28 = ($119.00 + $547.20)

    d. = **$665.20**

    Thus $665.20

    The income tax to withhold from each weekly pay is $665.20. **Note this is income tax only. Social Security, Medicare and Federal Unemployment Tax (FUTA) must be computed separately.**

How To Use The Income Tax Withholding Tables

Section 16. Example.

34. A married person claims two withholding allowances. She is paid **$3,650.00** weekly. Determine only, the **2013** weekly income tax withholding for this individual.
    (a) $694.20
    (b) $694.22
    (c) $694.24
    (d) $694.28

    Answer: See Section 16. How To Use the Income Tax Withholding Tables. Percentage Method Tables for Income Tax Withholding. Page 44/ (a) $694.20

    Solution: The Missing Steps.

    Wages = $3,650.00 - $150.00 (the dependent allowance deduction) this equals $3,500.00

    Go to **Table 1-Weekly payroll (b) Married person**—*If the amount of wages(after subtracting withholding allowances) is: If the amount is OVER $2,975.00 But Not Over —$4,449.00 The amount to withhold is: $525.00 plus 28% (0.28) of the excess over $2,975.00.*

    Check:
    a. $3,650.00 minus $150.00 = **$3,500.00**
    b. $3,500.00 - $2,975.00 = $525.00
    c. $525.00 **TIMES** 0.28 = ($147.00 + $547.20)
    d. = **$694.20**
    Thus **$694.20**

    The income tax to withhold from each weekly pay is $694.20.

Note this is income tax only. Social Security, Medicare and Federal Unemployment Tax (FUTA) must be computed separately.

The International Leader in Construction Technology Home Study

How To Use The Income Tax Withholding Tables

Section 16. Example.

35. A married person claims two withholding allowances. She is paid **$3,750.00** weekly. Determine only, the **2013** weekly <u>income tax withholding</u> for this individual.
    - (a) $722.20
    - (b) $722.22
    - (c) $722.24
    - (d) $722.26

    Answer: See Section 16. How To Use the Income Tax Withholding Tables. Percentage Method Tables for Income Tax Withholding. Page 44/ (a) $722.20

    Solution: The Missing Steps.

    Wages = $3,750.00 - $150.00 (the dependent allowance deduction) this equals $3,600.00

    Go to **Table 1-Weekly payroll (b) Married person**—*If the amount of wages(after subtracting withholding allowances) is: If the amount is <u>OVER</u> $2,975.00 <u>But Not Over</u> —$4,449.00 The amount to withhold is: <u>$547.20</u> plus 28% (0.28) of the excess over $2,975.00.*

    Check:
    a. $3,750.00 minus $150.00 = **$3,600.00**
    b. $3,600.00 - $2,975.00 = $625.00
    c. $625.00 **TIMES** 0.28 = ($175.00 + $547.20)
    d. = **$722.20**

    Thus **$722.20**

    The income tax to withhold from each weekly pay is <u>$980.08</u>. **<u>Note</u> this is income tax only. Social Security, Medicare and Federal Unemployment Tax (FUTA) must be computed separately.**

How To Use The Income Tax Withholding Tables

Section 16. Example.
36.   A married person claims two withholding allowances. She is paid **$3,850.00** weekly. Determine only, the **2013** weekly <u>income tax withholding</u> for this individual.
- (a) $750.20
- (b) $751.22
- (c) $752.24
- (d) $753.26

Answer: See Section 16. How To Use the Income Tax Withholding Tables. Percentage Method Tables for Income Tax Withholding. Page 44/ (a) $750.20

Solution: The Missing Steps.
Wages = $3,750.00 - $150.00 (the dependent allowance deduction) this equals $3,600.00
Go to **Table 1-Weekly payroll (b) Married person**—*If the amount of wages(after subtracting withholding allowances) is: If the amount is <u>OVER</u> $2,975.00 <u>But Not Over</u> —$4,449.00 The amount to withhold is: <u>$547.20</u> plus 28% (0.28) of the excess over $2,975.00.*

Check:
a. $3,850.00 minus $150.00 = **$3,700.00**
b. $3,700.00 - $2,975.00 = $725.00
c. $725.00 **TIMES** 0.28 = ($203.00 + $547.20)
d. = **$750.20**
Thus **$750.20**
The income tax to withhold from each weekly pay is <u>$750.20</u>.

<u>Note</u> **this is income tax only. Social Security, Medicare and Federal Unemployment Tax (FUTA) must be computed separately.**

The International Leader in Construction Technology Home Study

How To Use The Income Tax Withholding Tables

Section 16. Example.

37. A married person claims two withholding allowances. She is paid **$3,950.00** weekly. Determine only, the **2013** weekly <u>income tax withholding</u> for this individual.

    (a) $778.20
    (b) $778.22
    (c) $778.24
    (d) $778.26

Answer: See Section 16. How To Use the Income Tax Withholding Tables. Percentage Method Tables for Income Tax Withholding. Page 44/ (a) $750.20

Solution: The Missing Steps.

Wages = **$3,750.00 - $150.00 (the dependent allowance deduction) this equals $3,600.00**

Go to **Table 1-Weekly payroll (b) Married person**—*If the amount of wages(after subtracting withholding allowances) is: If the amount is <u>OVER</u> $2,975.00 <u>But Not Over</u> —$4,449.00 The amount to withhold is: <u>$547.20</u> plus 28% (0.28) of the excess over $2,975.00.*

Check:

a. $3,950.00 minus $150.00 = **$3,800.00**

b. $3,800.00 - $2,975.00 = $825.00

c. $825.00 **TIMES** 0.28 = ($231.00 + $547.20)

d. = **$778.20**

Thus **$778.20**

The income tax to withhold from each weekly pay is <u>$778.20</u>.

Note this is income tax only. Social Security, Medicare and Federal Unemployment Tax (FUTA) must be computed separately.

How To Use The Income Tax Withholding Tables

Section 16. Example.

38. A married person claims two withholding allowances. She is paid **$4,150.00** weekly. Determine only, the **2013** weekly <u>income tax withholding</u> for this individual.
    - (a) $834.10
    - (b) $834.20
    - (c) $834.25
    - (d) $834.30

    Answer: See Section 16. How To Use the Income Tax Withholding Tables. Percentage Method Tables for Income Tax Withholding. Page 44/ (b) $834.20

    Solution: The Missing Steps.

    Wages = $3,750.00 - $150.00 (the dependent allowance deduction) this equals $3,600.00

    Go to **Table 1-Weekly payroll (b) Married person**—*If the amount of wages(after subtracting withholding allowances) is: If the amount is <u>OVER</u> $2,975.00 <u>But Not Over</u> —$4,449.00 The amount to withhold is: <u>$547.20</u> plus 28% (0.28) of the excess over $2,975.00.*

    Check:

    a. $4,150.00 minus $150.00 = **$4,000.00**

    b. $4,000.00 - $2,975.00 = $1025.00

    c. $1025.00 **TIMES** 0.28 = ($287.00 + $547.20)

    d. = **$834.20**

    Thus **$834.20**

    The income tax to withhold from each weekly pay is <u>$834.20</u>.

How To Use The Income Tax Withholding Tables

Section 16. Example.
39. A married person claims two withholding allowances. She is paid **$4,500.00** weekly. Determine only, the **2013** weekly <u>income tax withholding</u> for this individual.
    - (a) $932.15
    - (b) $932.18
    - (c) $932.20
    - (d) $932.22

    Answer: See Section 16. How To Use the Income Tax Withholding Tables. Percentage Method Tables for Income Tax Withholding. Page 44/ (c) $932.20

    Solution: The Missing Steps.

    Wages = $4,500.00 - $150.00 (the dependent allowance deduction) this equals $4350.00

    Go to **Table 1-Weekly payroll (b) Married person**—*If the amount of wages(after subtracting withholding allowances) is: If the amount is <u>OVER</u> $2,975.00 <u>But Not Over</u> —$4,449.00 The amount to withhold is: <u>$547.20</u> plus 28% (0.28) of the excess over $2,975.00.*

    Check:
    a. $4,500.00 minus $150.00 = **$4,350.00**
    b. $4,350.00 - $2,975.00 = $1375.00
    c. $1375.00 **TIMES** 0.28 = ($385.00 + $547.20)
    d. = **$932.20**
    Thus **$932.20**

    The income tax to withhold from each weekly pay is <u>$932.20</u>.

    <u>Note</u> **this is income tax only. Social Security, Medicare and Federal Unemployment Tax (FUTA) must be computed separately.**

How To Use The Income Tax Withholding Tables

Section 16. Example.

40. A married person claims two withholding allowances. She is paid **$5,000.00** weekly. Determine only, the **2013** weekly income tax withholding for this individual.
    (a) $1092.19
    (b) $1092.21
    (c) $1092.23
    (d) $1092.25

    Answer: See Section 16. How To Use the Income Tax Withholding Tables. Percentage Method Tables for Income Tax Withholding. Page 44/ (d) $1092.25

    Solution: The Missing Steps.

    Wages = $5,000.00 - $150.00 (the dependent allowance deduction) this equals $4850.00

    Go to **Table 1-Weekly payroll (b) Married person**—If the amount of wages(after subtracting withholding allowances) is: If the amount is **OVER** $4,449.00 **But Not Over** —$7,820.00 The amount to withhold is: $959.92 plus 33% (0.33) of the excess over $4,449.

    Check:
    a. $5,000.00 minus $150.00 = **$4,850.00**
    b. $4,850.00 - $4,449.00 = $401.00
    c. $401.00 **TIMES** 0.33 = ($132.33 + $959.92)
    d. = **$1092.25**
    Thus **$1092.25**
    The income tax to withhold from each weekly pay is $1092.25.

The International Leader in Construction Technology Home Study

How To Use The Income Tax Withholding Tables

Section 16. Example.
41. An unmarried employee is paid **$1,200.00 Biweekly** ($1,200.00 divided by 80 hours = $15.00 per hour). This employee has in effect a Form W-4 claiming two withholding allowances. Using the percentage method figure the income tax as follows:
   1. Biweekly total wage payment = $1200.00
   2. One biweekly allowance = $150.00
   3. Allowances claimed on Form W-4 = 2
   4. Multiply line 2 by line 3 = $300.00 (Form W-4 claimed)
   5. Amount subject to withholding (subtract line 4 from line 1. $1200.00 - $300.00 = $900.00
   6. Tax to be withheld on $900.00 from Table 2 — (a) Single person, page 44 =

   Solution —The Missing Steps:

   7. Over $428.00 but less than $1,479.00 the tax is $34.30 plus 15% (0.15) in excess of $428.00.
   8. $900.00 - $428.00 = $472.00
   9. $472.00 times 0.15 = $70.80
   10. $34.30 + $70.80 = Biweekly Income Tax to be withheld $____

   (a) $104.98
   (b) $105.00
   (c) $105.05
   (d) $105.10

   Answer: See Section 16. How To Use the Income Tax Withholding Tables. Percentage Method Tables for Income Tax Withholding. Page 44/ (d) $105.10

Note this is Income Tax Only. Social Security, Medicare and Federal Unemployment Tax (FUTA) and additional taxes must be computed separately.

How To Use The Income Tax Withholding Tables

Section 16. Example.

42. An unmarried employee is paid **$1,500.00 Biweekly** ($1,500.00 divided by 80 hours = $18.75 per hour). This employee has in effect a Form W-4 claiming two withholding allowances. Using the percentage method figure the income tax as follows:
    1. Biweekly total wage payment = $1500.00
    2. One biweekly allowance = $150.00
    3. Allowances claimed on Form W-4 = 2
    4. Multiply line 2 by line 3 = $300.00 (Form W-4 claimed)
    5. Amount subject to withholding (subtract line 4 from line 1. $1500.00 - $300.00 = $1,200.00
    6. Tax to be withheld on $1,200.00 from Table 2 — (a) Single person, page 44 =

    Solution —The Missing Steps:
    7. Over $428.00 but less than $1,479.00 the tax is $34.30 plus 15% (0.15) in excess of $428.00.
    8. $1,200.00 - $428.00 = $
    9. $772.00 times 0.15 = $___
    10. $34.30 + $65.40 = Biweekly Income Tax to be withheld $___

    (a) $115.75
    (b) $115.78
    (c) $115.80
    (d) $115.85

    Answer: See Section 16. How To Use the Income Tax Withholding Tables. Percentage Method Tables for Income Tax Withholding. Page 44/ (c) $115.80

How To Use The Income Tax Withholding Tables

Section 16. Example.

43. An unmarried employee is paid **$1,600.00 Biweekly** This employee has in effect a Form W-4 claiming two withholding allowances. Using the percentage method figure the income tax as follows:

    1. Biweekly total wage payment = $1,600.00
    2. One biweekly allowance = $150.00
    3. Allowances claimed on Form W-4 = 2
    4. Multiply line 2 by line 3 = $300.00 (Form W-4 claimed)
    5. Amount subject to withholding (subtract line 4 from line 1. $1,600.00 - $300.00 = $1,300.00
    6. Tax to be withheld on $1,300.00 from Table 2 — (a) Single person, page 44 =

    Solution —The Missing Steps:

    7. Over $428.00 but less than $1,479.00 the tax is $34.30 plus 15% (0.15) in excess of $428.00.
    8. $1,300.00 - $428.00 = $___.
    9. $872.00 times 0.15 = $130.80
    10. $34.30 + $130.80 = Biweekly Income Tax to be withheld $____

    (a) $165.10
    (b) $165.12
    (c) $165.15
    (d) $165.21

    Answer: See Section 16. How To Use the Income Tax Withholding Tables. Percentage Method Tables for Income Tax Withholding. Page 44/ (a) $165.10

How To Use The Income Tax Withholding Tables

44. An unmarried employee is paid **$1,700.00 Biweekly** This employee has in effect a Form W-4 claiming two withholding allowances. Using the percentage method figure the income tax as follows:
    1. Biweekly total wage payment = $1,700.00
    2. One biweekly allowance = $150.00
    3. Allowances claimed on Form W-4 = 2
    4. Multiply line 2 by line 3 = $300.00 (Form W-4 claimed)
    5. Amount subject to withholding (subtract line 4 from line 1. $1,700.00 - $300.00 = $1,400.00
    6. Tax to be withheld on $1,400.00 from Table 2 — (a) Single person, page 44 =

    Solution —The Missing Steps:

    7. Over $428.00 but less than $1,479.00 the tax is $34.30 plus 15% (0.15) in excess of $428.00.
    8. $1,400.00 - $428.00 = $972.00
    9. $972.00 times 0.15 = $145.80
    10. $34.30 + $145.80 = Biweekly Income Tax to be withheld $____

    (a) $180.05
    (b) $180.10
    (c) $180.15
    (d) $180.21

    Answer: See Section 16. How To Use the Income Tax Withholding Tables. Percentage Method Tables for Income Tax Withholding. Page 44/ (b) $180.10

Note this is Income Tax Only. Social Security, Medicare and Federal Unemployment Tax (FUTA) and any additional taxes must be computed separately.

How To Use The Income Tax Withholding Tables

Section 16. Example.

45. An unmarried employee is paid **$1,800.00 Biweekly** This employee has in effect a Form W-4 claiming two withholding allowances. Using the percentage method figure the income tax as follows:

1. Biweekly total wage payment = $1,800.00
2. One biweekly allowance = $150.00
3. Allowances claimed on Form W-4 = 2
4. Multiply line 2 by line 3 = $300.00 (Form W-4 claimed)
5. Amount subject to withholding (subtract line 4 from line 1. $1,800.00 - $300.00 = $1,500.00
6. Tax to be withheld on $1,500.00 from Table 2 — (a) Single person, page 44 =

Solution — The Missing Steps:

7. <u>Over $1,479.00 but less than $3,463.00 the tax is $191 plus 25% (0.25) in excess of $1,479.00</u>.
8. $1,500.00 - $1,479.00 = $21.00
9. $21.00 times 0.25 = $5.25
10. $191.00 + $5.25 = Biweekly Income Tax to be withheld $____
    (a) $196.15
    (b) $196.25
    (c) $196.28
    (d) $196.30

Answer: See Section 16. How To Use the Income Tax Withholding Tables. Percentage Method Tables for Income Tax Withholding. Page 44/ (b) $196.25

The International Leader in Construction Technology Home Study

How To Use The Income Tax Withholding Tables

Section 16. Example.

46. An unmarried employee is paid **$1,900.00 Biweekly** This employee has in effect a Form W-4 claiming two withholding allowances. Using the percentage method figure the income tax as follows:

1. Biweekly total wage payment = $1,900.00
2. One biweekly allowance = $150.00
3. Allowances claimed on Form W-4 = 2
4. Multiply line 2 by line 3 = $300.00 (Form W-4 claimed)
5. Amount subject to withholding (subtract line 4 from line 1. $1,900.00 - $300.00 = $1,600.00
6. Tax to be withheld on $1,600.00 from Table 2 — (a) Single person, page 44 =

Solution —The Missing Steps:

7. Over $1,479.00 but less than $3,463.00 the tax is $191 plus 25% (0.25) in excess of $1,479.00.
8. $1,600.00 - $1,479.00 = $121.00
9. $121.00 times 0.25 = $30.25
10. $191.00 + $30.25 = Biweekly Income Tax to be withheld $____
    (a) $221.11
    (b) $221.21
    (c) $221.25
    (d) $221.30

Answer: See Section 16. How To Use the Income Tax Withholding Tables. Percentage Method Tables for Income Tax Withholding. Page 44/ (c) $221.25

How To Use The Income Tax Withholding Tables

Section 16. Example.

47. An unmarried employee is paid **$2,000.00 Biweekly** This employee has in effect a Form W-4 claiming two withholding allowances. Using the percentage method figure the income tax as follows:

    1. Biweekly total wage payment = $2,000.00
    2. One biweekly allowance = $150.00
    3. Allowances claimed on Form W-4 = 2
    4. Multiply line 2 by line 3 = $300.00 (Form W-4 claimed)
    5. Amount subject to withholding (subtract line 4 from line 1. $2,000.00 - $300.00 = $1,700.00
    6. Tax to be withheld on $1,700.00 from Table 2 — (a) Single person, page 44 =

    Solution —The Missing Steps:

    7. Over $1,479.00 but less than $3,463.00 the tax is $191 plus 25% (0.25) in excess of $1,479.00.
    8. $1,700.00 - $1,479.00 = $221.00
    9. $221.00 times 0.25 = $55.25
    10. $191.00 + $55.25 = Biweekly Income Tax to be withheld $____

    (a) $246.00
    (b) $246.11
    (c) $246.21
    (d) $246.25

    Answer: See Section 16. How To Use the Income Tax Withholding Tables. Percentage Method Tables for Income Tax Withholding. Page 44/ (d) $246.25

How To Use The Income Tax Withholding Tables

Section 16. Example.

48. An unmarried employee is paid **$2,500.00 Biweekly** This employee has in effect a Form W-4 claiming two withholding allowances. Using the percentage method figure the income tax as follows:

   1. Biweekly total wage payment = $2,500.00
   2. One biweekly allowance = $150.00
   3. Allowances claimed on Form W-4 = 2
   4. Multiply line 2 by line 3 = $300.00 (Form W-4 claimed)
   5. Amount subject to withholding (subtract line 4 from line 1. $2,500.00 - $300.00 = $2,200.00
   6. Tax to be withheld on $2,200.00 from Table 2 — (a) Single person, page 44 =

   Solution —The Missing Steps:

   7. Over $1,479.00 but less than $3,463.00 the tax is $191 plus 25% (0.25) in excess of $1,479.00.
   8. $2,200.00 - $1,479.00 = $721.00
   9. $721.00 times 0.25 = $180.25
   10. $191.00 + $180.25 = Biweekly Income Tax to be withheld $____

   (a) $371.25
   (b) $371.30
   (c) $371.35
   (d) $375.45

   Answer: See Section 16. How To Use the Income Tax Withholding Tables. Percentage Method Tables for Income Tax Withholding. Page 44/ (a) $371.25

How To Use The Income Tax Withholding Tables

Section 16. Example.

49. An unmarried employee is paid **$3,000.00 Biweekly** This employee has in effect a Form W-4 claiming two withholding allowances. Using the percentage method figure the income tax as follows:

   1. Biweekly total wage payment = $3,000.00
   2. One biweekly allowance = $150.00
   3. Allowances claimed on Form W-4 = 2
   4. Multiply line 2 by line 3 = $300.00 (Form W-4 claimed)
   5. Amount subject to withholding (subtract line 4 from line 1. $3,000.00 - $300.00 = $2,700.00
   6. Tax to be withheld on $2,700.00 from Table 2 — (a) Single person, page 44 =

   Solution —The Missing Steps:

   7. <u>Over $1,479.00 but less than $3,463.00 the tax is $191 plus 25% (0.25) in excess of $1,479.00</u>.
   8. $2,700.00 - $1,479.00 = $1,221.00
   9. $1,221.00 times 0.25 = $305.25
   10. $191.00 + $305.25 = Biweekly Income Tax to be withheld $____

   (a) $496.20
   (b) $496.25
   (c) $496.30
   (d) $496.34

   Answer: See Section 16. How To Use the Income Tax Withholding Tables. Percentage Method Tables for Income Tax Withholding. Page 44/ (b) $496.25

How To Use The Income Tax Withholding Tables

Section 16. Example.

50. An unmarried employee is paid **$3,500.00 Biweekly** This employee has in effect a Form W-4 claiming two withholding allowances. Using the percentage method figure the income tax as follows:

   1. Biweekly total wage payment = $3,500.00
   2. One biweekly allowance = $150.00
   3. Allowances claimed on Form W-4 = 2
   4. Multiply line 2 by line 3 = $300.00 (Form W-4 claimed)
   5. Amount subject to withholding (subtract line 4 from line 1. $3,500.00 - $300.00 = $3,200.00
   6. Tax to be withheld on $3,200.00 from Table 2 — (a) Single person, page 44 =

   Solution —The Missing Steps:

   7. <u>Over $1,479.00 but less than **$3,463.00** the tax is $191 plus 25% (0.25) in excess of $1,479.00</u>.
   8. $3,200.00 - $1,479.00 = $1,721.00
   9. $1,721.00 times 0.25 = $430.25
   10. $191.00 + $430.25 = Biweekly Income Tax to be withheld $____

   (a) $621.15
   (b) $621.20
   (c) $621.25
   (d) $621.34

   Answer: See Section 16. How To Use the Income Tax Withholding Tables. Percentage Method Tables for Income Tax Withholding. Page 44/ (c) $621.25

Note this is Income Tax Only. Social Security, Medicare and Federal Unemployment Tax (FUTA) and any additional taxes must be computed separately.

How To Use The Income Tax Withholding Tables

Section 16. Example.

51. An unmarried employee is paid **$3,800.00 Biweekly** This employee has in effect a Form W-4 claiming two withholding allowances. Using the percentage method figure the income tax as follows:

    1. Biweekly total wage payment = $3,800.00
    2. One biweekly allowance = $150.00
    3. Allowances claimed on Form W-4 = 2
    4. Multiply line 2 by line 3 = $300.00 (Form W-4 claimed)
    5. Amount subject to withholding (subtract line 4 from line 1. $3,800.00 - $300.00 = $3,500.00
    6. Tax to be withheld on $3,500.00 from Table 2 — (a) Single person, page 44 =

    Solution —The Missing Steps:

    7. **Over $3,463.00 but less than $7,133.00** the tax is **$687.95 plus 28% (0.28) in excess of $3,463.00**.
    8. $3,500.00 - $3,463.00 = $37.00
    9. $37.00 times 0.28 = $10.36
    10. $687.95 + $10.36 = Biweekly Income Tax to be withheld $____

    (a) $698.15
    (b) $698.20
    (c) $698.25
    (d) $698.31

    Answer: See Section 16. How To Use the Income Tax Withholding Tables. Percentage Method Tables for Income Tax Withholding. Page 44/ (d) $698.31

How To Use The Income Tax Withholding Tables

Section 16. Example.

52. A married employee is paid **$1,200.00 Biweekly**. This employee has in effect a Form W-4 claiming two withholding allowances. Using the percentage method figure the income tax as follows:

1. Biweekly total wage payment = $1,200.00
2. One biweekly allowance = $150.00
3. Allowances claimed on Form W-4 = 2
4. Multiply line 2 by line 3 = $300.00 (Form W-4 claimed)
5. Amount subject to withholding (subtract line 4 from line 1. $1200.00 - $300.00 = $900.00
6. Tax to be withheld on $900.00 from Table 2 — (b) Married person, page 44 =

Solution —The Missing Steps:

7. Over $319.00 but less than $3,108.00 the tax is $0.00 plus 10% (0.10) of excess over $319.00.
8. $900.00 - $319.00 = $581.00
9. $581.00 times 0.10 = $58.10
10. $0.00 + $58.10 = Biweekly Income Tax to be withheld $____
    (a) $58.10
    (b) $58.25
    (c) $58.35
    (d) $58.55

Answer: See Section 16. How To Use the Income Tax Withholding Tables. Percentage Method Tables for Income Tax Withholding. Page 44/ (a) $58.10

The International Leader in Construction Technology Home Study

How To Use The Income Tax Withholding Tables

Section 16. Example.

53. A married employee is paid **$1,500.00 Biweekly**. This employee has in effect a Form W-4 claiming two withholding allowances. Using the percentage method figure the income tax as follows:

1. Biweekly total wage payment = $1,500.00
2. One biweekly allowance = $150.00
3. Allowances claimed on Form W-4 = 2
4. Multiply line 2 by line 3 = $300.00 (Form W-4 claimed)
5. Amount subject to withholding (subtract line 4 from line 1. $1,500.00 - $300.00 = $1,200.00
6. Tax to be withheld on $1,200.00 from Table 2 — (b) Married person, page 44 =

Solution —The Missing Steps:

7. Over $319.00 but less than $3,108.00 the tax is $0.00 plus 10% (0.10) of excess over $319.00.
8. $1,200.00 - $319.00 = $881.00
9. $881.00 times 0.10 = $88.10
10. $0.00 + $88.10 = Biweekly Income Tax to be withheld $____

(a) $88.05
(b) $88.10
(c) $88.25
(d) $58.35

Answer: See Section 16. How To Use the Income Tax Withholding Tables. Percentage Method Tables for Income Tax Withholding. Page 44/ (b) $88.10

How To Use The Income Tax Withholding Tables

Section 16. Example.

54. A married employee is paid **$1,600.00 Biweekly**. This employee has in effect a Form W-4 claiming two withholding allowances. Using the percentage method figure the income tax as follows:
    1. Biweekly total wage payment = $1,600.00
    2. One biweekly allowance = $150.00
    3. Allowances claimed on Form W-4 = 2
    4. Multiply line 2 by line 3 = $300.00 (Form W-4 claimed)
    5. Amount subject to withholding (subtract line 4 from line 1. $1,600.00 - $300.00 = $1,300.00
    6. Tax to be withheld on $1,300.00 from Table 2 — (b) Married person, page 44 =
    Solution —The Missing Steps:
    7. Over $319.00 but less than $3,108.00 the tax is $0.00 plus 10% (0.10) of excess over $319.00.
    8. $1,300.00 - $319.00 = $981.00
    9. $981.00 times 0.10 = $91.10
    10. $0.00 + $91.10 = Biweekly Income Tax to be withheld $____
       (a) $91.00
       (b) $91.05
       (c) $91.10
       (d) $91.25
    Answer: See Section 16. How To Use the Income Tax Withholding Tables. Percentage Method Tables for Income Tax Withholding. Page 44/ (c) $91.10

Note this is Income Tax Only. Social Security, Medicare and Federal Unemployment Tax (FUTA) and additional taxes must be computed separately.
Section 16. Percentage Method. Table 2-BIWEEKLY Payroll Period (Example) (b) Married person

How To Use The Income Tax Withholding Tables

Section 16. Example.

55. A married employee is paid **$1,700.00 Biweekly**. This employee has in effect a Form W-4 claiming two withholding allowances. Using the percentage method figure the income tax as follows:

    1. Biweekly total wage payment = $1,700.00
    2. One biweekly allowance = $150.00
    3. Allowances claimed on Form W-4 = 2
    4. Multiply line 2 by line 3 = $300.00 (Form W-4 claimed)
    5. Amount subject to withholding (subtract line 4 from line 1. $1,700.00 - $300.00 = $1,400.00
    6. Tax to be withheld on $1,300.00 from Table 2 — (b) Married person, page 44 =

    Solution —The Missing Steps:

    7. Over $319.00 but less than $3,108.00 the tax is $0.00 plus 10% (0.10) of excess over $319.00.
    8. $1,400.00 - $319.00 = $1001.00
    9. $1001.00 times 0.10 = $108.10
    10. $0.00 + $91.10 = Biweekly Income Tax to be withheld $____

    (a) $100.10
    (b) $100.15
    (c) $100.20
    (d) $100.25

    Answer: See Section 16. How To Use the Income Tax Withholding Tables. Percentage Method Tables for Income Tax Withholding. Page 44/ (a) $100.10

How To Use The Income Tax Withholding Tables

Section 16. Example.

56. A married employee is paid **$1,800.00 Biweekly**. This employee has in effect a Form W-4 claiming two withholding allowances. Using the percentage method figure the income tax as follows:

1. Biweekly total wage payment = $1,800.00
2. One biweekly allowance = $150.00
3. Allowances claimed on Form W-4 = 2
4. Multiply line 2 by line 3 = $300.00 (Form W-4 claimed)
5. Amount subject to withholding (subtract line 4 from line 1. $1,800.00 - $300.00 = $1,500.00
6. Tax to be withheld on $1,300.00 from Table 2 — (b) Married person, page 44 =

Solution —The Missing Steps:

7. Over $319.00 but less than $3,108.00 the tax is $0.00 plus 10% (0.10) of excess over $319.00.
8. $1,500.00 - $319.00 = $1181.00
9. $1181.00 times 0.10 = $118.10
10. $0.00 + $91.10 = Biweekly Income Tax to be withheld $____
    (a) $118.05
    (b) $118.10
    (c) $118.15
    (d) $118.20

Answer: See Section 16. How To Use the Income Tax Withholding Tables. Percentage Method Tables for Income Tax Withholding. Page 44/ (b) $118.10

Note this is Income Tax Only. Social Security, Medicare and Federal Unemployment Tax (FUTA) and additional taxes must be computed separately.

How To Use The Income Tax Withholding Tables

Section 16. Example.

57. A married employee is paid **$2,000.00 Biweekly**. This employee has in effect a Form W-4 claiming two withholding allowances. Using the percentage method figure the income tax as follows:

   1. Biweekly total wage payment = $2,000.00
   2. One biweekly allowance = $150.00
   3. Allowances claimed on Form W-4 = 2
   4. Multiply line 2 by line 3 = $300.00 (Form W-4 claimed)
   5. Amount subject to withholding (subtract line 4 from line 1. $2,000.00 - $300.00 = $1,700.00
   6. Tax to be withheld on $1,700.00 from Table 2 — (b) Married person, page 44 =

   Solution —The Missing Steps:

   7. Over $319.00 but less than $3,108.00 the tax is $0.00 plus 10% (0.10) of excess over $319.00.
   8. $1,700.00 - $319.00 = $1381.00
   9. $1181.00 times 0.10 = $138.10
   10. $0.00 + $138.10 = Biweekly Income Tax to be withheld $____

   (a) $138.0
   (b) $138.05
   (c) $138.10
   (d) $138.15

   Answer: See Section 16. How To Use the Income Tax Withholding Tables. Percentage Method Tables for Income Tax Withholding. Page 44/ (c) $138.10

How To Use The Income Tax Withholding Tables

Section 16. Example.

58. A married employee is paid **$2,500.00 Biweekly**. This employee has in effect a Form W-4 claiming two withholding allowances. Using the percentage method figure the income tax as follows:
    1. Biweekly total wage payment = $2,500.00
    2. One biweekly allowance = $150.00
    3. Allowances claimed on Form W-4 = 2
    4. Multiply line 2 by line 3 = $300.00 (Form W-4 claimed)
    5. Amount subject to withholding (subtract line 4 from line 1. $2,500.00 - $300.00 = $2,200.00
    6. Tax to be withheld on $2,200.00 from Table 2 — (b) Married person, page 44 =

    Solution —The Missing Steps:
    7. Over $319.00 but less than $3,108.00 the tax is $0.00 plus 10% (0.10) of excess over $319.00.
    8. $2,200.00 - $319.00 = $1881.00
    9. $1881.00 times 0.10 = $188.10
    10. $0.00 + $138.10 = Biweekly Income Tax to be withheld $____
        (a) $188.00
        (b) $188.05
        (c) $188.08
        (d) $188.10

    Answer: See Section 16. How To Use the Income Tax Withholding Tables. Percentage Method Tables for Income Tax Withholding. Page 44/ (d) $188.10

Note this is Income Tax Only. Social Security, Medicare and Federal Unemployment Tax (FUTA) and additional taxes must be computed separately.

How To Use The Income Tax Withholding Tables

Section 16. Example.

59. A married employee is paid **$2,800.00 Biweekly**. This employee has in effect a Form W-4 claiming two withholding allowances. Using the percentage method figure the income tax as follows:

1. Biweekly total wage payment = $2,800.00
2. One biweekly allowance = $150.00
3. Allowances claimed on Form W-4 = 2
4. Multiply line 2 by line 3 = $300.00 (Form W-4 claimed)
5. Amount subject to withholding (subtract line 4 from line 1. $2,800.00 - $300.00 = $2,500.00
6. Tax to be withheld on $2,500.00 from Table 2 — (b) Married person, page 44 =

Solution —The Missing Steps:

7. Over $319.00 but less than $3,108.00 the tax is $0.00 plus 10% (0.10) of excess over $319.00.
8. $2,500.00 - $319.00 = $2,200.00
9. $2,200.00 times 0.10 = $220.00
10. $0.00 + $220.00 = Biweekly Income Tax to be withheld $____

(a) $220.00
(b) $220.05
(c) $220.10
(d) $220.15

Answer: See Section 16. How To Use the Income Tax Withholding Tables. Percentage Method Tables for Income Tax Withholding. Page 44/ (a) $220.00

How To Use The Income Tax Withholding Tables

Section 16. Example.
60. A married employee is paid **$3,000.00 Biweekly**. This employee has in effect a Form W-4 claiming two withholding allowances. Using the percentage method figure the income tax as follows:
1. Biweekly total wage payment = $3,000.00
2. One biweekly allowance = $150.00
3. Allowances claimed on Form W-4 = 2
4. Multiply line 2 by line 3 = $300.00 (Form W-4 claimed)
5. Amount subject to withholding (subtract line 4 from line 1. $3,000.00 - $300.00 = $2,700.00
6. Tax to be withheld on $2,700.00 from Table 2 — (b) Married person, page 44 =

Solution —The Missing Steps:
7. Over $319.00 but less than $3,108.00 the tax is $0.00 plus 10% (0.10) of excess over $319.00.
8. $2,700.00 - $319.00 = $2,381.00
9. $2,381.00 times 0.10 = $238.10
10. $0.00 + $220.00= Biweekly Income Tax to be withheld $____
    (a) $238.05
    (b) $238.10
    (c) $238.15
    (d) $238.20

Answer: See Section 16. How To Use the Income Tax Withholding Tables. Percentage Method Tables for Income Tax Withholding. Page 44/ (b) $238.10

Note this is Income Tax Only. Social Security, Medicare and Federal Unemployment Tax (FUTA) and additional taxes must be computed separately.

The International Leader in Construction Technology Home Study

Instructor's Manual Tax Test 15E-INDEX

The Tax Test for IRS Publication 15, Circular E, Employers Tax Guide is simple and straight to the point. This test is about knowing teaching students to where to look quickly and easily for the correct answer to any question. Each part of Circular E can be divided into half sections, quarter sections, thirds or whatever if the student knows where to look. Thus, a question about the tax rate for social security can be easily located on the front cover of Circular E. In a similar manner Where do you generally locate the Index of a textbook or the Table of Contents. Why must a student waste time searching for the correct answer when knowing here to look and find the answer will divide search time in a fraction of the time. The index test is an important tool of and for research and study. An important tool seldom taught.

DU VALL'S TEST'S™
Instructor's Manual Study Guide Series United States Tax Code
IRS Publication 15 Circular E, Employer's Tax Guide Tax Year 2013
Tax Test 15E-The INDEX [Multiple-Choice Questions With Answers]

Index—Tax Test

1. The Index for Circular E is located on page ____.
   - (a) 58
   - (b) 59
   - (c) 66
   - (d) 68

   Answer: See Contents, Front page, Circular E/ (c) 66

2. According to IRS Publication 15, 2013 Circular E, the employer tax rate for social security is ____%.
   - (a) 6.2
   - (b) 7.1
   - (c) 8.4
   - (d) 8.5

   Answer: See Cover, Index and page 23, Employer tax rate and the social security wage base limit/ (a) 6.2

3. According to the 2013 Circular E, the employee Medicare tax rate is ___%.
   - (a) 1.35
   - (b) 1.45
   - (c) 1.51
   - (d) 3.51

   Answer: See Cover, Index and page 19, Tax rates and the social security wage base limit/ (b) 1.45

© Copyright 2013. All rights reserved. Notice: United States Copyright Laws and International Treaties prohibit unauthorized publication, reproduction, distribution of this Work. Unauthorized use of this copyright in any form, format, publication or document may result in severe civil and criminal penalties. Violations of this copyright are investigated by the United States Department of Justice and carry, upon conviction of fines up to $250,000 and five years confinement. This Work is protected by United States Copyright Laws and International Treaties. Do not Copy, do not reproduce, do not distribute.

A Ficus Tree Publishing Educational-Technical Publications

The International Leader in Construction Technology Home Study

Index—Tax Test

INDEX Test:

4. Information about family employees can be located on page ___ of Circular E.
    (a) 3
    (b) 5
    (c) 10
    (d) 12
    Answer: See Contents, front page and Index of Circular E/ (d) 12

5. Information about payroll period can be located on page ___ of Circular E.
    (a) 9
    (b) 10
    (c) 15
    (d) 20
    Answer: See Contents, front page and the Index Circular E/ (d) 20

6. Information about depositing taxes can be located on page ___ of Circular E.
    (a) 11
    (b) 19
    (c) 20
    (d) 23
    Answer: See Contents, front page and Index. Circular E/ (c) 20

7. Employees are defined on page ___ of Circular E.
    (a) 3
    (b) 5
    (c) 9
    (d) 11
    Answer: See Contents, front page and Index. Circular E/ (d) 11

8. Information about filing of forms 941 and 944 is found on page ___, and the Index of Circular E.
    (a) 2
    (b) 27
    (c) 30
    (d) 37
    Answer: See Contents page 1/ (c) 30

9. The Accuracy of Deposits Rule, is described on page ___ of Circular E.
    (a) 13
    (b) 19
    (c) 23
    (d) 28
    Answer: See Index page 66/ (d) 28

© Copyright 2013. All rights reserved. Notice: United States Copyright Laws and International Treaties prohibit unauthorized publication, reproduction, distribution of this Work. Unauthorized use of this copyright in any form, format, publication or document may result in severe civil and criminal penalties. Violations of this copyright are investigated by the United States Department of Justice and carry, upon conviction of fines up to $250,000 and five years confinement. This Work is protected by United States Copyright Laws and International Treaties. Do not Copy, do not reproduce, do not distribute.

A Ficus Tree Publishing Educational-Technical Publications

601
The International Leader in Construction Technology Home Study

Index—Tax Test

Index Test Page 66

10. Backup withholding, is discussed on page ___ of Circular E.
    (a) 2
    (b) 4
    (c) 5
    (d) 7
    Answer: See Index, Circular E / (c) 5

11. Change of address is discussed on page ___ of Circular E.
    (a) 3, 6
    (b) 15, 8
    (c) 20, 23
    (d) 29, 31
    Answer: See Index, Circular E/ (a) 3, 6

12. COBRA premium assistance credit is discussed on page ___ of Circular E.
    (a) 5
    (b) 10
    (c) 15
    (d) 23
    Answer: See Index, COBRA/ (b) 10

13. FUTA tax, is discussed on page ___ of Circular E.
    (a) 6
    (b) 16
    (c) 28
    (d) 35
    Answer: See Cover, Index, Circular E/ (d) 35

14. Information about household employees, is found on page ___ of Circular E.
    (a) 2
    (b) 12
    (c) 25
    (d) 30
    Answer: See Index, Circular E/ (d) 30

15. International Social Security Agreements, are discussed on page ___ of Circular E.
    (a) 10
    (b) 19
    (c) 24
    (d) 25
    Answer: See Index, Circular E/ (c) 24

© Copyright 2013. All rights reserved. Notice: United States Copyright Laws and International Treaties prohibit unauthorized publication, reproduction, distribution of this Work. Unauthorized use of this copyright in any form, format, publication or document may result in severe civil and criminal penalties. Violations of this copyright are investigated by the United States Department of Justice and carry, upon conviction of fines up to $250,000 and five years confinement. This Work is protected by United States Copyright Laws and International Treaties. Do not Copy, do not reproduce, do not distribute.

A Ficus Tree Publishing Educational-Technical Publications

Index—Tax Test

Index Test Page 66

16. Lookback period, is discussed on page ___ of Circular E.
    (a)   7
    (b)   20
    (c)   25
    (d)   27
    Answer: See Index, Circular E/ (c) 25

17. Long-term care insurance, is discussed on page ___ of Circular E.
    (a)   16
    (b)   20
    (c)   30
    (d)   40
    Answer: See Index, Circular E/(a) 16

18. Medicare tax, is discussed on page ___ of Circular E.
    (a)   8
    (b)   10
    (c)   12
    (d)   23
    Answer: See Index, Circular E/ (d) 23

19. Government employers, are discussed on page ___ of Circular E.
    (a)   2
    (b)   4
    (c)   5
    (d)   9
    Answer: See Index, Circular E/ (d) 9

20. Medical savings accounts, are discussed on page ___ of Circular E.
    (a)   5
    (b)   13
    (c)   16
    (d)   18
    Answer: See Index, Circular E/ (c) 16

21. Mileage, is discussed on page ___ of Circular E.
    (a)   7
    (b)   10
    (c)   12
    (d)   15
    Answer: See Index, Circular E/ (d) 15

© Copyright 2013. All rights reserved. Notice: United States Copyright Laws and International Treaties prohibit unauthorized publication, reproduction, distribution of this Work. Unauthorized use of this copyright in any form, format, publication or document may result in severe civil and criminal penalties. Violations of this copyright are investigated by the United States Department of Justice and carry, upon conviction of fines up to $250,000 and five years confinement. This Work is protected by United States Copyright Laws and International Treaties. Do not Copy, do not reproduce, do not distribute.

Index—Tax Test

Index Test Page 66

22. Moving Expenses, are discussed on page ___ of Circular E.
    - (a) 3
    - (b) 6
    - (c) 7
    - (d) 16

    Answer: See Index, Circular E/ (d) 16

23. The Monthly deposit schedule, is discussed on page ___ of Circular E.
    - (a) 7
    - (b) 11
    - (c) 15
    - (d) 26

    Answer: See Index, Circular E/ (d) 26

24. Noncash wages, are discussed on page ___ of Circular E.
    - (a) 9
    - (b) 12
    - (c) 15
    - (d) 27

    Answer: See Index, Circular E/ (c) 15

25. Payroll period, is discussed on page ___ of Circular E.
    - (a) 13
    - (b) 14
    - (c) 15
    - (d) 20

    Answer: See Index, Circular E/ (d) 20

26. Reconciling Forms W-2 and 941 or 944 are discussed on page ____ of Circular E.
    - (a) 15
    - (b) 25
    - (c) 31
    - (d) 35

    Answer: See Index, Circular E/ (c) 31

27. Per Diem reimbursements, are discussed on page ___ of Circular E.
    - (a) 3
    - (b) 7
    - (c) 9
    - (d) 15

    Answer: See Index. Reimbursements. Circular E, 5. Wages and Other Compensation (reimbursements, per diem or other fixed allowance)/ (d) 15

Index—Tax Test

Index Test Page 66

28. Semiweekly deposit schedule is discussed on page ___ of Circular E.
    (a) 4
    (b) 21
    (c) 26
    (d) 31
    Answer: See Index, Circular E, (c) 26

29. Statutory employees, are discussed on page ___ of Circular E.
    (a) 4
    (b) 9
    (c) 11
    (d) 15
    Answer: See Index, Circular E/ (c) 11

30. Successor Employers, are discussed on pages ___ of Circular E.
    (a) 3, 15
    (b) 19, 29
    (c) 21, 30
    (d) 24, 35
    Answer: See Index, Circular E/ (d) 24, 35

31. The Trust Fund Recovery Penalty, is discussed on page ___ of Circular E.
    (a) 12
    (b) 17
    (c) 24
    (d) 29
    Answer: See Index, Circular E/ (d) 29

32. Wages, are defined on page ___ of Circular E.
    (a) 7
    (b) 14
    (c) 18
    (d) 21
    Answer: See Index, Circular E/ (b) 14

33. Withholding exemption is discussed on page ___ of Circular E.
    (a) 8
    (b) 14
    (c) 21
    (d) 25
    Answer: See Index, Circular E/ (c) 21

Index—Tax Test

Index Test Page 66

34. Pensions and annuities, are discussed on page ___ of Circular E.
    (a) 5
    (b) 8
    (c) 12
    (d) 16
    Answer: See Index, Circular E, a part of the withholding discussion (W)/ (a) 5

35. The percentage method, is discussed on page ___ of Circular E.
    (a) 12
    (b) 23
    (c) 35
    (d) 42
    Answer: See Index, Circular E (W)/ (d) 42

36. Seasonal Employers, are discussed on page ___ of Circular E.
    (a) 24
    (b) 30
    (c) 41
    (d) 65
    Answer: See Index, Circular E/ (b) 30

37. The Formulario W-4 (SP), Certificado de Exención de la Retención del Empleado may be used in place of the Form ____.
    (a) W-4
    (b) W-4A
    (c) W-4B
    (d) W-4S
    Answer See Form W-4, Forms in Spanish/ (a) W-4

38. For companies engaged in fishing and related activities the employer should see IRS publication ___.
    (a) 440
    (b) 489
    (c) 713
    (d) 334
    Answer: See Circular E, page 37, 15. Special Rules for Various Types of Services and Payments, Fishing and related activities, Tax Guide for Small Business/(d) 334

The International Leader in Construction Technology Home Study

DUVALL'S TEST'S™
2013 Circular E Employer's Tax Guide
2013 Tax Tables for Circular E.

For solving tax table problems use the Tax Tables of your free copy that you obtained with IRS Publication 15. Employer's Tax Guide.

Obtaining original IRS tax tables for each current year substantially reduces the cost of this publication. In addition, each progressive tax year publication of IRS Publication 15, Circular E, Employer's Tax Guide usually allows purchasers of this work to examine, reference and compare the annual changes for each tax year. A reminder: Always obtain and use the current IRS Publication 15, Circular E, Employer's Tax Guide when computing taxes. Further, DUVALL'S Tax Tests, Study Guides and Workbooks are <u>study guides only</u>, not Source Documents.

© Copyright 2013. All rights reserved. Notice: United States Copyright Laws and International Treaties prohibit unauthorized publication, reproduction, distribution of this Work. Unauthorized use of this copyright in any form, format, publication or document may result in severe civil and criminal penalties. Violations of this copyright are investigated by the United States Department of Justice and carry, upon conviction of fines up to $250,000 and five years confinement. This Work is protected by United States Copyright Laws and International Treaties. Do not Copy, do not reproduce, do not distribute.

A Ficus Tree Publishing Educational-Technical Publications

A Ficus Tree Publishing Quick Notes Page.

www.ingramcontent.com/pod-product-compliance
Lightning Source LLC
Chambersburg PA
CBHW081932170426
43202CB00018B/2920